Political

Oppositions

in *Western*

Democracies

POLITICAL

OPPOSITIONS

IN WESTERN

DEMOCRACIES

edited by

ROBERT A. DAHL

New Haven and London

Yale University Press

To the memory of Otto Kirchheimer

ACKNOWLEDGMENTS

This book was made possible through the generous support of the Rocke-feller Foundation. The authors are also indebted, singly and jointly, to Mr. and Mrs. John Marshall for their many gracious kindnesses at the Villa Serbelloni, Bellagio, Italy, where much of this book was formulated and discussed in a setting that could not have been more attractive or more hospitable; and to our rapporteurs at the two conferences there, Ian Budge and Mary Dahl.

We are obligated to Marian Ash for her skillful editing at the Yale University Press.

I should like to express my own thanks to Yale University and the Henry L. Stimson Fund for their generous assistance, and to my wife Mary for her help from the beginning of this undertaking to the end.

R.A.D.

April 1965
New Haven, Conn.

CONTENTS

PREFACE TO THE
PAPERBOUND EDITION

No doubt the safest forecast a student of politics can make is that any political system he observes will change with the passage of time. If the authors represented in this book were writing today, I have no doubt that with four additional years of political life to analyze each would possess a conception of the political system of which he writes different, in at least some respects, from the one he held in 1964.

The fewest changes seem to have occurred in the two representative democracies that could hardly be more contrasting in their patterns of government and opposition: Great Britain and the Netherlands. In several other countries the changes that have taken place only amplify what is already emphasized or foreshadowed here. In Italy, the coalition produced by a successful *apertura a sinistra*, which was created shortly before Samuel Barnes finished his chapter, fell apart after elections in May 1968, and was replaced, at least until the Socialists could agree either to enter or to oppose the government, by a Christian Democratic *monocolore* Cabinet. In Germany, the "vanishing opposition" portrayed by a much-missed and far-sighted friend (to whom this book was posthumously dedicated) finally reached the stage that Otto Kirchheimer speculated it might: "an Austrian-type combined operation of the two great parties." But since the advantages to the two parties of participation in the grand coalition will not indefinitely outweigh the advantages of a government by one party and opposition by the other, the coalition in Germany is unlikely to endure as long as the one in Austria. Meanwhile, the country that provided Germany with the model for "the pooling of opposition" terminated — at least for some time — its system of a Grand Coalition and *Proporz*. As Frederick Englemann points out, however, "the coalition ... brought a softening of oppositions" in Austria. For this and other reasons the antagonisms between the two great *Lager* of the First Austrian Republic have now cooled enough so that political conflict remains very much more moderate in the Second Republic than in the First.

In Norway, too, the more things change the more they remain the same. If the coalition of parties that after thirty years of opposition displaced Labor in 1965 (a change Stein Rokkan describes briefly in a postscript added while the book was in press) has continued, so has the Norwegian combination of "numerical democracy and corporate pluralism."

In other countries, conflicts between government and opposition have intensified, without, however, altering in any very basic ways the previous patterns. In Belgium, the rift described by Val Lorwin between French-speaking and Flemish-speaking Belgians has deepened. As I write, the French-speaking Socialists of Brussels refuse to join the governing coalition consisting of the majority of the Socialist Party and the Christian Social Party. The United States has been witnessing a phenomenon that, I suggested, has occurred about once every generation in the history of this country: a polarizing conflict of extreme severity. Alienated or disaffected groups "who reject some or most of the key elements in the dominant ideology and some or most of the major institutions" — what I referred to as "the neglected side of the American political system" — have been more active and significant than at any time, perhaps, since the period just prior to the Civil War. Yet — for better or for worse — my conclusion, I believe, still holds: "the tendency for opinions and beliefs to converge will probably continue. The center will then continue to dominate political life, and dissenters will continue to be frustrated and alienated."

The most dramatic confrontation between government and opposition has occurred in France, the classic home of "nothing but opposition," as Alfred Grosser puts it, where in May and June of 1968 France underwent an almost universal general strike and teetered close to the edge of civil war. After President de Gaulle was very nearly driven out of office, he regained the initiative and won a stunning electoral victory that gave his party an overwhelming majority in parliament and decimated the ranks of the opposition.

These events in France and the United States, like many events elsewhere, confirm, I think, the prophesy contained in the final pages of the Epilogue: that "political ideologies, far from waning, will be ascendant." New structural and ideological oppositions, I suggested, would arise because the Western democracies will continue to provide three sources of enduring conflict: disagreements over distribution, over international politics, and over "the new democratic Leviathan itself." The experiences of the intervening years also seen to confirm the forecast that these conflicting ideologies, demands, and opposition will not be related significantly to "the familiar social and economic characteristics that have done such yeoman service in social theory in the recent past."

There is every reason to conclude, then, as Lorwin does about Belgium: *Eppur si opone.*

Shelter Harbor   ROBERT A. DAHL
Westerly, R.I.
July 1968

PREFACE

Somewhere in the world, at this moment, a political group is probably engaged in the antique art of imprisoning, maiming, torturing, and killing its opponents. Somewhere, as you read these words, a government and its opponents are no doubt trying to coerce one another by violent means. For without much question the most commonplace way for a government to deal with its opponents is to employ violence.

Of the three great milestones in the development of democratic institutions—the right to participate in governmental decisions by casting a vote, the right to be represented, and the right of an organized opposition to appeal for votes against the government in elections and in parliament—the last is, in a highly developed form, so wholly modern that there are people now living who were born before it had appeared in most of Western Europe.

Throughout recorded history, it seems, stable institutions providing legal, orderly, peaceful modes of political opposition have been rare. If peaceful antagonism between factions is uncommon, peaceful opposition among organized, permanent political parties is an even more exotic historical phenomenon. Legal party opposition, in fact, is a recent unplanned invention that has been confined for the most part to a handful of countries in Western Europe and the English-speaking world. Even more recent are organized political parties that compete peacefully in elections for the votes of the great bulk of the adult population who can exercise the franchise under nearly universal suffrage. Universal suffrage and enduring mass parties are, with few exceptions, products of the past century. It should not be altogether surprising, then, that of the 113 members of the United Nations in 1964, only about 30 had political systems in which full legal opposition among organized political parties had existed throughout the preceding decade.

If political systems with legal opposition parties are a minority as we move into the last third of the twentieth century, what can we expect for the twenty-first century? Are the 30 systems that now exist merely the exotic flowers of a unique and passing historical climate? Or are they vigorous products of a long evolution, a political species now rugged enough to thrive in other, perhaps harsher, climes? In short, if systems with legal party opposition do not fully reflect the present world, do they merely reflect the past—or do they provide patterns for the future?

A Few Preliminary Assumptions

The fact that a system of peaceful and legal opposition by political parties is a comparative rarity means that it must be exceedingly difficult to *introduce* such a system, or to *maintain* it, or both. To explain how and why these systems start is difficult; historical explanations tend to dissolve into minutiae that do not altogether "explain," while ahistorical explanations remain on the surface or recede into shadowy uncertainties because the data needed for a satisfactory explanation do not exist.

The novelty of peaceful opposition does suggest, however, that governments have usually tried to prevent the development of opposition. One could convert this historical observation into a simple axiom about the behavior of any political group that controls the central government of any political association: A governing group will use the coercive powers of the government to deny opponents the opportunity to oppose it, in every instance where the governing group expects that coercion has a fair chance of succeeding *and* the gains of a successful denial will exceed the costs. The plausibility of this axiom, you will notice, gains from the fact that it does not say very much. But let us now turn the axiom around: Opposition is likely to be permitted in a political system if (1) the government believes that an attempt to coerce the opposition is likely to fail, or (2) even if the attempt were to succeed, the costs of coercion would exceed the gains.

This excessively simple axiom suggests two interrelated questions: What factors increase the chances that a government will fail if it tries to coerce its opponents? And what factors increase the relative costs of successful coercion?

Consider the first question. Ordinarily a government has access to much greater resources for coercing opponents than opponents have for coercing government. (Otherwise, the chances are that the opposition would soon control the government.) Our initial conjecture is, however, that peaceful opposition is more likely to be introduced and maintained in a system where there is a kind of limited preponderance, so to speak, in the government's access to resources of coercion: that is, where a governing group stands a significant chance of failure if it tries to coerce its opponents, and hence permits or even encourages the development of institutions for peaceful negotiation. Would systems of legal opposition ever have developed if governing groups had known that they could, unquestionably, coerce their opponents and get away with it?

Specifically, then, the nature of the military and police forces has a bearing on the prospects of opposition. The potential effectiveness of military or police forces as instruments for coercing opposition may be limited because the standing army is small and police forces are under local control as in eighteenth-century Britain where an insular position and a navy eliminated the need for a large standing army while the country gentry and the justices of the peace maintained law and order; [1] or because the military forces consist of a citizen militia, as in Switzerland; or because the loyalty and obedience of the military or the police would be doubtful if they were employed to put down the opposition. This last constraint on the coercive power of the government may develop because bonds exist between military elements and the opposition. Or tradition and even law may deny legitimacy to a government that uses military forces for settling internal political wrangles; norms of this kind seem to have developed in the Netherlands during the fifteenth and sixteenth centuries, in Britain following the Revolution of 1688, and in Sweden during the course of the eighteenth century.

The prospects of successful coercion also decline when opposition groups improve their own opportunities to resort to defensive violence if they are threatened with coercion. Defenses against coercion by the central government may be relatively strong because of equality or superiority in numbers; because efficient weapons and military skills are widely diffused, as in the United States during the eighteenth and early nineteenth centuries; or because an opposition receives the loyalty of a population in a region with good natural defenses, economic supremacy, or other advantages.

Thus it is plausible to think that the existence of a limited preponderance of coercive forces, as these are perceived by government [2] and opposition, plays a key part in the transition to a system in which government and opposition are both prepared to renounce the use of violence. I say "limited preponderance" to cover an inescapable vagueness in the formula. An opposition might renounce violence because it sees that in an outright conflict, given the enormous potential power of the government, it would have no chance at all; one thinks here of the strategy of nonviolent resistance in British India and in the American South in recent years. For its part a government may renounce violence because, though it *might* succeed, the strategy of coercion is heavily fraught with risks of failure.

1. Ernest Barker, *The Development of Public Services in Western Europe, 1660–1930* (London, Oxford University Press, 1944), pp. 28–34, 50–52.

2. For convenience, I use "government" here, as later, as a shorthand for the more cumbersome "groups that control the government." The context will indicate sufficiently whenever the term is used this way.

The element of coercion, the requirement for a limited preponderance of coercive potential, is worth stressing because it is not uncommon to understate the importance of violence and coercion in the evolution of democratic institutions. Nonetheless, even if some rough balance may help to initiate a phase of growing tolerance of opposition by government and of government by its opponents, it seems unlikely that the growth of full-fledged systems of legal opposition could have rested entirely, or even mainly, on such precarious foundations. Limited preponderance is, conceivably, a necessary condition, but it is hardly sufficient. What weight should we give, then, to the factors posed a moment ago in our second question: factors that increase the relative costs of successful coercion? For a governing group might believe that it could coerce its opponents, and yet not do so because the costs would be too great.

What turns "successful" coercion into costly failure? Among other things, one surmises, are matters of belief, ideology, values. Costs of coercion rise, one may assume, whenever elites and the general population of a country develop a sense of nationhood that includes the opposition; a distaste for violence; a commitment to a liberal ideology; or economic and social goals that require internal stability. Finally, once a system that permits peaceful party opposition is highly institutionalized and surrounded with legal protections, the costs of destroying it are likely to be extremely high. For a government can destroy the opposition only by wrecking the constitutional system. At this stage of evolution, to destroy the opposition requires a revolution. And the costs of revolution often run high.

These speculations as to the introduction and maintenance of a system of peaceful opposition suggest two further observations. First, the conjunction of the necessary factors depends heavily on historical developments over which it is difficult to exercise precise control. Second, the rise and conjunction of the appropriate factors take *time;* until now, stable systems with legal oppositions have evolved rather slowly. It is by no means clear whether or how the process can be deliberately contrived or greatly speeded up. Yet it would be hard to find other questions on which knowledge is more urgent.

A New Form: Opposition Parties

Political systems with organized political parties protected by law are, as I have already said, a modern development. Historical analogies can generally be found for any innovation; nonethless, the opposition political party as we know it today represents a radical break with older forms of opposition.

Because some conflict of views seems to be unavoidable in human affairs, political societies have always had to deal somehow with the fact of opposition. Nevertheless, that there might legitimately exist an organized group within the political system to oppose, criticize, and if possible oust the leading officials of government was until recently an unfamiliar and generally unacceptable notion. When the men at the American Constitutional Convention of 1787 expressed their fear of "factions" as the bane of republics, they spoke the traditional view. The most long-lived republic in history, the aristocratic republic of Venice, deliberately inhibited the formation of enduring political organizations. Venice, like Rome before it, sought to provide in its constitutional arrangements sufficient checks and balances among officials to prevent arbitrary decisions and to insure a large measure of consensus for the laws; thus organized opposition was seen as unnecessary and a danger to the stability of the Republic.[3] Not all the premodern democracies and republics went quite as far as Venice. Factions, coalitions, and alliances of one kind or another existed in and outside the popular assemblies of Athens,[4] and in the late Roman Republic political alliances sought votes both for candidates and for laws in the various popular assemblies. But evidently these groups were never highly organized, had no permanent structure, and even lacked definite names.[5] Moreover, like the Guelphs and Ghibellines of medieval Italy or the Piagnoni and the Arrabiati of Savonarola's Florence, factions typically settled their differences sooner or later, as they came to do during the last century of the Roman Republic, by bloodshed.

The system of managing the major political conflicts of a society by allowing one or more opposition parties to compete with the governing parties for votes in elections and in parliament is, then, not only modern; surely it is also one of the greatest and most unexpected social discoveries

3. All the more so because the aristocracy was acutely aware of the danger, particularly after the strife of the thirteenth century, that a split within the aristocracy would endanger its exclusive control over the constitutional machinery of the Republic. For a thoroughgoing description of this constitution and the preoccupation of the aristocracy with the prevention of internal conflict see Giuseppe Maranini, *La Costituzione di Venezia* (Venice, La Nuova Italia Editrice), Vol. 1, *Dalle Origini alla Serrata del Maggior Consiglio* (1927), and Vol. 2, *Dopo La Serrata del Maggior Consiglio* (1931), particularly Vol. 1, pp. 168–71; the description of the highly complex method for electing the doge at pp. 187–90; and 324–50, also Vol. 2, pp. 99, 115, 122.

4. "There were no parties in anything like the modern sense, either among the politicians or the general public. At the one end of the scale there were groups or cliques among the politicians. But such alliances were probably based on personalities rather than principles, and seem to have been temporary." A. H. M. Jones, *Athenian Democracy* (Oxford, Blackwell, 1957), pp. 130–31. Jones concludes, however, "that Athenian policy was really determined by mass meetings of the citizens on the advice of anyone who could win the people's ear." (p. 132). See also Fustel de Coulanges, *The Ancient City* (Garden City, N.Y., Doubleday Anchor Books, n.d.), pp. 340 ff.

5. Lily Ross Taylor, *Party Politics in the Age of Caesar* (University of California, Berkeley and Los Angeles, 1961). Also F. E. Adcock, *Roman Political Ideas and Practice* (Ann Arbor, University of Michigan Press, 1959), pp. 60–62.

that man has ever stumbled onto. Up until two centuries ago, no one had accurately foreseen it. Today one is inclined to regard the existence of an opposition party as very nearly the most distinctive characteristic of democracy itself; and we take the absence of an opposition party as evidence, if not always conclusive proof, for the absence of democracy.

Yet there are signs, as the essays in this volume show, that this new form, which was unknown before the nineteenth century and had spread to some 30 countries in the twentieth, is, nearly everywhere, undergoing profound changes. One task of these essays is to discover what these changes are.

The Meaning of Opposition

The term "opposition" is rather difficult to define precisely. This is not unusual with key terms in social theory, though it is often annoying. A preliminary definition will, I think, prove satisfactory enough for our purposes. Suppose that A determines the conduct of some aspect of the government of a particular political system during some interval. We need not specify the interval exactly; it may be a period in the past, the coming year, etc. Suppose that during this interval B cannot determine the conduct of the government; and that B is opposed to the conduct of government by A. Then B is what we mean by "an opposition." Note that during some different interval, B might determine the conduct of the government, and A might be "in opposition." Thus it is the *role* of opposition that we are interested in; we are concerned with A and B only insofar as they perform that role in different ways.

This preliminary definition can be clarified a little, at the price of adding logical embellishments of doubtful beauty. To begin with, the "conduct" of the government is deliberately broad and vague, and I propose to leave it undefined; it remains therefore what logicians sometimes call a primitive term. But it is intended to be comprehensive enough to include, for example, the mere fact that A comes from an ethnic, racial, or religious group that B is opposed to having in high government offices. What it means to "oppose" might also be left undefined, but a few comments may help to specify the meaning. As the term is used here, A is opposed to B's action or strategy S_b if A believes that S_b will prevent A from successfully pursuing his own preferred action or strategy S_a. In this sense one cannot speak of an "objective" opposition of "interests" that is independent of the perceptions or beliefs held by the parties themselves.[6] Nonetheless, it is useful to distinguish between *active* op-

---

6. To say that A and B are "objectively" opposed, even though they are not aware of it, presumably means, in our terms, either: (1) An observer can demonstrate, or believes he can demonstrate, that A's strategy makes it "objectively" impossible for B to pursue his preferred strategy S_b; or (2) given certain "objective" characteristics of A and B, such as occupation or class, an observer holds that he

position, which occurs when *B* undertakes a deliberate course of action intended to modify the conduct of government, and *passive* opposition, which exists when *B* recognizes the conflict but does not deliberately undertake any action directed toward a change in the conduct of government. In this volume we are almost entirely concerned with active opposition.

Second, in some political systems the role of opposition might be difficult to distinguish, either because one is uncertain whether it is *A* or *B* that determines the conduct of the government, or because both do. In systems like this, opposition is not distinctive; it dissolves into the system, so to speak. As we shall see later, something like this seems to happen so often in the United States that it is difficult or even impossible to locate "the opposition."

Third, you will notice that our preliminary definition is highly abstract. It refers to the government of *any* political system. In this volume, however, we are concerned with the national government of a territorial state. A study of patterns of opposition in other kinds of political systems —local governments or trade unions, for example—would be highly instructive; but we have nonetheless restricted our attention to national systems because the national patterns are of crucial importance, we have more information about them than about other patterns, and they provide some basis for comparison.

Finally, the definition does not explicitly restrict itself to "democratic" political systems. Admittedly, it would be important to know more about the ways in which opposition operates in nondemocratic systems, but in this volume we deliberately confine ourselves to the operation of oppositions in democracies.

Our preliminary definition need not be taken too seriously. It is not intended to serve as a rigorous definition in a deductive system; it will serve, rather, as a pointer. In the essays, the meaning of the term is usually clear enough from the context.

Questions and Problems

I had originally intended to provide an introduction to this volume that according to currently fashionable and sufficiently ambiguous jargon would probably be called an analytical framework—something, that is, rather more than a classification scheme and less than a tightly knit theory. But as the discussions among the contributors proceeded, our analytical framework kept changing—for the better, one hopes. A candid portrayal of the relation between the essays in this volume and the

---

can predict from certain theoretical or hypothetical conditions that *A* and *B* will come to believe that they pursue conflicting strategies; or possibly (3) both of these.

analytical scheme that eventually emerged would have to show the final scheme less as a format for the essays than as their product. I have therefore placed the whole comparative analysis in the final chapters.

Discussions of drafts and revised papers that ultimately led to these essays took place at the Villa Serbelloni, in Bellagio, Italy, first through a week in August 1962 and again during a week in July 1963. Between these meetings and after the second one, all the authors exchanged their revised essays for additional comments. Thus, more than is usually the case, the result is, I think, a joint product.

Our discussions and written exchanges continued to demonstrate that it was easier to dismantle our various "frameworks" than to build an enduring one. For one thing, the range of countries examined provided such a diversity of experience that generalization was all too easily torpedoed by its natural enemy, some stubborn fact that would not consent either to fit the generalization or to be ignored. Moreover, our attempt to understand modern democratic politics by examining oppositions provided a perspective that constantly produced new questions, hypotheses, tentative explanations, and reevaluations.

In these circumstances, the most profitable course, it began to appear, was to leave each author considerable leeway in describing and explaining the pattern of political oppositions in the country for which he was responsible. Some of the authors have placed a relatively heavy emphasis on the historical and developmental factors that seem to account for present patterns; others have given greater weight to more recent factors. The differences in treatment stem, I think, partly from differences in intellectual temperament, partly from differences in the character of the problem and the amount of knowledge the author can assume his readers possess about the country, and partly from unsettled differences, which mirror the current state of the social sciences, over the place of historical explanation in social analysis. Since these essays enter upon a domain that had not been well charted before we began, a tight, authoritative analytical scheme would have compelled our essayists to chop off a good deal of information and explanation that would not have fitted a Procrustean framework. I cannot help feeling that in the end both the reader and future progress on this subject would have been a good deal poorer.

Moreover, much of the experience described in these essays lies almost completely outside the main body of knowledge about the political systems of advanced countries. Knowledge of the political systems of Norway, Belgium, Holland, and Austria, for example, rarely enters into comparative political analysis: there are the major developed countries —Britain, France, Germany, the United States—and there are the developing countries, but we generally ignore the experiences of the smaller

European nations in an advanced state of social, economic, and political development. Because of our relatively greater ignorance about these countries, it seemed wise to permit more descriptive material, and perhaps more variation in treatment, than would otherwise be required. The result is that the number and variety of democratic systems examined in this volume are large in comparison with most comparative efforts.

Even so, there are important omissions. Some of these are accidental. The lengthy illness of a distinguished Swiss colleague prevented him from writing what would surely have been a highly important contribution to our understanding of oppositions in the unique and venerable democracy of Switzerland. Simple considerations of space and the availability of contributors eliminated many other potential chapters; thus only two of the five Nordic democracies are included, and only two of the English-speaking democracies; Israel, an outpost of democracy in the Middle East, has been excluded, along with all the non-Western democracies, even such important ones as Japan and India.

It would be grossly misleading, however, to leave the implication that each of the essays that follow takes off, without guide or map, into an unknown territory. For one thing, to examine the problem of oppositions is sometimes a matter of employing a new perspective to look at fairly familiar things—political parties, elections, legislatures, for example. For another, and this is the more important point, our discussions and the resulting essays do reflect our concern for a common set of questions that have confronted us from the outset.

These questions fall into two sets. As to the *patterns within countries*, what are the principal characteristics of political oppositions, particularly their goals and strategies? How has the prevailing pattern developed in each country? Has the pattern of opposition goals and strategies undergone important changes in recent years? How can this pattern, its development, and its changes be explained? As to *comparisons among countries*, is there a single more or less standard pattern of political oppositions in all countries examined here? If not, what are the main patterns? What factors seeem to account for variations? To what extent have there been general changes in the patterns of oppositions associated with the kind of economy and society emerging since the Second World War? In particular, to what extent have patterns of opposition been changing in Western Europe and the United States as a result of declining structural opposition, social cleavages, polarization, or political alienation?

The authors of the chapters on the individual countries were naturally concerned primarily with the first set of questions. The second set, which asks for comparisons among countries, I have tried to deal with in the concluding chapters.

R.A.D.

Political

Oppositions

in Western

Democracies

1

GREAT BRITAIN:
OPPOSITION WITH A CAPITAL "O"

Allen Potter

Peaceful political opposition has had a long history in Great Britain. It antedates the Industrial Revolution of the late eighteenth century and the series of Reform Acts, starting with those of 1832, which turned the parliamentary electoral system of an oligarchy into that of a representative democracy. Perhaps one in twelve adult males could vote before 1832, one in seven thereafter, one in three after 1868, and three in five after 1884. The Second Reform Acts, of 1867 and 1868, whose general effect was to enfranchise the male working-class householders of the towns, constituted the decisive step in the "transition to democracy." They increased the electorate proportionately more than any of the other nineteenth-century Acts. The Ballot Act of 1872 made voting secret.

The situation since the late nineteenth century has had the following features:

a mass electorate, including rural workers on the same basis as urban workers from 1884, almost all adult males and almost all females aged 30 and above from 1918, and women on the same basis as men from 1928;

a constitutional system in which there is, owing to the principle of parliamentary sovereignty, no formal limit to the power of a Government with a parliamentary majority and, when the two-party system is fully operative, no possibility between elections of a Government losing its majority;

a consensus, especially among political leaders, about the general nature of the rights, privileges, and duties of the Opposition, which makes the propriety of opposition as integral a part of the constitutional structure of conventions and understandings as the authority of government; and

a social cleavage along class lines, which is more or less institutionalized in the contest between the two major political parties for governmental power, and whose political effects are thereby contained within the

3

conventional structure restraining the governing of the Government and the opposing of the Opposition.

The British constitution, with its implicit recognition of the legitimacy of opposition, is an inheritance from aristocratic times. There were forebodings in 1867 that it would not be preserved by a democratic age. It would fall victim to the war between "the masses" and "the classes." That war seemed to begin in earnest in the politics of the early years of this century, but it was the crisis over Irish Home Rule that then seemed most likely to destroy the constitution. After the First World War the prospect of an uncomplicated and full confrontation between the proletariat and privilege opened, as the incubus of Ireland was lifted from internal British politics and the Labor Party with its socialist program replaced the Liberal Party with its measures of social reform. The conditions preserving the British constitution in an age of a mass electorate may be discerned in the failure of that straight class struggle for power to materialize.

The Situation

THE HISTORICAL BACKGROUND   In 1937 the Ministers of the Crown Act provided for the payment of a salary from public funds to the Leader of the Opposition in the British Parliament. In debate on the provision Kenneth Pickthorn, M.P., remarked that the position of Leader of the Opposition, in anything like the modern sense, was hardly older than the oldest member:

> it was not until the late sixties, when Mr. Gladstone threw his hat into the ring in competition with Lord Stanley, that there was a Leader of the Opposition in the sense not of a man who most criticised the Government on the way they were doing their business and hoped that, in the long run, his criticism would get the Government out; but in the sense of a man who put up a different programme, with different subjects on which to base his programme and upon which he fought, who looks round to see what is likely to interest the public—the Irish Church or the means test.[1]

As befitted a member for Cambridge University, Pickthorn thought it premature to give formal recognition to this constitutional innovation. The Home Secretary, Sir John Simon, agreed with Pickthorn's account, but added that "the conception that you were discharging a public duty when you were opposing is one of the oldest conceptions in the history of British politics."[2]

1. 323 H.C. Deb. 5s. 621.
2. Ibid., 642.

The constitutional settlement within which the institutions of cabinet government and official opposition eventually developed followed upon the civil war of the seventeenth century. The tendency thereafter to avoid pushing political differences to extremes reflected a similar tendency in religious controversy, which was more central in the politics of the seventeenth century than later; and the growth of religious toleration was in the first instance much less a matter of positive conviction or religious indifference than of a reluctant realization that the cost of imposing uniformity was too great. Charles II's Declaration of Breda in 1660, the acceptance of which by the Convention Parliament put Charles on the throne, stated:

> because the passion and uncharitableness of the times have produced several opinions in religion, by which men are engaged in parties and animosities against each other (which, when they shall hereafter unite in a freedom of conversation, will be composed or better understood), we do declare a liberty to tender consciences, and that no man shall be disquieted or called in question for differences of opinion in matter of religion, which do not disturb the peace of the kingdom.[3]

Although the ensuing Cavalier Parliament disquieted those who refused to take the sacrament according to the rites of the Church of England, in doing so it recognized dissent as lawful for the first time. The acceptance of the constitutional settlement was also for some time less than complete, with plots or rumors of plots disturbing the political conversation before and after the Revolution of 1688; as usual, Scotland was the last to lay the old aside, but the 'Forty-five was a political anachronism even there.

In the late seventeenth century the country was decidedly becoming a business nation, and intolerance was thought bad for trade. After the Glorious Revolution Britain engaged in long wars with France. By way of contrast with French intolerance and absolutism the British ruling class pointed with pride to British liberties. That class, the landed aristocracy, dominated society and politics in the century after the Glorious Revolution. Divergences of opinions and interests could be tolerated within and to some extent outside that class, which was in any case never defined with legal precision, because its position seemed unassailable.

The events of the French Revolution frightened the upper classes. In 1792 the Government embarked on a policy of outright repression of unrest in "the mob," though not of opposition to its measures among gentlemen in Parliament. The worst social tension was during the period of unsettled ecenomic conditions caused by the end of the Napoleonic wars. But it was followed by adjustments to changes in society brought about

3. S. R. Gardiner, *The Constitutional Documents of the Puritan Revolution 1628–1660* (Oxford, Clarendon Press, 1889), p 352.

by the Industrial Revolution which ensured, in the language of the day, that the "age of improvement" would not be suddenly transformed into an age of "disruption." [4] The outcome was the Victorian compromise in which social and political leadership remained largely in the hands of the hereditary but absorbent ruling class, though government policy was now more directly responsive to the interests and opinions of the middle classes; and, since social, political, and economic power was less concentrated in a single class than in the previous century, the working classes were also not without influence as long as they did not, as in the case of the Chartists, frighten all the classes above them.

"It has been said," Walter Bagehot wrote in the mid-1860s in *The English Constitution*, "that England invented the phrase, 'Her Majesty's Opposition'; that it was the first Government which made a criticism of administration as much a part of the polity as administration itself. This critical opposition is the consequence of Cabinet Government." [5] It might equally well be put that cabinet government is the consequence of critical opposition. Once the supremacy of Parliament was established in the constitutional settlement of the late seventeenth century, the problem arose of relating the conduct of administration to opinion in Parliament in some regular way. The ultimate solution was a cabinet controlling administration and commanding the confidence of a majority in the House of Commons against its opponents in the chamber. The solution was long in emerging, though rudiments of it were discernible almost from the start. It was not fully realized until the support of the electorate completely displaced the favor of the monarch as the determinant of who should govern.

The development of opposition in Parliament was essentially from an opposition to particular men or measures to an opposition offering an alternative government. From the Restoration the fact that the monarch needed at least to consider the ability of ministers to manage Parliament was an element in politicians' calculations. This made it worthwhile to attempt to marshal opposition in Parliament against particular ministers or their policies. Throughout most of the eighteenth century the king's ministers maintained themselves in Parliament as the "Court Party," against the active and hostile politicians of the "Country Party," the majority of whose members, however, were not playing for office and, though independent of the Court, were not generally unfriendly to ministerial policy. The Court and Country parties were kaleidoscopic combinations of family and other personal connections, "Whigs" and "Tories" alike, active politicians supporting or opposing the Court in accordance with the immediate political interests of the groups to which they be-

4. Asa Briggs, *The Age of Improvement* (London, Longmans, 1959), p. 259.
5. Fontana Library ed. London, Collins, 1963, p. 72.

longed. The originally opprobrious nicknames "Whigs" and "Tories" date from the time of Lord Shaftesbury's Country Party, in the 1670s and '80s, and, though they persisted as the main political denominators for a century and a half, soon lost most of whatever value they had had as differentiating indicators of political behavior.

The theory of parliamentary supremacy was combined with the practical leadership of the king and his ministers. They had the support of placemen in the House. They attached groups to themselves by patronage and contracts, and corruption also ensured that they gained more support from elections than did their opponents. But for their majority ministers had to obtain the approval of enough independent members. Opposition politicians sought to harass ministers sufficiently to be bought off or to induce the king to replace one or more of his ministers; or, looking to the future, they attached themselves to the Prince of Wales. There was neither a formed general majority nor a formed general opposition.

Both started to emerge in the 1780s. Differences of opinion about public policy grew more important. An increasing number of social and political interests articulated issues. Reforms reduced the influence of patronage and contracts. Ministerial policy began to be based on public political attitudes. This meant that the question of parliamentary reform was bound to be raised, for a ministerial policy more directly related to "opinion" than in the past would not necessarily be a policy that the monarch could be induced personally to accept: ultimate support must come from "the people." The First Reform Acts completed the transition to responsible government, which had in essence been demanded by the Long Parliament in the Grand Remonstrance of 1641; "in 1841, for the first time, the opposition won a general election and the Crown accepted the decision at the polls." [6]

A straightforward connection between elections and cabinets was not established, however, until after the electorate was almost doubled and the constituencies made more uniform by the Second Reform Acts. The parliamentary political parties thereafter took the lead in mass political organization; the party labels became increasingly important in elections, and the independence of M.P.'s was considerably reduced. In the period between the first two sets of Reform Acts, glittering as the golden age of parliamentary government in Bagehot's classic account of *The English Constitution*, it came to be accepted that neither Her Majesty's Government nor Her Majesty's Opposition was, in theory at least, any more or less the Queen's Friends than the other. But the absence of a simple two-party system meant that Her Majesty's Opposition was not the alternative government that it is now. When the Government fell, the Opposition might not be prepared to take its place, though the four successive Parlia-

6. John P. Mackintosh, *The British Cabinet* (London, Stevens, 1962), p. 17.

ments elected from 1841 began under one sort of cabinet and ended under another, indicating the degree to which the connection between elections and cabinets was broken by the interposition of the House of Commons.

With the development of a strong and disciplined two-party system after the Second Reform Acts, Her Majesty's Opposition became the alternative government, but now normally unable to displace the Government during the life of a Parliament. Its appeal must be to the electorate; and from the late 1860s the party leaders tended to base their campaign appeals on one or two issues. A generation later these were becoming "programs." The party contest of British representative democracy took form, an essential element of which is official opposition—opposition with a capital "O."

THE CONSTITUTION   The constitutional principles of contemporary British government are conceived in terms of the other classic account of the nineteenth-century English constitution, A. V. Dicey's *Introduction to the Study of the Law of the Constitution*. The basic principle of the British, or at least the English, legal order is simple: Parliament, by which in this context is meant the Queen, Lords, and Commons or, under the provisions of the Parliament Acts of 1911 and 1949, the Queen and Commons alone, is sovereign. That means, in Dicey's words, "that Parliament thus defined has . . . the right to make or unmake any law whatever; and, further, that no person or body is recognized . . . as having a right to override or set aside the legislation of Parliament." [7] The principle of parliamentary sovereignty describes legal competence, the conditions of whose exercise are determined, according to Dicey, by the conventions of the constitution. The queen acts on the advice of her ministers. Her ministers command the confidence of the House of Commons. The House of Commons is chosen in free elections, in which the Government and Opposition parties in effect contend for the control of the state. It is as the arbiters of this contest that the electors were described by Dicey as "the true political sovereign of the State." [8]

The last phrase is vacuous: the aggregation of the individual decisions of voters in a general election determines which team of party leaders becomes the Government, and this makes the leaders responsive to opinion in its various manifestations, in the parties, pressure groups, the press, and public opinion polls; but the electorate, *qua* electorate, is in no significant sense the ultimate source of the content of the laws. In the British political system with its two highly disciplined parties, the victory of one of them in a general election gives to its leaders governmental authority without formal limit. Its exercise is tempered by thoughts of the next free election.

---

7. 10th ed. London, Macmillan, 1959, pp. 39–40.
8. P. 429.

But the prior question is why in their relations with each other the Government and the Opposition behave so that the Government allows the next election to be free, or rather why that question does not overtly arise in British politics.

Under a constitution that permits the Government always to get its own way, the Opposition is not protected by any institutional arrangements of the state. But the legitimacy of opposition is incorporated in the structure of constitutional conventions and understandings, so that the conditions preserving legitimate opposition are in Great Britain the conditions preserving its constitution.

> We may say [Dicey wrote] that the constitution is pervaded by the rule of law on the ground that the general principles of the constitution (as for example the right to personal liberty, or the right of public meeting) are with us the* result of judicial decisions determining the rights of private persons in particular cases brought before the courts; whereas under many foreign constitutions the security (such as it is) given to the rights of individuals results, or appears to result, from the general principles of the constitution.[9]

As Dicey's examples indicate, the rights of private persons under the "rule of law" are essential to legitimate opposition. Dicey has been correctly criticized for attempting to derive the constitution from ordinary law, but he was fundamentally right in perceiving that no constitution is less a creator and more a creation of the arrangements it regulates than the British.

THE PARTY SYSTEM   That description of the constitutional position discounts the capacity of the House of Commons to check the actions of the Government, except insofar as the House is one of the media and sources of opinion to which the political leaders, in a system of free elections and competitive parties, respond. When its members belong to two disciplined parties, with too few M.P.'s outside them to hold the balance and with such dissident members of the main parties as there are usually on the extreme wings, and therefore more in disagreement with the other party than with their own, the House is not an independent factor in determining who governs and how. For that—for it to be the case that in bestowing its confidence in a Government the House "assumes the initiative, and acts upon its discretion or its caprice"—there must be a center element of independent and independent-minded members—as there was when Bagehot wrote the quoted words.[10]

It has been said that the Church of England is rightly named because it

9. Pp. 195–96.
10. *The English Constitution*, p. 151.

is the church that most Englishmen stay away from; likewise, even since the 1860s, the British two-party system has been the system from which the British have more often than not departed. The Liberal Unionists for two decades after 1885, the Irish Nationalists from 1874 to 1918, the independent Labor Party from 1906 to after the First World War, and the Liberals from then to near the end of the interwar period, provided elements of confusion in a parliamentary system whose conventions were increasingly institutionalizing the contest between the two front benches of the Government and the official opposition. But the Liberal Unionists soon were a few political leaders without independent voting support; and, like the Liberal Nationals (later National Liberals) who allied themselves to the Conservatives from 1931, became part of the Conservative side with little more than the pretence of independence. The Irish Nationalists provided the only parliamentary opposition of any significance that was unwilling to operate the British parliamentary system and, except for a couple of members among the representatives of Northern Ireland, were eliminated from the British Parliament by the establishment of the Irish Free State. The split in the Liberal Party in 1916 enabled the Labor Party to become the second party of the country by 1922, though it took another decade, during which there were two minority Labor governments, to settle that the only alternative governing party to the Conservatives was Labor. Once that was settled, any real resemblance to a three-party system came to an end.

The two-party system is the system to which the British return, and with which they have abided, in general elections, since the Second World War—as the table indicating the results of the elections from 1945 to 1964 shows. The increase in the Liberal percentage of the total vote in each of the last two general elections was largely accounted for by the increase in the number of Liberal candidates, of whom there were 110 in 1955, 216 in 1959, and 365 in 1964. However, the average Liberal vote as a percentage of the vote cast in the constituencies in which Liberal candidates stood rose from 15.1 per cent in 1955, to 16.9 per cent in 1959, and to 18.5 per cent in 1964 (just short of the 18.6 per cent of 1945).

The electoral system of single-member constituencies electing by simple majority favors a two-party system. The Representation of the People Act of 1918 introduced the requirement of a £150 electoral deposit, forfeited by all candidates failing to receive one-eighth of the votes cast in a constituency, in order to discourage "freak" candidacies. The average cost of contesting a constituency is a good deal higher than the amount of the deposit. The greatest financial problem of smaller parties is to raise funds for matching the services of the central party organizations of the major parties, especially the Conservative Party, which now include expensive advertising campaigns between elections that, unlike electioneering activities in the constituencies, are not subject to any legal limit as to the amount of money spent on them.

	General Election 1945		General Election 1950		General Election 1951	
	% of M.P.'s elected (640)	% of total vote (25.1 million)	% of M.P.'s elected (625)	% of total vote (28.8 million)	% of M.P.'s elected (625)	% of total vote (28.6 million)
Labor	61.4	47.8	50.4	46.1	47.2	48.8
Conservative	33.3	39.8	47.7	43.5	51.4	48.0
Two-party total	94.7	87.6	98.1	89.6	98.6	96.8
Liberal	1.9	9.0	1.4	9.1	1.0	2.5
Communist	0.3	0.4		0.3		0.1
Other	3.1	3.0	0.5	1.0	0.5	0.6

	General Election 1955		General Election 1959		General Election 1964	
	% of M.P.'s elected (630)	% of total vote (26.8 million)	% of M.P.'s elected (630)	% of total vote (27.9 million)	% of M.P.'s elected (630)	% of total vote (27.7 million)
Labor	43.9	46.4	40.9	43.8	50.3	44.1
Conservative	54.6	49.7	57.9	49.4	48.3	43.4
Two-party total	98.5	96.1	98.9	93.2	98.6	87.6
Liberal	1.0	2.7	1.0	5.9	1.4	11.2
Communist		0.1		0.1		0.2
Other	0.5	1.1	0.2	0.8		1.1

Besides the conservatism of party loyalties, the emphasis on choosing a Government in a general election buttresses the position of the existing major parties. The evidence for this lies not only in the way election campaigns are conducted, but also in the differences in voting behavior between general elections and by-elections, when non-major-party candidates often do comparatively well, and in the results of public opinion polls that compare how electors intend to vote in the next general election with how they would vote if "the Liberals had a chance." It is reasonable, therefore, to surmise that if the Liberals were thought to have gained a chance, the electoral system would aid and accelerate a shift of support to that party, but it has in the existing circumstances acted as a brake on the "Liberal revival."

Television is now the chief medium of mass communication and, unlike the press, subject to stringent regulation in party political matters. Both the British Broadcasting Corporation and the commercial Independent Television service are charged with maintaining political impartiality in their programming, and the latter cannot accept political advertisements of any kind. The services provide free facilities for a limited number of party political broadcasts, which are entirely under the control of the parties giving them. For 1965 the television allocation is five programs totaling 60 minutes to each of the two major parties, two programs totaling 20 minutes to the Liberal Party, and one five-minute program apiece to the Scottish National Party and the Welsh Nationalists. This is the first time that others than the three main parties have shared in the annual allocation. During the 1964 general election period the Conservative and Labor parties each had five programs of 15 minutes apiece and the Liberal Party three. There are similar arrangements for sound programs on the B.B.C. Since 1949 it has been agreed by the party managers of the three leading parties, who work out the arrangements with the broadcasting authorities, that any other party running 50 candidates qualifies for an election broadcast. In 1950 the Communist Party ran 100 candidates and was allotted one ten-minute sound program, at a time when there was no television electioneering. No party has qualified in that way since.

Until the advent of commercial television as provided for in the Television Act of 1954 led to a competition for audiences, a blackout had been imposed on news and comment about election campaign activities, apart from the party political broadcasts. It was ended by a commercial company during a by-election in 1958. There is now a good deal of coverage, though the broadcasting services must do nothing to promote the election of particular candidates. Between general elections the chief political beneficiaries of the change have so far undoubtedly been the Liberals, whose by-election candidates are treated on a par with those of the two major parties, and whose by-election gains have been well publicized. In general elections they and to some extent the small parties have been represented, along with the two main parties, on discussion programs put out by the broadcasting bodies. But the inevitable consequence of unbiased reporting of general election campaigns is on balance to call more attention to and thereby reinforce the tendency to reduce a general election to the contest for office between the leaders of the two main political parties.

The inertia of the present two-party system is large. But its continuance is conditional on the absence of strong and diverse political passions, which would burst out of a system that treats the political attitudes of electors as constituting a single linear distribution with the two parties competing for the "floating voters" at the mean point of the distribution: "offering bait to the same fish." [11] There seems little likelihood of a change in this respect. The system also assumes the occasional alternation of the

11. W. Ivor Jennings, *The British Constitution* (Cambridge, Cambridge University Press, 1946), p. 50. Cf. D. E. Butler and Anthony King, *The British General Election of 1964* (London, Macmillan, 1965), p. 54.

parties in office. After the third successive Conservative victory in 1959, it was fashionable to ask whether in the existing two-party alignment the Labor Party could ever win power again. But the Labor victory in 1964 and its narrowness ensure the continuance and probably the intensification in the immediate future of the present two-party contest.

The variations in the two-party system during the last hundred years ought not to obscure the fundamental and permanent change that took place in the latter part of the nineteenth century with respect to the influence of party on parliamentary voting. After 1832 the Government sought increasingly to guide the House: in 1836, the first year in which division lists were printed, Government whips acted as tellers on less than half the divisions, from 1851 to 1860 on seven-tenths, and in 1894 on nearly nine-tenths. But the percentage of divisions on which nine-tenths of the Conservative members who voted went into the same lobby was 56 per cent in 1836 and only 31 per cent in 1860; for members of the Whig-Radical or Liberal Party the comparable figures were 40 in 1836 and 25 in 1860; and the percentage of divisions in which nine-tenths of the members of each of the parties who voted went into opposite lobbies was 23 per cent in 1836 and only 6 per cent in 1860. In 1871 the figures under all three headings were greater than in 1836; and in 1894 the percentage of divisions on which nine-tenths of the Conservative and Liberal Unionist members who voted went into the same lobby was 91 per cent, that for Liberals and the two groups of Irish Nationalists taken together was 81 per cent, and that for nine-tenths of the members of each of the parties who voted going into opposite lobbies was 76 per cent.[12] Divisions in the House of Commons had become occasions on which the Government and the Opposition deployed their parliamentary forces against each other, and the only development since has been to perfect and institutionalize the change.

When the two-party system is fully functioning (as it was not in the two world wars as well as the periods of minority Government), it is politically impossible to bring the Government down by adverse votes or abstentions in the House of Commons. Backbench pressure in the majority party may more or less successfully be brought to bear on the Government off the floor of the House, though less successfully if the Government is determined to resist it. This pressure may mount if the Government seems unpopular among its supporters or the voters in the country. But it is not a force for preserving the rights of the Opposition.

OPPOSITION WITH A CAPITAL "O"   Like cabinet government, the official opposition is part of the conventional British constitution. The Leader of the Opposition, like the Prime Minister, holds an office that arose out

12. A. Lawrence Lowell, "The Influence of Party upon Legislation in England and America," in *Annual Report of the American Historical Association for the Year 1901, 1* (Washington, 1902), 321–29.

of practice. His position has no official functions according to legislation or the rules of the House of Commons. The rights, privileges, and duties of Her Majesty's Opposition are subjects in which the ambiguities of constitutional interpretation, with its mixture of descriptive and prescriptive elements, cannot be resolved by recourse to courts of law.

That the official opposition has privileges is evident in the practice of the House of Commons. Thus a convention of more than 60 years' standing permits the Opposition to select the topics of debate on days allotted to the consideration of the Estimates and the bills by which they are finally authorized. In general the two front benches of Her Majesty's Government and Her Majesty's Opposition between them set the great majority of topics of parliamentary debate. The Government's legislative program perforce determines most of the broad subjects, but the leaders of the Opposition have the greatest influence in deciding what specifically to discuss. This is mainly at the expense of backbench members on the two sides. In relation to their small numbers in the House of Commons the members of any minor parties and "rebels" are given at least proportionate opportunities to express their points of view.

More and more, the Leader of the Opposition is treated in effect as Her Majesty's alternative prime minister, in public ceremonies and in private conversations with the Prime Minister on confidential matters, though it is constitutionally improper to describe him thus, since the choice of a new Prime Minister is the personal prerogative of the monarch. There is disagreement about how far the possible future position of the Leader of the Opposition casts its shadow before. Leaders of the Opposition are cautious about receiving the confidences of the Government, of which their backbenchers are naturally suspicious. It is argued that the leaders of the Opposition have responsibilities, not to damage the security of the state and other public interests in their criticism and to keep themselves informed as potential advisers of the queen, which require them to receive confidential information; but once they have received it, they are not in a position to dispute with the Government about the value of imparting it in the particular case. They sometimes refuse it, when it seems likely to be incompatible with the constitutional function of criticism and without compensating advantages for themselves or the public interest as they conceive it.

Generally, while recognizing that the Opposition has duties as well as rights and privileges, Leaders of the Opposition resist attempts to impose restraints on their conduct. Near the end of 1937, a Conservative M.P. put down a motion inviting the House to pass a vote of censure on the Labor Leader of the Opposition for speeches Attlee had made during a visit to the Spanish Republican government. Attlee made a personal statement in the House of Commons, in which he said in part:

In his Motion, the Hon. Member . . . has specifically referred to me as 'the Leader of His Majesty's Official Opposition,' and seems to imply that this places me in a special category. The Leader of the Opposition is a private Member. He owes no allegiance to the Government. No action of his can in any way implicate the Government. He is responsible only to his constituents and to the Members from whom he derives his position. He is, I think, under a special obligation to defend the rights and privileges of private Members, particularly the right of every Member to express his opinion freely on all matters of public policy.[13]

That was the end of the matter.

Her Majesty's Opposition is not a "licensed" opposition: the status of being the official opposition is not in the gift of the Government. The payment of a salary to its Leader necessitated a legal definition of his position, which appears in the Ministers of the Crown Act of 1937: " 'Leader of the Opposition' means that member of the House of Commons who is for the time being the Leader in that House of the party in opposition to His Majesty's Government having the greatest numerical strength in that House." [14] But on the formation in 1940 of Churchill's Coalition Government embracing the Conservative, Labor, and Liberal parties, leaving only the four Independent Labor Party members and one Communist M.P. outside the government supporters, the Speaker ruled that "it cannot be said that there is now an Opposition in Parliament in the hitherto accepted meaning of the words; namely, a party in Opposition to the Government from which an alternative Government could be formed." [15] The Prime Minister announced that the provision of the Ministers of the Crown Act relating to the payment of a salary to the Leader of the Opposition was in abeyance for the time being. The practice of the House of Commons required that someone act as Leader of the Opposition. Some of the older Labor leaders had been left out of the Government and were, in Attlee's words,

> available to lead the Party in the House. By tacit consent, first Lees Smith and, after his death, Pethick-Lawrence . . .—although both were wholehearted supporters of the Government—performed the duties of a Leader of the Opposition, asking questions as to the business of the House and so on. The Labor Party continued to sit on the Opposition benches. The Front Bench was filled by leading members of both Parties who were sometimes found in temporary alliance.[16]

Opposition with a capital "O" is provided by a party—or parties,

13. 330 H.C. Deb. 5s. 824.
14. 1 Edw. 8 & 1 Geo. 6c. 38, s. 10 (1).
15. 361 H.C. Deb. 5s. 27
16. *As It Happened* (London, Heinemann, 1954), p. 116.

though the conception fits more naturally in a two-party than a multi-party system—prepared to become the Government; and that entails a willingness to govern as well as to oppose which is, however, not a willingness to govern, or to oppose, too much. Her Majesty's Opposition as well as Her Majesty's Government behaves so as not to call into question the structure of constitutional conventions and understandings regulating their relationship. "What we mean by the 'Opposition,'" wrote Lord Campion, formerly Clerk to the House of Commons, "is the party for the time being in the minority, organized as a unit and officially recognized, which has had experience of office and is prepared to form a Government when the existing Ministry has lost the confidence of the country. It must have a positive policy of its own and not merely oppose destructively. . . . Our system, alone," he added with insular pride, "can produce a responsible Opposition, one with a consistent policy known to the country in broad outline, one which is not anxious to win at the expense of ruining the game." [17]

THE SOCIAL SETTING   Great Britain is a populous, highly urbanized, and mature industrial country, whose class structure relates to disparities of income and wealth and also, both reinforcing and modifying the influence of money, differences in education, occupation, ancestry, and behavior. Class differences are politically the most significant social cleavages in a society whose people have perhaps an even stronger sense of their homogeneity than the facts warrant. This unity is partly accounted for by the greater homogeneity among the leaders of opinion than among the population as a whole.

The population of Great Britain in 1961 was 51.3 million, of whom 43.4 million lived in England, 2.6 million in Wales and Monmouthshire, and 5.2 million in Scotland. Eighteen and seven-tenths million lived in Greater London and six other conurbations. That was a smaller proportion of the population than lived in them in 1901, but the urbanization of the countryside continues: the percentage of the total occupied population engaged in agriculture or fishing was 9 per cent in 1901 and 4 per cent in 1961.

Estimating the distribution of income and wealth is an undertaking of great difficulty; and the data on personal wealth, derived mainly from estate duty statistics, undoubtedly underestimate the concentration at the top, owing to the ease with which the tax may be avoided. Even so, "the concentration of ownership of capital is much greater than the concentration of income. Out of total real disposable income the top one per cent of income units received in 1954 only about 7 per cent; out of total

17. "Developments in the Parliamentary System Since 1918," in *British Government Since 1918* (London, Allen and Unwin, 1950), p. 19.

personal net capital (excluding pension and trust funds) the top one per cent of persons aged 20 and over in 1954 owned 43 per cent. Wealth is much more unequally distributed in Britain than in the United States." [18]

To give a very rough idea of the educational situation in England and Wales in the late 1950s: of every 20 boys aged twelve, 19 were in state-supported schools, of whom 4 were in grammar schools providing the most academic education and the rest in schools from which the great majority left at fifteen. One of the 20 was in a "public" or other independent school. Not one in a hundred was in the 20 best-known public schools. One in 20 boys went on to a university. Oxford and Cambridge had more than a fifth of the university population, a quarter of the male and a tenth of the female full-time students. At least two-fifths of their intake were from the public schools.

Less than one per cent of the population have gone to one of the leading public schools or to Oxford or Cambridge. But social analysis of the top people in the City, in the Foreign Service, in the armed services, on the Bench, or in the Church shows that a majority of them have been educated at the leading public schools; and if they have attended an English university, it has almost invariably been Oxford or Cambridge.[19] Studies of managers and directors of larger public companies indicate that a third to a half have been to a public school, and "the advantages of being an old Etonian become more marked the higher up you go." [20] A large proportion of top managers have not attended a university, but recruitment by industry from the public schools and Oxford and Cambridge is increasing. A study of senior civil servants in 1958 showed that one-fifth had been educated at six leading public schools and two-thirds at Oxford or Cambridge.

Of 304 Conservative M.P.'s elected in 1964, 68 had been to Eton, 17 to Harrow, 12 to Winchester, and 132 to other public schools. Of 317 Labor M.P.'s, 2 had been to Eton, 2 to Winchester, and 52 to other public schools. Of the 192 Conservative members who had been to a university, 159 had been to Oxford or Cambridge. Of the 134 Labor members who had been to a university, 60 had been to Oxford or Cambridge.[21] In 1961 more than one-third of the incumbent Conservative ministers had been to Eton and Harrow, and two-fifths to other public schools. Of 34 Labor

18. H. F. Lydall and D. G. Tipping, "The Distribution of Personal Wealth in Britain," *Bulletin of the Oxford University Institute of Statistics, 13* (1961), 97. Cf. Richard M. Titmuss, *Income Distribution and Social Change* (London, Allen and Unwin, 1962).
19. There is a summary table with bibliographic references in W. L. Guttsman, *The British Political Elite* (London, Macgibbon and Kee, 1963), pp. 336–37.
20. Roy Lewis and Rosemary Stewart, *The Boss* (London, Phoenix House, 1958), p. 96.
21. Butler and King, *The British General Election of 1964,* p 237.

ministers who served in cabinets between 1916 and 1931, 6 had been to
public schools; of 34 who served between 1940 and 1951, 11 had been;
and of 23 entering the cabinet formed in October 1964, 8 had been. Of
Conservative ministers who have been university graduates, the overwhelming majority have always gone to Oxford or Cambridge Of Labor
ministers who served in cabinets between 1916 and 1931, 7 had been to
Oxford or Cambridge, 7 to other universities, and 20 to none; of those
who served between 1940 and 1951, 11 had been to Oxford or Cambridge,
6 to other universities, and 17 to none; [22] and of those entering the cabinet
formed in October 1964, 11 had been to Oxford, 1 to Durham, 1 to
Glasgow, and 10 to no university. By far the larger number of editors of
the quality national newspapers and periodicals, "the governors of culture
and the arts," [23] the leading satirists of "the Establishment" as well as the
leading members of it, if they have been to a university (and most of
them have), have been to Oxford or Cambridge.

Education, it seems, largely determines occupation and the chances of
success in it; but the occupation of parents tends to determine the education of their children even in the state system of free schools and free
places. In the generation educated in English schools after the Second
World War, fewer than one-sixteenth of the children admitted to grammar schools were children of unskilled manual workers, though one-eighth
of men aged 20–64 were such workers; and, while seven-tenths of men
aged 20–64 were manual workers of all kinds, their sons constituted only
half that fraction of the male entry to British universities from grammar
schools and only about a quarter of the total male entry. Among university entrants from grammar schools there were 62 children from white-
collar (professional, managerial, and clerical) homes for every child of
an unskilled manual worker. The state system, however, provides for
much greater social mobility than the independent system, which is most
closed at the top. Three-fifths of Etonians are sons of Old Etonians, and
the remainder are practically indistinguishable from them. Fewer than
an eighth of the male entrants to Oxford and Cambridge universities are
sons of manual workers.

Thus continues the process by which social mobility at the top of
British society is more or less contained within the established social
hierarchy. In the nineteenth century the landed aristocracy lost its economic dominance. There was a formal transfer of ultimate political power
to first the middle-class and then the working-class electorate. But the
landed aristocracy retained a large measure of its social leadership; and it
joined with the plutocracy in an alliance of old families and new wealth
to form a "governing class," set apart from "the masses" by ancestry,

22. Guttsman, *The British Political Elite*, pp. 313, 244, 103, 106.
23. Ibid., p. 346.

education, and affluence, and knit together by family and marriage connections, the leading public schools, Oxford and Cambridge, and continual contacts among its members. In this century the governing class has become looser and its social influence less pervasive: "the hereditary Establishment of interlocking families, which still has an infectious social and political influence on the Conservative party, banking and many industries, has lost touch with the new worlds of science, industrial management and technology." [24] It has never been a "power elite" organized to overcome the opposition of the rest of the population, but its members have on the whole had the greatest access to and command of what the British by their strivings define as the good things of life. When the process of absorbing new elements has worked smoothly, the standards of behavior of the established gentlemen have predominated; when it has not, the standards have succumbed to the pursuit of money and pleasure.

Throughout the period of mass party politics the bulk of the governing class have been in the Conservative Party and most working-class electors have usually voted against Conservative candidates. The middle classes were divided more evenly and less certainly between the Conservatives and Liberals, but have always been predominantly anti-Labor. Concerning recent years "all the published studies of British voting behavior support the same general conclusion: that the way a British elector votes is closely related to his social and occupational status and, more particularly, to the way in which he sees his own status." [25] In the 1950s the two-party vote of the manual working classes divided between 2 to 1 and 3 to 2 in favor of the Labor party; the two-party vote of the classes above them taken as a whole divided about 4 to 1, and that of the upper class overwhelmingly, in favor of the Conservative Party, with a shift in general toward the latter. This meant that about half the Conservative vote and about four-fifths of the Labor vote came from the manual working classes.

The social cleavage between the two parties can be traced from top to bottom, with manual workers disappearing from the Conservative Party before the top and being present in varying proportions at different levels of the Labor Party, though most preponderantly at the bottom. There are few manual workers among Conservative constituency party leaders and only two among the 304 Conservative M.P.'s elected in 1964, assessing the latter by their first or formative occupations. Manual workers are a smaller proportion of Labor constituency party leaders than of Labor voters. In 1918 they were over nine-tenths of 61 Labor and Co-

24. Anthony Sampson, *Anatomy of Britain* (London, Hodder and Stoughton, 1962), p. 632.
25. Graeme C. Moodie, *The Government of Great Britain* (New York, Crowell, 1961), p. 61.

operative M.P.'s elected, in 1935 nearly two-thirds of 154, and in 1964 a
little under one-third of 317. The great majority of them have always
been the "sponsored" candidates of trade unions affiliated to the Labor
Party. Officials of the working-class movement—trade unions, consumer
cooperatives, and the Labor Party organization—made up about half the
membership of every Labor cabinet before 1964, the rest of whose members, with a single exception in each of two cabinets, had come into
politics from non-working-class occupations and in the great majority of
cases non-working-class backgrounds.[26] Of the 23 members of the cabinet formed in 1964, 9 were from the trade union movement.

Other social differences are much less determinant of variations in
voting behavior. There is, however, an intrusion into a few localities of
Great Britain of the division—still exacerbating the politics of Northern
Ireland—between Irish Catholics and Orangemen among working-class
voters, the first being more Labor, the second less so, than the working
classes as a whole. In some places, too, Anglican working-class voters are
more Conservative than are non-conformists; and in the House of Commons after the 1964 election there were 30 known Jews and 47 known
nonconformists among 317 Labor M.P.'s as compared with 2 and 6 respectively among 304 Conservatives.

Only about a tenth of the adult population are Roman Catholics. Present
estimates put the number of colored people in Britain at between 750,000
and 1,000,000 (less than 2 per cent of the population). The Commonwealth Immigrants Act of 1962 was passed to check their influx. The
great majority of the British are of white Protestant stock. They set the
tone of British politics and life. The differences among them, of religious
belief and indifference, of regional or national sentiment associated with
the North or South of England, with Scotland, or with Wales, are not
only less important politically than what unites them but also less important than what otherwise divides them—class.

OPPOSITION WITH A LITTLE "o"   Mass political organization in Great
Britain first developed outside the parliamentary system. That was necessarily so at a time when the great majority of the masses were without
the vote. The Catholic Association founded by Daniel O'Connell in
Ireland as part of a campaign for Catholic Emancipation (which was
conceded in 1829) and Home Rule was the model for Thomas Attwood's
Political Union agitating for parliamentary reform. In the 1830s and '40s
the working-class Chartist movement failed to secure universal manhood
suffrage, annual parliaments, and the secret ballot. But the middle-class
Anti-Corn Law League led by Manchester men organized opinion so
successfully that its structure and methods were later adopted by the
political parties.

26. Guttsman, *The British Political Elite*, p. 242.

The Birmingham Liberal "caucus" proved the most effective device for organizing the enlarged electorate created by the Second Reform Acts; and in 1877 Joseph Chamberlain's supporters formed the National Liberal Federation of local associations to bring advanced Radical opinion in the country to bear on the parliamentary Liberal Party. Birmingham, with its small workshops making for less of a division between masters and operatives than the large factories of the cotton district around Manchester, was the natural center of the new Radicalism seeking to bring together the middle- and working-class electors of the industrial towns for—in Chamberlain's words—"the politics of the future . . . social politics." [27] Although the Federation was incorporated in the official party machinery after Chamberlain left the Liberals over Home Rule, it continued to reflect the opinions of militant Liberals in the constituencies. From 1867 the Conservative Party provided its constituency organizations with a National Union, which apart from a brief period in the 1880s, when Lord Randolph Churchill used it to further his own ambitions, has never played an important part in the counsels of the party.

At the turn of the century, trade unions were persuaded to join a simple organization for putting independent Labor representatives in Parliament. In 1918 the Labor Party outside Parliament was transformed into a national party of affiliated trade unions and individual members. The trade unions have always had a great majority of the votes at the extraparliamentary Labor Party conference, at which the individual members are represented through the constituency parties. But the notion, derived in part from the former necessity to organize working-class opinion outside the parliamentary system, that the party conference should guide the parliamentary Labor Party succumbed to the tradition, also coming from the time when the masses were beyond the pale of the constitution, that extraparliamentary efforts to instruct or coerce M.P.'s are unconstitutional. It is persuasively argued that in representing the electorate members of Parliament and the Government must not submit to the orders of any outside body, which however representative of its party cannot be so representative of the country as Parliament itself. On both the Conservative and Labor sides "the mass parties are primarily the servants of their respective parliamentary parties." [28]

During the last hundred years there has been an enormous increase in the number of bodies in the country organizing sectional interests and promoting causes. But the trend has been to separate the activities of these bodies as political pressure groups from party politics. Most of them maintain strict impartiality.

27. Donald Read, *The English Provinces c. 1760–1960* (London, Arnold, 1964), p. 181.

28. R. T. McKenzie, *British Political Parties* (2nd ed. London, Heinemann, 1964), p. 647.

The business community is closely identified with the Conservatives, but trade associations consult and bargain with any Government on behalf of their industries. They oppose any Labor proposals to nationalize their industries, but they insist that the opposition, which may take the form of extensive and expensive advertising campaigns asking electors to reject nationalization at the next election, is aimed only at the proposals. The connections between the trade unions and the Labor Party are more formal than those between business and the Conservative Party, but the trade unions likewise (and increasingly) insist that their prime function is to protect their members' interests under any Government. "It is our long standing practice," stated the General Council of the Trades Union Congress when the Conservatives were returned to office in 1951, "to seek to work amicably with whatever Government is in power. . . . On our part we shall continue to examine every question solely in the light of its industrial and economic implications." [29]

The system of disciplined political parties occasionally alternating in power deters groups whose concerns are mainly "defensive" from committing themselves wholly to one party, because if they do they are bound at some time to lose. Because the constitutional authority of a Government with a parliamentary majority is unlimited, groups behave so as not to invoke its full exercise against them; and this tends to remove much of the activity shaping public policy from electoral politics. It may be argued in any case, as it was by the Webbs about the time of the First World War and as it has been by many political commentators in recent years, that governmental policy is the resultant of a continuous political process only marginally affected by "who loses and who wins; who's in, who's out." This is a valuable corrective to the "mandate" theory of British politics which describes governmental policy as the direct result of the electorate's choice between alternatives.

But the argument should not be pushed too far. The ways in which groups press and persuade take into account that the Government wants to be popular and successful at the next general election. That the great majority of them forbear from intervening openly in the choice of a Government is to make a virtue of necessity. At close hand who's in, who's out often seems to matter, especially on questions of major importance, about which ministers may be reluctant, for various political, administrative, or diplomatic reasons, to consult outside bodies in advance of announcing their policies. "The result of all this," Sir Raymond Streat, a leading spokesman of the cotton textile industry for over a quarter of a century, pointed out, "is that new departures of a major kind are often made with little consultation whereas new departures of a minor and non-

29. *Report of the 84th Annual Congress* (London, Trades Union Congress, 1952), p. 300.

controversial type can be the subject of extremely detailed and adequate inquiry and consultation. This is a rather ironical consequence of government by politicians but it is hard to see how to avoid it." [30]

There is virtually no opposition in Britain with a little "o," in the sense of organized activity outside the parliamentary party system aimed at displacing the holders of governmental power. The last agitation by and on behalf of those without the vote was the woman suffrage movement. The only mass agitations against parliamentary authority to achieve any success among the enfranchised were those in Ireland, South and North, prior to the granting of Home Rule. There was a syndicalist strain in the trade union movement in the second decade of this century, and in 1920 the labor movement's threat of strike action to stop British intervention against the Russian Soviet government was effectual in a nation weary for peace. But the General Strike of 1926 was considered by the General Council of the T.U.C. to be for an industrial end: to resist the proposed worsening of miners' wages or hours. Neither the trade union leaders nor the Labor Party ever contemplated using the General Strike to displace the Government. There is not the slightest chance that direct-action nuclear disarmers, Trotskyists, or those few Scottish and Welsh nationalists prepared to use direct action will overturn the central government or achieve regional independence by either civil disobedience or force. Opposition in Great Britain, as well as government, is by politicians, offering an alternative government in accordance with the conventions of the parliamentary system—opposition with a capital "O."

The Conditions

THE CONSTITUTION IN PERIL   The one time in the last hundred years when the constitutional structure of conventions and understandings seemed in peril was just before the First World War. There was a series of constitutional crises, over the budget of 1909, the Parliament Bill, and Irish Home Rule. There was recourse to direct action by suffragettes in the woman suffrage movement, syndicalists in the trade union movement, and, above all, in Ireland where the crisis over Home Rule appeared to be leading to a civil war in Ulster.

By the beginning of this century the landed interest was breaking up and the national landed aristocracy merging with the capitalist plutocracy. "The apparently stable Edwardian society had in fact resolved upon a social revolution, the liquidation of the landed interest, whose full accomplishment was but deferred by the First World War." [31] Among "the

30. "Government Consultation with Industry," *Public Administration*, 37 (1959), 5–6.

31. F. M. L. Thompson, *English Landed Society in the Nineteenth Century* (London, Routledge, 1963), p. 326.

classes" accepted social distinctions were sapped by the influence of money. The result was class bitterness among all strata of society, but also an assimilation of the interests of the old and newer sources of great wealth. Among "the masses" the notion of the "laboring classes" or "working classes" in the plural tended in the last quarter of the nineteenth century to yield to the concept of a single "working class." "The Education Act of 1870 tended to separate the population more clearly into those who were educated at their parents' expense and those who went to the 'Board' schools or the church schools; nearly all the manual workers fell into the latter category." [32] Changes in industry and the new unionism of the 1880s among the unskilled also made for a more homogeneous industrial class.

In politics, the Whig landed families had been leaving the Liberal Party in reaction against concessions to Radicalism before 1885, when Gladstone's adoption of the policy of Home Rule for Ireland made their secession almost complete. The Liberal Government of 1886 was turned out of office on that issue; the Liberal Governments of 1892–95 were too weak and divided to fight the House of Lords, which rejected a Home Rule Bill in 1893 by a majority of 419 to 41; but the Liberal Government that won the general election of 1906 was strong. It was essentially a Government composed of the "educated and professional classes." For the first time the landed aristocracy might be effectually challenged by a Government in which it was not substantially represented. The Liberal politicians were, moreover, increasingly responsive to working-class claims, though they fought the 1906 election on other issues. Fifty-three Labor candidates were elected in 1906, 29 of them candidates of the Labor Representation Committee and the rest, 13 of whom were sponsored by the Miners Federation, more or less associated with the Liberal Party. A secret agreement between L.R.C. and Liberal leaders had also freed the great majority of the independent 29 from direct Liberal opposition.

In the eighteenth century "governmental power was never used to challenge the natural social order, in which family, property, rank and intelligence were the attributes which counted." In the absence of any apparatus of centralized administration the country was governed "not by 'politicians' or by a civil service, but by a miscellaneous collection of unpaid local authorities, all of which, efficient or inefficient, gave a paramount place to rank and property. Indeed it was rank and property which conferred authority and not the other way round." [33] In the course of the nineteenth century the apparatus of professional government was formed. By the turn of the century the administrators recruited from the reformed

32. Henry Pelling, *A Short History of the Labour Party* (London, Macmillan, 1961), p. 2.
33. Briggs, *The Age of Improvement*, p. 100.

universities as the result of Gladstone's reorganization of the civil service
in 1870 were reaching the top, and the importance of the central departments in the governmental process began to be recognized. In the country
the County Councils Act of 1888 brought to an end the rule of the justices
of the peace. It was now conceivable that a Government not representative
of the governing class might govern in opposition to the natural social
order. This was, however, a conception that the representatives of the
governing class were reluctant to accept. In an election speech in 1906,
A. J. Balfour, the Leader of the Unionist (Conservative) Party, declared
that it was the duty of everyone to see that "the great Unionist party
should still control, whether in power or whether in Opposition, the
destinies of this great Empire." [34]

The Lloyd George budget of 1909, a revolutionary departure from
Gladstonian public finance, epitomized the use of the ordinary operations
of government to attack the natural social order. For faced with the need
to raise more money, the Chancellor of the Exchequer proposed, among
other things, increases in death duties, more graduation of the income tax,
and the introduction of land taxes, of which the most spectacular was a
duty of 20 per cent on the unearned increment of value when land changed
hands. The Lords, many of whom were substantial landowners, rejected
the budget in a constitutionally questionable exercise of their legally equal
legislative power with the Commons, thereby putting themselves clearly
in opposition not only to the Irish but also to "the people." After a general
election in January 1910 the Government introduced a Parliament Bill to
remove the veto power of the Lords over money bills and to reduce it over
other legislation to a power to delay for two years. After a second general
election in December it was made known that the King had promised
Asquith, the Prime Minister, that he would create enough peers to ensure
the enactment of the Parliament Bill. Under that threat the Lords accepted
the Bill in August 1911 by a majority of 131 to 114. "The division lists
show most strikingly how complete had been the desertion of the Whigs":
"for the first time in the advance to political democracy . . . there was
hardly a patrician who would aid the process." [35]

From 1910 the Liberal Government was dependent on the Irish Nationalists in the House of Commons for its parliamentary majority. In the
December election the Liberals and Conservatives each won 272 seats. The
Labor Party (which the miners had joined in 1909) won 42 and the Irish
Nationalists 84. The Nationalists were resolved upon securing Home Rule
for a united Ireland. But the Protestants of Ulster were at least equally
determined that Home Rule would not mean "Rome rule" from Dublin
for them. This conflict between the Catholic and Protestant peoples of

34. Roy Jenkins, *Mr. Balfour's Poodle* (London, Heinemann, 1954), pp. 18–19.
35. Ibid., pp. 183–84.

Ireland was too intense to be contained within the conventions of the British constitution. It also had ominous repercussions in British society as a whole.

"I can imagine no length of resistance to which Ulster will go," Bonar Law, who had succeeded Balfour as Leader of the Conservative Party in the House of Commons and who was himself the son of an Ulsterman, declared publicly in July 1912, "which I shall not be ready to support and in which they will not be supported by an overwhelming majority of the British people." [36] In November he wrote to the King's Private Secretary that the results of the Government's policy would be the coercion of Ulster, civil war, and a situation in which the position of the Crown would be made impossible. "Well, if it is in our power to prevent it," he explained, "we shall not permit this; and sooner or later, if the tension does not come to an end in some other way, we shall have to decide between breaking the Parliamentary machine and allowing these terrible results to happen. When faced with the choice of such evils as these, we shall not, I think, hesitate in considering that the injury to the House of Commons is not so great an evil as the other." [37]

In 1914 the Conservative leaders considered amending in the House of Lords the annual Mutiny Act, the palladium of the subordination of military power to parliamentary authority, so as to prevent the use of the army against Ulster. Bonar Law had decided against that, when the Curragh incident in March made it unnecessary. General Sir Arthur Paget, the Commander-in-Chief in Ireland, upon being ordered to concentrate his troops in Ulster, extracted from the War Office permission to tell his officers who were Ulstermen that they would be allowed to "disappear" from Ireland and his other officers that they could elect to be dismissed from the service. Fifty-seven of 70 officers of the 3rd Cavalry Brigade, stationed at the Curragh, chose dismissal rather than accept orders that might involve the initiation of military operations against Ulster. This, to say the least, cast doubt on the readiness of the army to coerce Ulster, while Orangemen prepared to fight. What the consequences of provoking them would have been for British politics, had not the First World War led to the postponement of Irish self-government to a time when the Ulster claim was met, can only remain a matter of conjecture.

The Irish question was *sui generis* in modern British politics, but it is important to remember that it was not alone in giving rise to a constitutional crisis in the years just before the First World War, nor the only question to introduce an unaccustomed note of violence. The class cleavage both amplified and dampened the Irish crisis. Home Rule had always had class implications, with Irish landowners part of the United Kingdom

36. Harold Nicolson, *King George the Fifth* (London, Constable, 1952), p 199.
37. Ibid., p. 202.

landed interest. In the army "the class from which most officers came tended by 1914 to be overwhelmingly Conservative, whereas fifty or sixty years before it would probably have divided fairly evenly between Tory and Whig." [38] But if officers had little regard for, in a phrase reportedly used by General Paget in March 1914, "those dirty swine of politicians" in Asquith's Government, they were concerned for the natural social order. According to the major-general commanding the 5th Division in Ireland, Paget said that "it was reported by the Secret Service that great internal trouble was brewing in London, Liverpool, and other large towns, and that there was great anxiety on this score. I understood him to say that the Labour party was determined to make a big effort to advance their policy by taking advantage of the crisis." For the major-general, as for many other officers, the "king's order" was enough. But in succeeding in keeping most of his own officers from choosing dismissal he told them

> Logically, we Officers could not refuse to obey the present orders, and yet expect our men to obey orders when they, on strike duty for instance, were placed in difficulties similar to those now confronting us.
> I spoke of the far reaching consequences of a disruption of the Army. That the country without a disciplined and united Army would be at the mercy of the mob. I alluded to the probability of even bigger questions arising if the Army broke up, that the Monarchy, Society and Empire itself might be shattered. [39]

One of the considerations deterring Conservative leaders from amending the Mutiny Act was the dangerous precedent it might give in the event of labor unrest.

THE CONSTITUTION SECURE   In 1918 the Labor Party adopted a socialist program. In 1922 it replaced the Liberals as the second largest political party. In 1924, in a Parliament with 258 Conservative, 191 Labor, 159 Liberal, and 7 other M.P.'s, the Labor Party formed a minority Government with Liberal support. The King and the outgoing Conservative Prime Minister, Stanley Baldwin, who was not, however, consulted by the monarch as to who his successor should be, thought it desirable to give Labor a fair chance to learn the British way of governing. As Asquith, the Liberal Leader, pointed out, the Labor Government would be too weak without a majority in the House of Commons to introduce a socialist regime even if it wanted to. It lasted less than a year. The upper and middle classes were much more alarmed by the General Strike of 1926. On

38. Robert Blake, "Great Britain. The Crimean War to the First World War," in Michael Howard, ed., *Soldiers and Governments* (London, Eyre and Spottiswoode, 1957), p. 36.
39. A. P. Ryan, *Mutiny at the Curragh* (London, Macmillan, 1956), pp. 142, 137, 145–46.

May 3rd Prime Minister Baldwin told the House of Commons that the Government "found itself challenged with an alternative Government" and that the trade union leaders were "threatening the basis of ordered government, and going nearer to proclaiming civil war than we have been for centuries past." [40] On May 12th the King wrote in his diary that "the Government have remained firm & backed up by the people have won a great victory for law & order." [41]

The General Strike was a mistake, not a crime against constitutional government. The Labor movement focused its political efforts on increasing its parliamentary representation, and in 1929 the second minority Labor Government took office. In August 1931 it split under pressure from the City and American bankers to introduce drastic economies as a condition for receiving help to stop a run on sterling. The Prime Minister, Ramsay MacDonald, and a few of his colleagues joined Conservative and Liberal leaders in a "National" Government led by MacDonald and supported by the Conservative and Liberal parties. In October the new Government, in an unprincipled campaign for a "doctor's mandate," won an overwhelming victory at the polls which gave the Conservatives more than three-fourths of the seats in the House of Commons and disrupted the Labor parliamentary leadership still further.

After the events of 1931, it was not altogether implausible to argue, as Harold Laski did in his *Parliamentary Government in England* in 1938, that the propertied classes might use unconstitutional means to prevent a socialist Government with a majority from implementing its program. "What was possible over a relatively minor controversy like Ulster," he wrote, "is certainly not impossible over a major controversy like the foundations of the economic system." [42] The Labor Government of 1945, the first with a parliamentary majority, set about changing the economic system about as much as Laski seemed to have had in mind in 1938. But the constitutional conventions and understandings that he thought might be destroyed remained secure.

From the time when Labor leaders joined the Coalition Government of the First World War, the leaders of the party have sought to demonstrate their "fitness to govern" in the traditional manner. A second generation served in the Coalition Government of the Second World War. That was useful to a party whose continuity of leadership had been broken in 1931; and the experience gained enabled the Labor Government of 1945 to take over very much more smoothly than would otherwise have been the case. It also confirmed Labor's acceptance of the established ways of governing. Since these derive from an era when governing was the preserve of a small class, they tend to sustain elitist attitudes of which the governing class, as

40. 195 H.C. Deb. 5s. 70–71.
41. Nicolson, *King George the Fifth*, p. 420.
42. London, Allen and Unwin, 1938, p. 37.

the social elite, is inevitably a beneficiary, even though Labor Governments bring some people with other backgrounds into the governing circles. The traditional ways, for example, keep a great deal of information about the working of the decision-making processes from the wider public.

It is too simple to say that the Labor leaders have thus succumbed to the "aristocratic embrace." The Fabian strain of socialism has always been elitist: the "meritocracy" bestows social justice on the masses instead of teaching them to seek it for themselves. In this respect Fabianism has had an affinity with "Tory Democracy," in which the "aristocracy" is the counterpart of the "meritocracy." The convergence of the "political formulas" of the two parties is the ideological reflection of the fact that both the "meritocracy" and "aristocracy" are, increasingly, educated at Oxford and Cambridge.

Incorporating by far the greater part of the governing class, the Conservative Party tends to lay claim to rule as of right, and regards its periods in Opposition as contrary to the natural order of things. It tends, therefore, to be a more fractious Opposition than Labor, which accepts a decision of the mass electorate as conclusive on the question of who should govern. But the Conservatives opposed the Labor Government after the Second World War in a much milder fashion than they had opposed the Liberal Government before the First. During the Second War something like a socialist regime had come into being. There was a planned and controlled economy. Tax, rationing, labor, and other policies, together with full employment and inflation, produced a much greater measure of social equality. The parties were not far apart in principle about the need for social security, both major parties generally associating themselves with the plan of an eminent Liberal, Sir William Beveridge. The parties were not very far apart in practice about the need for the Government to reorganize the coal, rail, and utility industries; and the only nationalization measure of the Labor Government to which the Conservatives offered uncompromising opposition was that for the iron and steel industry.

Although attitudes toward economic planning and organization have shifted back and forth in the postwar years, the parties have generally moved in tandem. It was Harold Wilson who, as Labor President of the Board of Trade in 1948, lit the first "bonfire of controls." It was the Conservative Government of Harold Macmillan which set up the National Economic Development Council late in 1961. The nationalization issue now affects only a few industries. In the 1964 election Labor, Conservatives, and Liberals alike promised an expansion in public services based on greater economic growth to be achieved by "modernizing" Britain.

THE PLURALISTIC SOCIETY   In Great Britain a considerable concentration of economic and social privilege coexists with a mass electorate. Of the two major political parties, one is closely associated with the most privileged sections of the community and the other with the organized work-ing-class movement. The party that wins a general election obtains constitutional power without limit. Those points have been emphasized in this account because a class struggle for state power would end—in Laski's words—"the long habituation to peace which the party system has secured" the British people.[43]

The danger is now wholly illusory. The habituation to peaceful pro-cedures has been strengthened by further experience. The Irish settlement of 1921–22 left only class cleavages as a significant politically divisive force. Class distinctions, though still in many respects strongly felt, are much less raw than at the turn of the century. The condition of the people has been greatly improved since then and since Laski wrote *Parliamentary Govern-ment in England*. The British people are becoming more "middle class." The percentage of the occupied population engaged in manual work is falling at something like a rate of one-quarter of one per cent a year. Changes in consumption habits and self-images are assimilating large num-bers of manual workers to people in middle-class occupations. Because of its association with the organized working-class movement, the Labor Party has had difficulty in shifting its appeal from the "working-class" to the "classless" masses, though the Conservative Party lost the 1964 election through failing to continue to meet the rising expectations of the people. In the more fluid class structure neither party can afford to talk the political language of the 'thirties. There is also a growing awareness that the problem of political leadership is not simply to capture the "com-manding heights" of government but to make effective the social influence of political institutions.

A description of the British situation in terms of a class struggle for state power has always required qualifications. It is convenient in conclu-sion to indicate the general nature of the qualifications mainly by referring to present details. Together with the long habituation to peace, the quali-fications are the conditions preserving the British constitution: viz., there is not a sharply defined and unified class at the top of British society en-trenched against the mass electorate; the British political parties are not the agents of coherent bodies of interests and opinions; and the social power of British government is confined within the structure of a plural-istic society.

1. The landed aristocracy was not a class apart from others so much as the apex of a social order of extended families and connections cutting through the layers of society. It was always permeable to the heirs and heiresses and the opinions and interests of rising groups. Indefiniteness and flexibility are even more the characteristics of the broader governing class formed in the latter part of the last century. This is what makes

43. Ibid., p. 110.

serious discussion of "the Establishment" in Britain so difficult. If it is not equated with the hereditary but absorbent governing class, it is impossible to specify the attributes that distinguish its members from others except that they are at the top; but if it is equated with the governing class, there are many important people outside it. The widespread feeling in Great Britain that there is a single "Establishment" in positions of power is probably accounted for by the stable hierarchy of social prestige. The men of power are varied; but the "gentleman" is, for almost all of them, the exemplar—to be deferred to, imitated, or joined.

To say that there is a considerable concentration of economic and social privilege at the top of British society is not to say that the privileged groups are united. There are many diverse interests and real conflicts among them. A study of the "revolt" under a Conservative administration by the leaders of productive industry against the City's influence on national economic policy, which led eventually to the creation of the National Economic Development Council, would illuminate more of the inner workings of British capitalism than all the statistics of interlocking directorships in British finance and industry compiled by political sociologists and "New Left" polemicists.

2. The diversity of interests in the circles from which the Conservative Party draws its money, and with which its leaders have close personal connections, gives the leaders considerable freedom of action. So does the existence of the mass electorate. To win a general election the Conservative Party must be supported by the great majority of middle-class electors, and about half its vote must come from the working class. Rational policy requires concessions, and habit has taught the privileged classes reason. Dishing the Whigs and their successors is the oldest surviving Conservative principle.

The diversity of interests at the top is more than matched by the crosscurrents of opinions below. Members of both parties agree as to which occupational groups support each of the major parties, though the stereotypes regarding political allegiances are not always correct. The main conclusion to be drawn from studies of political attitudes "appears to be this: to the great mass of the British electorate, at all social levels, the party contest is seen primarily in terms of competition between two great classes of the population for material satisfactions." [44] But there are many working-class Conservatives. Studies of their attitudes indicate that they have tended to regard members of the governing class as the natural leaders of society, though this "deferential" support may be declining compared with support based on an assessment of Conservative performance in the national and for particular interests. Conservative values are indeed widely spread among working-class electors: many who vote

44. John Bonham, *The Middle Class Vote* (London, Faber, 1954), p. 94.

Labor are on many points more in agreement with Conservative than Labor Party positions.[45]

Studies of political opinions have indicated on the one hand that the ordinary members of each party disagree a great deal among themselves on political questions: "the Labour members, in particular, disagree with one another to such an extent that a common outlook on political issues can hardly be said to exist among them." [46] The studies have indicated on the other hand that "there is a broad measure of agreement on political matters among supporters of both parties" and that at least two-fifths of the supporters of both regard the other party as equally likely to deal satisfactorily with some important matters as the one they support.[47] A lot depends, however, on the questions in the sample surveys. When asked which party would do the best job for a particular class, the voters again refer to the stereotypes of party alignments, with a sizable fraction of Conservative working-class voters agreeing with Labor working-class voters that in terms of purely class interests the Labor Party would do best for the working class.

The attitudes of the electorate to the parties and the behavior of the parties toward the electorate reinforce each other in making partisanship in Britain more significant than in the United States, but about as moderate. A larger proportion of the supporters of each of the two main parties are harsh in their appraisals of voters for the other, as compared with Americans, but the majority of British party supporters who are indifferent to the marriage of a son or daughter across party lines is almost as overwhelming.[48] British party discipline makes differences in party programs usually seem more meaningful than in the United States. But in a two-party system in which there is habitually a large turnout in general elections, the parties are even more likely than those in the American two-party system, with its greater variations in turnout, to bid for floating voters between the parties with moderate appeals, instead of attempting to mobilize occasional voters on their extreme wings. There is some evidence to suggest that the parties' stereotypes of floating and occasional voters may be at least as incorrect as the voters' stereotypes of the parties' supporters. But erroneous beliefs of that kind can alter a situation so as to make them more correct.

3. In the past England lacked a centrally controlled police force and had a very small army. The eighteenth-century constitution was—in G. M.

45. Robert McKenzie and Allan Silver, "The Working-Class Tories," *The Observer* (September 6, 1964), p. 11.

46. A. H. Birch, *Small-Town Politics* (Oxford, Oxford University Press, 1959), p. 94.

47. Mark Abrams et al., *Must Labour Lose?* (London, Penguin, 1960), p. 19.

48. Gabriel A. Almond and Sidney Verba, *The Civic Culture* (Princeton, Princeton University Press, 1963), pp. 124–26, 135–36.

Trevelyan's phrase—"aristocracy tempered by rioting." [49] The police (and education) are still far from fully centralized, though the organized forces of the state are now adequate for imposing the Government's will as long as the forces remain loyal. But as a method of dealing with constitutional opposition that course is unthinkable among political leaders, who are not only imbued with British traditions but also well aware of the consequences of calling an army into politics.

In governing a modern industrial society, moreover, the administrative structure of the British state is hardly more than a shell, which would break if not supported by thousands of organizations—public bodies of all sorts, voluntary services, and affected interests. There are again "rules of the game," well understood by those who work them, which while recognizing that the Government always has the last word dispose it not to utter it as long as "there is not yet sufficient agreement among those concerned." [50] The formal authority to govern is unlimited. The effective power to manage is vitiated by the inadequacy of public administration for the task. The apparatus of professional government was developed in Britain without destroying the tradition that "public" arrangements are part of the natural social order rather than the function of "the state." The result is professional government without professionals: there is a distinct organization of full-time officials, and politics is also increasingly a profession, but administrative class civil servants as well as ministers are largely uneducated in fields directly related to the needs of running a modern industrial society. This "cult of the amateur" is currently a subject of controversy among those interested in public affairs. One of the arguments in defense of the present civil service is that its incompetence as an industrial management puts a limit on the potential tyranny of officials.

Any social and political system that is reasonably successful in meeting expectations tends to be self-sustaining. This means that the degree to which political power has been used consciously to mold society tends to define the limits of its exercise. In that sense the formal power of British government cannot be used instantly to make or prevent changes in the natural social order outside the broad limits set by the structure of that order and its development, in which the longer-term effect of governmental action is only one of the factors. Great Britain is, socially and politically, a pluralistic society, in which the government no more than any other group or institution is outside the interaction of social forces that constitute the society. British politics is by nature the politics of compromise.

49. *History of England* (London, Longmans, 1926), p. 533.
50. Words often used by ministers in Parliament. Allen Potter, *Organized Groups in British National Politics* (London, Faber, 1961), p. 233.

2

THE AMERICAN OPPOSITIONS: AFFIRMATION AND DENIAL

Robert A. Dahl

The normal pattern of oppositions in the United States is roughly this:

Oppositions seek limited *goals* that do not directly challenge the major institutions or the prevailing American system of beliefs.

Oppositions employ a wide variety of *strategies:* they combine a heavy emphasis on winning presidential and congressional elections with an equally heavy emphasis on bargaining, logrolling, and pressure-group activities in policy-making.

Oppositions are not usually very *distinctive;* they are not even clearly identifiable as oppositions; they melt into the system.

Oppositions are not combined into a single organization of high *cohesion;* they usually work through one or both major parties, each of which has rather low internal unity.

These two parties are highly *competitive* in national elections but in Congress members of different parties are both *competitive* and *cooperative.*

Oppositions try to gain their objectives by seeking out encounters with policy-makers at a great variety of official *sites*—bureaucratic, congressional, presidential, judicial, local, etc.

A distinctive, persistent, unified structural opposition scarcely exists in the United States. Overt and organized oppositions ordinarily affirm their support for the prevailing ideology and the basic social, economic, and political institutions; these oppositions concentrate on limited changes within the established framework of ideas and institutions. Oppositions, then, are typically opposed only to specific policies or the personnel of government. Thus it is nearly always impossible to refer precisely to "the" opposition, for the coalition that opposes the government on one matter may fall apart, or even govern, on another. To say where "the government" leaves off and "the opposition" begins is an exercise in metaphysics.

So far I have been speaking of "normal" oppositions. There are, however, other chapters in the story of oppositions in the United States. For example, groups opposed to existing policies and frustrated by their inability to achieve changes sometimes go beyond the conventional strategies of American politics: they defy national law, call the legitimacy of one or more major institutions into question, and even resort to individual or collective violence.

These oppositional groups shade off into an indeterminate collection of alienated Americans whose opposition is even more out of line with the pattern of normal opposition described a moment ago. Even if we put to one side the small radical or revolutionary parties and political movements that have existed from time to time on the fringes of American political life, commitment to the prevailing ideology and institutions among the general population is highly uneven. There are, and probably always have been, Americans who reject some or most of the key elements in the dominant ideology and some or most of the major institutions. The size and social content of this group probably varies from one generation to another. Since it is extremely difficult for these individuals and groups to express their opposition through the usual processes of American politics, they may either resort to other means or lapse into apathy and withdraw from politics. These Americans are the neglected side of the American political system.

To explain the normal pattern of opposition, and its dark underside, I propose to rely mainly on three sets of factors:

1. The characteristic pattern of consensus.
2. The characteristic pattern of cleavage.
3. The structure of government and politics.

Consensus

That American opinions tend to converge has been emphatically stressed by foreign observers ever since Tocqueville and Harriet Martineau visited the United States in the 1830s. If caution and even skepticism are justified in evaluating their assertions as to what Americans believe or once believed, it is nonetheless difficult to explain American politics without invoking the familiar proposition that a predominant number of Americans arrived fairly early in their national history at a rough concordance on attitudes on some important political questions—questions of a kind that have led to profound and enduring cleavages in other countries.

What usually strikes foreign observers is the extent to which Americans profess the virtues of a government ruled by the elected representatives of the people, that is, popular government or "democracy." Americans publicly disagree about liberty; they do not, in this strict sense, publicly disagree over "democracy." The question whether there might be alternatives open to Americans other than popular government was settled very early. When Hamilton stressed the virtues of monarchy at the Constitutional Convention of 1787 his views and proposals were looked on as irrelevant: not necessarily intrinsically wrong but simply irrelevant because so obviously unacceptable to the overwhelming majority of Americans. Federalists sometimes tried to accent the virtues of an aristocratic republic—but after 1800 they did so less and less frequently in public; and the demise of the Federalists as a party was a lesson to others. Consider the fate of John Adams, whose early works, "Defence of the Constitutions" and "Discourses on Davila," were widely interpreted (incorrectly, Adams later insisted) as defenses of monarchy and aristocracy. A dozen years after he had left the White House, Adams wrote to Jefferson, his old political enemy, now his personal friend: "In truth, my 'Defence of the Constitutions' and 'Discourses on Davila' were the cause of that immense unpopularity which fell like the tower of Siloam upon me. Your steady defence of democratical principles, and your invariable favorable opinion of the French Revolution, laid the foundations of your unbounded popularity."[1] Doubtless Adams exaggerated the effect of his writings, but there can be no doubt that his political opponents, the Republicans, hung his words about his neck like a millstone. Given his instructive example, no one seriously interested in a political career was likely thereafter to utter words—in public—that might be interpreted as favorable to any system other than popular government. Later, when the Whigs challenged Jackson's notions of presidential leadership, they did so in the name of popular government itself, and chose the very title of their party to emphasize the point.

If one excludes the Federalists (simply in order to ignore a controversial case that could not be analyzed properly in a few sentences), it is correct to say that no political party openly in favor of an alternative to popular government has ever elected a single representative to Congress or captured one electoral vote in a presidential election. Thus a question on which, in other countries, political elites and party followings have often generated opposition has been excluded in the United States.

Support for popular government was interwoven with support for specifically American forms of government. The tendency to identify republican government or, later, democracy with the particular American political system evidently developed quite early. Most of the men who attended the Constitutional Convention lived to see their patchwork of compromises, the American Constitution, become an object of veneration. Within a few years it had already become dangerous to attack the Constitution, perhaps even before it had become politically dangerous—and

1. Adams to Jefferson, July 13, 1813, quoted in Joseph Charles, *The Origins of the American Party System* (New York, Harper Torchbooks, 1956), p. 56.

futile—to attack popular government. An understanding quickly developed that all controversies, particularly constitutional controversies, must take for granted the overriding legitimacy of the Constitution and the superiority of American political institutions. Opposition groups were therefore restricted to changes that (so supporters would argue) were consistent with the Constitution. The view of the Massachusetts Antislavery Society and William Lloyd Garrison that the U.S. Constitution was "a covenant with death and an agreement with hell" was, even in the heat of the controversy over slavery, eccentric. Most opponents in this controversy assumed the legitimacy of the Constitution: the quarrel was over what the Constitution meant. Thus just as avowedly antidemocratic parties were effectively excluded from politics, so anticonstitutional parties also had little prospect of success.

Given the flexibility of the document and the political institutions it chartered, the worship of the Constitution was less restrictive than foreigners who encountered that fetish might suppose. Indeed one could even advocate changes in the Constitution itself provided these were shown to be in harmony with the principal institutions it established. The main outlines of the constitutional system and the principle that changes, including of course, changes in the Constitution, must take place within the limits of that framework, thus set imprecise but nonetheless important boundaries to the goals and strategies of the opposition groups.

The proposition that support for popular government, for the constitutional system, and for constitutional rather than revolutionary change has been widespread among Americans since the 1830s is about as reliable as any we are likely to get from historical evidence about attitudes. Two things seem reasonably certain: First, political leaders came to believe that they could not win elections without giving at least lip service to popular government, the Constitution, and constitutional change; second, opposition to these principles did not in fact flourish.

In the third place, there is the complex matter of American beliefs about "equality." Although the evidence for a wide commitment to "equality" is impressive, the nature and bounds of that commitment cannot be precisely described, for there were (and are) too many variations on the theme. The notes from Tocqueville's journey to America contain a record of his conversation with John Quincy Adams in which the former President remarked:

> Slavery has altered the whole state of society in the South. There the whites form a class to themselves which has all the ideas, all the passions, all the prejudices of an aristocracy, but do not be mistaken, nowhere is equality between the whites so complete as in the South. Here we have great equality before the law, but it simply does not affect our ways of life. There are upper classes and working classes. Every white man in

the South is an equally privileged being whose destiny is to make the
Negroes work without working himself ·. . . I remember a Southern
congressman who was dining with me in Washington, and who could
not conceal his surprise at seeing white servants serving us at table.
He said to Mrs. Adams: "I feel that it is degrading the human race to
have white men for servants. When one of them comes to change my
plate, I am always tempted to offer him my place at table." [2]

Complex and contradictory as they were, commitments to equality
encouraged a rapid expansion of the suffrage, facilitated the incorporation
of new groups (except Negroes) into the political system, and reduced
the influence of class and status as sources of political cleavages. As compared with some of the countries in our study, the development of oppositions was not significantly shaped by resentments, hostilities, memories,
and struggles of excluded groups to gain entry into political life.

   A fourth convergence of views is more difficult to assess; yet it is worth
stressing because it has probably been important in limiting the bounds of
successful opposition. This was a belief, evidently popular in the early
years of the Republic, in the virtues of private property. It is true that in
drafting the Declaration of Independence Jefferson and his colleagues
wrote "life, liberty, and the pursuit of happiness." Yet it was "life, liberty,
and property" that the men at the Constitutional Convention more obviously had in mind. And though small property owners quarreled with
large property owners, though landed property contested with commercial and banking interests, it is a fact that Americans were, from the
beginnings of national independence, a nation of small property owners.
They were, after all, a nation of small farmers; in 1820, 70 per cent of the
working population were farmers, and land was plentiful. Thus side by
side with the common ideology of popular government and constitutionalism there also developed an ideology favorable to private property. Even
after a great share of economic life came to be conducted by large corporations that had only a remote resemblance to the private property of the
small farmer, the ideology of private property proved to be extremely
durable.

   Emphasis on the virtues of private property may be one example of a
fifth and more general constellation of values that foreign visitors have
encountered in Americans: a relatively weak sense of social solidarity,
particularly among social "classes," and a strong emphasis on individual

   2. Alexis de Tocqueville, *Journey to America*, trans. George Lawrence, ed. J. P.
Mayer (New Haven, Yale University Press, 1959), p. 61. For another contemporary
observation on the nature of American beliefs in equality, see Francis J. Grund,
Aristocracy in America, from the Sketch-book of a German Nobleman (1839; New
York, Harper Torchbooks, 1959). S. M. Lipset has summarized and analyzed a wide
variety of nineteenth-century observations on the American character in *The First
New Nation* (New York, Basic Books, 1963), Ch. 3.

achievement, on personal success, on the desirability and the possibility of getting on in the world.[3] Tocqueville held that among Americans "the doctrine of self-interest rightly understood . . . finds universal accept-ance," that is, intelligent, reasonable self-interest bounded by vaguely Christian or humanistic standards. Indeed, according to Tocqueville, even religious commitments were seen as "self-interest rightly understood." [4]

This emphasis on individual achievement was not an emphasis on indi-vidual distinction, on individuality; quite the contrary, as Tocqueville, Harriet Martineau, and many others complained.[5] Americans were often so afraid of being different that they lived in terror of their neighbors' opinions. Nor—to avoid another common error—did Americans rely solely on individual action to get ahead. They were not at all averse to pursuing individual self-interest by means of voluntary associations; in-deed, according to Tocqueville, "the English often perform great things singly, whereas the Americans form associations for the smallest under-takings." [6] What is more, they quite freely used instruments of govern-ment; Tocqueville found that legislators were kept busy turning out laws to regulate the behavior of Americans.[7]

Nonetheless the constellation of values we are discussing undoubtedly did have some consequences highly relevant to our concern here with opposition. For the weak sense of social solidarity, the lack of class con-sciousness, and the concern for individual success made it difficult to

3. In 1889 Henry Adams wrote of America in 1800: "Reversing the old-world sys-tem, the American stimulant increased in energy as it reached the lowest and most ignorant class, dragging and whirling them upward as in the blast of a furnace. The penniless and homeless Scotch or Irish immigrant was caught and consumed by it; for every stroke of the axe and the hoe made him a capitalist, and made gentlemen of his children. Wealth was the strongest agent for moving the mass of mankind; but political power was hardly less tempting to the more intelligent and better-educated swarms of American-born citizens." *The United States in 1800* (Ithaca, N.Y., Great Seal Books, Cornell University Press, 1955), p. 115. This book consists of the first six chapters of Vol. 1 of Adams' *History of the United States of America During the First Administration of Thomas Jefferson, 1889.* This set of values has been reemphasized by sociologists, who find it a rich source of explanations for many different aspects of American behavior. For example, Robert K. Merton, *Social Theory and Social Structure* (rev. ed. Glencoe, Ill., Free Press, 1957), S. M. Lipset, *The First New Nation.*

4. Alexis de Tocqueville, *Democracy in America* (New York, Vintage Books, 1955), *1,* 130–35.

5. Ibid., *1,* 273 ff. Harriet Martineau, *Society in America* (New York, Anchor Books, 1961), pp. 251 ff.

6. Tocqueville, *Democracy in America, 2,* 115.

7. The common view that early Americans were implacably hostile to government regulation of the economy is without historical foundation and is largely (it would appear) an invention of later ideologues. As F. W. Coker observed, "In both our practice and our theory we have had, throughout our national history, a tradition of governmental intervention as well as of nonintervention." "Income Stabilization and the American Political Tradition" in Max Millikan, ed., *Income Stabilization for a Developing Economy* (New Haven, Yale University Press, 1953), p. 87.

appeal to Americans with political ideologies or programs based upon class gains. Americans, it appears, did not typically think of progress as the progress of a class or social stratum to which they belonged but of individuals or like-minded groups; they did not see conflict as the conflict of classes but of individuals, groups, or perhaps regions. Government therefore was not the central mechanism for social and economic progress but a regulatory instrument—not the moving force, the motor, but the regulator, the governor, or fly wheel. Government could be used to eliminate barriers and to even up the chances of personal success, but "success" was then a matter of action by individuals or voluntary groups. Even the conflict over slavery was in this sense a question of regulation, of laying down the terms under which free farmers and slaveholders could carry their institutions into the Western territories.

Sample surveys over the last several decades show that these attitudes so frequently ascribed to Americans in the nineteenth century remain widespread today.[8] The evidence from surveys indicates that:

1. It is very nearly impossible to find an American who says that he is opposed to democracy or favors some alternative—at least for the United States. On the contrary, nearly everyone professes to believe that democracy is the best form of government.[9]

2. Although substantial minorities see specific defects in the constitutional system, the broad elements of the system are widely endorsed.[10]

3. There is substantial agreement that if defects exist in the laws and the Constitution they should be cured by legal processes of change.[11]

4. Most Americans also display complacency about their economic institutions. Proposals for extensive reconstruction do not enjoy much

8. For analyses of greater breadth or depth than space permits here, the reader should consult: Clyde Kluckhohn, "The Evolution of Contemporary American Values," *Daedalus*, 87 (Spring 1958), 78–109; Robert Lane, *Political Ideology, Why the American Common Man Believes What He Does* (New York, The Free Press, 1962); Gabriel A. Almond and Sidney Verba, *The Civic Culture, Political Attitudes and Democracy in Five Nations* (Princeton, Princeton University Press, 1963); V. O. Key, Jr., *Public Opinion and American Democracy* (New York, Knopf, 1961); Herbert McCloskey, "Consensus and Ideology in American Politics," *American Political Science Review*, 58 (June 1964), 361–82.

9. James W. Prothro and C. W. Grigg, "Fundamental Principles of Democracy: Bases of Agreement and Disagreement," *Journal of Politics*, 22 (Spring 1960), 276–94.

10. The evidence is indirect. For example, "Should the Constitution be made easier to amend?" No, 69%, AIPO, March 1, 1937, in Hadley Cantril, *Public Opinion 1935–1946* (Princeton, Princeton University Press, 1951), p. 939. "Do you think the Constitution of the United States should ever be changed in any way?" No, 54%; Yes, 34%; Don't know, 12% (NORC, Nov. 1945, in ibid.)

11. One study provides as evidence the percentages of "political influentials" ($N = 3020$) and "general electorate" ($N = 1484$) *agreeing* to the following statement: "There are times when it almost seems better for the people to take the law into their own hands than wait for the machinery of government to act." Political influentials, 13%; general electorate, 27%. McCloskey, "Consensus and Ideology in American Politics," *American Political Science Review*, p. 365.

support. The great corporations, it appears, have regained rather wide acceptance. A minority holds that corporations should be more severely regulated; a smaller minority holds that they should be nationalized. The trade unions are somewhat more unpopular than the corporations; many would like to see them more severely regulated by the government; but few say that they would like to see trade unions done away with altogether.[12]

5. Although a majority of Americans seem willing to place themselves in the "working class," their sense of class is obviously weak. The key word seems to be "working," not "class." Few believe that class lines divide Americans into hostile camps.[13]

6. Most Americans continue to profess a strong confidence in the possibilities of personal achievement in the American milieu. A great many continue to believe that personal success is attainable by hard work and skill.[14]

7. Thus Americans tend to express satisfaction rather than discontent with their lot. Most Americans claim that life in the United States is the best they could attain anywhere in the world; almost no one wants to emigrate. They expect that their own material conditions will improve, and that for their children life will be much better, provided there is no war.[15]

These propositions concerning American attitudes suggest two questions:

How deeply are these attitudes sustained?
How did such an astonishing unity of views ever come about?

DEPTH AND DISTRIBUTION   How deeply these attitudes run, how firmly they are held, and how they are shared among Americans are questions on which historical data shed almost no direct light, and modern survey data

12. The Survey Research Center, Institute for Social Research, University of Michigan, *Big Business from the Viewpoint of the Public* (Ann Arbor, 1951), pp. 18, 20, 26, 44, 56. In the midst of the Great Depression, responses to the question, "Should the government attempt to break up large business organizations?" were: No, 69%; Yes, 31% (= 100%), No opinion, 10%. (AIPO, July 19, 1937, in Cantril, *Public Opinion 1935–1946*, p. 345). On government ownership, see polls #14 and 16, p. 345; #53, #54, #59, p. 349; and #73, p. 351.

13. See V. O. Key's analysis, "Occupation and Class," Ch. 6 in *Public Opinion and American Democracy*. See also Robert R. Alford, *Party and Society* (Chicago, Rand-McNally, 1963), Ch. 8.

14. The hypothesis that there has been a decline in the motivations for personal achievement is highly dubious. See: Lipset's discussion of "A Changing American Character?" Ch. 3 in *The First New Nation*; the data cited in Key, *Public Opinion and American Democracy*, p. 47 n. 2 and 4 and p. 48 n. 5; and Fred I. Greenstein, "New Light on Changing American Values: A Forgotten Body of Survey Data," *Social Forces, 42* (1964), 441–50.

15. William Buchanan and Hadley Cantril, *How Nations See Each Other* (Urbana, University of Illinois Press, 1953), p. 53.

only a little more. Survey data do, however, lend some support for the following hypotheses:

1. Though Americans are agreed on abstract, general propositions about popular government, majority rule, the Constitution, the virtues of individual liberty, and so on, an attempt to apply these generalities to concrete problems is likely to produce extensive disagreements.[16]

2. Statistically speaking, the more formal education an American has, the more likely he is to express support for the general views we have been describing. The greater his income, the more likely his support, though we cannot be sure about the very rich, who are too small a group to show up in surveys. Support also increases with the status or social prestige of one's occupation; it is higher among professional people, for example, than among skilled workers. Again, we cannot be sure about small categories—corporate executives or Wall Street brokers, for example. Finally, the more active and involved one is in political affairs, the more likely he is to support these views.[17]

3. The connection between the word and the deed is rather uncertain. In particular, to express disagreement with widely prevailing views does not at all mean that one will actually do anything more to act out his dissent. Many—perhaps most—Americans who express disagreement do not, it seems, try to change the attitudes of others by discussion or bring about changes by joining dissident political movements or trying to secure the nomination and election of candidates favorable to their views. The reasons for inaction include political apathy and indifference, lack of strong feeling, pessimism over the prospects of success, ignorance, etc.[18]

Thus the patterns of support, disagreement, and apathy help to sustain the prevailing views and weaken the effectiveness of opposition to them. Since support tends to increase with education, income, occupational status, and political activity, and since political influence is also to a considerable extent a function of these same factors, the influence of

16. The best evidence is found in Prothro and Grigg, "Fundamental Principles of Democracy: Bases of Agreement and Disagreement," *Journal of Politics;* McCloskey, "Consensus and Ideology in American Politics," *American Political Science Review;* and Samuel A. Stouffer, *Communism, Conformity and Civil Liberties* (Garden City, N.Y., Doubleday, 1955).

17. See the survey data reported and analyzed in Fred I. Greenstein, *The American Party System and the American People* (Englewood Cliffs, N.J., Prentice-Hall, 1963), Ch. 3, pp. 18–36. See also S. M. Lipset, *Political Man* (Garden City, N.Y., Doubleday, 1960), Ch. 4, "Working Class Authoritarianism," pp. 97–130, and Stouffer, *Communism, Conformity and Civil Liberties,* passim.

18. The evidence is indirect but strong. See Herbert McCloskey, "Conservatism and Personality," *American Political Science Review,* 52 (March 1958), 27–45; Robert Lane, *Political Life* (Glencoe, Ill., The Free Press, 1959), Ch. 5, pp. 63–79, and Ch. 12, pp. 163–81; A. Campbell, P. E. Converse, W. E. Miller, D. E. Stokes, *The American Voter* (New York, Wiley, 1960), Ch. 5, pp. 89–115.

supportive attitudes tends to be disproportionately increased while opposition tends to be politically ineffectual.

SOURCES   How one explains the development of such a high degree of unity in political attitudes depends on the point in time at which one starts his explanation and on the relations one assumes to exist between "ideal" and "material" factors, between cognitive activity and everyday life. I can do no more here than to suggest a few of the more evident factors.

In 1776 Americans were, in the main, Englishmen; during a century and a half of colonial experience they had adapted English political ideas, attitudes, and institutions to the conditions of life in America. Among the Englishmen living in English colonies, American colonial experience, it seems fair to conclude, strengthened attitudes favorable to constitutionalism, the virtues of written constitutions, the supremacy of law, the values of representative government. In the colonial legislatures the English-Americans learned the arts and skills of self-government, made and enforced many of their own laws, and developed political elites with a high degree of expertness in managing political institutions. Unlike many countries that have recently acquired independence, by 1776 the United States was, in a sense, already an "old" country; though it would be easy to exaggerate the point, the fact is that by the time of the American Revolution, Americans had had a long and varied experience in operating some of the institutions of representative government. And they shared a common political tradition.

Their colonial experience and their common political tradition would not account, by themselves, for the speed with which the United States was transformed into a democratic republic. For in the United States the length of about one generation was needed in order to arrive at political conditions that in Britain were to require still another century. In fact, by 1800 or thereabouts a high proportion of white males could vote in local, state, and national elections.[19] The Democratic-Republicans were rapidly becoming a mass-based political party highly organized at all levels of government from towns and villages to the United States Congress and the presidency.[20] By 1832, there existed two such parties. When Tocqueville visited the United States—from May 1831 to February 1832—the

19. Although the question is still somewhat unsettled, the older view which held that property qualifications greatly limited the suffrage in most states until a decade or two after 1800 apparently has to be revised in the light of more recent evidence. See especially Robert E. Brown, *Middle-Class Democracy and the Revolution in Massachusetts, 1691–1780* (Princeton, Princeton University Press, 1960).

20. Charles, *The Origins of the Party System;* Noble E. Cunningham, Jr., *The Jeffersonian Republicans, The Formation of Party Organization 1789–1801* (Chapel Hill, The University of North Carolina Press, 1957); and Noble E. Cunningham, Jr., *The Jeffersonian Republicans in Power Party Operations 1801–1809* (Chapel Hill, University of North Carolina Press, 1963).

credo and institutions of democracy had, it seemed to him, already gained
well-nigh universal acceptance among Americans.

Why this amazing speed? Given the background of traditions and
experience, one reason for the rapid transition is undoubtedly to be found
exactly where Tocqueville found it, in the "equality of condition" that
prevailed among Americans. "America," he wrote, "exhibits in her social
state an extraordinary phenomenon. Men are there seen on a greater
equality in point of fortune and intellect, or in other words, more equal
in strength, than in any other country of the world, or in any age of
which history has preserved the remembrance." [21]

If one prefers to go yet further back in order to account for this
equality of condition, that explanation too is surely to be found mainly
where Tocqueville and later F. J. Turner found it: in the vast supply of
cheap land. If the United States, like some recently independent countries,
was launched by revolution it became a stable republic only as a result
of a second silent revolution that accomplished what many new nations
struggle painfully and even violently to achieve: a wide distribution of
landholdings. For the land was there to be had. In 1803 the Louisiana
Purchase alone provided the equivalent of 90 acres of land for every man,
woman, and child then living in the United States. In 1850, the area of the
public domain was still equal to 50 acres for every person in the country.[22]
The problem of expropriation did not exist. The land did not have to be
taken from a preexisting set of feudal barons. At most the land had to be
obtained from foreign governments or seized from the Indians with the aid
of the new federal government; it could then be bought from speculators
or sometimes from the government itself. Everyone stood to profit by the
diffusion of landholdings (except the Indian, who had no representatives
in Congress): the would-be independent farmer, the speculator who sold
him the land, the banker who lent him money on his mortgage note, the
merchant and real estate dealer who thrived in the new towns.

The attitudes that developed out of the already existing traditions of
English and American political thought were perfectly harmonious with
the emerging structure of the American society, a nation of small independent farmers. Democratic ideas and institutions offered the farmers
substantial control over government and laws; given the distribution of
people, landed property, and muskets, and the state of civil and military
technology, no elite could have ruled the Americans without their assent.
Thus democratic ideas and institutions gave legitimacy to what was unavoidable, namely some kind of popular government. Once the constitutional equilibrium was established in their favor, the body of citizen

21. *Democracy in America, 1, 55.*
22. *Historical Statistics of the United States, Colonial Times to 1957* (Washington,
U.S. Government Printing Office, 1960), Series A 1–3 and Series J 3–9.

farmers naturally supported the Constitution and constitutional change, for these insured that elites could not easily change the rules of the game. To a nation of landholders, moreover, the virtues of private property were obvious; where so many people were of roughly the same socioeconomic condition—small farmers—and had no landlord class as an enemy, feelings of class solidarity were bound to be weak. With land to be bought, land to be sold, towns of be built, roads, bridges, canals, and railroads to connect the towns, opportunities for personal success were everywhere.[23] Government was needed only to make sure that the framework for individual competition seemed fair to the preponderant majorities.

Yet it is one thing to explain how the unity of views among Americans happened to arise and quite another to explain how it continued to exist when the United States ceased to be a nation of small independent farmers. By 1880 workers in nonfarm occupations exceeded those in farming. Thereafter the farmers were an ever smaller minority; by 1957 less than one out of ten persons in the labor force was in agriculture, and of these only about half owned their own farms.[24]

Probably the sheer inertia of an already venerable tradition helped the United States through periods of crisis. But the crises themselves may have helped even more. The inertial force of the traditional attitudes must have increased as each great challenge to the liberal democratic, privatistic, success-oriented ideology was turned back. Each challenge offered the possibility of a rival ideology—aristocracy, slavocracy, socialism, plutocracy. Yet in each case these potential rivals for the minds of Americans were defeated, and the older, victorious ideology then became thoroughly intertwined with traditionalism. To attack the conventional ideas meant more and more to attack the whole course of American national history, to imply that Americans had failed, long ago, to take the right path.

These challenges might not have been successfully overcome, however, if the "equality of condition" that Tocqueville had observed had vanished: if, in short, blatant contradictions had developed between the lives led by ordinary Americans and the aspirations offered in the dominant ideology. Despite increasing economic inequalities that accompanied industrialization, particularly in its early stages after the Civil War, enough of the old

23. "The possession of land," Harriet Martineau reported with some exaggeration, "is the aim of all action, generally speaking, and the cure for all social evils, among men in the United States. If a man is disappointed in politics or love, he goes and buys land. If he disgraces himself, he betakes himself to a lot in the west. If the demand for any article of manufacture slackens, the operatives drop into the unsettled lands. If a citizen's neighbors rise above him in the towns, he betakes himself where he can be monarch of all he surveys. An artisan works, that he may die on land of his own. He is frugal, that he may enable his son to be a land-owner. Farmers' daughters go into factories that they may clear off the mortgage from their fathers' farms; that they may be independent land-owners again." *Society in America*, p. 168.
24. *Historical Statistics*, Series D 1-12 and K 8-52.

"equality of condition" evidently survived—if not in reality, at least in expectations—so that the old ideas won converts even among the very people who were worst off under industrial capitalism.[25]

Two additional elements have helped to sustain the dominant traditional ideology in the twentieth century. One of these is the educational system, which from the primary grades through high school and even on in the universities, emphasizes the values and institutions expressed in the dominant liberal-democratic ideology. While the relationship between formal education and ideas is complex, most of all with any specific person, one simple and imposing statistical fact is that, in survey after survey of political attitudes and ideas among Americans, the amount of formal education appears as a highly significant variable; indeed, more often than any other, education shows up as *the* most significant variable, even when the effects of socioeconomic status and occupation are canceled out.[26] As we have already observed (and this is the important point), the greater one's formal education, the more likely one is to endorse the key propositions in the prevailing ideology.

The other influence, that of the mass media—radio, television, newspapers, and mass circulation magazines—is harder to assess. Concrete data are few. Critics on the Left argue that the great bulk of Americans are lulled by the mass media into a complacent acceptance of the values in the prevailing ideology, chiefly the emphasis on private property and personal success, and that these beliefs in turn protect the position of certain important elite groups, business leaders, men of wealth, and so on. Critics among the ranks of the radical Right tend to view the mass media in much the same way; they see them as major instruments (along with the educational system) by which the Liberal Establishment acquires and retains its dominance over American institutions and attitudes.[27]

25. Comparative studies of rates of social mobility are still too few for confident conclusions. The view of S. M. Lipset and Reinhard Bendix that "the overall pattern of social mobility appears to be much the same in industrial societies of various Western countries" (*Social Mobility in Industrial Society* [Berkeley and Los Angeles, University of California Press, 1960], p. 13) appears, in the light of later studies, to be doubtful. Perhaps the most that one can say at this point is that social mobility is or has been relatively high in the United States, as compared with such European countries as Britain and the Netherlands, in some but not in all respects. See S. M. Miller, "Comparative Social Mobility: A Trend Report, "*Current Sociology, 9,* No. 1 (1960), 1–5; and also Thomas Fox and S. M. Miller, "Intra-Country Variations: Occupational Stratification and Mobility," in Richard L. Merritt and Stein Rokkan, eds., *Comparing Nations: The Use of Quantitative Data in Cross-National Research* (New Haven, Yale University Press, 1966), pp. 217–38.

26. Key, *Public Opinion and American Democracy*, Ch. 13, "The Educational System," pp. 315–43.

27. The following quotation could as easily have come from a source on the Left as on the Right: "the mass circulation media in this country have virtually closed their columns to opposition articles. For this they can hardly be blamed; their business is to sell paper at so much a pound and advertising space at so much a line. They must give the masses what they believe the masses want, if they are to maintain their mass

Both views, I think, exaggerate the direct, manipulative influence of the mass media on American attitudes. The opposition of three-quarters of the daily newspapers of the United States may have reduced the amount of support for Franklin D. Roosevelt, but it did not prevent him from being reelected three times. Or, to take a more recent example, differences in attitudes toward a highly controversial issue like medical care were in 1956 related in a very weak way to the amount of exposure to the mass media. Moreover, some of the differences were the opposite of what one might expect from simple theories of the influence of the media on "mass man." Thus among persons with only a grade school education, both support for (76 per cent) and opposition to (15 per cent) a government program of medical care was higher among those *most* exposed to the mass media.[28]

The explanation is not mysterious. There is a good deal of evidence that the individuals and groups who might be most susceptible to positive influences from the media because of weak social, psychological, and political ties—"mass man"—also pay much less attention to the media; whereas the individuals who are most exposed to the mass media are in general those with the strongest social, psychological, and political barriers between them and manipulative efforts.[29] The views of Left and Right also underestimate, I think, the extent to which the mass media themselves reflect stable values in the American culture; for better or worse, culture and media reinforce one another.

What is essentially correct, however, is that the amount of time and space devoted by the mass media to views openly hostile to the prevailing ideology is negligible.[30] An American who wishes to find criticisms of the

---

circulation business; and there is no doubt that the promises . . . reiterated by the propaganda machine of the government, have made it popular and dulled the public mind to the verities of freedom." The source is, in fact, an editorial note in a right-wing publication, *The Freeman* (June 1955), cited in Daniel Bell, "Interpretations of American Politics," in Daniel Bell, ed., *The New American Right* (New York, Anchor Books, 1964), p. 68 n. 23. The editorial was attacking the mass media for lulling the public into socialism. The best-known criticism from the Left, sounding many of the same themes, is in the late C. Wright Mills, *The Power Elite* (New York, Oxford University Press, 1956) Ch. 13, "The Mass Society," pp. 298-324.

28. V. O. Key, *Public Opinion and American Democracy*, p. 398.

29. A sophisticated and skeptical attempt to assess the influence of the mass media is V. O. Key, *Public Opinion and American Democracy*, Chs. 14 and 15, "Media: Specter and Reality" and "Media: Structure and Impact," pp. 344-410. On the general problem of manipulating attitudes, see also R. E. Lane and D. O. Sears, *Public Opinion* (Englewood Cliffs, N.J., Prentice-Hall, 1964), Ch. 5, "Leaders' Influence on Public Opinion." See also Elihu Katz and Paul F. Lazarsfeld, *Personal Influence* (Glencoe, Ill., Free Press, 1955).

30. "Extraordinarily few [American] journals, either daily newspapers or magazines, act as agencies of political criticism. They may dig to find the facts about individual acts of corruption, but the grand problems of the political system by and large escape their critical attention." Key, *Public Opinion and American Democracy*, p. 381.

basic social, economic, and political structures can indeed find them; but he will have to search outside the mass media. And, naturally, the number who are strongly motivated enough to do so is relatively small. Hence the general effect of the mass media is to reinforce the existing institutions and ideology.[31]

Cleavage

The ambience of unity that has just been described is impressive. It is, nonetheless, something of an illusion. The traditional ideology, which appears so monolithic, is a patchwork of ambiguities and potential contradictions that not only permit but even encourage a wide variety of conflicts.

European (and American) observers have often underestimated the pervasiveness of conflict in American politics because political conflict in the United States does not follow the expected patterns of class and ideological politics. The American "working class" is obviously not arrayed against "the bourgeoisie." The sound of conflict is muffled by the outward consensus on ideology: everyone seems to be employing the same ideology, the same phrases, even the same words.

Nevertheless, an examination of cleavage patterns in American politics suggests three conclusions:

1. Certain types of questions or issues have been the subject of political conflict for relatively long periods of time.

2. These questions have led to extremely severe conflict about once every generation.

3. Ordinarily, however, the severity of political conflicts is greatly reduced by, among other things, the pattern of cleavage, which encourages conciliation rather than conflict.

THE PERSISTENT SUBJECTS OF CONFLICT   Dispute over specific, concrete policy questions tends to be of a rather short-run nature. The particular issues that provoke controversy in one decade are likely to be superseded in the next by other specific questions. Nevertheless, certain types of issues have been recurrent subjects of conflict in American politics.

One of these is the nature and extent of democratic processes. This question has persistently reappeared in American politics in a multitude of forms. It was one of the basic cleavages of the Constitutional Convention itself, where a question at issue was whether the republic to be established under the new constitution was to be democratic or aristocratic in character. The Convention and the Constitution left the issue unsettled. A major difference between the Federalists and the Republicans during the first several decades under the new Constitution was the way they

31. For a similar conclusion, see Key, *Public Opinion and American Democracy*, p. 396.

answered this question.[32] After the demise of the Federalists, aristocratic themes were muted—at least in public. But even if the outward form of the dispute changed, differences have persisted to the present day over the extent, distribution, and kinds of civil and political rights and liberties that should be guaranteed. On matters of this kind, the seemingly massive consensus about "democracy" quickly breaks down; as we saw above, although certain general propositions in the American ideology are given well-nigh universal lip service, any attempt to apply these general principles to concrete cases reveals sharp differences. Thus a problem on which there has never been much deep agreement is the proper balance between the rights and duties of majorities and minorities. Spokesmen for regional minorities (the South, for example) frequently challenge the constitutional or moral authority of the Congress, the President, or the Supreme Court (or all three) to impose a national policy on the whole country. The rights of dissident, radical, or revolutionary opposition groups are invariably in dispute. Although conflicts over liberties and rights almost always wind up in the courts, and often produce epochal Supreme Court decisions, these conflicts are inescapably political as well. A recent example was supplied by Senator Joseph McCarthy, who formed the nucleus of an opposition movement on the Right that challenged existing government policies and procedures for dealing with Communists, alleged Communists, and other individuals and groups who, it was charged, endangered the national security.

Another highly visible kind of issue that generates conflict is the specific or general role of the government in the regulation and control of the economy. The absence of a sizable socialist movement in the United States and any large-scale challenge to the basic economic institutions can easily be misleading. For consensus breaks down here too. Ever since Alexander Hamilton, the first Secretary of the Treasury, presented his economic programs to the First Congress, government economic policies have stimulated sharp controversy. Indeed, probably conflict in national politics has occurred more frequently in this domain than in any other.

The single most concrete, persistent, and explosive issue in American politics from the Constitutional Convention to the present has, however, been the place of the Negro in American life, whether as slave or as freeman. Although the question has sometimes been removed from national debate by tacit understandings among white leaders, it seems safe to say that no other issue has exerted such a steady force on the patterns of coalition and opposition in American politics. To protect its peculiar institution, whether slavery before the Civil War or white supremacy

32. Some historians would probably disagree with the preceding three sentences, which telescope a complex development into a few words. The relevant literature is too vast to cite here. I am developing each of these points at length in a forthcoming book on American politics.

afterward, the South has always had to maneuver so as to prevent the triumph of a majority hostile to the racial practices of the White South. The South has steadily and skillfully used its political strength in Congress and in presidential elections to bargain with the North and West for protection of—or at least acquiescence in—its treatment of the Negro. On only two occasions has this strategy failed. It failed (at least in the eyes of some Southern leaders) just before and after the election of 1860; as a result these leaders induced the South to choose the path of secession and finally war. The second failure occurred during the period beginning with the Supreme Court decision outlawing segregation in the schools in 1954 and culminating in the passage of the Civil Rights Act in 1964. The eventual results of this second failure may prove to have important consequences for American politics.[33]

Finally, foreign policy, though a dormant question for long periods, sometimes generates fairly sharp conflicts. During the early years from 1789 to 1815 foreign policy was an important source of conflict between Federalists and Republicans. During the century that followed, widespread acceptance of neutrality, isolationism, and the Monroe Doctrine tended to inhibit sharp and persistent controversy over foreign affairs. But from the First World War onward, American foreign policies have frequently been the subject of political conflict: neutrality, the arming of merchant ships, and entry into the First World War; the Treaty of Versailles and the League of Nations; neutrality and aid to the Allies prior to our entry in World War II; since then the dimensions of foreign aid, how to deal with Communist nations, the wars in Korea and Viet Nam—all have provoked controversy.

THE RECURRENCE OF INTENSE CONFLICT   One of the commonest beliefs about American politics (rather widely shared by Americans themselves) is that although conflict does occur over these issues, it is rarely if ever very intense. Because there are no precise ways of measuring the severity or intensity of a conflict, and it is therefore difficult to compare the severity or intensity of one conflict with that of another, the validity of this belief is not easy to challenge. Yet if one is prepared to accept as indices threats or moves to disrupt the constitutional system, threatened or actual violence against or on behalf of national policies, or expressions by sober and informed observers or participants that a given conflict will lead to disruption, revolution, or civil war, then the weight of historical evidence seems to offer solid support to a contrary proposition:

> From the very first years under the new Constitution American political life has undergone, about once every generation, a conflict over national politics of extreme severity.

33. See pp. 68–69.

To suggest the evidence for this proposition, let me review some familiar historical episodes.

1. Before the Constitution had completed its first decade, the Alien and Sedition Acts (1798), which threatened the very existence of any organized political opposition, were challenged by the legislatures of Kentucky (1798) and Virginia (1799) in resolutions that hinted for the first time (but definitely not the last) that a state government might deliberately refuse to enforce a federal law which its legislators held to be unconstitutional. The specters raised by the Alien and Sedition Acts on the one side, and by the Kentucky and Virginia resolutions on the other, were temporarily banished by what Jefferson called "the Revolution of 1800."

2. Within hardly more than another decade (December 1814), New England Federalists, driven to desperation by the embargo policies enforced by the Republicans, assembled at Hartford in a convention that not only adopted a set of resolutions calling for extensive constitutional changes but issued a report asserting among other things that "in cases of deliberate, dangerous and palpable infraction of the Constitution, affecting the sovereignty of a State and liberties of the people; it is not only the right but the duty of such a State to interpose its authority for their protection, in the manner best calculated to secure that end." [34]

3. Less than another score of years went by before the United States approached civil war over the tariff.[35]

4. Thereafter, the middle years of the century were occupied with various aspects of the controversy over slavery, particularly whether slavery should be permitted in the great unsettled areas of the West, a question that touched the most sensitive interests of Northerners and Southerners. Finally, as everyone knows, the issue no longer could be contained; and for four terrible years men died of wounds and disease to settle the question—or so it was supposed.

34. Richard B. Morris, ed., *Encyclopedia of American History* (New York, Harper, 1953), p. 153.
35. In 1828 the legislature of South Carolina adopted a set of eight resolutions holding unconstitutional, oppressive, and unjust the newly passed "Tariff of Abominations," which ultimately hit cotton exporters with what seemed to them undue severity; in an accompanying document written by John C. Calhoun the legislature espoused the view that a single state might, in such cases, "nullify" an unconstitutional law. Four years later, when the South Carolinians were still chafing under the protective tariff, a convention called by the state legislature adopted an ordinance that "nullified" the tariff acts of 1828 and 1832, prohibited the collection of duties within the state, and asserted that the use of force by the federal government could be cause for secession. The state legislature passed laws to enforce the ordinance, to raise a military force, and to appropriate funds for arms. President Jackson thereupon sought and gained from Congress the legal authority to enforce the tariff laws by military means if necessary. A compromise tariff was worked out in Congress, South Carolina rescinded its Ordinance of Nullification, and civil war was avoided—or rather postponed for thirty years. Morris, *Encyclopedia*, pp. 166–72.

5. In fact, the issue was only partly settled: slavery was abolished, to be sure, but the freed Negroes were not permitted for long to enjoy equal political rights, to say nothing of economic, educational, or social privileges. Ten years after Appomattox, the election of 1876 brought the country to the verge of civil war, but as so often before and after the outcome was compromise rather than war; yet a compromise that tacitly allowed the restoration of white supremacy throughout the South and thus adjourned the whole problem of effective citizenship for Negroes until the middle of the present century.

6. This adjournment allowed economic questions to take over. During the last third of the century, discontented farmers and urban workers formed a pool of recurring opposition to the policies of a national government that responded less and less to their demands and more and more to those of the new men of business, industry, and finance. Out of economic dissatisfaction radical and reformist movements developed: Socialist Labor, the Greenbacks, the Farmers' Alliance, Populism, the Socialist Party, the IWW. The trade union movement also had a turbulent growing period: the Knights of Labor, the AFL, the railway unions. Strikes, lockouts, and protest meetings frequently led to severe violence.[36]

7. In the presidential elections of 1896, William Jennings Bryan, a man of primitive intellect and beguiling eloquence, whom Democrats and Populists had jointly nominated as their candidate, and who in his simple and confused protests evidently evoked support among farmers and urban workers who were opposed to the "domination of Eastern capital," was defeated by McKinley after a campaign period of unusually high tension.[37]

8. Sixteen years later a new Democratic President, the second since the Civil War, was elected, and under Wilson's leadership many of the specific reforms that had been demanded earlier by Populists and Socialists were carried out. Although these reforms were sharply opposed, the conflicts seem to have lacked some of the earlier intensity; the country was not viewed as approaching another civil war.

9. The next generation witnessed the Great Depression, mass unemployment, extensive discontent, the election of the third Democratic

36. In 1886 during a demonstration near the McCormick Reaper Works in Chicago, six strikers were killed by the police and many more were wounded. The next day two thousand persons attended a protest meeting in Haymarket Square; policemen ordered the meeting to disperse; a bomb was thrown, killing a policeman; in the ensuing battle, seven more policemen and four workers were killed, sixty policemen and fifty workers were wounded. Six men who had addressed the meeting were sentenced to death; four were hanged the following year. In 1894, Grover Cleveland, the first Democrat elected to the presidency since 1856, now in his second term as President, called out federal troops in order to break a great nationwide strike of railway workers against the Pullman Company.

37. Bryan won 47 per cent of the two-party vote and carried 21 states—all of them, however, agricultural states of the South, Midwest, and West.

President since the Civil War, new outbreaks of violence, the rise of quasi-democratic or antidemocratic political movements on both Right and Left, and extensive changes in national policies, changes that from 1935 onward were fought with increasing bitterness. Driven to extreme measures by a Supreme Court dominated by conservatives who steadily rejected the major items of the New Deal as unconstitutional, President Roosevelt even tried to "pack" the court in 1937. It was his first important unpopular move, and he was defeated.

10. Less than thirty years later the unsolved problem of equal rights and opportunities for Negroes has produced a new eruption of demonstrations, discontent, and violence not only in the South but also in the Negro ghettos of the large Northern cities. And in 1964 the long-frustrated opposition of the Radical Right, capitalizing on white reactions to Negro discontent, temporarily captured the Republican Party and at last found national spokesmen in the Republican nominees for President and Vice President, Senator Goldwater and Representative Miller.

Whoever supposes, then, that American politics has been nothing more than a moving consensus, a sort of national Rotary Club luncheon, has not sufficiently reflected on the recurrence of intense conflict, crisis, and violence in American history.

THE PATTERN OF CLEAVAGE   If cleavages have been persistent, and if at times they have led to intense conflicts, why, one might inquire, has the system not been disrupted more often? Why have American oppositions been, on the whole, so moderate? Why don't oppositions "debate the great issues" and "present clear-cut alternatives," as critics so often demand? Why is it that "opposition" and "government" are often so hard to distinguish from one another?

One reason was discussed in the preceding section: the ambience of concensus in which government and oppositions operate. As long as oppositions employ substantially the same ideology and accept much the same set of values as the administration, it is difficult for them to force debate on the great issues (for there are no great issues) or to present clear-cut alternatives (for alternatives clearly outside the common ideology are excluded).

A second reason, which will be discussed briefly in the next section, is the structure of government and politics in the United States.

But a third reason is to be found in the very patterns of cleavage that lead to conflict. Even though, as we have seen, Americans divide quite often on questions of democratic rights and privileges, on the place of Negroes in American life, and on the economic role of the government, and divide somewhat less often on foreign policy, these and other issues do not ordinarily divide them into exclusive camps. For two reasons, it seems, American politics is almost never highly polarized.

1. Differences in political attitudes and actions are not highly related to

differences in socioeconomic characteristics—region, status, occupation, etc. Even though there is some relationship, it is usually weak: people in the same regions, or the same status groups, or the same broad occupational categories do not form distinct, homogeneous clusters of attitudes. Consequently, polarization of politics along socioeconomic lines is inhibited.

2. Differences in political attitudes and loyalties are not highly interrelated among themselves. That is, persons who hold the same attitudes on one question frequently hold different attitudes on other questions. To overstate the point, every ally is sometimes an enemy and every enemy is sometimes an ally. Thus polarization of politics along ideological lines is inhibited.

As to the first explanation, it is difficult to find any distinctive and persistent clusters of attitudes in different regions of the United States, except on the question of the Negro. Regional differences in political attitudes do, of course, exist; but the differences are, on the whole, weak. Southerners are not, for example, more conservative about the economic role of the government than people in other regions. In fact, on the basis of 1956 survey evidence, V. O. Key suggested that "on some questions the South turns out to be a shade more 'liberal' than other regions." Key also pointed out, incidentally, that "even with respect to the Negro the unity of the South varies from aspect to aspect of race policy. Southerners take a far stronger position on school segregation than on such questions as the protection of the economic rights of Negroes." [38] Nor, despite its reputation, has the Midwest remained (assuming that it once was) notably more isolationist or less internationalist than the rest of the country.[39] The reputation of the Midwest was created in part by its representatives in Congress, of whom a larger percentage opposed foreign aid in the period before and after World War II than among the representatives from other regions. Yet much of this congressional isolationism was more closely related to party than to region: Democratic congressmen from the Midwest have been, unlike their Republican colleagues, predominantly internationalist.[40]

Relationships are often found between political attitudes and various indices of occupation, socioeconomic status, and class. But strong relationships are rare, and often they are surprisingly weak. Thus in 1956

38. Key, *Public Opinion and American Democracy*, pp. 102–03.

39. On a scale of "internationalism," the percentages in each region which ranked high in 1956 were 53 per cent in the Midwest, compared with 59 per cent in the Northeast, 58 per cent in the Far West, and 56 per cent in the South. Key, *Public Opinion and American Democracy*, p. 107.

40. Leroy N. Rieselbach, "The Demography of the Congressional Vote on Foreign Aid, 1939–1958," *American Political Science Review*, *58* (September 1964) 577–88, esp. 582–83.

percentages of persons who ranked high on a scale of internationalism did not seem to vary a great deal according to whether the occupations were white-collar, blue-collar, or farming.[41] As in other countries, however, manual workers tend to diverge from nonmanual workers in their views on the proper economic policies of the government. The effects of class identification seem to be even greater than the effects of occupation; in 1956 a white-collar worker who identified himself as a member of the working classes was somewhat more likely to be in favor of government intervention in the economy on a variety of fronts than a blue-collar worker who identified himself as middle class. (See Table 2.1). Yet be-

Table 2.1. Socioeconomic Status and Support for Stronger Economic Role of Government*

Occupation of head of family	Class with which respondent identified himself	
	Working	Middle
White-collar	40%	22%
Blue-collar	50%	35%
Farm operator	41%	32%

* Entries are percentages ranking high in support for government aid to cities and towns for building more schools; to Negroes for fair treatment in jobs and housing; in guaranteeing everyone a job; for medical care; and in providing electric power and housing.

Source: Key, *Public Opinion and American Democracy*, p. 143.

cause class identity is weak, manual workers do not differ as sharply from nonmanual workers in their voting for candidates and parties as they do in a number of countries. Among the major English-speaking democracies, class voting seems to be lower in the United States than in Britain and Australia (though higher than in Canada).[42]

Ethnic and religious loyalties and identifications introduce heterogeneity into regions and status groups. The common belief that distinctive ethnic and religious identifications are weakening in the United States as the descendants of the various immigrants become assimilated into American life has been recently challenged in a study of ethnic groups in New York; the authors conclude:

Religion and race seem to define the major groups into which American

41. White-collar workers who identified themselves as middle class ranked a little higher in internationalism; otherwise, differences were negligible. See Key, *Public Opinion and American Democracy*, Table 6.11, p. 144.
42. "A number of public opinion surveys taken between 1952 and 1962 indicate that class voting is consistently higher in Australia and Great Britain than in Canada and the United States. The countries may be ranked in the following order: Great Britain, Australia, the United States, and Canada." Robert R. Alford, *Party and Society*, pp. 101-02.

society is evolving as the specifically national aspect of ethnicity [i.e., the specific nation from which one's ancestors came] declines. In our large American cities, four major groups emerge: Catholics, Jews, white Protestants, and Negroes.[43]

Yet, like region, status, occupation, and economic position, ethnic and religious loyalties do not as such produce sharp political cleavages. Voting patterns are very much more distinctive than political attitudes. Jews and Catholics vote more heavily Democratic than Protestants; Negroes vote more heavily Democratic than whites; and voters of Irish, Italian, Polish, German, and Scandinavian descent often seem to have somewhat distinctive voting patterns. The differences may be more apparent in local elections than in national elections, and most distinctive when a representative of their own ethnic group—or an enemy of their ethnic group—has a leading place on one ticket.[44]

The extent to which religious differences cut across class differences is revealed in a very general way by the data in Tables 2.2 and 2.3. In national elections over the past generation, among both manual workers and nonmanual workers, Catholics have voted Democratic in considerably higher proportions than Protestants. (Table 2.2) The discrepancy was

Table 2.2. Religious Voting by Occupational Categories, 1936–1960 (non-Southern whites only): 7 Presidential, 2 Congressional Elections

Religious voting: % Catholics voting Democratic minus % Protestants voting Democratic

	Manual workers	Nonmanual	Farmers
High	41% (1960)	59% (1960)	39% (1956)
Median	20% ('52, '54)	28% (1956)	14% (1958)
Low	16% (1956)	17% (1952)	− 5% (1954)

Source: Data taken from Table II, pp. 92–94, in Seymour M. Lipset, "Religion and Politics in the American Past and Present," in Robert Lee and Martin Marty, eds., *Religion and Social Conflict* (New York, Oxford University Press, 1964).

greatest between middle-class (nonmanual) Catholics and Protestants; many Catholics who had moved into nonmanual occupations maintained their traditional loyalties as Democratic voters. The differences between

43. Nathan Glazer and Daniel Patrick Moynihan, *Beyond the Melting Pot* (Cambridge, Mass., the MIT Press and Harvard University Press, 1963), p. 314.

44. See the evidence in Louis Harris, *Is There a Republican Majority?, Political Trends, 1952–1956* (New York, Harper, 1954), Ch. 6; Angus Campbell and Homer C. Cooper, *Group Differences in Attitudes and Votes, A Study of the 1954 Congressional Election* (Ann Arbor, Survey Research Center, 1956), Ch. 3; Alford, *Party and Society*, pp. 241 ff.; Campbell et al., *The American Voter*, pp. 319 ff. In the 1964 presidential election the fears aroused among Negroes by the candidacy of Senator Goldwater amplified to near unanimity their predisposition to vote Democratic.

Catholics and Protestants were smallest in the elections of 1952 and 1956, when General Eisenhower was the Republican candidate, and, as might be expected, greatest in 1960 when John F. Kennedy, a Catholic, was the Democratic candidate.

To look at the same data in another way (Table 2.3), Protestants split

Table 2.3. Class Voting by Catholics and Protestants, 1936–1960 (non-Southern whites only): 7 Presidential, 2 Congressional Elections

Class voting: % manual workers voting Democratic minus % nonmanual voting Democratic

	Catholics	Protestants
High	28% (1952)	29% (1936)
Median	16% (1948)	23% (1956)
Low	6% (1960)	18% (1954)

Source: See Table 2.2.

most sharply along class lines in 1936 in the midst of the Great Depression, when Franklin Roosevelt was running for a second term. Catholics split most sharply in 1952 when many middle-class Catholics succumbed to the appeal of Eisenhower; in 1960, on the other hand, Kennedy all but obliterated the appeal of class among Catholics by his appeal as a fellow Catholic.

Thus religion or ethnic identity may either amplify the effects of class and status on voting, as in the case of Negroes or working-class Catholics; or, conversely, religion or ethnic identity may depress the significance of class and status by providing a crosscutting cleavage, as in the case of middle-class Catholics and Jews or white working-class Protestants. Moreover, just as the impact of occupation and economic position on voting may vary depending on the state of the economy, so the impact of religion and ethnic identity is not a constant but a varying factor depending on current issues and on the candidates themselves.

More important, differences in voting and partisan loyalties among ethnic and religious groups do not seem to reflect significant differences in ideology or attitudes about policy. This is not to say that there are *no* discernible differences in political predispositions and beliefs among the different groups. It has been conjectured that "the sympathy which Catholic doctrine has had for trade union objectives, as contrasted with the greater emphasis on individualism inherent in Protestantism may in some part explain why even non-union middle-class Catholics are more supportive of union rights in this country."[45] In New York City, it has been

45. Lipset, "Religion and Politics," *The First New Nation*, p. 113. Lipset cites the following finding: "Ohio's counties were segregated (for analytic purposes) into twenty different levels of urbanism, income, and rural farm, and in all twenty of

said, "what attracts Jews is liberalism, using the term to refer to the entire range of leftist positions, from the mildest to the most extreme." [46] The kind of Christian pacifism exemplified by Martin Luther King's strategy of nonviolence quite possibly could not have succeeded with any other group of Americans as well as it did with Negroes.

Nonetheless, differences in attitudes and beliefs often reflect other factors like education and economic position; or else the differences are highly specific and depend on some particular issue that impinges directly on the group, as in the case of Catholic views on governmental aid to parochial schools or the views of Negroes on civil rights. On the whole, when these factors are removed it is difficult to find much distinctiveness in the political attitudes of the various ethnic and religious groups. [47]

In short, then, differences in political attitudes and actions are related to a number of different social and economic characteristics, but they are not highly related to any, and the variety of social and economic characteristics of any broad category of the population makes for a high degree of political heterogeneity. Hence polarization along social and economic lines is inhibited.

The second factor mentioned a moment ago—that differences in political attitudes and loyalties are not highly interrelated—contributes further to this process. Despite the relatively low level of differences in political attitudes and actions among people in different regions, occupations, classes, religions, and ethnic groups, it is conceivable that Americans might divide into two distinctive ideological blocs, each of which was internally a rather heterogeneous (though not random) mixture of socioeconomic groups. In a very rough way this might serve as a description of the Democratic and Republican parties. The difficulty is, however, that until the present the ideological distinctiveness of these blocs has been blurred because even on major issues persons who hold the same attitudes on one question diverge on others. Two issues of great recent salience—integration and medical care—furnish illustrations. One might speculate that at least in the North economic liberals who would favor medical care would also be civil libertarians who would favor racial integration in the public schools; conversely, the prosegregationists might also be economic conservatives. Doubtless there is some tendency of this kind. The relations are, however, very shaky. In a 1956 sample, among Northerners who favored medical care about half also favored racial integration

these groups the more Catholic counties exceeded the least Catholic in their opposition to right-to-work" (i.e. anti-union) legislation in a 1958 referendum. See also John H. Fenton, *The Catholic Vote* (New Orleans, Hauser Press, 1960), pp. 37–38.

46. Glazer and Moynihan, *Beyond the Melting Pot*, p. 167.

47. See, for example, the generalizations based on data from a survey made during the 1954 congressional elections, in Campbell and Cooper, *Group Differences*, pp. 79–80.

in the schools; but more than a third opposed it. Hence a Northern medical care coalition would, in the extreme case, lose a third of its support when it endorsed racial integration. Conversely, Northerners who opposed a federal medical care program were almost evenly divided on the question of racial integration; hence their coalition would (in principle) split wide open if it took any definite stand on the issue of segregation.[48]

Unless attitudes are highly polarized, it is impossible to divide a population into two like-minded collections of people. No matter what criterion is used for dividing people, as long as there are only two categories or collections, then within each category there will be many conflicting views. Given the existence of a two-party system, it follows inevitably that, unless attitudes are highly polarized, each of the two parties can hope to win only by constructing an electoral coalition made up of people whose views coincide on some questions but diverge on others. This is exactly what happens most of the time in the United States. And as long as (1) political attitudes are not polarized and (2) only two major parties exist, there can be no escape from two parties each with heterogeneous followings.[49]

Is the pattern I have been describing a recent one? It is difficult to say, for we have surveys and election studies only for the past quarter-century. Yet there is substantial reason for thinking that low polarization has been the usual condition of American politics, and that the reasons for low polarization have been about the same in the past as they are now: large socioeconomic groups have generally been heterogeneous in political attitudes, and persons who agree on one question disagree on others.[50]

Presumably there have been historical fluctuations; the tide of polarization ebbs and flows. Polarization has probably risen to high points during each of the major crises described earlier, and then receded. But polarization is rarely high in American politics and, it would appear, never persistent.

Structure of Government and Politics

After the patterns of consensus and cleavage, the third major factor that helps to account for the characteristics of oppositions in the United States

48. V. O. Key, *Public Opinion and American Democracy*, p. 170. In the 1964 election the voters in California supported President Johnson against Senator Goldwater by six to four and at the same time supported by two to one an amendment to the state constitution permanently nullifying all state legislation to eliminate racial discrimination in the sale of housing.

49. For some speculation as to the likelihood of a change, see pp. 68–69.

50. Although it covers only a limited period, a recent study of Jacksonian Democracy lends support to this interpretation. See Lee Benson, *The Concept of Jacksonian Democracy: New York as a Test Case* (Princeton, Princeton University Press, 1961), particularly Ch. 13, "Outline for a Theory of American Voting Behavior."

is the structure of government and politics: structure in large part prescribed by the Constitution but in some measure amplified by practice
and tradition.

One critical element in this structure is of course the two major parties.
Parties other than the two largest have less impact on politics in the
United States than in any other country examined in this volume. The
two parties are, however, decentralized; they do not command as high a
degree of voting support from their members in Congress as most
European parties seem to do; they tend to be pragmatic, even opportunistic, in approach; they seek and retain highly heterogeneous followings. Some of these characteristics, as we shall see, result from—or at any
rate are strengthened by—the kinds of factors discussed up to this point.
But the reasons an almost exclusive two-party system exists and persists
in the United States are too complex and debatable to enter into here. I
propose therefore to consider the two-party system as a given, and not
try to account for it. Its existence helps us explain the characteristics of
oppositions.

The other aspect of the structure of government and politics that bears
most heavily on the characteristics of oppositions is the fragmentation of
power that it facilitates. As everyone knows, the structure provides a
great many checkpoints at which one set of officials can block, slow up,
or significantly modify the actions of other officials—the White House,
the executive agencies, the independent commissions, the House, the Senate, the rules of procedure in each house, the standing committees,
conference committees of the two houses, the federal courts—and not
least the federal system itself, in which all these features are in greater or
lesser degree duplicated in 50 different states with a rather extensive
amount of authority and power.

These features reinforce the heterogeneous character of the parties,
primarily by providing to leaders who hold these offices, or can influence
officeholders, an extensive opportunity to bargain for advantages by
threatening to block, slow up, or modify the policies of other leaders
who need their support, constitutionally or from long-standing tradition,
practice, or law.

Illustrations abound. Ever since 1938 Democratic Presidents have suffered defeats at the hands of conservatives in Congress. In President Kennedy's first two years in office, a conservative coalition of Northern
Republicans and Southern Democrats voted together on about one-fourth
of the roll-call votes in the Senate and about one-sixth of the roll-call votes
in the House. Considering only these votes, the coalition defeated the
President by winning in the Senate more than half the time and in the
House nearly two times out of three. The victories of the conservative
coalition included measures dealing with foreign aid, farm laborers from

Mexico, mass transportation, and aid to depressed areas.[51] Or to take the example of civil rights: until 1964 opponents of laws designed to strengthen Negro rights regularly defeated these measures even when they had majority backing; the instruments were usually the House Rules Committee (controlled by a coalition of Southern Democrats and conservative Republicans) and the filibuster in the Senate. It was the Supreme Court, not the Congress, that ordered the principal changes in Southern patterns of segregation. Yet the Southern states, aided by the institutions of federalism, generally refused to comply; with relatively weak presidential leadership and enforcement under President Eisenhower, their opposition was on the whole successful. Southerners who defied the Court argued, moreover, that they were only obeying the law: the law of their own state.

Consequences for the Strategy and Tactics of Opposition

The strategy and tactics of opposition in the United States have been largely determined, I have suggested, by

1. The characteristic pattern of consensus
2. The characteristic pattern of cleavage
3. The structure of government and politics

Let me now describe some of the consequences in more detail.

First, a group opposed to existing American institutions is unlikely to gain much support if it mounts a comprehensive attack on the prevailing American ideology, or if it is widely perceived as doing so. To the extent that such a group is pragmatic and realistic in orientation, it will try to reduce its apparent divergence from the prevailing ideology by stressing aspects more consistent with its own ideology and objectives. Since the prevailing ideology is not all of one piece, it lends itself fairly readily to such treatment. However, the result within a radical opposition group is to create an esoteric ideology and an exoteric one; and this produces difficulties when naïve followers attracted by the exoteric ideology are repelled by the esoteric one. To some extent this has been a problem with the Communist Party.[52] Alternatively, an opposition that does not accommodate itself to the prevailing ideology is likely to be so unrealistic in its general behavior that its following is minuscule and made up of a disproportionate number of individuals low in political skills, realism, and effectiveness. The result is that few Americans are ever exposed to a

---

51. *Congressional Quarterly, Weekly Report, 21* (Week Ending April 17, 1964), "On Conservative Coalition," pp. 737–40. It should be pointed out that the victories of the conservative coalition were sometimes only marginal changes in the President's proposals, not outright defeats of the whole measure.

52. Irving Howe and Lewis Coser, *The American Communist Party, A Critical History* (New York, Praeger, 1962), pp. 538 ff

presentation of an alternative ideology that involves extensive criticism of the prevailing institutions or the belief-system that legitimizes these institutions.

Second, opposition is likely to be successful in bringing about the changes it seeks only if it affirms its support for the prevailing ideology and the basic institutions of American life, and concentrates its fire on some specific aspect of existing institutions, practices, or beliefs, e.g., free land for homesteaders, slavery, national regulation of banks, child labor, the sale of alcoholic beverages, and so on.

Third, given the dominance of two parties, low polarization, and the particular structure of government and politics, opposition is likely to be successful only if it enters directly into one of the two parties or bargains with both parties.

Although the option of forming a new party is theoretically open, there is not a single case in American history where an opposition has formed a third party, pushed one of the major parties aside, and subsequently won a national election. The electoral record of third parties in the United States is one of nearly total failure.[53] Of all the party systems in the world, the American two-party system has the longest continuous history of rivalry between the same two major parties. To anyone contemplating the formation of a third party, this historical fact should be (though evidently it not always is) a melancholy prospect to contemplate.

The upshot is, then, that to be effective in a concrete way an opposition will usually have to operate in league with, and make concessions to, leaders of groups whose attitudes on some questions will be in conflict with attitudes among its own followings.

Fourth, it is difficult or impossible to make a sharp distinction between "loyal opposition" and "government." Both merge imperceptibly into a system of coalitions, bargaining, and compromise in which no one coalition can be said to "govern" and none is definitely and persistently in opposition. Significantly, in Congress, in the state legislatures, and with rare exceptions in the press, Americans do not speak of "the loyal opposition" or even "the opposition." The closest terms are "the majority party" and "the minority party"; and even these terms cannot refer to both President and Congress during those periods when President, Senate, and House are not of the same party, which has been the case one-fourth of the time since 1789.

53. One might object that the Republicans began in 1854–56 as a third party, but the point is only technically true and of little relevance. For the Republican Party did not destroy the Whigs and take their place. The Whigs were destroyed by the slavery controversy, and the Republicans built their party, like Phoenix, on the ruins of the Whigs. This could perhaps happen again. The leaders of some third parties have impatiently awaited their Phoenix for a very long time. But after a full century the phenomenon has not yet been repeated.

Some Consequences for the System

Thus, just as the pervasive ideology provides support for the political system, so too the operation of the political system, in the ways I have just examined, provides support for the prevailing ideology.

To overstate the point somewhat: opposition cannot change the institutions because of the ideology; yet opposition cannot change the ideology because of the political institutions. Since most of the electorate accepts roughly the same ideology, it is possible (with the assistance of institutional factors such as presidential elections and single-member districts) for a two-party system—of a kind—to exist. Yet given the existence of only two major parties competing for votes, and given the initial acceptance of a single ideology among the electorate, competition between the two parties in turn undoubtedly reinforces the ideology.

This familiar process of reinforcement might be illustrated in the following way. Suppose we were to classify American adults according to the number of major propositions in the prevailing ideology with which each person disagrees: for example, support for popular government, for the constitutional system, for change by constitutional means, for private property, and for the desirability and possibility of personal success. Although we do not have the exact data we need, the evidence presented earlier suggests that most voters would not disagree with any of the major propositions; some, however, would disagree with one; a few with two or three; almost none with all five. A distribution would look something like Figure 2.1.

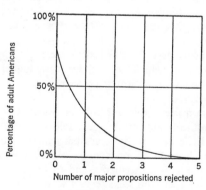

Figure 2.1

In conditions like these both parties direct their appeals to the great body of voters piled up on the left of the distribution. For either party to make any other appeal is to run the risk of losing a vast number of votes in order to gain a much smaller number among the political deviants.[54] When a party or a presidential candidate misreads the distribution, as Senator Goldwater did in 1964, the election confirms the risk of "extremism" by producing a resounding defeat. Further, the very fact that both parties are driven by the logic of numbers to adhere to roughly the same ideology means that the ideology is constantly reinforced, or, at the very least, that alternative ideologies are severely handicapped. Thus a typical election, far from generating long-lasting ideological tensions and conflicts as in many other countries, instead tends in the long run to strengthen the traditional ideology. For both major parties emphasize the virtues of that ideology and their faithful adherence to it.

The result is, then, that Americans have solved over long periods the problem of national unity that has weakened and even destroyed many other attempts to operate representative government. If the price for this success is high, the costs of failure could be even higher. Americans have their Civil War to remind them what failure can cost: one out of every dozen males of military age dead, an entire section of the country devastated, and the major question at issue, the place of Negroes in American life, given no more than a superficial, unstable, and morally intolerable solution. The twentieth century has revealed once more what enormous costs may be imposed on the people of a country, and on the world, when representative institutions fail from internal conflicts: Italy, Spain, and Germany, to mention only the three major European examples. The American achievement is all the more significant because of the differences in race, ethnic group, religion, and national origin of the American people, their sheer numbers, the vast size of the country, and the degree of economic specialization that has much of the time existed in the different regions.

Yet the costs of success (in this sense) are high—higher than most Americans are aware of, I think, and quite possibly higher than they need to be. For there are several additional consequences that must, I think, be weighed in the balance.

First, the system makes it easy for political leaders to ignore groups of people whose problems lie outside the attention, loyalties, values, and identifications of the great mass of voters, particularly if these groups lack bargaining power because of poor organization, low status, isolation, ignorance, lack of political incentives, and so on. In practical political terms, the political leader who seeks to find solutions for the problems of marginal groups runs the risk of gaining less support than he loses. It seems highly unlikely, for example, that the deprivation of Negro rights could have gone on so long, with so little national attention, if the United

54. This point was strongly stressed by E. E. Schattschneider in *Party Government* (New York, Rinehart, 1942).

States had had cabinet government, proportional representation, three or four major political parties, and more sources of ideological dissent. To say that this alternative would also have generated costs (costs that many of us would regard as excessive) does not gainsay the costs of the present system.

Second, criticism of the major structures and institutions of the United States tends to be rather limited, and examination of structural alternatives is ordinarily rather slight. The point is, no doubt, a familiar one; yet to weigh the balance of advantage and disadvantage flowing out of this consequence is not as easy as it is sometimes made to appear. Extensive, severe, and persistent criticism of the major social, economic, and political structures would put a serious strain on any democratic polity. Moreover, comprehensive and persistent criticism is almost inevitably grounded in ideologies; yet ideological controversy, like religious controversy, is rarely conducive to rational presentation, consideration, and appraisal of alternatives. Although nationwide shouting matches put a heavy burden on a democracy, they do not even compensate for that disadvantage by improving the grasp of the alternatives among citizens and leaders. Is it, as a practical matter, possible to have a rational, orderly examination in national politics of great structural alternatives? The question poses, I think, an unsolved problem. But to say that it is unsolved does not mean that the American solution is desirable. At one extreme, Italy, France, and Germany have in the past all incurred very high costs from implacable ideological controversy. At the opposite extreme, the immunity from comprehensive criticism that the major structures of American social, economic, and political life seem to possess may also impose heavy costs.

Third, if severe ideological cleavages often stimulate irrational controversy, it seems more than likely that the overwhelming ideological consensus of the kind I have described in this essay also encourages irrationalities. It may do so by compelling political dissenters to choose between futility and the two-party politics of compromise, thereby increasing their sense of frustration and political alienation. One enters here a doubtful terrain, and what follows is speculative. It is usually assumed that pragmatic, two-party politics American-style encourages reasonable compromises that mitigate frustration by yielding something to all the parties to a conflict. Yet this is surely not the whole story. Consider the lot of the political dissenter in the light of all that has been said up to this point. If he enters into a third party, he is condemned to political impotence. If he enters into one of the two major parties, he constantly sees his principles compromised or even forfeited. He has no satisfactory choice among candidates in elections. From his point of view, the relevant policy alternatives are rarely posed; national leaders, it seems, are unwilling to take his alternatives seriously. Differences among national leaders that are im-

portant to voters closer to the center of the political spectrum are, to our
political dissenter, too small to be noticeable. It is natural for him to interpret political conflict among national leaders as sham battles within a
unified power elite—or, as the American Right often calls it, taking a leaf
from the British Left, the Establishment (Eastern, Liberal).

For the political dissenter, continued political impotence and rejection
breed frustration. Frustration may produce apathy and withdrawal from
politics, but frustration may also turn to hostility, resentment, vengeful-
ness, and even hatred for national leaders in both parties. The political
dissenter, then, is likely to become alienated from the political system—
from its prevailing practices, its institutions, its personnel, and their assumptions. "Betrayed" by the leaders who dominate the system of politics,
the politically alienated dissenters look to some new leader for deliverance
—a leader who, like them, will shake off the shackles of two-party, pragmatic, compromising politics and offer a radical and uncompromising
alternative. In 1948 Henry Wallace may have briefly tapped a reservoir of
politically alienated voters on the Left; an alienated Right evidently responded to a Joe McCarthy in 1952, to a Barry Goldwater in 1964.

It is reasonable to surmise (if one continues this line of speculation)
that from the defeat of Populism in 1896 until the New Deal, the largest
alienated group in the United States was on the Left. Populism was in
many ways the American equivalent of European social democracy.[55] And
when it went down to defeat in 1896, the Left was confronted with the
familiar alternatives of supporting a separate socialist party that could not
win elections or entering one of the two major parties and compromising
with all the heterogeneous elements that made up these parties.

Since the advent of the New Deal, however, it is evidently the Right
that has been alienated, perhaps increasingly. Except for the fact that this
new Right is almost exclusively white, its composition seems to be socially
and economically heterogeneous. Attempts to locate the new Right in
particular social, economic, or educational strata have on the whole proved
unsuccessful. What distinguishes the new Right most sharply is not its
social-economic position but simply its dissenting ideology; and its alienation stems from a total inability to win national elections or, until 1964,
even to secure presidential candidates who would espouse its obviously
deviant minority views.[56]

55. Norman Pollack argues: "Had Populism succeeded, it could have fundamentally
altered American society in a socialist direction." *The Populist Response to Industrial
America* (Cambridge, Harvard University Press, 1962), p. 12.
56. This interpretation deliberately stresses the political sources of the radical Right.
Attempts to locate the socioeconomic sources of the new Right have been unsuccessful. In the first edition of *The Radical Right*, ed. by Daniel Bell (New York, Criterion
Books, 1955), the authors suggested such sources as anxieties over status and the new
rich. But the evidence for these hypotheses was slight; in the second edition (New

In national elections, the Right has had to look, in the North, to the Republican Party; in the South, to the Republicans or to a Southern third-party "Dixiecrat" movement. The Dixiecrats, like other third parties, have proved to be a political failure. As for the Republican Party, until 1964 it refused to nominate a presidential candidate wholly satisfactory to its right wing. The defeat of Senator Taft at the Republican convention in 1952, and the nomination and election of General Eisenhower, were dramatic and unmistakable victories for the moderates—the "Eastern, Liberal Establishment." Because Eisenhower was a Republican President, his attitudes and policies were perhaps all the more displeasing to the Right, since they demonstrated the ineffectiveness of the Right within its own party. In 1964, the Right at last had its way in the nomination of Barry Goldwater. The consequence was—as most responsible observers outside the Right predicted from the outset—overwhelming defeat.

In the conventional liberal-democratic theory of politics, political dissenters are a valuable source of enlightenment; by posing currently unpopular alternatives they force citizens and leaders to examine possibilities they could otherwise ignore. In the United States, however, it is doubtful whether the process has worked quite this way. Frustration and alienation seem to encourage paranoid interpretations of political life,[57] emotionalism and styles of thought that do not produce debate and discussion but

York, Anchor Books, 1964) the authors themselves are inclined to doubt them. As Lipset remarks, efforts to test their hypotheses about the effects of status incongruities "with the data now available proved unfruitful." (*The Radical Right*, p. 402) Oddly, in the first edition the authors all but ignored the most obvious possibility: the frustration of conservative Republicans unable to win elections. In 1960 Nelson Polsby called attention to the fact that the most significant distinction between those who supported and opposed McCarthy in various surveys was party identification: his supporters were mainly regular Republicans, while most Democrats opposed him. ("Towards an explanation of McCarthyism," *Political Studies, 8* [1960]). Lipset, after acknowledging Polsby's finding, says that two surveys "suggest that the most important single attribute associated with opinion of McCarthy was education, while a 1954 national study . . . indicated that religious affiliation was of greater significance than party." (*The Radical Right*, p. 398. The findings were: the more educated the respondents, the more anti-McCarthy they were, and Protestants were more anti-McCarthy than Catholics.) In a more recent study of persons who attended a "San Francisco Bay Region School of Anti-Communism" (an extreme right-wing group) in 1962, the authors found that this particular group of right-wingers were Republicans of relatively high socioeconomic status and education. Their most salient characteristic was their support for Republican candidates. Ninety-two per cent of those who voted in the 1960 presidential election supported the Republican candidate, Richard Nixon, and two-thirds identified themselves as Republicans, 19 per cent as independents, and only 8 per cent as Democrats. Raymond E. Wolfinger, Barbara Kaye Wolfinger, Kenneth Prewitt, and Sheila Rosenhack, "America's Radical Right: Politics and Ideology" in David E. Apter, ed., *Ideology and Discontent* (New York, The Free Press, 1964), pp. 262–93.

57. Richard Hofstadter, "The Paranoid Style in American Politics," *Harper's Magazine* (November 1964), pp. 77–86.

hostility and rejection. The moderates close ranks against the threat. In the end, the attack of the political dissenters, far from clarifying alternatives by debate and discussion, may actually reinforce the prevailing ideology.

Changes

In emphasizing the recurring patterns of the American system, I have inevitably portrayed that system as more static over the long run than in fact it is. The system does change. Opinions change as to what the government should be doing in the issue-areas mentioned earlier—democratic rights and privileges, the Negro, the role of the government in the economy, foreign policy. And the policies enforced by the government also change.

An attempt to explain changes in political opinions and policies would take us into a vast area, important but not well charted. However, it might be useful to conjecture whether there are likely to be any important changes in the three main sets of explanatory factors discussed earlier. Of these three kinds of factors, the pattern of cleavages seems to offer the greatest likelihood of significant changes.

The pattern described earlier seems likely to change in two ways. First, it is reasonable to project a trend of gradually declining salience of objective differences within the American population as a result of affluence, widespread education, mass communications, the expansion of white-collar employment and declining proportions of farmers and manual workers. If this trend continues, then objective differences will become even less related than they are at present to differences in voting patterns and, more important, to political attitudes. Subjective factors only related in a loose way to these objective characteristics—values, ideology, psychological predispositions—may then become relatively more important. To the extent that this occurs, the appropriate strategy for the political parties will be to pay less attention to the presumed desires of particular socioeconomic categories in the population and more and more to general attitudes, aspirations, and policy-oriented views that cut across socioeconomic categories to like-minded voters in each of these categories. In this sense, American politics may become more, not less, "ideological." As a result of this change the parties may be even more heterogeneous than at present in the socioeconomic characteristics of their support, and at the same time less heterogeneous and more unified in the policies for which they can secure the support of their voters. To put it another way, one's political allies and opponents today would remain one's allies and opponents tomorrow.

This change might well be the result of two other changes that are very likely to occur in American politics: the removal of the ancient issue of Negro rights from its central (if not always public) place in politics by defeating the South on this question and providing such powerful juridical guarantees for the Negro that the process cannot be reversed, as it was after 1876; and the development of a two-party system in the South.

For one condition above all created the pattern of cleavage that has dominated American politics in which today's allies are tomorrow's opponents. This was the power of the one-party South in elections and in Congress and its virtually unbreakable unity on the institutions of white supremacy in the South. A party that would not do business with the South on its own terms, i.e., yield to white supremacy in the South, has for nearly a hundred years stood in perpetual danger of being defeated in elections or in Congress, or both, by a party that would. Both parties yielded to this imperative. As a result, the South was at once a permanent opposition (on all questions involving racial segregation) and a permanent partner in government.

If, however, the issue that has made this inevitable is removed from politics, and if the Republican Party gains an increasingly strong foothold in the South (not merely in presidential elections but also in elections to Congress and the state legislatures), there will be little left to distinguish Northern liberals and progressives from Southern liberals and progressives, Northern moderates from Southern moderates, or Northern conservatives from Southern conservatives. The parties may then regroup along lines of greater ideological and programmatic consistency.

Should this take place, however, it is not likely to produce two sharply differentiated parties with distinct ideologies. The kind of consensus, even pseudo-consensus, discussed earlier, makes this unlikely. The content of the beliefs at the center may—indeed, undoubtedly will—change. But the tendency for opinions and beliefs to converge will probably continue. The center will then continue to dominate political life, and dissenters will continue to be frustrated and alienated.

3

NORWAY:
NUMERICAL DEMOCRACY
AND CORPORATE PLURALISM

Stein Rokkan

28 Years In, 28 Days Out:
The Labor Government Is Ousted but
Returns to Power After a Brief Interlude

An extraordinary crisis was triggered off in Norwegian politics by the resignation of the Minister of Industrial Affairs on June 20, 1963. A disaster had occurred in a state-owned coal mine in Spitzbergen some months earlier and the Commission of Inquiry appointed by the government to look into the mining operations had concluded that the disaster was likely to have been caused by gross negligence on the part of the management and the government inspectors. The report of the Commission had not yet been published but the members of the Cabinet knew its conclusions. The mining company was administered by a board under the Department of Industrial Affairs, and the minister responsible for the Department decided to resign, apparently without consulting his colleagues in the Cabinet. His letter of resignation set off the first serious crisis in domestic politics since the early 1930s. The letter was made public the day before the Storting was to be prorogued; this was the first time anyone in the opposition had been given any information about the conclusions of the Commission of Inquiry. The rumor spread that the Cabinet had deliberately withheld the report from the Storting in order to gain time during the summer recess. The five opposition parties—the 2 Left Socialists (formally, the Socialist People's Party) as well as the 74 Liberals, Christians, Agrarians, and Conservatives to the right of the government—united in defense of their right to full information and decided to keep Parliament in session through the summer to allow detailed consideration

This chapter was written while I held a Simon Visiting Professorship at the University of Manchester. I am much indebted to William Mackenzie for support, encouragement, and advice and to Richard Rose for stimulating discussions. I also wish to record my indebtedness to Robert Dahl, Harry Eckstein, Egil Fivelsdal, Val Lorwin, Jens Arup Seip, Nils Stjernquist, Ulf Torgersen, Henry Valen, and Jörgen Westerståhl for comments on and criticisms of an early version of the chapter.

of the action to be taken on the report. This was a direct threat to the Labor government: if the Left Socialists sided with the four nonsocialist parties, there would be 76 votes for a motion of no confidence, the 74 Labor representatives would be outvoted, and the government would have to go. All hinged on the 2 Left Socialists: they could repudiate the Labor government, but they might make life equally impossible for a new government formed by the 74 nonsocialists.

Few political leaders had any holiday that summer. The Liberals, Christians, Agrarians, and Conservatives developed a united front and agreed to do their utmost to carry out the threat and, if they were successful, form a coalition government. The Labor Party rallied massive support behind the government and encouraged the trade unions to put heavy pressure on the Left Socialists to keep them from any act of disloyalty toward the working class. The young Socialist People's Party was indeed caught on the horns of an acute dilemma: the party might lose its raison d'être if it kept giving in to the Labor Party, but it might lose a lot of its electoral support among dissident trade unionists and other workers if it helped the "bourgeois" parties to power after 28 years of Labor rule.

The party leadership decided to follow a novel strategy: the 2 Left Socialists in the Storting would vote for the motion of no confidence but would not support a new government of what the Norwegians call the "bourgeois" parties. The implication was that they were prepared to support a new Labor government after appropriate changes in personnel and in policy: they wanted a more socialist and perhaps also more neutralist government, and they wanted to use their two strategic votes to force such a change.

When it was first announced, this strategy met with derision and scorn in the Labor Party. But when the Labor government was ousted from power after a memorable debate on August 23, this was in fact the strategy its leaders adopted in their counteroffensive. They forced the new Cabinet of the four opposition parties to present its policies in a broad program statement on September 16, and then immediately counterattacked with a far more radical and far more socialist program of their own: they proposed a comprehensive scheme of service pensions of the type the Swedish Social Democrats had introduced, and they also suggested a series of moves to strengthen the role of the state in the economy. The Storting was faced with two alternative programs of action: one moderate and emphasizing balanced welfare state policies very similar to those followed by Labor in the years after World War II; the other distinctly more radical, more socialist. The result was a foregone conclusion: the Left Socialists thought they had had their way and voted with Labor. The four-party coalition government was out, and Labor was again in power.

The opposition still had hopes, however. The debates in the Storting

had taken place during local election campaigns and had been televised to
a national audience of unprecedented size. The local elections were held
only two days after Labor's return to power and in fact took the form of
a national contest between the opposing political groups. The result came
as a shock to all those who had hoped that the crisis had weakened the
Labor Party. It gained more votes than any other party and kept the Left
Socialists in check: Labor had mobilized its working-class electorate to a
maximum in moving leftward and at the same time had held the dissidents
to a minimum.[1]

1. Local elections since World War II have given these results:

*Per cent of total
votes cast for*

	1945	1947	1951	1955	1959	1963
Communist Party	11.4	10.0	6.1	5.3	3.9	1.9
Socialist People's Party	—	—	—	—	—	2.8
Labor	39.8	38.2	42.4	43.4	43.7	45.8
Middle parties (Liberal, Christian, Agrarian)	19.8	22.2	22.7	22.8	24.2	25.4
Conservatives	9.7	13.9	15.3	16.7	18.6	19.8
Joint "burgher" lists	6.2	8.2	6.2	4.3	2.3	1.2
Local, nonpartisan lists	13.2	7.6	7.4	7.5	7.3	5.1
Per cent voting	*65.5*	*71.6*	*72.7*	*71.5*	*72.9*	*81.0*

The 1959–63 gains registered for the Socialists in general (+2.9 per cent) and for
Labor in particular (+1.9 per cent) seem to have resulted from two movements
within the electorate: first, the increased turnout (+8.1 per cent), and second, the
reduction in the number of votes for local nonpartisan lists (−2.2 per cent). Direct
comparison with the results for national elections is difficult for three reasons: (1)
differences in turnout levels between the two types of elections, (2) the presence of
nonpartisan and joint "burgher" lists in local elections, and (3) variations in the
number of constituencies and communes in which the new Socialist People's Party
presented its own lists. To get around the first difficulty one can calculate party
votes in per cent of the electorate rather than of the total valid vote. A comparison
for two national and two local elections give these results:

	1957 national	1959 local	1961 national	1963 local
Total electorate in '000s = 100%	*2,298*	*2,314*	*2,340*	*2,363*
Turnout (incl. rejected votes)	77.9	72.9	79.1	81.0
Per cent for:				
Communist Party	2.6	2.8	2.3	1.5
Socialist People's Party	—	—	1.9	2.3
Labor	37.7	31.5	36.8	36.8
Middle	22.8	17.4	21.9	18.9
Conservative	14.7	13.4	15.7	15.9
Joint "burgher" and nonpartisan lists	—	6.9	—	5.1

The Socialist gains from 1959 to 1963 were indeed considerable: they advanced from
34.3 to 40.6 per cent of the electorate. But this was essentially due to the "nationalization" of the local elections of 1963: by comparison with the preceding national elections in 1961 there was very little change indeed. For details on traditional differences
between local and national elections in Norway, see S. Rokkan and H. Valen, "The
Mobilization of the Periphery," in S. Rokkan, ed., *Approaches to the Study of
Political Participation* (Bergen, Chr. Michelsen Institute, 1962).

The four-party opposition to the right had again been reminded of a stubborn fact of Norwegian political life: the numerical majority of the mobilized citizens has been to the left in all elections since the war and a crisis such as the one of the summer of 1963 could only have been brought about through dissidence and splinter movements within this majority.

The Norwegian Party System:
Four Minor Parties Face One Major Party

The Norwegian party system hovers at some point halfway between the Anglo-American and the Continental. There are one "in" party but four "out" parties: the Labor Party has been close to the majority point for three decades; throughout this period the opposition has been divided into several organizationally distinct parties, each with its particular clientele. There is no possibility of regular alternation between major parties as in Britain or in the United States, yet there is no discernible trend toward an "all-party" or "most-party" coalition as in Austria, Switzerland, the Netherlands, and several German Länder. There is no great enthusiasm for this halfway system, and there have been assiduous advocates of change in one direction or the other: toward an Anglo-American system of alternation between major parties or toward a Continental system of proportional sharing of responsibilities among all national parties.

The pleas for an Anglo-Saxon solution have no doubt been loudest and most persistent: calls for unity among all antisocialists have been heard ever since the introduction of manhood suffrage in 1900, and the need for a broad alliance in opposition to Labor has been a central theme in all election debates since the early 'twenties. The idea of a merger into one great antisocialist opposition party has survived an endless series of setbacks. The brief period of coalition in the summer of 1963 gave fresh impetus to efforts in this direction, but subsequent debates over the rights and wrongs of the joint program of action made it clear that there was no basis yet for an organizational merger across the historically given lines of cleavage.

Pleas for a Continental solution have been fewer and more academic. The idea of shared government gained momentum during the years of war, occupation and resistance from 1940 to 1945 and was argued fervently by several leading publicists and one or two active politicians in the years that followed. The notion of a *Proporz* solution was never a central issue of public debate, however, and the bitter experiences of the summer of 1963 made the possibility of agreement on an all-party national government more remote than ever.

The advocates of change in the established halfway system, whether toward the Anglo-American or toward the Continental model, have tended to ignore the hard structural facts of Norwegian politics; they have underestimated the difficulties of introducing workable alternatives to a system of gradually formed alignments along inherited lines of cleavage in the national community. A realistic analysis of the problems and prospects of effective opposition in such a system must start with an account of the succession of conflicts, divisions, and realignments which led to the current constellation of parties, and seek to pinpoint the conditions for the continued functioning of this system.

A leading academic historian recently reviewed the history of Norway from 1814 to 1964 and divided this time span into three distinct periods: first, the *regime of the officials*, the 70 years of centralized bureaucratic rule from 1814 to 1884; second, the *multiparty regime*, the 60 years that followed of rapidly changing governments and frequent shifts in parliamentary constellations and alignments; and finally, from 1945 onward, the *one-party regime*, the rule of the Labor leaders and their allies in the central bureaucracy and in the giant interest organizations.[2] Paradoxically, this dialectical interpretation of the cyclical movement of Norwegian history appeared only a month after the greatest upheaval in national politics since the early 'thirties: the theory of the one-party state was propounded in the immediate wake of a severe, if unsuccessful, challenge to the continued dominance of the Labor movement in the affairs of the nation. In a sense the theory functioned as a self-falsifying prophecy: it was one item in a broad movement of Left Socialist opposition to the rigidities of the regime, and it was this very movement of Socialist dissent which had put the Labor leaders to their severest test since the victory in 1945.

The historian had joined the ranks of the *terribles simplificateurs* but in doing so had pointed to three crucial sets of factors in the development of the Norwegian polity: firstly the deep-rooted tradition of *centralized bureaucratic rule*, originally inherited from the absolutist regime under the Danish kings but later developed and reinforced as the farmers, the fishermen, and the workers rose to state their claims and pressed forward the twentieth-century service state; second, the heritage of *territorial and cultural opposition* to the governing officials and the allied urban elites of academics, merchants, and industrialists; and third, the intensification of *class contrasts* with the spread of the money and market economy throughout the national territory and with the development of industrial centers both in the traditional urban settings and in the peripheral countryside.

Norway was granted internal independence in the wake of the Napoleonic wars: it had to accept personal union with Sweden and the dominance of Stockholm in all external affairs, but it was granted full autonomy in the organization of its domestic administration and its internal political life. The Constitution of 1814 gave the new nation the most democratic

2. Jens Arup Seip, *Fra embedsmannsstat til ettpartistat og andre essays* (Oslo, Universitetsforlaget, 1963).

system of representation in Europe: all freehold peasants and most lease-holders were given the right to vote.[3] In practice, however, the government of the country continued to be in the hands of a small elite of officials and patricians; for decades after the grant of the franchise the great majority of peasants deferred to their "betters" and were content to leave the affairs of the nation in the hands of the educated administrators and the privileged burghers of the cities.

The peasantry was not to remain in this state of obedient apathy, however. A slow process of social, cultural, and religious mobilization got under way in the wake of independence and gradually prepared the ground for a political breakthrough. The decisive marshaling of forces against the regime of the officials took place from the 1860s onward. The peasants finally organized themselves for political action and established their allies among reformers and radicals in the cities—artisans, teachers, lawyers, and other groups—in opposition to the central administrative elite. This alliance soon gained the upper hand in the Storting and launched a long series of skillfully organized attacks against the supremacy and independence of the Cabinet and the administration.[4] The struggle was long and protracted but the opposition stuck to the rules of the game and was at every point careful to establish its rights through due process of law. Before every major decision it insisted on consulting the people in duly organized elections. The result was an unprecedented mobilization of new voters on each side in the struggle. The *Left*, as the alliance of rural populists and urban radicals came to be called, won overwhelming victories at the polls in 1879 and 1882, but its very success forced the official establishment to mobilize all the electoral counterforces it could command and to organize clubs and societies for the defense of the Constitution: this was the origin of the *Right*, the Conservative Party.

The final struggle between the forces of the Left and the forces of the Right was ugly and bitter. The country was on one or two occasions on the verge of civil war: there were rumors that the Swedish king was preparing to mobilize the army for a coup d'etat against Parliament, and the Left on its side organized a network of riflemen's associations to serve as a popular militia against the forces of the officials.[5] In the end, however,

3. For detailed estimates of the size and composition of the electorate under the original franchise criteria see S. Rokkan, "Geography, Religion and Social Class," in S. M. Lipset and S. Rokkan, eds., *Party Systems and Voter Alignments* (New York, Free Press, forthcoming 1967). The fullest discussion of early electoral arrangements is found in Alf Kaartvedt's volume of *Det norske Storting gjennom 150 år* (Oslo, Gyldendal, 1964), *1*, 51–138.
4. The best analyses of these struggles are found in J. A. Seip, *Et régime foran undergangen* (Oslo, Tanum, 1945); Alf Kaartvedt, *Kampen mot parlamentarisme 1880–1884* (Oslo, Universitetsforlaget, 1956); and in Rolf Danielsen's volume of *Det norske Storting gjennom 150 år* (Oslo, Gyldendal, 1964), *2*.
5. Kaartvedt, *Kampen mot parlamentarisme*, pp. 131–37, and 304–13.

both sides agreed to proceed within the law. The struggle ended in 1884 in a series of dramatic impeachment proceedings against the King's Council. The Left used its overwhelming majority in the Storting to pack the Court of Impeachment and the verdict itself was never in doubt: the members of the Cabinet had acted contrary to the Constitution and were to be divested of their offices. But what would the King do? This was the real issue: would he appoint another Cabinet of the Right from among his own officials or would he give in and accept the supremacy of the Storting? After much soul-searching, the King and his advisers took the safer course: they asked the leader of the Left majority to form the Cabinet and thereby took a decisive step toward the establishment of the principle of parliamentary rule in Norway.[6]

The critical contest for power between the Left and the Right generated a process of mass mobilization into politics, and this process soon acquired its own dynamics. It changed the conditions for political activity and set the stage for new alignments and new cleavage lines in the system. The system had lost its equilibrium, and each party was continuously pressed to bring in new allies on its side to achieve some balance. The result was an unprecedented expansion of the political arena: first through increased turnout among those already registered and through increased registration of those qualifying under the old franchise rules, later through a series of extensions of the suffrage.[7]

In 1876, at the last of the "prepolitical" elections, the total number of citizens on the electoral rolls was only 84,000 out of an adult male population of close to 400,000. In 1900, at the first election after the introduction of manhood suffrage, the total number on the rolls had risen to five times the 1876 figure even though the adult population had only increased by some 20 per cent. These masses of new entrants into the political system could not easily be absorbed by the original contestants; new lines of cleavage came to the fore in the body politic, new alliances were tried out, and an increasingly complex system of party constellations emerged.

In oversimplified structural terms we may say that the Norwegian multiparty system was generated by regional differences in the timing of the two decisive waves of mobilization: the mobilization of the peasants and the mobilization of the workers.

The original struggle between the Left and the Right was triggered off by the mobilization of the peasantry. The decisive lines of cleavage tended to be territorial and cultural. The provinces resented the dominance of the capital. The awakening rural communities resisted the influence of an alien and foreign-oriented urban culture. The peasantry found it more and

6. Ibid., Chs. 8, 10–12.
7. For statistical details of this process of mobilization see S. Rokkan, "Geography, Religion, and Social Class."

more difficult to accept the standards set by the officials and the patrician establishment: the urban language, the *riksmål,* so remote from the inherited dialects of the countryside, the rationalist Lutheranism of the State Church, the foreign manners, the tolerant morals, and the convivial drinking prevalent in the open urban society. The Left gained strength through the convergence of these resentments against the urban establishment: the Left did more than open up channels to influence political power—it met a widespread demand for cultural self-assertion and identification. In the early decades after independence, the peasantry had generally accepted the language and the cultural traditions of the king's officials and the educated bourgeoisie as superior to their own, but increasing contacts with urban manners and urban realities led to widespread frustration and alienation. The peasants felt awkward and uncertain when communicating with officials and others in authority; they felt inferior and exploited in their dealings with city folk; and they found little comfort in the teachings of the established Church. Mobilization did not lead to cultural integration; instead it produced a widespread breakdown in human communication and generated a number of "countercultures" essentially hostile to the established standards and models of the original elite.

The movement for a new national language, the *landsmål,* was the most direct and most forceful of these expressions of resistance against urban influence. The new language gave the peasants a concrete symbol of their historical identity and inspired pride and confidence in their national mission. The movement accentuated the regional contrasts in the nation; it entrenched itself firmly in the inner valleys of the East and in the fjords and on the coast of the South and the West but remained in a minority in the central rural areas and the cities of the East, in the Trøndelag and in the North.[8] The conflict over the language forms deepened the cleavage between city and countryside throughout the national territory but it was only one among a number of polarizing issues. Religious divisions often reinforced, sometimes cut across linguistic cleavage lines. Pietistic and fundamentalist doctrines and practices entrenched themselves in many rural districts early in the nineteenth century and prepared the ground for a broad movement of religious protest against the established Lutheran Church.

A number of educational endeavors helped to give the young peasantry

8. *Riksmål* was the name given to the language of the educated urban strata. This was, at least until 1907, essentially Danish in orthography and structure but East Norwegian in pronunciation and vocabulary. The contrast between the written and spoken form was reduced through a series of linguistic reforms in the twentieth century. The *landsmål,* later *nynorsk,* was originally the creation of a linguist of peasant origin, Ivar Aasen. It represented an attempt to reconstruct a common Norwegian standard language on the basis of the rural dialects least affected by the 400 years of Danish rule. For an attempt at a sociological interpretation of these cultural contrasts see S. Rokkan, "Geography, Religion, and Social Class."

a deeper consciousness of their historical mission and trained them for
active citizenship: the Folk High Schools established from the 1860s onward became important recruiting stations for militants and leaders within
the rural Left.[9] Even such essentially philanthropic and practical movements as the teetotal organizations fitted into this alignment of countercultures: the total rejection of alcohol was part of a general movement of
protest against the moral disintegration brought about by urbanization. All
these movements reflected deep divisions in the national community. There
was no single acceptable medium of communication; there was only
fragmentary consensus on national standards and national values and there
were many built-in barriers against informal social contacts across the
many cultural enclaves. Foreign observers have often found it difficult to
understand the importance of alcohol as an issue in Nordic politics. It is
tempting to interpret the strength of the teetotal movement within the
Left as another expression of a basic refusal to accept communications from
the established elite: the refusal to take part in convivial drinking was
tantamount to a refusal to mix freely within the community and helped to
maintain a multitude of local cultural enclaves from erosion through informal social contact with other milieux.

The Left offered a common platform for these varieties of cultural
enclaves, whether linguistic, religious, or moral. The party did not stand
for one integrated counterculture but was a temporary alliance of several,
some in close communication with each other, others far apart. The unity
of the heroic years of struggle did not last long. The first split came only
four years after the victory in 1884: the fundamentalist wing of the party
could no longer cooperate with the nationalist radicals. The two wings
came together again after the settlement with Sweden in 1905, but the
unity of the party was always precarious. The failure of the policy of
alcohol prohibition in the 'twenties increased the strains between the
fundamentalist and the nationalist factions of the party, and in 1933 led to
the next split in the ranks of the defenders of rural cultural traditions:
a Christian People's Party was formed by a dissident wing of the old
Left and established itself as a serious competitor for votes, first in the
West only, later, from 1945 onward, throughout the country.

However fragile the unity of the old Left, the territorial-cultural cleavages have persisted in Norwegian policies throughout the 80 years since
the downfall of the old regime. The mobilization of the working class in
the years after the introduction of manhood suffrage produced new lines
of conflict within the system, but there was no polarization along any
single dimension: the old center-periphery axis cut across the new upper-

9. For a lively description and comparison of the Danish, Swedish, and Norwegian
Folk High School movements see Erica Simon, *Réveil national et culture populaire
en Scandinavie* (Paris, Presses Universitaires, 1960).

lower axis and produced an increasingly complex system of alignments. The conflicts between the capital and the provinces, between the urban culture and the rural, were far from resolved at the time the workers entered the political arena, and the old issues of cultural policy proved distinctly more divisive than the new issues of class conflict throughout the period up to 1918. The core of the old Left continued its fight for the rural countercultures: it championed the recognition of *landsmål* as a standard national language, it fought for a reorganization of the established Church, it advocated stringent legislation against the sale of alcohol. There was no basis for an understanding with the Right: even the threatening specter of a giant working-class party could not bring the two cultures into close communication with each other.

This conflict between rural claims and urban dominance goes far to explain the difference between the Scandinavian multiparty system and the English two-party system. In Scandinavia there were few and only tenuous ties between the rural and the urban elites; in Norway this chasm was even deeper than in Denmark or Sweden as a result of centuries of foreign dominance channeled through the cities. In England the original conflict between Tories and Liberals pitted landed interests against commercial and industrial, but the great estate owners soon found allies in the boroughs and from 1885 onward there was a distinct trend toward a merger between rural, suburban, and urban elites.[10] This realignment brought about a polarization of English politics and paved the way for the rise of a distinct lower-class party, first under the wings of the embattled Liberals, later on its own. In England the decisive struggles between rural and urban interests came long before the mobilization of the lower classes for political action. In Scandinavia the two waves of mobilization came close on each other's heels and one set of issues had not come anywhere near settlement before the next set forced itself on the body politic. The result was a very different system of party constellations: there was the same tendency toward class polarization as in England, but it did not come through with equal force in all regions and the poles of the class conflict were not the same in the rural as in the urban areas.

In the Norwegian case the crosscutting of the two axes produced a complex system of regionally differentiated party oppositions along the lines indicated in the table on page 80.

The new wave of mobilization triggered off by the extension of the suffrage to the landless, the propertyless, and the wage earners accentuated the territorial differences in the system, not only between the central and the peripheral areas but also between the regions.

The equalitarian communities of the South and the West had long been

10. See especially James Cornford, "The Transformation of Conservatism in the Late 19th Century," *Victorian Studies,* 7 (1963), 35–66.

Territorial axis	*Functional-economic axis*	
	Least polarized: South, West	*Most polarized: East, Middle, North*
Center: cities, suburbs, industrialized, rural	Labor vs. Left, Right	Labor vs. Right
Intermediate rural: market farming, forestry	Labor weak, Agrarians, Liberals, Christians dominant	Labor vs. Agrarians
Periphery: marginal farming, fisheries	Labor weak, Liberals, Christians dominant	Labor vs. Right

the strongholds of the movements of cultural defense against the influences from the cities and from the economic and administrative center of the nation. In these communities the old Left and its offshoots remained in dominance and offered stubborn resistance against the trend toward a class polarization of local politics. This was the case not only in the isolated periphery but even in areas of incipient urbanization and industrialization: the territorial opposition to the influences from the cities was stronger than the contrast between the old established electorate and the lower-class entrants, and the Labor Party found it very difficult to enlist support outside the few core groups of unionized industrial workers.[11]

In the other regions the spread of the money and market economy undermined the earlier traditions of cultural defense and created new alignments on functional lines. The result was another split within the ranks of the old Left—this time not on issues of religious orthodoxy but over questions of economic policy. The farmers and the forest owners felt increasingly unable to support the diffuse politics of cultural defense so central in the program of the Left, and insisted on action to protect their prices and to ensure regular government support for their efforts to expand and modernize. They were also worried about the rise of the rural lower classes and the entrenchment of the Labor Party among the agricultural wage earners and the forestry workers. They could not ally themselves with the Right: the age-old traditions of suspicion and distrust against the urban elite were too strong, and there were also direct clashes of interest between the producers of primary commodities and the managers of free enterprise commerce and industry. The market farmers and the forest owners were among the first to establish vigorous interest organizations, and the leaders of these organizations soon exerted heavy pressures both on nominations of candidates for the Storting and on the decisions of the representatives once they had been elected. It did not take

11. For details see S. Rokkan and H. Valen, "Regional Contrasts in Norwegian Politics," a chapter in E. Allardt and Y. Littunen, eds., *Cleavages, Ideologies and Party Systems* (Helsinki, Westermarck Society, 1964).

long, however, before they felt the need to go further and to establish their own party: steps in this direction were first taken in a few constituencies in 1915 and a full-blown nationwide Agrarian Party emerged in 1921. The crosscutting of the two axes had produced four parties: the old Left still remained culturally opposed to the Right, but the rise of the Labor Party had added another dimension to the system and pitted the lower classes against the Right in the cities and the industrialized countryside, but against the Agrarians in the majority of the farming and forestry communities.

The enfranchisement of the lower classes had brought about a profound change in Norwegian politics. The cities and the industrial centers were the first to be polarized between the middle and the lower strata, but the movement gradually spread to the traditional rural communities and to the coastal peripheries: very slowly, as we have seen, in the South and the West, surprisingly rapidly in the poorest of all the provinces, the North. The Labor Party, originally an offshoot of the burgeoning trade union movement in the cities, cut across the earlier territorial lines; it established alliances between rural and urban, peripheral and central forces and stimulated a series of moves toward the development of "nationalized" politics. It is deeply significant that the party had its decisive breakthrough not in the capital or in any of the larger cities but in the Northern periphery: it had built up its initial organizational strength in the central areas of the East, but the Socialist message spread much more quickly and with much more effect among the crofters, the fishermen, and the "navvies" of the far North. The first five Socialists to be elected to the Storting all came from the North: four from the fisheries districts of Troms and Finnmark, one from the new industrial center at Narvik. Class resentments in the traditional primary economy in fact proved as important for the growth of the Labor Party as the new cleavages within the industrializing centers. The waves of rapid industrialization after 1910 radicalized the party, and the experiences of inflation and unfettered speculation during the First World War strengthened its revolutionary wing. But the party remained an alliance between rural and urban interests, and the broad popular appeal of the movement in fact acted to restrain its ideologists and its leaders.

The Norwegian Labor Party went further to the revolutionary left than any of the other Scandinavian working-class movements. The radical wing gained the upper hand in the wake of the Russian Revolution and mobilized a majority for the Third International: the result was a split-off on the right. The Norwegians proved highly insubordinate in their relations with the Comintern, however, and the alliance was broken in 1923.[12] The result was another split-off, this time on the left. This anarchic state of

12. For details see K. Langfeldt, *Moskvatesene i norsk politikk* (Oslo, Universitetsforlaget, 1961)

affairs lasted for four years. By 1927 the majority party and the right-wing
Social Democrats had finally decided to unite again and to build up a
broad national organization for effective electoral action. The election that
year proved decisive: the united Labor Party advanced from 32 to 59 seats
in the Storting and constituted the largest group of representatives in the
legislature. The divisions between the old, established parties, the Left and
the Right, were still deep and bitter and in the Cabinet crisis that followed
the election the King decided to ask the leader of the Labor Party to form
an administration.[13]

This decision marked a turning point in the history of democratic
politics in Norway. A revolutionary party representing hitherto underprivileged strata of the national community was admitted to power in
accordance with the established rules of the parliamentary game. The party
was not immediately domesticated as a result of this gesture of acceptance:
there was widespread distrust of all varieties of "Ministerial Socialism"
and a great deal of reluctance to take power without a clear parliamentary
majority.[14] Nevertheless, the party decided to accept the challenge: its
leaders presented a straight socialist program of action to the Storting and
were voted out of power nine hectic days later.

Labor had had its first brief taste of power. Did the experience prove
that the revolutionaries were right, that the fight for a socialist society
could not be won through electoral and parliamentary procedures? Or did
it only show how little could be achieved before a numerical majority had
been won in people and Parliament? The Labor Party was rocked by
debates over this question for the next three years: should it build itself up
as a strong class party ready to fight the capitalist forces directly or should
it broaden its appeal to the people at large and seek power through the
regular channels of elections and majority voting? The revolutionaries
again won out, and the party went into the 1930 election with a program
even further to the left than the 1928 declaration. The result was a massive
mobilization of the available counterforces in the community. The turnout
rose to the highest level reached since the introduction of universal
suffrage, and large numbers of women voting for the first time in their
lives threw their weight against Labor. The party maintained most of its
strength in absolute numbers but it lost grievously in the competition for
new votes. To the revolutionary wing of the party this was not necessarily a loss; it wanted an organization of convinced Socialists, not a mass
of mobilized sympathizers. But to the majority of the party leaders the
defeat was a call for action: they wanted to win mandates, and they wanted
to broaden the appeal of the party. The economic crisis of 1930–31 forced

13. An illuminating analysis of the background of these developments is given in
Ivar Roset, *Det norske Arbeiderparti og Hornruds regjeringsdannelse i 1928* (Oslo,
Universitetsforlaget, 1964).
14. Ibid., Ch. 3

them into concrete political action in their localities, and they became increasingly convinced that the revolutionary strategy of the party could only lead to despair and disillusionment. The world crisis, the disenchantment with the Soviet system, the threatening specters of Fascism and National Socialism made more and more of them rally to the defense of parliamentary democracy and made them willing to cooperate with other parties in the solution of concrete problems of policy. A fundamental change of orientation took place in the leadership during 1930–33: the party was about to enter the national political community and was preparing itself for its ascent to power.

This process of domestication was accelerated by the strains between the urban and rural wings of the party. Two young party ideologists, Dag Bryn and Halvard Lange, analyzed this contrast in great detail in a path-breaking article in 1930.[15] They pointed to the marked imbalance between the cities and the countryside in the member–voter ratios of the party and saw in this an expression of the strain between the two models of organization, the class party and the people's party. Their figures, in the accompanying table, are indeed striking.

	Members 1927 (in '000s)	Voters 1927 (in '000s)	Ratio of members to voters
Oslo	26.1	63.5	1:2.4
Other cities	15.4	79.1	1:5.1
Rural communes	26.5	225.6	1:8.5

In the capital the party came close to having direct organizational ties with at least one voter in every household on its side. In the rural districts the party had gathered votes from a great number of households without any such membership ties to the organization. In the capital and some of the larger cities the party could count on an organized body of committed members ready to support the Socialist cause not only in elections but also in demonstrations, in strikes, and in other forms of direct action. This core of convinced Socialists offered the best basis for the development of a centralized elite party on Leninist lines. In the provinces and in the rural areas the party was weak in organization but strong in votes. The steady worsening of conditions in the primary economy had rallied more and more fishermen, smallholders, and casual laborers behind the party, but only a few of these were swayed by considerations of ideology and long-term strategy. They wanted immediate relief from their economic difficulties, and they cast their votes for Labor because they trusted the party to defend their interests. This set the dilemma for the party leaders after

15. Dag Bryn and Halvard M. Lange, "Klasse eller folk," *Det 20de århundrede, 31* (3) (March 1930), 67–75.

1927: should they give priority to ideology and organization and keep away from involvement in practical decision-making, or should they broaden the electoral appeal of the party and enter into cooperation with other parties in the solution of day-to-day problems of immediate urgency?

The events after 1930 in fact made the decision for the party: the revolutionary wing lost out and the parliamentary democrats took over. The party went all out for electoral victory in 1933 and came very close indeed: it won 69 out of the 150 seats in the Storting. The leaders immediately declared themselves willing to take over the government of the country. The old, established parties, the Right and the Left, resisted to the end, but the Agrarians finally agreed to back a Labor government under a guarantee of support for the primary economy. Again it is significant that a decisive change in the political system came about through an alliance in defense of the rural interests: the Agrarians represented a higher socioeconomic stratum than the rural Labor leaders, but this class cleavage proved less important in the concrete situation of economic crisis than the traditional conflict between the primary economy and the commercial and industrial interests centered in the cities.

The Labor Party acceded to power in 1935 and has dominated Norwegian politics ever since. The new government presented a cautious program of concrete action to relieve the current crisis—it did not want to risk a repetition of the brief intermezzo of 1928. The party wanted to establish its parliamentary trustworthiness and was concerned to discourage as far as possible any trend toward a merger of the opposition on its right. It still needed allies and was most likely to find these among the representatives of what were now called the Middle parties: the old Left and the emerging Christian People's Party no less than its current partner, the Agrarian Party. These parties helped to keep the system in balance under the strains of the transfer of power: the polity was not torn between two poles but was kept within bounds through the crosscutting of a number of cleavage lines.

Figures 3.1 and 3.2 give the strength of the parties on each side of the principal conflict line from the decisive election of 1882 to the latest contest in 1961. The most striking characteristic of this long sequence of electoral decisions is the continuity of alignments. From 1882 to 1924 the principal cleavage line in the system was between the Left on the one side and the Right on the other. The character of the opposition between the two changed fundamentally after 1900: the Left remained essentially a party of cultural and territorial defense but the Right was gradually transformed from a party of the official "establishment" to a party defending the broadening community of commercial and industrial interests. The extension of the suffrage to all adults accentuated class divisions: the rise of the Labor Party, the transformation of the farmers' interest groups into

The Balance of Power in the Storting

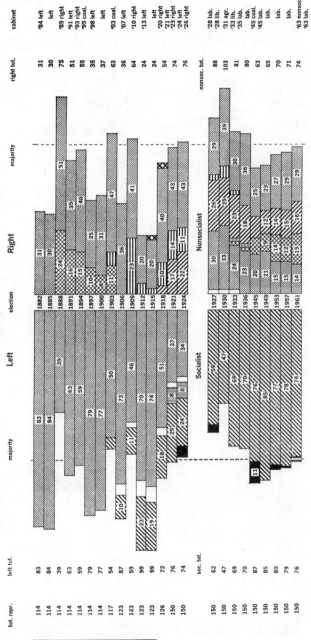

Figure 3.1 The Political Composition of Parliaments and Cabinets in Norway, 1882–1963

Party Strengths in Percentage of Valid Votes

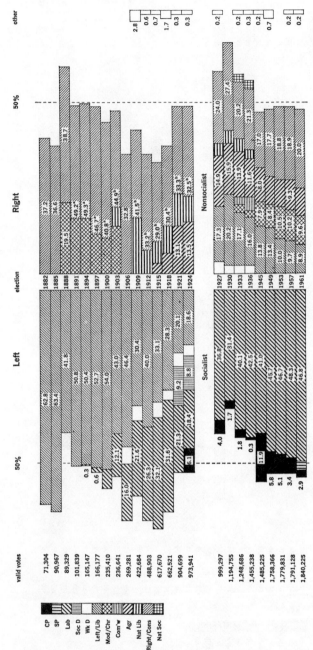

Figure 3.2. The Voting Strengths of the Parties, 1882–1961

a. For these elections the statistics do not distinguish Moderate and Right votes: The percentages given therefore refer to the Moderate plus Right total.

b. For these elections the statistics do not distinguish National Liberal and Right votes.

Notes to Figures 3.1 and 3.2

This ordering of the parties from a working-class left to a nationalist-elitist extreme right is not based on any detailed analysis of the dimensions of policy disagreements and the likelihood of coalitions. In its basic structure this ordering has been confirmed through analyses of differences in attitudes toward Labor policies (cf. Table 3.4), but the placement of some of the minor parties in the middle range of the spectrum is questionable and should not be interpreted to reflect detailed research on the "dimensionalities" of Norwegian politics.

Separate figures for the votes cast for the Moderates and Right have only been established for 1888, see *Indstilling S.XX* (1890). For subsequent elections through 1903 the combined percentage strength of the two groups has been entered under "Right" in Figure 3.2 and only approximate distributions have been indicated on the basis of the known ratios of seats.

Separate figures for the National Liberals and the Right are not given in the statistics from 1909 to 1924. In Figure 3.2 the percentages given for the Right therefore refer to the totals for these two parties.

Norwegian name	Elections	English translation	Abbreviation
Norges Kommunistiske Parti	1924–	Communist Party	CP
Sosialistisk Folkeparti	1961	Socialist People's Party	SP
Det Norske Arbeiderparti	1894–	Labor Party	Lab.
Norges Socialdemokratiske Arbeiderparti	1921–24	Social Democrats	Soc.D.
Arbeiderdemokratene	1906–18	Worker Democrats	Wk.D.
Radikale Folkeparti	1921–36		
Venstre	1882–	Left 1882–1924 / Liberals 1924–	Left. / Lib.
Moderate	1888–03	Moderates	Mod.
Kristelig Folkeparti	1933–	Christian People's Party	Chr.
Samfunnspartiet	1933–49	Commonwealth Party	Com'w.
Landmandsforbundet	1915–18		
Bondepartiet	1921–53	Agrarians	Agr.
Senterpartiet	1957–		
Frisinnede Venstre	1909–30	National Liberals	Nat.Lib.
Frisinnede Folkeparti	1933–36		
Høire (Høyre)	1882–	Right 1882–1924 / Conservatives 1927–	Right / Cons.
Nasjonal Samling	1933–36	National Socialists	Nat.Soc.

an Agrarian Party, the change in the ideology of the Right—all these
developments cut across the earlier territorial-cultural cleavage line and
produced new constellations of opposition and alliance. From 1927 the
principal cleavage line was no longer between Left and Right, but between the Socialists and all the offshoots of the parties established before
the extension of the suffrage: the Left, now better rendered into English
as the Liberals, the Agrarians and the Right, now better translated as the
Conservatives (for details on the party names and their translation, see the
notes to Figures 3.1 and 3.2). The rise of the Labor Party to its position of
dominance in the 'thirties did not decisively change this structure of party
alignments. Nor did the five years of war, occupation, and resistance from
1940 to 1945. There was much talk of a broad coalition based on the experiences of cooperation in the exile government and in the resistance
movement, but when it came to brass tacks in the summer of 1945 the old
parties proved their vitality.[16] The election of 1945 did not produce any
major changes in the system. The war had strengthened the working-class
parties: the Communists made a spectacular comeback after their near
disappearance in the 'thirties, and Labor won its first clear majority of
seats, if not of votes. On the opposition side there was very little change:
the Christian People's Party was transformed from a regional to a national
movement but otherwise the alignment remained roughly as before. The
subsequent elections of 1949, 1953, and 1957 produced little in the way of
structural change: the Communist Party lost out after the coup in
Czechoslovakia, and Labor consolidated its position. It is true that the
party lost seats in 1953 and 1957; this did not reflect a loss in votes, however, but a change in the electoral law—the switch from the d'Hondt to the
Sainte-Laguë allocation procedure lowered the threshold for the small
parties and increased the number of votes required for additional seats for
the largest party.[17] The first sign of potential change came in 1961: a
dissident group of Left Socialists decided to move into competition with
the mother party and won two seats in the Storting, one in the capital and
one in the North. The Labor Party found itself in a minority position for
the first time since 1945. The situation in the Storting became highly unstable: the two representatives of the Socialist People's Party held the
balance between the 74 Laborites and the 74 members of the traditional

16. See T. Chr. Wyller, *Frigjøringspolitikk* (Olso, Universitetsforlaget, 1963).
17. Under the d'Hondt system the total number of votes cast for each party list is
divided successively by 1, 2, 3, 4, and so on. This means that each new seat costs a
party the same number of votes as the first seat gained. The Sainte-Laguë procedure
is to divide successively by the odd numbers 1, 3, 5, 7, etc. This makes further seats
progressively more expensive and gives the advantage to the one-seat parties. To
increase the threshold of representation without favoring the large parties, the
Scandinavian electoral systems have since 1952 set the first divisor at 1.4 instead of 1,
but kept the subsequent Sainte-Laguë divisors. For details on the mathematics of
these procedures see C.-G. Janson, *Mandattilldelning och regional röstfördelning*
(Stockholm, Idun, 1961).

opposition. There was much soul-searching but the final outcome was clear: the Gerhardsen Cabinet stayed in power under a tacit agreement that it could rely on support from the opposition in carrying out major policies. The nonsocialist opposition had very little choice in the matter: it could not muster a majority for an alternative government and it was seriously split over a central issue of foreign policy—the stormy issue of Norwegian entry into the European Economic Community, which broke out shortly after the election. In this fight, the antagonists on the functional-economic axis of the political system, Labor and the Conservatives, were united in their advocacy of entry while the offshoots of the old party of territorial-cultural defense were either deeply split or entirely against any application for full membership in the EEC. Our reanalysis of Gallup data for the peak period of the campaign for and against entry [18] suggests a resurgence of the old alliance of the 'seventies and 'eighties: alienated urban radicals, primarily on the left wing of Labor and among the Eastern Liberals joined with the peasantry of the provinces in an attack on the "establishment." But the central authorities they attacked were very different: the radical-peripheral alliance was no longer directed against the King's administration and its ties with Swedish interests but against a complex of trade unions, business organizations, and public bodies, and their ties with the organs of European integration. The stakes of the game had indeed changed, but the conflict had retained something of its old structure.

The fight over the EEC issue kept Labor in power. Entry would require a change in the Constitution, and to bring this about the pro-EEC Liberals and the Conservatives had to cooperate actively with the majority faction within Labor. These unusual cross-party agreements lost their objective after January 14, 1963: General de Gaulle called off the campaign, and in fact changed the structure of Norwegian politics. The result was the Cabinet crisis of the summer of 1963—the point where we started our story.

The Sociology of Norwegian Politics:
The Struggle for the Majority Narrows the Range of Alternatives

Two blocs of voters have been pitted against each other in Norwegian politics at least since 1927: an "established" bloc essentially recruited from the strata already enfranchised under the *régime censitaire* and an "underprivileged" bloc recruited from the urban and industrial working class and the landless rural proletariat after the introduction of manhood suffrage in 1898. The registered electorate more than doubled from 1897 to 1900. If the Labor Party had been able to mobilize all these new voters it would have risen to a majority position right away. But the process of mobilization was slow and irregular, and the subsequent extension of the suffrage to adult women on the same terms as men in fact delayed the process of

18. See S. Rokkan and H. Valen, "Regional Contrasts," pp. 199-201.

polarization between the two blocs. The Labor Party came very close to
one-third of all votes cast at the first election under universal suffrage for
both sexes in 1915. Only half the women had voted, however, and in the
subsequent struggle to mobilize this potential, the working-class parties
clearly lost out, at least in the first round. The "underprivileged" bloc
stayed at the 30 per cent level until 1924. The first breakthrough toward a
majority position came in 1927 in the wake of the widespread economic
crisis in the countryside: the Socialist parties for the first time polled beyond the 40 per cent mark. The "underprivileged" again lost out in the
scramble for further electoral reserves in 1930 but continued the march
toward the majority point in 1933 and 1936. The movement culminated
in 1945, at the first election after the war: the two working-class parties
reached 52.9 per cent of all votes cast and won a decisive majority of the
seats in the Storting. The voting majority was only slightly reduced in the
elections that followed: it never moved below 51.5 per cent in the period
1945 to 1961.

These majorities said a great deal about the balance of orientations in the
electorate, but they were essentially socioeconomic, not political majorities. The working-class parties were deeply split over core issues of foreign
policy and could not cooperate with each other at any level of political
action. The dominant Labor Party could only hope to govern as long as it
was in a position to marshal parliamentary majorities of its own. Any move
toward a coalition with the left splinters would bring the entire system out
of equilibrium. In terms of *Koalitionsfähigkeit* the Norwegian system was
split in three, not two blocs of parties: the alienated Socialists to the left,
the domesticated Labor Party in the center, the four parties of the "established" bloc to the right.

In this situation the strategies of the governing Labor Party were largely
determined by two sets of concerns: it must hold the left splinter movements to a minimum, and it must keep its appeal broad enough to attract
the votes of the less committed masses halfway between the poles of the
political system. The programs and campaign messages of the party reflected the difficulties of reconciling these two strategic objectives: the
old strains between class and nation, between ideology and policy, were
still there. The Communists posed a real problem for the party until the
Czechoslovak coup d'état in 1948 and the subsequent Stalinist-Titoist
quarrels. The decline of the Communist Party from 1949 onward secured
the left flank of the governing party for 12 years. Power and responsibility
brought Labor closer to the established institutions of the nation, and
agreement with the nonsocialist opposition on entry into the Western
alliance system gradually brought about an ideological détente between the
two blocs.[19] The four parties of the "established" bloc found themselves in

19. For a review of these tendencies toward "deideologization" in the 'fifties, see

Norway

91

agreement with the government over a wide range of issues of domestic policy, and the steadily expanding system of functional representation on decision-making boards within the central government tended to "depoliticize" much of the debate and to blunt the edges of the ideological conflict.[20]

Not everybody, of course, was equally happy with this drift toward the political center: there were highly articulate, and sometimes very influential dissidents both on the right and on the left.

The remarkably dynamic *Libertas* movement [21] mobilized widespread support in the business community for a radically antisocialist program and sought to infiltrate both the Conservative and the Agrarian party organizations in an effort to create a strong front against the Labor government. The nonsocialist parties fought off these attempts, however, and retained their welfare-state platforms: ironically, when in 1963 the broad opposition front did what Libertas had fought for, and defeated the government, it did not present a strong antisocialist counterprogram but a remarkably balanced plan for a continuation of agreed-upon policies at the center of the political spectrum.

The dissidents on the left flank of the Labor Party had much more success. A vigorous neutralist movement had been active within and on the fringes of the party ever since the decision to join NATO in 1949. For a number of years the Labor leaders nevertheless felt sure that these dissidents would continue to vote for the party or at worst simply abstain; the system did not give them any real alternative. This was true as long as the movement remained small. Even though the change-over in 1953 from the d'Hondt to the Sainte-Laguë procedure had lowered the threshold for the first seat in all the multimember constituencies, it still required a sizable number of core members and an extensive organization to launch a new party. The neutralist movement grew during the late 'fifties, however, and in 1961 a group of dissidents in Oslo took the decisive step of launching a party of their own, the Socialist People's Party. The party was able to present lists in only 6 of the 20 constituencies; against the predictions of all experts it succeeded in crossing the threshold in two of them. What was even more astounding was that these two members were to become the arbiters in an unprecedented deadlock between the government and the "established opposition": the additional crack in the old

Ulf Torgersen, "The Trend Towards Political Consensus: the Case of Norway," in S. Rokkan, ed., *Approaches to the Study of Political Participation* (Bergen, Michelsen Institute, 1962), pp. 159-72.

20. For accounts of these developments see J. Moren, *Organisasjonene og forvaltningen* (Bergen, Norges Handelshøyskole, 1958), and Per Stavang, *Parlamentarisme og maktbalanse* (Olso, Universitetsforlaget, 1964), Ch. 10.

21. The tactics of this movement have been analyzed in a comparative perspective by Arnold Heidenheimer, whose book on patterns of political finance in Germany, Japan, and Norway will be published in 1965-66.

bloc of the "underprivileged" had made rule by the routine procedures of parliamentary decision-making an impossibility, and the system was faced with its first serious crisis since the early 'thirties. The leaders of the Labor Party, after a long period of complacency, were face to face with a basic dilemma of electoral strategy: they could not continue to broaden the appeals of the party without risking losses on the left and they could not satisfy their clients on the left without risking defeat in the battle for the middle ranges of the electorate.

The government–opposition game in Norway might up to a point be analyzed in terms of the Downs model of two-party competition: [22] the votes at the center of the political spectrum decide the struggle for power, and each of the contestant blocs tends to focus its appeals on the uncommitted citizens halfway between the poles of the system. But this holds only up to a point: the low-threshold proportional representation system opens up possibilities of splinters at the extremes, and the leaders of the dominant parties have to temper their eagerness for indiscriminate, catchall electioneering with concern for dissidence and defection among the militants and idéologues in each bloc. The Downs model assumes that the voters at the tails of the frequency distribution of policy positions have no real alternatives: however centrist the party strategy, the cost of dissidence would be greater than any conceivable payoff. In a PR system this may not hold: the lower the threshold of representation, the greater the likelihood of splinter movements.

The crucial electoral battles since 1945 have not been fought at the extremes, however, but over the middle ranges of the system. The Downs model would not take us far in the analysis of the strategies and counterstrategies of these battles. We have seen how the Norwegian party system was generated by a succession of crosscutting cleavages and how the earlier divisions persisted through lags in the processes of change from locality to locality. To fit all these dimensions of conflict into one model would be very difficult and probably not very illuminating. At the level of functional-economic conflict the simplest model would have to posit three poles of electoral attraction: the unions, the farmer organizations, and the business community. Figure 3.3 spells this out in further detail. The decisive electoral struggles have taken place at the halfway ranges between these three poles:

> at the L-F front the fight has been for the votes of the declining population of subsistence farmers, smallholders, and fishermen in the peripheries of the nation;
>
> at the L-B front it has been for the votes of the rising new middle class of salaried employees in the private and public bureaucracies;

22. Anthony Downs, *An Economic Theory of Democracy* (New York, Harper, 1957).

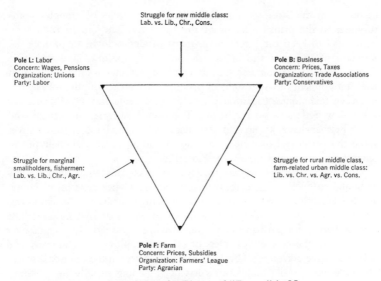

Figure 3.3. A Model of the Electoral "Fronts" in Norway:
The Functional-Economic Dimension

and at the *F-B* front it has been for the votes of the owners, the managers, the organizers, and the professionals at the intersections between the primary and the secondary-tertiary economies.

The fights at the *L-F* and the *L-B* fronts have decided the balance between the government and the "established" opposition. The fight at the *F-B* front has essentially concerned the balance among the four opposition parties: it has been of minor importance both numerically and strategically. To the governing Labor Party the fights on the *L-F* and the *L-B* fronts have been of equal importance strategically but the numerical stakes have been rapidly changing.

The party rose to power through an alliance between the rural proletariat and the industrial working class. The continuing exodus from the rural peripheries and the primary economy has reduced the numerical weight of the smallholder-fisherman wing of the party but in a tight majority-minority situation the votes from this wing will still remain of strategic importance for years to come. Survey data for 1957 indicate that the Labor Party derives some 20 per cent of its votes from the primary economy: 12 per cent from farmers, smallholders, and fishermen and 8 per cent from agricultural and forestry workers.[23] Any move likely to alienate this clientele could have disastrous consequences for the balance

23. Calculated from Table 2.7 in S. Rokkan and H. Valen, "Regional Contrasts."

94 *Stein Rokkan*

of power in the Storting. The result has been a series of complex compromises in the primary sector of the economy. The unions have been concerned to keep the prices of primary products down to protect the standard of living of the industrial and urban working class and have favored measures to increase the efficiency of farming and fishing through the establishment of larger units of production and the adoption of capital-intensive techniques. Electoral pressures have made it very difficult for the Labor leaders to go far in this direction, however; the farmers and the fishermen have strong and articulate lobbies, and the representatives from the peripheral provinces have again and again proved their power against the urban and industrial leadership.

With continuing economic growth, however, this wing of the party is bound to decline in electoral weight; about 26 per cent of all households were still in the primary economy in 1950 but by the 'seventies this proportion, it is estimated, will be down to only half that figure.[24] The crucial battles for parliamentary control will increasingly be fought over the votes of the new middle class of salaried employees, technicians, and administrative personnel. This broad stratum between the industrial working class and the old middle class has been gaining steadily in numerical weight since the beginning of the century and will soon number one-third of all the households in the nation.[25] No single political party has been

24. A classification of the active population in three sectors shows these trends since 1875:

	Total active (in '000s)	Primary sector (agric., forestry, fish.)	Secondary sector (mining, industry, construction)	Tertiary sector (services)
		Per cent in		
1875	736	52	18	30
1900	887	42	26	32
1930	1163	36	26	38
1950	1388	26	36	38
1960	1409	20	36	44

Sources: *Population Census 1950*, Vol. 4 (Oslo, N.O.S. XI 323, 1959), Table 12, p. 31, and *Statistisk ukehefte* 3 (40) October 1962.
The remaining population in the primary sector is much older than the national average. This suggests a rapid decline in its share of the total during the 'seventies.
25. A classification of the active population by occupational status from 1875 to 1950 gives these trends (figures are percentages):

	Independents Primary	Other	Salaried	Workers	No information
1875	28	10	5	52	5
1900	23.5	10	8	55.5	3
1920	19	8.5	13.5	48.5	0.5
1950	15.5	9.5	19.5	54.5	0.5
1960	19.4		24.9	55.7	—

Source: *Bidrag til en sosiologisk beskrivelse av norsk næringsliv* (Oslo, Institute of

able to stake any exclusive claim to this stratum. The new middle class emerged as a political force after the parties had organized themselves around their core groups of supporters and was too split, both in terms of its socioeconomic origins and its political loyalties, to produce a distinctive nucleus of electoral action all its own. An expanding middle ground was left open in the system and offered great opportunities for mass electioneering. The new stratum became a major target of party propaganda, and the efforts to attract scarce additional votes brought about a convergence of policy lines and a softening of ideological oppositions.[26]

The new middle class divided its votes among Labor, the Liberals, the Christians, and the Conservatives (see the detailed distributions in Table 3.1) but at the same time exerted a unifying influence on the system. Two claims tended to unite the new middle class: the demand for explicit recognition of training and experience in a system of differentiated economic rewards, and the concern for long-term security through the provision of collective and compulsory pension schemes. The one claim went counter of the egalitarian ideology of the labor movement and the policy of severely progressive taxation pursued by the government. The other claim implied opposition to the ideology of individual self-reliance and the belief in a beneficent free enterprise economy so strongly entrenched among the Conservatives. To meet these claims the Socialists had to move closer to the recognition of a hierarchical structure of rewards and the Conservatives closer to the acceptance of the principles of collective solidarity underlying the welfare society.

The result was a softening of class appeals and a greater emphasis on the role of the state as an arbiter between economic interests: in fact a convergence toward the position of the old Left. In the nineteenth century the opposition to the regime had recruited a high proportion of its local leaders in the salaried middle class: sheriffs, teachers, newspapermen. Once in power the Left had placed increasing numbers of its loyal supporters in public employment, and through a natural process of entrenchment it became a defender of the apparatus of national government

Sociology, 1961), Tab. A 2.100.5, and, for 1960, E. Fivelsdal, *Funksjonærenes syn på faglige og politiske spørsmål* (Olso, Universitetsforlaget, 1964), Tab. 1.1.

Exactly comparable figures for the 1960 census are not yet available. Interestingly enough, the great number of intermediary positions between "workers" and "salaried" forced the Central Bureau of Statistics to abandon this overall distinction in its 1960 census tabulations; see *Population Census 1960*, Vol. 3 (Oslo, N.O.S. XII 129, 1964), p. 9. An extrapolation from social security data gives roughly these proportions by 1970: under 20 per cent independents, over 30 per cent salaried, and 50 per cent wage earners (calculations by K. G. Åbyholm, Norwegian School of Economics and Business Administration, 1959).

26. For a detailed development of this point see S. Rokkan, "Geography, Religion, and Social Class," sect. V.

Table 3.1. Party Choices Within Major Occupational Groups
(survey data for 1957)

	N	Socialist (CP/ Lab.)	"Left" (Lib./ Chr.)	Agr.	Cons. (incl. joint lists)	Unclear, nonvoter
Primary economy						
All	407	21	15	22	7	25
farmers	171	14	19	38	9	20
smallholders, fishermen	138	35	15	12	7	31
workers	98	57	9	6	3	25
Secondary and tertiary economy						
Wage earners	644	61	7	1	7	23
manufacturing	285	65	7	1	4	23
others	359	58	8	1	10	23
Self-employed	53	21	13	2	24	40
Salaried	319	28	19	2	28	23
public	130	30	27	2	22	19
private	189	26	13	2	33	26
Employers	92	10	12	0	46	32

Note: Dependent respondents have been classified by the occupation of the head of the household (current or, if retired, past occupation).

against the private interests of the unions no less than of the capitalists. The rise of the Labor Party did not change this overnight. The offshoots of the old Left, the Liberals and the Christians, still retain much of their hold on the salaried employees and officials of the public sector, most markedly so in the South and the West but also in the more polarized regions of the country. Table 3.1 shows a remarkably even division of allegiances within the public sector: the Conservatives, the heirs of the old defenders of the regime of the officials, can count on some 22 per cent of these votes, the offshoots of the old Left on 29 per cent, and the Labor Party on 30 per cent. A breakdown by region tells us a great deal about the conditions for the politicization of public bureaucracies: in the South and the West, the strongholds of the Middle parties, the Labor Party still gets as little as 5 per cent of the votes in this sector while in the rest of the country it reaches 40 per cent. The dominance of the old Left in public employment is especially marked in the least industrialized communes of the South and the West; in these areas the strong traditions of territorial and cultural defense have given particularly important leadership positions to such public employees and officials as teachers and clergymen and have served to contain the spread of polarized class politics from the cities and the centers of industry. Table 3.2 shows this clearly: in the cities and towns the South and West differ very little from the other regions in the level of class polarization, while in the typical

Table 3.2. *The Distinctiveness of the South and West: Differences in the Politics of Major Occupational Groups in Communes at Different Levels of Industrialization Within Two Contrasting Divisions of the Country* (1957)

Occupation	Community	Region	N	Intended vote (percentage of N)			Un-clear, non-voter
				Soc.	Middle	Cons.	
Worker	City, town	South, West	77	61	8	9	22
		Rest	230	63	7	9	21
	Industrialized	SW	31	45	30	3	22
		Rest	161	65	6	5	24
	Other rural	SW	70	35	24	4	39
		Rest	173	64	10	4	22
Farmer, smallholder, fisherman	Industrialized	SW	25	4	68	8	20
		Rest	40	32.5	30	2.5	35
	Other rural	SW	86	10	58	6	26
		Rest	228	32	35	11	22
Middle class	City, town, industrialized	SW	84	13	25	29	33
		Rest	228	26	11	39	24
	Other rural	SW	77	16	72	18	25
		Rest	108	29	18	25	28

primary-economy communes the contrast is most marked indeed. The Labor Party has throughout its history remained an almost exclusively industrial movement in the South and the West: it found only minimal support in the primary economy (the L-F front in Figure 3.3) and it has been much weaker than elsewhere on the expanding front of the salaried middle class (the L-B front).

In the rest of the country, however, the Labor Party was not only successful on the rural front but also—and this has become increasingly important—in the battle for the votes of the new middle class. Several factors were at work in this process of "bourgeoisification." First of all,

there was the increasingly frequent upward mobility from the rural proletariat and the industrial and urban working class: many of the sons and
daughters who moved into the new stratum from below had been
brought up in the politics of Labor, and at least half remained loyal to the
family party even after the change from the parental milieu.[27] In many
cases there was indeed very little cross-pressure between the old working-
class and the new middle-class environment. This was especially the case
when the son or daughter had entered a salaried position in the public
sector or was a member of the Labor-oriented trade union movement,
the Norwegian Federation of Labor (Landsorganisasjon, LO). To a large
extent the growth of the middle-class wing of the party was in fact a
direct consequence of Labor's rise to power; not only had the party placed
an increasing number of workers' sons and daughters in municipal and
central government employment at the salaried and professional levels
but the very growth of the public sector since the 1930s had created a
number of new openings for such upward mobility. The LO kept a close
watch on this process of change and succeeded in unionizing remarkably
large proportions of the public employees and the civil servants.[28] The
LO was in fact able to cut across traditional class lines, and this opened
up important possibilities for a broadening of the appeal of the Labor
Party. In Sweden the new middle class had achieved a much higher level
of organizational unity and built up strong, distinctive unions for the
defense of its interests. In Norway the new middle class is much more
split—perhaps one-third is affiliated with the working-class movement
within the LO, around one-third has joined independent bargaining organizations without any overall federative ties, and the rest, mainly employees in the smaller units of family businesses, remain unorganized.[29]

27. For further details see S. Rokkan, "Geography, Religion, and Social Class,"
Tables 5.3 and 5.4, and H. Valen and D. Katz, *Political Parties in Norway* (Oslo,
Universitetsforlaget, 1964), Table 6.23.
28. Egil Fivelsdal, *Funksjonærenes syn*, Tab. 3.2, reports these results of a nationwide survey carried out in 1961–62:

Percentage of salaried employees (excl. professions) in service of

	National government		Municipalities		Cooperatives		Private firms	
	Men	Women	Men	Women	Men	Women	Men	Women
Member of LO union	70	31	71	27	75	(76)	21	17
Member of other union	15	28	9	29	9		17	8
Not unionized	15	41	20	44	16	(24)	62	75
Total	100	100	100	100	100	100	100	100
$N =$	*344*	*85*	*196*	*48*	*44*	*17*	*469*	*208*

Parentheses indicate too few cases for safe computation.
29. The membership figures published by the unions and the professional associations do not allow uniform breakdowns in conformity with the distinctions between

The result has been a steady strengthening of the middle-class wing of the Labor Party. Table 3.3 represents an attempt to gauge the generational changes in the party's clientele since the introduction of manhood suffrage.[30] In the early phase of growth the party was essentially a coalition of workers, smallholders, and fishermen without any appeal to the middle-class voters, whether of the new or the old stratum. The decisive change came in the 'thirties with the rise of the party to a position of political dominance; in this generation the party not only retained its important smallholder-fisherman wing but also developed a strong middle-class wing in the cities and the urbanized countryside. In the 'fifties the continuing processes of urbanization, industrialization, and bureaucratization brought about further changes in the structure of the party clientele: there is now very little recruitment in the primary economy but a steady influx of voters from the new middle class.

---

wage earners and salaried in the official occupational statistics. Rough estimates for 1959 give 30 per cent LO, 30 per cent other unions and professional associations, 40 per cent unorganized. Nationwide surveys have not produced exactly comparable results either:

Percentage of salaried employees

	LO	Other	Not organized
(a) NGI survey, 1954	29	20	51
(b) Election survey, 1957	24	27	49
(c) Fivelsdal survey, 1961 (excludes higher civil servants, teachers, academically trained employees but includes fixed-contract manual workers in the public services)	42	16	42

Sources: (a) Norsk Gallup Institutt, *Funksjonærenes og tjenestemennenes organisasjonsforhold* (Oslo, Funksjonærsambandet, 1954); (b) unpublished data from the nationwide election survey carried out in 1957; (c) Fivelsdal, *Funksjonærenes syn.*

Fivelsdal's Table 3.4 shows a very clear relationship between the size of work organization (firm, department) and unionization:

Percentage of employees organized

	In units of less than 5	In units of more than 150
Men		
Governmental	75	88
Municipal	56	100
Private	14	59
Women		
Public	41	65
Private	14	33

30. This analysis has been developed in further detail in S. Rokkan, "Geography, Religion, and Social Class," sect. V.

Table 3.3. Changes in the Occupational Composition of the Socialist Vote,
1890s–1950s (estimates based on survey data for 1957)

	N	Manual workers	Farmers, small-holders	Salaried em-ployees	Inde-pendent, self-employed
			(percentage of N)		
1890s–1920s Resp. born before 1907: occupational distribu-tion for fathers voting Socialist	119	76	13	3	8
1910s–1930s Resp. born 1907–27: occupational distribu-tion for fathers voting Socialist	267	74	15	6	5
1930s–1940s Resp. born 1907–27: occupational distribu-tion for respondents voting Socialist at their first election	372	65	13	15	5
1950s Resp. born after 1927: occupational distribu-tion for those who said they had voted or would vote Socialist	128	72	5	20	3

This change in the structure of the clientele might have had very little
influence on the policies pursued by the party if it had been in a clear
majority position. In a tight situation at the 50 per cent mark, however,
every vote counts and the party was forced to pay more for the uncertain
votes at the margin than for the safe votes within its core groups of
traditional support. The equalitarian policies of economic austerity came
under heavy pressure after 1949 and the government gave up its attempt
to control in detail the wage and salary settlements between the unions
and the employers' associations.[31] The stringent policies of investment
controls were gradually relaxed, and there were even some adjustments in

31. Wages were settled through a system of compulsory arbitration up to 1952. For
an account of problems of union–government relations during this period see W.
Galenson, Labor in Norway (Cambridge, Mass., Harvard University Press, 1949),
Chs. 12–13. For further developments see M. W. Leiserson, Wages and Economic
Control in Norway 1945–1957 (Cambridge, Mass., Harvard University Press, 1959),
Chs. 4, 5, and 10. For partisan analyses see A. Berglöff, Trenger vi en funksjonær-
bevegelse? (Oslo, FSO, 1952), and "6 års historie," FSO-nytt (June 1958), pp. 4–6,
and Aake Anker-Ording, Funksjonæren i går, i dag og i morgen (Oslo, Funksjonærs-
ambandet, 1962).

the steeply progressive taxation schedules.[32] Taxation proved a vexing
area of policy pressures: the rural and the industrial wings of the party
were concerned to maintain the high tax levels for the middle- and upper-
income brackets while the salaried and professionals within the party
pressed forward their claims for increased rewards for their training,
skills, and responsibilities. With continuing inflation a number of better-
off industrial workers came within the reach of progressive taxation, and
adjustments were reluctantly made, but taxation still remained a core
issue within the party.

Survey analyses of voter positions on crucial issues between the parties
may help us to pinpoint this process of change. Unfortunately we do
not have at hand any time series data for stands on policy issues, but an
analysis of responses from a nationwide survey carried out in 1957 may
at least help us to map the major dimensions of conflict and consensus
within the system. Table 3.4 gives estimates of the range of differences
in positions between the supporters of the governing Labor party and
the voters for the four "established" opposition parties. To guard against
overinterpretation each party clientele has been divided into an "active"
group of members and campaign participants and a "passive" group of
citizens who reported no political activity beyond voting. The results tell
us a great deal not only about the divisions within the Labor Party but
also about the conditions for a coalition of the opposition parties.

On all the issues of income distribution and government-enterprise conflict we find a distinct polarization between Labor and the Conservatives.
Whatever the level of Labor discontent with the government, the Conservatives tend to unite in outright opposition against its equalitarian and
dirigiste policies. There is one significant exception, however: only 50 per
cent of the Conservative "actives" and 37 per cent of the "only-voters"
find fault with the rigidity of the tax controls for independents reporting
their own incomes. On this score the Agrarians take the clearest stand
against the government: almost without exception they are self-employed
or employers and consequently oppose measures designed to ensure detailed controls of income statements. The Conservative Party also speaks
for a clientele of independents but in addition counts a large wing of

32. Detailed comparisons between rates of income tax progression for a number of
countries are given in *Innstilling om progresjonen og andre spørsmal i forbindelse med
statsskatten* (Olso, Finans- og tolldept., 1964), Tab. III, 1–4. The following extract
illustrates the extreme equalitarianism of the Norwegian system of taxation:

*Marginal taxation for family with two children
(percentages of added income of Nkr. 1000)*

Income level in Nkr.	Denmark	France	Nether-lands	Norway	Great Britain	Sweden
20,000	25.8	12.0	21.9	27.3	23.3	26.4
50,000	47.3	20.0	47.5	66.3	30.1	47.6
100,000	50.4	30.0	59.2	77.3	34.4	56.0

Table 3.4. Differences in Policy Positions Among the Voters for the Five Major Parties: "Active" vs. "Only-Voters" (survey data for 1957)

Policy area Direction of statement	Ranking of parties from lowest to highest per cent opposed to government policy									
	Actives					Only-voters				
	Least opposed to govt. policy			Most opposed to govt. policy		Least opposed to govt. policy			Most opposed to govt. policy	
Taxation	Lab.	Lib.	Chr.	Agr.	Cons.	Lab.	Lib.	Chr.	Agr.	Cons.
Taxes too high	58	67	77	78	93	66	80	82	90	91
Too much control of income reports (independents)	Lab. 4	Lib. 17	Chr. 24	Cons. 50	Agr. 60	Lab. 4	Chr. 18	Lib. 23	Cons. 37	Agr. 46
Control of economy										
Too much restriction of house building	Lab. 23	Chr. 37	Agr. 50	Lib. 67	Cons. 78	Lab. 29	Agr. 48	Chr. 51	Lib. 67	Cons. 67
Too much interference with enterprise	Lab. 5	Chr. 57	Lib. 67	Agr. 78	Cons. 83	Lab. 12	Agr. 38	Chr. 44	Lib. 60	Cons. 69
Too little to encourage private saving	Lab. 18	Chr. 70	Lib. 70	Agr. 78	Cons. 89	Lab. 29	Agr. 60	Chr. 65	Lib. 76	Cons. 79
Too little done to stop inflation	Lab. 12	Chr. 43	Lib. 55	Agr. 66	Cons. 80	Lab. 15	Chr. 44	Agr. 50	Lib. 56	Cons. 62
Protection of primary economy										
Too little support for agriculture	Cons. 7	Lab. 9	Chr. 23	Lib. 33	Agr. 63	Lab. 11	Cons. 12	Chr. 17	Lib. 19	Agr. 62
Religion										
Too little done to strengthen Christian faith and morals	Lab. 18	Lib. 44	Cons. 56	Agr. 59	Chr. 97	Lab. 26	Cons. 42	Lib. 44	Agr. 65	Chr. 90
Defense										
Military budget too high	Cons. 33	Chr. 50	Agr. 53	Lab. 66	Lib. 72	Cons. 49	Agr. 63	Lab. 63	Chr. 71	Lib. 71
N	Lab. 164	Lib. 18	Chr. 30	Agr. 32	Cons. 54	Lab. 407	Lib. 75	Chr. 68	Agr. 52	Cons. 120

readily taxable salaried employees, and these tend to resent the income deductions of the self-employed and the employers just as much as the middle-class Labor voters.

To put it very schematically, Labor and the Conservatives will be at opposite poles on issues within the advanced corporate economy of the cities but will tend to take their stand on the same side in the territorial-cultural conflicts within the system. They take very similar positions on the level of support for the primary economy, and they do not differ much in their reactions to the religious activism of the Christian People's Party. These are the basic issues of conflict within the "established" opposition: the Agrarians defend the rural economy against the industrial and commercial interests in the cities and will therefore often conflict with the Conservatives; the Christians fight the tolerant secularism and tepid Lutheranism nourished in the urban bourgeoisie and will therefore often find it difficult, if not impossible, to cooperate with the Conservatives. The third of the Middle parties, the core group of Liberals still sticking to the old Left standard, is much more difficult to place in the political landscape of the 'fifties. The party is split in several wings, but the average positions registered through the analysis of survey data place its voters in the middle range on almost all issues. The one exception is defense: on this issue the Liberals rank first in the proportion expressing outright opposition to the policies of the government. But this is not a very distinctive reaction. There was widespread rank-and-file resentment against the heavy burden of the defense budget in all parties, and on this score the governing Labor Party had as much of a problem controlling its clientele as any of the other parties.

If we compare the stands taken by Labor voters toward the policies of their government we find remarkably low levels of disaffection on all issues but two: taxation and defense. These two exceptions tell us a great deal about the problems of electoral strategy facing the party: Labor leaders have not only had to cope with increasing pressures for a recognition of income differentials and hierarchies of economic status but have also found themselves in a great quandary over their commitment to pursue the foreign and the military policies agreed on with the "established" opposition parties in 1949. Their concern to attract the middle class softened their ideological stands and brought them closer to the "bourgeois" opposition, but this very détente, and especially the cross-party agreements on a common policy of defense within the Western alliance, triggered off articulate splinter movements and endangered the majority position of the party. The events of 1963 forced an agonizing reappraisal of this dilemma: how could the party crush the left splinter and still retain its appeal to the rising middle class?

The Swedish Social Democrats had pointed to a possible solution. They had seen the dangers of a "soft" strategy in the mid-'fifties and found a powerful alternative: instead of continuing a policy of general détente they were gradually driven to accentuate a new line of potential conflict in the system and made a·major effort to polarize the electorate over this conflict. They came to the conclusion that it was time to break down the old status division between manual wage earners and salaried employees and to try instead to establish a joint platform for the defense of the employed against the employers and the economically independent. Their strategy was to focus on issues that united the workers and the new middle class against the employers and the owners. They found a perfect answer in the proposal for publicly administered retirement pensions based on average earnings during the peak period of the work career. This plan met a widely felt need for improvements in old age benefits and at the same time recognized the principle of a hierarchy of rewards reflecting differences in training, skills, and responsibilities. The issue was fought out in a national referendum in 1957 and later in the Riksdag, and there is a great deal of evidence that this strategy actually paid off. The Social Democrats strengthened their overall position and broadened their appeal to the new middle class.[33]

The Norwegian Labor Party took much longer to make up its mind. There was no urgent need for a change in strategy before 1961, and the Common Market issue delayed the effect of the elective defeat of the government that year. The decisive change came in September 1963: in its radical counterprogram the Labor Party not only proposed a system of state-administered service pensions along Swedish lines but at the same time put forward a comprehensive plan for investments in the backward peripheries of the nation from the huge capital fund to be established through employer and employee contributions toward the pensions. Whether economically defensible or not, this program revealed a deliberate strategy of electioneering: its ambitious aim was to secure the party's position on all its difficult fronts in one move. The pension plan was designed to strengthen the appeal to the new middle class (the *L-B* front in Figure 3.3); the investment plan was designed to secure the rural wing of the party (the *L-F* front); and the whole program was designed to strengthen the role of the state in the national economy, and might therefore help mend the fences to the left of the party.

To many observers this program indeed appeared to be a master stroke of electoral strategy. In the first round, the strategy clearly paid off: in moving leftward the Labor Party clearly kept the dissidents at bay without seeming to lose any of its middle-class appeal. Whether the gains registered at the local elections in 1963 heralded an upward swing for

33. Details of the policy discussions and strategic considerations behind these developments will be found in B. Molin, *Jjänstepensionsfrågan* (Gothenburg, Akademiförl., 1965). A lively, but obviously subjective account of the pensions issue is given in Herbert Tingsten's autobiography *Mitt Liv.* (Stockholm, Norstedts, 1964), 4, 221–59. For survey statistics on the resultant changes in electoral alignments see Bo Särlvik, "The Role of Party Identification in Voters' Perception of Political Issues: a Study of Opinion Formation in Swedish Politics 1956–1960," paper, Fifth World Congress of the International Political Science Association, Paris, 1961.

Labor or simply reflected a short-term success in the mobilization of marginal voters it is still difficult to say: the opposition parties, possibly guided by the Swedish experience, have not offered outright battle over the pension issue, and Labor leaders seem unlikely to be able to polarize the electorate over this issue as their Swedish counterparts did. What is certain is that the new situation will force continued reappraisals of party strategy and prompt a variety of efforts to break the deadlock between government and opposition.

Numerical Democracy and Corporate Pluralism: Votes Count but Resources Decide

By 1965 the four parties of the "established" bloc will have been in opposition for 30 years. They had a brief spell in office in the summer of 1963, but that was poor consolation for so many years in the wilderness. Such protracted opposition raises a series of problems in a political system: How can citizens opposed to the government keep up their partisan enthusiasm when their votes seem to make so little difference? How can the parties recruit dynamic leaders when the chance of ever gaining office appears so remote? How can the interests and values seen to be threatened by the government be defended when the opposition parties are continuously outnumbered in the fight for electoral votes?

These questions have not yet been subjected to detailed research in Norway. Survey data for 1957 give evidence of widespread defeatism among the voters for the opposition parties: When asked whether they thought Labor would lose its majority in the election that year only 10 per cent of the Middle parties and 20 per cent of the Conservatives saw any such likelihood. Only a minority of the voters for the opposition in fact seemed motivated by a desire for a change in the government. When asked whether they would vote for the nearest party if the chances of their own proved very small, only about one-third of the voters in the middle and about half of the Conservatives declared themselves willing to pool forces. To large masses of citizens in the "established" bloc, elections clearly were not occasions for choosing between alternative governments but simply opportunities for registering loyalties to particular parties—elections were held to decide on territorial representation in the legislature, not to make a choice between competing teams of potential governors. The only opposition party seriously concerned to establish a basis for an alternative government was the Conservative Party: it took the lead in the campaign for a united opposition front and showed great willingness to join in electoral alliances against Labor. Even in this party, however, the drive for government office was rarely a dominant motive among party workers and candidates. It is perhaps significant that when the Labor government, after its return to power in September 1963, offered high positions in the civil service to two Conservative leaders they did not hesitate to accept: they knew that this might take them out of politics, but they preferred the certainty of appointive position to the uncertain prospect of ministerial power.

There has been much talk, particularly among the right-wing activists, about the possibility of setting up a "shadow cabinet" of representatives of the four parties of the nonsocialist opposition, but this has not come to anything: the middle parties have been wary of any such commitment and have been anxious to keep doors open to other alternatives. One wing of the Liberal party has indicated potential willingness to join in a coalition with Labor if the government should not regain its majority. This has caused a great deal of worry and resentment within the other parties of the opposition and has made the prospects for a clear-cut solution of the parliamentary situation very dim indeed.

How can rights be defended and interests protected in such a halfway system? Clearly if voters in the "established" bloc really felt oppressed by the Labor regime they would forget their traditional differences and rally to the defense of their cause in a broad antisocialist front. But so far there have been few signs of such a development. The explanation is very simple: the opposition may have been losing in the fight for votes but the interests it represents and the causes it stands for can still be defended through other channels of influence on government decision-making. Votes count in the choice of governing personnel but other resources decide the actual policies pursued by the authorities.

The extension of the franchise to all adults and the maintenance of a strict majoritarian rule of decision-making in the legislature made it possible for a movement of the hitherto underprivileged to rise to power. But the parallel growth of a vast network of interest organizations and other corporate bodies made it impossible to rule by any simple "50 per cent plus" principle. To understand the strategies and counterstrategies of government and opposition we have to analyze the bargaining processes between the giant alliances of such associations and corporations. The vote potential constitutes only one among many different power resources brought to bear in these bargaining processes: what really counts is the capacity to hurt or to halt a system of highly interdependent activities. In the triangular conflict between labor, the farm interest, and business no single group dares to rely exclusively on its electoral machinery. The efforts on the electoral front are paralleled at the level of organizational action and at the level of the mass media. The workers and employees rely on their capacity to call strikes and to paralyze recalcitrant industries and service sectors. The farmers and fishermen have given top priority to the establishment of an efficient machinery for the control of production and marketing: one obvious purpose has been to increase their ability to withhold needed primary goods from the consumers and to force decisions on prices and subsidies. The managers, owners, and financial interests rely on their power to call off investment plans, to withhold skills, and to channel their initiatives to areas beyond the control of the unions and the national government. We have seen how these groups of organizations constitute the major poles in the system of electoral alignments and how the fates of the parties tend to be decided at the fronts between these poles (Figure 3.3). But none of the groups can rely exclusively on the verdict of one citizen, one vote contests. Even if they lose out in the competition for votes and seats they can still bring their organizational resources to bear on the actual policy decisions of the government. They need not actually use the weapons at their disposal, but the very fact that they can claim a measure of control over central factors in the national economy acts as a deterrent in the bargaining process. The crucial decisions on economic policy are rarely taken in the parties or in Parliament: the central area is the bargaining table where the government authorities meet directly with the trade union leaders, the representatives of the farmers, the smallholders, and the fishermen, and the delegates of the Employers' Association. These yearly rounds of negotiations have in fact come to mean more in the lives of rank-and-file citizens than the formal elections. In these processes of intensive interaction, the parliamentary notions of one member, one vote and majority rule make little sense. Decisions are not made through the counting of heads but through complex considerations of short-term or long-term advantages in alternative lines of compromise.

This two-tier system of decision-making places the Cabinet in an intricate position: it stands at the top of the electoral hierarchy but it is only one of four corporate units at the bargaining table. The Labor leaders *could* of course decide to throw all their weight behind the claims of the trade unions, but this could hurt them electorally—they need votes beyond the households of the unions to stay in power. Despite the close organizational ties between the unions and the party, the Labor Cabinet has consequently been anxious to divorce itself from the triangular conflict in the national economy. The responsible ministers have of course not tried to conceal their sympathies with the wage earners and the employees, but they have had to balance these interests against their stake in the electoral resources in the primary economy and their concern as employers of a major sector of the nation's labor force. The Cabinet has increasingly had to take on the role of mediator between the conflicting interests in the national community. At least in matters of internal policy it can rarely if ever force through decisions solely on the basis of its electoral power but has to temper its policies in complex consultations and bargains with the major interest organizations. To guard against difficulties and reversals in these processes of bargaining the government has over the years built up a large network of consultative boards and councils for the representation of all the relevant interests.[34] This has worked very well at the lower level of sectoral interest representation, but an attempt to establish a Board of Economic Coordination on the lines of the Dutch Sociaal-Economische Raad (SER) failed miserably in the early fifties: the partners felt that such a formal body made them hostages of the government and committed them to policies they could not defend within their constituent organizations.[35] The bargaining at the top still takes place in a constitutional vacuum. There is an efficient government machinery of mediation and there is also the possibility of instituting compulsory arbitration in cases of deadlock and of threatened strikes or lockouts, but no serious attempt has as yet been made to establish anything approaching a corporative framework for decisions on the distribution of incomes between the three principal sectors of the economy.

The Labor Party has clearly lost a great deal of leeway for its policies through the development of this two-tier system, but perhaps for this very reason has strengthened its position in the nation. At least in private, many business leaders will express relief that there is a Labor government to keep the unions in check: if the Labor Party were to lose power, strikes might become a major weapon of political struggle. Whether this argument is realistic or not, it points to an historically important dilemma of Labor strategy. In the doctrinal controversies of the 'twenties the revolutionary wing advocated the development of a strong organization for direct action against the established economic system, while the reformists wanted to mobilize for power through the existing electoral and parliamentary channels. When the first Labor government was voted out of office in 1928, there was evidence that the decisive opposition move had originated not within the parties but in the financial circles concerned to protect the currency and the position of the banks.[36] The revolutionaries concluded that parliamentary action was futile; the reformists concluded that everything would change once the party had won its majority. Events proved both wrong: parliamentary action was not futile, but even when Labor had a clear majority it could not introduce major changes in the structure of the economy. The labor movement has throughout its history kept up its two fronts: it has mobilized for industrial action against employers and for political action against other parties. The strategies chosen on the two fronts could not always be reconciled: the very success of the movement on the electoral front restricted its freedom

34. See J. Moren, *Organisasjonene og forvaltningen.*
35. For an analysis of the reasons for the dissolution of the early Board of Coordination and of the arguments for its reestablishment in the form of an Economic Planning Council see S. Lindebrække, "Samarbeid mellom staten og det private næringsliv." *Næringsrevyen Norges Handel, 12*(29) (August 1964), 470–74, 479.
36. See Roset, *Det norske Arbeiderparti,* pp. 134–37.

of action on the industrial front. Whether losses on the electoral front would make for increasing industrial unrest is difficult to say: it seems likely that the many years of uneventful bargaining will have set precedents that will be hard to break.

Whatever happens in the electoral and organizational channels of decision-making will again be affected by the balance of influences in the third channel—the mass media. During the crisis in the summer of 1963 the Prime Minister stated in one of his speeches that the press, not the other parties, was the real opposition in Norway. There is a great deal of evidence of the importance of the newspapers in Norwegian politics.[37] The burgeoning press played a crucial part in the early partisan struggles between the Right and the Left. Newspapers speaking for each of the parties were established in practically all the urban localities and in many rural centers. The papers became the principal organs of public debate and established links of close communication between the parties and the articulate citizenry and between the politicians and the local and national authorities. The press acquired a number of community functions beyond the purely political, however, and many newspapers became economic enterprises of great strength and independence. When the Labor Party rose to power it was rarely able to challenge the power of the established Liberal or Conservative press. With the help of the local trade unions it managed to establish some 40 dailies throughout the country, but these have never reached more than about one-quarter of all households. Survey data for 1957 [38] indicate that only about 30 per cent of the Labor voters read the party press exclusively while practically one-third are completely unexposed to Labor newspapers. This means, of course, that loyalty to the Labor Party is more likely to be maintained through primary group channels and in unions and other organizations, but it also means that a sizable proportion of the voters come under regular cross-pressure between their party spokesmen and the newspapers they read. Newspaper reading may not convert them from their basic Labor allegiance, but it does expose them to the arguments of the opposition. It is not possible to trace in any detail the effects of this exposure, but survey data indicate more agreement with government positions among the party-loyal readers than among the party-indifferent. To what extent this openness to opposition pressure finds direct reflection in decisions at the top of the party hierarchy is of course difficult to estimate, but the very lively debates in the newspapers indicate a great deal of awareness of counter-arguments to policies proposed.

The disproportionality between votes and newspaper copies simply

37. See S. Rokkan and P. Torsvik, "Der Wähler, der Leser und die Parteipresse," *Kölner Zs. Soziol.*, *12* (1960), 278–301, and S. Høyer, "Pressens økonomiske og politiske struktur," *Tss. for samfunnsforskning*, 1964 (4), 221–42.
38. Rokkan and Torsvik, "Der Wähler," p. 293.

reflects the lag between the two crucial moves of mobilization: the press flourished after the mobilization of the peasantry and was too firmly entrenched to be affected by the subsequent mobilization of the workers into politics. The development of the electronic mass media—radio and TV—came after the second wave of mobilization and took place under the exclusive sponsorship of the government. The Broadcasting Corporation has tried to adhere to strict rules of neutrality in politics and has adopted very rigid principles of time allocation among the parties. In a multiparty system, however, this means that more time is allocated to the opposition than to the government. Even the provision for double time for Labor—one unit for the government and another for the party—does not change this. There is no proportionality between the voting strength in the electorate and the share in the total mass of political messages sent out. This party-parity rule is not seen as an injustice but again functions to counteract the effects of strict adherence to the majoritarian principle in the choice of government.

Are There Alternatives?

Are there any realistic alternatives to the current deadlock between government and opposition?

Changes might come about through a variety of internal strains and external pressures, but whatever their origins the changes would have to be channeled through one or the other of the two channels of decision-making: the electoral-legislative and the organizational-corporate. Fluctuations in the electoral fates of the parties open up a variety of alternative futures for the regime, but changes in the electoral procedures may increase or decrease the possibility of each alternative. Much of what happens in the electoral-legislative channel will depend, however, on the outcome of decisions within the "second tier" of the system, at the level of corporate bargaining. To map all these possibilities of change is impossible within the present context, but it may help us gain perspective on the conditions of opposition in one Western democracy if, by way of conclusion, we review some of the major alternatives to the current arrangements. Let us look first at the alternative electoral outcomes and their likely consequences for the regime.

1. *Labor returns to the majority position in Parliament.* This would break the current deadlock but face the nonsocialist parties with the bleak prospect of another spell of protracted opposition. There would be increasing bitterness among the frustrated aspirants to power and a real danger of widespread alienation from a system offering so few hopes for the opposition.

2. *Neither Labor nor the nonsocialist bloc gains a majority of the seats and the balance of power is held by left-wing splinters.* This would mean

a continuation of the current deadlock: a repeat of the 2–74–74 situation
in the current Storting or some equivalent situation without a workable
positive majority but with a constant threat of negative majorities against
any government based on one of the competing blocs. Variants of this
situation tend to occur with increasing frequency in Scandinavia: the
Swedish election in September 1964 produced the constellation of 8
Communists, 113 Social Democrats, and 112 nonsocialists, and the Danish
election a week later produced 10 Left Socialists, 76 Social Democrats, 10
Radicals, and 81 outright nonsocialists. Several solutions are possible in
such situations. One may opt for a minority government and keep it afloat
on tactical majorities varying from issue to issue; one may prefer a
minority government based on a longer-term agreement with one supporting party; or there will be a coalition government. In the current
situations in the three countries the Social Democrats have all opted for
the first solution: minority government without direct ties to any other
party. The Swedish Social Democrats used to enter into bargains with
the Agrarians, but this so-called "Red-Green" agreement broke down in
1956. The Danish solution was for a number of years a coalition between
Social Democrats and Radicals, but this did not work after the 1964
election. If future elections in Norway continue to produce deadlocked
situations, the only likely alternatives are two: Labor will decide to stick
to the minority government arrangement or it will strike a bargain with
one of the Middle parties, most likely the Liberals, either for parliamentary
support or for a share in the government. An arrangement or coalition
with the Left Socialists seems very remote and a broader coalition toward
the right is not very likely except in a situation of national emergency.[39]

3. *The nonsocialist bloc gains a majority.* If this were to happen, the
alternative nearest at hand would be a coalition of the four "established"
opposition parties—a continuation of the experiment made in the summer
of 1963. How long such a coalition could be kept together is anyone's
guess. Difficulties over incomes policy might soon make for strains between the Agrarians and the Conservatives and so would any proposal
to enter into European agreements on primary products. A Labor-Liberal
coalition might prove an alternative, but how far the two parties would
be willing to go in agreeing on a joint policy would depend on a number
of factors.

The majority-minority situation in the electorate is very tight, and no
amount of sociological trend analysis could generate reliable predictions
of the outcome. The fate of the last seat hangs on a few hundred votes

39. The possibility of a Norwegian *Proporz*, or all-party government, is discussed
in D. Flem, *Det sveitsiske demokrati* (Oslo, Aschehoug, 1945); L. S. Oftedal, "Stort-
ingsmakt og regjeringsmakt," *Samtiden*, 62 (1953) 169–76; G. Garbo, *Samregjering. Et
parlamentarisk alternativ* (Oslo, Norges Venstrelag, 1960); and P. Stavang, *Parlamentarisme og maktbalanse*, pp. 212–17.

in most of the constituencies and very small movements in the electorate could bring one bloc or the other over the 75-seat mark. In this situation, changes in the electoral law may make for a great deal of difference and have therefore been much discussed. The crux of the situation is this: the nonsocialist parties have an interest in increasing the likelihood of a split in the Labor Party and may therefore propose to lower the 1.4 threshold to 1.3 or 1.2, but this very move will of necessity also make it highly unprofitable for the four opposition parties to merge. The largest of the opposition parties, the Conservatives, has an inherent strategic interest in higher thresholds but seems ready to forego this advantage in order to encourage splinters from Labor. The Swedish proposal [40] to ensure greater parliamentary stability through a provision for moderate overrepresentation of the largest party has been received with little enthusiasm in Norway. Several proposals have been made for the addition of members-at-large for each region, but the stated purpose has in this case been to increase overall proportionality, not to ensure a premium for the near-majority party. The Labor Party has on occasion ventured to suggest a switch to the Anglo-American system of plurality decisions, but this would give it such overwhelming majorities in the first phase and cause such bitter quarrels among the opposition parties that even the party most likely to gain from it in the long run, the Conservatives, have shown no inclination to accept the idea. The Sainte-Laguë procedure fits the party system very well: it favors the one-seat Middle parties in the multi-member constituencies and discourages mergers of party lists.[41] Any

40. See Författningsutredningen, *Sveriges statsskick. Del 2. Motiv* (Stockholm, SOU, 1963), *17*, 57–80.
41. An example from the Bergen elections of 1957 and 1961 illustrates this very clearly:

List	Candidate votes	Seat allocation				Votes per seat
	(5 candidates)	Divisors			Total	
1957		1.4	3	5		
Labor	146,871	104,907 = I	48,957=III	29,374=V	3	48,957
Conservative	75,653	54,037 = II	25,217		1	75,653
Liberal	47,658	34,041 = IV			1	47,658
Christian	29,440	21,028			0	
Communist	12,921	9,229			0	
1961						
Labor	154,753	110,537 = I	51,584=III	30,950	2	77,376
Joint Conservative-Christian	97,043	69,316 = II	32,347=V	19,408	2	48,521
Liberal	50,752	36,251 = IV			1	50,752
Communist	12,250					

The joint Conservative-Christian list produced a gain of one seat for the nonsocialist front despite a decrease in the relative voting strength of this bloc. This happened

change toward a strengthening of the chances of the larger parties at the poles of the system would disturb the current equilibrium. It would increase the likelihood of a return to clear-cut Labor majorities, and it would threaten the survival of the Middle parties as separate units in many constituencies. The success of the joint "Bourgeois Front" list in one of the Southern Swedish constituencies in 1964 strengthened the arguments for closer electoral cooperation among the four opposition parties, but there is little likelihood that this solution will be uniformly adopted in the near future. Considerations of electoral tactics will force different solutions in different constituencies.

All these speculations concern arrangements within the electoral-parliamentary channel of influence. What happens in this channel, however, will in great measure depend on the tensions, conflicts, and solutions in the other channel, the corporate-organizational. So far there has been no tendency to fuse the two channels. The Finnish attempt to bring union representatives directly into the Cabinet would not make sense in Norway. There has been a great deal of discussion of the possibility of establishing a policy coordination body along the lines of the British National Economic Development Council, but no question of developing a corporate chamber on the lines of the Dutch SER.[42] The protagonists in the triangular conflict over incomes do not want to bind themselves within a common framework and prefer to take their chances in an uncertain bargaining market. The corporatism of the "two-tier" system of decision-making is implicit and latent, not formal and institutionalized. The Constitution recognizes only one type of representation: the territorial. Functional representation is channeled implicitly through the parties and explicitly through boards and councils under the central administration, but there is no instituted procedure of legitimation for such representatives —no constitutional provision for the definition of functional electorates, for rules of nomination, and for procedures of election. Any move toward explicit corporatism would require some such regularization of the government of private organizations and associations and, at least at present, this seems to be too high a price to pay for the uncertain gains in stability and accountability to be achieved through a merger of the two "tiers." The overlap in personnel, the criss-crossing of role relationships, the interdependence of strategies at the two levels all create complex

---

because the below-threshold votes for the Christians could be added to the Conservative surplus. If all three nonsocialist parties had presented one joint list, however, the result would have been a clear-cut loss (147,795 for the joint list vs. 154,753 for Labor): the first seat for the Liberals cost much less than the third seat for a joint list.

42. See J. Moren, *Staten og næringslivet* (Bergen, Chr. Michelsen Institute, 1962); S. Rostoft, *Samarbeidet mellom staten of næringslivet* (Bergen, Norges Handelshøyskole, 1963); and S. Lindebrække, "Samarbeid."

constraints on the actions of the participants, and these may be more effective in integrating the system than any formal framework of institutional arrangements.

The great danger of these complex systems of interdependent decision-making is that representatives get tied into charmed circles of negotiators and administrators and become immune to communications from their rank and file. The loose and informal two-tier system may leave them more exposed to backbench pressure than formal provisions for functional representation in a corporative assembly. Whatever the institutional setting, this is a problem of crucial importance in advanced mass societies. The survival of democratic pluralism may depend as much on provisions for effective channels of opposition and protest within the private associations and the corporate bodies as on the chances for a regular alternation of governments at the top.

Postscript September 1965

This attempt at an analysis of forces and counterforces in Norwegian politics was written under the impact of the deadlocked constellation created in 1963: the first draft was written at the University of Manchester in May 1964, and the final version was completed in October of that year (a few footnotes were added later).

At the time the chapter was written it was expected that the volume would appear shortly before the next contest of forces in Norwegian politics: the election of representatives to the Storting scheduled for September 12–13, 1965. Instead, this analysis is now destined to appear a number of months *after* what turned out to be a major upheaval in the affairs of an otherwise stable and circumspect polity: Labor lost out after thirty years of near-continuous government and the four cooperating parties of what we have termed the "established opposition" were finally confronted with the task of forming a regular majority cabinet. Time and space will not allow any detailed discussion of the background and the implications of this dramatic change in political fortunes but the reader is at least entitled to a quick summary of the new situation.

By American standards the 1965 election could hardly qualify as a "landslide" but with so many lists so close to the thresholds of representation even minor defections from Labor could produce significant changes in the majority-minority balance.

The decline of the Labor Party can be seen in this comparative table for the last general elections:

Party	1961 % of electorate	% of votes cast	Total seats won	1965 % of electorate	% of votes cast	Total seats won
CP	2.3	2.9	0	1.2	1.4	0
SP	1.9	2.4	2	5.1	6.0	2
Labour	36.8	46.8	74	36.7	43.1	68
Liberal	7.0	8.9	14	8.8	10.4	18
Christian	7.6	9.6	15	6.9	8.1	13
Agrarian	7.3	9.3	16	8.4	9.9	18
Conservative	15.7	20.0	29	17.9	21.1	31
Turnout	79.1			85.4		

Comparing 1965 and 1961 we see that the Labor Party retained its share of the *electorate* (36.7 vs. 36.8%) but lost out in the contest for *votes* (down 3.7 points to 43.1%). The net losses flowed leftward as well as rightward: the Socialist People's Party had lists in all the 20 multimember constituencies and nearly tripled its strength while the Liberals, the Agrarians, and the Conservatives all made significant progress. The balance in the system was disturbed but not quite disrupted: the three competing Socialist parties still polled 50.5 per cent of all votes cast and the four cooperating parties of the old opposition had not quite reached the magical 50 per cent point.

But the Socialist majority of votes was again without political significance: what counted was the fate of each list and this time as many as 34 Socialist lists (16 CP and 18 SP) did not reach the threshold. The result was a clear victory for the cooperating nonsocialist parties: they gained six more seats and could command a clear-cut majority of 80 over 70.

Could the four parties actually pull together and make effective use of this majority? This was the question asked among politicians and analysts throughout the Nordic countries the day after this "turn of the tide." The four parties had shelved their differences during the campaign: would they be able to reach workable compromises when confronted with the long-standing policy issues of the Norwegian system? Our analysis has pointed to the principal sources of strain and *malaise* among the four parties, but it is very difficult to predict how far it will prove possible to keep these tensions within bounds under the paramount pressure for unity in the face of embittered opposition. Much will depend on external forces. Will the European issue come up again? Will the negotiations over the continuation of NATO strain the established unity in matters of alliance policy? Whatever the outcome, aficionados of comparative politics will watch with fascination the behavior of this curious system at the half-way point between straight Anglo-Saxon "ins–outs" alternations and mixed Continental coalition and *Proporz* manipulations.

4

SWEDEN:
STABILITY OR DEADLOCK?

Nils Stjernquist

In Sweden the Social Democratic Party has been in power almost without interruption since 1932. To the right of the government are three nonsocialist parties, often called the "bourgeois" parties; the Conservative Party, the Liberal Party, and the Center (until 1959, the Farmers') Party. To the left of the government is the Communist Party with only a few members in the Riksdag. The Center Party has sometimes collaborated with the Social Democrats on the governmental level. During the Second World War there was a coalition government consisting of all parties except the Communists.

The nonsocialist parties sometimes comment that the opposition is, or soon will be, without importance. As the Conservative leader, Gunnar Heckscher, stated in 1963:

> In fact the concentration of power in the government and in the governing party is the most characteristic feature of Swedish politics just now. We are rapidly moving away from the politics of compromise based on reciprocal concessions which was typical of our country from the mid-thirties to the mid-fifties. The Social Democratic government is more and more impatiently dictatorial, and the Social Democratic Party is concentrating on an unceasing and indisputable possession of power . . . The chief risk is that we really might end up by having a kind of one-party system by which the opposition is allowed, in principle, but care is taken to see that it never has any political importance.[1]

Even some Socialists have said that the opposition finds it difficult to carry out its function. As early as 1951 Prime Minister Tage Erlander asked what would happen to "an opposition that represents almost half of the citizens but which never has an opportunity of trying its strength

1. G. Heckscher, *Trygga folkstyret!* (Stockholm, 1963), pp. 12 ff.

For comments and criticism I wish to acknowledge my debts to Pär-Erik Back, Robert A. Dahl, Agne Gustafsson, Val R. Lorwin, Hans F. Petersson, Stein Rokkan, Bo Särlvik, Torbjörn Vallinder, and Ernst Wigforss.

as the government and which never has practice in assuming the responsibility which this involves." [2]

Other observers, however, argue that the opposition *is* worthwhile and does have influence. The Liberal leader, Bertil Ohlin, said in 1963:

> The opposition, as we all know, has had a great influence on the development of society in Sweden since the war by putting an end to the Socialist "harvest-time" before it began, by speeding up and influencing a number of reforms, and, furthermore, by criticizing the government's mistakes and bringing about corrections. [3]

Some spokesmen even suggest from time to time that the Socialist government gets its ideas from the opposition.

These diverse opinions are not academic evaluations but part of a national political debate. They may therefore represent tactical moves and appeals to various electorates as well as candid observations or fears.

What really is the role of the opposition in the present political system?

Constitutional Provisions [4]

The Swedish Constitution, dating from 1809, provides for a distribution of power between king and Parliament (called the Riksdag). According to the Constitution the king has the executive power, Parliament the powers of taxation and budget-making. The legislative power is divided between king and Parliament. Parliament also has control of the executive power.

The Constitution did not lay down the parliamentary system. When this system was decisively accepted in 1917, the change took place without any alteration in the constitutional provisions, which still give the king, not the ministers, the governmental power and still permit the king to choose his ministers without regard to party support or majorities in Parliament.

The Swedish Parliament has been divided since 1866 into an Upper House and a Lower House, which in all matters have equal competence and powers. If the houses disagree on legislative matters and their opinions cannot be reconciled, the question is dropped. If they differ on matters concerning state expenditure or taxation, each house has to vote on the different decisions. Then by the method of "joint division" the votes of the two houses are put together and the opinion that receives a majority of the aggregate number of votes constitutes the decision of the Riksdag.

---

2. *Reformer och försvar. En bok till Per Edvin Sköld* (Stockholm, Tidens förlag, 1951), p. 172. Cf. *Tiden* (1963), pp. 449 ff.
3. B. Ohlin, *Liberal utmaning* (1963), p. 18.
4. See N. Andrén, *Modern Swedish Government* (Stockholm, Almqvist and Wiksell, 1961). See also L. Frykholm, "Swedish Legal Publications in English, French and German 1935–60," *Scandinavian Studies in Law, 5* (1961), 196 ff.

If the aggregate number of votes is evenly divided, the issue is finally decided by drawing lots.

Universal and equal suffrage for men in the elections to the Lower House was introduced in 1909. At the same time proportional representation came into being. In 1918–21 universal suffrage was introduced for women too and for both sexes in municipal elections. The members of the Lower House are elected directly, the members of the Upper House indirectly by the county councils and, in the largest cities which are not represented on the county councils, by the city councils. The term of members of the Lower House is four years; that of members of the Upper House, eight years; every year one-eighth of the memberships in the Upper House are renewed.

The bicameral system has been and still is effective, even though some people argue occasionally that the Lower House should be more influential than the Upper House.[5]

The Socioeconomic Structure

A century ago Sweden was largely agrarian. Almost 75 per cent of the total population was engaged in agriculture and only about 13 per cent lived in the towns. Today the situation has changed completely. In 1960 only 13.8 per cent of the economically active population was occupied in agriculture and forestry, and people have at an increasing rate since 1945 moved into urban areas, especially to the three largest cities.

During the process of industrialization, which began slowly in the 1870s and increased rapidly in the 1890s, both the total and relative number of wage earners increased. In contrast, one of the most important changes in the last few decades has been the increase in the number of salaried employees, chiefly as a result of new methods in industry and the expanding activity of state and local government. In 1960 salaried employees constituted about 35 per cent of the economically active population, wage earners about 51 per cent, and employers about 14 per cent.

The occupational groups have built up local and national organizations with far-reaching influence. The wage earners are organized in trade unions with the LO (Landsorganisationen) at the top, the farmers in producers' associations with the SL (Sveriges Lantbruksförbund) at the top. For most of the salaried employees the TCO (Tjänstemännens Central-organisation) is their top organization. Salaried employees with a univer-

5. In 1963 a royal commission presented a draft for a new constitution to replace the constitution of 1809. The commission proposed that the parliamentary system be incorporated in the written constitution. The majority of the members of the commission preferred a unicameral system. (See *Statens offentliga utredningar* [1963], No. 16–18.) At the beginning of 1965 two special commissions were appointed, one to examine technicalities of the electoral procedure and one to investigate the interdependence between national politics on one hand and regional and local politics on the other. In the meantime the party leaders continued their discussion of basic features of a new constitution. Cf. n. 62, below.

sity degree have built up the SACO (Sveriges Akademikers Central-
organisation), some public servants' groups the SR (Statstjänstemännens
Riksförbund), while a large group of low-salaried employees have joined
the LO in a section of their own (Statstjänarkartellen). On the other side,
employers in the private sector are organized in the SAF (Svenska
Arbetsgivareföreningen).

By the time the bicameral Parliament came into being in 1866, the
division of the population into the Four Estates (nobles, clergy, burghers,
and peasants) was outmoded. Instead the population could be divided in a
rough way into three social groups: the upper, middle, and lower classes.
To the upper class belonged the senior bureaucracy and the big industrialists, to the middle class the small businessmen, salaried employees, and
farmers, to the lower class the wage earners and farm laborers (overwhelmingly the largest part of the population at that time). Although the
distribution has been changed by the urban shift mentioned above, the
division into these social groups is still used.

The Cleavages and the Party System [6]

Sweden covers a vast area (450,000 sq. km.) but has a population that is
small (about 7.7 million in 1965) and highly homogeneous. Regional
differences for the most part are not of real importance in politics, and
religion has not played a role in politics comparable with that in the
Catholic countries. The overwhelming majority of the population belongs
to the Lutheran State Church. Friendly relations exist today between the
State Church and nonconformists. The nonconformists have generally
supported the Liberals, while a majority of the active members of the
State Church vote with the Conservatives or the Center Party. The
Socialists were, to begin with, opponents of the State Church. By and
large, however, as they began to assume responsibility as the government,
their attitude became more neutral.[7] Among the Socialists there is an
organized group that is actively religious, and religious interests today are
probably protected by a majority in Parliament. In the 1964 elections to
the Lower House a new party appeared, called the Christian Democratic
Union (KDS), to a large extent supported by the Pentecostalists. It got
about 75,000 votes mainly at the expense of the Liberals and the Socialists,
but did not win a seat.

THE OLD SOCIETY   As early as the eighteenth century, during the so-
called Era of Liberty, Sweden had a highly developed parliamentary
system with two parties, the Hats and the Caps. They were mainly or-

6. I. Andersson, *A History of Sweden* (2d ed. Stockholm, Natur och Kultur, 1956);
D. A. Rustow, *The Politics of Compromise: a Study of Parties and Cabinet Government in Sweden* (Princeton, Princeton University Press, 1955); D. Verney, *Parliamentary Reform in Sweden* (Oxford, Clarendon Press, 1957).
7. C. A. Hessler, *Statskyrkodebatten* (Stockholm, Almqvist and Wiksell, 1964),
with an English summary.

ganizations inside Parliament, which at that time consisted of the Four
Estates. This old parliamentary system was abolished by a coup d'etat by
the king in 1772.

After the parliamentary reform of 1866 the cleavage between the two
well-established classes on the one hand and the lower class on the other
was for a long time not a real political problem, because the lower class
was excluded from the suffrage. The dominant cleavage was between the
farmers and the bureaucracy.

In accordance with the provisions of the Constitution of 1809, Parliament for a long time had no influence upon the king's choice of ministers,
and they were recruited from the ranks of the senior bureaucrats. It was
impossible, however, to avoid opposition to the government in Parliament
and quite naturally a party system developed inside Parliament. Suffrage
restrictions made it possible for the upper class to control the Upper
House and for the middle class to control the Lower House; in the latter
the farmers won a majority. The Agrarian Party in the Lower House
formed the opposition to the government. In appointing ministers, the
king was eventually obliged to take into consideration how Parliament
would react, although in 1887 he still characterized parliamentarism as a
foreign practice unknown to the Constitution.[8]

In the 1880s the tariff question deeply involved all interests in economic
life and led to large cleavages both inside and outside Parliament and also
among the farmers. As a result, politics began to interest the voters as well
as those who were not entitled to vote, and from then on real election
campaigns took place.[9]

In the 1890s a new political issue, the move for universal suffrage, came
to the fore.[10] At the end of the nineteenth century only one-quarter of the
men over 21 had the vote. The question of universal suffrage deepened the
cleavage between those who were comfortably off and the poor. People
with a liberal ideology demanded universal suffrage. The adherents of this
ideology in the Lower House formed the Liberal Party in 1900, and two
years later this party started a national organization. The Socialist Party
had come into being as early as 1889, when a national organization was
started, and the Socialists too demanded universal suffrage, which offered
them their only hope of gaining a strong representation in Parliament. In
1897 the first Socialist representative, Hjalmar Branting, entered Parliament. On the opposite side the Conservatives, in defense of their position,
organized a national party in 1904 and then organized themselves in

8. Letter from Oscar II to his ministers, Nov. 21, 1887, published in T. Petré, *Min-
istären Themptander* (Uppsala, 1945), p. 296.
9. E. Håstad, "Tullstridens val och folkmeningen," in *Festskrift till Axel Brusewitz*
(Uppsala, 1941), pp. 105 ff.
10. T. Vallinder, *I kamp för demokratin: Rösträttsrörelsen i Sverige 1886–1900*
(Stockholm, Natur och Kultur, 1962), with an English summary.

Parliament.[11] The demand for universal suffrage was in fact a demand for a change in the fundamentals of the existing society and for a transfer of political power to new strata. The main lines of the present party system were established during the struggle for universal suffrage.

Universal suffrage was introduced gradually from 1909. At the same time, to protect the interests of the established classes, the PR system came into being. Closely allied to the suffrage question was the issue of parliamentarism and ministerial responsibility. The Liberals demanded parliamentarism and were supported by the Socialists. The king and the Conservatives were against parliamentarism. After the elections to the Lower House in 1917, when the two parties on the left got a strong majority, the king finally had to accept the parliamentary system and appoint a government consisting of both Liberals and Socialists. The Conservative Party still held a majority in the Upper House, until the democratization of the county councils in 1918 changed this situation.

The PR system made it possible for more than two parties to compete effectively in elections. Thus from 1911 a real three-party system—Conservatives, Liberals, and Socialists—developed.

MINORITY PARLIAMENTARISM, 1920–32   Universal suffrage and the growing number of wage earners made it possible for the Socialists to become the largest party. One problem for them was that for a long time the lower class did not participate as actively in elections as the other classes. Another problem was that the left wing of the Socialists had in 1917 formed their own party, from which different Communist parties developed in the 1920s. The Liberal Party declined in size and between 1923–34 was split into two factions. In 1921 the Farmers' Party, now called the Center Party, was formed.[12] Thus when democracy was fully established Sweden had a multiparty system with five parties which are still represented in Parliament. Appendix Table 4.1 shows the distribution of seats in the Riksdag since 1922.

Universal suffrage and parliamentarism were soon accepted in the 1920s by those who had previously opposed them. Having realized their constitutional program, the Liberals and the Socialists found it no longer possible to continue their collaboration in the government, for they had contrary views on how society ought to be constructed from the socioeconomic point of view. The Socialists demanded nationalization in principle, while the Liberals together with the Conservatives and the Center Party, all following their own ideologies, acted as guardians of the prevailing system. Nationalization now created the deepest cleavage

11. There was in the beginning one Conservative group in the Upper House and one in the Lower House.
12. The party was formed by the amalgamation of two smaller parties originating from the 1910s.

between the parties, and it was obvious that the dividing line on the party scale was between the Socialists and the Communists on the one side and the nonsocialist parties on the other.

During the period of minority parliamentarism from 1920–32 no party held a majority position (Appendix Table 4.2). A coalition between the Socialists and one of the nonsocialist parties was hardly possible,[13] nor could the nonsocialist parties collaborate with each other in the government. Sometimes, indeed, all the political parties actually preferred to be out of power. Each election to the Lower House led to a defeat for the governmental party and to a change of government. During this period Sweden changed its government at least every other year. Since the government was without a parliamentary majority, political issues were solved in each separate case by compromises by at least two parties. Political power was concentrated in Parliament, especially in the committees, where the political compromises were made. The Liberals were no doubt in the best position to control the situation and to form a stronger government than could be formed under the leadership of the Socialists or the Conservatives. Sometimes a Liberal government tried to find support from the right, sometimes from the left, but sometimes the Conservatives and the Socialists made a united stand against this system of fleeting majorities.[14] Socialists and Conservatives, but not Liberals, today quite naturally have unhappy memories of minority parliamentarism.[15]

MAJORITY PARLIAMENTARISM FROM 1933   In the development of the parliamentary system the year 1933 forms a dividing line. Since that year one party has been dominant—the Socialist Party. A main feature of its policy has been collaboration with the Center Party. In elections to the Lower House the distribution of votes for the Socialists and Communists on the one hand and for the three nonsocialist parties on the other has been very stable, oscillating since 1940 between 58–42 per cent (1940) and 49.6–50.3 per cent (1956).[16] Among the three nonsocialist parties, however, there have been considerable fluctuations (Appendix Table 4.3).

The Socialists took over the government in the autumn of 1932 when the depression and unemployment were at their worst. In this situation the majority of the party had decided to drop the demand for nationalization and instead concentrate on a social welfare policy.[17] Thus the most im-

13. At the end of the 1920s negotiations between the Socialists and the Liberals took place but without result.
14. A Conservative review could boldly characterize the Liberal government as a dictatorship. See *Svensk tidskrift* (1929), p. 327.
15. See G. Andersson, "Regeringar utan riksdagsmajoritet," in *Ekonomi, politik, samhälle; en bok tillägnad Bertil Ohlin* (Stockholm, 1959), pp. 15 ff.
16. In the 1958 elections the figures were 49.6–50.4 per cent. At that time, however, the Communists were active in only a few constituencies.
17. H. Tingsten, *Den svenska socialdemokratiens idéutveckling, 1–2* (Stockholm, Tidens förlag, 1941).

portant cleavage between the Socialists and nonsocialists was eliminated. However, to say that the Socialists accepted the socioeconomic structure of society would not be correct. Social welfare programs were seen as another means of leveling incomes.[18] Furthermore, influenced by Keynes, the Socialists wanted a higher level of state activity and an economy planned by the state. The Conservatives and the Liberals still acted as protectors of the structure of society and opposed state regulation. The Center Party, however, was able to accept state regulation in agriculture. This explains to a large extent why it was possible in 1933 for the Socialists and the Center Party to work out a common program for economic policy. As a result of the agreement the government was able to rely on a majority in both houses. Thus the period of minority parliamentarism came to an end and was succeeded by a system that can be called majority parliamentarism, although the Center Party had not yet entered the government. Political power moved from Parliament to the government.

In 1936 the defense question caused an open cleavage in Swedish politics. For a short time the Socialists let the Center Party take over the government. After the elections to the Lower House in the autumn of 1936, the Socialist leader, P. A. Hansson, formed a new government, this time in coalition with the Center Party.

The nonsocialist parties, taken together, held a minority position in the Lower House in 1937. In 1941 the Socialists acquired a majority in the Lower House and in 1942 also in the Upper House. During the war political power was highly centralized in the Cabinet, which at that time also included representatives of the Conservatives and the Liberals. Only the Communists remained outside the government. As in other countries in wartime, the government was given far-reaching authority, and Parliament functioned only as an apparatus for registering what the government had already decided. A prerequisite for the all-party government, however, was an understanding that nothing be decided in matters involving internal cleavages.

After the peace in Europe in 1945 the all-party government was dissolved and the Socialists formed a new government. They were still in a strong position, with almost half the votes in the Lower House and a majority in the Upper House and in joint divisions. In 1944 they had made their party program more radical, and the cleavages between them and the nonsocialist parties were now more sharply emphasized. When Sweden's foreign exchange position became difficult in 1947, the nonsocialist parties criticized the government for its economic policy and what they called "misrule." In the 1948 elections to the Lower House, the Liberals more than doubled their seats, though this was mainly at the expense of the

18. E. Wigforss, *Ha vi råd till sociala reformer?* (1937), pp. 17 ff.

Conservatives and the Center Party; the Socialists lost three seats. The nonsocialist parties did not succeed in gaining a majority in the Lower House.

The Socialists found it troublesome, however, not to control the majority in the Lower House and for that reason the Center Party was invited to enter the government after the elections of 1948. After some hesitation it declined the invitation. In 1951 new negotiations resulted in a coalition government of the two parties. They had a common program concerning economic policy and agriculture. The issues between the government and the opposition now involved primarily economic and tax policies. By this time the extensive social welfare program, which was passed from 1946 to 1950, was supported as energetically by the non-socialist parties as by the Socialists. On defense policy,[19] foreign policy,[20] and educational policy, there was almost complete unanimity.

In the elections to the Lower House in 1956 the government parties both suffered setbacks. The situation seemed especially dangerous for the Center Party, which lost about one-quarter of its seats. Its supporters were mainly farmers, and the agrarian population was decreasing rapidly. Furthermore, many of the party's supporters were dissatisfied with its collaboration with the Socialists. As a result of the elections, the three nonsocialist parties together obtained a majority in the Lower House. The coalition between the Socialists and the Center Party continued, however.

In 1957 the pension question became a major political issue. The Socialists were planning a general supplementary pension that would be compulsory and involved building up large funds. The nonsocialist parties opposed the plan, but they did not express their opposition in joint action. The Conservatives and the Liberals sponsored a voluntary system of agreements between employers' organizations and employees' organizations; the Center Party's attitude was that the system had to be founded on "personal voluntariness." In the autumn of 1957 the electorate was asked to help settle the question by a consultative referendum. About 46 per cent of those who participated preferred the Socialist approach, about 35 per cent the plan of the Conservatives and the Liberals, and—the most interesting development—15 per cent supported the Center Party. The problem was not solved by the referendum. Immediately afterward the Center Party declared that it could no longer remain in a coalition with the Socialists, and as a result the entire coalition government resigned. The King first explored the possibility of forming a government consisting of all parties except the Communists, a solution recommended by Conservative leader Jarl Hjalmarson and Liberal leader Bertil Ohlin. After discus-

19. Cf. T. Erlander, "Försvaret över partierna," in *Fred och försvar under 60-talet* (Stockholm, 1961), pp. 11 ff.

20. Cf. H. Tingsten, "Issues in Swedish Foreign Policy," *Foreign Affairs*, 37(1959), 474 ff.

sions with the leaders of the nonsocialists parties, Socialist leader Tage Erlander, who had already said that the Socialists were against this solution, refused to join an all-party government. Ohlin and Hjalmarson were then asked by the King to investigate the possibility of forming a government supported by the nonsocialist majority in the Lower House. However, the leader of the Center Party, Gunnar Hedlund, said that he did not want to enter into a government with the other two nonsocialist parties or to support a Liberal-Conservative government. He underlined the fact that the Socialists still had the majority in the Upper House and that from a political point of view it was impossible for him to start collaborating with the Conservatives and the Liberals immediately after having left a coalition with the Socialists. Erlander then formed a government consisting only of Socialists.

In the spring of 1958 the nonsocialist majority in the Lower House rejected a pension proposal made by the Socialist government, which then ordered elections to the Lower House. The Socialist Party won five more seats and the nonsocialists lost their majority. The most striking fact was that the Liberals lost 20 seats and the Center Party won 13. The pension question gave the Center Party an opportunity to reestablish its strength and appeal to groups other than the agrarian population.

The pension question was solved in 1959 mainly along the lines advocated by the Socialists. But neither the Socialists nor the nonsocialist parties controlled a majority in the Lower House or in joint divisions. At the end of 1959 a government proposal for the introduction of a general sales tax brought harsh criticism from the opposition and could be put through only with the help of the Communists, who abstained from voting in the joint divisions.

After the elections to the Lower House in the autumn of 1960 the Socialists had one seat more than the three nonsocialist parties together and still controlled a majority in the Upper House. But because of the Communist members they were one seat short of a majority in the joint divisions. The municipal elections in 1962 strengthened the position of the Socialists in the Upper House, and in 1964 they regained their majority in joint divisions. On the eve of the elections to the Lower House in 1964 it was generally expected that the Socialists would win a stable majority; in the municipal elections in 1962 they had received 50.5 per cent of the votes, an increase of 2.7 per cent in comparison with the elections to the Lower House in 1960. But in fact they did not win more than 47.3 per cent of the votes; they lost one seat in the Lower House, and lost their majority in the joint divisions.[21]

21. The number of Socialist seats in the Upper House will increase by one in both 1966 and 1967, hence from 1967 the Socialists will regain the majority in joint divisions.

Two new parties participated in the 1964 elections—the Christian Democratic Union (KDS), which did not receive a sufficient number of votes to be represented in Parliament, and the Citizens' Union (MBS), which appeared in only one constituency (Malmö) and won three seats. The purpose of the MBS was to unite the three nonsocialist parties and overthrow the Socialist government. It acted against the national organizations of the nonsocialist parties and was supported primarily by people who had previously voted Conservative and by two big Conservative newspapers. It was successful in that one of its representatives was a Conservative, one a Liberal, and one a member of the Center Party. Each one tried to join his original party in Parliament; the centrist, however, was not accepted by his parliamentary group. Although the Socialist Party lost a little ground—both absolutely and relatively—the three non-socialist parties and the MBS taken together also lost ground. The Liberal Party, it is true, won two seats and the Center Party one, but the Conservatives lost seven seats and all three parties received relatively fewer votes. As a result of the efforts of their new leader, Carl-Henrik Hermansson, the Communists won three seats and increased their percentage of the electorate from 4.5 (in 1960) to 5.2.

The margins between the Socialists and nonsocialists have been small since 1960, and illness or refusal to follow the party line can unexpectedly change the situation. This nearly equal balance has invited agreements behind the scenes. A far-reaching agreement of this type was made on the taxation question in the autumn of 1961 between the Socialist government and the Center Party. The policy of the Center Party shows that it prefers to have contacts both with the Socialists and inside the nonsocialist sector, especially with the Liberals, and to utilize the advantages of being the balancer (see below).

PARTY AFFILIATION   There is an obvious correlation between party affiliation and occupational group and, on the whole, socioeconomic status. Table 4.1 shows the 1964 voters by party affiliation and nonvoters in different occupational groups. Table 4.2 shows them by occupational groups.[22]

The majority of the wage earners support the Socialists and the majority of the farmers the Center Party, while the salaried employees are split up, primarily among the Conservatives, the Liberals, and the Socialists. It may, however, be emphasized that actually among the Socialist voters the relative number of lower-salaried employees is increasing while the

22. The tables and figures are from a Political Science Institute of Gothenburg Survey by B. Särlvik, published in *Official Statistics of Sweden, The Elections to the Riksdag During the Years 1961–1964, 2* (Stockholm, 1965). See also B. Särlvik, "Politisk rörlighet och stabilitet i valmanskåren," *Statsvetenskaplig tidskrift,* 67 (1964), 185 ff.

Table 4.1 *The 1964 Voters by Party Affiliation in Occupational Groups*

	Cons.	Lib.	Center	KDS	MBS	Soc.	Comm.	No answer	Non-voters	Total	N
					(in percentages)						
Larger employers, higher-salaried employees	42	27	3	2	6	7	—	4	9	100	160
Farmers	12	11	58	2	0	6	0	2	9	100	297
Smaller employers	12	28	14	2	1	20	1	4	18	100	255
Lower-salaried employees, shop assistants	13	22	5	1	2	41	2	3	11	100	740
Farm and lumber workers	3	12	17	1	—	42	3	4	18	100	171
Other workers	3	6	7	1	0	64	4	2	13	100	1226

Table 4.2 *The 1964 Voters by Occupational Groups in the Political Parties*

	Larger employers, higher-salaried employees	Farmers	Smaller employers	Lower-salaried employees, shop assistants	Farm and lumber workers	Other workers	Total	N
				(in percentages)				
Cons.	25	13	12	36	2	12	100	265
Lib.	10	8	18	40	5	19	100	408
Center	1	48	10	11	8	22	100	359
KDS	10	12	12	30	5	31	100	41
MBS	29	3	7	45	—	16	100	31
Soc.	1	1	4	25	6	63	100	1248
Comm.	—	1	3	18	9	69	100	67
No answer	8	6	13	30	9	34	100	77
Nonvoters	3	8	13	23	9	44	100	353
Total	6	10	9	26	6	43	100	2849

Table 4.3 The 1962 Voters by Their 1964 Votes

Voting in 1962	Voting in 1964 (in percentages)									Total	N
	Cons.	Lib.	Center	KDS	MBS	Soc.	Comm.	No answer	Non-voters		
Cons.	74	8	3	1	7	1	0	1	5	100	254
Lib.	4	77	4	4	2	1	1	1	6	100	372
Center	2	1	88	1	0	2	0	0	6	100	290
Soc.	0	1	2	1	0	88	2	1	5	100	1155
Comm.	0	0	3	3	0	12	76	0	6	100	34
No answer	9	10	6	1	1	18	2	33	20	100	154
Nonvoters	7	10	8	2	0	31	2	2	38	100	459
Not entitled to vote	5	15	8	2	2	37	0	4	27	100	131

Table 4.4 The 1964 Voters by Their 1962 Votes

Voting in 1964	Voting in 1962 (in percentages)								Total	N
	Cons.	Lib.	Center	Soc.	Comm.	No answer	Non-voters	Not entitled to vote		
Cons.	71	6	2	2	0	5	12	2	100	265
Lib.	5	71	0	3	0	4	12	5	100	408
Center	2	4	71	7	0	3	10	3	100	359
KDS	7	32	7	21	3	5	20	5	100	41
MBS	55	19	3	3	0	3	7	10	100	31
Soc.	0	1	1	81	0	2	11	4	100	1248
Comm.	2	3	2	37	39	4	13	0	100	67
No answer	3	3	0	10	0	66	12	6	100	77
Nonvoters	3	7	5	16	0	9	50	10	100	353

relative number of workers is possibly decreasing. In the 1930s and 1940s it might have been possible for the Liberal Party to be transformed into a party for salaried employees. In the old days and even in the 1950s all parties appealed to the farmers; the percentage of farmers among the members of Parliament has always been higher than among the electorate.

Stability within the electorate is generally rather high. There has been more mobility among the nonsocialist parties than between these parties on the one hand and the Socialists on the other. The net fluctuations between the two blocs were (at least from 1954 to 1962) chiefly due to fluctuations in participation in elections. Table 4.3 shows voters and nonvoters in the 1962 municipal elections distributed by voting behavior in the 1964 election. Table 4.4 shows voters and nonvoters in the 1964 election distributed by voting behavior in the 1962 municipal elections.

About 70 per cent of those interviewed voted in both elections for the same party, while 7 per cent of those entitled to vote in both elections did not participate either in 1962 or in 1964. About 8 per cent of those entitled to vote both years changed over from one party to another—4.3 per cent from a nonsocialist party to another nonsocialist party, 0.6 per cent from a nonsocialist party to a socialist (Socialists and Communists) party, 2.1 per cent from a socialist to a nonsocialist party and 1.1 per cent from one socialist to another socialist party.

FROM CLEAVAGES TO CONSENSUS AMONG THE PARTIES   The two most widely discussed issues in recent years, the pension question and the sales tax question, were solved in a manner not endorsed by the opposition. The solution to the pension question, however, was soon generally accepted, although in the 1964 elections the Conservatives criticized the funds for being too large. The sales tax alignment was astonishing, for in a reversal of traditional roles the Socialists introduced the tax while the nonsocialists opposed it. On the whole the cleavages between the parties have decreased since the beginning of the 1930s, for many reasons.

Before the introduction of universal suffrage the socioeconomic and ideological cleavages were very deep, and the society was in fact a class society.[23] As democracy was gradually accepted these differences were modified. Considerable further leveling took place when the Socialists abandoned their demand for nationalization and all the nonsocialist parties accepted a social welfare policy. Universal suffrage gave political power, in principle, to the "little man," whose interests, by and large, the nonsocialist as well as Socialist parties tended to look after. To a large extent he achieved the same income and the same standard of living as the middle class. It is significant that while 2.5 per cent graduated from secondary school (gymnasium) in 1932[24] and 6.5 per cent in 1950, the figure had

23. Cf. S. M. Lipset, *The First New Nation* (New York, Basic Books, 1963), pp. 235 ff.
24. The average age of graduation is 20.5.

increased to 17.1 in 1964 and is, according to the secondary school reform
of 1964, expected to increase to 30 per cent by the end of the 'sixties, a
figure that is probably too low.[25] The concept of class is in fact not very
useful in politics today. The Socialists do not appeal only to wage earners,
nor does the Center Party appeal only to farmers. The Conservatives have
used the idea of "the common citizen" as a political slogan. The political
parties often appeal to all groups in society, and modern mass-media have
certainly made people feel less like members of a particular class.

Swedish society today is highly pluralistic.[26] The organizations favor
compromises; they try to avoid state regulation and strikes and to come to
terms with each other by bargaining. Since 1947, there have been practically no strikes. The top organization of the employers and the top
organization of the industrial workers came to a major agreement at
Saltsjöbaden in 1938; labor relations are now said to be characterized by
"the spirit of Saltsjöbaden." There are channels between political parties
and socioeconomic organizations, for instance between the Socialists and
the trade unions and between the Center Party and the farmers' organizations. But the fact that the interest groups are not organized along party
lines has caused overlapping memberships and cross-pressures, so cleavages
are not polarized and political parties are inclined to compromise. Interest
groups in many fields bargain directly with the government; in matters
such as salaries and wages for state employees the agreements between the
government and the organizations result in the Riksdag being presented
with a fait accompli.[27] The organizations and not the political parties
actually deal with problems of distribution of income. It has been said that
cooperation between the government and the big organizations—which
has been characterized as "Harpsund-democracy" [28]—means that the opposition is passed over, and this is dangerous for the parliamentary system.[29] On the other hand it has been stressed that the organizations are of
vital interest to individuals and give them channels to political decision-
making other than voting on election day.[30]

25. The percentage of members of the Lower House with a university degree increased from 10.9 to 20.3 (in the Socialist group from 7.7 to 11.4) from 1933 to 1963.
26. See G. Heckscher, "Interest Groups in Sweden," in *Interest Groups on Four
Continents,* ed. by H. W. Ehrmann (Pittsburgh, University of Pittsburgh Press, 1958),
pp. 154 ff.; H. Zetterberg, "National Pastime: Pursuit of Power," *Industria International* (1960), pp. 105 ff. Zetterberg overestimates the role of the organizations.
27. In order to strengthen the position of Parliament, a parliamentary salary delegation was introduced in 1965. The delegation will follow the bargaining process and
be able to accept an agreement concerning salaries for state employees on behalf of
Parliament.
28. Harpsund is the summer residence of the Prime Minister, where top-level meetings between politicians and leaders from big business and the organizations take
place.
29. N. Elvander, "Organisationerna och statsmakterna," *Industriförbundets tidskrift*
(1963), pp. 424 ff.
30. B. Östergren, "Organisationsväsen och demokrati," *Tiden* (1962), pp. 206 ff.

The main aim of Swedish economic policy has been to secure social welfare and full employment and to raise the standard of living. Democracy has become equated with social services.[31] To realize this aim it has been necessary to give priority to actions that can lead to an increase in production.[32] On this point the government, the opposition, the organizations, and big business are united. Another important factor is that a country like Sweden, which is greatly dependent upon its exports and imports, cannot act independently of big business or independently of other countries. It can be argued that a Socialist government is advantageous for big business, since it is best fitted to put pressure on the trade unions in the bargaining process. All these considerations taken together have many times made the nonsocialist parties and the Socialists accept the same policy. In the process ideological differences have been pushed aside.

Up to 1933 the great political issues—universal suffrage and nationalization—were easy for the electorate to understand. But the issues of economic policy since 1945 have been very complicated for politicians and more so for the man in the street. Both from the economic and the technical points of view modern society is so complicated that the power of the bureaucracy and technocracy[33] has increased at the expense of politicians and political parties. The decisions on principle, the long-term planning, and the far-reaching authority now in the hands of the government have in fact restricted the power of Parliament and thus the power of the political parties. This has been a problem for the opposition parties in particular.

The electorate has become more apolitical because of the complicated structure of modern society and the decrease in cleavages. Depoliticization must not be overestimated, however. Party identification is still rather strong, and about one-quarter of the adult population are members of a political party.[34] Moreover participation in elections has increased rather than decreased (see Appendix Table 4.4).

Compromises between the parties and their bargaining tactics have no doubt helped to decrease the cleavages.

The present parliamentary situation invites the parties to concentrate on groups in the middle, on people who are likely to be among the floating vote—at one time primarily farmers but today more often salaried em-

---

31. J. Westerståhl, *Dagens Nyheter*, Aug. 4, 1956.
32. A specific problem is that further rises in the standard of living would become more and more expensive, relatively speaking. Cf. Prime Minister Erlander, *Upper House Minutes* (1956), *2*, 23 ff.
33. The civil service is on the whole traditionally not appointed according to party lines and neutral on political issues.
34. Cf. U. Himmelstrand, "A Theoretical and Empirical Approach to Depoliticization and Political Involvement," *Acta Sociologica, 6* (1962), 96 ff.

ployees. Because they must appeal to identical interests, the proposals the parties put forward to each such group must therefore be similar.[35]

The parliamentary situation has long been one of an almost even balance between the Socialists on the one hand and the nonsocialist parties on the other. The Socialists have as a rule had a majority, but even a slight shift in the electorate has been and still is enough to alter this. The 50-50 balance makes both blocs and all the four parties cautious, and therefore has a leveling effect.[36]

Do cleavages no longer exist? The development just mentioned has led to the opinion, especially underlined by Herbert Tingsten,[37] that ideological cleavages have disappeared. Cleavages of today, it has been said, are restricted to the question: Which persons ought to be in power? The cleavages are certainly latent or potential, however, to a greater extent than is often recognized. For example Socialists and the nonsocialist parties still differ concerning the role of the state in economic life. But such differences are not generally brought before the public.

Cleavages sometimes occur *within* the parties. During the last few decades, however, the parties have been so well established and party identifications among the electorate so strong that new political issues have not produced changes in the party system. The emergence of the KDS and the MBS in the 1964 elections is interesting from this point of view. The MBS may be seen as a protest against the party system on the nonsocialist side.

The Conditions of the Opposition

In the debate within Sweden on parliamentarism and the role of the parliamentary opposition one school of thought has taken the English parliamentary system as a model, calling it the pure form of parliamentarism.[38] Characteristic of this form, as it has been understood in Sweden, are majority elections and hence a two-party system consisting of one majority party, which forms the government, and one minority party, which forms the opposition and is entirely out of power. The aim of the opposition party is to replace the government party by presenting alternatives with which it hopes to win the confidence of the majority of the electorate in the next election. It has often been maintained that the

35. In 1948, 3 per cent of the private members' proposals in the Lower House were signed by members from all parties except the Communists. In 1964 the figure had increased to 8.3.

36. It may be added that the members of both houses are seated by constituency, not party affiliation.

37. A leading Swedish political scientist, Tingsten was chief editor of the Liberal newspaper *Dagens Nyheter* from 1946 to 1960.

38. See e.g. C. A. Hessler, "Parlamentarismens begrepp," in *Studier tillägnade Fredrik Lagerroth* (Lund, 1950), pp. 172 ff.

English form of parliamentarism also implies alternations in office between the two parties, which presupposes a considerable proportion of floating votes among the electorate. In recent years Conservatives and Liberals have emphasized that alternation in office is necessary so that a one-party system will not emerge de facto and so that democracy can function in a satisfactory way.[39] A very long period of one-party rule would lead to a process of degeneration in the governing and alienation in the governed. The party in power would find it increasingly difficult to resist the temptation to regard itself as the *only* party able to serve society.[40] The primary task of the party system, it has also been said, is to facilitate a transfer of power from the incumbents to the opposition.[41] In rejoinder it is argued that the rules of the game in democracy positively presuppose a good chance of a change; but this again presupposes a lively opposition with a well-defined policy which it is prepared to put into effect should it come into power.[42] Obviously a democratic system cannot in itself guarantee alternations in office from one party to another.[43]

In this view of the English system, the function of the government is to govern, the function of the opposition is to oppose the government exclusively by criticizing government policy and presenting alternatives. Criticism provides in fact a most valuable and necessary brake on the government.[44] With all the efforts of the opposition directed toward victory in the next election, its strategy might be called an electoral strategy.

On the opposite side in the Swedish debate on parliamentarism and the role of the opposition, there has been another school of thought which has argued in favor of another system, also called a pure one. Fundamental to this system are PR elections and hence a multiparty system. The basic justification for PR is a belief that each party ought to be represented in Parliament in proportion to its strength among the electorate. In a democratic system, it is argued, this principle ought to be applied, too, in forming the government. Thus the government ought to be an all-party government, and the ministries and political power should be divided among the parties in proportion to the number of their seats in Parliament. The main aim of an opposition in a system of this kind would be to influence the policy-making process. The means available to the opposition would be compromises; its tactics, bargaining. But this aim is incompatible with the basic aim of the opposition in the English approach. For partici-

39. Cf. B. Ohlin, *Liberal utmaning* (1963), p. 18; G. Heckscher, *Trygga folkstyret!* (1963), pp. 12–14; *Svenska Dagbladet*, Aug. 4, 1964; *Dagens Nyheter*, Aug. 23, 1964.
40. S. Wedén, *Samhällsåskådningar och partier* (1963), p. 59.
41. *Dagens Nyheter*, July 16, 1963.
42. Cf. H. Adamsson, *Industritjänstemannen*, December 1963.
43. Cf. K. C. Wheare, *Legislatures* (London, Oxford University Press, 1963), p. 120.
44. Cf. O. Dahlén, *Stärk demokratin* (1964), pp. 46 ff.

pation in the policy-making process means that the opposition assumes a share of responsibility for government policy. By entering an all-party government the opposition would attain its goal of influencing the policy-making process, but it would weaken not only its claim to replace the government but also its role as the parliamentary opposition as such. With an all-party government there would be no alternative, no shadow government—indeed ought not to be any opposition at all among the parties. Instead the opposition would have to come from inside the parties and from groups outside the parties. The electorate would be stable. The fundamental structure of society could hardly be changed or attacked. The system could not function without a general sharing of common fundamental values.

The idea of joint work by all "good" parties has had a strong appeal in Sweden, and the all-party-government system, like the PR system, has been called just. Proponents of a permanent all-party government often emphasize that the English approach only increases dissatisfaction among the electorate and the politicians.

The two forms of government mentioned here are both "pure," ideal types at opposite ends of the scale.[45] However, facts have only in exceptional cases corresponded to either of the extremes on the scale. Generally there has been a mixture or a combination of the two systems. How then has the opposition functioned?

In the last few decades of the nineteenth century the opposition cannot be characterized as an opposition in the parliamentary sense. It had no desire either to replace the government or to collaborate with the government. Its main aim was to cut down state expenditure.[46] But the method of solving great political issues through compromise laid the basis for a political tradition.

In the period 1900–20, irrespective of which party formed the government the Liberals in fact acted as an opposition against the prevailing structure of society, while the Conservatives served as guardians of that structure. The Liberal Party, and especially its leader Karl Staaff,[47] believed in the English concept of the role of the opposition. Thus, when they were out of power the Liberals tried to replace the Conservative government, and when they were in power they were in principle not

45. The arrangement in the beginning of the 1920s, when no party wanted to be in government either alone or in coalition with another party and the government was therefore composed of high officials, is also the opposite of the all-party government but is antiparliamentarian. It was never considered a normal solution.

46. See N. Stjernquist, "The Swedish Constitution and the Budgetary Principles," *Scandinavian Studies in Law,* 6 (1962), 222.

47. See L. Kihlberg, *Karl Staaff, 1–2* (Stockholm, Bonniers förlag, 1962–63).

open to compromises with the Conservatives. In the beginning the Socialists were against any collaboration with a nonsocialist party on the government level, and among them were many who preferred revolutionary to electoral tactics. At the end of the period, however, the Socialists found it possible to collaborate with the Liberals even on the government level.

The crucial decisions, however, when universal suffrage for men and the PR system were introduced in 1907–09, were a typical political compromise. The PR system removed the real basis for the English system, though politicians did not embrace the idea that any other concept of an opposition party should be adopted. By the 1920s the main goal of the Socialists was not revolution but nationalization, the changing of the economic structure of society. From then on their opposition was entirely parliamentary, but they were still in opposition to the socioeconomic structure of society, while the nonsocialist parties tried to maintain this structure. The Socialists, however, did not hold sufficient power to achieve their objective.

Independent of whatever party formed the government, the opposition was in practice directed toward influencing the policy-making process. But the opposition parties sometimes hesitated to seek office. Generally it was assumed that it was undesirable to be in power during elections. The government party lost every election in the 1920s. The tactics of the opposition parties were electoral, but at the same time directed to a high degree toward bargaining with the government party or with other parties. Thus a system of majorities changing from question to question was developed. Government power was weak. On the other hand, because there were several opposition parties, each was weak. Politics was characterized by compromise between the parties, not primarily between the government and the opposition. Thus the system diverged markedly from the English one.

During the period of minority parliamentarism, when the political system was discussed the discussion generally started from the weakness of the government, not from the role of the opposition. The remedies proposed, however, would all have affected the role of the opposition. One remedy proposed by some Socialists was to change the electoral system to a majority system.[48] Tage Erlander, then a student at Lund University, argued in favor of the American system with a directly elected president.[49] Nils Herlitz, later a Conservative member of the Upper House and a lead-

48. See especially Motion No. 239 (1930) in the Upper House by G. Möller, R. Sandler, and K. Schlyter. P. A. Hansson, however, was in favor of the PR system.
49. *Arbetet*, July 4, 1928; reprinted in *En verklig folktidning, Arbetet 1887–1962* (Malmö, 1962), pp. 126 ff. As a comment, Erlander declared in the reprint that after 1932 parliamentarism had functioned well, on the whole, in Sweden.

ing authority on constitutional law, recommended in 1929 a system with an all-party government.[50]

The position of the government was strengthened by the collaboration between the Socialists and the Center Party from 1933. Instead of occasional cooperation between two or more parties in order to solve special issues, as the practice had been in the 1920s, an organized and permanent collaboration took place between two parties with a common program and control over a majority in both houses. Neither one opposition party nor all opposition parties together could any longer meet the government party as an equal.

Did the new situation change the aims, the tactics, and the role of the opposition? In principle, the opposition parties still wanted to replace the government party. They still criticized government policy and the trend to increase the state sector, and they still acted as guardians of the socio-economic structure of society. But in fact the aims and tactics of the opposition did change. After the coalition government came into existence in 1936, the opposition parties had to face openly the new situation of a majority government. The Liberal leader, Gustaf Andersson, then made the following declaration for his parliamentary group:

> Our conduct toward the government and its majority in the Riksdag can of course have various forms. One way is to sit back and let things take their course. Another is to oppose at every turn just for the sake of opposition. Finally, the third way is to take an active part in dealing with and deciding on the matters in hand to the best of our ability, and on every occasion act as if we had a part in the responsibility for what happens. Obviously we ought to take the last-mentioned course.[51]

The Conservative leader, Gösta Bagge, also offered collaboration and said that his party was delighted at each real decrease in party cleavages.[52] Prime Minister Hansson compared the statements from the Conservative and Liberal parties with statements from these parties during the election campaign in 1936 and said that he was somewhat astonished. But

> an opposition that wants to come and cooperate with us in order to make the parliamentary decisions as good as possible, and as a basis for these make opinion in the Riksdag as wide as possible, this kind of opposition can always count on its points of view receiving a good deal of consideration.[53]

50. N. Herlitz, "Regeringsproblemets svårigheter," *Svensk tidskrift* (1929), pp. 177 ff.
51. *Svenska Dagbladet*, Jan. 12, 1937.
52. *Lower House Minutes* (Jan. 20, 1937), pp. 1 ff.
53. Ibid. p. 25.

Obviously the opposition had now adopted a new policy: in election campaigns, the English approach; in parliament and elsewhere, collaboration with the government in order to influence the political decision-making as much as possible.

The period of all-party government in World War II, when there was no place for a parliamentary opposition, was important for the development after the war. Prime Minister Hansson, it is said, would not have disliked having the all-party government continue after the war, but what he really wanted has been open to discussion.[54] What is certain is that the leaders of the Conservative and Center parties were against the dissolution of the all-party government at that time.

Since 1945 the Conservative and Liberal parties have said in each election campaign that it was time for a change, that the Socialists should be out and the nonsocialist parties in. To this extent they have clearly accepted the English approach. This pursuit of office was especially conspicuous in the 1948 elections, in the pension campaigns in the 1950s, and in 1957, when the Center Party left the government. The recent efforts to unite the nonsocialist parties in one party (see below) are motivated by the hope of getting a nonsocialist government.

The acceptance of the English approach has been clearer in the Conservative Party than in the Liberal Party. In an article in a weekly journal in 1962 Conservative leader Gunnar Heckscher underlined the fact that the opposition had two tasks: keeping a guard on the government and presenting alternatives. He also argued for real opposition which in his opinion often gave better results than going along with the government. In the same journal Liberal leader Bertil Ohlin stated, in words reminiscent of the period of minority parliamentarism, that the most important thing was that in critical situations no party should have a majority (including votes from supporting parties). Thus all parties would be obliged to take into account the views of different groups of people.[55]

On the other hand, spokesmen from all three nonsocialist parties have often made statements in favor of an all-party government.[56] Since 1946, the most prominent advocate of this system has been Herbert Tingsten. But, it has been asked, would the result not be the disappearance of parliamentary opposition? Who would take on its task of criticizing? Effective opposition is as important as effective government. In answer to this objection, it has been argued that if an all-party government were to come about, party discipline would have to be slackened, opposition

54. See for instance E. Wigforss, *Kan dödläget brytas?* (Stockholm, Tidens förlag, 1959), pp. 16 ff.
55. *Vecko-Journalen* (1962), No. 31. Cf. Ohlin in *Dagens Nyheter*, Oct. 22, 1964.
56. Conservative Party leader Gunnar Heckscher did not recommend the system. G. Heckscher, *Trygga folkstyret!* (1963), p. 22.

would have to be released inside the parties, and the electorate would have to be revitalized by use of the referendum.[57] The Socialists have been against all-party government except in times of crisis.[58]

In Parliament, however, the opposition parties are still anxious to look after their "right" to proportional influence in the political process and to see that the government is in contact with them in all important matters and really takes their interests into consideration. To a large extent there has been consensus, collaboration, and compromise between the government and the nonsocialist opposition parties. The opposition, however, has not had an influence proportional to its relative strength in Parliament. And, further, it is significant that the Center Party, even when out of government, has been more influential than the Conservatives and the Liberals. When an opposition party has been left out, it has protested. Thus the Conservatives and Liberals reacted against the agreement between the Socialists and the Center Party on the taxation question in 1961.

The tactics of the opposition in Parliament have to a high degree been those of bargaining. The opposition parties have often made proposals that would increase state expenditure, yet they have also been eager to reduce taxes and hence have restricted their proposals for higher state expenditure. But universal suffrage and the widespread acceptance of social welfare programs have resulted in Parliament's abandoning its nineteenth-century tradition of trying to cut down state expenditure. Today this job is primarily a duty of the government and especially of the Minister of Finance. Only the Conservative Party—in opposition to the claims of the Socialists that the government ought to have "sufficient" resources—has sometimes upheld the old tradition but at the same time abandoned the tactics of bargaining. As the Conservative leader, Jarl Hjalmarson, said in 1960, "The government and the Riksdag must have so little money that they are always obliged to live according to the stern principle of scarcity."[59]

The comments made here all have to do with opposition from the nonsocialist parties. The opposition from the left, from the Communist Party, has been carried on mainly inside the trade unions. On the parliamentary level the Communists have not played a significant part. Between 1945 and 1951 and from 1961 onward they held the balance between the nonsocialist opposition and the Socialists in the Lower House and between 1958 and 1963 and between 1965 and 1966 in joint divisions. But not being in the middle of the party scale they could not join the nonsocialist parties in

57. H. Tingsten, *Argument* (Stockholm, Bonniers förlag, 1948), pp. 196 ff. Cf. T. Vallinder in *Modern demokrati* (Lund, Gleerups förlag, 1963), pp. 73 ff.
58. Prime Minister Erlander in *Radio*, Oct. 28, 1957. E. Wigforss, *Kan dödläget brytas?* (Stockholm, Tidens förlag, 1959), pp. 16 ff.
59. *Svenska Dagbladet*, Aug. 14, 1960.

any action that would have overthrown the Socialist government. As previously mentioned, they abstained from the final vote on the sales tax question in 1960 and in this way helped the government. They did not dare to act in the same way as the People's Socialist Party in Norway did in 1963.[60]

Why Has Compromise Become So Important in Politics?

With the decrease in the cleavages between the parties and the increase in consensus, better conditions for compromise and agreement have, on the whole, been created. The effect has often been cumulative: every compromise probably tends to reduce existing cleavages.

Compromise is traditionally considered the Swedish technique in politics,[61] and the word "compromise" evidently sounds pleasing to Swedish voters. Even when the cleavages were deepest at the beginning of the century, the great political issues of universal suffrage, the election system, and the bicameral system were solved by compromise. The days of minority parliamentarism in the 'twenties necessitated cooperation and compromise between at least two of the parties. The periods of coalition government—despite the conflicts that arose toward the end of the war—helped to cement this tradition.

The proportional representation system fixed the multiparty system and laid the institutional basis for compromise politics. This trend has been strengthened by the fact that the political parties are proportionally represented on the parliamentary committees. Moreover, in a multiparty system the middle party—in Sweden the Liberals in the 1920s and the Center Party after 1932—has a key position since it can act as a balance, and it is generally inclined to make compromises.

National politics have been influenced by local politics. Entry into national politics and into membership in the Riksdag is normally by way of local politics. The member of Parliament often retains his membership on local commissions. Moreover, the members of the Upper House are elected by local bodies.[62] In local politics compromise is the normal way of dealing with differences of opinion, and the practice is institutionalized by proportional representation in the local authorities and the local committees.

National politics have been influenced by the politics of the large

60. Cf. p. 71.
61. Cf. F. Lagerroth, "Staaff eller De Geer? *Statsvetenskaplig tidskrift, 46* (1943), pp. 1 ff.
62. In the present discussion concerning a change-over to a unicameral system, Prime Minister Erlander has emphasized the importance of the connection between national politics and local politics. To maintain this connection and to keep participation in the local elections at a high level it is necessary in his opinion that local elections influence the composition of Parliament and thereby national politics. Cf. n. 5.

organizations: the trade unions, employers' associations, and so on. Bargaining and compromise are the tactics of these organizations, and "the spirit of Saltsjöbaden" has spread to the relations between political parties.

The opposition's desire to cooperate in the decision-making process leads it toward compromise. The opposition, to quote Hedlund, wants to have a policy of results, e.g. a policy that gives it a reasonable influence. Moreover, the expansion of state activity and long-range planning during the last few decades means that it is now more important for a political party to be in the government than it was in the 'twenties.

The government, wishing to act for all classes and interests and to have a wide following when solving great political issues, is usually inclined to compromise.

The party leaders' strong position and the increased discipline within the parties have facilitated compromises. Particularly interesting are the party leaders' conferences. They have been used for making agreements on issues that are troublesome from the political point of view, for instance on defense and the budget [63] and on the question of driving on the right.[64] It is believed that conferences and agreements help the parliamentary system to work smoothly. The contrary view, however, is that questions are taken out of politics.

All this evidence suggests the difficulty that parties have today in presenting the electorate with clear alternatives. When they seek to persuade the electorate in election campaigns that there *are* important differences among parties, they often go back to the cleavages of the old days. They carefully watch the proposals of the other parties in order to make it clear to the electorate that they are eager to look after the interests of the people. This is especially conspicuous in the field of social welfare.

The Influence of the Opposition

Although the opposition parties ordinarily have close to half the votes in Parliament, their influence on the conduct of government is relatively small. How can we account for the fact that their influence is so disproportionate?

63. See I. Amilon, "Partiledarkonferenserna, en studie i parlamentarisk praxis," *Statsvetenskaplig tidskrift,* 66 (1963), 278 ff
64. Parliament decided in 1963 to change over from left-hand traffic on the roads to right-hand traffic. In a consultative referendum in 1955, about 83 per cent of the participants had said "no" to a change. The pressure from those who were in favor of a change continued, with support on the whole from all the newspapers. The political parties were afraid that the issue would come up as a political issue. It was therefore taken out of politics by a party leaders' agreement in 1963 in favor of a change. In this process the party groups in Parliament were consulted, and guarantees were given of a majority in each group for a change. It was further guaranteed that no new referendum would be demanded.

In trying to criticize the government in order to replace it and at the same time collaborate with it in order to participate in the decision-making process, the opposition has fallen between two stools. For the two objectives are incompatible.[65]

The opposition has been divided. For this very reason, however, some claim, it has been able to win more votes in elections (see below).

Because of the increasingly complicated structure of society, the party that acts as the government has a superior position. The government has all the ministries, agencies, and royal commissions at its disposal. It may be stressed that the Center Party, with its special interest in agricultural policy, when in a coalition government has always held the Ministry of Agriculture. The opposition's resources for working out alternatives to the government's proposals or for taking the initiative are greatly inferior to the government's. The fact that the opposition parties are represented on the more important royal commissions certainly guarantees that they have some opportunity for observation and control, but they can by no means neutralize the government's advantage. The opposition parties, particularly the Liberals and the Center Party, lack economic resources to build up a sufficiently big party secretariat of their own.

Long-term planning, broad decisions on principle, the delegation of authority, and the government's own negotiations with the great organizations have all pushed the Riksdag to one side with the result that real decisions are made in the Riksdag less frequently than previously. Thus opportunities for observing and taking action have diminished for the opposition parties.

In some cases, in the opposition's view, the government has acted without due reference to the Riksdag or to the opposition.

Finally, an unproved and subjective observation offered by some critics is that the opposition has not been able to attract peeople of talent and ability because it has little hope of ever being in power.

Why No Change?

Why has the opposition not managed to oust the Socialists from their position? In other words, why has the parliamentary majority not swung over to the nonsocialist side?

This can be explained partly by the reasons just given as to why the opposition has not obtained more influence. The opposition has fallen between the two stools of opposing and participating. It has been divided

65. U. Himmelstrand ("A Theoretical and Empirical Approach," p. 93 ff.) states the hypothesis "that the opposition parties in Sweden, particularly the Liberal Party, are more depoliticized than the Socialist Party in the sense that they have more clearly dissociated ideology and practical politics. Being caught on the horns of this dilemma, ideological faithfulness and political effectiveness both being sought, a dissociative solution . . . is ready at hand for a permanent opposition party."

and thus weak. It has insufficient resources. In addition, with the expanding economy since World War II there has been prosperity and practically
no unemployment. This situation favors the government party, especially
insofar as the Communists have got only a few seats.

The opposition has not been able to present alternatives that would give
it a distinctive character of its own in the opinion of the electorate.
Neither have their alternatives been attractive enough in comparison with
those of the Socialists to make the majority of the electorate support the
opposition parties. The Socialists have also done a better job of organizing
their election campaigns.

The Center Party has not wanted to overthrow the Socialist government. This party prevented a change in 1957, when the nonsocialist
parties together held a majority position in the Lower House.

The Communists have not wanted and have been virtually unable to
vote against the Socialist government in crucial decisions.

Toward Better Conditions for the Opposition?

There is a strong feeling in Sweden that the opposition is too weak. On
the other hand, it is emphasized, especially by the Socialists, that in these
days when society has a complex economic and technological structure a
strong government is essential; the electoral method ought to be such that
it favors the formation of a strong government. In general discussions of
the means of governing, it has been pointed out that the political parties
taken together are too weak in relation to the socioeconomic organizations
and bureaucracy, and that political discussion and consequently the vitality
of the democracy are too weak.[66]

The problem put here is basically insoluble. There is no way of getting
an electoral system which at the same time would result in a strong government and a strong opposition. But it may be of interest to try to
analyze the measures that have been proposed to strengthen the opposition.

An improvement in the financial resources of the opposition parties
would undoubtedly help them. The Center Party has proposed that each
opposition party should be granted money to finance a secretariat for
parliamentary and research work in order to create a better balance between the government and the opposition.[67] The royal commission on
the Constitution has proposed that every party should have a government
appropriation for one full-time secretary. The commission has also called
for reorganization of the working conditions of the Riksdag, which would
favor the opposition parties in particular.[68] In the recent debate there has

66. Cf. H. Tingsten, "Stability and Vitality in Swedish Democracy," *The Political
Quarterly, 26* (1955), 140 ff.
67. Lower House, 1961, Motion No. 58.
68. *Statens offentliga utredningar* (1963), No. 18, pp. 211 ff.

been a call for considerably more aid to the political parties.[69] In fact, however, a real reorganization of the opposition's resources and the formation of a "shadow secretariat" that can match the ministries presupposes a two-party system.[70]

Another topic that has aroused lively discussion is the suggestion that an amalgamation of the nonsocialist parties would strengthen the opposition's position and in fact give it a chance to come to power. Since the nonsocialist parties have been out of power for a long time, two of them for a very long time, there is today, quite naturally, a tendency toward unification of the opposition. Those adherents of the Center Party and the Liberal Party who feel close to the Socialists would probably dislike such an amalgamation and to a large extent abstain from voting or change over to the Socialists.[71] Whether an integration would in the long run help the nonsocialist bloc has been widely discussed. Interest is higher among the Conservatives than among the Liberals and the Center Party, and higher in the newspapers and among the general public[72] than inside the political machines.

In October 1962 a Swedish weekly journal asked the three nonsocialist party leaders: Is organized collaboration among the nonsocialist parties to be desired and is such collaboration possible? Conservative leader Heckscher answered that collaboration was to be desired and perhaps possible. Liberal leader Ohlin replied that the forming of a nonsocialist bloc was the best help the Socialists could receive, because then the Liberals and the Center Party could be suspected of condoning the sins of the Conservatives. Center Party leader Hedlund said that unification was unrealistic and that a nonsocialist bloc would only favor the Socialists.

69. L. Andersson, I. Carlsson, A. Gustafsson, *Författningsreform—nytt alternativ* (Stockholm, Tidens förlag, 1963), p. 82; O. Ruin, "Kanslihusets ställning," in *Morgondagens samhällsproblem* (Stockholm, 1963), p. 94; P. Ahlmark, *Vår fattiga politik* (Stockholm, 1964), pp. 121 ff.
70. Cf. O. Ruin, "Kanslihusets ställning," p. 94.
71. Cf. *Idun-Veckojournalen* (1965), No. 2.
72. Public opinion polls (Svenska Institutet för Opinionsundersökningar, SIFO) taken in 1961 and 1963 show that interest in a united nonsocialist party was greater among electors who voted for these parties than among the Socialists. But the interest seems to have declined somewhat on all sides in the intervening period.

Voted in the last election for

	Socialists		One of the non-socialist parties	
	1961	1963	1961	1963
	%	%	%	%
Prefer 2 parties	31	18	59	48
Prefer 4 parties	44	49	25	29
Doesn't matter	13	9	4	4
Doubtful	12	24	12	19
Total	100	100	100	100

For that reason the three parties ought to be independent of one another.[73]
On later occasions Hedlund has repeatedly said "no" to an amalgamation
of the opposition parties. It is obvious that such a move would make it
impossible for the Center Party to keep its position as the balancer. The
Socialists have asked from time to time why the opposition parties do not
get together and agree on *one* alternative. In July 1962, when Prime Minister Erlander was asked which he preferred—a single opposition bloc
with a clear alternative or three divided small parties—he answered:

> A single nonsocialist bloc would probably give Swedish politics a
> firmer contour, and it is possible that the formation of a bloc of this
> kind would make it easier for the Socialists to convince the electorate
> of our political advantages. Therefore, a bloc of this kind would prob-
> ably bring about some advantages of a tactical and propaganda nature
> for Social Democracy. From the point of view of the nation the non-
> socialist parties can be divided as long as they form the opposition. If
> they are aiming at taking over the government, then they had better
> work out a unanimous program.[74]

The amalgamation issue and the best way to realize the amalgamation
were widely discussed in the 1964 elections, when the MBS Party competed in the Malmö constituency with both the Socialists and the three
nonsocialist parties. The Malmö constituency is entirely urban, has a
strong Conservative Party, a weak Liberal Party, and a diminutive Center Party. The leaders of the new party emphasized that the MBS was the
first step toward an amalgamation. People who were in favor of an amalgamation in principle argued, however, that the first step should not be
taken on the local level. The discussion continued after the elections.
More probable than an immediate amalgamation of the nonsocialist parties
may be a more intimate collaboration or an amalgamation of the Liberal
Party and the Center Party.

A unification of the nonsocialist parties can be arranged by changes in
the electoral legislation. One method proposed is a change-over to the
system of a simple majority in elections, which might automatically create
a two-party system. Within the royal commission on constitutional reform there was a majority in favor of such a system in principle.[75] But
the introduction of a two-party system would not in fact bring about a

---

73. *Vecko-Journalen* (1962), No. 40. The nonsocialist party leaders made the same
statements in the Lower House, Jan. 22, 1964.

74. *Stockholms-Tidningen*, July 15, 1962. See also Erlander, *Upper House Minutes*
(1956), *2*, 18. Gunnar Myrdal, who was a member of the Socialist Cabinet in the
1940s, criticized, in a speech of May 1, 1964, the inability of the opposition to amal-
gamate and said that it would be useful for the "strong, conservative" Socialist Party
to compete with a united opposition.

75. *Statens offentliga utredningar* (1963), No. 16, pp. 51 ff.

change in the fundamentals of the present situation—the tug of war for the marginal votes—and hence the same policies would remain.

A return to the proportional method (d'Hondt) which was applied up to 1952 would make it necessary for the nonsocialist parties to cooperate in elections as they were obliged to do before 1952. Such cooperation, however, would be inconvenient for the Center Party in its role as balancer. The d'Hondt method was abandoned when the Center Party entered a coalition government with the Socialists in 1951, and it was then replaced by the present proportional method (Sainte-Laguë), which makes it possible for the nonsocialist parties to stand alone in elections. It is characteristic of the attitude of the leader of the Center Party, Gunnar Hedlund, that he is said to have described the Sainte-Laguë method as "a miraculous formula." [76]

A change-over to a permanent all-party government would probably give the opposition parties greater influence.

A weakening of the position of the interests groups would strengthen that of the parties.

If the cleavages were more clearly distinguishable, there would be more intense political discussion.[77] It would make compromise politics more difficult and would therefore decrease the opposition's influence, but at the same time it would give the opposition a chance to strengthen its position in the electorate. It is in fact a problem for the political parties to find new issues that emphasize the cleavages and stress the differences between one party and another. On the other hand, it is of vital importance to a party that its stand on a new political issue does not antagonize marginal groups. From all these points of view, the pension question was a successful one for the Socialists.[78]

How can the present situation of the opposition best be described? Some representatives of the nonsocialist opposition will certainly characterize the situation as a stable deadlock, as there are no changes in the government. Other representatives will probably say that the 50–50 balance between the Socialists and the nonsocialist parties is a good thing, as it obliges the two blocs to respect each other and especially the groups in

---

76. *Sydsvenska Dagbladet*, June 18, 1963.

77. Cf. H. Meijer and O. Ruin, "Ny författning?" *Tiden* (1963), p. 336.

78. According to S. M. Lipset, "Class Structure and Politics," *Daedalus* (Winter 1964), p. 287, the Socialists introduced the pension reform largely because their electoral research had suggested that such a proposal would be popular not only with their traditional supporters, the manual workers, but with many white-collar workers. This statement can be argued. Cf. B. Särlvik, *The Role of Party Identification in Voters' Perception of Political Issues: a Study of Opinion Formation in Swedish Politics, 1956–1960* (mimeo., paper for the International Political Science Association Congress, Paris, 1961). See also B. Molin, *Tjänstepensionsfrågan* (Gothenburg, 1965), with an English summary.

the middle. The Socialists, on the other hand, will probably emphasize the stability, since they have been in power practically since 1932, but at the same time underline the instability that results from their not being able to command a majority either in the Lower House or in the joint divisions and from the fact that small fluctuations in the electorate can change the situation.

The viewpoints described here are largely a part of the political debate among the various parties. The idea that a proportional election is a fair election is deeply rooted, and the same is true of the attitude toward compromise. Moreover, the present party organizations act as built-in stabilizers in the system. Institutional changes are therefore difficult to achieve. The socioeconomic organizations are so consolidated that they too have a stabilizing effect in the present situation. Finally, it could probably be said that in many circles even outside the government party people are more pleased than displeased with the present arrangements. From those points of view the situation is best characterized by "stability" or, if you wish, "a stable deadlock."

This stability or deadlock, however, is promoted by a number of contributory factors. An alteration in one or several of these could bring about changes. Shifts in the structure of society and in the composition of the population could transform the party system. A deterioration in the economic situation or in the international situation could result in an all-party government. A further expansion of the influence of interest groups or of technocracy will probably make it necessary for the political parties to reconsider their situation. A change-over to a two-party system, however, with one Socialist and one nonsocialist bloc, or an amalgamation of two of the nonsocialist parties will, as previously mentioned, hardly alter the basic feature of the present political system, as the parties will still appeal to the floating votes in the middle of the party scale. A considerable increase in the number of Communist votes and seats would be more important. It would oblige the Socialists to conduct a war on two fronts, which is always difficult, and to make their program more radical, thereby emphasizing the differences between their views and those of the nonsocialist parties—but at the risk of neglecting the floating votes in the middle.

5

BELGIUM:
RELIGION, CLASS, AND LANGUAGE
IN NATIONAL POLITICS

Val R. Lorwin

An energetic Belgian Prime Minister described the policy of his Catholic-Socialist coalition government in 1962 as an attempt at "dialogues" between Catholics and anticlericals, between labor and employers, and between the two linguistic-cultural communities of the nation.[1] If Théo Lefèvre did not mention a dialogue between the government and the parliamentary opposition, it was not forgetfulness or disdain for a numerically small formal opposition. It was a recognition of the way in which the chief cleavages in Belgian society have cut across government and party lines more often than they have divided government from formal opposition.

The three dialogues that Théo Lefèvre sought recall the three oppositions which have dominated Belgian political life. The oldest opposition arose from differences over the relationships of Church and State and the role of Catholic and public schools. This is the only form of dialogue in which each party has spoken with a single voice. It is the only one in which a sort of two-party system has existed, pitting the Catholics first against the Liberals and later against the Socialists as well.

The second opposition is that which brought into being a Socialist Party and the labor wing of the Catholic Party. Strong employer associations and well-organized trade unions carry on a continuing dialogue, with an occasional assist or call to desist from the government. The dialogue of these "social partners" is paralleled by the political dialogue be-

1. Senate, *Compte-Rendu Analytique*, June 13, 1962, p. 480.

I gratefully acknowledge the help of the Center for Advanced Study in the Behavioral Sciences, the Social Science Research Council and its Committee on Comparative Politics, the Graduate School of the University of Oregon, the Rockefeller Foundation Constitutional Democracy Program, and the Ford Foundation. To friends and acquaintances in Belgium and elsewhere, I am so deeply (and happily) indebted that I must wait until a full-length book on Belgian politics permits me, however inadequately, to thank them.

tween the Socialist Party and the Catholic left wing, on the one hand, and the Catholic right wing and the Liberal Party, on the other.

The third opposition to which Lefèvre alluded, that of the "cultural communities," has not been essentially party-forming. It has confronted the Flemish-speaking and French-speaking ethnic-linguistic communities, and now also the regions of Flanders and Wallonia, sometimes with Brussels as a third interlocutor.

The system of parties has been remarkably stable for eight decades. It has withstood two world wars and two enemy occupations, changes in social structure, the rise of regional-linguistic movements, the introduction of universal suffrage and of proportional representation, the Great Depression, the tides of international communism, the surge and collapse of European fascism, the shifts from Belgian neutrality to international commitment and back and forth again, the acceptance of the welfare state, the forced abdication of a monarch, and the loss of a vast colony. It has withstood changes of name and structure by each of the parties. (For simplicity, I shall sometimes speak of the "Catholic Party" in a context that includes the years since 1945, when it was reborn as the Christian Social Party; of the "Socialist Party" to signify what was until 1940 called the Belgian Workers Party; and of the "Liberal Party" to denote the group which in 1961 reorganized as the Party of Liberty and Progress.)

On the surface the party system has been simple, stable, and even logical. There have been only three national parties since the 1880s, each associated with one of the nation's "spiritual families," and each with its network of socioeconomic organizations. There has been a fairly stable balance of voting strength among the three parties since the introduction of universal equal suffrage. Obligatory voting has almost done away with fluctuations in electoral participation. A large measure of proportional representation has caused voting strength to be fairly well reflected in parliamentary representation, with a rather close correspondence in party balance between the two houses of Parliament. And—oh, miracle for the American beholder—there have been frequent readjustments of parliamentary representation to reflect population changes.

The loyal oppositions appeared early in national history. Oppositions of principle appeared much later, but they did not long challenge the legitimacy of the regime. The Constitution slowed the process of democratization of the suffrage, but this prevented such shocks as France experienced with the sudden acquisition of universal suffrage.

The regular course of constitutional government has been stimulated or deflected by an occasional general strike. But it has been suspended only by enemy occupation. Only islands of disadvantaged groups remain alienated from the community, and most people share its essentially middle-class values. The rapid pace of industrialization has had a slower reflection in social structure, because many villagers have been able to become industrial workers without losing their attachment to the soil, thanks to the dispersion of factories and subsidized low railway fares for workers.

The regime has never suppressed the right of the opposition to oppose, except in the wake of wartime treason. Parliament invests, formally controls, and occasionally even overthrows cabinets. In both houses, the outs confront the ins and, except for a few minor parties, can look forward to sharing power. The parties aggregate the demands of social groups and bargain them out in Parliament and government. Political and ideological oppositions pervade voluntary associations as well as all of public life. They are even projected into education and the bureaucracy, but does that not again show how logical, or at least consistent with cultural reality, the system is?

The reader will of course have understood that the political system of Belgium is more complex, and the political history richer, than these orderly appearances suggest. But first let us see the political system as it emerged in the critical early years of national existence.

The Union of Oppositions

The Belgian state was born parliamentary, and with the concept of opposition as legitimate. It was a self-conscious "union of the oppositions" which made the national revolution of 1830 against William I, king of the Dutch-Belgian "amalgam" created by the Congress of Vienna. These "oppositions" were groups—not yet parties—which thought of themselves as Catholics and as Liberals. They went back to the experience of an earlier national uprising, the Brabant Revolution of 1789, in which the Austrian Netherlands momentarily shook off the rule—and the reforms— of Joseph II. The Statists, or Van der Nootists, opposed the reforms of Joseph II; they sought to maintain the customs and privileges of the established Catholic Church and the narrowly based oligarchy of landowners, masters of urban crafts, and nobles who dominated the sclerosed provincial assemblies or Estates. For a moment they worked with the followers of François Vonck, members of the higher business and professional classes and intellectuals, who welcomed the rationalization Joseph II sought at the expense of the Church and the provincial Estates, but upheld Belgian autonomy against the aloof and impolitic, if enlightened, Habsburg despot.

Together the Statists and the Vonckists swept out their Austrian rulers and tried to establish a decentralized, oligarchic, federal republic. But they soon set upon each other; chiefly, the Statists set mobs upon the Vonckists as enemies of the Church. In this civil strife, the Habsburgs easily reconquered the "United Belgian States."

It was the successors of these two groups who found themselves, for different reasons, in opposition to Dutch King William. The Catholics rallied to defend the Church and its educational system against the lay, centralizing hand of William I, whom they saw as a Dutch-speaking Protestant version of Joseph II. The Liberals, although in sympathy with the anticlerical and centralizing measures of William, felt threatened by his restrictions on freedom of the press, his favoring of Dutchmen over Belgians in appointments, and his promotion of the Dutch language against the French which was by now the language of almost all the Belgian elites.

In an unusual effort of tolerance and comprehension, Belgian Catholics and Liberals agreed in 1827–28 on a "union of the oppositions" against William's innovations. This union of the oppositions launched the constitutional protest that preceded the sudden revolt that won national independence. Then the Unionists went on, in the "National Congress" of 1830–31, to write a constitution with freedoms of speech, press, and religion liberal indeed in the Europe of Metternich and Wellington. The suffrage provisions were less ungenerous than those of Britain or France at the time. But a minimum direct-tax requirement for voting left room within the constitution for only a modest expansion of the national electorate.

To avoid the chaotic decentralization of the Brabant Revolution, the Constitution created a unitary state. But it left place for extensive local autonomy and thus for the communal (municipal) politics which soon produced vigorous party oppositions. The members of the National Congress had in their minds, as their president said, "the hatred of the last king and the fear of the next one." Not free to set up a republic, which would have alarmed the Great Powers too much, they created a "republican monarchy." The monarch was restricted to specified powers, and his ministers were declared responsible to Parliament. All powers were identified as emanating from the nation.

The Constitution did not separate Church and State, as many Belgians like to say. But it set new patterns of freedom for both. There would be no established Church, but all recognized religions would be supported by the State. The State would not intervene, however, in the operations of the churches or their appointments. With Protestants and Jews no more than one per cent of the population, the Catholic Church thus obtained a rare combination of material support and freedom from state control. The guaranties of freedom of education and of association left the Church free to carry on its educational efforts, its training of the priesthood, its charities and social services.

If for Catholics the Church was to be free of control by the State, for Liberals the State had to be free of control by the Church. The Constitution set forth a number of the liberal freedoms that were anathema in other Catholic lands, where error was not permitted to compete with revealed truth. Rome grudgingly recognized the "liberal hypothesis" of the special "Belgian case" as the best it could obtain.[2] Not until Leo XIII, however, did Rome fully accept the Belgian constitutional charter and its modern liberties.[3]

From Unionism to Party Government

The principle was soon established that a cabinet had to have the support of a majority not only in the House of Representatives, the predominant chamber, but also in the Senate, an elected body with a highly restrictive direct-tax qualification for membership. If there was doubt about the government's ability to govern or about its still representing a majority of the enfranchised minority (the *pays légal*), one or both houses were dissolved, and the voters were called upon to decide. There might also be a dissolution in the event of serious differences between the two houses.

Leopold I promoted "unionism," or government that declared itself impartial—above party and without reference to parties. In unionism he saw the best hope of protecting the new nation's existence from evident external threats and potential internal threats. It also gave him the largest personal role under a constitution written, as he grumbled, "when the King was not there to defend the monarchy." Grumble he did, but he was too shrewd to flout the Constitution openly or clash head on with a parliamentary majority. From 1831 to 1847, Leopold presided over unionist cabinets. Most were mixed cabinets of Catholics and Liberals; a few were one-party cabinets, but based on unionist majorities in Parliament.

Unionism was conservative. It was better for business, its advocates thought, than "sterile discussions" of "vain ideological questions." [4] The example of France was always there to show how dangerously such discussions might agitate the masses. Anyway, social and economic issues hardly intruded yet upon that organized political life which a leading moderate Liberal termed "the diplomatico-juridico-Catholico-baroquo-political fracas." [5] Even before Parliament began to vote on party lines, there was considerable awareness of political group identification. Local

---

2. See the admirable and fascinating series of books and articles by Msgr. A. Simon on the relations between Church and State, between the monarchy and the Vatican, in the nineteenth century, especially *Le Cardinal Sterckx et son temps* (2 vols. Wetteren, Scaldis, 1950); *La Politique religieuse de Léopold I* (Brussels, Goemaere, 1953); *Catholicisme et politique: Documents inédits (1832–1909)* (Wetteren, Scaldis, 1955); and *L'Hypothèse libérale en Belgique: Documents inédits, 1839–1907* (Wetteren, Scaldis, 1956); *Le Parti Catholique Belge, 1830–1945* (Brussels, Renaissance du Livre, 1958); *Le Cardinal Mercier* (Brussels, Renaissance du Livre, 1960), and *Léopold I* (Brussels, Renaissance du Livre, 1963).

3. K. Van Isacker, S.J., *Werkelijk en Wettelijk Land: De Katholieke Opinie tegenover de Rechterzijde, 1863–1884* (Antwerp, Standaard Boekhandel, 1955), pp. 248–50.

4. Quoted by Colette Lebas, *L'Union des catholiques et des libéraux de 1839 à 1847* (Louvain, Nauwelaerts, 1960), p. 38.

5. Joseph Lebeau, quoted by Carlo Bronne, *Joseph Lebeau* (Brussels, Renaissance du Livre, 1944), p. 60.

electoral associations, many of them run by the Masonic lodges, opposed the clergy in local elections, many of which were more partisan than national elections.

In 1838 the Belgian bishops forbade the faithful to be Masons any longer. This brought the Vatican condemnation of Freemasonry onto the Belgian scene for the first time, and it created a crisis of conscience for many hitherto obedient Catholics. As the Masonic lodges had not yet become anti-Catholic, the crisis of conscience was not in all cases resolved in favor of the Church. This was the first, but far from the last, time the Church was to drive out believers in the name of the political unity of Catholics. To the bitterness of ideological difference was now added fear of international secret organization, which the Liberals saw in the Church of Rome and the Catholics saw in Freemasonry.

The bishops' action gave a powerful impetus to the formation of the Liberal Party in 1846 and its move toward homogeneous one-party cabinets. The Liberals who broke with unionism were among the moderates, not the extremists, of the party. Offering both alternative personnel and alternative policies, they put forth cogent views of the role of parties in government and in opposition. Said Paul Devaux in 1839:

> A practical opposition . . . tries not only to destroy, but knows what it will put in place of what it overthrows. This opposition has its extremes, its agitators, but they constitute neither its essence nor its base . . . In a state organized like ours, the real and lasting alternative is not between the existence and the absence of an opposition, but rather between a violent, exaggerated opposition and a practical, moderate opposition, a friend of order; or even between parliamentary opposition and an extraparliamentary opposition.[6]

With the passing of the foreign threat to the nation's existence, unionism had lived its hour. The King had to recognize the impossibility of unionist cabinets or even unionist majorities for cabinets of a single party. The Liberal Joseph Lebeau affirmed the need for party government:

> The inauguration of one-party cabinets is the end, and the irrevocable end, of an overly long political hypocrisy which not only altered the principles of representative government, but struck unfortunate blows at the morality of the administration . . . Mixed ministries are the exceptional state of power; they are never its normal state.[7]

But he promised that if Belgian peace was threatened from without or from within by "a frantic demogogy menacing public order and our institutions," the nation would go back to "mixed cabinets." It was not to

6. Quoted in Lebas, *L'Union des catholiques et des libéraux*, pp. 241–42, note.
7. Bronne, *Joseph Lebeau*, pp. 92–93.

do so until the German invasion of 1914, except for a few years in the 1850s.[8]

If party government was ineluctable, Leopold I hoped at least to prevent a division of the nation's conservative forces. He had always seen the union of throne and altar as natural and necessary.[9] Now he tried to build up a party of "dynastic men and religious men" to support the political and social order against the threats of democracy. In this hope the old king was disappointed. To conservatives, the threat of political democracy was remote, and the threat of social and economic democracy even more remote. The very ease with which the monarchy survived the European storm of 1848—at the small price of extending the suffrage to its modest constitutional limits—lessened the force of Leopold's argument. The division between Liberals and Catholics had hardened.

Liberals and Catholics: The Classic Model

In his plea for moderate and responsible opposition, Paul Devaux had not foreseen the bitterness that would come to characterize the opposition of the two conceptions of public life and of the roles of State and Church. To Catholics the liberty proclaimed by the Constitution was the liberty to build certain of the nation's institutions, notably of education and welfare, aided by a "mutual benevolence" between Church and State.[10] (While a national system of public education was only slowly and painfully being organized, Catholic educational institutions were functioning at all levels. To this day, they have continued to have more students at every level than the public system.[11]) In these Catholic aims, and in the pressure of the hierarchy and parish priests to produce "good elections," the Liberals saw a threat to the independence of the State and to the diffusion of Liberal notions among future generations of Belgian voters. Liberalism took on an anti-Catholic tone absent in its early years. Pressed by the now-embattled Masonic lodges and the rationalist societies, the Liberals moved on after mid-century to an even more anticlerical posture and sought not only independence of the State from the Church, but its supremacy: the neutralization—that is, the laicization—of all education, welfare work, and even burial grounds.

What was neutral or secular to the Liberals, especially in education, was antireligious to Catholics. As the contest waxed more bitter, many priests

8. Of De Decker, head of the unionist ministry of 1855–57, it was said by some fellow Catholics that he was like "a double-barrelled gun, which went off by itself, one barrel against the enemy and the other against his friends." Frans van Kalken, *La Belgique contemporaine (1780–1949)* (2d ed. Paris, Colin, 1950), p. 87.

9. Largely indifferent to religion, Leopold himself remained a Protestant, shrewdly judging that he could be of more use to the Church, and the Church to him, if he did not become a converted Catholic. All his successors have been Catholics.

10. The phrase is that of Simon, *Le Parti Catholique Belge*, p. 73.

11. For numbers of students in the two systems in 1960–61, see Appendix Tables 5.1 and 5.2.

led the faithful in the prayer: "From schools without God and from teachers without faith, deliver us, O Lord." [12] Not indolently leaving all the work of deliverance to the Lord, the clergy urged the faithful on to political activity and, after 1863, to political unity within the Catholic Party.

The pattern of opposition emerged in the debate over the school law of 1850, and reached its zenith after the Liberals' 1879 school law. The clergy literally drove out of the Church many of those who tolerated the public schools. The Catholic parliamentary delegation (far more reasonable than the clergy, the violent Catholic press, and most of the faithful [13]) implored the new Pope to restrain the hierarchy and through it the parish clergy. But this was more than Leo XIII and his Nuncio could do.

The extremes of opposition were not in electoral tactics but in attacks on the intimate beliefs and social relationships of Liberals and Catholics. The rationalists ridiculed religious ceremonies and sometimes attacked funeral corteges. Priests used their spiritual powers to enforce—or so they thought—the political unity of the faithful: from the pulpit they attacked Liberals present in church and denied the sacraments to public school teachers and parents of their pupils.[14]

Religious and antireligious manifestations were thus not only sources of cleavage, but also forms of propaganda and constraint. As in other old Catholic countries, believers confronted unbelievers with no third choice that might diffuse hostilities. The appearance of the Socialist Party only reinforced this dichotomy. For the one thing about which the Socialists long remained sectarian was their opposition to religious sectarianism.

These tactics of opposition did not attack the regime. But they poisoned the atmosphere of social life and political discourse in many communities. The Dreyfus case in France and the Ulster issue in England perhaps cut more deeply and polarized opinion more sharply. But both were shorter-lived, and neither involved so many people's daily lives for so long a period as did the church-school issue in Belgium.

The Liberal-Catholic opposition produced a classic alternation in national government between 1846 and 1884, with the Liberals dominant most of the time. In 1884 the Catholics began an unparalleled 30 years in control of the central government. The balance of strength among the taxpaying voters was fairly close. But the small number of voters and the quirks of the electoral system before proportional representation made for occasionally sharp swings in electoral results.[15]

12. Henri Pirenne, *Histoire de Belgique*, 7 (2d ed. Brussels, Lamertin, 1948), 234.
13. Van Isacker, *Werkelijk en Wettelijk Land*, passim.
14. Simon, *Le Parti Catholique Belge*, and Van Isacker, *Werkelijk en Wettelijk Land*.
15. On the electoral system, see John Gilissen, *Le Régime représentatif en Belgique depuis 1790* (Brussels, Renaissance du Livre, 1958). For the electorate and results of elections under the *régime censitaire*, see Appendix Table 5.3.

Despite the ideological alignment, there were floating voters. Ideological lines might be broken—or reinforced—by economic-interest appeals, social pressures or fraud. Even after the secret ballot act of 1877, electoral irregularities were widespread among those happy few whose fiscal contributions marked them as independent, intelligent, and interested enough in the commonweal to rate the franchise.[16]

The depth of opposition did not reflect polarization along lines other than Church-State issues. Social and economic issues hardly appeared as yet on the political agenda. There was some difference, but no polarization, in the parties' social bases among the voters and among the voteless masses whom they brought onto the stage in mob scenes from time to time. The Catholics could call upon the rural masses more than upon the city masses, upon Flemish more than upon Walloon or Brussels crowds. Catholic voters comprised the largest part, though far from all, of the great landowners, including those of the hereditary nobility. The Liberals' chief strength was in the industrial, commercial, and professional bourgeoisie.

Neither of the two "spiritual families" was monolithic in opinion or in electoral behavior. No sooner did the Liberal Party achieve a precocious national structure in 1846 (31 years before England's National Liberal Federation) than splits developed. The Progressives favored suffrage extension, which the Doctrinaires heartily opposed. This and other conflicts —over the degree of antireligious action and over personalities—often produced competing Liberal electoral slates, notably in the capital.

The Catholics, served politically by the structures of the Church, began to build a special party structure only in the 1860s and firmed it up only in 1884. Meanwhile they were divided in their attitudes toward the liberties protected by the Constitution. The ultra-right Catholics criticized the parliamentary Catholic Party for taking part in the governance of a state that tolerated error and evil impartially with truth and good. These "Ultramontanes"—the sense of this word in Belgian history is different from its meaning elsewhere—formed no party or organization and elected no one to Parliament. At no time did they attack the political regime as such. There was no such hopeless pursuit of an outworn system as the French Catholic devotion to a royal restoration. But they harried the Catholic M.P.'s—the parliamentary Right.

The Ultramontanes had a very large following because of their support in the lower ranks of the clergy, their press, and the social or intellectual eminence of a number of their spokesmen. Leo XIII felt that the divisions in the Catholic community and the opposition of some Catholics to the Constitution had contributed to Liberal political victories. No sooner did he become Pope than he told the Belgians that even

16. In 1890–91, almost 23,000 votes were challenged. That was the record year for election appeals. Gilissen, *Le Régime représentatif*, p. 111.

if their Constitution, like all man-made works, was imperfect, half a century's experience showed that "in the present state of modern society, the system of freedom in Belgium is favorable to the Church. Belgian Catholics must not only refrain from attacking, they must also defend, the Constitution." [17]

The "social question" came to be an issue in Catholic political circles only slowly. Despite the efforts of the socially conscious Catholic politicians, many of them aristocrats, of the "New Right" after the turn of the century, the demands of Christian Democracy [18] did not become urgent until the Flemish masses had votes equal to their numbers.

The Socialist Party

Church-State issues had prevented a concentration of the possessing classes in the conservative party which Leopold I had wanted. Religious differences prevented the socialist political organization, formed in 1885 and prudently named the Workers Party, from representing more than one section of the working class. Within that section, the Socialists created a subculture—"a state within the State," their leader Emile Vandervelde called it—of consumers' cooperatives, friendly societies (mutual insurance groups), trade unions, and party which set a pattern for Catholic, and even Liberal, organizations.

The party settled down to the role of a loyal opposition even more rapidly than most other so-called Marxist parties. It concentrated on winning universal suffrage rather than fighting the class war. The Belgians were almost all revisionists, and showed little taste for the doctrinal debates that raged in other continental parties. "They have nothing to revise, for they have no theory," sneered Karl Kautsky in the typically un-Marxist statement of an orthodox Marxist.[19]

The strategy of universal suffrage called for the tactic of alliance with the Progressive wing of the Liberal Party. To the electoral and parliamentary fight, the Socialists added the thrust of the general strike.[20] The French syndicalists of the pre-1914 generation made a fetish of the revolutionary general strike, but never tried it. The Belgian Socialists carried out four general strikes before 1914 to advance political democracy.

The grant of universal manhood suffrage, although with plural voting,[21]

17. Speaking to a delegation of the Belgian Catholic press, 1879. Van Isacker, *Werkelijk en Wettelijk Land*, p. 249.
18. This term refers in Belgian history only to the labor, socially progressive currents within the Catholic community and the Catholic Party.
19. Kautsky to Victor Adler, May 23, 1902, in Adler, *Briefwechsel mit August Bebel und Karl Kautsky*, ed. Friedrich Adler (Vienna, Weiner Volksbuchhandlung, 1954), p. 400.
20. For an excellent discussion, see Carl Landauer, *European Socialism* (2 vols. Berkeley, University of California Press, 1959), *1*, 478–80.
21. The new constitutional provision gave all men the vote at age 25, with supple-

brought the Socialists into the parliamentary arena with a rush in 1894.[22] There they fought for equal manhood suffrage and for other reforms, notably universal free primary school education and equality in military service. The effect of all these would be to help integrate the industrial working classes and the peasantry into the social and political order.

The Liberals were the great victims of the enlargement of the franchise, for they were unable to compete with the Socialists for the votes of industrial workers and with the Catholics for the votes of the Flemish masses. Proportional representation, introduced in 1900, saved them from the sort of parliamentary catastrophe that later struck the British Liberals.[23]

The Catholic Party introduced proportional representation to avoid a government–opposition duel with the Socialists alone. The Liberals represented substantial political traditions in the cities and in some rural areas, and a middle-class and upper-middle-class political temperament which could not be accommodated either in a confessional party or in a workers' party. Proportional representation did not lead to a multiplication of small parties; except for a brief period in the 1930s and in 1946, the three-party system endured.

Compulsory voting was instituted along with universal male suffrage. Abstentions immediately dropped from an earlier 20–30 per cent to the 5 or 6 per cent customary since then (with spoiled ballots a smaller percentage). The performance of the duty has entered into the customs of the nation.

In 1890, at a great mass meeting of Socialists, 70,000 manifestants had vowed that they would struggle "with neither rest nor relaxation till the day when, by the introduction of universal suffrage, they had in truth won a fatherland." [24] The weighted voting of the universal suffrage they had obtained a few years later, after the general strike of 1893, was a reminder of inequality and inequity still to be overcome. Paradoxically, it was the German conquest of the fatherland in the First World War that finally won the workers their full political membership in it.

In the common suffering and opposition to the occupying Germans, conservatives acquired a new respect for the patriotism and good sense of the Belgian Socialists. Cardinal Mercier was only the most illustrious

---

mentary votes for heads of families over 35, for property owners, and for those with certain educational attainments. The new electorate of 1894 numbered some 1,371,000 men with 2,111,000 votes. About 850,000 voters cast only one vote; 290,000 had two votes; 220,000 had three votes, the maximum permitted. For the voting system, see Gilissen, *Le Régime représentatif*, pp. 119–32.

22. For results of elections to the House from 1894 to 1914, see Appendix Table 5.4.
23. Maurice Duverger, *Les Partis politiques* (1st ed. Paris, Colin, 1951), Fig. 29.
24. Julien Kuypers, *Bergop!* (Antwerp, Ontwikkeling, 1957), Plate XLII. The famous "oath of St. Gilles."

example of this new attitude. King Albert had long shown tolerance toward the party and sympathy with workers' problems.

With liberation, this remarkable monarch showed that he knew when to depart from strict constitutionalism. The long-mounting pressures for equalization of the suffrage had been pent up during the war. If the constitutional amending process had been followed, a Parliament with amending powers would have been elected under the old plural voting system. Workers and peasants who had suffered in the trenches or in deportation could have cast one ballot each, while war profiteers could have cast two or three. Instead the King and the government called the voters to the polls on a one man, one vote basis. The Parliament they elected legitimized the change by constitutional amendment. Conservatives grumbled that it was not legal, and indeed it was not. But any other course would have been a flagrant, needless injustice straining the constitutional and civic consensus far more, at a time when moderates and conservatives all over Europe (and the United States) feared revolution.

In Belgium alone of the belligerent nations, Socialists continued in the Cabinet after the war. Well could King Albert tell a friend, "I made of Socialism a party of government." [25] That governmentalism was confirmed by the extensive reforms of three years of post-war national union government. By 1921, when Belgian Socialists were ready to go back into opposition, they could contrast the realization of all their old minimum demands with the political reaction and social conflict in postwar Britain and France, and promise a constructive opposition.

It is high time, now, to go back to the third of the dialogues of which Théo Lefèvre spoke—that of the two communities which we may call linguistic or ethnic or regional.

The Flemish Question

The nation born in 1830 was bisected by an internal linguistic frontier which had hardly shifted since the fifth century A.D., running from west to east just south of Brussels. It separated the French-speaking southern provinces (whose masses spoke chiefly the Wallon dialect) from the Flemish-speaking northern provinces. But within Flanders itself there was a more complex and provocative frontier, a linguistic-social barrier between the Flemish-speaking masses—peasants, workers, and lower middle classes—and their French-speaking native elites, some of whom hardly even knew Flemish.[26] "French in the parlor; Flemish in the kitchen," ran the telling, scornful phrase.

25. Tschoffen, in Institut Belge de Science Politique, *Aspects de la Société Belge* (Brussels, Librairie Encyclopédique, 1958), p. 23.
26. A single example: Msgr. Dechamps, cardinal-archbishop of Malines from 1867 to 1883, did not know Flemish, the language of the majority of his diocese. A. Simon, *Catholicisme et Politique*, p. 64.

This could pass as long as "one spoke as sang the bird." [27] Then came the linguistic patriotism of national or regional consciousness, in Flanders as in so many parts of Europe in the nineteenth century. The advocates of the Flemish cause first saw it only in linguistic and sentimental terms. "The language is the whole people," was their slogan. "Language is more than an instrument; it is the soul of a people. To outrage it is more than a misdeed; it is a sacrilege." [28] The Flemish people must be free to learn and to use their own language; their language must have equal standing with French. But the protagonists of Flemish had to define and to spread the language of cultured speech, for the rich tongue of medieval literature had fallen into a degraded and divided state. Most Flemings spoke one of a number of often mutually incomprehensible local dialects. Only a tiny minority spoke a correct Flemish, or *Nederlands* (Dutch), the name by which it is now legally called. And first its defenders had, as Jan-Frans Willems said, literally to "teach their people to read."

The cultural backwardness of the Flemish masses reflected the economic backwardness of Flanders. After the heyday of its medieval communes, after the glory of sixteenth-century Antwerp, Flanders had fallen far behind Wallonia. While Wallonia paced the continent's industrial revolution, Flanders had only its agriculture, its textiles, and the port of Antwerp. In its overpopulated villages, a wretched peasantry long tried to keep cottage industries alive, while many of its sons went off to work in Walloon coal mines and steel mills, in Brussels, in France, and the United States. The Flemings had the doubtful consolation of being more numerous [29] —and more Catholic.

Differences in the pace of industrialization accentuated regional contrasts. In Wallonia, as in many other industrializing areas of Europe, most of the new working classes turned away from, or grew up outside, the church of their fathers. Not until well into the twentieth century did a modernized Catholicism stay the loss of workers' support brought on by industrialization, displacement, and urbanization.

In the Belgian self-image, Wallonia has become dechristianized while Flanders has remained Catholic. The reality is more nuanced, although the self-image is one form of reality. The contrast is chiefly between industrial-and-urban and rural-and-small-town populations. Walloon rural areas have retained their Catholicism but in the large Flemish cities the Church has lost most industrial workers.

The dominance of French reflected the political and social dominance of the French-speaking property holders and professional elites of nine-

27. Godefroid Kurth, *La Nationalité belge* (Namur, Picard-Balon, 1913), p. 196.
28. Alfons Willems, in *Beschryf van de Betooging en Het Banket van den 25 April 1859, ter Eere der Vlaamsche Tael-Commissie* (Brussels, Verbruggen, 1859), p. 14.
29. The first census, in 1846, showed 2,471,000 Flemish-speaking and 1,827,000 French-speaking Belgians.

teenth-century Belgium. Naturally they carried on the national government and most local government in their own tongue. Some, moreover,
saw the French language as a vehicle of national unification and centralization. So Parliament and all but three city councils debated in French;
the army commanded in French; the courts judged in French. For several
generations, education in Flemish stopped with the primary schools; secondary schools and universities taught exclusively in French. Only in
French could one make a professional or civil service career. "To be
Belgian," complained Flemish intellectuals, "we have to cease being
Flemish."

The first leaders of the Flemish movement came chiefly from modest
strata of the intelligentsia—lower civil servants, school teachers, priests.
To many of these, especially the lower clergy, the tide of godlessness that
threatened pious Flanders was peculiarly associated with the French language and literature, which "oozed crime and demoralization." [30] It was
associated with the French nation, persecutor of the Church, with French-
speaking industrial Wallonia, where Flemish immigrants lost their faith,
and with the *francophone* (French-speaking) Liberal bourgeoisie of
Flanders itself.

The emphasis on language diverted the attention of the Flemish movement from the social and economic bases of Flemish inferiority in Belgian
life. "The myth that 'the language is the whole people' " for a long time
dominated the thinking of leaders of the Flemish movement.[31] That movement took form first in literary and cultural associations. There were
occasional political forays at the municipal level, notably in Antwerp,
where they were associated with antimilitaristic activity. But no regional
political parties appeared before the First World War.

Among the national parties, the Liberals were the most nationally
minded, including as they did in Flanders so many of the French-speaking
bourgeoisie of the region *(Fransquillons)*. Individual Liberals, however,
were among the leaders of the early Flemish cultural movement. The
Socialists at first insisted on seeing in Flanders only the same economic and
social evils they saw in Wallonia, accentuated by the economic backwardness and clerical domination which they associated with each other. The
Catholic Party showed some interest, but the democratic side of the Flemish movement clashed with the conservatism that long dominated the
party. In the immediate prewar years, Flemish representatives of all three
parties began some concerted action, notably in favor of a Flemish-
language [32] university. Meanwhile, as all aspects of public life tended to

30. M.J.J. van der Voort, *Coup d'oeil sur la langue et la littérature flamandes* . . .
(Antwerp, 1837), p. 18, cited by Pirenne, *Histoire de Belgique*, 7, 274.
31. Telemachus, "De Spanning tussen de Taalgroepen: een sociologische benadering," *De Maand*, *6* (1963), 332.
32. The "proper" language of cultivated usage is referred to variously as Dutch
("Nederlands") or Flemish; the dialects as Flemish.

become politicized the Flemish cultural movement split into Liberal and Catholic and Socialist organizations.

Only at the very end of the century had the government come around to requiring an official text of its laws in Flemish as well as French. By the First World War it had made some place for Flemish, alongside French, in secondary education, administration, and criminal justice in Flanders.

The war gave new dimensions and new urgency to the Flemish problem. If it deepened national feeling among many Belgians, it also deepened the opposition between the Flemish and "the others." Military sacrifice was glaringly unequal, by the direction of invasion and the nature of Belgian social structure. The Germans overran the country too fast for the Walloon contingents to be mobilized as fully as the more distant Flemish. When skilled workers were taken out of the lines and sent to jobs in French industries, most were necessarily Walloons. Remaining in the trenches were mostly Flemings, with a majority of their officers French-speaking. Serious incidents in some units in the trenches and in punishment camps behind the lines pitted Flemish soldiers against often uncomprehending commanders.

The Germans encouraged Flemish separatism, leaving a train of political booby traps for the Belgian nation after the war. The Flemish "activists," as they were called, who accepted measures of autonomy from the occupation authorities, were not political leaders for the most part, but literary and cultural figures. Only the national government's long indifference to their just cause was responsible for their collaboration with the enemy, they claimed; it was "now or never."

After the years of suffering in the trenches, in occupied Belgium, and in deportation, the old demands for Flemish equality could no longer be put off. Equal suffrage, moreover, gave a new political weight to the masses of Flemish peasants and workingmen. But the war had also called forth a surge of Belgian nationalism, which brought a stiffening against Flemish claims. The prosecutions of the activists after 1918 caused some French-speaking Belgians, consciously or unconsciously, to identify not only the men on trial, but the entire Flemish movement, with treason. By a comparable reflex many loyal Flemings felt resentfully that not just the "activists" but the entire Flemish people were being put in the dock.

The Interwar Years

The prewar government-versus-opposition relationship disappeared with the first elections under universal equal suffrage. The 1919 elections produced a balance of voting strength which, *grosso modo,* has continued to the present: the Catholics in the lead, with their chief strength in Flanders and rural Wallonia; the Socialists a very close second and occasionally overtaking the Catholic Party vote between the wars, strongest in

Wallonia, Brussels, and the largest Flemish cities; the Liberals, the victims of equal suffrage, a distant but significant third, strongest in Brussels and holding some traditional "fiefs" elsewhere. Flemish nationalist parties and, soon, a Communist Party became permanent minor actors on the national scene.[33]

Since there was no backing for minority governments or cabinets made up of nonparliamentary figures, coalition cabinets became the rule. Between the wars, the most frequent combinations were Catholic-Liberal and tripartite cabinets. The term "tripartite" should not conjure up an impression of anything like unanimity. With party discipline poor in Catholic and Liberal ranks, all cabinets faced serious oppositions within their own parliamentary delegations, even on their votes of investiture. Most often they received what Emile Vandervelde called "a vote of short-run confidence or of delayed no-confidence."[34]

One government was unique—formed in 1925 by the Catholic Party's Flemish laborite wing with the Socialists. It fell in less than a year because of a threatened monetary crisis. But it gave the Socialists the tantalizing hope, not to be realized, of a breakup of the Catholic Party on socio-economic lines, whereby the Socialists would emerge as the largest party, allying with the Catholic labor wing or absorbing some of it.

The Catholic Party's internal difficulties encouraged such hopes. With the growth of its allied social movements, it had become a *standen-organisatie*, to use the Flemish term, a party of corporate membership of its several "estates." It held together, in loose and quarreling federation, the organized *standen* of Catholic labor, Flemish farmers (the Boeren-bond), the "middle classes,"[35] and the party's original political circles, primarily aristocratic and bourgeois in composition, and now of steadily declining importance. By 1936, under the pressures of Flemish nationalism, the party also reorganized in two nearly autonomous regional wings.

Despite the repeated crises of parliamentary government in the 1930s, the three traditional parties surmounted their rivalries sufficiently to meet several of the nation's hardest challenges. In 1935 they formed the tripartite Van Zeeland Cabinet which, despite some Catholic and Liberal defections in Parliament, set the nation on the way to economic recovery.

The parties also suspended their oppositions long enough to fight the

33. For election results since 1919, see Appendix Tables 5.5 (votes for the House) and 5.6 (seats). For electoral system, Gilissen, Ch. 6. Women did not receive the vote in national elections until 1949. For regional distributions of votes and of party support, see Tables 5.7 and 5.8.

34. *Annales Parlementaires, Chambre,* Feb. 21, 1933, p. 370, cited by Carl-H. Höjer, *Le Régime parlementaire belge de 1918 à 1940* (Uppsala, Almqvist, 1946), p. 341, n. 5.

35. Following Belgian usage, I use the term "middle classes" here to mean self-employed business and professional people, artisans, and small employers.

one successful flash party in Belgian history, the Rexists of Léon Degrelle.[36] In the 1936 elections, six months after its birth, this nationalist,
anti-Marxist, anti-Semitic party won a ninth of the nation's votes (and a
sixth of those of French-speaking Belgians). Degrelle had dropped the
specific Catholic appeal of "Christus Rex" to summon all Belgians to the
good cause. Along with its negative aspects, Degrelle's whirlwind oratory
and writing stirred many people, especially young Catholics and some
young Liberals, with its appeal for a purer, radiant Belgium. For all its
demagogic vagueness and ugly menaces, his appeal was not quite fascist
until the war.

Degrelle himself did not run in 1936. A year later, with his deputies
revealing Rexist ineptitude and emptiness in Parliament, the leader himself stood for the House in a Brussels by-election which he forced [37] as a
sort of national plebiscite. In the face of the clear and present danger, the
three national parties united behind the candidacy of the Prime Minister,
the Catholic Paul van Zeeland. On the eve of the vote, the Cardinal-
Archbishop of Malines spoke out against Degrelle as a "danger to the
country and to the Church." The alternatives stood forth with rare
clarity: Rex or the regime. Van Zeeland received 80 per cent of the vote.
Rex was a punctured balloon; in the 1939 elections, it sank from 21 to 4
House seats.

The Linguistic Laws of the 1930s

It was a long time before Parliament enacted the equality for the Flemish
language King Albert had promised from the throne on the liberation of
the country in 1918. The Flemish showed increasing bitterness at the
delays in giving effect to solemn promises, while the *francophones* showed
irritation at the aggressiveness of Flemish leaders.

Specific Flemish parties had made their appearance in 1919, rising to a
modest peak in 1936 and 1939, when they elected 16 and then 17 members
out of 202 members of the House. In the Flemish cantons alone, however,
they reached 15 per cent of the votes cast in 1939. Their threat to the
established parties, especially to the Catholic Party, moreover, was much
greater than their percentage of the electorate. They functioned in effect
mostly as pressure groups attempting to affect action by the government
and by major parties.[38]

The Flemish movement had been essentially democratic in style, with

36. See essay by Jean Stengers on the extreme right in Belgium, in Hans Rogger
and Eugen Weber, eds., *The European Right: A Historical Profile* (Berkeley and Los
Angeles, University of California Press, 1965).

37. By having a Rexist deputy and all the Rexist alternates resign.

38. Jan Dhondt, "De evolutie van de partijen tussen de twee wereldoorlogen," *Res
Publica*, 4 (1962), 370–80; A. W. Willemsen, *Het Vlaams Nationalisme, 1914–1940*
(Groningen, Wolters, 1958), and Willemsen, "Sociologie als Therapie?" *De Maand*, 6
(1963), 493.

important elements of social radicalism and pacifism. In the 1930s, however, its extremists took on a totalitarian style, in two movements (to which we cannot devote space in an essay concerned with the "legitimate opposition"): the Dutch-speaking National Solidarity League (Verbond van Dietsche Nationaalsolidaristen, Verdinaso) and the Flemish National League (Vlaams Nationaal Verbond, VNV).

The main Flemish agitation, however, went on outside the extremist groups. Though even the loyal opposition often overflowed peaceful channels, the riots and bloodshed were far less than in any one of a large number of strikes in the United States at the time. But preoccupation with linguistic issues in the 1930s kept Parliament in a state of recurring turmoil. It rendered laborious the formation of cabinets and made their maintenance difficult. It took the attention of parties, governments, and electorate from the challenges of the Depression and European fascism.[39]

A series of laws in the 1930s finally enacted a long-delayed equality for the Flemish language in education, administration, justice, and the army. As it turned out, the laws were implemented only partially, most successfully in the courts, where there were sanctions for noncompliance. By this legislation Flanders and Wallonia would be unilingual; only in Brussels would there be some attempt at bilingualism. There would be instruction in the second national language in the schools, but that language would be a foreign tongue to almost all. Many Flemings, and a few rare *francophones*, would be more or less bilingual, but only as the result of personal effort or family circumstances. The hopes for French as a national unifying factor had failed. But it continued in national economic life and in the higher ranks of public administration to hold a predominance which, diminishing and precarious as it was, roused the opposition of many Flemings.

The Communist Party

History denied the Belgian Communists opportunities such as their brethren in less fortunate lands exploited. The first years were critical. In the political democracies where a left opposition failed to win a strong position in the Socialist movement before the rise of international communism, the Communist Party never became a major force on its own. The entering wedge in the major continental belligerents was the reaction against Socialist and trade union support of the war. But in the long-neutral little nation which, as King Albert said, had been "driven to heroism," revolutionary defeatism and postwar recrimination against social patriotism were absurd.

39. In 1939, for example, a tripartite government fell and Parliament had to be dissolved in a dispute over the government's naming a convicted and amnestied activist to the Flemish Academy of Medicine—this within half a year of the outbreak of war.

The political and social reforms of the immediate postwar government justified Socialist participation in it against criticism from the extreme left. Among the working class, the tightly meshed organizations of the Socialist world supported each other against Communist penetration. Even in the Depression, the Communists failed to emerge from political isolation. The Socialists rejected Popular Front proposals—which would not have made sense anyway, given the strength of the Catholics and Liberals. Instead the Socialists joined with the other two major parties in national union cabinets, as they had in previous emergency situations.

The Aftermath of World War II: Class Relations

The Second, like the First, World War diminished certain oppositions, created new ones, and sharpened others. If the First War marked the full acceptance of the Socialist Party, the Second marked that of the labor unions. Under the Nazi occupation, clandestine personal contacts among leaders of industry and Catholic, Socialist, and Liberal trade unionists produced a "pact of social solidarity" of symbolic and practical importance. The pact was implemented after the Liberation by wide advances in social legislation and collective bargaining. Leaders of employer associations and trade unions developed the habit of periodic meetings, with government leaders and without them, to regulate the labor market and consider national social policies. Wages, relatively low before the war, were raised more above prewar levels than in any other Western country. Social generosity was possible because of the relatively fortunate state of the national economy. Meanwhile, the government's vigorous currency contraction and stabilization measures kept the money wage increases meaningful and saved Belgium from the social tensions of galloping inflation.

Employers as a group were not discredited as they were for a time in France and Italy. The transition to a welfare state was made with their cooperation and hence without the resentments and conflicts of postwar industrial relations in France and Italy.[40]

Union and industry representatives came to exercise powers of administration in a number of quasi-public social welfare agencies. They sit together in advisory councils on national social and economic policy and on the boards of public and semi-public industrial and financial institutions. A few leading figures of the employer associations and Socialist and Catholic unions now frequently decide social policies in face-to-face contacts remarkably close for an otherwise stratified society. Sharing power in social affairs with labor unions, the employers have preserved

40. For a comparison of this and earlier historical experience with that of France, see Val R. Lorwin, "Labor Organizations and Politics in Belgium and France," in E. M. Kassalow, ed., *National Labor Movements in the Postwar World* (Evanston, Ill., Northwestern University Press, 1963), pp. 142–68.

most of their economic power and gained a high degree of social peace. Industrial conflict has been of mild proportions since the war; the two big general strikes were both directed at the government, not at employers.

The Parties

The postwar scene has been dominated by the three traditional parties. They broke with traditional names and structures, however. The Catholic Party was reborn as the Christian Social Party (Parti Social Chrétien, PSC [41]). It declared its "deconfessionalization" and its intention to be less conservative and more social-welfare-minded. In structure it was to be unitary, based on individual membership instead of the prewar federation of "estates" (*Standen*), and national instead of a federation of Flemish and francophone wings.

So it looked in the new dawn of 1945. The party did indeed become more "social." It soon forgot about "deconfessionalization," however. It avoided the head-on oppositions of the interwar *Standen,* but found new methods of informal recognition and even rather formal aggregation of the claims of its "estates." [42] While recognizing the regional wings in the party, it has been a force for national unity. At the war's end, the party found itself in the opposition for the first time in 61 years. Several experiences of opposition only confirmed it in its "governmental calling." But that "calling" it shares with the other two national parties; since 1918, all three have spent much more time in government than out (see Appendix Table 5.9).

The old Workers Party was reborn too in 1945, resuming the Socialist name (Parti Socialiste Belge, PSB) its forebears had prudently laid aside six decades earlier. The party adopted individual membership instead of the old collective affiliation of unions, cooperatives, and friendly societies.

The Communist Party represented a significant opposition only—paradoxically—when its tactics were those of cooperation and identification with the national interest in resistance and reconstruction. In 1944, for the first time, it had members in the government, a sizable labor union following, and much public sympathy or at least friendly curiosity. Even though national elections were postponed until 1946, when the party was already

41. Each national party obviously has both French and Flemish names. I have used only the French name and French initials.

42. There is no space here to discuss some of the interesting methods of reconciliation of divergent socioeconomic groups within the Catholic political community. One is the Agenda Committee, a body not even provided for in the party statutes, which has brought together leaders of the social groups (the old *Standen*) and the political heads of the party in periodic meetings of great policy importance. Another is the balancing of candidates from, or acceptable to, interest groups in the various constituencies. Multimember constituencies facilitate such slate-balancing. Agreed slates may be submitted to the party primaries for expected confirmation. Disagreements may be fought out in the primaries or finally decided by national leaders.

in decline, it obtained one-eighth of the total vote. For the first and last time since universal equal manhood suffrage, a fourth party surpassed the Liberals in votes and House seats.

The Socialists had fused their unions with those which emerged under Communist leadership at the liberation. Contrary to widely accepted opinion, trade union fusion was possible without suffocation by the Communists. The conditions were a vigorous Socialist leadership, Socialist union ties with other Socialist working-class organizations, and freedom from the myth of "no enemies to the left." There were enemies to the alleged left, but they seemed less dangerous as an internal minority than as an external opposition.

Eliminated from the Cabinet early in 1947, the Communists staged unsuccessful strikes against the government and the Marshall Plan a year later. Their popular vote dwindled steadily to a postwar low of two per cent in 1958, recovering slightly in 1961. The party retained some following in Walloon industrial centers and among Brussels white-collar and public service employees. Weak in numbers, leadership, press, and intellectual support, the Communist Party was almost pathetically mild and colorless. It shuffled along in the wake of the Socialist Party, halfheartedly claiming to be in advance of it.

The Liberal Party merged in 1961 with a few minuscule right-wing splinter parties to create the Party of Liberty and Progress (PLP). The PLP's chief innovation was an explicit repudiation of historic Liberal anticlericalism.

Immediately after the war, an attempt was made to break out of the mold of religious and antireligious opposition. A group of Catholics and Socialists, influenced during the war by the British experience, attempted to launch a Labor Party form of political action. They hoped for a realignment of parties, more modern and less emotional, primarily on social and economic issues. But the old parties reaffirmed themselves too soon for that. Especially among its original Socialist sponsors, old loyalties and calculations were too strong for the new Belgian Democratic Union (Union Démocratique Belge, UDB). When the UDB entered the election campaign of 1946, it was chiefly a mildly left and laborite Walloon Catholic group. To many, therefore, it looked like only a dissident Catholic formation. Perhaps it had too high a percentage of intellectuals. Certainly it lacked the mass base its orientation required, for the Catholic and Socialist trade unions returned to their old party affinities. The UDB went into its first and last election with two Cabinet ministers. It came out with a mere 2.2 per cent of the vote and a single deputy. The experiment came to an abrupt end. Its failure confirmed the confessional character which Catholic political action once again assumed.

The Royal Affair

The first great cleavage of postwar national life arose from the passionate debates over the constitutionality and wisdom of Leopold III's wartime behavior: his refusal to follow his Cabinet into exile after his surrender of the army in May 1940, his own and his entourage's hesitating or hovering attitude toward the German occupants, and the circumstances of his wartime remarriage.

At the end of the war Parliament declared the sovereign "unable to reign." While the King's brother Charles efficiently and discreetly performed the functions of regent, governments comprising both the pro-Leopoldist PSC and the anti-Leopoldist PSB and/or Liberal Party agreed to disagree on the issue. In 1950 a PSC parliamentary majority was able to carry through an advisory national referendum.[43] With some 10 per cent of the ballots blank or invalid, some 52 per cent of the eligible electorate pronounced for the exiled King's return. Taking account only of valid ballots, as most favorable to the King's cause, he had a 58 per cent majority. But was there a national majority or only a conflict of regional majorities? Flanders showed a Leopoldist majority (of valid ballots cast) of 72 per cent. But Wallonia gave him only 42 per cent, and Brussels 48 per cent.

The Leopoldist cause was strong enough to prevent any Flemish nationalist or dissident Catholic tickets in the national election of 1950, and the PSC won a majority in both houses, the only such majority since universal equal suffrage. Parliament ended the King's "inability to reign," despite Socialist threats of a general strike. When the monarch set foot on Belgian soil again, the Socialists launched a determined strike movement. It ended quickly, with the first victims—upon the death of several strikers at the hands of gendarmes, the King and the PSC government gave in, and the King made way for his young son Baudouin.

Once again the Socialist labor movement, with considerable middle-class support, had used the general strike for a political purpose, with complete victory for the first time. An hereditary sovereign and a duly constituted cabinet with an intact parliamentary majority had given way to avert further bloodshed and perhaps civil war. Their restraint at the eleventh hour preserved both the monarchy and national unity.

Why had this limited and sentimental issue provoked such violent opposition? The long debate kept alive opposing wartime memories. It gave a dramatic new, personal emphasis to the existing regional and party and religious divisions. (For a picture of the Catholic political pre-

43. The referendum was not sanctioned, but it was not specifically prohibited, by the Constitution. This was its first and only use; it was thinly veiled as a "consultation of the people." As in elections, voting was compulsory. On the votes, see E. R. Arango, *Leopold III and the Belgian Royal Question* (Baltimore, Johns Hopkins Press, 1963), pp. 189–90.

dominance in Flanders, and the Socialist predominance in Wallonia and Brussels, see Appendix Tables 5.7 and 5.8.) Only a class alignment was lacking to make polarization complete. There was no compromise possible, only postponement, and—Leopold's health being good—the issue would not die down. The referendum had merely exacerbated regional antagonisms, for it reopened the disagreement on whether the unit of decision was the nation or the region. A Liberal had asked before the referendum, "What will happen to the unity of the country when the Walloons can say that the Flemings imposed a king on them or the Flemings can say that the Walloons kept them from having a King?" [44] As it turned out, the Walloons said the first, and then forced the Flemings to say the second.

The School Issue

Five years later the Catholic political leaders, who in 1950 had yielded to force, themselves threatened force against a parliamentary majority, this time on the school question. After World War I the old issue of government support had been settled in favor of the Catholic primary schools. Now the issue that flared up, once the royal question had been settled, involved the secondary schools. The PSC majority legislated in favor of the Catholic secondary schools in 1952. A few years later (1955) a Socialist-Liberal government reversed that policy. Thereupon the Catholic opposition attempted a series of extraparliamentary pressures. The party president's call to boycott the government's postal savings and checking accounts and its bond issues was ineffective. In a march on Brussels—classic tactic of national protest—Catholics had their heads clobbered by tough gendarmes. With sporadic hooliganism by schoolboys and some acts of violence by adults, the Catholic protests were a long way in both style and aims from the Socialists' general strike.

Catholics were too wedded to tradition and order to feel at home in this kind of opposition activity. Moreover, unlike the Socialists in 1950, they knew they had another remedy. Indeed, at the next general election they won in the conventional political arena the victory they had failed to win in the streets.[45]

The dialectic of government-opposition-new government did produce a temporary and perhaps a permanent synthesis. After their electoral success in 1958, largely on the school issue, the PSC leaders took the initiative to get agreement with the two national parties supporting the public schools. The heads of the three parties negotiated the "school pact" of 1958, a 12-year truce that hopefully offered to take the school question out of

44. Blum, *Annales Parlementaires, Chambre des Représentants*, Jan. 18, 1950, p. 3.
45. The 1958 victory did not give them a majority: there are no landslides in Belgian politics. Its gains permitted the PSC to turn out the Socialist-Liberal Cabinet and to form the next government.

politics at last. The Catholics accepted the principle that where neither the communes nor the provinces (nor private initiative) organized nondenominational elementary or secondary schools, the national state should do so. The Socialists and Liberals accepted the principle that public subsidies should cover teachers' salaries for private (i.e., Catholic) schools. In good collective bargaining manner, the pact provided for a permanent tripartite panel to settle the conflicts of interpretation and implementation bound to arise under any such long-term accord.

All opposition over schools did not abruptly dissolve. There were thorny questions of allocations of funds to the competing educational systems, appointments to teaching positions in the public institutions, and the meaning and observance of "religious and philosophical neutrality" in public schools, questions the tripartite panel has so far settled.

Each party had reasons for wanting the pact, but it was the PSC that risked most, for it gave up the issue that had so often cemented the political unity of Catholics of different regions and classes.

The Flemish Problem Again

The occupation authorities had not deliberately favored Flemish autonomism in World War II as they had a generation earlier.[46] Contrary to the belief of many Walloons and Bruxellois, the *francophones* had no monopoly on resistance to the Nazis nor the Flemings on collaboration. Contrary to the belief of many Flemings, the widespread and perhaps excessive purge after the war struck many French-speaking as well as Flemish Belgians.[47] But as after the First World War, the demand for an amnesty came from the Flemish, and again aroused long and heated debate.

Flemish nationalist action resumed slowly, at first only under the cautious form of cultural and youth movements. From 1949 on, the Flemish Volksunie (People's Union) showed that a Flemish regionalist party had a permanent, if small, place in national politics. By 1961, with six per cent of the vote in Flemish districts, it elected five (out of 212) House members. Its importance was less as an opposition party than as a pressure group, weighing especially upon the PSC's action.

Unlike the VNV and the Verdinaso, neither the Volksunie nor the related Flemish People's Movement (Vlaamse Volksbeweging) is authoritarian, let alone totalitarian, in structure or style. In Parliament, the Volksunie has conducted itself generally as a loyal opposition. Its members are too few to practice any serious obstruction, but they do not even vote in systematic opposition.

Outside Parliament, Flemish organizations are not above troubling the

46. The Germans did release Flemish prisoners of war soon after the surrender, while holding most Walloons to the bitter end.

47. John Gilissen, "Étude statistique sur la répression de l'incivisme," *Revue de Droit Pénal et de Criminologie, 31* (1950–51), 513–628, especially summary 624–26.

public order now and then. The Flemish Action Committee for Brussels and the Language Frontier organized marches on Brussels and other demonstrations whose force impressed public opinion. For a time the Volksunie maintained a paramilitary youth organization. But whatever the latent threat to democratic processes from some "hard" elements, in the early 1960s they did no more than interrupt services in the several Antwerp and Ghent churches having French-language sermons, deface French-language highway markers and business signs on Flemish soil, and rough up bystanders in occasional "border incidents" around Brussels.

Meanwhile, the course of economic development was slowly eliminating some of the old Flemish disadvantages. An overwhelming percentage of postwar investment in new industries, especially by foreign capital (notably American), was in Flanders. The structural unemployment which had so long plagued Flanders was finally being absorbed by the region's and the nation's demands for labor. Flanders, like Wallonia, was now calling upon foreign laborers to do some of its hardest, dirtiest, and poorest paid work. These changes would take time to produce their full social and psychological and political effects among Flemings. Walloons, however, soon regarded them as marking the irrevocable passing of control to the once-backward northern provinces.

The Walloon Problem

There has never been a Walloon consciousness as strong as the Flemish consciousness. Walloons have thought of themselves in local terms—as Liégois or men of the Borinage, as people of Namur or Charleroi—more than in regional or linguistic terms.

As long as Wallonia prospered and *francophones* ran the nation, there was no "Walloon problem." A few people manifested inquietude about the region's prospects even before the First World War, but until recently the only regional interest groups were small sentimental movements of a literary or folklore character and minor economic-interest organizations.

With the end of World War II, the shift in the relative position of Wallonia began to alarm an area once confident of its economic destinies. To the continued experience of demographic decline (see Appendix Table 5.10) was joined the newer, more harrowing experience of economic stagnation due to superannuated coal mines, old factories and equipment, and an industrial structure still reflecting the first industrial revolution.

Frustrations and fears came to a head in a general strike of 34 days' duration in December 1960 and January 1961, which broke out despite the opposition of the national leaders of the Socialist unions and party. The stoppages began as a protest against the PSC-Liberal government's omnibus economic retrenchment bill after the loss of the Congo. Then they turned into a violent protest against government policies toward Wallonia. For in the heat of the strike, as their immediate national demands were getting nowhere, some Walloon Socialist leaders—chiefly of a left orientation—launched federalist demands and a regional organization. With the founding of the Walloon People's Movement (Mouvement Populaire Wallon, MPW), Walloon federalism for the first time had a mass backing.

Flemish federalists sought regional autonomy for its own sake or chiefly for cultural reasons. Walloon federalists sought regional autonomy to improve their region's economic prospects and to carry out the economic and social reforms they could not win on a national basis. The MPW called itself a pressure group—not afraid of a term that disturbed many citizens—but it represented a threat of independent political action that could come only at the expense of the Belgian Socialist Party.

Walloon Socialists might optimistically foresee an absolute majority for themselves in their own region. But the Flemish Socialists opposed a federalism that would leave them so clearly a minority in their region. The national PSB leadership responded vigorously and (so far) successfully to contain the MPW threat by their less disciplined Walloon comrades. But the general strike and the MPW had exacerbated divisions between Walloons and Flemings. Even more it had exacerbated divisions between the right-wing majority (Flemish and Walloon) and the small but significant left minority (Walloon and Bruxellois) which has been a permanent feature of the Socialist trade unions and party.

The Problem of Brussels

Brussels and its environs supply the leading issue of Flemish-Walloon contention. Here is a special form of the metropolis–provincial opposition to be seen in many nations. A pole for Flemish immigration and the center of the nation's French-speaking dominance, Brussels became for *Flamingants* (militant pro-Flemish elements) both an obstacle to overcome and a *terra irredenta* to recover.

Near the capital the fifteen-centuries-old language frontier has shifted visibly and significantly. The once-little Flemish city in the last century became a French-speaking metropolis. Here not even Dutch, let alone the Flemish dialects, could compete with French. The culturally stronger language was also the language of upward social and economic mobility in the capital. Most Flemish immigrants, or at least their children, were lost to Flemish culture. The 1932 language law seeking to make Brussels bilingual was honored in the breach by the authorities of a number of communes of metropolitan Brussels. Flemish citizens, more numerous in the nation than their *francophone* compatriots, complained that they did not feel at home in their national capital.

Another dimension of the problem was the migration of Brussels families to the suburbs and rural communes of surrounding Flemish Brabant. Naturally they wanted to use their own language and have their children taught in it. *Flamingants,* however, could not view this merely as a local manifestation of a universal urban–suburban migration. Some called it a "robbery of Flemish soil." For the proximity of French speech brought an increasing, intolerable competition for Flemish. In other ways too they saw an "oil stain" spreading out from Brussels over the Flemish country-side. Some of the newcomers were indifferent Catholics at best, and some freethinkers, and they disturbed the political balance in hitherto over-whelmingly Catholic Flemish communes. Even when the newcomers were good Catholics there were conflicts—often within parishes—with old settlers.

By the early 1960s, language and regional issues again dominated national politics. In 1962 and 1963, the Lefèvre-Spaak (Catholic-Socialist) govern-ment managed with the greatest difficulty to put through a series of laws on these issues, some giving greater force to old principles and some enacting new principles.

The new principle was that of fixity of the language frontier. The law scrapped the 1932 principle of administrative conformity, in various com-munes along the language frontier, to language practices as determined by a periodic language census. The census had become something of a refer-endum of preferences rather than a finding of facts about existing linguistic knowledge and use.[48] The new law fixed the existing language frontier [49] and administrative practices along it, in theory permanently. Here was a long step toward an undeclared federalism.[50]

In behalf of Flemish rights, another law sought to give more reality to official bilingualism in the Brussels metropolitan area by creating sanctions and a mechanism for enforcement. In behalf of the *francophones,* it recog-nized some of the facts of migration out of the capital to its outskirts by concessions in administrative practices in certain Flemish communes with large French-speaking minorities.

The third in the triptych of language laws confirmed the principle, accepted in the 1930s, of unilingualism in the schools of Flanders and Wallonia. But it made a greater effort to improve quality and augment the amount of instruction in the second language in each area, and in metro-politan Brussels to provide more Flemish schools in *francophone* communes, while making it harder for Flemish parents to send their chil-dren to French schools.

48. See Paul M. G. Lévy, *La Querelle du recensement* (Brussels, Institut Belge de Science Politique, 1960); Vlaams Aktiekomitee voor Brussel en Taalgrens, *Geen talentelling* (Brussels, 1959).

49. A few administrative transfers were made (with considerable political furor) to give homogeneity of language to each of the two language zones and to each province except bilingual Brabant.

50. Cf. Lode Claes, "Het federaliseringsproces in België," *Streven* (April 1963), and in English in "The Process of Federalization in Belgium," *Delta* (Winter 1963–64), pp. 43–52.

Why Linguistic-Regional Opposition Remains So Intractable

The linguistic-regional conflict appears more intractable than class conflict or the religious-ideological conflict. For this there are many reasons.

1. The sentimental and practical interests of the two linguistic communities are not effectively organized, and the geographical regions have no administrative or formal political existence. There are no recognized representatives qualified to formulate demands, to negotiate, and to fulfill commitments.

2. Flemings know little of Walloon thinking; the Walloons know less of Flemish thinking. People on each side therefore tend to see and to resent the others as a solid bloc arrayed against them.[51] Actually each linguistic community, each region, is far from monolithic on any relevant issue.

3. Inequality—bane of the relations between man and man—poisons the relations of the two cultural communities. Flemings are aware of *francophone* snobbishness toward the Dutch language,[52] a snobbishness still touched with old assumptions of social superiority.

French-speaking Belgians, always a numerical minority, now fear that they will become a sociological minority. They are aware that they lack the feeling of community (some would say "national" feeling) of their Flemish-speaking compatriots. Neither Walloons nor *francophones* have any concept or—significantly—any phrase comparable to the powerful Flemish *"ons volk"* ("our people"). And *"ons volk"* embraces the Flemish-speaking people of Brussels as well as those of Flanders. There is no such identification between Walloons and French-speaking Bruxellois.

4. Many of the Flemish elite pass their days in an environment that keeps linguistic sensitivities raw. If they work in, or deal with, national institutions in Brussels, they find French still the dominant language. They may assert the rights of their own language to equality, at the cost of friction with *francophones*. Or they may, as good fellows, carry on in a language few of them command as they do their mother tongue,[53] and at the cost of friction with more punctilious Flemings.

5. In the arguments over the Brussels area, the thorniest complex of linguistic opposition now, Flemish and *francophone* spokesmen keep appealing to different values. The contrast is classic. The Flemish appeal to the rights of the collectivity; the *francophones* to those of the individual.

51. Differences in ways of thinking and feeling are at least as important as differences in language. For difficulties of understanding by people speaking more or less the same tongue, see Anton van Duinkerken, "Two Ways of Looking at Flanders: A Dutch View," *Delta* (Winter 1963–64), pp. 39–42.

52. The "Walloon View" of Flanders, in ibid., pp. 33–39, is an example of the persistence of stereotypes and snobbery, culminating in an oft-repeated joke (sic) at the expense of Flemings comparable to some of the unfunny "darky" stories in the United States.

53. Common parlance calls people "bilingual" if they have a fair working knowledge of the second national language. If bilingualism means perfect command of the two tongues, there are few bilingual people even among Flemings.

The former, socially still at a disadvantage in Brussels, ask the state to protect their language and the continuity of their culture even against members of their own community who wish to be assimilated, at least through their children, into the other linguistic community. The socially dominant group wants the state to protect the individual's right to choose his cultural medium, but does not recognize the social and economic pressures and "silent intolerance" [54] weighing upon the Flemish in the Brussels environment.

6. There is an incongruity between many of the grievances and the remedies sought. Legal equality for the Dutch language cannot of itself make up for a lack of precision, uniformity, and style in Flemings' use of their own language. No official policy can preserve for the Walloons an equal share of responsible government posts when their numbers are so much fewer than those of the Flemish and when comparatively few of them make the effort to learn the other national language. Official policy alone cannot restore the Walloon birthrate. In fact, the Flemish birthrate has been falling, with a generation's lag, to meet that of Wallonia.

7. The Flemish still see themselves as oppressed, despite the political weight of their numbers, the progress in use of the Dutch language everywhere except in the Brussels area, and a recent economic growth in Flanders that is much more rapid than that of Wallonia. What Michael Balfour might call "the reflexes of underdogs" [55] continue far beyond the conditions that created them. So do the reflexes of "overdogs" or former overdogs. The Walloons look backward too, but only to contrast past security with fears for the future. They forget that the Walloon economy, even if relatively unprogressive, still yields wage rates and incomes well above those of most of Flanders. If Dutch is advancing, the French language still dominates in the higher echelons of the economy, finance, and administration.[56]

The *francophones* have a far higher percentage of students at university-level institutions than their percentage of the university-age Belgian population (See Appendix Table 5.11), even when allowance is made for foreign students taking courses in French. Although Brussels still determines and administers much, perhaps too much, of the nation's life, many Bruxellois feel threatened between Flemish aggressiveness and Walloon indifference to their special interests. In this unique national triangle of one oppressed majority and two oppressed minorities, rational and tolerant discourse is not easy.

8. Local and regional leaders and interest groups compete for public

---

54. The phrase is that of Telemachus, "De Spanning tussen de Taalgroepen," p. 334.
55. Michael J.L.G. Balfour, *States and Mind* (London, Cresset Press, 1953), p. 97.
56. On the latter, see Edw. Van Leuven, *De Evolutie van de Personeelseffectieven in Overheidsdienst* (Brussels (?), 1962 or 1963), pp. 25–27, offprint of two articles from the *Tijdschrift voor Bestuurswetenschappen en publiek Recht*, 1962, nos. 4 and 5, pp. 230–37, 304–19.

and private investment and for other advantages in public policy. Too often these normal clashes of local or regional economic interest are intensified because they are seen in the sentimental light of ethnic-linguistic conflict.

9. Money has met many of the historic demands of the working classes. More money has made the school pact acceptable to Catholic and public institutions. Money helps to meet regional economic demands. But it can do little to solve the linguistic demands and counterdemands.

10. The national sentiment that might offset centrifugal tendencies is weaker—for good or for ill—than in any other European nation. Political socialization in most cases emphasizes the particularistic, not the national. Belgians know a Flemish culture and a Dutch culture, a French culture and in folklore a Walloon culture—but hardly a Belgian culture. Except for the king, few national symbols [57] have power to move or to hold. And the monarchy, though generally accepted, is far from universally popular. The army suffers as a symbol from the antimilitarism traditional among the Flemish in general and among the Socialists in Wallonia. Each culture has its own historic memories, and those of Flanders are regional rather than national. In Flanders the anniversary of the Battle of the Golden Spurs in 1302 is more lively than the national holiday, and the Flemish lion evokes more enthusiasm than the national flag. In what other capital of a democratic nation would federalists give the unfurling of the national colors as an excuse for assault and battery? [58]

The Factors of Unity

We should examine consensus as well as conflict.

1. The Constitution is, to be sure, no longer venerated as once it was. But except for the federalist proposals its institutions are accepted with little question. If there is a "crise de régime," as Belgians frequently say, it is in the demands for modernization, for greater efficiency and authority, more participation by citizens in civic life, and forms of decentralization in the working of the existing institutions—fine but often contradictory demands—which are the staples of discussion in Western democracies, as well as in linguistic-regional tensions.

In the royal question, both sides appealed to the Constitution, while taking opposing views of the constitutionality of the king's acts. In the school conflict, neither side questioned the constitutional provision for

57. Among the rare discussions see Roger Mols, *Bruxelles et les Bruxellois* (Louvain, Société d'Etudes Morales, Sociales et Juridiques, 1961), pp. 121–33; Léo Moulin, "Les Liturgies nationales," *Revue Générale Belge* (January 1962), pp. 21–34.
58. In Wemmel, Flemish suburb of Brussels, in June 1963, Flemish nationalist demonstrators assaulted some citizens who flew the national colors from their windows. A Volksunie leader did not hesitate to say, publicly and privately, that the flags had been "a provocation" to the demonstrators.

freedom of education, while each asserted that only its own approach could realize that freedom in practice.[59]

2. Born with the nation, the monarchy is a symbol of its existence and unity. Except for the decade of the 1940s, the kings have been not only symbols, important as that role is, but mediators. The royal function has had "some of all three of Max Weber's ideal types of power: the traditional, the charismatic, and the rational." [60] That function is more important in a multi-ethnic than in an ethnically homogeneous state. Even in the heat of the fight against the return of Leopold III there was relatively little attack on the institution of a monarchy which, said the Socialist Achille Van Acker, "the nation needs as it needs bread."

3. Communal politics, on the whole, is a factor of unity. The commune is the normal ladder to national political office, and a high percentage of M.P.'s continue to hold communal office. Communal councils are elected by proportional representation. Electoral arithmetic requires administration by coalition in most of the larger communes. Municipal coalitions form and fall apart, most often with scant reference to ideology, and generally (at least before 1964) with little reference to national coalition patterns. Politicians thus are likely to have considerable experience of alliance at one level of government with people they oppose at another level. On balance, this experience tends to diminish hostilities by making the reasons for opposition seem relative rather than absolute.

4. Brussels has a "national vocation." Its very existence as a metropolis depends upon the performance of national political, administrative, commercial, financial, and cultural services. Out of interest and sentiment, Brussels wants (even if it fails to show the necessary linguistic tolerance) to maintain the unitary state. Conversely, advocates of regional separation *à deux* find Brussels a stumbling block.

5. Economic life reflects the national experience and helps to shape it. Most large industrial and financial enterprises are national. Exports and the transit trade, upon which Belgium is so heavily dependent, call for national action. The highly structured system of collective bargaining is essentially on a national, industry-wide basis.

6. Most social and economic interests, except those of a specifically local or regional character, are organized nationally. National organizations preserve their unity by recognizing diversity. Almost all of them have either formal bifurcation or informal recognition of the two linguistic communities or of the two (or three) geographic regions.

7. If all the lines of cleavage ran in the same direction, the tensions in the nation might become unbearable. Comparisons with Austria and

59. See the excellent discussion in André Mast, "Une Constitution du temps de Louis-Philippe," *Revue de Droit Public et de la Science Politique* (November-December 1957), pp. 987–1030.

60. "La Couronne et le Pays," *Revue Nouvelle, 30* (July 15, 1959), 57.

France may be helpful. The Fourth Republic collapsed in part because, in what Maurice Duverger called a "superposition of dualisms," [61] its many divergent lines of cleavage made impossible any continuing or cohesive majority in public opinion or Parliament. In Belgium the "superposition of dualisms" has not led to anything as paralyzing as the political fragmentation of the Third or Fourth Republics. On the other hand, further polarization along the same lines as those of ethnic-linguistic differences in Belgium might disrupt a territorial unity less deeply rooted than that of the French nation.

In *Austria infelix* between the wars, polarization was the prelude to civil war. To be sure, the oppositions of ideologies, social groups, and regions in Belgium (or in the Second Austrian Republic) are not of the armed ferocity of those of the First Austrian Republic. Some Belgians, with emotion or coolly, envisage a dissolution of the national state. But they do not envisage civil war for regional independence.

Each great factor of division—religion, class, party—is also a factor of national cohesion across regional and language boundaries. The leaders of the Church and the national labor and employer organizations are conscious of national responsibilities. In the political parties, although secondary leaders defend chiefly Flemish or Walloon or Brussels interests, the top leaders are highly conscious of their role in the aggregation of regional claims. In their own ways, and no doubt generally in their own interests, all these organizations work to surmount the tendencies toward further polarization.

Opposition Style

Between the wars, most governments were either Catholic-Liberal coalitions or tripartite. The Liberals were not ready to join with the Socialists except in the presence of the Catholics. Since the war, there have been no more "national union" cabinets. All possible coalitions of two major parties have governed. Any combination remains politically possible, although arithmetically, most of the time, only a coalition of the PSC with one of the other two has been possible.[62] This general availability for cabinet coalitions we might, for the sake of a short and catchy name, call *Allgemeinkoalitionsfähigkeit*. It contributes elements of stability and of instability.

The possibility of a reshuffling of partners in the coalition dance leads to some instability, which is not always dysfunctional. There is no single pattern of majority-minority relations. But on balance a certain stability results from the interchangeability of majority and minority roles and the

61. *Les Partis politiques*, p. 262.

62. Since the Second World War the Socialists and Liberals together have had a majority in both houses only in the 1954–58 legislature. On the recurrence and duration of various combinations, see Appendix Table 5.9.

continuity of personnel [63] and of role expectations. As a Liberal Vice-Premier remarked, "We have all had the experience of being in the government and that of being in the opposition." [64] The considerable stability of cabinets since the war, as compared with the troubled interwar years, also reflects a greater cohesiveness of all three parties.

Shifts in the weight of the various Catholic social groups in differing government combinations help make *Allgemeinkoalitionsfähigkeit* possible. As the largest party (in all but two legislatures since 1918), the PSC has most freedom in the choice of coalition partners. But the very existence of choice may heighten internal strains. Each coalition formula is identified with different social and regional groups and leading personalities within the party. Switches from one partner to another, or from government to opposition and vice versa, extend those strains from party cadres to social constituencies. [65]

Within the Socialist Party the duration of national government participation tends to bring protest from a left opposition based on doctrine, temperament, and—most recently—Walloon restiveness. To this tension the party contributes by the special socialist form of ancestor worship which consists of intoning ancient slogans believed to keep the ghosts of departed leaders from haunting the scenes of a briefly revolutionary youth.

The Socialists have been pulled by contradictory hopes and strategies. Most have ceased to nourish the old confidence, supported by Marxist analysis and the disaffection of industrial workers from the Church, that continuing industrialization would give them an absolute majority. Never since 1925 have they even reached the 39.4 per cent of the vote they won that year. Unless the PSC breaks up, they cannot expect a majority, perhaps not even a plurality.

Prime Minister Spaak announced his coalition with the Catholics in 1947 as one to last a generation. The royal affair blew it up two and a half years later. In 1954, Prime Minister Van Acker announced his coalition with the Liberals as the "alliance for a generation." During that generation, his coalition's school policy was to reduce what was regarded as a

63. The latter is based in part on the many safe seats in multimember constituencies and on party cooptation in the Senate.

64. A. Lilar, *Annales Parlementaires, Sénat*, Nov. 18, 1958, p. 15.

65. One switch will illustrate these problems. Its 1958–61 coalition with the Liberals gave weight to the PSC's conservative social groups and its Walloon constituency. In the 1961 electoral campaign, the PSC defended its government by attacking the Socialists for violence and lawlessness in their recent general strike. The election returns in, the PSC invited the "Reds" it had just been denouncing to replace the Liberal Party as its coalition partner. The PSC loss of votes made it quite natural, under the rules of the game, for it to change its coalition partner. But many conservative PSC activists and voters felt betrayed by the sudden shift after 12 years of frequently hard opposition between their party and the PSB. The outgoing Prime Minister was naturally bitter about his successor's public appeals for a change of coalition partner.

major source of Catholic political recruitment. Such a policy put economic reform on the shelf, for the Liberals had all the economic ministries.
The coalition collapsed with the voters' rebuke in the election of 1958.

The current "grand alliance" of the two mass parties adds to the weight
in the PSC of the Catholic Labor Movement and of the party's Flemish
wing, of which labor is the chief component. In the present constellation
of Belgian politics, this alliance gives the maximum possibilities of social
and economic reform. Yet it is acceptable to many influential business
people.[66] For it minimizes the incentives for either Socialist or Catholic
unions to outbid the others in militancy of industrial tactics or political
demands, and maximizes the interest of their leaders in government
stability.

National leadership having passed from them, the Liberals have long
consoled themselves with the role, in their self-image, of "balance wheel
of the nation's politics." [67] But their participation in governments led by
the Socialists and the Catholics failed to prevent the bitter dualistic confrontations of the royal affair and the school fight.

In creating the new Party of Liberty and Progress, the Liberals (for
there is still no other name for the men and women of the PLP) modernized and centralized a traditionally loose political organization. Where
the UDB had failed to surmount religious cleavages on the left, the PLP
sought with considerable success to surmount them on the right. By the
municipal elections of 1964, the PLP had attracted enough candidates of
known Catholicism to cover up the old Liberal image of anti-Catholicism.

Like the Liberal Party, the PLP seemed to find its chief support among
middle-class business and professional people, who as individuals and in
their interest groups are for the most part less effectively organized and
less committed politically than workers or Flemish peasants. In opposition
since its formation in 1961, the PLP could combine the frankest "catch-all"
economic-interest appeals in all sections of the country [68] with uninhibited
francophone linguistic appeals in Wallonia and Brussels.

Whatever the outgoing majority-minority alignment, parties fight
national elections alone and not in tandem.[69] The direction and relative

66. Of course many business leaders, quietly or openly, have supported measures
of recent reform, e.g. of the tax system.

67. Others have applied harsher terms, including that of the world's oldest profession, to the Liberals' ability to bargain for much more than their proportionate share
of Cabinet posts in any coalition they enter.

68. Said a Liberal Minister of the Middle Classes (a Ministry which may be a
Belgian Liberal contribution to the science of public administration), in laying down
the burdens of a long public career: "In my first political speech, I said that my
ambition was to become a 'merchant of happiness.' And this is what I have tried to
be all through my career." L. Mundeleer, *Le Soir*, Brussels, Jan. 29, 1958.

69. Joint Socialist-Liberal slates were of importance in the pre-World War I days,
when both were in semipermanent opposition. Of small consequence have been such
joint slates in some overwhelmingly Catholic provinces since 1946. See Appendix
Tables 5.4 and 5.5.

weight of any leading campaigner's attack on his opponents reflect his postelection coalition preferences. (The vocabulary of coalition possibilities runs: "My coalition is a marriage of reason. Your coalition is an unstable combination. His coalition is an alliance against nature.")

In Parliament, members of the opposition, even the Communists, have the right of the floor, including the (unwritten) right of interruption. They can usually have items placed on the agenda, although the government has priority for its business. Their verbal and written interpellations impress constituents more than cabinets.

Effective scrutiny of the budget, classic locus of the opposition, is difficult now in any parliamentary democracy. Yet Belgian budget debates are often the occasions for meaningful expositions of policy by ministers and criticism by various oppositions, including those within the majority.

In general, however, the opposition does not exercise most of its formal rights in budget matters, for lack of time and competence or out of a feeling of hopelessness.[70] Budgets are often submitted late; functional divisions of ministerial allocations are in many cases inadequate and confusing; supplemental budgets come in after expenses have been incurred, sometimes including expenses rejected in regular budgets. The reports to Parliament by the Court of Accounts on the legality of past expenditures are years behind. The important public activities carried on by the quasi-public or "parastatal" agencies are beyond parliamentary budget control.

The chief aim of party opposition is dislocation of the governing coalition. Dislocation tactics seek to increase the strains between the two partners of any coalition and within each of the governing parties. Each party out of office can focus special appeals and electoral threats on those elements of a party in government which chafe at their own party's choice of coalition partner. The Liberals can threaten the PSC right wing and vice versa. The Catholic trade union wing can embarrass the Socialist unionists and vice versa. These dislocation tactics we might see as "negative bargaining."

The Socialists face a special paradox in their relations with the PSC as a coalition partner. In the long run, they would like to see the PSC fall apart on socioeconomic issues. But in the short run, they can have the legislation they want only if their PSC partners prevent too many of their right-wing M.P.'s from breaking party ranks in committee and floor votes. If they fail to show legislative gains, the Socialist managers of the coalition face criticism within their own party.

When the two mass parties are together in the "grand alliance," the official opposition is small in numbers. In the legislature chosen in 1961, the recognized opposition in the House mustered only 20 Liberals, plus 12

70. An informal group may use its power not by pruning a budget but by holding it up entirely to get a policy or administrative change, as Flemish deputies did in 1962 with the education budget in order to obtain a measure of federalism in the Ministry of National Education and Culture.

from the minor parties, against the government's 180. For part-time M.P.'s, with no staffs of their own, this makes a heavy burden for the opposition, especially as committee meetings may go on simultaneously with floor debates, interrupted only for votes on the floor.

The larger the nominal majority, however, the more safely may the oppositions within the governing parties manifest themselves in debate, committee action, and floor votes without bringing down the government. Usually they wish to avoid doing that, and that is a government's strength.[71]

Public employment has been an arena of opposition. Employment and promotion in national, provincial, communal civil service and the quasi-public bodies have reflected party, religious, regional and linguistic cleavages and competition. A reduction of partisanship in national civil service hiring after the war brought an increased political pressure on promotions. This is, however, an old and civilized society, which respects vested interests. The rules of the game do not permit political dismissals; in fact, they hardly permit dismissals at all. But responsible officials are often sidetracked when a minister of a different party takes over a department.

Does it make the civil service more representative, more in tune with the rest of society, to have it reflect the religious and political and linguistic affinities of Belgians? The reflection is not candid, however. Everyone pays lip service to politically neutral professional competence, and each successive Cabinet's declaration of policy deplores the politicization of the bureaucracy. But it is always necessary to repair past inequities. Always in the name of restoring equilibrium, therefore, the balance in the civil service reflects the changing of partners in the saraband of coalition formation and opposition. But alternations of favoritism and discrimination do not secure anything recognized as equilibrium by the contending political, religious-ideological, and linguistic groups. For a long time, the contrasts between principle and practice have diminished public esteem for the public service, adversely affected work and personal relationships within the service, and discouraged initiative among all but the boldest.[72]

71. In 1963 Flemish PSC opposition to a major language bill caused the PSC Prime Minister to tender his government's resignation. Only when the King had refused it (as no doubt Lefèvre expected) was the Prime Minister able to hammer out a compromise among the members of his own party and the majority, enabling the government to carry on.

72. Among the few discussions in the literature, see especially the admirable essay by André Molitor, "L'Administration dans la société belge," in Institut Belge de la Science Politique, *Aspects de la société belge*, pp. 113–34; J. Vandendries, "L'Influence de la politique dans la vie de l'administration en Belgique," *International Review of Administrative Sciences*, 24 (1958), 512–22; Victor Crabbe, "Les Commissions de réforme administrative en Belgique," ibid., *20* (1954), 869–903, and the reports of the commissions of inquiry cited in that article: Edw. Van Leuven, *De Evolutie van de Personeelseffectieven in Overheidsdienst;* also Val R. Lorwin, "The Politicization of the Bureaucracy in Belgium" (Stanford, Center for Advanced Study in the Behavioral Sciences, 1962).

In 1964 the Lefèvre government proposed the most serious and comprehensive steps in a generation toward a reform of the civil service. But it was unable to achieve much of its program in its own weakened state at the end of the term of the legislature.

The courts are not a channel of policy opposition. There is no judicial review of parliamentary action. The Constitution bids the courts enforce only those administrative regulations (royal decrees) which are in conformity with the laws, but they have hardly used that implied power. Appeals are often taken to the Council of State against specific arbitrary acts of administration—for example allegedly political promotions made without due regard for the forms of civil service procedure. But such appeals constitute only a minor form of political opposition.

A party out of power or a locally entrenched interest may use its control of communal or provincial government to counter national policies. Most frequently it works within the law, though at times it operates beyond the law's margins. Many Socialist burgomasters and police chiefs gave support to strikers and condoned violence in the general strikes of 1950 and 1960–61. They were following the tradition of the Liberal burgomasters of large communes who in the nineteenth century abetted anti-Catholic manifestations and riots. Most significant in its continuing consequences, perhaps, was the refusal in 1960 of several hundred Flemish burgomasters, of all parties, to administer the government's bilingual forms for the national census. (Their disobedience reflected their concern that the responses would show the progress of French in some communes.) The government yielded to this defiance and sent them only Flemish forms.

In this nation of extensive commercial publicity efforts, appeals to general public opinion by both government and opposition are surprisingly bland and ineffectual. The principle of a party press is accepted, but neither of the two mass parties has a press comparable to its numerical importance, especially among *francophone* readers.

Newspapers in many lands are farther to the right than the voters. The Belgian phenomenon of the continuing opposition of the *Libre Belgique* may be almost unique. This well-informed, well-written but heavily slanted Brussels French-language daily has a national circulation which even includes many thousands of *bien-pensant* Flemish. Nominally very Catholic but with no spirit of charity, it is also aggressively conservative, nationalistic, and *francophone*. Its insistence on treating the Socialists as the "enemy brothers" of the Communists has helped keep alive Socialist anti-Catholicism. It directs its biting criticism at the progressive wing of the PSC as much as at the party's rivals. In a small country, the opposition of one such powerful journal is equal almost to that of another opposition party.

The Brussels boulevard press (especially *Pan* and *Pourquoi Pas?*) plays

a minor but occasionally significant opposition role by its revelations. The
weekly *Pan* is a Belgian analogue of the Paris *Canard Enchaîné*. It is
notably well informed about the Court and about the law courts. It is one
of the few French-language sheets to mock *francophone* as well as Flemish
excesses, and was courageous enough to defend the Lefèvre-Spaak government in its most unpopular hour. The Liberal-oriented *Pourquoi Pas?*
meanwhile has moved toward the right and engaged in bitter anti-Flem-
ish and antigovernment diatribes.

The public corporation that runs the nation's radio and television networks allocates equal time in campaigns to each of the three national
parties, but in driblets. To recognized minor parties it gives some, but
much less, time. None of the parties has yet made effective or significant
use of such time as it has had. The corporation fills positions in terms of
the proportional representation so widespread in Belgian life. Its job
allocation among the parties leaves out the minor parties in favor of the
exclusive rights of those a Volksunie deputy called "the Holy Trinity." [73]

Congo

In what was perhaps the nation's greatest responsibility—its vast colony—
the opposition had not fulfilled its role for four decades. There had been
strong and often well-informed and thoughtful criticism of Leopold II's
Congo administration. After the nation acquired the King's former personal domain,[74] the Socialists at first continued a vigorous opposition
which gave reality to parliamentary control. After the First World War,
however, by indifference and by more or less common consent, the Congo
was insulated from the scrutiny of the Belgian political process. Congo
policies were decided by a paternalistic administration, the Church, and
large industrial and financial interests. All parties shared responsibility for
it; if only Catholics and Liberals held the ministerial portfolio of colonies,
Socialists were also responsible as prime ministers. No party in opposition
turned the light on the nation's imperatives and choices in the Congo.
Belgians knew little about the colony, naturally, and neither parliamentary
debates nor election campaigns enlightened them. The task would have
been difficult. And indifference made it easier to release the Congo—but
too suddenly, once the decision was taken.

The internal rivalries of the homeland were, however, projected
onto the screen of the Congo: the school fight, the competition of the
trade unions, and the linguistic issue. The latter created a final echo in
the parliamentary discussion of the organic statute giving the colony its

73. Daniel Deconinck, *Annales Parlementaires, Chambre de Représentants,* June 6,
1961, p. 16.
74. For a fascinating description of the political process of that acquisition, see Jean
Stengers, *Belgique et Congo: L'élaboration de la charte coloniale* (Brussels, Renaissance du Livre, 1963).

independence. A leading Flemish Socialist deputy protested against the undue importance of the French language and the slight to Flemish: he saw it as "intolerable that the two languages should not leave the Congo on an equal footing."

Eppur Si Oppone

As I hope the preceding pages have indicated, there are still lively oppositions in Belgian life. They are not what they were in the classic system of an ideological two-party taxpayers' suffrage elite, nor are they those of the three-cornered party stage onto which the Socialists first advanced the cause of the working classes. As for the opposition of principle, it has receded almost beyond sight or sound. Politics have settled down chiefly into an opposition of center-right and center-left, capable of regrouping in response to old ideological concerns, to bursts of general antigovernmental feeling, and especially to linguistic fears and resentments.

The ideologies are largely *Privatsachen*, to be sure. But they have left their structures of institutions and attitudes. The heritage is clearest in the institutions of Catholicism, whose renewed vitality may be due as much to the tensions among the different social groups within the Catholic community (which a more socially homogeneous Socialist community does not experience) as to the renewal of Catholic social doctrine and the advent of Catholic lay action.

A great complex of organizations asserts the positive values of Church and school, of Catholic social and political action. But also, complain some earnest Catholics, it minimizes "dangerous outside contacts." It is possible to live most of one's life in a Catholic world: parish, school, youth movement, trade union or farmers' league or other occupational group, family association, consumer cooperative, friendly society, clinic and hospital, cultural organization, women's movement, and pensioners' organization. There are few meaningful personal contacts between most Catholics and non-Catholics. As the Catholic Center of Socio-Religious Research said in one regional study, "People of each group know people of the other groups only through stereotypes. These are usually simplified and deformed images of reality, of which a chief aim is to disparage the people of the other group." [75]

The old phenomenon of *Verzuiling*, or compartmentalization of life within "spiritual families," is in some ways decreasing. There are many more contacts among the elites of the Catholic, Socialist, and Liberal worlds. Ideologies have been losing their thrust and their rancor. But the organizations based upon them have become increasingly well established in most of organized social life. In the United States, multiple

75. Jean Remy, *Charleroi et son agglomération, 1: Unités de vie sociale* (Brussels, 1961?), 494.

memberships in voluntary associations may tone down hostilities. In Belgium, they reinforce them, as the memberships are all ordinarily within one spiritual family and one language group.

A thoughtful writer in the lively journal of a Catholic "ginger group" finds the old idea of "philosophical and religious barriers" laughable—"as if Belgium were peopled with philosophers and theologians!" [76] And one might add that philosophers and theologians have advanced beyond the structures their predecessors created. But people remain conditioned by those structures. "These ruins are inhabited," as the American boy discovered in running about Oxford.[77]

Most interest groups are not free to shop around from one political party to another because they are tied to a single spiritual family. But they may be more or less active during a political campaign, depending both on the care shown for their interests and even more on the threat to their sentiments. The Catholic unions have been most active politically in response to the threat against the Catholic schools. To be sure, interest groups usually do not have to shop around. Each mass party will meet the offers of the other party. Thus the PSB and the PSC competed with each other through the 1950s, election after election, in promises (and performance) to raise old-age pensions and to reduce the term of military service.

The major interest groups ordinarily have rather good access to decision-making centers, whoever is in office. A dramatic clash in April 1964 between the doctors and the government was in part due to the almost total inexperience of the former in lobbying and bargaining on economic, as distinct from purely professional and ethical, concerns. Despite the close powers of regulation of the profession by the Ordre des Médecins, with its compulsory membership, the doctors had almost no organizations for bargaining with the government and the friendly societies under the revised health insurance law. That inexperience was a major cause of the breakdown in negotiations which resulted in the doctors' strike. An immediate result of the conflict was the new, modern, and exigent organization of this small but strategically placed interest group. If its members sympathized with the party in parliamentary opposition at the moment, they seemed to recognize the advantages of maintaining a nonpartisan stance.

Most Belgians do not yet accept the full implications of pluralism, despite the slackening of anticlerical passions and the growth of tolerance and ecumenical feeling in the Church. Partisans of public and parochial

76. *La Relève,* March 7, 1964, p. 2, untitled article on Guy Cudell, unsigned (by F. Coupé).
77. Muriel Beadle's book by that name (concerned with other matters) (Garden City, New York, 1961).

Belgium   187

schools may tolerate each other; not many yet fully accept the other
system's legitimacy. Catholics and non-Catholics have similar reservations
in their attitudes toward each others' hospitals.

Governments, wiser than their constituents, have enshrined pluralism
in a representation for all recognized interests in every aspect of life
affected with a public interest or expenditure, from elected local and
national political assemblies, the Central Economic Council and the joint
collective bargaining commissions, down to the three brass bands—Liberal, Catholic, and Socialist—which sound forth, with the aid of public
subsidies, in any large city.

The institutionalization of all these particularisms helps to maintain the
attitudes to which they once gave more militant expression. The attitudes
may remain long after the ideologies have lost their force, as in Austria.
In Belgium in normal times the attachments and antipathies of the spiritual
families are pervasive but not virulent, brooding rather than aggressive. If
meaningful personal contacts with people of other subcultures are few,
so are the occasions for personal hostility. Normal man will not be political man much of the time. Joining a trade union or even a party may
be—rather than an act of commitment and participation—merely conformism to a social milieu, an insurance policy for a career, a key to a
housing project. For many, organizational membership is a dull gray rather
than a militant Red or a faithful Black.

Listen to the advice to civil service aspirants by the leader of a Flemish
nationalist organization, which has no trade unions of its own: "Join the
union connected with the party of the Minister in whose department you
want a job." For other limiting cases, look at some commuting Flemish
workers who join a Catholic union to have peace in the Flemish village
where they live and a Socialist union to have peace in the Walloon mill
where they work.

Yet even the antiheroes of these limiting cases respond to demands for
support of an opposition, on the set occasions of political balloting or
occupational elections, or on the unpredictable occasions when a royal
affair or a regional strike sends gusts of new passion flooding through old
canals. The classic opposition has indeed waned, as Otto Kirchheimer has
so well demonstrated.[78] But the waning of that opposition has left the
attitudes and the institutions of many oppositions, manifest and latent.
Eppur si oppone.

78. Otto Kirchheimer, "The Waning of Opposition in Parliamentary Regimes,"
Social Research, 24 (1957), reprinted in R. C. Macridis and B. E. Brown, eds., *Com-
parative Politics* (Homewood, Ill., Dorsey, 1961), pp. 216–27. Cf. Gabriel A. Almond,
"A Comparative Study of Interest Groups and the Political Process," *American
Political Science Review, 52* (1958), 270–82.

6

THE NETHERLANDS:
OPPOSITION IN A SEGMENTED SOCIETY

Hans Daalder

Legal parliamentary opposition has been a permanent feature of Dutch political life for over a century. By definition, it could not have arisen earlier: there was plenty of opposition previously, but no parliament. One could argue that there was not even a Dutch state until 1795. The Republic of the Seven United Provinces which existed from around 1579 to 1795 was merely a loose confederacy of practically sovereign polities, so much so that even at the end of the eighteenth century the States of Holland still addressed the States of Zeeland as: "Honorable High Mighty Gentlemen, Favored Friends, Neighbors and Allies." A parliament proper was only introduced in 1814 when central authority was securely established. Direct elections for the lower house did not come until 1848.

Neither the rise nor the role of oppositions could be explained adequately, however, without careful attention to the enduring effects of previous experiences. Pluralism and certain kinds of legitimate opposition predated parliamentary government and democracy in the Netherlands. Older elite characteristics and traditional modes of interelite conflict and accommodation have had a lasting influence. Even present-day social cleavages, between classes and masses and between latitudinarian Protestants, orthodox Protestants, and Catholics have their roots in sixteenth and seventeenth-century divisions.

Roughly speaking, Dutch experience with opposition can therefore be summarized as follows:

First, medieval traditions successfully resisted central authority. Political power, if strictly oligarchical, thus remained highly dispersed in the seventeenth and eighteenth centuries. There was no recognition of opposition as a justifiable attempt on the part of the outs to replace existing rulers. But factionalism was a well-understood phenomenon. The need

---

I am much indebted for criticism to Robert A. Dahl, Hans Daudt, Robbert P. van den Helm, Val R. Lorwin, Ivo Schöffer, and Ed van Thijn.

to adjust conflicting interests fostered a tradition of compromise and an acceptance of disagreement and diversity.

Second, the imposition of central government after 1795 provoked a conflict about the scope of government. Slowly, a democratic, reformist opposition developed in Parliament which successfully enforced ministerial responsibility after 1848.

Third, a dominant liberal elite became confronted with policy-oriented and even democratic structural opposition from orthodox Protestants and Catholics. This led increasingly to mass politicization. Shortly afterward, a Socialist opposition developed which was at first in total conflict with the society, then became a democratic structural movement, then turned increasingly toward policy-oriented or even office-seeking opposition. Neither of these successive emancipationist groupings achieved an independent majority. Rather than destroying the previously established political order, they came to form highly segmented subcultures which strengthened the pluralist character of Dutch society.

Fourth, the main political parties have learned to operate within a system of political bargaining in which separate ideological traditions are carefully respected and protected, but in which a considerable measure of practical cooperation is achieved. Most articulate interests have an opportunity to make themselves felt. But the effective foci of decision-making have tended to become rather centralized (though remaining collegial and pluralist). All parties engage in policy opposition and in office-seeking opposition. But while opposition is thus continuous, it is often fluid. While there is no strong opposition of principle to the system, there appears to exist a considerable gap between leaders and led. Survey and other data reveal a high degree of satisfaction with living standards and little interest in politics. While the ground plan of the party system has changed little since World War I, the modern electronic mass media subject the prevailing segmentation to increasing strains.

Throughout the last centuries there has been comparatively little violence in public life. Governments have been relatively secure and comparatively seldom repressive, while oppositions have been on the whole moderate if persistent. Both rulers and ruled have jealously insisted on their own autonomy. Governments have tended to enjoy a rather free hand, but have used authority on the whole in rather responsible fashion. Otherwise, the words of a British minister at the Hague, written over a hundred years ago, would still seem pertinent:

> The Dutch are little disposed to take a busy and sustained part in politics. They enjoy their liberties rather than exercise their rights. Some vital question must be at stake, affecting the conscience, the heart, or the purse of the nation, to rouse them to exertion. The Pope, or the

House of Orange, the finances, or the colonies, must be in question; then the masses are stirred to an active participation in public affairs.[1]

Central Government and Persistent Pluralism

As Robert Dahl observes in the introduction to this volume, a formal opposition is likely to be permitted in a political system if (1) the government believes that an attempt to coerce the opposition is likely to fail, or (2) even if the attempt were to succeed, the costs of coercion would exceed the gains.[2] Both circumstances have prevailed in the Netherlands from an early date. The Dutch political community itself was born of successful resistance against attempts at coercive centralization by the Burgundian and Hapsburg overlords in the fifteenth and sixteenth centuries. In the *Placaet van Verlatinge* of 1581, the Dutch States-General solemnly renounced their legal prince, Philip II, justifying their opposition on two grounds: "the liberties of men, wives and children and of future descendants, for which the Law of Nature bade them to sacrifice even goods and blood" and the circumstance that of old princes had ruled in the Low Countries, "after recognition of privileges, customs and ancient traditions, on condition, contract and agreements breaking which a Prince is deprived by right of the rule of the land." [3]

For a while the States-General looked around for a new sovereign. But before long they came to be satisfied with the peculiar construct of the United Provinces of the Netherlands established in the *Unie van Utrecht* in 1579 as little more than a temporary alliance. Thus at a time when absolutism and the divine right of kings came to dominate in most European countries, Dutch particularist interests successfully sought to arrest the further growth of central government.[4]

What emerged was a highly pluralist, decentralized political society. The States-General stood technically at the pinnacle of the political hierarchy. But this assembly was itself made up of strictly mandated delegates

1. Report from Lord Napier to the Foreign Secretary (1860), published in full by J. C. Boogman in *Bijdragen en Mededelingen van het Historisch Genootschap, 17* (1957) 213.
   2. This volume, p. xii.
   3. The last Orange Stadholder, William V, greeted the American Declaration of Independence as "a parody of the document which our ancestors made public against King Philip II of Spain." See P. Geyl, *Geschiedenis van de Nederlandse Stam, 5* (Amsterdam, Wereldbibliotheek, 1962), 1203. His statement was, of course, highly anachronistic; even Madisonian democracy would have been far too progressive for a man of his small caliber, who was himself at one time reinstated in power with the aid of Prussian troops.
   4. For full treatment in English, see especially G. J. Renier, *The Dutch Nation: An Historical Study* (London, Allen and Unwin, 1944), and Pieter Geyl, *The Revolt of the Netherlands, 1555–1609* (2d ed. London, Benn, 1958), *The Netherlands in the Seventeenth Century*, Part I (London, Benn, 1961), Part II (London, Benn, 1964), and *History of the Low Countries: Episodes and Problems* (London, Macmillan, 1964).

from the seven provincial states who were in turn dependent on the various nobilities and cities that composed them.[5] What resulted was a curious amalgam, in which central authority was severely restricted. Althusius and others provided the new structure with a suitable political formula based on the concept of sovereignty from below through a pyramid of freely established *consociationes*. Authority was thus theoretically circumscribed by the prior claims of ancient privileges and contractual undertakings. Aristotelian preferences for the mixed state and natural law theories of legitimate resistance to unlawful authority thus came to solidify what was in fact a highly oligarchical, loosely jointed confederacy.[6]

Within the Republic, the most powerful and richest province, Holland, tended to play a paramount role. Holland alone paid more than half the confederal budget. Its Grand Pensionary tended to be the most powerful official in the Republic, apart from the Orange stadholders. But Holland was at the same time extremely jealous of its independence. Its maritime and commercial interests often conflicted with those of the other provinces which it tended to regard mainly as protective bastions against invasion on land. Consequently Holland had an interest in maintaining the confederacy, but preferably at minimal strength.[7]

The Orange stadholders, too, provided something of a central focus in the Republic. They inherited some of the truncated functions of the traditional princely overlords and enjoyed a very high social and political prestige. Their main immediate powers were of a military nature. They occupied the offices of Captain-General and Admiral of the United Provinces. But they never succeeded in obtaining absolute control over the armed forces, even though they sometimes used them to promote political purposes by methods little short of those of a coup d'état. Administrative control over the Admiralty was divided among five Admiralty Boards, residing in different maritime cities. As to the army, the States-General appointed the highest officers and sent their own political deputies with the Captain-General to determine joint strategy. Army control was further decentralized by the so-called repartition system: each of the provinces was made directly responsible for financing the troops garrisoned within its boundaries. Troop movements were subject to approval

5. See I. Schöffer, in *500 Jaren Staten-Generaal in de Nederlanden* (Assen, Van Gorcum, 1964), pp. 64–98.
6. See E. H. Kossmann, "Politieke Theorie in het Zeventiende-eeuwse Nederland," *Verhandelingen der Koninklijke Nederlandse Akademie van Wetenschappen*, Nieuwe Reeks, 67 (Amsterdam, 1960). For a shorter version in English see Kossmann, "The Development of Dutch Political Theory in the 17th Century," *Britain and The Netherlands*, papers delivered at the Anglo-Dutch Historical Conference, 1959 (London, Chatto and Windus, 1960), pp. 91–110.
7. J. C. Boogman, "Achtergronden en Algemene Tendenties van het Buitenlands Beleid van Nederland en België in het Midden van de 19e Eeuw," *Bijdragen en Mededelingen van het Historisch Genootschap*, 76 (1962), 50 ff.

of the provincial states concerned. Individual cities, which often claimed a measure of direct control over parts of the army, could normally rely on their own *schutterijen*, armed guards of independent burghers who gave substance to the strong independent stand many cities chose to take. Thus the tradition of divided control remained strong enough to prevent the development of a strong autochthonous military establishment. Most troops were mercenary soldiers from abroad. Toward the end of the eighteenth century there was only one factory in the Dutch Republic that could make rifles.[8]

The confederal structure of the United Provinces also militated against the establishment of a powerful central bureaucracy. All the more important bodies of the Generaliteit were filled by delegates from all the provinces under a rotating chairmanship. They were served by only a handful of permanent officials who might attain considerable personal influence,[9] but had no means to coerce. Effective political power at the center depended therefore on the ability to balance carefully widely varied particularist interests. Within the restricted circle of effective decision-makers each man took part in the discussions as the representative of a quasi-independent province or city. All therefore learned to live in a climate of constant reciprocal opposition, which fostered the habit of seeking accommodation through slow negotiations and mutual concessions. This also caused a measure of public debate. Within each city or province, citizens were usually prevented from criticizing their rulers. But at the same time these rulers might well see profit in strengthening their case through a public airing of their views and a deliberate attack on the opinions of potential adversaries elsewhere in the Republic. Throughout the life of the Dutch Republic an unending stream of pamphlets and books on controversial issues (so-called *libellen* or *paskwillen*) poured forth from the printing presses.[10]

International considerations tended to further the growth of a spirit of laissez faire in the spiritual as in the economic field. The city oligarchs

8. S. J. Fockema Andreae, "De Nederlandse Staat onder de Republiek," *Verhandelingen der Koninklijke Nederlandse Akademie van Wetenschappen*, Nieuwe Reeks, 68 (Amsterdam, 1960), 117. Since 1848 the Dutch Parliament has dismissed 28 defense ministers (out of 47 ministers who lost their jobs over a conflict with Parliament), usually over trivial financial matters. Dutchmen accord high professional military officers a rather low prestige; according to a recent study generals and colonels are ranked 15th among 57 possible professions, below veterinarians, mayors of small communities, clergymen, and high school teachers; see F. van Heek and E.V.W. Vercruijsse, "De Nederlandse Beroepsprestigestratificatie," in *Sociale Stijging en Daling in Nederland, 1* (Leiden, Stenfert Kroese, 1958), 25–26.

9. In addition to Fockema Andreae's thorough study (see n. 8), see also A. M. Donner, "De Geschiedenis van het Bestuur," in *Nederlands Bestuursrecht* (Algemeen Deel, Alphen, Samson, 1962), pp. 11–42.

10. G. J. Renier used these writings as the basis for his interesting *The Dutch Nation*, passim.

were particularly well aware of the economic benefits which emigré groups brought to the country by promoting industry and trade. They were also highly conscious of the unfavorable effects of ideological partisanship on international trade. Consequently they deliberately sought to de-emphasize ideological conflict at home. A "political" preparedness to live with existing cleavages has ever since gone hand in hand with a relatively peaceful outlook in international affairs. International law and political neutrality enjoyed widespread support as providing a happy combination of high ethics and economic profit. To quote John de Witt, one of the foremost leaders of the Dutch Republic: "The interest . . . of this State [is] posed in this that calmness and peace be everywhere and that commerce may be carried on unhindered." [11]

Does all this mean that pluralism made opposition a recognized feature in Dutch politics as early as the seventeenth or eighteenth century? The answer depends on the way one defines the word "opposition." There was considerable regional conflict which found institutionalized expression in the complex deliberative procedures that prevailed at the center of the Republic. There was ample strife on many issues: international, constitutional, economic, financial, social, and religious. There was often an attempt made to build up partisan support throughout the territory of the Republic, in order to carry special decisions through the cumbersome confederal organs. In addition, more or less lasting groupings tended to coalesce around the Orange dynasty and the *Staatsgezinden* (the leading city oligarchs, called *Heeren* or *Regenten*) respectively. As neither of these groupings were strong enough to completely subjugate the other, they were forced to live with one another, enjoying at most a temporary predominance at any given period. But what was lacking was a view on either side of accountability toward a sovereign people. Active politics was carefully reserved to small, privileged, generally hereditary segments of the population. "Ins" and "outs" were not thought of as complementary forces that might both contribute to good government, but at most as self-seeking factions. A changing of political personnel only occurred through political intimidation, such as the high-handed *wetsverzettingen* (literally, changing of the laws) by which various Orange stadholders replaced too independent *regenten* by more congenial ones, or through manipulated or spontaneous rebellions by the multitude in time of war or economic depression. If it is true that the Dutch Republic knew comparatively little political violence, it is yet well to remember that two of its leading statesmen, Oldenbarnevelt and John de Witt, died in conditions little short of judicial murder. Grotius, the able advocate of Dutch particularism, was himself forced into exile. For considerable periods of time, the regents did without stadholders. And toward the end of the eighteenth century, domestic conflict

11. Cited by Boogman, "Buitenlands Beleid," p. 51.

reached such tension that it was only temporarily restrained by Prussian arms.

The Dutch Republic lasted until the country was overrun by French troops in 1795, long enough to have a profound and lasting influence on political behavior. Dutch *Unitarissen* and French administrators then laid the administrative framework for a unitary state which was retained by the first Orange king, William I (1813–40). William's activist regime was the nearest experience to royal absolutism the Netherlands ever had. Since then the country has had a relatively strong central administration. But the imposition of new central government machinery on what had hitherto been a highly particularist society did not destroy the effect of earlier political styles. Some older regent groups continued to take a fairly independent stand, and regional diversities retained considerable importance. Centralization did induce a change in the site of opposition, however. Whereas oppositions had formerly tended to be restricted to particularist bases even when they fought on the national scene, activist centralization now caused them to shift their attention almost entirely to the center itself. Henceforth political oppositions perforce addressed a national audience and carried their battles into the national arena. Unlike the old Republican days, oppositions could no longer agree to differ, being relatively secure in their quasi-independent sovereignties. They could only achieve their aims through changes in the personnel, the policies, and even the structure of government. Organized political opposition, in the sense of regular endeavor to change the rules of the game, and with it the persons and policies pursued, must therefore be dated in the Netherlands from this period.

Dissatisfaction with the King's expensive mishandling of the Belgian Separation (1830–39), among other things,[12] led to increased political activity, both in Parliament and in the country at large. Liberal opposition gained increasing force, while simultaneously Calvinists and Catholics came to protest against the Josephist attitude of William I in matters of church organization. In 1840 the King abdicated, unwilling to rule after a mild constitutional change. Eight years later his successor, William II, agreed to a much more drastic constitutional revision. It restrained royal power and made possible a considerable extension of political activity to all groups and areas.

Since 1848 central government and a rejuvenated system of local self-government have existed side by side. While improved communications have led to a relatively peaceful interpenetration,[13] regional factors have

12. See Lorwin, this volume, pp. 149–50.
13. For a fuller discussion of the relevance of this factor to problems of general political development, see Hans Daalder, "Parties, Elites and Political Development(s) in Western Europe," in J. LaPalombara and M. Weiner, eds., *Political Parties and Political Development* (Princeton, Princeton University Press, 1966), pp. 63–77.

remained of considerable importance for the working of opposition in the Dutch system.

Distinct regional interests have clashed, for instance, in matters of central government expenditure. In the nineteenth century in particular, various governments fell because they did not placate articulate regional interests in Parliament on matters of railways, canals, or even the physical location of courts of justice.[14]

Later opposition parties partly owed their chance to develop to continued social and geographic diversity. Elements of peripheral protest played a substantial part in the rise of Liberal, Catholic, Calvinist, and Socialist opposition. D. Hans and M. Litten [15] have shown how both Liberals and Socialists drew most of their earliest strength from the northeastern provinces. Similarly, the rise of a separate Catholic movement was greatly encouraged by the circumstance that most Dutch Catholics live in two quite heavily Catholic southern provinces; they almost invariably elected Catholic deputies long before there was a Catholic Party. The orthodox Protestants, too, owed much of their electoral strength and social stamina to attitudes of protest in clearly defined orthodox regions against the nonfundamentalist influences from the nation's cultural centers. Differences within the orthodox Protestant camp can to some extent be traced to deep-rooted historical factors, such as the particular way in which the Reformation struck root and variations in the challenges which local Protestants faced from other confessions, and from special social and economic situations.[16]

Finally, the persistence of strong local government traditions has eased the pressure from nationally dominant elites.[17] New social groups have

14. There have always been a considerable number of judges and mayors and other local government officials in the Dutch Parliament, reminiscent of the days before 1795 when the States-General was nothing but an assembly of local interests. (For the period 1848–79, see S. J. Fockema Andreae, *500 Jaren Staten-Generaal in de Nederlanden*, pp. 217 ff.) This has continued to be true, although there were no residence requirements during the period of the district system and even though proportional representation has made the arrangement of party lists a highly centralized affair since 1917. The percentage of representatives actually living in the two provinces, North and South Holland, has declined from three-fourths in 1913, to two-thirds in 1933, to about one-half at the present time; see N. Cramer, "Portret van de Parlementariër," *Het Parool*, September 19, 1964.

15. D. Hans, *Het Nederlandsche Parlement* (Amsterdam, Van Kampen, 1911), pp. 146–48 and M. Litten, "De geografische verdeeling der politieke partijen in Nederland vóór den wereldoorlog," *Mensch en Maatschappij, 12* (1936), 50–59 and 126–39.

16. Generally speaking, the militant *Gereformeerden* tend to be concentrated more heavily in the maritime provinces and in the cities, the *Orthodox-Hervormden* who form the backbone of the Christian Historical Union in the traditional rural areas of the center and east of the country, and the theocratic supporters of the Staatkundig-Gereformeerde Partij in rather isolated regions like Zeeland and the Veluwe.

17. See Robert L. Morlan, "Central Government Control of Municipalities in The Netherlands," *Western Political Quarterly, 30* (1959), pp. 64–70. Fear of particularism has resulted in central government appointment of burgomasters for over a

been able to acquire positions of responsibility in local and provincial
government long before they have acceded to power at the center. All
manner of coalitions between rival groupings have proved practicable at
the local level without immediate reference to the political situation in
the national capital. The existence of various levels of government has
thus widened the opportunities for positive political action and participation by different groups. This has facilitated cooperation among all kinds
of political groups within one constitutional order. While governments
have been far from all-powerful, oppositions have rarely been completely
without power.

To conclude: persistent pluralism has been a powerful factor in allowing
the rise of formal oppositions without violent reversals of the constitutional
order. Central power developed relatively peacefully and gradually and
became an integral and accepted part of society, not its alien overlord. This
facilitated the transfer of older traditions of compromise and the continued recognition of the value of diversity to the modern state. Regional
variations in turn came to fit relatively easily into the new political system,
becoming sufficiently part of the whole so as not to fragment the political
order.

Classes and Masses

THE ENDURING IMPACT OF OLDER CLASS RELATIONSHIPS   Until late in
the nineteenth century Dutch politics tended to be the exclusive domain
of the classes rather than the masses. The styles of older elites have therefore exerted a substantial influence on present-day political behavior.

At an early date in Dutch history the more important provinces came
to be dominated by burgher elements. Both in Holland and in Zeeland,
towns formed the backbone of government in the time of the Republic:
in the states of Holland the nobility had only one vote, against 18 votes for
the cities; in Zeeland, too, the towns had all the votes but one. Within the
towns political power was concentrated among self-contained and self-
recruiting oligarchies consisting, in the words of an old city charter, of
the "richest, most honorable, notable and peaceful." [18] These oligarchies
became more exclusive in the eighteenth century and adopted all the styles
and titles of an hereditary aristocracy. But if the city regents became, in
the words of Renier, more and more "bourgeois gentilhommes," intermar-

---

century. But though central government appointees, burgomasters have in fact often
become the champions of local government against the central government itself;
mayors are frequently elected to Parliament where they readily criticize their nominal
superiors.

18. These words are taken from the *Privilege* of Delft, 1445; see Renier, *The Dutch
Nation*, p. 17. The supreme bodies in Dutch cities were called *vroedschappen*, the
"wise men." To this day *vroede mannen* are often considered capable of settling
painful political conflicts.

riage between newer and older aristocracies at the same time made the latter more and more into "gentilhommes bourgeois." [19]

This pervasiveness of bourgeois values has had important consequences. It saved the Netherlands from the bitter antagonism between the nobility and the *tiers état* which had such explosive effects in France. The Dutch elites retained considerable political, social, and economic prestige. This tended to help them in maintaining their legitimacy; it also dampened working-class militancy, and eased the integration of the working class into the national political community.[20]

Political security made it easier for the ruling classes to permit considerable social freedom to the citizens at large. Mass interference with politics was not permitted; on several occasions in Dutch history rebellious actions by the masses have been quelled by arms and rather heavy-handed "justice." The Dutch regent class did not consider itself in any way responsible to the population at large; affairs of state have traditionally been settled in considerable secrecy.[21] But at the same time, city folk were left a fairly wide autonomous sphere in which they could privately shrug their shoulders over their rulers.[22] This has fostered a rather peculiar mixture of both deference and indifference which has tended to characterize the attitude of most Dutchmen toward authority.

Further, the self-reliance of the regent class has tended to be a factor in the preservation of political liberties. Even after the arrival of central government, the Dutch elites were never completely absorbed into the state apparatus. Memories of old freedoms have helped to ward off autocratic government. Representative government was obtained in 1848 long before the full effects of the Industrial Revolution and rising pressure on the part of the masses were felt.

Finally, the Dutch political elites have never identified completely with one state church. Calvinist pressure in the sixteenth century ensured that the Dutch Reformed Church was officially recognized as the "true religion," and offices were in principle reserved to its adherents. But even in the time of the Republic the city fathers tended to be fairly permissive toward dissenters, Jews, and Catholics. Since 1795 all citizens have formally enjoyed equal civil rights irrespective of religious allegiance. In other

19. Renier, *The Dutch Nation*, p. 104.
20. See Val R. Lorwin, "Working Class Politics and Economic Development in Western Europe," *American Historical Review, 63* (1958), 338–51 and S. M. Lipset, "The Changing Class Structure of Contemporary European Politics," *Daedalus, 93* (1964), 271–304, for general analyses along these lines.
21. I have elsewhere attributed the comparatively little interest of Dutchmen in politics (and the displacement of political studies by legal studies which took place in the nineteenth century) to this special relationship between relatively secure ruling elites on the one hand and rather free citizens on the other; *Leiding en Lijdelijkheid in de Nederlandse Politiek*, Leiden inaugural address, 1964, pp. 10 ff.
22. Renier, *The Dutch Nation*, pp. 180 ff., and 253 ff.

words, the ruling elites, divided themselves in their religious sympathies, have tended to be relatively tolerant. Orthodox Calvinists and Catholics consequently have had to fight an uphill battle against latitudinarian traditions. Rather than upholding a reactionary status quo, they have represented emancipationist movements.[23]

From the end of the eighteenth century, the monopoly of the regent class slowly waned. But upper-class elements retained considerable influence, and even after the introduction of full parliamentary government and ministerial responsibility in 1848 the franchise remained highly restricted. Parliamentarians owed their selection for a long time mainly to small coteries of local patricians, and party organization was practically absent.[24] The power of Parliament thus tended to be somewhat negative. The *Grand Bourgeois* deputies were usually satisfied to hold cabinets and ministers accountable. They used legislative and budgetary powers to ensure adequate consideration for their private rights and interests, but rarely sought to force a particular ministerial *équipe* on the Crown. The king thus maintained substantial influence on ministerial appointments, and many ministers continued to be chosen from outside the parliamentary circle. The influential Liberal leader Johan Rudolf Thorbecke, himself often a minister but also a redoutable opposition leader in Parliament on other occasions, thus characterized the resulting system:

> A free and independent monarchical government with unlimited parliamentary responsibility of ministers, a freely elected representative assembly, independent, deciding according to its own views and judgment, without any link with the voters; exercising general legislation jointly with the monarchical authority, but without participating in the executive power, whose working it controls through the means of ministerial responsibility.[25]

This careful equilibrium was broken up from the 1870s onward by a series of issues that led to more intensive mass participation: the school issue, the conflict about franchise extension, and what an earlier generation termed "the social problem," i.e. the relation between the state and the new industrial proletariat. These issues broke the practical autonomy of the upper classes and gave rise to the establishment of well-organized opposition parties.

23. The failure to grasp this point has faulted Duverger's analysis of Dutch experience on almost every point. It may also account for the fact that the Netherlands does not really fit Almond's typology of a continental European political system; Gabriel A. Almond, "Comparative Political Systems," *Journal of Politics, 18* (1956), 391–409.

24. See S. J. Fockema Andreae, in *500 Jaren Staten-Generaal,* pp. 215 ff. and J. C. Boogman, "De Britse Gezant Lord Napier over de Nederlandse Volksvertenwoordiging (in 1860)," *Bijdragen en Mededelingen van het Historisch Genootschap, 71* (1957), 189 ff.

25. J. R. Thorbecke, *Parlementaire Redevoeringen, 10,* xii–xiii.

THE SCHOOL ISSUE AND THE FORMATION OF RELIGIOUS PARTIES From the early part of the nineteenth century on, both orthodox Protestants and Catholics had felt uneasy about the increase in secular influences in the Netherlands. But they had tended to find themselves at opposite political poles. The orthodox Protestants were for long practically indistinguishable from the Conservatives, who shared their abhorrence of the French Revolution and, to some extent, their belief in the natural Protestantism of the Dutch nation. The Catholics, on the other hand, resented the Protestant habit of linking together God, Calvinism, the Netherlands, and the House of Orange. After their long condemnation to practical oblivion in the seventeenth and eighteenth centuries, they tended to be hesitant in political action, and at most to expect favorable consideration from the Liberals, whose secular outlook made for a comparatively tolerant attitude toward Catholic demands.

For a long time neither orthodox Protestants nor Catholics were very militant in politics, though for different reasons. The orthodox Protestant elite was so much a part of the upper-class Establishment that most leaders hoped to reverse the "modernist" trends in church and state from the inside.[26] They pointed to past history as witness to the need to return to the ways of the fathers, and generally expected the Orange dynasty to be sympathetic to this cause. Had not the Orange stadholders traditionally been the champions of the Calvinist masses against the latitudinarian regents? Against a predominantly non-orthodox Parliament, they often put their trust in executive privilege.[27] They denied the representativeness of the Liberal *pays légal* and appealed over the head of Parliament to the "people behind the electorate" who had preserved Calvinist orthodoxy with greater purity. But when lower-class elements walked out of the Dutch Reformed Church in fundamentalist protest in 1834, the orthodox

26. Orthodox Protestants divided into roughly three religious groups around the middle of the nineteenth century: (1) the *Ethisch-Irenischen*, who stressed individual conscience and direct missionary activities from one believer to another; (2) the *Confessionelen*, who wished to restore orthodoxy by stricter church organization, and (3) the later *Gereformeerden*, who put great stress on freedom for the local churches; they wished to maintain strict adherence to established doctrine among like-minded individuals but rejected state enforcement. Although Ethical Irenicals and Confessionals were opposed to each other's methods, they usually agreed on the value of preserving a national church, in contrast to the *Gereformeerden*, who did not hesitate to break up the Dutch Reformed Church in the name of true doctrine. The *Gereformeerden* organized partly as a subdivision of the Dutch Reformed Church where they enjoyed local preponderance, partly in separate Gereformeerde Kerken; they have formed the backbone of the Anti-Revolutionary Party, while Ethical Irenicals and Confessionals have associated on the whole with the Christian Historical Union.

27. Anti-Revolutionary spokesmen sought to make a clear distinction between "counterrevolutionaries" who would wish to reverse history and "antirevolutionaries" who, while rejecting the entire spirit of 1789, would yet recognize change. Groen van Prinsterer was strongly influenced by the German political theorist Friedrich Julius Stahl.

elites had sympathized rather than followed suit. Catholics, on the other hand, were afraid to jeopardize their newly gained legal freedoms and thus treaded very carefully and timidly, preferring the safety of isolation to active political participation.[28]

This situation changed, however, from about the 1860s as a result of various factors. Improved communications made for more intensified central government action. The outlook of the dominant Liberals (as well as a number of Conservatives) came to be more secular, and in some cases even frankly anticlerical. Events abroad, such as the German *Kulturkampf* and the conquest of the Papal State in 1870, added further fuel. The smouldering conflict finally broke into the open over the control of education, which assumed increased importance in the wake of social and economic modernization. Schools were vital to religion, culture, and political power. The issue touched not only the elites, moreover, but parents in all walks of life. It thus contributed to a thorough politicization of the still disenfranchised masses.

This new situation had different effects on orthodox Protestants and Catholics. The latter for a time withdrew further into isolation, severing such tenuous links as had previously existed with the Liberals. The orthodox Protestants, on the other hand, found themselves faced with the question whether to break away from what were after all influential positions within the elite. Many hesitated or even refused, preferring compromise to the doubtful pleasures of the political wilderness. But others reasoned as the first prominent orthodox Protestant political leader, Guillaume Groen van Prinsterer, a former private secretary to the king, who held: "In our isolation lies our strength" or, to use a Dutch word: "In our *onafhankelijkheid* (independence), our firmness of principle, lies our force." Opposition to the Liberals thus reduced the Catholics to a fairly passive isolationist stand under the protection of the newly established church hierarchy, while the orthodox Protestants became increasingly activist and even mass-oriented.[29]

The architect of the Calvinist mass movement was a clergyman, Abraham Kuyper.[30] Within a score of years he organized (or helped to organize) a militant daily newspaper (1872); an Anti-School Law League (1872) consciously modeled on the British Anti-Corn Law League; a

28. Catholic emancipation in all its aspects has been brilliantly analyzed by N. de Rooy and L. J. Rogier, *In Vrijheid Herboren* (The Hague, Pax, 1953).

29. Unlike the Catholics, the orthodox Protestants could not rely on a church organization to fight their battles; this partly explains the much greater and earlier development of the Anti-Revolutionary Party as compared to the Roman Catholic Party. Only in 1896 did Catholic deputies underwrite a common program; a federation of constituency parties was not formed until 1904; not until after the arrival of proportional representation and universal suffrage was an articulate national party organization developed (1926).

30. See D. Jellema, "Abraham Kuyper's Attack on Liberalism," *Review of Politics*, *19* (1957), 472–85.

massive petition movement against a new Liberal School Bill (1878) which obtained over 300,000 signatures at a time when the electorate was only a little over a third of this figure; a political party, the Anti-Revolutionary Party (1879), which proclaimed resistance against the world of 1789 and pioneered modern mass-party organization techniques in the Netherlands; an independent Calvinist University (1880) which provided the new movement with its future intelligentsia; and finally a separate church organization, formed after a walk-out of Calvinist fundamentalists from the Dutch Reformed Church in 1886, which then merged six years later with most of the earlier separationists of 1834 into the Gereformeerde Kerken. Through the aid of careful electoral and parliamentary organization, the Anti-Revolutionaries soon came to replace the Conservatives as the main anti-Liberal opposition party.[31]

Their organizational onslaught nothwithstanding, the Anti-Revolutionaries were too weak numerically to destroy the Liberal domination without Catholic support. It took Catholics quite a while to realize that they shared with the Calvinists, as Groen had phrased it, "community of injustice, of faith, and of danger." But a common oppositional stance in Parliament, and common interests in the school issue, slowly led to increased cooperation, first in parliamentary tactics, then at the ballot box, and finally after a constitutional revision of 1887 (during which the religious groups threatened a policy of noncooperation unless the Liberals agreed in principle to the constitutionality of school subsidies) in a joint cabinet (1888–91). From then on, until 1913, Dutch politics witnessed an almost classical alternation between Liberal and (religious) coalition cabinets (see Figure 6.1).

The line between government and opposition became clearly drawn. Though parliamentary bargaining between the parties remained of some importance, ultimate power was increasingly shifted to the constituencies that gave fairly clear verdicts about personalities and policies. The religious parties used their power, first and foremost, to obtain recognition of their common claims on matters of school subsidies, fully accepted in a great national compromise between all parties in 1916–17 during the First World War. Ever since 1918, the religious parties have jointly obtained a majority of seats in Parliament.

Several features of the opposition campaign of the religious groups between 1870 and 1916 should be noted.

Their impact made itself felt only gradually. For a long time their leaders hoped to achieve their aims by action within the elite, through persuasion, petition, and protest. They sought to convert existing authority rather than challenge it. This slow pace was made possible on the one

31. Conservative seats in the lower house declined from 1868 to 1888 as follows: 19, 16, 9, 6, 1, 1; during the same years the Anti-Revolutionaries rose from 7, 16, 9, 15, 19 to 27.

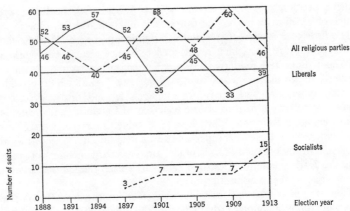

Figure 6.1. Alternating Governments in the Netherlands: The Lower House of Parliament, 1888–1913

Note: *Religious coalitions governed from 1888–91, 1901–05, and 1908–13; Liberal cabinets of somewhat different shades from 1891–1901, 1905–08, and 1913–18. The last two Liberal cabinets were minority governments relying on support from the Socialists and/or one or more religious parties. The 1905 Cabinet was dismissed by Parliament over a defense budget, and was followed by a new minority cabinet of the religious parties which subsequently obtained a majority in the 1909 elections.*

hand because of the diversified character of the governing elites, on the other because the existing social pluralism tended to soften grievances and for a long time kept the masses from political action.

The movement assumed dimensions of real political importance only when the dichotomy of classes and masses was broken. Yet the entry of the masses also took place only gradually and resulted as much from proselytizing activities by existing elite groups downward as from the organization of new counterelites upward. For a long time, moreover, mass action was carefully tempered by a strong insistence on the need to respect public authority and to follow leadership. Toward the end of the nineteenth century, this situation even forced a break between two wings of the orthodox Protestant movement. Kuyper was willing to make all-out use of the organizational weapon to capture government power, but the leader of the Anti-Revolutionary parliamentary group, A. F. de Savornin Lohman, insisted on the need for the extraparliamentary party to leave government and Parliament alone so that it could work out the necessary compromises free from mass pressure. This led to a breakup of the party in 1894, and the continuous existence since then of two orthodox Protestant parties: the more highly disciplined mass organization of the Anti-Revolutionary Party and the more loosely organized Christian Historical Union, formally established in 1908.

The coalition of the religious parties proved mainly a *mariage de raison* in favor of the parallel promotion of minority interests. Catholics and orthodox Protestants shared the desire to promote their own subcultural freedoms against the strong cultural dominance of the Liberals. But in the last analysis this was not so much a claim for exclusive power as a demand for equal rights and social recognition. Catholics, Anti-Revolutionaries, and Christian Historicals disagreed with one another in paradoxical ways, moreover. The Christian Historicals came nearest to wanting the restoration of orthodoxy as the official state religion. They derived their support almost exclusively from adherents of the Dutch Reformed Church who were angered at Kuyper's exodus of 1886.[32] But this church traditionally also organized a very large number of nonfundamentalist Protestants. Consequently, the Christian Historicals tended at one and the same time to identify the Dutch nation with Protestantism (which made for strained relations with the Catholics) and to assume a relatively conciliatory attitude to less fundamentalist elements. The Anti-Revolutionaries, in contrast, preferred the subcultural isolation of true believers, if necessary, to what they feared would at most be an empty official theology. Kuyper rejected all thought of theocratic compulsion and put great store on the independence of local churches. The more militant and mass-based orthodox Protestants, in other words, consciously opted for the lesser evil of a permanent minority position. From this vantage point they found it easier to use hard political tactics, including cooperating with the Catholics against the Liberals. The Catholics, finally, were the most numerous but at the same time most passive supporters of the religious coalition. Afraid to expose themselves to antipapist reaction, they were generally satisfied to be a follower rather than a leader in the religious coalition.

The minority position of each of the religious groupings within the nation as a whole strengthened the introverted orientation of each of them. The lines of political division came to coincide roughly with denominational boundaries. This gave the Dutch party system considerable stability, especially after proportional representation was introduced. But the potential automatism of the expression of electoral opinion led at the same time to some degree of dissociation between electorate, Parliament, and government.

THE IMPACT OF THE ELECTORAL SYSTEM AND OF SUFFRAGE EXTENSION   The potential mass mobilization effect of the school issue was diminished by

32. From 1889 to 1960 the Dutch Reformed Church declined from about 48.7 per cent of the population to 28.3 per cent while the number of those belonging to no church rose from 1.5 per cent to 18.4 per cent. During the same period the number of *Gereformeerden* remained a fairly steady 9 per cent of the population. (See Appendix Table 6.5.) About half the members of the Dutch Reformed Church must be assumed to belong to the various orthodox groups, including those *Gereformeerden* which for local reasons stayed within the Dutch Reformed Church (see n. 26). The latter group appoints roughly a quarter of Dutch Reformed ministers.

certain features in the electoral system which existed until 1917: a district system requiring an absolute majority on the first ballot, with a second ballot between the two top candidates in case no candidate won in the first round.[33]

The geographic element in electoral representation worked to the disadvantage of the more militant sections of the religious opposition groups. As shown by Hofstee,[34] social modernization has tended to spread from the more internationally, commercially oriented north and west of the country to the more traditional regions in the east and south. Among the restricted electorate of the north and west, the Liberals for a long time obtained a majority, so that relatively few Catholics and Anti-Revolutionaries were elected from these regions. The religious groups thus drew most of their earliest strength from more traditional areas where a strong measure of paternalism tended to dominate.[35] Differences in the franchise between urban and rural areas tended to reinforce this situation. Generally speaking, the franchise requirements were considerably higher in the cities than in the rural districts. But they were kept high enough in both to give an advantage to the upper classes, which were disproportionally Liberal in orientation. Gerrymandering further strengthened this overrepresentation of Liberals. The religious groups were thus reduced to their more conservative bastions. They did not fully profit from their massive pluralities in the Catholic south nor could they derive proportionate strength from their sizable minorities in the north and northwest and in the larger cities generally. They only slowly overcame this handicap when Catholics in mixed areas learned to vote for orthodox Protestant candidates.[36] But not

33. Until 1887 members were usually elected in two-member districts, each member being elected at large for a four-year period at alternate two-year elections. From 1887 most members sat for single-member districts, which were also introduced for the larger cities in 1897. For details, see chapter on the Netherlands in Stein Rokkan, ed., *An International Guide to Electoral Statistics* (forthcoming), and M. Albrecht, *De Invloed van het Kiesstelsel op de Samenstelling van de Volksvertegenwoordiging en op de Vorming van de Regering* (Amsterdam, De Arbeiderspers, 1960). It is a pity that the inaccurate interpretation of Dutch electoral experience by Enid Lakeman and James D. Lambert, *Voting in Democracies* (London, Faber, 1955) has been given a wider circulation in Harry Eckstein and David E. Apter, eds., *Comparative Politics: A Reader* (New York, Free Press, 1963), pp. 292–95.

34. E. W. Hofstee has documented this hypothesis with a careful study of the Dutch birthrate; see his "De Groei van de Nederlandse Bevolking," in *Drift en Koers: een halve eeuw Sociale Verandering in Nederland* (Assen, Van Gorcum, 1962), pp. 13–84. See also Litten, *Geografische Verdeeling,* passim.

35. Between 1848 and 1870 Catholic districts of the south were often represented by Liberal Catholics from the West, dubbed Papo-Thorbeckianen. This was no longer possible after 1870 when a highly conservative Catholic Electoral Association *Noord-Brabant* captured the nomination process for local candidates.

36. It proved easier to persuade Catholics to vote for Protestant candidates than vice versa. Profits from electoral cooperation thus accrued almost exclusively to the Anti-Revolutionaries, which strengthened their leadership posture in Dutch political life.

until the introduction of proportional representation in 1917 was this disadvantage fully overcome.

The franchise itself was extended slowly. (See Appendix Table 6.1.) Until 1887 it remained at the same level, effectively restricting the suffrage to one in eight adult males. In 1887 the electorate was expanded to about a quarter of the adult male population; it was doubled to about half in 1896. For the next twenty years no further changes in the electoral law proved politically possible. But the electorate slowly grew from about 52 per cent in 1897 to about 68 per cent in 1913 as a consequence of automatic enfranchisement through economic prosperity.[37] Universal suffrage was only obtained in 1917 as part of the national compromise which also resulted in equal subsidies for religious schools. This slow expansion of the electorate prevented the sudden inrush of the masses in the *pays légal* and facilitated the careful elaboration of compromises.

Mass influence made itself felt even more slowly in Parliament and in government than at the ballot box. Between 1850 and 1870, no less than 66 per cent of the Anti-Revolutionary parliamentary group in the lower house [38] were members of the nobility (as against a much lower 36 per cent for the Conservatives, 15 per cent for the Catholics, and 10 per cent for the Liberals). This percentage declined to 63 per cent for the period 1871–87, and 45 per cent from 1888–96. Even after Kuyper broke with De Savornin Lohman and "all the men with the double names" in 1894, the number of Anti-Revolutionary deputies belonging to the aristocracy remained comparatively high (17 per cent, as against 53 per cent for the Christian Historicals and 23 per cent for the Catholics for the period 1896–1917).[39] Similar tendencies prevailed in ministerial recruitment.[40] Obviously even noblemen could be activist politicians, and some were. But at all times potential Anti-Revolutionary militancy was further restrained by the need to govern with the support of the much less activist Catholics and Christian Historicals and to keep the confidence of the constituencies. Figure 6.2 shows that the religious coalition gained or lost power mainly through votes for or against Anti-Revolutionary candidates.

---

37. See Appendix Table 6.1 and G. M. Bos, *Mr. S. van Houten* (Purmerend, Muusses, 1952), pp. 117–18.

38. Until 1917 the provincial states (which elect the upper chamber in Holland) were constitutionally bound to make their choice from a list of those who paid the highest direct taxes (until 1887 this list contained at most one name for every 3,000 people living in a province, and from 1887 to 1917 one name for every 1,500). From 1887 to 1917 eligibility was extended to those who had served in high political or administrative office. See J. Th. de Ruwe, *De Eerste Kamer der Staten-Generaal* (Dissertation, Nijmegen, 1957), pp. 4–6.

39. Calculations by J. J. de Jong, as published by A. Hoogerwerf, *Protestantisme en Progressiviteit* (Meppel, J. A. Boom, 1964), p. 176–77.

40. See the excellent study by Mattei Dogan and Maria Scheffer-van der Veen, "Le Personnel Ministériel Hollandais," *L'Année Sociologique* (1957–58), pp. 95–125, in particular pp. 103 ff.

Kuyper might harangue the unprincipledness of the *kleurloze middenstof* (the colorless floaters); he could not obtain a majority at the ballot box without their support.

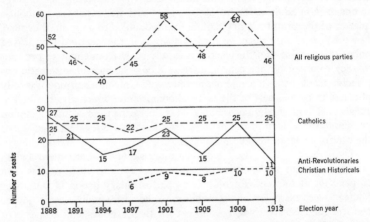

Figure 6.2. Number of Seats for the Three Religious Parties in the Lower House of Parliament, 1888–1913 (total number of seats = 100)

The slow process of franchise extension thus blunted the edge of the religious opposition groups. But it had considerable influence on the internal structure and relative strength of the parties. Generally speaking, the religious parties handled the participation crisis with more success than the Liberals. Perhaps the most crucial date in Dutch politics is 1894. A fairly radical Liberal Cabinet had proposed extending the franchise to all men who could read and write and did not live on charity (this would have amounted in practice to about 74 per cent of all adult males). The proposal met with serious parliamentary resistance. It was first whittled down and then provoked a dissolution of Parliament in which the Cabinet was defeated and all parties split. The Catholics recovered their unity with little difficulty. As we saw above, internal conflict led to a lasting separation between Christian Historicals and Anti-Revolutionaries, but the need for electoral and government coalition-building tended to hold these parties fairly closely together even so. The Liberals, however, who had only barely achieved a measure of party organization, were split into no less than three groups: a right, a center, and a radical left. The latter actively propagated universal suffrage, sometimes in direct cooperation with Socialists who were campaigning for the same end inside and outside Parliament. This stand of the Radicals must have strengthened reformist tendencies among the Socialists. But as a whole the Liberal movement was too elitist and too little organized to manage the demands of the rising working classes. This inevitably reduced it to a relatively small, mainly upper- and middle-class party once universal suffrage was introduced in 1917.

Universal suffrage was accompanied by proportional representation and the compulsory vote. This was decided partly as a matter of abstract justice: it seemed the natural corollary of the principle that each vote should have equal value. But at the same time it also had practical political meaning. It was thought right that Parliament should present a perfect mirror of the different groups that composed the nation. This fitted in well with the isolationist tendencies of the various minority cultures. It also underlined the historic separation of government and Parliament. While Parliament represented the nation, and government was fully responsible to it, as a more "national" institution the government yet stood somewhat apart from particular cleavages.[41] But it followed from this that future elections were mainly to choose parliamentary representatives, not governments.

THE CHALLENGE OF THE WORKING CLASSES   The potentially alienating effect of the long-delayed extension of the franchise was partly offset by the circumstance that the full effects of the Industrial Revolution were felt comparatively late in the Netherlands. This affected the development of the Dutch labor movement in a number of ways.

First, the lesser orders of society had for a long time been the passive objects of paternalism and philanthropy. The position of the existing elites seemed invulnerable, and they ruled with considerable confidence. The poor thus lived under strong outward and inward social control and in such poverty that little energy was left to raise themselves out of this position.[42]

Second, the growth of a modern labor movement was preceded by the emancipation movement of Calvinists and Catholics. For a considerable time, both Calvinist and Catholic reaction to the "social problem" tended to be one of moralization and negative antisocialism. Initially, many lower-class people outside the more traditional areas were thus lost to the churches, especially in certain parts of the rural areas in the north and west where the churches themselves had become highly rationalistic, and in the industrializing cities to which many workers from the more traditional countryside emigrated. But at the same time a sense of historic grievance and political and ecclesiastical organization tended to keep many other

41. See C. W. de Vries, *Cort van der Linden: de visie van een groot staatsman,* (The Hague, Nijhoff, 1952).

42. See in particular I. J. Brugmans, *De Arbeidende Klasse in Nederland in de 19e eeuw* (3d ed. Utrecht, Het Spectrum, 1958), and L.G.J. Verberne, *De Nederlandse Arbeidersbeweging in de Negentiende Eeuw* (Amsterdam, Van Kampen, 1950).

would-be proletarians within the religious groups. Within both the Calvinist and the Catholic subcultures, effective working-class organizations soon
developed. Though these may have been instruments of continuing social
control, they also eventually helped to democratize the religious parties
from the inside and to force them to take a more positive attitude toward
the claims of the new working classes.[43]

Third, as a consequence of late industrialization the first working-class
movements did not stem from an industrial proletariat. Roughly speaking,
three early groups may be distinguished.

Artisans were first in establishing crafts unions, which sought mainly
to provide their members with a measure of social security and intellectual
enlightenment. Their political orientation tended to be either Radical-
Liberal or Anti-Revolutionary according to their religious outlook. They
helped to strengthen the more radical wings of both movements and thus
to prevent their too close identification with the existing social order.
They did not resort to revolutionary action, but put their trust in suffrage
extension, for which they campaigned actively.

In the second place, the agricultural depression of the latter part of the
nineteenth century, led in certain parts of the country (notably in
Groningen, Friesland, and Noord-Holland) to a highly radical outlook
among impoverished farmers and agricultural laborers. The earliest Radical and Socialist deputies were elected from constituencies in these areas,
which have preserved a fairly left-wing voting record to this day.

Finally, some manual laborers acquired an early socialist consciousness,
due to a special combination of religious and socioeconomic factors. Some
of the older cities, especially Amsterdam, had an autochthonous proletariat, eking out a precarious living in the harbors, warehouses, and inland
transport. In some other regions, sweatshop industries (textiles, potteries,
etc.) provided an easy target for socialist propagandists. Finally, canal-
and peat-digging led to unusual working conditions that tended to nourish
both rebelliousness and a strong sectarianism. Most of these groups devel-

43. See R. Hagoort, *De Christelijk Sociale Beweging* (Franeker, T. Wever, 1956);
W. G. Versluis, *Beknopte Geschiedenis van de Katholieke Arbeidersbeweging in
Nederland* (Nijmegen, Dekker and Van de Vegt 1949); and M. Ruppert, *De Nederlandse Vakbeweging* (2 vols. Haarlem, De Erven F. Bohn, 1953).
In both Calvinist and Catholic circles considerable conflict broke out between those
who considered the "social problem" above all a moral issue and those who demanded
effective working-class organization. For a time, militant elements in both camps
combined to form an antisocialist, but interconfessional union. The Catholic Bishops
eventually permitted the establishment of autonomous working-class unions on the
condition that these would be exclusively Catholic. From then on the *Christelijk-
Nationaal Vakverbond* (CNV) became a purely orthodox Protestant organization.
Oddly enough, the word *Christelijk* is now often used interchangeably with orthodox
Protestant in the Netherlands. Membership in the (overwhelmingly Socialist) NVV
was until recently forbidden to Catholics; but the controversial pastoral letter *De
Katholiek in het Openbare Leven van deze Tijd* (Utrecht, 1954) was rescinded on this
point in 1965.

oped an anarchist outlook, which was easily fostered by the absence of the vote, and a belief in the possibility of a drastic reversal of the socio-economic system through spontaneous revolutionary action which tends to be typical of small-scale economic organization.[44]

Fourth, late industrialization exposed the Dutch working-class movement to considerable influence from abroad where socialist ideologies and union organization had developed much more strongly. The influence of French syndicalism, German Marxism, and British New Unionism are all easily traced. They led to a certain amount of fragmentation of political action, to highly doctrinaire debates among socialist intellectuals, and to various organizational splits in both the political and union wings of the working-class movement.

The first effective Socialist leader was an ex-clergyman, F. Domela Nieuwenhuis. He had great oratorical influence, and was elected to Parliament in 1888 (after a short imprisonment for *lèse-majesté*). Once there, he was completely cold-shouldered by his bourgeois opponents. After that he turned increasingly anarchist. When he committed the first Socialist Party, the Sociaal-Democratische Bond, to a rejection of parliamentary methods, a number of his followers broke away and established the Sociaal-Democratische Arbeiderspartij (SDAP, 1894).[45] It adopted an orthodox Marxist line, taking its program almost literally from the Erfurt Program of the German Social Democratic Party. Marxism provided a particularly useful formula: it helped to foster the class consciousness of the Dutch workers, so exposed to diverting political traditions; it "scientized" hope, and thus made life more bearable in what was otherwise a relatively weak social and political position; and it vindicated concentration on the immediate political battle, seemingly sanctified by long-term revolutionary ideology.

Participation in electoral and parliamentary battles soon led the SDAP to acquire a vested interest in the existing regime. Had not the old Socialist slogans: "The Vote or Revolution!" and "Voting Right or Fist Right!" been a fitting portent? Franchise restrictions led the party into a highly un-Marxian wooing of poorer but enfranchised farmers in the north. Conscious of the need to attract Calvinist and Catholic workers, the party went on record as early as 1902 that it did not oppose in principle the granting of subsidies to religious schools. It entered into informal electoral agreements with the Liberals to promote the common cause of

44. See Lorwin, "Syndicalism," in the forthcoming *Encyclopaedia of the Social Sciences,* and Lorwin, "Working Class Politics." The relation between syndicalism and small-scale economic organization has been stressed particularly by H. B. Wiardi Beckman in his excellent study, *Het Syndicalisme in Frankrijk* (Amsterdam, Em. Querido's Uitg.-mij., 1931).

45. See D. J. Wansink, *Het Socialisme op de Tweesprong—de geboorte van de* S.D.A.P. (Haarlem, Tjeenk Willink, 1939).

universal suffrage. Participation in Parliament gave ample opportunity for
informal pressures and coalition building on specific issues. In 1913 the
Socialists were even offered some seats in a Liberal government; some
parliamentary leaders were tempted, but the offer was rejected by a more
militant party congress. World War I, in which the Netherlands remained
neutral, nevertheless led to a further rapprochement with the bourgeois
parties and to the critical assumption of a measure of executive responsibility, notably in local government. The Socialists fully shared in the great
national compromise of 1916–17 in which full parity for the religious
schools, universal suffrage, and proportional representation were accepted
by all the major parties.

Full integration in the political system took much longer, however,
than these developments seemed to forecast. This was due partly to continuous opposition from the left, but mainly to the continued powerful
position of the religious and Liberal parties.

The decisive break with the anarcho-syndicalists had come in 1903 after
a somewhat lukewarm attempt at a general strike had foundered on a
resolute stand by the (Kuyper) government.[46] This led to bitter recrimination within the working-class movement. The anarcho-syndicalists accused the Socialist officials of having betrayed proletarian solidarity. The
Socialists countered with the argument that there was little value in badly
organized action in behalf of unclear political and economic goals. Some
of the better organized industrial unions went on to establish a new Trades
Union Congress (NVV, 1906) as a rival to the earlier, mainly syndicalist
Nationaal Arbeids Secretariaat (1893). The new federation was given a
powerful lift by the now fast-arriving large-scale industrialization. The
NVV unions concentrated on effective organization and collective bargaining, and soon became part of the system rather than a threat to it.[47]

In 1909 a group of left-wing Marxists were expelled from the SDAP
for having published an opposition journal within the party. For a number
of years they remained a minor sect. But during World War I they made
common cause with pacifist, anarchist, syndicalist, and other revolutionary
groups who jointly organized Revolutionary-Socialist Committees against
Mobilization, High Prices, and Rationing. In 1918 the party renamed itself
Communistische Partij Holland. It obtained a small but fairly constant
vote, notably in those regions which had acquired an anarchist outlook
before the workers were given the right to vote.

But the SDAP's greatest setback came in 1918. Its hope for a large increase in votes under universal suffrage was dashed when it obtained only

46. For a model analysis, see A.J.C. Rüter, *De Spoorwegstakingen van 1903* (Leiden,
Brill, 1935).
47. See Fr. de Jong Edz., *Om de Plaats van de Arbeid* (Amsterdam, De Arbeiderspers, 1956).

22 per cent of the national vote (against 2.3 per cent for the Communists). Revolutionary rumblings in Germany and in some Dutch army camps then led the Socialist leader, P. J. Troelstra, into an impromptu statement that the revolution would not stop at the Dutch border, and that the time had come for the Socialists to take over the reins of government. No effective steps were taken to carry out this threat, but the Cabinet (composed mainly of the religious parties) reacted by mobilizing its religious and bourgeois supporters in a clamor of national indignation which culminated in a mass demonstration around the Queen in the Hague. Troelstra's rashness was strongly criticized by other Socialist leaders, and he tried to retreat as far as possible from the implications of his statement. Nevertheless, the Socialist movement was again effectively isolated from the other political parties.

Between the wars, the SDAP tended to live a fairly lonely life in Parliament. Conflict among other parties might occasionally give it a chance to influence proceedings and even to help defeat a Cabinet. But its strength never rose above a quarter of the national vote. None of the other parties (with the sole exception of a small radical party) seriously considered forming a governing coalition with the Socialists. Although the party opposed the government, it was not an opposition that could seriously hope to replace it. On both sides relations were somewhat strained: for a considerable time the Socialists refused to attend the opening of Parliament and to cheer the Queen; the bourgeois parties retaliated by continuing to exclude the Socialists from certain official posts. Inevitably the Socialist movement assumed a somewhat introverted character. The party built up a large number of ancillary organizations and gave its supporters the fullness of life which their estrangement from the churches prevented them from getting elsewhere. The movement succeeded in raising the cultural level and political consciousness of Dutch labor to a considerable degree. But it added to the characteristically strong ideological segmentation of Dutch social life. The party found itself in a kind of ghetto, from which it could not free itself without outside help.

Not until the Depression of the 1930s and the rise of Nazism sapped erstwhile democratic certainties did a change occur. In the early 1930s some left-wing elements in the SDAP attempted to steer the movement back into revolutionary channels. They proposed to organize mass campings of the unemployed outside the cities and to engage in active street demonstrations. The SDAP leadership rejected these schemes and the leftist opposition was ejected from the party in 1932. After this the SDAP turned increasingly to Plan-Socialism. In 1935 it put forward an elaborate national plan that sought to relieve unemployment by large-scale public works and other injections of purchasing power in the slack economy. The *Plan van de Arbeid* signaled the wish of the Socialists to cooperate with other classes and political groups for the rehabilitation of the existing economy. A similar attitude developed in other parties and facilitated a slow rapprochement. Also, the threat of Nazism turned most Socialists away from their earlier pacifist leanings. National defense and national symbols, including the monarchy, were more readily accepted. Finally, the long-standing coalition of Catholics (who had moved to the left under the pressure of universal suffrage and new economic insights) and the Anti-Revolutionaries (who had assumed a very conservative position under their leader H. Colijn in the 1930s) broke up in 1939. The Socialists were invited to enter a Cabinet composed of Catholics, Christian Historicals, and assorted Liberals. The Socialist leader, J. W. Albarda, advocated entering the Cabinet in a confidential memorandum to the party executive that throws a clear light on the party's quandary.[48] Albarda argued first that Socialists had traditionally overestimated the numerical significance of the proletariat by wrongly including in it small peasants, petty bourgeois, officials, and so forth:

> These groups live on economic and social bases different from those of the working classes; they also have other social ideologies and ideals, to a certain extent anticapitalistic, it is true, but not socialist.
>
> Secondly, many of our old theses and dogmas, which had unrivaled value in bringing the working class to consciousness and organization, have now become a liability for further growth of the socialist movement.

Albarda pointed particularly to the need to abandon dogmatic insistence on the class struggle and on the conflict between religion and socialism, which he called "a liberal prejudice garbed in Marxist dress." If such a change did not occur he prophesied doom for the party, because traditional allegiance alone would not suffice and would inevitably lead to eventual demoralization. The only hope, he argued, was to penetrate the traditional clienteles of the religious parties:

> It is quite understandable that all bourgeois parties, not least the Catholics, are afraid of the arrival of a Cabinet with Social Democrats. . . . For from the very day that the SDAP becomes a governing party (provided this is on a firm footing), its position changes. Then a bridge will have been built over the abyss that now yawns between the religious and the socialist part of our nation. Then traffic will begin over this bridge . . . A new growth will start for our movement, and this growth will not be easily halted. The hitherto impregnable voting masses of the religious part of the nation will become potentially available for our efforts.

48. This memorandum has been printed in full in the dissertation of H. M. Ruitenbeek, *Het Ontstaan van de Partij van de Arbeid* (Amsterdam, De Arbeiderspers, 1955), pp. 249–54.

Two Socialist ministers entered the government in 1939, later than in any other Western European country. The new government was soon to be the Dutch government in exile.

During the occupation many Socialists hoped for drastic changes through a complete restructuring of the party system. In 1945 the SDAP merged with the Radical Party, a number of left-wing Catholics and Christian Historicals, and some independents in a new Partij van de Arbeid (Labor Party). But the 1946 elections killed its extravagantly high hopes: it won only 28.3 per cent of the vote. Catholics, Christian Historicals, and Anti-Revolutionaries remained on the whole faithful to the traditional parties, and a Communist upsurge nibbled away at the Socialist Left. From 1945 to 1958 the Socialists nevertheless formed a leading element in coalitions otherwise composed of Catholics and, after 1948, also of some representatives of the smaller parties. For ten years, the popular Socialist leader, W. Drees, was Prime Minister. The party edged slowly upward, thanks to gains from both Communists and the religious parties, until it reached its all-time high of 32.7 per cent in 1956, for a while outranking the Catholics in size. Its electoral fortunes turned again in 1958, however, and the party was excluded from the government. It did not do very well in opposition and fell back in 1963 to its 1946 level. (For full data see Appendix Table 6.1.) But the Socialists returned to the Cabinet after an interim crisis in the spring of 1965.

Cleavages and Consensus in the Dutch System

The simultaneous emancipation of minority groups resulted in an exceedingly rigid segmentation of Dutch society. At least three distinct subcultures coexist: an orthodox Protestant one (comprising some 20–25 per cent of the nation); a Catholic one (numbering over a third); and a "general" one. The latter comprises less than half the population and, being composed mainly of Dutchmen who are neither orthodox Protestant nor Catholic, it tends to assume a rather special place on the political continuum. The "general" subculture is moreover further subdivided into various groups. On the religious side it contains more or less latitudinarian Protestants, humanists, and agnostics. Politically, it is divided between Liberals on the one hand, and various Socialist groups on the other. The latter form in many respects a special subculture of their own. It should be stressed that the religious subcultures hardly answer to Gabriel Almond's description of "significant survivals, 'outcroppings,' of older cultures and their political manifestations," remnants that are attributable only to "uneven patterns of development" and "failure on the part of the middle classes in the nineteenth century to carry through a thorough-going secularization of the political culture." [49] On the contrary, far from being traditionalist remnants, they themselves pioneered modern political tech-

49. Almond, "Comparative Political Systems," pp. 405 ff.

niques and have on the whole adjusted well to the processes of modern industrial development. The threat of secularization has been countered by a large number of burgeoning social organizations *within* each sub-culture that seek to cope with the complex social problems of the modern industrial era and do so successfully on an explicitly religious basis.

The pattern of subcultural isolation comes out most clearly in the educational field. Since the school pact of 1916–17, churches and parent organizations of every religious outlook have been entitled to full state subsidies (determined on the basis of the cost of normal public schools), provided they meet certain legal requirements as to qualified teachers, curriculum, and number of pupils. Whereas two-thirds of Dutch children still went to government schools in 1900, the proportion today is only a little over one-fourth. (See Appendix Table 6.6.) Separate schooling has spread from elementary to secondary and technical education, and for some years both the Calvinist and Catholic universities have been subsidized practically on a par with the older national universities. Organizations for recreation and culture are generally split along denominational lines. Unions, employers, workers, farmers, and *Middenstanders* reflect a tripartite division, of general, Catholic, and Calvinist organizations, while hospitals, old people's homes, and to a lesser extent government-subsidized cooperative housing projects show even greater pluralist divisions. A Dutchman can live an isolated life within a homogeneous ideological environment from the cradle to the grave, meeting people of different outlook only in the street, the army, and perhaps in factory or office and more recently on television screens. The technical term used for this segmentation is *Verzuiling*. The image is one in which the national state is supported by a variety of pillars (*zuilen*). The word has become slightly pejorative, however, as if "pillari-zation" inevitably meant "compartmentalization" or, in another metaphor, as if "columnization" meant in practice "colonization" by a tight ideological cadre.

J. P. Kruijt, a Dutch sociologist who is the recognized elder statesman of *Verzuiling* studies, has constructed a table (Table 6.1) to indicate the extent to which segmentation has moved forward in different social spheres. The interpretation of this table is complicated by the fact that the Dutch Reformed Church continues to organize both fundamentalist and non-fundamentalist elements; since there are many shades of both it is difficult to quantify the real degree of *Verzuiling* within this denomination.[50]

From all available data it appears that the extent of segmentation is still increasing both with respect to the number of formal organizations on

50. Although most orthodox Protestants within the Dutch Reformed Church have been drawn into separate organizations, some groups have resisted this trend on principle; they have not wanted to see the nation and the church surrendered by default to the less fundamentalist or agnostic elements of the population.

Table 6.1 Degree of Segmentation (Verzuildheidsgraad) in the Netherlands (percentage of persons belonging to different churches, or to no church, organized in subcultural associations or participating in subcultural activities)

	Catholic	Calvinist (Gereformeerd)	Dutch Reformed	Other[a]	No church[a]
Census (1960)	40.4	9.3	28.3	3.6	18.4
Elementary school (1957)	90[b]	90[b]	50[b]		10[b]
Farmers unions (1953)	95[b]	90[b]	37[b]		practically nil
Labor unions (1958)	90[b]	90[b]	30[b]		practically nil
Membership in Radio Association (1955)	89	94	32	18	4
Party vote, lower house (1959)	84.3	95[b]	32[b]	very few	very few
Newspaper reading (exclusively religious dailies) (1955)	79	58	9	8	1
Active membership associations (1955) religious, plus other	77	80	43	40	14
exclusively religious	71	73	36	33	13
Book reading (last book read exclusively religious) (1955)	16	39	19	18	15

a. For Other and No church, the figures represent percentages of membership in Catholic or Protestant organizations or activities in a Catholic or Protestant context.

b. Approximate figure.

Source: J.P. Kruijt, *Verzuiling* (Zaandijk, Heynis, 1959), p. 40.

explicitly ideological lines and the hold of Catholic and Protestant organizations, as contrasted with "general" ones, on their members.[51] This trend
is strengthened by the current practice of distributing government subsidies indiscriminately to organizations of all three subcultures and carefully balancing government advisory bodies in all walks of life with
representatives from each.

In view of these sharp divisions, what have been the factors that have
prevented the social system from flying apart? What has restrained any
subculture, or any two subcultures in coalition, from destroying potential
adversaries by political weapons? The answers must be sought partly in
historical factors, partly in certain system-sustaining forces still at work
to this day. The following historical explanations seem to me suggestive.

To reiterate a point made previously: throughout Dutch history the
leading political groups have tended to occupy a strong position. None of
the fundamental opposition movements have been able to displace the
existing power holders in one stroke. The ruling groups have had little
fear that this might happen. Consequently, they have tended to adopt a
relatively permissive attitude toward political opposition. There have been
little violence and little political repression in Dutch public life. There
have also been practically no attempts at conspiratorial activity, which
would have seemed somewhat ridiculous in the face of certain failure and
also somewhat superfluous because less violent means were generally
available for the expression of political discontent.

At no time have the Dutch ruling circles been completely closed or
homogeneous. Power resources have usually been spread so widely that
single groups have had little chance to impose their will without serious
friction. This has nurtured a feeling of mutual tolerance, strengthened a
mutual willingness to seek accommodation, and made people ready to
leave others alone provided they were left alone themselves.

This natural pluralism caused differences of opinion to generate relatively little heat, strong reciprocal prejudices notwithstanding. Protest
groups tended to become politicized only slowly. Political militancy was
tempered at all times by those sympathizers who wished to work from
within rather than against the existing regime, while even the more
militant thought in terms of increased influence rather than of actual
monopoly of power. Consider a typical passage from that great mass
organizer, Abraham Kuyper, addressing the party faithful of the Anti-
Revolutionary Party on the eve of the election that was to carry him into
the prime ministership (1901):

More than a quarter of the Chamber, we [that is, the Anti-Revolutionaries, without Catholic support] can never win; in this situation all the clamor for a ministry of our own can make no other impression on insiders or outsiders than foolhardiness, rooted in nothing, which we as Christians should resist. It is easy to blind ourselves to the question where to find men prepared and able to solve the big questions which our policy, based on our principles, faces . . . In practically all bureaus, in all organs of the state, in all prominent posts, the leaders are able and influential, I readily admit, but not given to our principles.[52]

Slow accommodation made for a gradual domestication of opposing groups in the pre-existing pluralist system and facilitated a transfer of older traditions of compromise to political newcomers.

The strong divisions into which the successive waves of emancipationist action by Calvinists, Catholics, and Socialists split Dutch society never extended to all government institutions. The electorate and Parliament came to be divided much more than the Cabinet, the judiciary, and the bureaucracy.

If elections and political conflict drove parties apart, the need for government forced them together. Government cooperation could be achieved only on matters of common concern, not on behalf of too particularist demands. Once in government, former opposition groups could not always convert their nominal powers into concrete action; lack of experience and internal dissension might give older government groups the opportunity to continue to exercise power even when they were reduced to a minority position in Parliament. Between 1848 and 1887, for instance, domestic squabbles often forced the Liberals to leave the reins of government to Conservative statesmen even though the number of Conservative deputies dwindled rapidly. The Liberals, in turn, could still form cabinets in the first decades of this century, although their forces were by then on the decline, because the remaining seats in Parliament were divided between the rising Socialists, on the one hand, and the religious parties on the other. When the coalition of Anti-Revolutionaries, Catholics, and Christian Historicals broke up in 1925, statesmen from these parties continued to preside over quasi-national "extra-parliamentary," "business," "personality," or *intermezzo* (caretaker) governments because they at least agreed on the undesirability of entering into a coalition with the Socialists.

Similarly, the bureaucracy has tended to be a political stabilizer. For a long time educational advantage made the Dutch bureaucracy something of a Liberal cum Christian Historical reserve; Anti-Revolutionaries, Catholics, and Socialists initially found it easier to secure specific concessions

52. Cited by P. A. Diepenhorst, in *Schrift en Historie—gedenkboek bij het vijftigjarig bestaan der georganiseerde Anti-Revolutionaire Partij* (Kampen, Uitg.-mij. J.H. Kok, 1929), p. 255.

from it than to try to take it over. More recently a political element seems
to have become more prominent in appointments and promotions. But a
spoils system has at no time been desired or countenanced in Dutch
administration. Newcomers, even from partisan milieus, have generally
accepted the view that the national interest should prevail over party
concerns. Party appointments have therefore not led to increased bitterness among the various groups, but rather to new forms of brokerage and
collaboration among them.

The monarchy, too, has tended to play a substantial integrating function.
For a considerable time Liberals (in the nineteenth century) and Socialists
(until well into the twentieth) thought the Crown too much a part of the
Conservative Establishment. Catholics have often resented the habit of
orthodox Protestants of claiming the House of Orange as their private
property. But as each subcultural group became more fully emancipated,
it found less difficulty in accepting the Crown as a symbol of political community above party—a development made easier by the long tenure of
Queen Wilhelmina (1890–1948), who deliberately broke away from the
Court ghetto in which she found herself immured [53] to become eventually
the great personal symbol of national resistance in 1940–45. More recently
certain personal developments in the royal family jolted the complacency
of those who thought the Crown could retain its earlier symbolic value
while the members of the "national family" still had complete freedom to
live their lives according to their own ideas and wishes. But these events do
not seem to have lessened the confidence of the great majority of the nation
in the value of monarchy as an institution. The Netherlands Institute for
Public Opinion found a drop in expressed preferences for monarchy from
86 per cent in favor in February 1964 (after the first intimation of difficulties in connection with the intended marriage of Princess Irene), to 74 per
cent in June 1965, when the engagement of the Crown Princess to a German commoner, Claus von Amsberg, was announced. But at the same time
the number who favored a Republic remained practically stationary at
9 per cent, the difference being made up of an increased number of "don't
knows." Disenchantment with the monarchy seemed to be increasing,
however, in intellectual circles and may acquire political significance in the
long run. But even there, and much more so among political leaders, there
was considerable reluctance to lose the Crown as a symbol of Nation
above party.

But perhaps the greatest contribution of the past has been the effect of
accumulating experience. Even staunch isolationists have learned that a
strong insistence on subcultural rights need not prevent day-to-day cooperation with representatives from rival groups. Each subculture has

53. See Queen Wilhelmina's Memoirs, *Lonely, but Not Alone* (London, Hutchin-
son, 1960).

gained considerable recognition for its special claims and has obtained practically all that can be had through state action. All groups are reasonably certain that future claims will be honored as far as possible through a compromise sharing of state benefits. They have learned from painful experience that other issues are not negotiable and hence not enforceable through state action. Unfulfilled demands (like special Sunday legislation for the Calvinists or permission for public processions throughout the country for the Catholics) may be brandished as signs of party identification, but they have proved to be so much *hors concours* that they no longer block practical cooperation on other matters.

All these historical factors would count for little, however, if there were no contemporary forces sustaining the system. Of course there are.

The divisive effects of segmentation are softened by the circumstance that none of the subcultures has much chance of acquiring an independent majority, while there is at the same time little advantage to any two of them in forming a lasting coalition against the third. Calvinists and Catholics have been united in their demand for separate schools and recognition of other common subcultural interests, but many historical sentiments and contemporary issues divide them. Both may well silently acknowledge the value of the "general" subculture as a potential counterweight against rival religious groups. Calvinists and "generalists" combine to resist too explicitly Catholic wishes, while Catholics and "generalists" share a distaste for too puritan attitudes on the part of the more outright orthodox Protestants and together reject their claim that Calvinism is (or should be) the foundation of Dutch national life.

This circumstance is reinforced by tactical considerations on the parliamentary scene. For many years now numerical relations have been such that neither the combined religious groupings nor the nonconfessional ones have had an adequate working majority in the lower house. Ever since 1939 the Netherlands has therefore been governed by cabinets of a mixed religious-nonreligious character. This has tended to lessen old antagonisms. Anticlericalism has practically disappeared from Dutch politics for reasons of both conviction and political expediency. Both Liberals and Socialists learned long ago that they are individually and jointly powerless. They can obtain a share of government power only by the grace of one or more of the religious parties. They are also well aware that their long-term electoral chances depend on their ability to gain votes from traditionally religious quarters. Ever since the war, they have therefore consciously sought to de-emphasize their earlier restrictive *Weltanschauung* traditions. Both have recognized publicly the positive value of Christianity. The Labor Party has even arranged for explicitly Catholic, orthodox Protestant, and humanist working groups within its fold.

Coalition politics has in the same way contributed to a lessening of socioeconomic tensions. The three religious parties have a much more heterogeneous social following than either Liberals or Socialists. This has tended to draw the religious parties toward a centrist position and to make them natural brokers between conflicting interests, first within their own ambit, but indirectly also in society at large. Tactical and electoral considerations have simultaneously pushed the Socialist and Liberal parties in the direction of what Otto Kirchheimer has called the catch-all type of political party.[54] A recent study has documented the observation that party programs of the main Dutch parties have increasingly converged on some points since 1946; it appears that elite groups tend to be in closer agreement on policy issues than potential party clienteles.[55]

Interest group politics have made for many links across ideological boundary lines. So far the more specific industrial associations, as well as individual enterprises, have most successfully resisted the *Verzuiling* trend. But even where interest groups have themselves been subject to ideological divisions, the need for effective promotion of joint interests has usually made for frequent confederal contacts among them. This has kept communications between the *zuilen* more open than they might otherwise have been. At the same time, it has had a significant influence on the way policy is made in the Netherlands. On any one matter there are usually a great number of interest groups involved. This leads to very complex consultations· and maneuverings. To operate in this complex situation with any chance of success usually necessitates considerable discretionary authority for the leaders of the interest groups involved. This encourages strong centralization of power at the top. But such leaders are therefore also able to take the responsibility for far-reaching decisions (which may be of strategic importance to the government). Complex compromises usually emerge from these deliberations. To make them digestible for widely different ideological groupings, they are often couched in highly abstract, quasi-scientific terms. Thus many issues are consciously depoliticized, paradoxically as a result of ideological divisiveness, but also as a means to offset its centrifugal tendencies.

Government, the Five Main Parties, and Policy Opposition

GOVERNMENT AND PARLIAMENT   With the exception of the Catholic Party, all parties have been outside the government for some period since 1946 (the Liberals from 1946 to 1948, from 1952 to 1958, and again since 1965; the Anti-Revolutionary Party from 1946 to 1952; the Christian Historical Union from 1946 to 1948 and since 1965; and the Socialists from

54. See Otto Kirchheimer, "The Transformation of the Western European Party System," in LaPalombara and Weiner, eds., *Political Parties and Political Development*, pp. 177–200.

55. A. Hoogerwerf, "Sociaal-Politieke Strijdpunten: Smeulend Vuur," *Sociologische Gids, 10* (1963), pp. 249–63.

1958 to 1965). (See Appendix Table 6.2.) Whether parties have been inside or outside the government has obviously made for substantial differences in their influence and political attitudes. Yet the importance of this circumstance has been reduced by certain factors: first, even when a particular party has not been in the government, this has not prevented its allied subcultural interest groups from being closely involved in the making of government policy; second, although a party may have been outside the government, this has not necessarily induced it to engage in hard opposition tactics against the government; and conversely, when a party has been a member of a government coalition, this has not necessarily implied warm support. The explanation must be sought in the peculiar historical nature of Dutch Cabinet–Parliament relations and in the intricate coalition politics that have maintained these.[56]

As we saw earlier, the Dutch Parliament has never insisted that ministers be chosen exclusively or even chiefly from among its members, even though it has held ministers at all times fully accountable to it. The complexities of coalition politics and the withdrawal into subcultural isolation have made Dutch parties often willing to compromise on persons who are experts in a particular field rather than strong political personages. Since 1848 almost two-thirds of Dutch Cabinet ministers have assumed their posts without previous parliamentary experience.[57] Only in two or three cases have ministers combined ministerial portfolios with parliamentary seats, and since 1938 this has not been permitted by the Constitution. Even one-time "politicos" readily assume a posture of "above party" once they have attained ministerial office. The government as a whole tends to preserve some detachment from Parliament. Ministers have access to Parliament and are in charge of their own bills. They may be dismissed by a simple adverse vote, and many individual ministers as well as entire cabinets have indeed been sent from office in this way.[58] But the exceeding complexity of the process of Cabinet-making in the Netherlands has made Cabinet crises highly unpopular. Few parties see an easy

56. See H. Daalder, "Parties and Politics in The Netherlands," *Political Studies, 3* (1955) 1–16; Daalder, *The Relation Between Cabinet and Parliament in The Netherlands,* report to the International Political Science Association, Rome, 1958; E. van Raalte, *The Parliament of the Kingdom of The Netherlands* (London, Hansard Society, 1959).

57. Dogan-Scheffer, "Le Personnel Ministériel Hollandais," p. 100.

58. Since 1848 (not including the period 1939–46) the average Dutch Cabinet lasted for somewhat over two years and eight months. Between 1848 and 1888 no less than nine cabinets resigned after conflicts with Parliament. But of twenty-four cabinets between 1888 and 1963, fourteen served during the entire session of a Parliament, while only six ended prematurely through internal dissension or an adverse parliamentary vote (often the same thing!). The dismissal of individual ministers, too, has become much less frequent in recent times: whereas some forty-three ministers resigned over parliamentary conflicts between 1848 and 1922, only four have done so since then.

way to replace a Cabinet once it has been formed, and they have generally allowed it to live out the four-year parliamentary period (not infrequently after an intermediate crisis, "solved" by a return of the old *équipe*). In only a few cases has a real *renversement des alliances* taken place, as in 1939, 1958, and 1965. The Netherlands is therefore in the paradoxical situation that complex party relations make for protracted periods of Cabinet-making, but that this very long duration of Cabinet crises reinforces the stability of governments once formed.[59]

But if cabinets enjoy considerable discretion, so does Parliament. Their nominal participation in the government does not prevent Dutch parties from acting like Pontius Pilate toward any specific government proposal. Parliamentarians like to give the impression that they can treat Cabinet proposals entirely as objective matters on which they are still free to make up their minds. No one party adopts the posture of all-out government— or all-out opposition—party. Each seeks to reserve its opinion, and to make it dependent on a careful assessment of the specific situation or pro-posal at hand. If particular government proposals are the immediate out-come of a Cabinet program which was negotiated when the Cabinet was formed, participating parties usually, if at times grudgingly, feel bound to honor their obligations. If it is evident that an adverse vote would lead to an undesired ministerial crisis, these parties also tend to comply in Parlia-ment, if often only under protest and not until after some give and take between ministers and parliamentary groups. In all other matters, the outcome remains an open question. Parties may more readily oppose if they know for certain that other parties will see a particular bill through. Issues that would arouse too strong a protest from any five of the bigger parties, or at least from one whose participation in the government is indispensable, are touched upon quite hesitantly. Certain issues are held as long as possible in cold storage, and are removed only by *force majeure*. A long delay may not make the matter easier to handle, but if necessary Dutch parties will act jointly, though belatedly, to remove a matter from political debate by arriving at a mutually acceptable solution. They usually find it easier to compromise than to make a final and definite choice among alternatives.

To a considerable extent, opposition in Dutch politics tends therefore to dissolve inside the system rather than to assume a distinct character. There is often hidden conflict between ministers, whether on party, de-partmental, or personal grounds. Individual ministers know that they are linchpins in a carefully constructed Cabinet structure; they are sometimes

59. Even when party relations were relatively simple, as they were between 1888 and 1913, only one Cabinet was formed in *less* than one month. The record so far has been the period of 122 days taken up by the formation of the 1956 Cabinet. For full data on the length of Cabinet crises, see Georg Geismann, *Politische Struktur und Regierungssystem in den Niederlanden* (Frankfurt, 1964), Appendix, p. 289.

not beyond exploiting their positions for highly individualistic policies. There may be a fairly steady *Nervenkrieg* between such ministers, or the Cabinet as a whole, and significant sections of Parliament. There is considerable rivalry among the parties, both in debate and at the polls. But they also bargain continuously, and often a nominal opposition party has helped to save a government from its own "friends."

THE MAIN OPPOSITION PATTERNS   What are the usual opposition patterns within this general framework? As the three main religious parties are tied rather closely to specific denominational groups, there is relatively little electoral competition among them. There is much talk of Christian Democratic affinity and cooperation i.e. between the Catholics and the two orthodox Protestant parties, and at times there has been definite nostalgia for the good old days of an exclusive coalition of the religious parties. The sharpest opposition tends to be between the Liberal and Socialist parties, which represent the greatest polarization on the socioeconomic scale. Since 1952 these parties have not sat in the same government, and both have at various times indicated that this is as it should be. Of decisive importance are the relations between the religious parties and their nonconfessional rivals, because these will determine the specific orientation of the government. Both Liberals and Socialists eye the religious parties with something of a love–hatred complex. They should like to make further inroads on their rather steady electoral clienteles, and both stand to profit if they can polarize political conflict in such manner that left-wing elements in the religious parties find it necessary to move over to the Labor Party and more conservative groups toward the Liberal Party. But the necessity of coalition-building forces them at the same time to tone down their most explicit demands. Hard electoral tactics may jeopardize their future bargaining position, while their present bargaining position is weakened by awareness on all sides that it is possible for the religious parties to govern without Liberals or Socialists, but not for Liberals or Socialists to govern without the religious parties.

Internal relations among the religious parties are therefore of decisive importance for Dutch politics. Their members and various elite groups tend to disagree among themselves about which nonconfessional party is the more eligible partner for a *mariage de raison*. Too close identification with any one of them might in the long run prove to be the worst choice, for those most in sympathy with the specific policies advocated by the nonconfessional ally might decide next time to go all the way and vote for the latter which, by virtue of government participation, is now apparently respectable and certainly offers more clear-cut choices on socioeconomic issues. At the same time, religious supporters on the other wing may bolt the party and join the nonconfessional opposition party in order to force a future coalition of a different character. Consequently, the religious parties attempt to keep the nonconfessional parties at arm's length, and to prefer friendly relations with both but intimacy with neither. To effect this, they stress the ideological differences that separate all of their followers from those in the nonconfessional camp.

The outcome is a curious paradox, which may be best illustrated by the specific position of the Catholic Party. Since 1918 the Catholic Party has been invariably represented in all regular cabinets. Its numerical importance (a third of Parliament, at its center!) is such that it can prevent the formation of any other coalition, but cannot escape government responsibility (unless it wishes to provoke an anti-Catholic coalition against itself, which it does not). But at the same time it is faced with a non-Catholic majority that prevents it from exploiting its political position for too specifically Catholic demands. On matters on which it is internally united it therefore tends to lack power, and on matters where it has power it is not united. This results in a very special position. Catholics have tended to be more outspoken and active in Parliament, where they can be fully themselves and use their voting strength as they think fit, than in the Cabinet, which is likely to have a non-Catholic majority and where even Catholic prime ministers have to tread carefully.[60] This dual position has tended to widen the division between Cabinet and Parliament, and thus to allow for a wide range of carefully played opposition tactics all round.

The historic separateness of Dutch parties has strengthened their unity at the parliamentary level; they have usually achieved a fair measure of success in maintaining a common front, even without formal disciplinary action. Reasonably strong group cohesion has facilitated interparty bargaining and enhanced Cabinet stability. The detachment of Cabinet from Parliament lessens the scope for personal ambition. Parliamentarians are far from certain that they will ever be called to ministerial office. They are therefore often as much, or perhaps even more directly interested in successful policy opposition than in the displacement of government personnel.

The wish to maintain external unity shifts the burden of policy decision to consultations *within* each of the parties, where the center of gravity tends to lie with the parliamentary group and to a lesser extent with the extraparliamentary party organization. The intensity of intraparty conflict may be considerable. But it is lessened by at least three factors: the desire not to offer hostages to competing parties; the considerable leverage which central party authorities can wield through the highly centralized nomination procedures (encouraged by the list system of proportional repre-

---

60. Comparatively few Dutch prime ministers have been Catholic. On the other hand the most prominent Catholic Party leaders have generally stayed outside the Cabinet in strong control of their parliamentary group. The first two great Catholic leaders, Schaepman and Nolens, were priests; typically this was thought to rule them out for ministerial appointment, unlike their Protestant counterparts such as Abraham Kuyper.

sentation); and the widespread awareness of the need to preserve a working relationship among all groups within the party and its potential electoral clientele if total parliamentary strength is to be maintained intact.[61]

At the same time the system offers considerable opportunity for special interest groups to make their weight felt. The attempt to balance electoral slates has led to direct representation in Parliament of a host of interest group executives (whether employers, farmers, workers, or *Middenstand* organizations). These representatives gravitate toward specialized parliamentary committees, where they cooperate easily with representatives of similar interests in other parties. This situation seems to invite a degree of tacit collusion between such specialized parliamentary committees, extra-parliamentary interest groups, and special bureaucratic interests, and tends to strain the resources of those who are responsible for welding a coherent policy under disparate pressures: the Cabinet, the Prime Minister, the Minister of Finance, party leaders, budget officials, etc. Their efforts are not facilitated by the strong particularist strands in Dutch political and bureaucratic life, where individual ministers insist jealously on their autonomy and where civil service recruitment is practically entirely in the hands of individual departments, or even of department sections.

The Strains of Segmentation

Strong segmentation and sharp political divisions provoke certain dysfunctional strains in the system. One can distinguish these in three categories: first, the occurrence of small splinter parties that carry the logic of segmentation to organizational extremes; second, mounting criticism of the *Verzuiling*, which according to some is symptomatic of a deeper-lying political malaise; and finally, the (admittedly somewhat marginal) existence of explicit antisystem groups.

INTEGRALISM AND OVERLAPPING   Strong segmentation has fostered the establishment of small parties which unwittingly confirm its basic pattern. On the one hand, certain integralist groups within each *Zuil* have adopted an extreme ideological position, in isolationist opposition to what they regard as the unprincipled attitudes of their larger subcultural brethren. Sometimes such groups have been satisfied to operate within the ambit of the larger party and merely to sermonize the official leadership. But especially in the case of the Calvinists, the Socialists, and to a lesser extent the Liberal Party, such groups have also often gone beyond and established separate political parties. Besides the Anti-Revolutionary Party and

61. There has been little systematic study of intraparty relations, but see J. J. de Jong, *Politieke Organisatie in West Europa na 1800* (The Hague, Nijhoff, 1951) and I. Lipschits, "De Politieke Partij en de Selectie van Candidaten," *Sociologische Gids*, 10 (1963), 273–81.

the Christian Historical Union, there are now two sectarian Calvinist parties represented in Parliament (with three seats and one seat respectively). They are supported by small denominational groups and tend to favor an undiluted, at times even theocratic Calvinism. The larger Staatkundig-Gereformeerde Partij has been represented in Parliament since 1922, and has become a nationally cherished antiquity. Some revolutionary socialist groups falling between the Socialists and Communists occasionally secured parliamentary seats between the wars. They have not done so since, but a Pacifist Socialist Party emerged in 1957 and successfully sought representation: the PSP secured 3 per cent of the national vote in 1963 and now has as many deputies in the lower house as the Communists (four seats). On the far right, a host of disparate anti-dirigiste movements have formed and reformed, usually with little success; two of the more important ones will be mentioned later as antisystem oppositions.

These integralist movements have not been very strong in the aggregate. But they have served as gadflies, forcing the larger parties not to stray too far from their ideological positions lest they lose votes. They have reinforced the tendency of Dutch party leaders to honor their subcultural traditions, if not in deed then at least in word. And the ever-present threat they have represented has been a constant element in the determination by the main parties of long-term strategy, restricting possible tendencies to seek closer forms of collaboration among them.

Integralist parties are the logical opposite of *overlapping* parties. I use this term to describe groups that seek to combine otherwise distinct forces in the political system. Attempts to straddle existing political boundaries have historically occurred particularly on the following fronts:

1. *Between orthodox Protestants and Socialists:* From the early days of the twentieth century there have been numerous groupings that sought to deduce a more radical program from Christian principles than either the Anti-Revolutionary Party or the Christian Historical Union has done. Some of these obtained occasional seats in Parliament. The most prominent example was the Christian Democratic Union (1926–40; two seats in 1937), which merged with the Socialists in the Labor Party in 1946. The orthodox Protestant working group within the Labor Party and the Pacifist Socialists continue to cater specifically to this clientele;

2. *Between Catholics and Socialists, on the one hand, and Catholics and Liberals, on the other:* Dissident groups sometimes arose out of either wing of the Catholic Party to give expression to progressive and conservative programs, respectively. They have always disappeared again under the combined pressure of history and the bishops. The most important recent example was the Catholic National Party (one seat in 1948, two seats in 1952), a conservative movement that originated in protest against the government's policies over Indonesia and did much to wean the Catholic

Party away from the explicitly progressive stand it had adopted after 1945.

3. *Between Liberals and Socialists:* Between 1901 and 1940 a radical party maintained itself with a steady strength of 5–7 per cent of the national vote and a highly articulate intellectual leadership. It, too, fused with the Socialists in the Labor Party in 1946 (its most prominent leader, P. J. Oud, was soon to bolt to the Liberals, however). Left-wing Liberals continue to have some nostalgic feeling for it, and occasionally reach a measure of organizational unity trying to offset right-wing pressures within the party by a threat of reviving the old radical separateness.

4. *Between two or more religious parties:* There have been some movements which have sought to bridge the gap between Anti-Revolutionaries and Christian Historicals, or, more ambitiously, all three religious parties. So far this drive has led only to further splintering in the name of unity. Public opinion polls suggest a considerable measure of grass-roots support for the idea of amalgamation (though not for any special party that has yet appeared).[62] Political expediency has so far militated against such moves, however. Long ago a wise Christian Historical argued that one could catch more fish with two nets than with one. A CDU on the German model would seem likely to get fewer votes than the present three parties separately. The electoral system provides all possible encouragement to those who might wish to resist such an amalgamation by the establishment of new parties, and many present supporters of a religious party might well bolt to a nonreligious party once tight historical and denominational links were broken.

CRITICS AND CRISIS?   The *Verzuiling* phenomenon has recently come under increasing attack. In all camps there are strong pleas for a more "open" attitude toward other subcultures and for greater cooperation across traditional dividing lines. But "national" solutions rather than organized ideological pluralism are more confidently advocated by Liberals and Christian Historicals than by Catholics and Anti-Revolutionaries, while the Socialists tend to be somewhat split between isolationist memories and a desire for "national" assertion.

These underlying attitudes have recently come to an open test over the control of radio and television. At present, radio and television time have been carefully proportioned among four large associations (of Catholic, Calvinist, Socialist, and "general" members respectively), and a much smaller latitudinarian Protestant one. The five organizations are in addition

62. According to investigations of the Netherlands Institute of Public Opinion (NIPO), around 90 per cent of those who indicated support for either ARP or CHU declared recently in favor of one unified Protestant party. This view is not shared by the CHU leadership, which has consistently rejected Anti-Revolutionary overtures over the last twenty years. Relations were further embittered when the two parties went different ways in the Cabinet crisis of 1965.

jointly responsible for some broadcasts and special time is reserved for the government, political parties, and some specialized cultural organizations. This pluralist structure has been criticized from various sides. Some Liberals and Socialists, as well as latitudinarian Protestants, have advocated a more "national" system on the B.B.C. model. Others have pleaded free access for independent commercial stations. The expansion of television facilities, and the question how to finance them (whether by advertising or increased levies on the public), have made the issue more and more urgent during the early sixties. But it only came to a head in the summer of 1964 when a private company erected an artificial platform in the North Sea, just outside Dutch territorial waters, and began broadcasting both radio and television programs. The company attempted to increase its popular appeal by floating a large number of small shares which found a willing public. Although in opinion polls some 70 per cent of the Dutch people declared themselves opposed to government measures against this new station, and although opposition also came from the Liberals, who were at that time represented in the government, the Dutch Cabinet and the majority of Parliament passed special legislation declaring Dutch laws applicable to artificial installations on the so-called continental plateau outside territorial waters. In December 1964 officials of the Department of Justice accordingly silenced the station.[63]

The issue caused lively political debate. Whereas Catholics, Calvinists, and Socialists tended to lean toward a defense of the existing system (supplemented by carefully controlled television and radio advertising that would benefit the existing organizations), this was much less true of the Dutch press. The attitude of the press is easily explained. "Neutral" newspapers (i.e. newspapers that are not Catholic, Socialist, or strongly Calvinist, hence are generally apolitical, Liberal, or vaguely Protestant) have long had a disproportionate influence in the Netherlands, partly because they were first in the field, partly because strong adherents of any subculture find it easier to read a so-called "neutral" newspaper than one strongly identified with an alien ideology. Some newspaper interests have looked with covetous eyes on the possibility of extending their sway in the new electronic mass media, whereas others have at least wished a measure of newspaper influence on television to offset feared losses in advertising income. It looked for a time as if a typical Dutch concert composed of some quasi-ecumenical elite groups, both high-toned and strident newspaper interests, candidates for commercial television, and assumed mass pressure for less ideology and more pop programs might break through the existing radio and television organization.

63. But when the government did silence the station, 43 per cent expressed approval, only 33 per cent continued disapproval, and 24 per cent no opinion. NIPO data, January 1965.

But in March 1965 disagreement between Liberals and Christian Historicals on the one hand, and Catholics and Anti-Revolutionaries on the other, led to a breakup of the nonsocialist coalition which had been in office since 1959. The Liberals demanded access for independent companies, and attacked the alleged *Zuilen* monopoly. Catholics, Anti-Revolutionaries, and soon the Socialists too resisted this Liberal drive. They rejected all forms of commercial television and demanded as a condition of entry for newcomers not unsubstantiated "nationalist" or "populist" claims, but a hard numerical following consisting of dues-paying members adequately registered. They jointly formed a new government in April 1965, the Liberals and Christian Historicals reverting to opposition. All clamor notwithstanding, there were no signs of a popular uprising against the new coalition in local elections for the Rijnmond authority in June 1965, when some 10 per cent of the Dutch population went to the polls: the Labor Party gained slightly, but the Liberals actually lost some votes as compared with 1963. It remains to be seen, however, whether the coalition of subcultural groups can permanently resist the leveling influence of an increasingly general culture and the decline of ideological certainties on the part of large masses of the population.

There is much talk about political malaise, generally, in the Netherlands. Frequent complaints are uttered against the existing government system: Parliament is thought to be no longer in a position to control the Executive; ministerial and civil service recruitment is believed to have declined in quality; parties are accused of oligarchy and rigidity; interest groups are said to be too prominent; elections are felt to be insufficiently meaningful; mass apathy is thought to be spreading, etc.

It is difficult to disentangle fact from fancy in these discussions. Underlying value judgments are not always made clear. Opinions are freely expressed without much hard evidence. Available evidence seems to be somewhat contradictory, and fundamental data are often lacking. But the following indications may be given about the stability (or instability) of the political and social system:

1. *Electoral participation.* In spite of indifferently enforced compulsory attendance at the ballot box, both the number of people voting and the number of people casting valid ballots has increased fairly steadily over the past forty years (see Table 6.2).

2. *Aggregate strength of the five main parties.* Increased electoral participation notwithstanding, the share of the combined vote for the five larger parties has, on the whole, increased since 1945 as compared with the interwar period. The Dutch electoral system provides every encouragement for splinter parties: the entire country is for all practical purposes treated as one constituency; financial deposits required of new

parties are low; and the threshold for representation in the Parliament has at no time been higher than 1 per cent of the valid national vote (since 1956 when the membership of the lower house was expanded from 100 to 150 members it has been only two-thirds of 1 per cent). Even so, all other groups *combined* (whether integralist, overlapping, or antisystem parties, or just ephemeral oddities) have at no time obtained more than 16 per cent (in 1933) of the valid national vote. In only a few cases have the five main parties had less than 90 per cent of the seats in the lower house (i.e. in 1918, the first year of universal suffrage; in 1933 and 1937 during the Depression; and in 1946 and 1948 when the Communists obtained a sizable share of the national vote, see Table 6.2).

3. *Increasing electoral mobility*. The fairly stable distribution of votes among the main parties since 1918 (see Appendix Tables 6.3 and 6.4) is, in fact, somewhat deceptive: it is a result not of stable electoral preferences but rather of the circumstance that certain crosscurrents have tended to cancel one another out. The apparent stability of the Catholic Party, for instance, masks a secular loss to both Labor and Liberals, compensated for by the advantage the party derives from the increasing number of Catholics in the electorate.[64] The Anti-Revolutionary Party has lost a third of its strength since 1950, apparently to the Christian Historical Union as well as to the Liberals and Socialists. The number of votes for the Liberals, Socialists, Pacifist Socialists, and Communists combined has increased from 36 per cent in 1937 to a postwar record of 47.3 per cent in 1959, while the total vote for all religious parties declined from 56.4 per cent to 52 per cent in the same period, despite their differential advantage in the birthrate. (See Appendix Table 6.4.) These facts attest to an increased electoral mobility in the Dutch electorate, as does the appearance of strong crosscurrents between the Liberals and Socialists, and of more incidental borderline traffic between the religious parties on the one hand and the nonreligious parties on the other.[65] It is difficult to say whether this increased sensitivity points to heightened political awareness on the part of the electorate or to alienation from the existing party system. There is no doubt that the leaders of all parties are becoming more concerned with the images of their parties and tend to rely less on traditional clientele relationships. Yet the movement is not yet of such dimension that a breakup of the traditional alignments seems at all likely (whether through a reorientation from the top down or from the grass roots up).

64. Actual Catholic voting records are better measured by the so-called Index of Political Orthodoxy, i.e., the percentage of recorded Catholics who actually vote for the Catholic Party. According to data from the Catholic Institute for Social Research, this index has declined from 92 in 1948, to 88 in 1952, 87 in 1956, 85.9 in 1959, to 84.9 in 1963 (albeit with considerable regional variations). See for an interesting analysis W.J.J. Kusters, "Stembusgedrag en Maatschappijstructuur," *Sociologische Gids, 10* (1963), 226–38.

65. Cf. the discussion between Kusters and Van Thijn, ibid., pp. 228–48.

Table 6.2 Extent of Electoral Participation and Share of Large and Small Parties in National Vote and Seats for Lower House of Parliament (1918–1963)

	1918	1922	1925	1929	1933	1937	1946	1948	1952	1956	1959	1963
Electoral participation												
Percentage of eligible voters voting	Data not available		91.4	92.7	94.5	94.4	93.1	93.7	95.0	95.5	95.6	95.1
Percentage of valid votes	Data not available		95.3	95.4	95.4	96.3	96.9	96.9	97.0	97.9	97.7	97.5
Valid votes in % of eligible voters	88.6	88.8 (estimates)	87.1	88.4	90.2	90.9	90.2	90.8	92.1	93.5	93.3	92.8
Share of Large Parties												
Percentage of valid votes [1]	87.2	87.8	88.4	89.1	83.9	84.6	86.2	87.0	86.7	91.5	91.6	87.5
Number of Seats [1]	87	94	94	92	87	89	88	89	90	94	142 (95%)	135 (90%)
Share of Small Parties												
Percentage of Religious splinters [2]	2.0	4.1	5.1	4.6	6.2	5.8	2.8	3.7	5.8	3.4	2.9	3.1
Percentage of left-wing socialists and communists [2]	3.6	2.2	2.4	3.0	5.2	4.1	10.8	8.1	6.5	4.8	4.8	5.8
Percentage of right-wing and interest parties [2]	7.2	5.9	4.1	3.3	4.7	5.5	0.2	1.2	1.0	0.3	0.7	3.6
Number of seats [1]	13	6	6	8	13	11	12	11	10	6	8 (5%)	15 (10%)
Percentage of votes cast for parties that did not obtain representation [3]	2.2	7.1	4.9	3.3	4.0	3.9	1.1	1.6	2.0	1.4	2.0	1.5

1. Number of seats in lower house: 1918–56, 100; 1956 to date, 150. Allocation of remainder of seats: 1918–33, largest remainder (Roget system); 1933 to date, highest average (d'Hondt system).

2. The assignment of political groups to categories (religious parties, left-wing socialist parties, and right-wing and interest parties) is necessarily somewhat arbitrary; percentages are therefore approximate only.

3. Threshold formulas: 1918, 50% of electoral quotient; 1922–33, 75% of electoral quotient; 1935 to date, electoral quotient (1% of valid national vote between 1935–56, and two-thirds of 1% of national vote since 1956).

Source: Central Bureau of Statistics and calculations by R. P. van den Helm.

4. *Survey evidence.* The evidence from such surveys as have been published is also somewhat unclear.[66] Interest in and knowledge of the field of politics are apparently at a low level, yet for lack of comparable data for historical periods it is not clear whether this situation was really much different, say, forty years ago. Many people feel that they have little influence on politics, but they do not seem very anxious to become actively involved in political life. The image of politicians is not always flattering, and quite a few respondents regard them as mainly self-seekers. At the same time, many seem to think that party politics are not overly important for government policy; quite a few seem to consider it relatively unimportant whether a particular political party is in the government or not, and many opine freely that parties should quarrel less and cooperate more. The suggestion that small parties complicate the workings of government finds frequent assent, but most people think it undemocratic to raise the threshold for representation. Most respondents say that they regard parties and party principles as more important than personalities, but they often reveal an uncritical admiration for particular ministers, which if not expressed in party votes then at least shows up in public opinion polls.[67] Does all this point to fundamental dissatisfaction? Other data reveal a very high degree of satisfaction with present living standards and future economic prospects. Younger people sometimes seem to take a more positive attitude toward politics than older ones, and rising educational levels tend to make for greater knowledge of political affairs. Perhaps the best conclusion one can draw is that most people are neither much worried nor much interested at the present time, and many realize that Dutch politics is not actually so important in view of the overwhelming role of international factors.

ANTISYSTEM OPPOSITIONS   It was mentioned earlier that the total electoral strength of antisystem opposition groups has tended to be low in the Netherlands. Both Communists and National Socialists scored their best results, moreover, when they offered a moderate, "national" image, and they declined greatly in importance when events abroad cast a dark

66. The most convenient collections of data are in: Wiardi Beckman Stichting, *Verkiezingen in Nederland* (Amsterdam, 1951); *De Nederlandse Kiezer, Een Onderzoek naar zijn gedragingen en opvattingen,* with English summary (The Hague, 1956); J. J. de Jong, *Overheid en Onderdaan* (Wageningen, Zomer and Keuning, 1956); L. van der Land a.o., *Kiezer en Verkiezing* (mimeo., Amsterdam, 1963) also in a much shortened English version: *Voting in The Netherlands, A Panel Study in an Amsterdam Suburb,* report to the International Political Science Association, Geneva, 1964; H. Daudt and H. Lange, "Welvaart in Nederland," *Ariadne, 18* (1963), 360–65; Hans Daudt and Henk Lange, *Youth and Politics in The Netherlands,* report to the International Political Science Association, Geneva, 1964; and A. Hoogerwerf, *Protestantisme en Progressiviteit.*

67. When NIPO pollsters asked Dutchmen recently what man (living or dead) they most admired, by far the largest number (about a quarter of all respondents) spontaneously named Joseph Luns, the Dutch Minister of Foreign Affairs, who can be very amusing in TV broadcasts.

shadow over them. Yet their existence has some importance, both as a measure of potential dissatisfaction in the system and as a yardstick with which to judge the attitude of democratic government to fundamental oppositions of principle.

The Communist Party [68] has represented the oldest and steadiest opposition of principle, having had seats in the Dutch Parliament ever since 1918. The hard core of its strength is found among alienated groups in Amsterdam and some other regions where, as we saw, a rebellious, mostly anarchist kind of socialism crystallized very early in Dutch social history. The party obtained its largest following in 1946, when its vote temporarily soared above 10 per cent, mainly under the influence of Russian victories, a strong resistance record, and the simultaneous refashioning of the SDAP into the Labor Party. At the same time the Communists also seemed to ride high in the trade union field. They became the chief sponsors of an Eenheidsvakbeweging (EVB, later EVC) that was established in 1945 to unite workers whatever their religious or political allegiance in one common union organization. But the Socialist and religious unions soon struck back, and the government and employers refused to deal with the EVB. When a few political strikes petered out, it soon declined in importance. Communist strength has gone down ever since, both at the ballot box and in union organization. Rock bottom was touched in 1959 when internal divisions destroyed the remnants of the EVC, and the Communist Party received only 2.4 per cent of the national vote, almost entirely in its most traditional areas.

Ever since its inception, the Communist Party has remained completely isolated in politics.[69] Known Communists are disqualified for most types of government employment. After the Prague coup of 1948 other parties refused to accept Communists as partners in local government executive organs. Communists were excluded from certain parliamentary committees, notably in defense and foreign affairs. Although they could publish and campaign freely, they were not allotted radio or television time. It is a moot question whether this discrimination was effective or superfluous. In any case, the new 1965 Cabinet decided to change this practice and to admit the Communists to radio and television on a par with other parties represented in Parliament. Generally speaking, the Communist movement has remained a sect in a sectarian country. True to this tradition, it has done itself considerable harm through internal heresy hunting.

---

68. Cf. F. Kool, "Communism in Holland—A Study in Futility," *Problems of Communism, 9* (1960), 17–24. The most convenient, though inadequate, data in Dutch are in W. van Ravesteyn, *De Wording van het Communisme in Nederland, 1907–1925* (Amsterdam, Van Kampen, 1948), and M. Perthus, ed., *Voor Vrijheid en Socialisme, Gedenkboek van het Sneevliet Herdenkingscomité* (Rotterdam, Gramo, 1953).

69. The Communists were invited to nominate one of their leaders for Cabinet membership in 1945; they demanded the Ministry of Agriculture and Food but were only offered the post of Minister Without Portfolio, which they refused.

Fascist groups were formed from the early 1920s onward, followed later by National Socialist groups that sought their inspiration in Germany. Most of these movements were exceedingly small and hardly worth attention but for the role which some of their members were to play later during the German occupation.[70] The most important group was the Nationaal-Socialistische Beweging of Anton Mussert. It won an unexpectedly large victory during the provincial elections of 1935, when it secured almost 8 per cent of the national vote, mainly at the expense of the nonconfessional bourgeois groups. (During the same period the Communist Party never rose much above 3 per cent.) Originally a somewhat petty bourgeois protest movement, it turned increasingly radical. In competition with some other fascist groups, it attempted to organize the beginnings of a private militia. This in turn provoked similar militant behavior from Communists and left-wing Socialists. The government of the time (under the Anti-Revolutionary leader Colijn) reacted by banning uniforms and public insignia on public streets and by other measures relating to public order. After that the NSB dwindled in strength, and received only 4 per cent of the vote in 1937 and slightly less in 1939.[71] Its decisive hour was to come only with foreign invasion.

Since 1945 extreme right-wing parties have been even less influential than they were in the interwar period.[72] Small financial interest groups, veterans and repatriates from the colonies, authoritarian orthodox Protestants and old-fashioned reactionary Liberals have sometimes formed fleeting political parties that never succeeded in passing the very low threshold for representation. The only movement that has done so is a more Poujadist-oriented Boerenpartij (Peasant Party) that obtained three seats in Parliament in 1963. Its main strength lies with small peasants and small shopkeepers who cannot keep pace with the impersonal forces of economic rationalization in both agriculture and retailing. In addition, it may have received a certain popular support for its efforts to stand up to the dominant political and administrative system. Its ideology is a curious mixture of authoritarianism, individual self-reliance, direct interest appeal, and considerable demagogy. Its fame is partly dependent on the earthy appeal of its leader, H. Koekoek. Interestingly, when Dutchmen were asked in 1964 to give the names of Dutch politicians, the names most

70. See W. Warmbrunn, *The Dutch Under German Occupation, 1940–1945* (Stanford, Stanford University Press, 1963), passim.

71. For an attempt to investigate the social roots of National Socialist strength and its consequent decline in the Netherlands, see G. A. Kooy, *Het Echec van een 'Volkse' Beweging—Nazificatie en Denazificatie in Nederland, 1931–1945* (Assen, Van Gorcum, 1964).

72. National Socialist parties have been proscribed in the Netherlands since 1945. The courts stopped one attempt to refound a National Socialist movement in 1954. After 1945 most Quislings lost both the active and passive franchise, usually for a period of ten years. The return to the electorate of a number of former Nazis may have been a factor in the increased vote for the extreme right in 1963.

frequently given were those of the then Socialist opposition leader, A. Vondeling, and of Koekoek, who symbolizes opposition to the system as a whole.[73]

GOVERNMENT AND OPPOSITION   The Netherlands is now, as it always was, a small but highly pluralist society. There is considerable friction and opposition whether from explicitly political groups or others. Ministers, parliamentarians, bureaucrats, interest groups, mass media, promotional associations, individual capitalist enterprises, and independent academic experts all seek to influence specific government policies. Tactics are equally varied: they comprise public criticism, propaganda campaigns, formal and informal petitions, threats to withhold services, informal pressure on strategically placed persons or groups, consultation, bargaining, legislation, and what not. The central objects of such pressures are ministers, parliamentarians, and bureaucratic agencies, the key means the securing of regular access, especially via representation in advisory bodies and party slates.

These processes have been little studied in the Netherlands, partly because of their fugitive quality, partly because a legalistic tradition has long preempted attention for the more formal institutional elements of policy-making. This same tradition has made for considerable secrecy about affairs of state, which in turn complicates the problem of gaining true insight.

Even without further inquiry it seems likely, however, that the situation would bear out Stein Rokkan's statement:

a proliferation of sectional and functional organization . . . tended to soften the overall strains in the system and to reduce the level of polarization. What we tend to find is a cumulation of forces making for a narrowing of the alternatives for national politics, a fragmentation of the networks of policy-influencing organizations, and a consequent decline in the importance of the decisions of the electorate-at-large. This may tend to lower the level of general political participation and to alienate from politics sizeable sections of the once-enfranchised citizenry, leaving the basic decisions to a bargaining process between interest organizations, parties and agencies and departments of the national bureaucracy.[74]

If this is true, the question whether opposition is distinct or dissolves into the system assumes a new importance. Presumably the complexity of modern society automatically produces enough countervailing forces to make for a considerable amount of intergroup opposition on all policy matters, whether highly specialized or not. Yet it seems that only a definite

73. See Daudt and Lange, *Youth and Politics,* p. 10.
74. Stein Rokkan, "Mass Suffrage, Secret Voting and Political Participation," *European Journal of Sociology,* 2 (1961), 152.

and powerful Opposition in Parliament can secure regular accountability and guarantee the openness of the system. It is on this point that the Dutch situation seems most vulnerable. The need to defer to many interests, the tradition of collegial rule, the constant quest for compromise, encourage careful consideration of policy questions. But they lead at the same time to some measure of deliberate depoliticization,[75] which makes it difficult for the common man to identify himself with particular policies or with the somewhat transcendental game of general politics. The presence of many oppositions is therefore not a real substitute for the absence of a strong Opposition that challenges government wherever possible— on the basis of its own strength, not from the need to ingratiate itself with future coalition partners. The absence of a real Opposition potentially weakens every government. A strong Opposition can provide a government with strength as it increases the confidence of the citizenry at large that government actions can bear scrutiny and can be challenged in specific instances. Even if this may not increase the measure of direct citizen participation, it may lessen the danger that government becomes too distant for the ordinary citizen, leaving him a helpless object of diverse pressures and possibly even of what Gabriel Almond termed "a Caesaristic breakthrough" from above.[76]

75. A former Clerk of the First Chamber drew the "logical" conclusion from the Dutch situation when he proposed the inclusion of all democratic parties in every government as a matter of course; he argued that the traditional detachment between government and Parliament would guarantee a sufficient measure of opposition on specific issues. See A. L. De Block, *Samenwerking in Nederland als Staatkundig Vraagstuk* (The Hague, Centrum voor Staatkundige Vorming, 1955). For a highly critical analysis of the Dutch situation, see J. F. Glastra van Loon, "Kiezen of Delen," *Nederlands Juristenblad* (1964), pp. 1133–42 and 1161–67. Glastra van Loon attributes the simultaneous existence of a tepid conformism and an irresponsible criticism of all politics and all politicians to the absence of a strongly articulated Opposition. He would like to see this changed by a system of direct popular election of the Prime Minister.

76. See Almond, "Comparative Political Systems," p. 409. The closest experience to a movement against the old party system was the Nederlandse Unie in 1940–41. Led by a triumvirate of younger men who had been quite critical of prewar politics, the Unie sought to present a national platform. It called for the cooperation of all Dutchmen in a new movement toward regeneration of Dutch society. Though boycotted by most old party leaders who thought or found political action during the German occupation impossible, it attracted a very large mass following, mainly because of its strong stand against the Dutch National Socialists. The Germans proscribed the movement in 1941 when it no longer served any purpose for their occupation politics. See Warmbrunn, *The Dutch Under German Occupation*, pp. 133–36.

Some of the Unie's leaders were later active in the Nederlandse Volksbeweging, a movement of a relatively large number of politicians from all parties which called for a reorientation of the party system in 1945. But old party ties soon reasserted themselves so that the NVB left little trace in Dutch politics; it did however provide a catalytic effect on the fusion of a number of left-wing forces into the Labor Party.

7

GERMANY:
THE VANISHING OPPOSITION

Otto Kirchheimer

In the particular context of the German experience, the terms with which we are concerned may be defined as follows:

1. We shall refer to "political competition" if political jobs are filled by selection from candidates whose number is in excess of the places to be filled.

2. We shall speak of "loyal opposition" if the political competition involves some form of goal differentiation between available candidates in harmony with the constitutional requirements of a given system.

3. We shall speak of "opposition of principle" if the competitor's behavior indicates the desire for a degree of goal displacement incompatible with the constitutional requirements of a given system.

Any form of political opposition necessarily involves some kind of competition. The reverse does not hold true: political competition does not necessarily involve opposition.

Our problem, in German terms, is about 100 years old. The Bismarck constitution functioned in a society split into two major camps. On the one hand was the military-bureaucratic complex which dominated Prussia, monarchic in principle; on the other, the up-and-coming bourgeoisie. While the monarchy represented the state, officially identified with the moral order, the bourgeoisie stood for the sum total of what the Germans would call *die bürgerliche Gesellschaft*. Executive power remained concentrated with and at the disposal of those in control of the state, while legislative power had become a joint enterprise of those controlling the state and the forces of the *bürgerliche Gesellschaft*. Since Bismarck's grant of federal universal suffrage in 1868, the urban proletariat had been brought to political notice as an independent and rapidly swelling section of Germany's *bürgerliche Gesellschaft*. Bismarck had not meant to integrate the working class into the official order as both the Liberal and Conservative parties had done in England. Rather he thought to keep the liberal bourgeoisie at bay in its own bailiwick, the parliamentary assembly, by utilizing the working-class franchise. But, as with so many of his domestic political schemes, he was unsuccessful. Through Bismarck's grant of federal universal franchise, the long-standing cleavage between the official state power and the *bürgerliche Gesellschaft* acquired more disturbing dimensions as Social Democratic Party (SPD) opposition of principle increased.

This opposition of principle grew by leaps and bounds during the halcyon days before the First World War. It was both a political party and a chapel. Some of its leaders were intent on nudging out the incumbents gently from the seats of both social and political power. Yet these tacticians, who were concerned with the parliamentary impact of tomorrow's elections, had to contend with fervent adherents certain of an impending millennium and scornful of any compromise that might obtain only a bit of daily progress. Yet, kept at arms' length and intermittently harassed by an official state organization which rejected the SPD as unpatriotic, the SPD's executive body could comfortably straddle the issue of tomorrow's policies by dilatory formulas.

The Weimar Period

The Weimar settlement presumably eliminated the cleavage between the state and the *bürgerliche Gesellschaft*, between the executive and parliament. Can we then, for the lifetime of the Weimar regime, speak of political competition beginning to develop along lines in any way familiar in America or England? Could the Weimar system be understood as a political game played by alternating leadership groups with the tolerance, acquiescence, and electoral consent of the population at large? Such a description would cover only a segment and not the most important one of the Weimar political reality.

There was rather a threefold system of political competition in this severely transfigured heritage of the previous constitutional period. There was the struggle between those parties which, half by inclination, half by political necessity, had become upholders of the constitutional order (most important of them, at least in numbers, the SPD), and the parties of opposition of principle, divided into Communist and nationalist components (including the Nazis), digging in for a siege of the establishment from two directions.

Opposition of principle had undergone mutations of thought and action as a consequence of and reaction to several developments. The left revolution which had failed at home had succeeded abroad to the East. There were drastic changes in conditions of existence among proletariat and bourgeoisie. Opposition of principle was no longer characterized by a state of mind patiently waiting to take over society's accumulated store of resources in the fullness of time but by the spirit of conquest here and now. The parties of opposition of principle were now very different from the half-political, half-chapel opposition of the benign pre-World War I days. They considered elections a ready-made battleground, where they might integrate and exploit their gains and then proceed to more far-reaching political action.

Between the parties operating within (or at least not clearly outside) the parliamentary system, there was a certain amount of political competition, genuine though slack and sporadic. These competitors were more intent on picking up pieces of disintegrating parties than in competing for each other's more or less well-established clientele. This intrasystem competition did not lead to clear-cut positions of majority versus minority, government versus loyal opposition.

The SPD had from the outset contributed to the frustration of such solutions by opting for proportional representation in January 1919. Whether a majority election system would have led to a much different outcome is unclear, because the heritage of the Empire had left strong traditional and religious cleavages superimposed on social class differentiations in German society. The SPD option for proportional representation was probably only partly due to loyalty to an outdated party program, only partly inspired by the battles of yesteryear's lopsided imperial election districts. A more important motive was probably the SPD leaders' fear of facing undivided governmental responsibility and their incapacity for making any attempt at implementing the central core of their party program.

At any rate the results were clear enough. There was never a chance to establish a government–loyal opposition relationship during the decade in which, in constitutional theory at least, a sort of parliamentary government existed. The difficulties of a multiparty regime, the job interests of each party's members, the socioeconomic interests of each party's clientele, and above all each party's urge for self-preservation as a political unit in the face of the precarious existence of the whole republican state machine almost forced the major parties, loyal to the system, to try to hang on to some pieces of the central state apparatus, or at least to some strategic administrative positions in the strongest political component, Prussia.

Yet if elections were also a means to determine to what pieces of the executive and the administrative machine a loyal party could manage to hang on, the total amount of and the structure of executive and administrative power accessible to the parties were scarcely determined by shifting election results. This power depended (memories of the previous regime) on the relative strength of the military and civilian bureaucracy and the political apparatus proper. And here we face a certain level of highly significant political relations involving little competition: the interrelation between all military and certain bureaucratic power holders and those officeholders emanating from and legitimized by the confidence of

Parliament. Certainly the military considered itself an independent establishment willing to negotiate contracts with rival sovereignties but otherwise serving the political establishment only on its own terms.

Therefore, from the very outset, opposition of principle against the existing constitutional system and the power of the bureaucratic and especially the military officeholders narrowed down the significance of electoral competition as a political basis for the determination of policy. There was little room left for the development of a concept of loyal opposition resting on alternative policy choices propounded by parties working within the constitutional framework.

Toward the end of the regime a continuing process led to the rapid disappearance of both political competition and loyal opposition. First, any attempt of the parliamentary establishment to contest the military-bureaucratic power of decision ceased to exist. Then the parliamentary establishment was ignored during the bureaucratic and military rearguard action against the growing forces of the opposition of principle of the Right. Finally, after Hindenburg's death in 1934, any idea of the military establishment's continuation as an independent factor in possible opposition to the National Socialist power was eliminated.

Nazism and the Occupation

The Third Reich permitted shared sovereignties as well as some sort of intrasystem competition. In the economic realm competition went on surreptitiously by quality differentiation or battle for administrative preference. In the political realm the system used an amount of intensive subleadership competition for the favor of the supreme leader. This intrasystem leadership competition might sometimes be artfully exploited to enlarge the interstitial space for opposition. Yet, and this is decisive: there was otherwise no bridge or easy communication between both competition and opposition. Opposition had to shed the purely competitive garb, and it became the banned and hunted opposition of principle, the only form of opposition meaningful or possible under the conditions of that regime.

The immediate afterwar and occupation period, 1945–49, brought an interesting separation of the functions of competition and opposition. There was a certain amount of competition among the various groups admitted to the classes for political reeducation put up by the Western Allied authorities, which included trial-run elections. The programs of these parties did not have much relation either to government decisions of the day, which were monopolized by the occupiers, or to the parties' own policies two or three years later, determined as they were by the swiftly changing political realities. Yet these programs served as posters for reassembling the various prewar party general staffs, reestablishing communication lines with old clienteles, and giving prospective recruits for political jobs a chance to look around. In addition they opened up to the public at large devices for getting reacclimatized to a sort of competitive politics, allowing them to show some innocuous preference for one or the other duly licensed competitor.

To the extent that there did exist an element of opposition it had nothing to do with the incipient German party or governmental structure but was opposition without any element of competition. This was an abnormality to be explained by the distorted focus of responsibility in occupation government; General Clay's customers were the Germans, but his responsibility and responsiveness ran to Washington. Opposition consisted of the open or subterranean resistance which indigenous leaders, most effectively those without jobs in the occupation-installed governments, such as Kurt Schumacher, put up to some of the policies of the occupation authorities. This opposition rested on different vistas of Germany's future role and organization, all related to the divergent national interests that separated foreign occupiers and incipient German political operators. The opposition became more effective as more discord between Western and Eastern occupiers necessitated close attention to German susceptibilities.

Social Democratic Opposition

The end of the Western occupation regime shades over into the beginning of the Bonn establishment. The new regime was put into the saddle by the Western occupation powers after the American authorities in early summer 1948 had taken the decision that was to determine much of the future course of German politics: to carry through a drastic currency reform without tying it in any way to a change in the distribution of property or in the ownership of the means of production. The new political regime, whose political viability was vouched for by the continued presence of the occupiers (now turning protectors and allies), rested on the acceptance of periodic elections carried on by competing parties. The whole apparatus was in the traditional Western style. It was tied up with and constitutionally answerable to a Parliament whose activities, in the long run, became at least as problematic as those of similar European institutions. The 1949 elections had given no party anything approaching a majority. But the future perennial chancellor, Konrad Adenauer, the leader of the catch-all Christian Democratic Union, managed to squeeze into office with a one-vote majority.

Both the narrowness of the government coalition's original parliamentary basis, the contrasting personalities of the two leaders involved (Konrad Adenauer and Kurt Schumacher), and the initially sharply drawn issues made it appear that Germany now for the first time had a parliamentary opposition, performing in the classic parliamentary tradition. Kurt Schumacher characterized his party's role in this sense when he opened the debate after the first government declaration by Chancellor Adenauer on September 20, 1949: "The essence of opposition is a permanent attempt to force the government and its parties by concrete proposals tuned to concrete situations to pursue the political line outlined by the opposition." [1] Such opposition seemed grounded on both domestic and foreign policy issues.

On the domestic front the SPD had already lost the first round in 1948 before the establishment of the Bonn government. After the currency reform, Ludwig Erhard, the economic delegate in the bizonal governmental structure who became the indefatigable propagandist of the so-called "social market economy," had his policy of doing away altogether with economic restrictions and rationing adopted, over the protest of the Social Democratic Party, which was representative of the urban consumer at large. Under the new establishment, Schumacher would come back to the same charges with increased vigor, becoming the sharpest critic of what he called the authoritarian state defending the interests of the property owners.

In foreign policy Schumacher tried to fight a two-front war. As a participant witness of Weimar history he wanted above all to avoid having his party again labeled defeatist and unpatriotic. First and foremost, therefore, he was firmly set against the slightest attempt to compromise with the regime in the Eastern zone. But at the same time he initiated the fight, persevered in by his party for only a short while after his death in 1952, against making Western Germany a partner of the various initial European integration endeavors. He described them not as praiseworthy efforts at a union of all democratic European peoples, but as the suspicious and undesirable enterprise of the momentarily ruling capitalist and Roman Catholic forces of little Europe. To his mind European integration was not only a conspiracy against the revival of the German nation but also against the people of the largely socialist-oriented nations of northern Europe. Instead, his policy stood for a conscious effort to reunite Germany at the earliest conceivable moment as an independent national community outside the framework of Eastern domination or Western mortgages.

Both by the choice of its leaders and the orderly, not to say conservative, background of its party members, this Schumacher policy of opposition was, however, to be exercised only within the strict limits of parliamentary procedure as prescribed by the Basic Law which the Social Democratic Party had prominently helped to shape. Opposing the present administration the SPD would steadfastly stand by the Bonn setup as established

1. *Bundestag Stenographische Berichte, 1,* (1949), 32.

under the Basic Law. From the outset it might have looked as if the chance of unfolding such a type of loyal opposition was to be enhanced not only by the tenuous parliamentary hold of the government, but also by the insignificance of any element of opposition of principle.

Under the harsh climate of economic deprivation prevailing in 1949, both the left- and right-wing oppositions of principle had managed to return to the first Bundestag a small band of followers, in spite of the recent experience with National Socialism and the current unfolding of the Communist regime in East Germany. But, totaling in the first Bundestag only about six per cent of the membership, these groups at no time had any appreciable influence on the work of assembly or government. Even at that early time, there was at no point a need for the parties loyal to the Basic Law to suspend their government–opposition battle in order to repulse the onslaught of destructive forces. Later, after the first apparent success of the Erhard economic policy, which was materially helped by the Korean boom, the opposition of principle disappeared completely from the Bundestag. It dwindled to a trickle among the public at large, even before the government read it completely out of the circuit of official party competition by courtesy of two Constitutional Court decisions.

But the disappearance of the Communist and rightist opposition of principle, which might have enlarged the scope for a loyal SPD opposition within the democratic framework, had no such invigorating effect. We might rather be tempted to say that disappearance was one element among others in the steady erosion of the potentialities of loyal opposition. Schumacher's initial attempt to force the will of the opposition on the government revealed itself through the years as a complete fiasco on all fronts. Two successive electoral defeats were instrumental in the SPD's ardent desire long before the start of the 1961 election campaign to disentangle itself clearly from any notion of opposing major governmental policies. The SPD consciously strove to eliminate parliamentary opposition as a desirable pattern for the conduct of political business.[2]

Let us first look at the stages of this breakdown of parliamentary opposition before trying to assess its reasons and its impact on the larger political scene. In 1947 suspicion was general against the German entrepreneurial class—a consequence of its support of the rising Hitler regime and its close association with it during the war. Even the Christian Democratic Union (CDU) had to make some genuflection, in its Ahlen program exercise of 1947, to public ownership. Scarcely more than six years later the tables had turned. The seeming success of the Erhard brand of eco-

2. I am intentionally dealing here mainly with the SPD because it stood, at least for some time, for alternative policy goals. The smaller parties, including the still fully operative third party, the Free Democratic Party, never had anything but a tactical motivation to enhance its competitive position, at no time making the slightest discernible attempt to sponsor alternative policies.

nomic liberalism, proudly acclaimed at the 1953 Hamburg pre-election congress of the CDU, served to rehabilitate the image of the German entrepreneur.

The SPD, after its first election defeat in 1953, started the long road of retreat on all fronts. Immediately the SPD relegated the socialization of the means of production to an inconspicuous place. By 1959, when redrafting its program in Godesberg, its social and economic clauses had become a collection of vistas and projections for an expanding society designed, à l'Américaine, to play up to nearly all segments of society by the proper insertion of strategically chosen, yet vague enough recognitions of group positions. If somewhat greater concern was given to the party's traditional labor clientele, great ingenuity was exercised to refrain from recommending any definite form of societal organization. Explicit condemnation hit only those systems restricting the free development of the human personality. Attitudes regarding the government of the day became a matter of purely tactical concern.

In such a tactical exercise, interparty competition still has an important role. On the domestic front, for example, the party continues to make a special effort to gain the ear of groups whose sympathies may be in relatively easy reach, such as Protestants in general and Catholic workers in particular. Both are supposed to be attracted by the unconditional shelving of the last vestige of the traditional "religion is a private affair of the individual." In the 1959 program, collaboration with the churches comes before a short reference to freedom of thought. Yet the 1959 program still took the view that children should be educated in common rather than in separate denominational state schools; three years later, in the light of modified tactical needs, such a clear-cut position had already again become outdated.[3] Catholic workers, for whom the party competes with the CDU, are also to be attracted by the heavy emphasis on the regressive character of government fiscal policy. The demand for exten-

3. See the instructive discussion at the Cologne SPD Parteitag (Protokoll, Bonn, 1962, pp. 391–92, 405–12), and the recent pamphlet, "Katholik und Godesberger Programm Zur Situation nach *Mater und Magistra*," published by the SPD party executive in March 1962; the pamphlet tries to show the similarities of approach between the Papal encyclical and the Godesberg program of the SPD. However, in the guise of interpretation, it offers the Catholic Church compromises on the school question which would not be smaller than those promised by other parties (pp. 47–51, esp. p. 51). The first postwar *Konkordat* concluded in February 1965 between the Vatican and the SPD-led Lower Saxony state government kept this promise. It is, as a matter of fact, more favorable to the church in regard to educational policies than the provisions so far applying in areas under CDU-led state governments. What is relevant from our viewpoint is the intent. It matters little that an element of self-deception is involved in such tactics of accommodating the churches at any price. At any rate, the *Konkordat* aroused a certain amount of resentment, especially among teachers. It also led to the withdrawal of the FDP from the Land government and the substitution of the CDU.

sion of existing social welfare and pension schemes is also an ever recurrent theme.

All this then remains on the purely competitive level. The same social policy themes and suggestions will recur in the propaganda of the CDU's labor wing. The economic and social organization (in the form it has taken since the early '50s) is no longer challenged in principle. The present interplay between economic liberalism and oligopolistic power of individual firms, and between various economic and social groups may not work out satisfactorily. In that event, the SPD, along with other parties, might be glad to accept changes suggested by experts to meet the new conditions. Yet the SPD's present program is an attractive sales prospectus for desirable group futures, and is neither designed to provide concrete answers for special contingencies nor, in contrast to the discarded old formulas, a total scheme for societal development.

The SPD not only shuns any frontal attack on the economic system but through the mouth of its 1964 convention keynote speaker on economic affairs paid special tribute to "the dynamics of market economy as an inalienable part of a libertarian economic order." [4] At the same time, however, in good catch-all party platform style the acceptance of the market economy is counterbalanced by an affirmative nod toward all those dirigiste policies required by modern industrial society. With an eye on the competitive advantages to be obtained it will press with a more lusty voice the claims of an actual and potential clientele. It has urged the continuation of a publicly sponsored housing program in spite of an overheated economic situation, and upheld, to a certain degree at least the job interests of miners threatened by cheaper fuel resources.

In matters of economic policy, then, the SPD simply yielded to the overwhelming success of the German economy of the '50s. But the foreign policy picture is by no means as clear-cut. In spite of the SPD's initial resistance, a measure of Western economic integration came off as planned. Rearmament too has been carried through within the framework of the Western alliance. This policy has paid off in economic terms and has enhanced German status within the Western community. Yet the policy has brought Germany no nearer the goal proclaimed by the SPD and echoed by the government: reunification in freedom. Nevertheless, the SPD's policy of opposition has caved in on this front more unconditionally than on any other. Until the middle '50s the SPD fought a rearguard action to delay Western integration. Under Schumacher's initial impetus it opposed the Schuman Plan and the setting up of the Council

4. See, e.g., Dr. Karl Schiller in SPD Parteitag, 1962 Protokoll, pp. 256–58, and his statements on the need for "cautious accommodation of the coal industry to the changed consumption structure" in the 1964 Karlsruhe party convention, quoted in *SPD Parteitag Arbeitsgemeinschaft B*, November 24, 1964 (uncorrected Protokoll, pp. 12–13).

of Europe. With the full support of its adherents and other large groups it fought in Parliament and in the Constitutional Court against the incipient rearmament effort. Its line faltered in the mid-'50s when it started to uphold the need for national defense and fully collaborated in implementing defense policies. In 1957 and 1958, however, it used the general abhorrence of atomic war for a vigorous parliamentary action. In 1959 it sponsored a so-called "German Plan" of foreign policy. To the need for accommodation with the Soviet Union to obtain a Western-style unity of Germany it tied a form of acceptance of a demilitarized zone in Europe. Yet by mid-1960 it had dropped the attempt at developing an independent foreign policy line. It solemnly abjured any thought of forcing the will of the opposition on the government; it now became its task "to find a common understanding to see what can be done, both in concrete situations and as a long-term proposition." [5] It condemned the idea of a third way between freedom and Communism which was still inherent in the "German Plan." To show their prospective political partners the seriousness of their intentions, the SPD leadership, dragging along the reluctant party chairman, Erich Ollenhauer, rammed a resolution through the 1960 Hannover party convention which whittled down the blunt rejection of German production, stationing, or use of atomic weapons contained in the otherwise tame enough Godesberg program of the previous year.[6]

By 1964 there were too few clear-cut foreign policy lines and initiatives left to allow one to speak of "the SPD foreign policy." A few distinctive emphases are still discernible—some continued opposition to the unnecessary dependence on nuclear weapons for European defense and vigorous resistance to the further spread of strategic nuclear weapons (in line with American strategy concepts) and special concern for both the needs and the propaganda possibilities inherent in the party's predominant position in Berlin. Yet none of these emphases is far from the tactical line of a broadly based interparty foreign policy, and none offers either basic criticism or alternative positions.[7]

The concept of opposition as a framework for presenting policy alternatives was officially abandoned in the speech given by the SPD's candidate-designate for the chancellorship, Willy Brandt, with the 1961 elections in mind: "In a sound and developing democracy it is the norm rather than the exception that the parties put forward similar, even identical demands in a number of fields. The question of priorities, of the

5. Herbert Wehner as official speaker in the foreign policy debate on June 30, 1960, *Bundestag Stenographische Berichte, 46,* 7055.

6. The Hannover debate was a tactical exercise. Two years later the same leaders were to emphasize a maximum of restraint concerning independent Western European atomic weapons.

7. See, e.g., Fritz Erler in the foreign policy debate of October 12, 1962, in *Bundestag Stenographische Berichte, 51,* 1773–80.

rank order of tasks to be solved, and of methods and accents thus becomes ever so much more the content of opinion formation." [8] This statement sees the reduction of opposition to its purely competitive elements as both necessary and desirable.

The basic factors in this change of political style, which have operated in most advanced industrial societies, have in recent years been discussed extensively.[9] They may be summarized as follows: the modern welfare state can now provide solutions to problems of many social groups without in this process worsening the situation of competing social groups. This weakens the old clashes of immediate interests and converts them into mere conflicts of priority in the time sequence of satisfactions. This has freed political parties of the necessity of concentrating their electioneering efforts on specific groups while antagonizing others. It allows them now to compete simultaneously for the electoral allegiance of a great variety of social strata. This situation allows their policies to be determined by tactical requirements of the moment, relegating ideologically determined long-range goals to a remote corner.

Foreign policy considerations work in the same direction. An opposition party may tactically exploit unpopular government decisions, especially those whose full meaning is slow to unfold. But first, such tactical advantage is balanced by the authority and prestige which the conduct of foreign policy bestows on the responsible statesman. Secondly, the interstitial changes which an opposition party operating within a framework of national consensus may propose are either too technical and complex or too vague and general to have an appreciable impact on the voter's attitude. By the same token, the revolutionary social implications of technological progress—the threat of mass unemployment—are cushioned by major power competition with the corresponding armament efforts of the big and medium-sized powers. Such "prophylactic" expenditures prevent the pressures on major parties both from the outside and from within their own ranks for new and radical solutions of major foreign and domestic problems. They allow them to avoid raising the more important problems of our time (threat of universal atomic destruction, dispropor-

8. Willy Brandt, *Plaidoyer für die Zukunft* (Frankfurt, Europaisch Verlags Anstalt, 1961), p. 17.

9. See, for an early succinct statement, Herbert Tingsten, "Stability and Vitality in Swedish Democracy," in *Political Quarterly*, 26 (1955), 140–51; for my own views, see "The Waning of Opposition in Parliamentary Regimes," in *Social Research* (Summer 1957), pp. 128–56, reprinted in John W. Wahlke and Heinz E. Eulau, *Legislative Behavior* (Glencoe, Free Press, 1960). Most recently the point has been taken up in considerable detail in Manfred Friedrich, *Opposition ohne Alternative* (Cologne, Verlag Wissenschaft und Politik, 1962), and with an added request for a revision of political style in "Politik ohne Alternative? Zur Profilneurose der Parteien," in *Neue Zuercher Zeitung*, April 21, 1963, p. 7. See also the articles by Karl Dietrich Bracher and Seymour Martin Lipset in "A New Europe?" *Daedalus, 93,* No. 1 (Winter 1964).

tion between the living standards and the expectations of advanced and former colonial countries, impact of technological change on social and economic structure of advanced nations), or, to the extent they cannot be disregarded, to handle them in vague, carefully modulated and, above all, noncontroversial ways, thus barring them from the field of national party competition. Major interparty differences lose their raison d'être when overriding technological, international, and military problems are not debated among the parties.

In modern industrial societies, the parties loyal to the regime in addition carry on a certain amount of competition with each other. The wider and more diversified the appeal they try to make, the greater their competition; the more they restrict their appeals to specific social groups, the less their competition. If the potential clientele is as broad as the electorate, there will be a more concerted effort than if it is known in advance that the structure and goals of the organization militate against reaching more than a regional, religious, or occupational segment. But as long as comparative electoral standing in the population is by common consent a yardstick for allocating spheres of political influence, some competition has to go on. The verdict may not actually be related to the performance of the competitors, as the electoral outcome is likely to depend mainly on the voters' reactions to events outside the control of the political actors. But political convention has sanctioned this yardstick in preference to more complicated and less clear-cut ones.

Now in a figurative sense this competition involves some element of opposition, if for no other reason than that the party representatives take their places on opposite sides of the moderator in their TV contests. To what degree their competition involves an actual element of opposition in the sense of our definition—sponsoring differential goals in one or the other major field of political contention—is a different question. Different historical backgrounds, traditions, and ideologies and varying objectives of their leaders and their clienteles may lead to variations in emphasis in the vague proposals on how to face tomorrow's still undecipherable reality. At any rate, opposition and competition timetables do not necessarily jibe. The more closely the dates of elections correspond to a prearranged constitutional schedule, the less the likelihood that interparty competitive pressures will coincide with situations crying out for alternative political solutions. The candidates' fights may be more in the nature of a collision between people obliged to squeeze through the same narrow thoroughfare to punch the clock before 8:45.

Competition and opposition are related techniques for obtaining political power. Competition performs a sort of selection among those eager to arrive, unless the candidates take their precautions. They may come near to distributing the prizes beforehand by a combined operation, depriving the public of the essence, though not the fun, of its role of selection. An element of opposition makes a collusive agreement less likely. Goal differentiation may transcend the mere accumulation of personal, organizational, or social-status defense positions.

In democratic politics competition and opposition easily intertwine. Political practitioners may shuffle back and forth between competing and coalescing, refurbishing traditional goals to look like new ones and putting up new signposts while trying to minimize the shock of goal displacement.

To these general reasons for the waning of opposition in advanced industrial societies should be added at least one German phenomenon unknown to any other European nation—the imposed division of the country into two parts. There is the all-pervasive fact that what used to be the Communist opposition of principle has now become a hostile state organization, which is master of a considerable part of Germany's former territory. From the German Democratic Republic's offices flows an un-interrupted stream of criticism—always prejudiced, often inane, and on rare occasions revealing—of West German institutions, policies, and personalities. This criticism is coupled with attempts to exploit every false step of the West German antagonists both in Germany and the world at large, but especially to set the West German population against its political establishment. The reaction in West Germany has been to play down divisive elements and internal criticism and to look with suspicion on any type of criticism which is parallel with, even if or-ganizationally independent of, that coming from East Germany. The mere fact of the existence of two mutually exclusive regimes transforms any opposition into opposition between the two regimes, emptying strictly domestic conflict of much of its substance and meaning.

This overriding conflict has had an abiding effect on the internal structure of the SPD. Both Communist foes and domestic competitors of the SPD, each for their own propaganda reasons, like to point out the common root of Communism and Social Democracy in nineteenth-century Marxism. Naturally, then, the SPD seeks in thought and action to make clear its radical departure from these suspect origins, even if this leads to the opposite result of making it look nearly indistinguishable from its main domestic competitor, the CDU. The SPD endeavors to eliminate the picture of the political party as a community of true believers.[10] It substitutes the image of an association of people who have banded to-

10. The Cologne 1962 SPD party convention was presented with a motion (55–56) asking it to abandon the habitual form of greeting, "Comrade" (*Genosse*), and sub-stitute "party-friend" (Protokoll, pp. 466, 648). This motion might have arisen from the acute embarrassment caused the party when the late Chairman Erich Ollenhauer was not firm enough in his response to Khrushchev, who, upon meeting Ollenhauer said, "We call each other 'comrade,' don't we?" While the motion was tabled without discussion, it seems symptomatic that the issue was raised.

gether for the pursuit of goals lying exclusively in the political field and left themselves complete freedom in all other fields. This development, officially emphasized at all times, is in line with the disappearance of intra-party debate. As long as alternatives to official policy persisted, internal party discussion and the democratic party structure played a significant role in policy elaboration. This party democracy was safeguarded not only by tradition, but by the realities of the political process. Under Weimar, many voters shifted back and forth between an extreme party, such as the Communists, and a party which worked within the constitutional frame-work, such as the SPD, each of which promised satisfaction of partly identical claims. (The same situation prevailed between the German Nationalist Party and the National Socialist Party.) The very possibility of such a switch gave the internal party opposition some leverage in com-batting the official party line. The demise of the Radical Left has thus become one element in the change of the internal style of the SPD. There are scarcely any remnants of such internal opposition left.[11]

Another element is the nature of present discontent and ensuing internal party discussion. Discontent now does not lie principally within the socio-economic sphere; no crying needs of important segments of the popula-tion clamor for immediate action. Discontent revolves around more abstract problems of foreign policy and German unity. These generate a flood of professional and subprofessional comment, but neither heat nor popular pressure for immediate solution. This situation allows the party executive to ride roughshod over deviationists—mostly violators of reso-lutions which declare participation in other organizational activities, such as anti-atomic bomb marchers or support of left-wing student organiza-tions, incompatible with party membership—and to carry out swift policy shifts with a minimum of intraparty fuss and friction.

The reduction of the opposition to its competitive element does not determine whether such competition will emphasize electoral or bargain-ing elements. Electoral and bargaining tactics are not mutually exclusive but the two opposite poles of a continuum. Bargaining strength will, to a degree varying with the democratic propensities of a given polity, be underpinned by electoral success; on the other hand, electoral tactics may be modulated by interest in striking political bargains.

The SPD, exactly like its Austrian sister party, only so far less success-fully, has laid more stress on bargaining than on electoral tactics. This may be due simply to a lack of self-confidence evidenced by its still holding on to a slightly modified system of proportional representation.

11. Some of these problems have been perspicaciously treated by a meanwhile ejected academic representative of the intra-SPD party minority, Wolfgang Aben-droth: *Aufstieg und Krise der deutschen Sozialdemokratie* (Frankfurt, 1964), pp. 50 ff., and "Innerparteiliche und Innerverbandliche Demokratie als Voraussetzung der politischen Demokratie," in *Politische Viertel-Jahresschrift*, 5, No. 3 (1964), 307–38.

While PR makes it more difficult for the party to hope ever to obtain a clear-cut majority, it does serve as a guarantee against electoral reverses taking a catastrophic turn. However, its conversion into a catch-all popular party organization has produced some second thoughts in SPD ranks on this point. During the December 1962 coalition negotiations the SPD turned down tentative advances by the CDU in the direction of adopting a straight majority electoral system. Yet the feeling of having successfully engineered the transition to a multiclass organization is making the SPD slightly more hospitable to the idea of a majority system as perhaps an additional, though by no means exclusive, approach toward gaining governmental positions.

The importance of the election system as a factor influencing the preference for electoral versus bargaining tactics should not be overrated. The political style of a country's elite may be equally if not more significant. Unlike the British situation, the fate of a German politician is influenced only mildly by his party's ability to obtain a majority or a plurality at election time. Due to the ways of access to politics in Germany, neither his livelihood nor his social standing will depend on the outcome of the electoral battle. Some major and middle-level politicians, irrespective of whether they want to escape the frustration of the intraparty politics of the CDU or the dampening of their ambitions through the SPD's prolonged failure to gain federal office, have a good chance to find berths with financial and status rewards in the top echelons of the state governments. The switch will allow them still to share some of the political limelight and perhaps make a comeback on the federal level. More important, political personnel on the intermediate level more often than not has entered Parliament as major officeholders of semi-autonomous public or private organizations (cities, counties, employer or trade union groups, agricultural associations, etc.); in other instances they may have status as civil servants or judges. In a handful of cases their party's hold on the reins of the federal government may give such men a chance at federal office. Neither their professional standing nor their financial security depend upon such preferment. In view of the relatively limited number of top political officeholders on the federal level (about 20) and the slow turnover in Cabinet jobs, such careers would anyhow be rare. Major federal political office is at the same time only a mildly attractive prize in a country which provides for its professional, intellectual, and civic elite many comfortable berths requiring less exertion and furnishing sufficient pay and security. Hankering for the spoils of government by impatient politicians is not a major element in political party life, nor does it force what one may call an electoral style on political competition.

A major element in the prevalence of bargaining-type politics is the country's federal structure. From the outset no single party has ever been able to dominate all state governments. Consequently the federal and state administrations must be prepared to work with each other on a close and continuous basis in all matters pertaining to finance, legislation, and administration irrespective of the particular administration's political complexion. Even if the effect of election victories—never spectacular under proportional systems—were not diffused by the staggering of the dates of the federal and state elections, the permanency of different interest constellations as between the states and the federal government deprives the party label of much of its meaning. Any federal government must periodically try cajoling the states into abandoning part of their constitutionally sanctioned hold over income and corporation taxes. Conversely, any state wants to keep maximum administrative and financial powers against the expanding claims of both the federal intruder and the formally subordinate cities and counties. This situation puts a constant premium on bargaining tactics.

Such conflicts are in most cases handled through purely bureaucratic channels. While the professional skill and experience of one or the other politician or administrator-politician may be decisive for the outcome of such a bargain, such activity has low political visibility and little value for electoral debates. The parties function as one element, and not necessarily the most important one, in an interbureaucratic equilibrium in which central, state and, local bureaucracies all play their roles.[12] As a rule state politics and even state–federal relations are crowded out of voters' minds at the time of state elections by issues or sentiments of a more general nature. This makes it easy for all participants in the political game to keep many subjects exclusively within bureaucratic channels. In cases of patent inability to reach an agreement, the terms of the federal–state bargain may be redefined [13] by a *deus ex machina* decision of the Constitutional Court. Electoral expectations or results figure only at infrequent intervals as determinants of action in this wide area of financial and administrative policy.

Another, and final, point on the decline of the opposition concerns the popular understanding of the concepts of party and state. The Bonn establishment was designed as an antidote to an adventurous and disorderly one-party government. In this establishment Adenauer himself— and this is part of his success story—embodied both the pragmatic virtues

12. Related viewpoints might be found in Edward L. Pinney, *Federalism, Bureaucracy and Party Politics in Western Germany: The Role of the Bundesrat* (Chapel Hill, University of North Carolina Press, 1963).

13. As happened in the 1962 television controversy, when a number of Land governments successfully sued the federal government for its attempt to put up a federal television station with privately financed programs. See *Entscheidungen des Bundesverfassungsgerichts, 12* (1962), 205.

of an interest-compromise-oriented party politician and the traditional type of state authority, functioning above and beyond the day-to-day struggles and firmly directed toward national goals.

Thus there have been two political images operative in German minds. The one perceives the turning of the German political parties from ideologically oriented gatherings of loyal adherents into bureaucratic machines soliciting individual votes and the assistance or benevolent neutrality of interest congeries. The party here is a machine for receiving and sorting out claims on the state; it is thus one more instance, belated but significant, of the turn of Germany into a Western-style business society. The party that performs these functions of processing claims most efficiently is then rewarded with office by a perspicacious electorate.

The competing image of the state as an objective value structure above and beyond all interest organizations and all parties has not disappeared, however. It is vivid not only as a somewhat idealized description of their own social functions among bureaucrats and members of the academic profession, but among the population at large. The near-general acceptance of the welfare state—in spite of the official German trappings of the so-called "social market economy"—involves a community obligation to take care of the citizens' minimum needs. This mental climate reinforces already existing inclinations to stress administrative continuity behind the gyrations of the players on the political scene. It is more than likely that the expectation of orderly and continuous government performance was held against the Adenauer regime, once the prolonged uncertainties and incessant rivalries of the succession crisis had become public knowledge.

The parties themselves are by no means averse to looking on their own role in administrative-bureaucratic terms rather than in competitive-electoral terms.[14] To some extent this tendency rests on apparent or real

14. Here is an example of bureaucratic-type state authority in the practices of what, in federal terms, is still the "opposition" party. The Socialist majority of the Diet of the city-state of Bremen in December 1957 passed a bill referring differences between a legally instituted personnel representation and the state government over personnel policies, including appointments and dismissals of less than top-ranking state officials, to an arbitration board. The board was to be manned by representatives of both state employees and the state government, and the decisive vote would lie with the chairman, the Social Democratic President of the City Assembly. The state government, also headed by a perennial Social Democratic Lord Mayor, unwilling to tolerate such diminution of state authority, first took its grievance to the state Constitutional Court. After having narrowly lost the case in the Bremen jurisdiction, it resorted to the federal Constitutional Court, which promptly vindicated its position and voided the law. (*Entscheidungen des Bundesverfassungsgerichts, 9* [1959], 268.)

Nobody will be astonished that a German Constitutional Court manned by people with judicial, bureaucratic, and university professors' backgrounds would look with jaundiced eyes at an attempt to treat the state as an employer exactly on the same level as any other party to a collective contract. The court would see in such a law

necessities of relations between the Federal Republic and East Germany, which, e.g., has led Federal Republic jurisprudence to assimilate party documents and papers to state secrets. This tendency also appears in the patterns of party financing, which recently has been shifting from exclusive reliance on membership fees (mainly in the SPD) and business contributions (mainly in the CDU and Free Democratic Party, or FDP) to federal treasury financing. At present the federal government distributes 38 million DM a year to the parties mainly according to the electoral strength of the federal party organizations.[15]

It is only logical that under such circumstances the SPD visualizes the goal of interparty competition more as that of universalizing bargaining practices than removing the stronger competitor from office.[16] That goal

only the possibility of diminishing state authority beyond the critical point rather than visualizing the potentiality that a compromise effected by a strategic person with a position midway between the interest groups and the formal state authority could maintain the uninterrupted functioning of public services. What is revealing, however, is that a socialist-led state administration felt an irresistible urge to go to such pains to teach its own majority the sanctity of the principle that state authority transcends groups claims.

15. As the law stands now 20 per cent of the total sum is distributed in equal shares to the CDU, Christian Social Union (CSU), FDP, and SPD; the other 80 per cent is allocated to the various parties according to the number of seats they hold in the Bundestag, which presently nets the SPD slightly over 13 million DM. The total election outlay for the 1961 Bundestag election may have come to 70 to 80 million DM. See Ulrich Dübber, *Parteifinanzierung in Deutschland 1962* (Cologne, Westdeutscher Verlag, 1962) and Ulrich Dübber and Gerard Braunthal, "West Germany" in *Comparative Political Finance*, ed. R. Rose and A. J. Heidenheimer (*Journal of Politics*, 1963). However, under a three-party agreement concluded in January 1965 *central* expenditures for the 1965 elections will be both supervised and kept to a prearranged maximum level of 16.5 million DM for the CDU-CSU and 15 million DM for each of the other two parties. The SPD has protested the increasing reliance on state financing for political organizations—more favorable to the CDU and FDP with low membership receipts than to the SPD which in 1963 received 14 million DM in membership fees. It has therefore been able to spend part of the federal bonanza, which is augmented by various similar outlays in the individual states, for educational rather than for straight political purposes. The whole institution of official party finance underlines the degree to which German parties turn increasingly into quasi-official machines.

16. Recently Wolfgang Kralewski and Karlheinz Neunreither (in *Oppositionelles Verhalten im ersten Deutschen Bundestag, 1949-1953* [Cologne-Opladen, Westdeutscher Verlag, 1963]) have studied in detail SPD participation in federal legislation during the first legislative period. We reprint part of an instructive tabulation which shows how many bills, at the time of the final vote, were passed against SPD opposition. The percentage relates to the number of total statutes passed in the respective fields during the first legislature (page 92):

Budget—78.9%	Internal affairs, police, culture, etc.—14.8%
Foreign affairs—55%	Labor, social legislation—11.8%
Agriculture—19.4%	Economics—7.4%
Finance—15.4%	

In evaluating these percentages it has to be taken into consideration that SPD rejection of the budgets of most individual ministries is a pure matter of form, indiis in accord with popular ideas. An early 1963 poll indicated that a majority of those expressing an opinion considered a coalition of the two major parties, CDU and SPD, "a favorable solution in the interest of the Federal Republic." [17] What does this approval mean? As the poll did not ask how many people would have preferred clear-cut majority party rule, its meaning is open to doubt. But in conjunction with other inquiries (see Appendix 7.1) it may signify some popular knowledge of the declining level of interparty controversy as well as some popular groping for orderly and steady government performance under conditions of maximal popular consent. A broad interparty compact may fulfill the same psychological function as the objective and independent state power for which people still hanker. Thus the enlarging of case-to-case, interstitial, and administrative bargains to the level of permanent political bargaining in the form of a major party coalition government might seem just a question of time.[18] Before it happens, however, the CDU, which still has a national plurality, has to be convinced that such a coalition would be both desirable and profitable for it.

The circle is nearly complete: the SPD now shuns the very idea of an opposition role, and multiplies both demands and offers of unconditional participation. All the government can do to protect itself from this impetuous urging is curtly to recall that no way exists to force the government to accept the SPD as a partner.[19] Such rebuffs only make the

---

cating the official opposition status of the party. The rather substantial number of rejections in the foreign policy field is, as explained in our text, a matter of the past. The removal of foreign policy from the field of party politics, so much desired by the authors (pp. 93, 99) has long since taken place. On the other end of the scale we find the field of economics indicating that most reconstruction legislation, even at the height of SPD opposition under the Schumacher regime, was noncontroversial from the outset or mutually satisfactory compromises had been obtained before the final vote. Interestingly enough the book, which contains among other things exhaustive studies of the legislative process in regard to three particular subject matters (boundary police bill, bill protecting youth against obscene literature, and the Constitution Court bill), comes to the conclusion that the effectiveness of the opposition in the legislative process has depended mainly on the varying quality of the opposition experts in the respective committees (p. 213). The substance of the policy differences seems to have played a much smaller role.

17. *Emnidinformationen*, No. 13 (1963) of March 25, 1963, p. 2, lists 36 per cent favoring an SPD-CDU coalition, 23 per cent favoring a CDU-FDP coalition, 9 per cent an SPD-FDP coalition, with 32 per cent uttering no clear-cut preference.

18. The details of the German variants of the demise of political opposition have recently been described, though with some ideological somersaults, in Waldemar Besson, "Regierung und Opposition in der deutschen Politik," in *Politische Vierteljahresschrift, 3* (September 1962) 224–41.

19. See the explanation of the CDU speaker, Von Brentano, in the debate on the government declaration of December 6, 1961, *Bundestag Stenographische Berichte, 50,* (1961) 65–73. The argument proffered by the same speaker that if the SPD were to join the government no controller would exist seems a bit tortured. The SPD had already on its own volition abandoned any thought of exercising a control function.

SPD strategists redouble their efforts to minimize their differences with the government and follow what is now commonly referred to as the "embracement" strategy. SPD energies are all bent to enhancing the chances for a permanent cut-in on the governmental organization.[20]

Competition with the goal of participation in the competitor's enterprise can make only marginal allowance for criticism. Conduct in Parliament must be modulated to express identity of thought patterns in all major affairs, but allow enough for small-scale needling to keep the advisability of joining forces steadily before the competitor. It may not be easy to keep about 200 M.P.'s always in line with the tactical requirements of the hour. Yet following both the listless general debates and the mass of trivia which the backbenchers pour out during oral questioning time impresses one with the lack of controversial issues or their studied avoidance. At question time there is universal eagerness to plead local and special interest group causes dear to the individual member or, at times, to prove one's loyalty and patriotic eagerness, to publicize German concerns and grievances throughout the world. The oral question remains by and large in the realm of the backbencher's title to recognition; it becomes an auxiliary weapon for political criticism only on special occasions.

One such rare flareup happened in 1962 when the question period was utilized for ventilating the *Spiegel* affair.[21] But one must immediately note the self-imposed tactical restrictions. Neither at that time nor in its written interrogatories submitted to the federal government did the SPD venture to raise the problem of freedom of critical opinion versus treason legislation which has aroused public concern. Instead it sought, successfully, to trip Minister of Defense Franz Josef Strauss on his inconsistent and incomplete statements and his unwarranted assumption of powers outside his own jurisdiction. The CDU's tactical retort—publicizing SPD members' irregularities in handling army committee material—was apparently sufficient to restrain the SPD from taking major parliamentary initiatives. Thus the SPD tacitly agreed to have the whole problem settled in the political no-man's-land where the judicial branch tries to figure out how to handle pernicious political dissent. It remains to be seen to what extent the quite recently introduced "currents events hour," during which members may speak extemporaneously on recent events for five minutes up to

20. All arguments for cooperative government by all parties may be found in endless variation in W. Brandt's keynote speech at the Cologne 1962 party convention. *Protokoll*, pp. 56–86; see also the characteristic discussion "Es hätte auch Schlimmer werden können" between party boss H. Wehner and some *Spiegel* editors in *Der Spiegel*, September 25, 1963.

21. Bundestag session of November 7, 8, and 9, 1962. *Bundestag Stenographische Berichte*, pp. 1949–2091; see also Otto Kirchheimer and Constantine Menges, "The Spiegel Case," in *Politics in Europe*, ed. G. M. Carter and A. F. Westin (New York, Harcourt Brace, 1965)

a total of one hour, will relieve the boredom pervading the entire institution.[22]

This, then, is a society which started out to practice party government and at first attempted to make it work within the grooves of the government–opposition system. The trappings of party government are there. They may be used to establish government formulas ranging from government by the strongest party alone, via interstitial stages of coalition between a major party and satellite parties, to the so far unrealized aim of the SPD—an Austrian-type combined operation of the two great parties. Whatever the particular form of party government, both those forces operating everywhere in advanced industrial societies and those forces arising out of the specific contemporary German situation have led to the steady erosion of goal-oriented opposition. What remains is a certain level of interparty competition, whose edges are blunted by all-pervasive bargaining carried through on a bureaucratic rather than a political level. Permanent institutionalization of such a bargaining style on the political level would mean an interesting attempt to stabilize political relations. In the last analysis such an endeavor at a watertight political cartel can be successful only if every outside or potential competitor is eliminated.

This raises the question: To what extent does the German political system allow for legal opposition outside parliamentary and party channels? The question coincides with the problem of constitutional limitations on extraparliamentary opposition. The Bonn Basic Law has privileged the parties as organizations that take part in the creation of the political will. It has penalized parties that want to impede the working of the free democratic order or endanger the existence of the Federal Republic. It allows the Constitutional Court (Art. 21, para. 2) to ban them altogether. The same rule holds for any other organization whose activity is in contradiction with "the Basic Law, the constitutional order or the idea of peaceful understanding between nations" (Art. 9, para. 2). With this exception, so far applied to the Socialist Reich Party and the Communist Party, and that of the impractical rule of Article 18, allowing an individual to be divested under the same conditions of some specifically mentioned basic rights, extraparliamentary opposition is legal. It is fully protected by the freedom of conscience, freedom of opinion-forming, and freedom of association provisions (Arts. 4, para. 1, Art. 5, para. 1, and Art. 8) of the Basic Law. If the Basic Law narrows freedom of opinion by adducing the limitations of the general laws,[23] "those which protect youth and personal

---

22. The first current events discussion of February 10, 1965, is reported in *Das Parlament*, February 17, 1965, together with the introductory remarks of Bundestag Vice-President Carlo Schmid.

23. According to the interpretation of the Constitutional Court, these "general laws" have to be interpreted from the "value-creating impact of the free democratic order and therefore themselves be restricted again in their effectiveness as limits on

honor" (Art. 5, para. 2), this does not create any government prerogative for supervising questions of political style.[24]

Boundary-line cases may, as they do in the United States, involve weighing priorities between freedom of opinion and protection of the interests of either the individual or of state security. This task devolves in the main on a federal Constitutional Court, inclining in a number of situations toward preferred freedom doctrines. Beyond such areas of possible conflict and choice there exists a guaranteed area for legal, yet extraparliamentary, opposition. The boundary-line cases, however, demonstrate that there may exist a considerable gap between constitutionally sanctioned legal extraparliamentary opposition and widespread public assumptions as to the legitimacy of such extraparliamentary opposition. Due to the increasing desiccation of parliamentary opposition, this question of the boundary lines of legitimate opposition has increased in importance. There is no doubt that uninvited suggestions, memoranda, and public discussion policy statements, emanating from academic or loosely church-connected groupings, on atomic policy, foreign affairs, inter-German policy, or social policy problems are considered appropriate even though they may often be considered unwelcome and inopportune in official circles. More and more general policy debates are taking place these days within the framework of such extraparliamentary groups rather than within political party organizations. Beyond this arena there is a grey zone of doubt.

There exists some tendency to look at systematic deviationism from official policies, especially in the field of East–West or inter-German relations, as illegitimate. This does not always involve condemnation of an advanced or deviant viewpoint, but simply a not uncommon conviction that such difficult problems should be handled by experts officially selected for the purpose. Consequently a television producer or a deviant press organ, like *Der Spiegel*, which does not observe these invisible boundaries may run into hostility. To what extent such hostility can be translated into action depends both on the legal situation and on community support for the attacked person or institution. The deviant producer's show may be put off the air by the public broadcasting corporation, as recently happened in the Panorama case. Putting legal impediments in the way of *Der Spiegel*, as the authorities found out too late, is much more involved and difficult. On the other hand, if it can be alleged with some degree of plausibility that the person or group involved

---

the basic right" (of free opinion formation). *Entscheidungen des Bundesverfassungsgerichts*, 7 (1957), 198, 208, and Professor H. Ehmke in his arguments in support of the constitutional complaint of the Spiegel Publishing Company filed with the federal Constitutional Court on May 1, 1963, pp. 66–79 (Verfassungsbeschwerde 1 BvR586/62 privately printed, Hamburg, 1963).

24. See A. Hamann, "Das Recht auf Opposition und seine Geltung im ausserparlamentarischen Bereich" in *Politische Vierteljahresschrift*, 3 (September 1962), 241, 255.

not only wants to exercise unhealthy influence on the general opinion-forming process but also strays into the field of political organization proper, both the established competitors—the parliamentary parties and the administrative organs of the state—will scan the records of the new-comers with magnifying glasses to discover improper motivations and unconstitutional connections. While deviant opinion is to some degree tolerated, legitimacy is not easily granted to movements and parties moving outside recognized channels in a country where the devastating memories of the '20s and '30s are still vividly in the minds of the older generation and where present conditions do anything but invite radical reorientation. Legality and legitimacy are not altogether identical in the German order of things. But prevalent legitimacy notions have a tendency to narrow down the radius of action left for legal, but extraparliamentary, opposition.[25]

25. The best introduction to this vast theme may be found in *Bestandsaufnahme Eine Deutsche Bilanz,* ed. H. W. Richter (Munich, Kurt Desch Verlag, 1961). For the most typical recent case see R. Schmid, "Auf dem Weg zum Überwachungsstaat" in *Die Zeit,* March 19, 1965, p. 3.

8
AUSTRIA:
THE POOLING OF OPPOSITION

Frederick C. Engelmann

The Prerepublican Background

Prior to 1889, the Austrian half of the Austro-Hungarian monarchy had neither a politically organized urban proletariat, nor widespread suffrage, nor responsible government. The Emperor had granted basic political freedoms in the 1860s, and in 1873 an unrepresentative Parliament was created, to which deputies were sent by landowners, burghers, chambers of commerce, and villagers. The Emperor continued to reign quasi-absolutely through ministers responsible to himself. The strongest political group was the German Liberals, who governed until 1879; after that the Emperor preferred to trust the advice of elements of the German and Polish nobility, the high clergy, and the high bureaucracy. The Germans formed only one-third of the population of "their" half of the monarchy, and the Emperor chose to give governmental responsibility to those who were not as intent on promoting a German hegemony as were the Liberals. The regime was not truly multinational, however, as the interests of Czechs, southern Slavs, and Ukrainians met with relative neglect. After 1879 the German Liberals formed the principal opposition. Soon they split into several groups, ranging from aristocrats to moderately progressive intellectuals (many of them assimilated Jews). Because of these splits, liberalism disintegrated organizationally and survived as an attitude rather than as a movement. Some former Liberals formed a German nationalist movement, which included even racist anti-Semites.

Organized legal opposition in Austria[1] dates from 1889. In that year, the Social Democratic and Christian Social parties were founded. The former was a typical party of the urban proletariat; the latter began as a movement of small tradesmen and soon developed into a party of the lesser non-class-conscious population, especially the smaller peasantry. Between them, these parties preempted the support of the not as yet enfranchised elements of the German-speaking population. In 1896 about

1. For the period prior to 1918, the term Austria denotes the western half of the Austro-Hungarian monarchy.

one-fifth of the parliamentary seats were given to representatives elected by universal suffrage, and a few Social Democrats and Christian Socials entered the Parliament. The Christian Socials achieved a notable success one year later—the capture of Vienna's municipal government.

In 1907 the Emperor granted universal and equal manhood suffrage, and the Social Democratic and Christian Social parties became the leading German-speaking parties. The Christian Socials formed the strongest single parliamentary party in the ensuing election. The next election (1911) brought a Social Democratic plurality. But because of the absence of responsible government neither party became an influential opposition. Obstructive parliamentary tactics, originally used by German radicals against Czechs, became the order of the day as the nationalities struggle drowned out any normal government–opposition dialogue. During these years, the Emperor did most of his ruling by decree, and Parliament became increasingly impotent. The monarchy disintegrated under the impact of the First World War, but the two young German mass parties—Christian Socials and Social Democrats—maintained their identity and were ready to play their roles in the future small republic of German-Austria.

The First Republic—Institutions, Parties, Cleavages, and Opposition

The establishment of the First Republic in 1918 brought representative government with a responsible executive to Austria. Only from this point on did Austria have true parliamentary opposition—an opposition legitimately capable of replacing the government. While the First Republic lasted from 1918 to 1938, the period of normal operation of opposition extended only from 1920 to 1933. From 1918 to 1920, the two major parties, Christian Socials and Social Democrats, formed a government coalition. The last five years of the First Republic were taken up by the Patriotic Front[2] dictatorship of Dollfuss and Schuschnigg.

German-Austria—the lands that were, according to Clemenceau, "left over" once the other nationalities had carved their states out of the Habsburg monarchy—adopted a constitution in 1920. There was responsible government, with the Cabinet elected by the Parliament, and a weak President. Amendment in 1929 provided for a strong President elected by popular vote (the first actual popular election took place only in 1951), who appoints the Chancellor and his government, who in turn must enjoy the confidence of the Parliament.

The country was left with its prewar political forces. The major ones, in terms of electoral support, were the Christian Socials and the Social Democrats. The German Liberals and Nationals, both weak ever since the introduction of universal suffrage, were further handicapped by the

2. The Patriotic Front consisted of Christian Socials, Catholic and fascist paramilitary organizations, and assorted anti-socialist elements.

severing of their heartland, the Sudeten areas, from German-Austria. They
survived in two rather weak political organizations: the largely urban petit-
bourgeois Pan-German People's Party, and the anticlerical Agrarian
League. The only other political group, the Communists, never even
achieved parliamentary representation in the First Republic. Their weakness was due to the organizational and ideological efforts of the Social
Democrats, who successfully prevented the political splitting of the workers that took place nearly everywhere else.

The three major groupings—clerical-Catholic,[3] Marxist-socialist, and
Liberal-National, true representatives of Almond's three subcultures [4]—
were more than political organizations. They were veritable subcultures,
with their own ideologies, interest groupings, and manifold ancillary party
organizations. The strong involvement in the politics of these subcultures
of hundreds of thousands of individuals made for inflexible voting behavior, resulting in a static electoral picture. The use of paramilitary
organizations by the groupings made particularly apt the Austrian term
used to designate them: *Lager* [5] (armed camp). Instead of giving their
political energies to the young and frail state, Austrians squandered them
on their respective *Lager*, which provided spiritual guidance, economic
representation, and avocational direction. The young state was, in fact,
not wanted by most of its citizens. The Liberal-National *Lager* was of
course dedicated to union with Germany. Even many Social Democrats
desired *Anschluss* to the Weimar Republic; and postwar plebiscites indicated that some of the provinces with strong Christian Social majorities
wanted it too. Many Austrians continued to feel that the state, proclaimed
in 1918 to be part of Germany, was nothing but the product of a dictated
peace settlement.

In 1919 and 1920 an attempt was made to make the weak state viable by
having it governed jointly by its two main political groups. But Christian
Socials and Social Democrats were too hostile to one another to permit
this coalition to succeed. The Social Democrats, confident that some day
they would be voted into power, unburdened themselves of governmental
responsibility and went into opposition. Until the elimination of Parliament in 1933 they remained the principal opposition group.[6] Some Liberal
and agrarian groups, mainly splinters, temporarily joined them in opposi-

3. During the First Republic, the Christian Social Party expanded its base, adding
to Catholic artisans and shopkeepers larger business interests that cannot be called
clerical.

4. Gabriel Almond, "Comparative Political Systems," *Journal of Politics, 18* (1956),
391–409.

5. The first systematic discussion of the *Lager* is contained in Adam Wandruszka,
"Oesterreichs Politische Struktur," in Heinrich Benedikt, ed., *Geschichte der Republik Österreich* (Vienna, Verlag für Geschichte und Politik, 1954), pp. 289–485.

6. See Appendix Table 8.1

tion, but their presence did not at any time affect opposition strategy and tactics. The government was formed from 1921 to 1930 by the *Bürger-block* (bourgeois bloc) consisting of the dominant Christian Socials and their allies, the Pan-Germans, and operating on the basis of an agreement entered into in 1921. Schisms in the bourgeois camp after 1930 reduced the government majority to one seat and strengthened those Christian Socials who eventually decided that the way to fight Hitler was to subdue the Social Democrats and abolish democracy.

The nature of Social Democratic opposition in the First Republic was democratic-structural.[7] The Social Democrats accepted the political institutions of representative democracy and the rules of free party competition—in fact they were the only party to do so consistently—but they were committed to bring about structural changes in the socioeconomic order. Some of these had been achieved prior to 1920. Tenants' protection had been granted by the Imperial government during the war, and the Social Democrats had utilized the short-lived coalition to place basic social security legislation on the statute books. In these fields, the main role of the opposition was to fight a holding operation, particularly against rent increases. The main policy achievement of the *Bürgerblock* government—currency stabilization through a deflationary loan from the League of Nations—met with heavy Social Democratic opposition throughout the period.

Much of the opposition of the Social Democrats was waged territorially. The city of Vienna, made a province early in the First Republic, had the first socialist government west of Russia, and the party made it a laboratory and showcase for socialist policies of welfare, housing, and taxation. These policies themselves formed the main, and certainly the most publicized, aspect of the Social Democrats' structural opposition. As policy objectives realized in Vienna, they were constantly before the Austrian voter as a set of policy alternatives.

Policy and territorial opposition was heavy enough; but its weight was increased by other factors. The Social Democrats integrated all of their opposition in their Austro-Marxist ideology, which took the place of religion with most Austrian workers. They also preempted political control of workers' economic representation: on the side of formalized policy advising through control of the Chamber of Labor, on the side of labor organization through control of the free trade unions. They achieved a degree of political organization unequaled in free parties through their

7. Charles A. Gulick, *Austria from Habsburg to Hitler* (Berkeley, University of California Press, 1948), is a monumental catalog of the nature and tactics of First Republic opposition (with a strong socialist bias). A concise summary of party warfare is contained in Mary MacDonald, *The Republic of Austria, 1918–34* (London, Oxford University Press, 1946), pp. 63–81.

system of cadres (*Vertrauensleute*). Finally they controlled the workers' leisure time by providing them with a full set of avocational organizations for everyone from cyclists to antialcoholics.

Throughout this period, opposition tactics were hard. Only twice did bargaining between opposition and government succeed. In 1927 education laws with mild social reforms, barely acceptable to the Social Democrats, were passed, and structural changes in the Constitution were agreed upon by both parties in 1929. The normal relationship between the parties was much less friendly. In Parliament the Social Democrats occasionally made use of walkouts or other obstructive tactics. Elections were fought with hard slogans. Some of the leaders felt that the party could hope to capture workers' votes only, but that victory would be theirs if it could capture virtually all of them.[8] A notable exception to class-based electoral tactics was the rent control issue; it appealed to many non-homeowners among the petit-bourgeois.

Outside Parliament, the Social Democratic opposition made use of a paramilitary organization, the Republican Defense League (Republikanischer Schutzbund). Born in the days of postwar free corps activities, the Defense League had the mission of protecting the Republic and the position of workers in the society. It was a useful counterweight to fascist groups (politically allied to the government) as long as it remained under the discipline of the party executive. But uncontrolled mob action after a typical class-justice situation (the acquittal of murderers of demonstrating workers in 1927) did irreparable damage to the Defense League's reputation among the uncommitted part of the population. The 1927 riots were the beginning of continuous paramilitary warfare between government and opposition. The rise of National Socialism after 1930 made this warfare three-cornered.

Hitler's rise to power united the Social Democrats in opposition to the *Anschluss* and made them staunch defenders of Austria's integrity. However, the Christian Socials, in facing the rising "brown" tide, turned not to them for aid, but to Mussolini. Exasperated by its one-vote majority in Parliament, and lacking a basic faith in democratic institutions, the government allowed itself to drift into the elimination of Parliament in March 1933. Dollfuss, the Christian Social Chancellor, subsequently founded the Patriotic Front and made clear that he was setting up a dictatorship. Terror activities of the tolerated *Heimwehr* (progovernment paramilitary organization) against the now outlawed Defense League led to resistance by the latter, bringing on the brief civil war of February 1934. The result was the "capture" of "red" Vienna and the outlawing of the Social Democratic Opposition. On May 1, 1934, a corporatist constitution was proclaimed,

---

8. Robert Danneberg, *Die Entwicklungsmöglichkeiten der Sozialdemokratie in Österreich* (Vienna, Verlag der Wiener Volksbuchhandlung, 1924).

and legal opposition, in fact any political organization outside the Patriotic Front, was at an end. Four years later the country itself ceased to exist, becoming a part of Hitler's *Reich*.

The Second Republic

INSTITUTIONS, PARTIES, CLEAVAGES   In 1945 the reconstituted Republic was governed initially by an antifascist concentration in which the People's Party (ÖVP), Socialists (SPÖ), and Communists were equally represented. There were no other legal parties, and therefore there was no legal opposition. The Constitution of 1920, with its 1929 amendments, was put in force once again. The country was divided into Russian, U.S., British, and French zones of occupation.[9] A free election, held in all zones, for a central parliament resulted in a parliamentary majority for the People's Party, a strong Socialist delegation, and only four Communist deputies. This election reduced the Communist government delegation to one member, who resigned in 1947. The government was left in the hands of the People's Party and Socialists, whose coalition is still in office.

Under this coalition the makeup of the government, and the representation of the two coalition parties within it, is decided in negotiations following each parliamentary election. Changes in the electoral picture in the elections of 1949, 1953, 1956, 1959, and 1962 have been slight.[10] Despite the fact that negotiations have become increasingly long (two months in 1959, four and one-half months in 1962–63), few portfolios have ever changed hands in these negotiations. The coalition operates on the basis of a coalition pact; these pacts are ratified by the two partners after each renegotiation of the coalition. The pacts of 1949 and 1953 were kept secret, though the latter has since been published. The pacts of 1956, 1959, and 1963 were made public. According to each of the pacts, decisions arrived at in the coalition committee (consisting of the top leaders of the two partners) are enacted by the unanimous vote of the parliamentary delegations of both partners. A complex clause of the pact of 1963 allowing some exceptions to this unanimity rule soon became the subject of controversy between the partners, but no legislation has been passed as yet by means of this clause. The *Proporz*—a system of two-party patronage exercised in proportion to the most recent election results—is used in government corporations and nationalized industries only. Within the regular departments of government, the party controlling the particular department has the major voice in bureaucratic appointments. The conventional stories according to which every government job in Austria is held by

9. An official at headquarters of one of the coalition parties emphasized to the writer that until the end of the occupation in 1955 much of the potential opposition energy was diverted into opposition to the occupation.

10. See Appendix Table 8.2.

three people—one "black," one "red," and one doing the work—are inaccurate.[11]

The coalition regime operates under the Constitution of 1920, as amended in 1929. Coalition pact and coalition committee (called "working committee" since 1963) are extraconstitutional institutions. The pact, with its provision for mandatory parliamentary support for bills on which the coalition committee agrees, has been attacked by leading constitutional authorities as contrary to the constitutional guarantee of the free exercise of the parliamentary mandate.[12] This particular issue, pitting the realities of the party state against a constitutional provision of dubious meaning, need not be resolved here; at any rate, the coalition practice cannot in fact be contested by any agency in a position to overrule the coalition committee.

Another provision of the Constitution however is of supreme importance in the operation of the coalition, and particularly in the exercise of intracoalition opposition (*Bereichsopposition*). This provision, Article 76, makes individual ministers responsible to Parliament. The authoritative interpretation of this provision, by both constitutional authorities and the Council of Ministers, has been that this individual responsibility imposes the unanimity rule on the Council of Ministers. On the policy-making side this means that a coalition government can act only on proposals cleared by the leaders of both coalition partners, i.e. the coalition committee. As regards opposition the interpretation means that either partner can render effective his opposition to policy proposals to the point of preventing their enactment. The requirement of unanimity prevents the coalition regime from adopting the Swiss model of decision-making by majority vote of the executive, also in use in the Austrian provinces.[13] Under this scheme, all or most parties are represented in the executive—in Switzerland by arrangement, in most Austrian provinces by right.

The parties of the Second Republic were fathered by the three *Lager* of the First Republic. The Liberal-National *Lager,* already weak in the First Republic and then bloated by National Socialism, is definitely of modest significance in the Second. Its party, the "Fourth Party" admitted by the Allies in 1949, was originally called League of Independents, and became known in 1955 as the Freedom Party. It not only lacks a common ideology, but, more importantly, the allegiance of a major interest group.

The coalition parties are of course the successors of the political representatives of the two major *Lager.* The chief reasons for continuation of the coalition beyond Austria's liberation from foreign occupation by the

11. John MacCormac, "The Improbable Coalition That Governs Austria," *Reporter,* January 23, 1958, pp. 33–37.

12. *Bundes-Verfassungsgesetz,* Art. 56.

13. Despite this constitutional difficulty, elements in the ÖVP favored the adoption of the provincial system on the federal level in 1963.

State Treaty of 1955 are (a) an inertia brought on by nearly two decades of multifaceted collaboration of the two parties and allied interests, and (b) the heritage of the *Lager* situation. The latter expresses itself in the fear of both subcultures of being governed by the other. This fear was—until 1962 at least—greater on the part of the Socialists who constituted the opposition *Lager* of the First Republic.

In the Second Republic, the subcultures have maintained their political as well as their socioeconomic bases. The Socialist Party was rebuilt quickly after 1945 and soon reached its First Republic membership strength. The organizational cadres have lost some verve, but they continue to exist; the ancillary organizations show less intensive activity, but they maintain their membership. The People's Party has a looser federal organization; yet its aggregate membership is as numerous as that of the Socialists. Such *dépolitisation* as has taken place, then, affects party life but not party membership. The latter maintains itself through spoils; there are on both sides *Proporz* jobs and *Proporz* franchises; in addition, membership in the Socialist Party is the easiest way to a municipal apartment.

The tie-up within each subculture among party, socioeconomic chambers, and interest groups reflects the rigidity of the First Republic nexus. The overwhelming majority of business and agriculture is in the camp of the ÖVP, and a very substantial majority of labor with the SPÖ. A system of compulsory membership in the chambers of commerce, agriculture, and labor, and partisan elections within all three of these chambers, gives conclusive evidence of the continued party-interest tie-up.[14] Among the voluntary interest organizations, the business and peasants' leagues of the ÖVP dominate in business and agriculture; on the labor side there is a suprapartisan Trade Union Congress, but all of the major unions, and therefore most Congress offices, are under Socialist control.

Ideological differences between the subcultures have subsided. In 1945 the church left politics. Clericalism has played a continually diminishing role in the People's Party. The Socialists found themselves after the war without their chief ideological element. In 1958 they adopted the largely de-ideologized Vienna program. Austrian society shows some of the conditions on which Kirchheimer bases his theory of the waning of structural differences,[15] and Austria is of course the home of Bednarik's shallow youths.[16] Yet despite all these developments, the two major subcultures remain socially and psychologically separated. *Lagermentalität* (*Lager* feeling and identification) persists. It has lost much of its philosophical basis, but retains its psychological reality; having lost much in ideology, it

14. See Appendix Table 8.3.
15. "The Waning of Opposition in Parliamentary Regimes," *Social Research*, 24 (1957), 127–56. See also his chapter in this volume.
16. Karl Bednarik, *Der junge Arbeiter von heute* (Stuttgart, Gustav Kilpper Verlag, 1953).

yet remains as mentality.[17] Most individuals' identification with their party remains strong.[18] The mutual distrust engendered by *Lagermentalität* goes far in explaining the persistence of the coalition, as well as the continuing peculiar condition of opposition under the Second Republic. Paradoxically, the second major explanation for the persistence of the regime is the convenience that the collaboration, so well established in years of coalition practice, has for parties, chambers, and interest groups.

NATURE OF THE OPPOSITION   Legal opposition in the Second Republic dates from 1947, when the Communist Party left the government. The Communist Party has remained as an organized opposition party, never surpassing its initial strength and losing its parliamentary representation in the aftermath of the Hungarian Revolution. It continues as legal but rather ineffectual opposition, and its few remaining islands of support are some of the industrial plants that had been under Russian control prior to 1955.

In 1949 the Socialists, intent on breaking the parliamentary majority of the ÖVP, persuaded the Allies to license a fourth party, which they hoped would split the non-Socialist vote. The licensing coincided with the enfranchisement of one-half million minor Nazis, most of whom supported the new party initially. The fourth party is now in its second incarnation. Having been variously called League and Electoral League of Independents, it has been the Austrian Freedom Party since 1955.

While it is unable to transcend the national subculture, it must share it with the major parties. ÖVP and SPÖ, identified with postwar reconstruction and aided by the *Proporz*, have gained the allegiance of many nationalists. The Freedom Party has been interested more in the representation of interests excluded by the coalition than in opposing coalition policies. These excluded interests are varied. First of all, there are those

17. The writer is indebted to Juan J. Linz ("An Authoritarian Regime: Spain," paper delivered at the 1963 Annual Meeting of the American Political Science Association, New York City, pp. 9–11 and notes) for the suggestion of Theodor Geiger's distinction between ideology and mentality (*Die soziale Schichtung des deutschen Volkes*, Stuttgart, 1932, pp. 77–79). Linz quotes "Mentality is *subjektiver Geist* (even when collective), ideology is *objektiver Geist*. Mentality is intellectual attitude, ideology is intellectual content. Mentality is psychic predisposition, ideology is reflection, self-interpretation, mentality is previous, ideology later, mentality is formless, fluctuating—ideology however is firmly formed . . . Ideology is a concept of the sociology of culture, mentality is a concept of the study of social character."
18. In a 1962 poll of the Sozialwissenschaftliche Studiengesellschaft (Vienna), respondents were asked to identify the three policy positions to which they objected most strenuously. They were then asked to say what they would do if the party with which they identified were to adopt these three policy positions. 38 per cent of the Socialists questioned said they would vote for the SPÖ anyway, while 23 per cent said they would consider voting for a different party. These figures show nearly as much inflexibility as those obtained from Communist respondents (49 per cent would vote Communist anyway, 27 per cent would consider voting for a different party). People's Party voters showed more flexible attitudes (26 per cent would vote ÖVP anyway, 28 per cent would consider voting for a different party).

ex-Nazis who did not find a ready home in either of the major parties. There are also some academic groups, some minor groupings that are anticlerical as well as anti-Socialist, and some interests based on war events; the latter includes those people who were bombed out and not properly compensated and prisoners of war who returned years after the end of the war. While the party does show staying power, it has some similarities with the German Refugee Party (BHE): as the excluded interests become assimilated to the major parties, the Freedom Party has diminishing appeal. The lack of expandability of the Freedom Party's electorate can be seen when it is recognized that it steadily commands only a small vote in the face of the fact that voting for the Freedom Party is just about the only way in which an anticoalition vote could be cast by a non-Communist. A possibly expanded role open to the party under the slightly looser coalition pact of 1963 may enable it to help one partner to out-vote the other on some issues in Parliament (as it actually did during the Habsburg crisis of that year), but it will hardly strengthen it as an opposition party.

Yet the Freedom Party does maintain a monopoly of parliamentary partisan opposition. Another party, the European Federalists, has been in evidence only in the parliamentary election of 1962 and the presidential election of 1963. The new party was launched by liberal intellectuals, a tiny group in Austria. It received only a minimal vote in 1962. The four per cent it gained in the presidential election of 1963 does not seem significant when it is realized that the European Federalist candidate was the only candidate not nominated by a coalition party.

More important than the opposition parties are elements of opposition to the coalition found either within the realm of the coalition parties themselves or at least close to one of them. Among these elements is, first, the so-called independent press. In addition to the so-called "boulevard" press we find included here two of Austria's major newspapers, the Vienna *Presse* and the *Salzburger Nachrichten*. Both of these papers occasionally flirt with the Freedom Party, but they consider themselves bourgeois papers and recognize the ÖVP as the major bourgeois party. They find fault, however, with the organizational leadership of the ÖVP, and with those elements in the ÖVP who give voice to their sympathy with the coalition regime.[19] The second anticoalition element within the general framework of the coalition is much of Austria's remaining private in-

19. The independent press has one continuous field day in opposing the coalition. Its main rival, the party press, is interested more in attacking the coalition partner than in upholding the cause of the coalition. The latter is done only in infrequent editorials in the *Wiener Zeitung*, the dry official gazette, and was done occasionally in the daily *Neues Österreich*, under suprapartisan management until 1963. On the other hand, the government is not generous toward this type of opposition where it controls the situation. When it took over operation of the radio from the occupation powers after the State Treaty, the first victim was the *"Watschenmann,"* a free-wheeling program of public criticism previously produced by the U.S. radio station.

dustry.[20] Industrial circles feel that in their representation both in the Business League of the ÖVP and in the Chamber of Commerce they are outnumbered by small business interests, which are generally friendly to the coalition. Much of private industry therefore, though its leaders are often identified with the ÖVP, will oppose the coalition regime, which it considers stifling to the development of large-scale free enterprise. Third and most important, there is the anticoalition wing of the ÖVP. This wing, which calls itself liberal or "reformist," is only partly opposed to the coalition. Most of the members insist only on major reforms in the mode of policy-making, hoping that a less rigid coalition will remove the Socialist veto over economic policies. It is linked closely with the industrial interests just mentioned and finds support also among originally anticlerical groups within the ÖVP. This wing is therefore particularly strong in the anticlerical province of Styria. However, not everybody in the wing is anticlerical; its chief exponent, Hermann Withalm, the ÖVP's general secretary, comes from the Catholic fraternity world. Finally there are anticoalition elements in the SPÖ. These came to the fore only in 1963 in the wake of the Habsburg crisis (the proposed return of the pretender). Since the SPÖ is more tightly organized than its partner, these elements had not been easy to locate. Even before the Habsburg crisis, they had flirted with the notion of forming a "small" coalition with the Freedom Party. Since the fall of Franz Olah as Minister of the Interior and his expulsion from the SPÖ (late 1964), the Socialist anticoalition elements have lost most of their strength.

The main opposition in the Second Republic is still the opposition between the two major parties. Within the coalition regime, it has taken the shape of *Bereichsopposition*—the opposition of one partner to those aspects of the regime governed by the other partner, and vice versa. Every department of government is subject to this *Bereichsopposition*. Its most prominently visible means is the institution of the secretaries of state. A secretary of state holds the constitutional position of a parliamentary secretary whose ostensible function is to assist his minister in parliamentary business. In reality however the secretary of state is a spy of one party implanted in a ministry administered by the other party. Secretaries of state are not provided for in every department. In fact, secretaryships of state are prizes the parties contend for in the postelection government negotiations.

The two coalition parties hold vastly different views of *Bereichsoppo-*

20. In 1962 Alexander Vodopivec (*Wer regiert in Österreich?* [2d ed. Vienna, Verlag für Geschichte und Politik, 1962, p. 255]), a hostile but knowledgeable observer of Austria's nationalized industry, reports: "A recent investigation has shown that 75 per cent of the total corporate capital is directly or indirectly in the public domain" (i.e., nationalized; "indirect" nationalization is administration by nationalized banks).

sition. To the People's Party, *Bereichsopposition* is a Socialist trick enabling the SPÖ to try its hand simultaneously at playing government and opposition.[21] The Socialist view of *Bereichsopposition,* on the other hand, is that it is the function of the party not holding a portfolio to oppose those in charge of its administration.[22] There are at least two reasons for these differing points of view. The first is historical. As the successor of the Christian Socials, the ÖVP continues to see itself as the party of government and the SPÖ as the party of opposition, despite the coalition. Secondly, in every coalition government so far the ÖVP has held the chancellorship and the Ministry of Finance. The holding of these portfolios has meant that the party has been concerned more than the Socialists with overall management and policy initiative. In the eyes of the ÖVP, *Bereichsopposition* in the realm of the chancellorship and the Ministry of Finance is outright opposition, irresponsible on the part of a cogoverning party.

While on the positive side the coalition regime constitutes a pooling of policy-making, *Bereichsopposition* amounts to a pooling of opposition. Policy initiatives are taken by the party holding the portfolio. Even the government declaration following the formation of each government— the Austrian equivalent to the Speech from the Throne—is an uneasily coordinated amalgamation of departmental policies, originating with the party controlling the department in each case. All policies are bargained over in meetings of the coalition committee. The policy veto of the coalition partner enables him to make effective a good part of his opposition to a policy. The unanimity rule in the committee, coupled with the fact that the real leaders of the coalition partners are present on the committee, means that bargains arrived at in the coalition committee can normally be made to stick. It should be noted here that the SPÖ, with better internal discipline, is in a better position to commit itself to a policy than is the ÖVP with its federal structure dividing it into business, agriculture, and employees and with its vociferous anticoalition element. The administration of every department is under constant attack from the party press, the parliamentary group, and organizational spokesmen of the coalition

21. Statements on this by ÖVP leaders and publicists are legion. For the classic version, see Wilhelm Boehm, "Koalition als Problem," *Osterreichische Monatshefte,* July-August 1950, pp. 479–83. Julius Raab blamed the defeat of 1959 on this alleged Socialist duplicity (*Österreichische Monatshefte,* May 1959, p. 1).

22. The leading Socialist writer on this point is Friedrich Scheu (*Zukunft,* February 1956, pp. 36–39; October-November 1956, pp. 305–08; April-May 1959, pp. 99–102). See also the statements by Oscar Pollak (*Zukunft,* February 1952, pp. 33–36) and Franz Olah (*Forum,* June 1959, pp. 211–13). Several party leaders impressed the virtues of *Bereichsopposition* on the writer in interviews in 1960. Before his retirement from active politics, Adolf Schärf presented the position of vice-chancellor, which he held for 12 years, as that of a virtual leader of the *Bereichsopposition* (SPÖ, *Bericht an Parteitag, 1956,* p. 21).

partner. While all this *Bereichsopposition* takes place, the anticoalition press and the other anticoalition elements listed above carry on a continuous opposition to the coalition itself, and to many of the bargains that have been arrived at in the coalition committee.

Parliamentary elections, which must be held at least once every four years and may be held earlier only by mutual agreement of the coalition partners, feature the employment of electoral tactics primarily between the two coalition partners, *who are the chief antagonists in every election.* These tactics will be described briefly in the next section. What should be emphasized here is the fact that the electoral efforts of the opposition parties proper (Freedom Party, Communists) involve only a minor part of the total campaign effort—the campaign looks to the observer, quite properly, like one which is fought between ÖVP and SPÖ. Throughout the campaign, the continuation of the coalition after the election is assumed by nearly everyone, though the anticoalition elements in the ÖVP make this assumption most reluctantly (especially in 1956, 1959, and 1962). In 1959 the mode of policy-making within the coalition was made a major issue by the ÖVP.[23] In the ensuing negotiations, however, the issue was once again resolved by the maintenance of the status quo, the rigid coalition.

The continuation of the coalition is favorable to the organizations of both coalition parties and to at least two of Austria's three major interests. The *Proporz* system is and continues to be a convenient patronage vehicle for both major parties. It is of course deleterious to the organizational workings of the opposition parties. The labor-socialist subculture prefers (or preferred at least until 1962) political codetermination to the risk of an alternation between government and opposition. Agriculture and small business, though before 1963 they would have had a better chance than labor to be on the government's side in a system of alternation, have come to prefer the social peace of the coalition to the potential hazards of the alternation pattern. On the other hand, large business and private industry at least consider taking chances with the potentialities of the alternation pattern in preference to a coalition with what amounts to a built-in labor veto.

Until 1963 ÖVP reform circles were the only ones that publicly discussed the possibility of forming a "small" coalition with the Freedom Party in preference to the existing "great" coalition. The Habsburg crisis spurred intentions on the part of some SPÖ leaders to form such a small coalition with the Freedom Party, without the People's Party. As might be expected, the chambers and interest groups on both sides responded to

23. For the fate of the issue in campaign and negotiations, see Frederick C. Engelmann, "Haggling for the Equilibrium," *American Political Science Review, 56* (1962), 656, 660–61.

the worsening coalition climate with pleas for continued collaboration. Certainly the 1963 crisis shows that mutual feeling between the partners continues to be poor, and that distrust and tension between them is real. The growing together of the coalition parties seems out of the question —there is no reason to believe that Austria will ever be governed by one "black-red" coalition party. After 20 years of coalition, one of the salient facts of Austrian political life is the continuing opposition attitude between the two major parties.

OPPOSITION STRATEGY AND TACTICS   Because of the coalition, opposition in Austria is sui generis. The nature of its strategy differs among the various opposition elements. Communist opposition, no longer revolutionary, is a structural one. The opposition of the Freedom Party, and of anticoalition elements within the coalition parties, is of the policy opposition type. But the facts of life in the coalition make it difficult to express this policy opposition clearly. No one has stated a set of alternative policies should the coalition cease to govern.

Opposition of one partner to the other can, within limits, be termed an office-seeking opposition. The two coalition parties are clearly vying for the presidency and the chancellorship (which goes to the party with the parliamentary plurality). Up to 1965 the SPÖ invariably won the former,[24] the ÖVP the latter (twice with fewer votes, though one more seat, than the SPÖ). Electoral competition is also reflected in the distribution of other executive offices. Any advantage gained in an election is registered in the redistribution of these offices after the election (though the extent of the shift indicates not only the magnitude of the electoral success, but also the relative negotiating skills of the delegations of the two parties). During the first 20 years of coalition, competition for office has involved only foreign affairs, nationalized industries, and the secretaryships of state. Education, finance, commerce, agriculture, and defense have always been "black." Justice, interior, social welfare, and transport have always been "red."

In general, the coalition has brought about a softening of opposition; yet statements about policy opposition in Second Republic Austria are difficult because the makeup and intensity of the opposition vary from issue to issue. The majority of issues is dualistic, yet the parties do not always oppose one another on them. In the period 1955–62, the main antagonists, in varying constellations, have been the following four elements: the SPÖ, the ÖVP, anticoalition elements (primarily the independent press, industrial interests, and anticoalition segments of the ÖVP), and the Freedom Party.

Externally, Austria was faced during this period with the twin prob-

24. See Appendix Table 8.4. President Schärf having died in office, a presidential election was held on May 23, 1965. Franz Jonas (SPÖ) won narrowly.

lems of its own neutrality and of European integration. Both parties have been backing a strict observance of the obligations of the State Treaty of 1955 (the SPÖ with greater enthusiasm). Anticoalition elements and the Freedom Party have been pursuing a pro-Western (primarily pro-German) policy, presumably to the degree of jeopardizing neutrality.

In regard to Austrian symbols and coalition styles, the main issues have been the proposed return to Austria of the pretender to the former throne, Otto von Habsburg, and the numerous scandals of the coalition regime. In the former case, ÖVP and anticoalition elements supported the Administrative Court ruling permitting Otto's return to Austria (1963); SPÖ and Freedom Party outvoted the ÖVP on the issue in Parliament, while Socialist ministers issued orders nullifying, at least temporarily, the effect of the court ruling. The scandals of the 1955–62 period aroused strong antagonism between the partners; the recurring charge against the ÖVP is shady dealing to finance the party; against the SPÖ, mismanagement of nationalized enterprises.

In the internal policy field the main economic issues, collectivism and fiscal management, have been clouded for want of a definite ÖVP position; in regard to these issues, there has been pronounced hostility between Socialists and anticoalition elements. On rent control the SPÖ, defending the status quo, has been facing all the other elements. In such noneconomic fields as agriculture, education, and church-state relations, the coalition has succeeded in substituting some consensual policies for earlier, usually heavy, opposition between the partners. Compared to the First Republic, the coalition has definitely brought about a softening of issue-opposition between the two major parties.

To the issues should be added another factor responsible for a general softening of the objective aspects of opposition: the *Proporz*. The civil service in the First Republic was made up of Imperial holdovers, of Nationalists (especially in the judiciary), and, as a major group, of members of Catholic fraternities. Socialists had been barred from the conventional recruitment channels, and very few were in the federal service between 1918 and 1934. The main sociopolitical effect of the *Proporz* has been the assignment of part of the recruitment channels to the SPÖ. In the Second Republic, difficulty in finding enough qualified Socialists was encountered at first. The League of Socialist Academicians, founded by Karl Waldbrunner (Minister for Nationalized Industries, 1949–56), initially took in academicians who were not members of the CV (overall organization of Catholic fraternities), whether Socialist or national. After nearly two decades of *Proporz*, the Austrian bureaucracy is no longer the conservative force it was prior to 1938. There is no more need for socialists to engage in structural opposition to the civil service and thereby to the apparatus of the state.

In regard to opposition tactics, the Communists tried violent tactics at first, but the failure of their 1950 *Putsch* reduced them to rather in-effectual electoral tactics. The Freedom Party uses electoral tactics pri-marily. Since 1953 it has been approached regarding collaboration by one or the other coalition party, more often by the ÖVP. Neither party ever held out much of a bargain to them until a confidential offer by the Socialists in 1963 reputedly envisioned giving electorally lucrative min-istries (commerce, agriculture) to the Freedom Party if there were a "small" coalition with the SPÖ. In Parliament, the Freedom Party engages in the electoral tactics normally employed by an opposition party with a greatly limited constituency.

The coalition itself is of course a grand effort to replace the hard tactics of the First Republic with bargaining. The effort has not been without success; after all, bargains between the partners are the sine qua non of policy-making. But these bargains come about only in the confidential arena of the coalition committee. Public discourse between the parties, whether in Parliament, in the party press, between the two party head-quarters, or at the hustings, continues to be hard. Parliamentary debate easily slides into name-calling between ÖVP and SPÖ, often involving civil war memories of the First Republic. The writer witnessed how these memories were evoked in 1960 during a trivial patronage incident. Any-one observing the chamber in session is bound to feel that he is witnessing two hostile party blocs. Positive feelings between the delegations of the coalition parties are evoked only when Freedom Party deputies launch their regular, though hopeless, attacks on the coalition. Many of the editorials in the party press are devoted to attacks on the coalition partner. Such editorials—assailing leaders, organization, and policy stands of the other party—are by no means restricted to election campaigns. The party press services invariably place sharply diverging interpretations on cur-rent internal events, and statements emanating from party headquarters tend to be hostile to the coalition partner.

Parliamentary election campaigns bring hard opposition tactics between the parties to a peak. The tone of the campaigns, while not as ideological as during the First Republic, is hostile, more so than in a number of coun-tries in which it is not known beforehand which parties will form the next government. In substance, however, Austrian elections differ from those in alternation countries. Only in Austria does it make sense for parties openly to purport to aspire to an electoral equilibrium with the opponent, and to accuse the opponent of desiring to rule by himself.[25]

The move to bargaining tactics has been and continues to be slow be-cause of the lag in perception of the diminishing socioeconomic differ-ences between the two subcultures. It is this lag in perception which helps

25. For the equilibrium theme in the 1959 election, see U. W. Kitzinger, "The Austrian Election of 1959," *Political Studies, 9* (1961), 119–40; Engelmann, "Haggling for the Equilibrium."

to perpetuate *Lagermentalität*.[26] So far there has been a vicious circle here: Many Austrians fail to perceive diminishing socioeconomic differences because they were born into a *Lager*. They continue to identify with their subculture exactly because they fail to perceive diminishing socioeconomic differences. Thus these subcultures continue to persist despite progressing de-ideologization, and they continue to be reinforced by belief. Some Socialists become managers, but they continue to be known and to identify as *Socialist* managers. Switches in party allegiance occur primarily when workers who become employees are switched to a Catholic union, or when villagers begin to commute to an industrial job and become members of a Socialist union.

Sizable elements in each subculture feel that the other subculture is solidifying. Some Socialists feel quite seriously that a new form of *Bürgerblock* is in the making. This time presumably the bourgeois elements would form *one* political organization, combining the clerical and liberal camps as they are defined by Almond.[27] There is some evidence that this development is taking place; just as in the German CDU, national and capitalist elements in the ÖVP exist next to clerical ones. On the other hand, groups in the ÖVP and anticoalition elements close to the ÖVP continue to see the specter of a Marxist unity front consisting of Socialists and Communists. They point out correctly that Communists have consistently supported Socialist presidential candidates, though of course outside support from Communists alone could not have elected these candidates. It is true that even after de-ideologization the Socialist subculture continues its efforts to maintain organizational rigidity. For proof of such rigidity in the Socialist camp, critics like to point to the much-discussed disciplinary cases within the movement. These however are now more than a decade past, and the most striking, the Erwin Scharf case, dealt with Communist infiltration.[28] A more relevant example of organizational rigidity is the case of the weekly paper *Heute*. Since all but the official Socialist party publications were essentially anti-Socialist, it had been felt by groups within the party that the party ought to subsidize an independent-looking weekly. *Heute*, the weekly so launched, occa-

---

26. S. M. Lipset writes: "nations that have experienced a continuing long-term conflict among social classes may take much longer to recognize the declining need for ideology." ("The Changing Class Structure and Contemporary European Politics," paper delivered at the 1963 Annual Meeting of the American Political Science Association, New York City, p. 3). As noted above, in the case of Austria "mentality" should be substituted for "ideology."

27. Almond, "Comparative Political Systems." For the Socialist view mentioned here, see Norbert Leser, *Begegnung und Auftrag* (Vienna, Europa-Verlag, 1963), pp. 224–32.

28. Franz Olah was expelled in 1964 because of clear indications that he was placing personal ambition above party interest; the official reason for his expulsion was breach of party discipline.

sionally also *acted* independently. Under repeated attacks from some quarters within the party, its life was snuffed out at the age of three and one-half years, and Austrian papers once again were either officially Socialist or anti-Socialist.[29] The fact that the Socialists still organize their subculture as though it were a First Republic *Lager* continues to have a tendency to unite all those outside it. This tendency in turn provides a bit of a true ring when the independent press continues to call "bourgeois" everyone who is not a Socialist or a Communist.

Elites and Opposition

The leaders of the major *Lager* in the First Republic did not differ in socioeconomic position as sharply as the populations of these two *Lager*. Few of the political leaders on the side of the Christian Socials were former aristocrats or leaders in business or industry, and few of the leaders of the Social Democrats were workers. Most of the Social Democratic leaders, among them a number of Jewish intellectuals, equaled or bettered their political opponents in education, and few leaders on either side were wealthy. They were however fundamentally different in two ways: (a) in their belief systems, and (b) in their religion (most Social Democratic leaders, whether from Catholic or Jewish families, were militant Free-thinkers). The parties' principal leaders were an actual "black" priest, Ignaz Seipel, and a virtual "red" priest, Otto Bauer. The elites conceived of their roles as leaders of armed camps, which needed to be completely mobilized. Seipel felt that all potential allies needed to be kept on the side of the anti-Marxist; not just shopkeepers, peasants, and intellectuals with a distinct Catholic orientation, but all anti-Marxist business groups, and of course the *Heimwehr*, the fascist paramilitary organization. The Social Democrats, having reduced the Communists to a negligible force, felt they were the masters of the workers' *Lager*: if only all workers could be mobilized there would be a Socialist government. The attitude of both elites hardened the discourse between government and opposition.

In the Second Republic, socioeconomic similarities between the two major elites are more pronounced, and their ideological differences are not as great. If anything, elites were more similar, certainly friendlier, prior to the ÖVP reform of 1951, when the party was dominated by concentration camp victims who felt a strong affinity with those Socialist leaders who had been concentration camp victims themselves.[30] From

---

29. The fact that the daily "boulevard" paper *Express* is now owned by the Socialist publishing concern hardly constitutes an exception; *Express* does not usually editorialize.

30. Of the elites in the Second Republic, an acute anticoalition journalist writes: "The oligarchy is still a fairly homogeneous circle. Observers at receptions, cocktail parties, and other official functions by no means have the impression that representa-

the beginning, both parties have come under the control of interest spokesmen. These interest spokesmen, used to interest bargaining, transferred their skills to the chief policy-making arena, the coalition committee. To this body the parties send their five or six principal leaders. In this way the keeping of bargains is assured, for the committee consists of the real leaders of the parties' constituent groups. Also, the work of the committee, although often hampered by an unfriendly atmosphere and by real differences of interest, is facilitated by the habituated bargaining ways of its members.[31]

Robert Dahl has suggested that incumbent elites, once industrialization is accomplished, try to minimize differences among the voters, while opposition elites try to emphasize them.[32] During the First Republic, both sides emphasized these differences precisely because the Christian Social elite was not truly an incumbent one, but one whose place at the seat of power dated only from 1921. Today both elites attempt to work along the lines suggested by Dahl for the advanced industrial stage —by seeking electoral support from all quarters—yet the shackles imposed by continued *Lagermentalität* and by the static party-interest nexus keep them from doing so singlemindedly.

There are clear examples of depolarizing efforts by both elites. The very founding of the ÖVP symbolizes the effort to create a true people's party. The founders set up a federation in which workers and employees were to be equal in influence with businessmen and peasants—a far cry from the Christian Social Party of the First Republic. The party began its role in the coalition by agreeing to the nationalization of key industries and banks. The Catholic Church withdrew from politics, and efforts to construct a new Catholic ideology were all but abandoned. On the Socialist side, it became obvious immediately that the party was no longer in the hands of the Austro-Marxist followers of Otto Bauer, but of Karl Renner and his moderate associates. Yet until Adolf Schärf exchanged the leadership of the party for the federal presidency (1957), there was hesitation in abandoning a basically anticlerical stand. The new party program (1958) and Bruno Pittermann's leadership are depolarizing agents. After some initial anguish,[33] the party has done its share to take

---

tives of two hostile camps are facing one another. They mix easily like acquaintances with similar income, equal prestige, the same cars, and basically not too strongly opposed interests." Vodopivec, *Wer regiert in Österreich?*, p. 321.

31. Several former members of the coalition committee told the writer that they had perfected their bargaining skills in negotiations with the Russian occupiers.

32. In an unpublished memorandum prepared for the Bellagio conference.

33. For a brief flare-up of antireligious feelings, see SPÖ, *Parteitag 1959, Protokoll*, pp. 121–29. The ideological front against the church has crumbled. Josef Hindels, one of the leading neo-Marxists in the SPÖ, wrote in 1963: "The deep and far-reaching changes in Catholicism demand an unprejudiced reexamination of our relations with the Catholic Church." (Quoted in *Furche*, July 6, 1963, p. 6.)

religion out of politics, and it is wooing the votes of churchgoers. The new policy is aided by the progressive and nonpartisan attitude of Cardinal König, Austria's chief prelate since 1956.

But there is also resistance to depolarization on both sides. When leadership of the ÖVP moved from the peasants to the Business League (1951), there began to be talk of re-ideologization in an economic direction. Reinhard Kamitz, Minister of Finance from 1952–60, followed the "social market economy" of his big cousin Erhard. Efforts were made to reestablish a bourgeois camp under the principle of a socially tempered economic individualism. These principles were emphasized in the ÖVP's successful 1956 campaign. Among the loosely connected leaders of the new direction are Kamitz, a national liberal himself, the clerical Hermann Withalm (who became the ÖVP's general secretary in 1960), Josef Klaus, first governor of Salzburg, then Minister of Finance, who became federal chairman of the ÖVP in 1963 and Chancellor in 1964, Josef Krainer, governor of anticlerical Styria, and Fritz Molden, former editor of the independent Vienna *Presse*. Some of the driving forces are organized in the anti-Socialist *Akademikerbund*. Spokesmen permeate the independent press (*Presse, Salzburger Nachrichten, Berichte und Informationen*); among them is the author of the only up-to-date book on Austrian politics, Alexander Vodopivec.[34] On the Socialist side there has been less resistance to depolarization. However, pressure from the cadres persuaded the leaders that it would be unwise to give up the annual May Day parade in Vienna. Also, the noisy stand taken by Bruno Pittermann and Franz Olah, the chief party leaders, in the Habsburg crisis indicates that the elite is not beyond resorting to an old-fashioned class appeal. Paradoxically, this one was accompanied by a flirtation with the Freedom Party.

The historical sequence of the genesis of opposition in Austria follows the German pattern. The urban proletariat developed first, dating from before 1848 (as an organized political movement from 1889), general suffrage dates from 1907, and representative government from 1918. During the coalition of 1918–20, the "opposition," i.e., the Socialist element within the coalition, gained several achievements by bargaining, especially in the fields of social welfare and housing; but because of the establishment of the *Bürgerblock*, the attractiveness of strong opposition and hard tactics was not reduced, and there was in fact a recurrence of them after 1920, leading eventually to civil war and the breakdown of the system.

Austrian Socialists have learned from their First Republic experience that they cannot hope to obtain and sustain a political majority on the basis of a class appeal. If the party they oppose, though the bonds of the coalition "marriage" now unite the two, were led by the old ruling group

34. Vodopivec, *Wer regiert in Österreich?*

from Imperial days, a Socialist class appeal might be more successful. But the ÖVP is the party of peasants, shopkeepers, and white-collar workers—segments of the population whose political power was as dependent on the grant of universal suffrage as was that of the industrial workers. Because of the persistence of the national subculture, the ÖVP also cannot hope to gain a majority on a static group appeal. The coalition is of course reinforced by the probability that *each* partner will remain in a permanent minority situation (though the ÖVP had 82 of 165 seats from 1956–59). Therefore both parties use electoral tactics to gain a plurality which puts them into a favorable position for bargaining within the coalition. In the interelection period the parties bargain within the coalition for the enactment of policies and for the protection of interests. In this bargaining process, the parties pool both government and opposition.

Opposition tension within the coalition is outliving the objective conditions that make for such tension in these days when advanced industrialism and the Cold War tend toward a lessening of opposition.[35] The circular nature of *Lager* structure and subjective perceptions accounts for this lag. At the same time there are lingering psychological inequalities between the partners, all favoring the ÖVP: (a) the ÖVP is identified (though hardly in fact) with the pre-1918 state; (b) the ÖVP is identified with the government of the First Republic; (c) the ÖVP is identified with such high-ranking elite groups in the Austrian society as the former nobility, the owners of private industry, and leaders in the professions (though it is not *led* by members of these elites); (d) the ÖVP is identified with the holding of the chancellorship and the Ministry of Finance. These factors appear to justify the party in referring to itself as the "state-bearing party." This self-appellation in turn brings on a continued identification of the Socialist Party with opposition, and continued demands by the Socialists to gain recognition as an equal partner within the coalition.

Socialists in turn have taken advantage of this psychological inequality within the coalition. Since those thinking of discontinuing the coalition have been thinking of an ÖVP or an ÖVP-Freedom Party government, the SPÖ has been holding on to the coalition as a guarantee of codetermination for labor. Alternation, Socialists say, would mean the recurrence

35. In view of the great extent of nationalization of Austria's industry, the blunting of issues in advanced industrial societies (see Otto Kirchheimer's chapter in this volume; also Kirchheimer, "Waning of Opposition") is partially counterbalanced by the issue of nationalization itself. Yet this issue should not be overemphasized. Socialists do not appear to be greatly concerned with further nationalization. A 1962 poll made available privately to the writer indicates that 40 per cent of the Socialist respondents expected further nationalization in case of a Socialist victory, while 21 per cent expected no changes. However, 67 per cent of ÖVP respondents expected the Socialists to nationalize further, and only 6 per cent did not.

of a *Bürgerblock;* to borrow from Orwell's *Animal Farm:* "Jones would come back." Only the Socialist negotiating success after the electoral defeat of 1962, and the overwhelming Socialist victory in the presidential election of 1963 (the first clear victory ever won in any election since free elections have been held in Austria) made it appear to the SPÖ that *it* might be able to govern without the ÖVP. The Habsburg crisis, following President Schärf's reelection by only one month, provided the opportunity to present to a baffled Austrian public the possibility of a "small" coalition of Socialists and Freedom Party.

This development did not come about; but the coalition, an external and internal necessity during the occupation and an internal necessity since 1955, may yet be moving toward a third stage, one of at least partial loosening.[36] Such a loosening would run counter to the continuing party-interest tie-up. If it could be accomplished (which no longer appears likely) by pushing the ÖVP into opposition, or by at least outvoting it in Parliament, it would not violate the maxim: no government against the industrial worker. The cavalier position taken by some Socialist leaders toward the coalition in 1963 may actually have reduced the psychological inequality between the partners and thus weakened even further the lingering *Lagermentalität.*

Speculations about the future of the coalition are particularly hazardous in the post-1963 situation;[37] they are also unnecessary for an evaluation of the nature of opposition under the Austrian coalition regime. Such an evaluation can be undertaken on the basis of the experience of the coalition's first 18 years.

In a different chapter of this book, Nils Stjernquist points to the tension between two basic opposition aims: displacing the government and influencing the policy-making process. If there were an all-party coalition, the opposition could realize the second aim at the expense of the first,

36. The loosening of the coalition, long a demand of the ÖVP, was implemented by the 1963 coalition pact in the following fashion: If the partners fail to agree on a specific policy, either partner may introduce a motion regarding it three months after the date of disagreement. Parliament is to vote five months later. The losing party may demand a plebiscite. Not the ÖVP, but rather the SPÖ threatened to make use of the above provision in early 1964. Motions were then in progress amending the electoral law and proposing a law against corruption. Efforts to enact either measure, with the aid of the Freedom Party, against the votes of the ÖVP were subsequently abandoned.

37. In September 1963 Josef Klaus, a "reformer" who earlier in the year had resigned as Minister of Finance because he refused to enter into further (and to him unsound) bargains with the Socialists, replaced Alphons Gorbach, the Federal Chancellor, as leader of the ÖVP, and in April 1964 as Chancellor. The Socialist attitude toward the ÖVP hardened in early 1964, and threats to form a "small" coalition between SPÖ and Freedom Party became more frequent. However, the "small" coalition idea apparently died with the dramatic purge of Franz Olah, Socialist Minister of the Interior, by his party in the fall of 1964.

and indeed at the expense of its opposition role proper. Has Austria solved Stjernquist's dilemma by, on balance, doing away with opposition?

The argument of this chapter has been that the duopolistic construct known as the Austrian coalition does maximize opposition influence without giving up the aim of displacement entirely. There is, to be sure, no complete replacement. As long as the coalition continues in its present form, neither ÖVP nor SPÖ will capture the government in its entirety, neither will be pushed out entirely, and no third party will be admitted. But displacement remains a constant operational aim. The People's Party attempts every six years to displace the Socialist President (unsuccessfully so far), and the Socialists have so far made five attempts, equally unsuccessful, to displace the People's Party's Chancellor. The presidential election of 1957 and the parliamentary elections of 1953 and 1959 came very close to achieving this displacement. Displacement has in fact occurred in the Foreign Ministry, the Ministry for Nationalized Industries, and indirectly through the creation and abolition of secretaryships of state. It is the knowledge that displacement is a realistic possibility which makes real struggles out of Austrian elections, despite the limited risk imposed by the coalition regime. Thus the electoral tactics employed are real opposition tactics, as are the bargaining tactics on which all policy-making in the coalition is based.

Even at the bargaining stage, the coalition does not hopelessly comingle the functions of government and opposition. Opposition goes on constantly as the delegates of one party veto some of the policy proposals of the other. True, both sides share the responsibility of government. But no one is truly responsible for the government as a whole. The Constitution, as noted earlier, makes each minister responsible directly to Parliament. But each minister only carries out such policies as have been approved by his party. Thus the functions of government and opposition remain separated in coalition bargaining. No one needs to accept governmental responsibility for what he opposes. Opposed policies simply are not enacted. Enacted policies reflect mutual consent of the parties; that is at best, though rarely, true agreement, but at least opposition that has been given up voluntarily in the bargaining process. This opposition is of course cast in a peculiar shape by the coalition regime. Everyone opposes: the Communists, the Freedom Party, the independent press, the anticoalition factions and interests, and, most importantly, the coalition parties themselves. The partners have not given up their mutual distrust. Neither wants to give up his share in the government, and neither wants the partner to govern freely and uncontrolled within his sphere. Therefore opposition is and remains pooled, along with government.

While everyone opposes, everyone is opposed. Every policy and every officeholder faces opposition. Except for impurities in the system, nothing and nobody goes unexamined. Through its secretaries of state, and through its probing into policy and administration in the process of coalition bargaining, the examining party has access to information going beyond that available to opposition parties in systems with normal government and opposition parties or coalitions.

The comingling of government and opposition functions within Austria's limited liability coalition has not been particularly conducive to policy-making. The *Junktim (do ut des* horse trading in policy-making) is not an Austrian invention nor an Austrian monopoly; yet its formalization and frequent use has made it impossible to govern Austria according to any kind of integrated program. The *Proporz*—as a system of patronage also hardly an Austrian monopoly—increases partisan emphasis in personnel matters when the interest of the country calls for less partisan emphasis. In contrast, *Bereichsopposition*, while not conducive to responsible opposition, gives to opposition a fullness, strength, and mode peculiar to Austria. Of the various aspects of this stormy marriage of convenience, here is one where a virtue has been made of necessity.

9

FRANCE:
NOTHING BUT OPPOSITION

Alfred Grosser

As Bertrand de Jouvenel in *The Pure Theory of Politics* distinguishes between *potestas* and *potentia*, between "Authority" and "authority," so in principle it is desirable to distinguish between Opposition and opposition. The first implies a rather precise role in a pluralistic political system, clearly defined by constitution or custom. The second suggests a variety of attitudes and behavior of which the only common characteristic is hostility to power. Unhappily this distinction, useful as it may be in other countries, is without much utility for studying opposition in France. Answers to apparently simple questions, such as "Who opposes?," "To whom is one opposed? to the government? to the regime? to the state?," "How is opposition carried on?" require so many careful distinctions that the question whether Opposition with a capital "O" has meaning in France must be reserved for the conclusion of our inquiry.

What we must do, then, is to study all the methods of opposition in French politics to the extent that these are employed in ordinary political life. Coups d'etat, civil wars, techniques of subversion are not in our domain, even though we shall have to try to specify what the limits to the existence and legal action of opposition are in France.

Legality and Legitimacy

THE LIMITS OF LEGALITY   In France, opposition is scarcely restricted at all by legislation. Until 1958 the political parties were not covered by any special statute and were, in general, ordinary associations defined by a law (1901) which provides that: "Every association founded for the purpose or aim of an illicit object, contrary to the laws or to decent practices, or which would have the aim of weakening the integrity of the national territory and the republican form of government, is null and void."

The Constitution of the Fifth Republic carries an article (Article 4), rather directly inspired by a provision in the Constitution of West Germany, of which the last sentence, obscure in itself, has never had to be given precise meaning since no party has been accused of violating it: "Political parties and groups assist in the expression of the franchise. They are formed and conduct their activities freely. They must respect the principles of national sovereignty and democracy."

Although radio and television are largely under government control,[1] the free exercise of opposition by the press is without doubt better respected than in a large proportion of the other pluralistic democracies, since the right to question the validity of the regime, and even the values on which the political society rests, is completely accepted. The law on the liberty of the press (1881), however, makes it punishable as a crime or misdemeanor to provoke various illegal actions by public utterances, whether oral or written. Thus it is punishable to provoke by public utterances, crimes of murder, pillage, incendiarism, sedition, and various crimes against the security of the state; to dissuade members of the armed services from performing their duty; to utter seditious cries or songs in public places; to publish false news if it is done in bad faith and disturbs the public peace; and (Article 26) to give offense to the President of the Republic in various ways.

Illegal seizures of newspapers stopped with the end of the war in Algeria. However, because of the ambiguity of the constitutional situation under the Fifth Republic, the application of Article 26 continues. Whoever displays his disapproval when the head of state passes by can be condemned for "offense to the President of the Republic." Article 26 makes this a misdemeanor and is rather frequently applied. The President of the National Assembly interrupts any deputy who attacks General de Gaulle; for the members of Parliament must not call the President of the Republic into question, since he is not responsible to Parliament. The courts and the President of the Assembly are perfectly right, since General de Gaulle embodies the collectivity and assures the continuity of state, like the Queen of England or the President of the Republic in Italy and in Germany. The difficulty is, however, that General de Gaulle is also the President of the Republic in the American sense, that is to say, the real head of the executive. But the President of the United States can be hooted at by any ordinary citizen and attacked by any member of Congress.

Tolerance with respect to the opinions and even the attitudes of opposition has remained much the way it was under the preceding republics. Thus the recruitment of future high officials is based solely on their capacities. To be sure, the government has the right to determine the list of candidates competing for entrance to l'Ecole Nationale d'Administration. But it cannot invoke the political opinions of a candidate in order to prevent his access to the public service. By a decision of 1954, annulling

1. See below.

a refusal to admit five supposedly Communist candidates, the Council of State affirmed that the administration could not invoke adherence to any political party that has a legal existence, much less refer to the opinions of the candidate. In 1962 the simultaneous admission to l'Ecole Nationale d'Administration of the one-time president of the National Students Union (Union Nationale des Étudiants Français, UNEF) who had been criticized by the government for having had contacts with the Algerian Nationalists, and of a student who had been interned for his activities on the extreme right, symbolized a liberalism for which one scarcely finds an equivalent in other countries, even in those generally supposed to be the most democratic. It has happened in France, but in what other Western democracy would an anti-Communist government impose on reluctant colleagues a university professor who is a member of the central committee of the Communist Party?

RECOURSE TO VIOLENCE   Opposition must not, however, resort to violence. The principle is simple to formulate; its application is more difficult. Certainly a coup d'etat is not permitted, at least when it fails, and the attempts of the Organisation d l'Armée Secrète have normally mobilized against their authors the forces of the police and a virtually unanimous opinion among the public.

But these are extreme cases. What is normal is a rather broad acceptance of pressures exercised by the most diverse means on the institutionalized authorities. The police and the courts have been indulgent toward gatherings of Poujadists who have mauled tax inspectors, merchants who have prevented the seizure of the furnishings of a fellow merchant condemned for fraud, peasants who have barred roads or surrounded prefectures. All these forms of violent opposition to legislative, judicial, or administrative decisions an indulgent opinion regards as demonstrations rather less extreme than the right to strike.

The right to strike was guaranteed by the preamble to the Constitution of 1946, which was reaffirmed in the Constitution of 1958: "the right to strike may be exercised within the framework of the laws that govern it." Such laws are practically nonexistent. The most recent (1963) and the most discussed is a law "relative to certain forms of the strike in the public services." This mainly imposes a strike notice of five days. But while this law regulates striking, it nonetheless affirms the legality of strikes on the railroads and in the electric power industry (which are publicly owned), and by teachers, whereas a half-century ago Briand considered that he had both the right and the duty to break a railroad strike by mobilizing the railroad workers. The total defeat of the procedure of requisition utilized against the miners in 1963 has shown that the right to strike has practically no limits, whether it is a question of opposing the state in its role as an employer, or the state as a representative of the general interest, or even the application of a law voted by Parliament, that is, by representatives of the whole peeople.

There are several reasons why resort to means not foreseen by the classical rules of liberal democracy has to some extent become normal. In the first place, organized groups are numerically and financially rather weak in France. The power to mobilize supporters constitutes an essential criterion of their representativeness: many strikes and demonstrations are undertaken solely to exhibit the influence and therefore the representativeness of the group that organizes them. Furthermore, the use of threats is the commonest form of group action. How is it possible to establish a precise boundary between a peaceful threat and a violent threat? During election periods a group will demand that candidates and parties take a position on questions that interest the group. While Parliament is in session, a group will threaten the parliamentarian that it will oppose his reelection if he does not satisfy their demands. Faced by the government or by the chief of state, a group will more or less overtly tie its "yes" on a referendum to the satisfaction of an occupational or regional demand. In an even more specific way, a group that is financially or economically powerful can obtain results by affecting the finances and credit of the state. In the case of open threats, as in demonstrations by peasants or strikes by employees, it is a matter of seeking satisfaction for the demands of a group by threatening disorder or slowing up or impeding the functioning of the economy or the public services.

For a great many years, two aspects of the strike have led to impassioned discussions: their "politicization" and the right of employees of the state to strike. What is a political strike? The answer is difficult even if one puts to one side the question of the legitimate or illegitimate character of a purely political strike. A work stoppage designed to obtain safer and healthier working conditions is assuredly not political. A strike that has as its avowed end stopping the war in Indochina is without question political. But there are many shades between these two extremes. Is a strike "political" if it seeks to bring pressure to bear on Parliament at the moment of a vote on a law? The conceptions vary according to the climate of the times.

In West Germany, for example, the law on workers' codetermination in the steel and coal industries was obtained in large part by a threat to strike. Some years later the dominant tendency in Germany was to speak retrospectively of *Parlamentsnötigung,* or "violence to Parliament." In France one tends to distinguish between pressure exercised on the government and on Parliament in relation to a social or economic decision and in relation to a political decision. But where is the boundary between the two? Doubtless one would regard as political any attempt to mobilize opinion against a decision made by political institutions. However, that is one of the aims of a strike: for a strike will fail if opinion is sharply hostile to it. It seems clear that disorder flows as much from the weakness, the poverty, the internal divisions of a trade union, from its inability to impose respect for its agreements on its own members, from unions outbidding one another for support, from the need to strike in order to prove that the union is strong, and from the difficulty of arbitrating among the divergent interests of members, as from obstacles to a reasonable and organized use of the threat to strike.

In any case, the trade unions will always resort to the threat that a strike constitutes as long as two elements in public life continue. The first is the fact that half the workers are blocked from an effective voice in government by the existence of a strong and isolated Communist Party. Since these workers normally express an attitude of opposition, why would the majority or the government take into account peaceful pressure they might try to exert on a particular issue? In the second place trade unions are not on a footing of equality with financial or business groups in negotiating with the administration. Whatever the orientation of top officials may be, between them and managers in banking and industry there is a community of background, language, and intellectual attitudes that creates a certain amount of understanding and sympathy for the managers.

To the conviction (in our view justified) that the various social groups are not on a plane of equality in influencing the decisions of power, and that a strict respect for the rules of classic democracy favors the most powerful, another consideration should be added. Political life has changed in content since the rules of pluralist democracy were enunciated. This change has posed a problem which constitutional law and political science have not yet clearly considered. Today law serves more and more as a means for transforming the society; that is to say, the majority has the right to decide the future of a minority group and the right to change radically the conditions of life of a socially or geographically determined group. The traditional democratic rule required that such a minority group should yield without complaint after having sought to make its own point of view prevail. But can one realistically expect a group that feels itself to be victimized by a change not to resort to violent forms of opposition if its members feel themselves deprived of rights to which they are deeply attached? The strike of the Belgian doctors in 1964 constitutes the most spectacular case. It is deplorable that nowhere, as little in France as in Belgium, has the basic issue been adequately debated: what changes in social conditions can the collectivity impose on individuals and on groups in the name of the common good? As long as that question has not been frankly attacked, one cannot really examine *au fond* the problems presented by peasant demonstrations or even the Poujadist actions of merchants.

CONFLICTS OF LEGITIMACY   In any case, however, it is not a question of the nonclassical forms of "bargaining opposition" nor even of "policy opposition." Ever since 1789, French political history has known oppositions much more profound than these, since the oppositions in France challenge the legitimacy of the regime itself.

One can speak of legitimacy only in countries and periods where it is contested. In Switzerland, in the United States since the Civil War, in Great Britain for an even longer time, it is enough that a government respects the law. As long as it does not transgress the law, its legitimacy is not questioned: the obedience of citizens is founded on the common belief that it is their duty to consent to the exercise of governmental authority. It is entirely different in France. We do not need to go back to the Revolution and to the attempt to replace royal legitimacy by the legitimacy of popular rule, for you may recall that the Third Republic was challenged for a very long time, notably by many Catholics and workers.

In 1940 the drama unfolded. Was the Vichy regime legitimate? If legitimacy is founded on the adherence of a large majority of citizens, reinforced by the legal character of the transmission of power and the act of formal recognition by foreign states, the answer should be in the affirmative. But the legitimacy of Vichy was contested from the outset in two distinct though related ways. The appeal on June 18, 1940, by De Gaulle opposed the legitimacy of the nation to the legitimacy of the majority. That the adversary was called Hitler and that the French government was exposed to the possibility of contamination by Nazism mattered little at the beginning. For other opponents, on the contrary, the challenge was above all moral: first the arbitrariness, then the impress of Nazism disqualified Vichy even more than the signing of the armistice.

The Fourth Republic witnessed a multiplicity of denials of legitimacy. In the long quarrel over German rearmament, one part of the Left denied at the outset the legitimacy of any regime that would accept the European Defense Community, which was held to be immoral: the majority decision, it was said, would not bind the citizens. On the Gaullist side, the same conclusion was based on the abandonment of sovereignty which the treaty entailed. Again, the wars in Indochina and Algeria were challenged on a moral ground: a regime that tolerated tortures and summary executions, that violated its own principles in opposing the liberty of other peoples, unquestionably lost its own legitimacy and no longer enjoyed the right to be obeyed, even if its governments issued from a majority of the elected representatives of the people. With respect to Algeria, a challenge on national grounds was particularly important: no government, no majority, it was asserted, has the right to abandon one piece of the national patrimony or to expel from the national community those who wish to remain within it. It was in the name of this challenge that the Fourth Republic was overthrown. The "week of the barricades" in January 1960, the "putsch of the generals" in April 1961, the terrorist action of the OAS in 1962, all invoked the same principle in order to overthrow the Fifth Republic.

There are other ways of denying the legitimacy of the majority. The distinction, which everyone admits in theory, between the *pays légal* (the majority that expresses itself through electoral and institutional devices) and the *pays réel* (a true but invisible majority) is very old. Formulated in these terms on the extreme right by *L'Action Française*, it has often been utilized by others: occasionally by the anticlerical Left against the laws involving government aid to Catholic schools; as a doctrinal matter by the Communist Party, which holds itself to be a minority solely because the people have not yet been liberated from "alienation"; finally, in an entirely personal fashion by General de Gaulle. In a speech on radio and television which constituted the turning point of the "Algérie Française" revolt (January 19, 1960), he declared: "By virtue of the mandate which the people have given me and of the national legitimacy which I have embodied for 20 years . . ." He has often returned to that simple idea: the majority only represents the *pays réel* if it is faithful to him.

It is worth reflecting for a moment on the persistence of conflicts over legitimacy in the political society of France. To say that it is a question of a "conflicted" society, while American society is "consensual," is to distinguish but not to explain. It seems to me that there are several contributing causes. For one thing, in France the Constitution, lacking age and that prestige which quasi-sacred texts like the Constitution of the United States possess, is considered only a procedure of government. Political society in France is defined not by the rule of law but by the rule of the majority. It is here, in the rule of the majority, that some of the most characteristic aspects of French life are revealed: absence of respect for the minority, refusal of a dialogue, identification of the current government with the state. And also the confusion between the current government and the regime: the minority finds it easy to attribute to the institutional system the defects it thinks it finds in the attitude or in the actions of the majority. Under the Fourth Republic, General de Gaulle found fault with the "system." Under the Fifth Republic, the opponents find fault with the "regime." If the Constitution is only a mechanism, why in fact establish a clear distinction between the institutions and the majority? This question is even more pertinent when the absence of a distinction allows you to escape from the very rule which you had previously claimed for yourself. You can be favorable to the rule of the majority, but to denounce the "system" or the "regime" allows you to challenge the legitimacy of any majority you oppose.

In addition, from a taste for language and a pleasure in ideas, political conflicts are so thoroughly rationalized and ideologized that compromises are rendered nearly impossible. Finally, the fact that the economic and social structures are subjected to constant critical examination, to basic questioning, means that the power of the state, if not indeed the law, appears even in the eyes of many non-Marxists as the reflection of a power situation which it is perfectly normal to contest. These last two phenomena are inseparable from a set of opposition attitudes which we need to examine in detail.

Opposition—A Principle of Political Life

THE CITIZEN AS OPPONENT   For a very long time, the typical French citizen has considered his participation in political life as a means of weakening the state. The title of Alain's book, *The Citizen Against the Authorities,* nicely expressed, between the two world wars, a fundamental attitude. Noted by sociologists and humorists, the distrust of Frenchmen for authority—evidenced by everything from verbal criticism to refusing statistical information to the government—is real and profound.

This attitude has at least two causes, one historical, the other pedagogical. For hundreds of years one regime after another in France has had one common feature: centralization. Decisions are taken in Paris even on local matters. Even today, a loan made to the mayor of a village by the state savings bank of the neighboring city must be approved by a government bureau in the capital. Thus the state, the Power, has never been looked on with a sense of belonging, with the idea that one participates in it, but as a distant power from which one has to demand advantages and to which one has to be opposed. Since participation even in the most local decisions is limited, how can one conceive political life as participation in shaping the future of a community?

Moreover, education in the primary school in France rests on two essential principles: it is authoritarian and it appeals to the individual qualities of the students. The school child and the student at the lycée are never called upon to participate; the infallibility of programs and teachers is an axiom; but the ranking of the individual student is the basic pedagogical stimulus, and from his first compositions to his dissertation for the baccalaureate, the student is invited to express his personal reactions. The combination of the absence of participation and individualism necessarily gives birth to a spirit of criticism, of opposition.

Le civisme du refuse has its advantages. Under both the German occupation and Vichy, the spirit of rebellion was the most elementary and the most widespread form of resistance. Even under a regime presenting some authoritarian characteristics like those of the Fifth Republic, respect for the state is limited. In October 1963 the Council of Administration for the Franco-German Office of Youth (a product of the treaty of January 22, 1963) met for the first time. To the surprise of the German participants, the representatives of the French youth movements continued throughout the conference to object to all of the proposals of the minister who had appointed them. It was the Germans, who live in a regime that seeks to be completely liberal and founded on citizen participation, who did not dare go too far against their *Obrigkeit*. One should not push this analysis of the spirit of opposition too far, however, for the French have always gladly granted to their country what they have refused to the state.

The unfortunate consequences are nonetheless numerous. The most evident is the systematic vote of opposition. Neither the ephemeral success of Poujadism nor the permanent implantation of the Communist Party can be explained without taking into account this attitude of a general denial of Power. And even the claims of legitimacy, even the ideological structures of noble facade, are only disguises for that denial.

Another consequence is something of a paradox: the opposition of principle results in a confusion between state and government, a confusion from which the largest beneficiary is the governing majority of the moment. In that respect the case of the French radio and television network is particularly significant. In France this network is the monopoly of the state. Private chains cannot broadcast on French territory even if (as with Radio-Luxembourg and Europe I) they are allowed to install their principal offices in Paris. This monopoly has been established, like the other nationalizations, by virtue of a conception which is expressed in the preamble to the Constitution of 1946 reaffirmed in that of 1958: "All property and all enterprises that now have, or subsequently shall have, the character of a national public service or of a monopoly in fact, must become the property of the community." The importance of radio and television in matters of information is such that the formula can be applied to them, the principal objective being to avoid the influence of money, notably by means of advertising. The doctrine of every French government since 1945 has been that "community" and "government" are synonymous. However, in Great Britain or in Germany the government is taken to mean the majority of the moment, while the national community comprises all of the tendencies which are expressed in public life. In France it was necessary to wait until 1964 for a statute on radio and TV, still imperfect, that reduced the confusion born indirectly from the wholesale hostility of citizens to the state.

PARLIAMENT AND THE PARTIES AS COLLECTIVE OPPONENTS   In most pluralist countries, to speak of opposition is to evoke the idea of parliamentary opposition, a provisional minority facing the government majority. Under the Third and Fourth Republics, the French situation was that only in appearance. In reality the principle of parliamentary sovereignty was so firmly implanted in the minds of the French that the Parliament, one might say, constituted very nearly a sort of permanent and collective opposition to the government of the moment. Its distrust of the Cabinet was a measure of citizen distrust of Power. The role of the parliamentary committees was thought of largely as a technique for weakening government authority. Both houses were masters of their own proceedings, a fact that prevented the Cabinet from ensuring that bills would be discussed in the form in which it presented them. The principal preoccupation of the government was not to fall; thus the Chamber or the National Assembly found itself solidly established in its function of sovereign—a judge nearly always malevolent toward the executive. It was all the more malevolent because the majority of parliamentarians perceived themselves as having the right in turn to become ministers which, even in the hearts of members of parties in the government, made them opponents in part, impatient to see a new ministerial combination give them the chance to obtain or to regain a portfolio.

Another factor helps to make the deputy or senator a demanding interlocutor of the government. Even more than in other countries, the parliamentarian in France is not only a representative of the people in the noble sense but a veritable solicitor, charged with obtaining specific advantages for the individuals and groups in his constituency. In this case the centralism of France exercises a particularly unfortunate influence. Since decisions on local affairs most often have to be taken in government offices in Paris, it is in Paris that one has to intervene in order to make sure that the slow movement of the relevant papers is accelerated. And who is better charged with this task than the parliamentarian? Rather indifferent to Parliament as an institution, full of distrust for parliamentarians as a collective group, the French citizen tends to appreciate his representative insofar as he is an intermediary between himself and Power, insofar, that is, as the deputy serves as a spokesman for his own special claims. The deputies of the majority have no less work; they must negotiate and solicit as much as the others. They simply have a better opportunity to get results for their clients who thus have their initial ideas reinforced: the state is an enemy from which you must seize whatever advantages you can.

Under the Third and Fourth Republics the nature of relations between Parliament and government, combined with the multiplicity of parties and the frequency of changes in the majority coalition, also had a particularly important repercussion on the idea of opposition in France. In Great Britain, the United States, and present-day Germany, elections constitute in large measure less a designation of representatives than the ratification or the rejection of the policies practiced by the incumbent government, by the dominant party. One might say that the French situation is the inverse of the Austrian. In Austria the voter, in going to the polls, virtually has a choice only between two parties which have been jointly in power for several legislatures. In France every party takes up, during the electoral campaign, the language of opposition.

Take for example the last elections of the Fourth Republic, those of January 1956. Naturally the Communists, out of power since 1947, and the Poujadists criticized the total activity of a legislature that had begun in 1951. The Socialists had been in opposition since the preceding election, but they had sustained the Mendès-France government in 1954–55. The MRP had violently fought this last government for two-thirds of its term and had participated in eight other cabinets during that period. Radicals, moderates, and Gaullists were often divided, some participating in, others opposing the same government. But all the parties presented themselves before the electors deploring the overall balance sheet of the legislature. The mildest oppositional language consisted in saying for a party: "Excellent things were done, at such and such a moment, thanks to the action of our ministers. But I recognize that the net result was not brilliant, even for the cabinets in which I participated: but after all I was not alone in office." The speaker ought then to have added: "I cannot tell you if, after the elections, I shall be in power or in opposition, nor with whom. What I ask of you, dear voter, is to give me your vote and leave the rest to me." How can the voter avoid having his spirit of systematic opposition reinforced when no one asks him to approve the balance sheet of the legislature or any one cabinet with its credits and debits?

TRADE UNIONISM AS OPPOSITION OF PRINCIPLE   In the United States as in Germany the trade unions, like other groups, accept the common ideology and take as given the fundamental principles that govern the political, economic, and social organization. It has never been thus in France, nor is it now. As a recent example one could take the new draft of rules which the leaders of the Confédération Française des Travailleurs Chrétiens (CFTC), the most important trade union organization after the Communist-dominated Confédération Générale du Travail (CGT), had adopted by their congress on November 7, 1964, when the CFTC became the Confédération Française et Démocratique du Travail (CFDT). Among other things the draft states that:

> Every struggle of the workers' movement for liberation and collective advancement of the workers is based on the fundamental notion that every human being is endowed with reason and conscience and that he is born free and equal in dignity and in rights.
>
> In a world in evolution marked by the progress of techniques that should serve his fulfillment, the worker is more than ever threatened by

dehumanizing or technocratic structures and methods which make him an object of exploitation and subjection . . .

The Confederation unites trade union organizations open to all the workers resolved—in mutual respect for each other's personal, philosophical, moral, and religious convictions—to defend their common interests and to battle to establish a democratic society of free and responsible men . . .

The Confederation challenges every situation, every structure, every regime which ignores these demands. It therefore challenges every form of capitalism and totalitarianism . . .

It intends to carry out this action not by erecting into a system the principle of the development of class antagonisms, but rather by favoring the growth of the consciousness by the workers of the conditions for their emancipation.

The key word is "challenges" (*conteste*): The unions never cease to reaffirm the importance of the function of "challenging" or "contesting." And to challenge is to oppose not merely the government of the moment but the very economic and social foundations of the political system.

However the time has long since passed when the trade unions refused to enter into the slightest relationship with the state. On the contrary, the unions participate more and more in consultative organs. From the Planning Commission and the Social and Economic Council to the departmental technical committees, the councils (national or lower), committees, offices, and bureaus, the consultative organs are innumerable. Their real audience varies enormously, as does the role played by the representatives of the unions. But to what extent does participation in one of these councils render the unions accountable for a decision or a policy of which they disapprove? Is not consultation basically in conflict with the function of "challenging" which the unions attribute to themselves? Can they simultaneously participate in organs established in and by a given society and challenge the overall structure of that society? Today the trade unionists tend to deny that this presents them with a dilemma: they speak of a permanent tension between challenging the system and participating in it. In reality, however, the second gradually seems to overtake the first in the unions not Communist-dominated. The result is a noticeable change in the conduct of the trade unions as systematic opponents. For them as for the other organized groups a process of integration is taking place which is clearly transforming the nature of opposition in present-day France.

The Forms of Present-Day Opposition

REFERENDUMS AND ELECTIONS   The Fourth and Fifth Republics were born under conditions that were almost exactly inverse. While all the parties in power that jointly submitted a constitution to the country in

1946 represented more than 70 per cent of the voters and 55 per cent of the registered voters, the constitution was accepted by only 53.5 per cent of the voters, and only 36 per cent of those who were registered to vote. In September 1958 on the other hand, 78 per cent of the voters (66.4 per cent of the registered voters) adopted the constitution proposed by the government headed by General de Gaulle, while in the elections that followed two months later candidates who claimed his exclusive support obtained only 20.4 per cent of the votes (15.2 per cent of the registered voters).

Two conclusions can be drawn from this comparison. On the one hand, the dominant parties were more legitimate in 1946 than the regime, whereas in 1958 General de Gaulle was more popular than his party, which was about to constitute the axis of the majority. On the other hand, citizens clearly made a distinction between the different methods of voting. We need therefore to distinguish the nature of approval and opposition which the votes under the present regime reflect.

Excluding the vote on the Constitution, the Fifth Republic has experienced three referendums: on January 8, 1961, on the policy of self-determination in Algeria (75.2 per cent yes); on April 8, 1962, on the agreements of Evian giving independence to Algeria and the delegation of the power to execute them (90.6 per cent yes); October 28, 1962, on the adoption of a proposed law providing that the President of the Republic be elected directly by universal suffrage (61.7 per cent yes, or 46.4 per cent of the registered voters.) In the eyes of many of the opponents of General de Gaulle, these three referendums and the adoption of the Constitution have been no more than plebiscites. The reality is much more complex.

The personal element has obviously played a large role. How many voters had read the Constitution in 1958? The President of the Republic has done everything to assure that the referendums would take on the appearance of votes of confidence in him personally. But it would be inexact to say that the partisans of the General have each time hoped for a "yes" vote and his adversaries for a "no" vote, and even less correct to say that the vote was independent of the stated purpose of the referendum. In fact, even if the chief of state maneuvered for a long time to lead public opinion to the point of accepting a change in Algeria, in the minds of the electors the referendums of January 1961 and April 1962 turned quite as much on the Algerian policy itself as on General de Gaulle's personal qualities; hence many citizens who opposed the idea of charismatic power nonetheless voted "yes." And in October 1962 both the content of the question posed and the procedure itself were subject to lively debate.

That referendum, however, had a quite special character. In the three preceding referendums various parties had campaigned in behalf of a "yes" vote. In April 1962 the only appeal for "no" came from the extreme Right. Thus in order to separate the good Gaullist wheat from the chaff of the "partisans," General de Gaulle with considerable skill provoked the conflict of October which put all the parties in the "no" camp, with the single exception of those who claimed unconditional fidelity to his person, even though an appreciable part of the "yes" vote finally did come from men who simply approved the direct election of the future President or who considered that the camp of the "no's" represented a return to a detestable past.

Four examples are insufficient for arriving at definitive conclusions on the procedure of referendum, even if one adds the three constitutional referendums of 1945–46. However, they permit one to make some specific points. The French citizen values direct consultation and submits himself to it with discernment, as witness the variety of results. In a referendum, even the Communist voter largely loses the systematic oppositional behavior that traditional analysis tends to attribute to him. The referendum appears largely as a means of fostering positive participation in large part because it simplifies the consultation. At the same time, all the risks of excessive personalization of Power are increased by the referendum procedure. The duality Power/Opposition tends to reduce itself to the duality approval/disapproval of a man. But the exceptional historical character of General de Gaulle allow one to think that this danger is smaller than the advantage gained in France by an evolution toward a conception of political life founded more on participation than on refusal.

It will doubtless be the same for the election of the chief of state. A typical voter will doubtless vote *against* certain candidates in casting his ballot, but at least in 1965 the citizen will have the impression of giving a mandate directly to the future chief executive, once it is taken for granted that even without De Gaulle the precedent he has created as a President who wields power and employs the Premier as an assistant will be imposed on his immediate successor.

The desire of the electoral body for a homogeneous unity among President, government, and parliamentary majority clearly appeared in the election of November 1962. To be sure, the Gaullist party (Union pour la nouvelle République, UNR) obtained only 31.9 per cent of the votes on the first ballot. But this was the greatest percentage ever obtained by any French party; and what is more, the triumph on the second ballot completely demonstrated the decline of the opposition vote. Nothing demonstrates, however, that this situation will last beyond General de Gaulle, although it does throw a totally new light on electoral phenomena.

THE FALSE TRIANGLE The Assembly elected in November 1962 had the composition indicated in the following table. Because the UNR/UDT benefited from a disciplined vote, and because the Pompidou government received the united support of this group and of the independent Republicans, France finally arrived at the situation which, in principle, all its political theorists had dreamed of: a disciplined and stable majority consistently supporting a government which, in principle, lasts through a whole legislature.

Union pour la nouvelle République, Union Democratique du Travail,[a] and affiliates	233	
Independent Republicans and affiliates [b]	35	
		268
Communists	41	
Socialists and affiliates	66	
Rassemblement Démocratique and affiliates [c]	39	
Centre Démocratique [d]	55	
Deputies not belonging to any group	13	
		194
Total		462

a. Somewhat left- and labor-oriented Gaullists.
b. Friends of M. Giscard d'Estaing, Minister of Finance.
c. Radicals and Union Démocratique et Socialiste de la Résistance (U.D.S.R.) of M. Mitterrand.
d. Movvement Républicain Populaire (MRP) and UDSR of M. Pleven.

Unhappily the very real progress toward a solution of the French problem of government stability which this state of affairs constitutes is considerably attenuated by three deviations that keep the present mechanism from truly resembling either the British or German system.

First, the "corset" that M. Debré wanted to impose on Parliament with the constitutional mechanisms of 1958 is too tight. Made in order to compel an Assembly with an inclination toward permanent opposition to allow the government to survive and to work, these mechanisms tend to render parliamentary life uninteresting by preventing the minority from actually controlling the Cabinet's action. The mechanisms include the principle of the "blocked vote," which permits a government to avoid putting troublesome amendments to a vote, limitations on the domain of the law (the Constitution specifies what belongs to the Parliament, all other issues belonging to the executive), the possibility of having a text that has not had a favorable vote adopted by making it a question of confidence [2]—all of them means of reducing the normal role of Parliament.

2. Under Article 49 the Premier can, after the Council of Ministers has deliberated, take the existence of the government before the National Assembly on the vote of a text. In this case the text is considered as adopted unless a motion of censure, put down within the following 24 hours, is voted in the conditions set forth in the preceding paragraph. An example of the application of Article 49, taken from the con-

Second, both the opposition and the majority have great difficulty getting used to the existence of a stable situation. In Great Britain, the opposition understands that its role in Parliament excludes the possibility of making the government fall. The most it expects to do is to modify the actions of the government, possibly by giving publicity to the positions taken by the opposition. At the Palais-Bourbon, the opposition benches are generally empty because debates that cannot result in the overthrow of the Cabinet do not interest the deputies. The oral questions on Friday, which in principle are a means of controlling the government (at Bonn, it was the play of this mechanism that forced Franz Josef Strauss to resign because of the *Spiegel* affair) generally have no weight and attract only a few members. For its part the majority does not yet understand that democracy also consists of a dialogue with the minority. "Since we can do what we wish, what good is it to discuss the matter?" The majority benches therefore are also deserted.

Third, the major reason why the game is not played by the British or German rules is this: In appearance France exhibits today the normal situation of parliamentary regimes with a dominant party: tension among the three points of a triangle formed by the government (drawn from the dominant party) the leadership of the party, and the majority in Parliament. But the fact is that these three points all depend on the same force outside the triangle: General de Gaulle. This in large part explains the malaise that troubles relations between the majority and opposition: the first is never certain whether the position it defends today may not change tomorrow; the second tells itself that it is not very useful to attack the government or the parliamentary majority since they simply reflect a will that is not under parliamentary control.

THE OPPOSITIONS   If one neglects for a moment the social forces of opposition, what today are the political opposition forces in France? In our view, it is convenient to distinguish three kinds:

First, the opposition desiring to share in government: These are all the parties which extend from the Socialists of Guy Mollet to the Independents, whose great man remains M. Pinay. Even if one part of this opposi-

---

clusion of the debate on the French nuclear striking force, the famous *force de frappe:*

> *The Speaker.* Here are the results of the votes on the motion of censure:
>   Majority required for the adoption of the motion   277
>   For adoption   214
>   (Applause from the Right and extreme Left)
> The required majority not having been attained, the motion of censure is not adopted. (Applause from the Left and the Center)
> In consequence the bill for the program relating to certain military projects is considered adopted . . .

(*Journal Officiel, Assemblée Nationale,* November 23, 1960, p. 3972.)

tion—Socialists or Radicals—sometimes speaks in opposition to the regime, they all voted yes in 1958 and since then have sometimes been in power, sometimes in opposition. Tomorrow Socialists, Radicals, MRP, and Independents could participate anew in a government without changing their basic inclinations or habits.

Second, the opposition of sheer protest: On the extreme right, this comprises those who are nostalgic for Vichy and those who are nostalgic for "Algérie française," two categories composed often but not invariably of the same persons. Despite the existence of several particularly violent weeklies, this opposition no more represents an effective political force under the Fifth Republic than it did under the Fourth, which was not overturned by it. It was only the decolonization (Indochina but mainly Algeria) that led to an alliance between this extreme right and part of the Army.

Badly organized after the frequently ephemeral regroupings of which the PSU (Parti socialiste unifié—even though hardly at all *unifié*) has, since 1961, been by far the most representative, the importance in the electoral body of the left opposition of protest is almost negligible, but it exercises a certain influence on the minority of Frenchmen who seek a militant cause or who are searching for a political commitment. It is situated between the Communist Party, which it regards with a mixture of blame, envy, and optimism and which disdains it, and the Socialist Party, which it considers opportunistic and a traitor to the people's cause. Its pleasure in political rigor and doctrinal purity produces a rather distinct behavior: courage and clarity of analysis have led its militants, notably in the matter of decolonization, to protest, to bear witness in the name of values neglected by the great majority of Frenchmen and by their representatives. And often the respect for these values has constituted its political wisdom. But at the same time a certain incapacity to think of themselves as governing, to understand the demands of reality, has always pressed the largest proportion of its members to condemn even the men to whom they feel closest.

Third, the Communist Party: One should reserve to the Communists a special place, not only because since 1945 they have gathered more votes than any other party of alliance in every election except those of June 1946 and November 1962, but also because the behavior of the voters and of the non-Communist parties is in large measure determined by its existence: because its very presence contributes a certain number of particular characteristics to the political game in France. Even if since 1947 a gulf has existed between the Communist Party and other political groups, one should not forget that the party does not appear in the eyes of French opinion as a systematic and eternal opposition force, as a permanently destructive element. Even if one were to ignore its important role in the Resistance from 1941 to 1944, the Communist Party held an important place in the two greatest periods of social progress that France has known in the twentieth century: the Communists supported the Popular Front government in 1936–37 and they participated in the governments of the Liberation under the direction of General de Gaulle from September 1944 to January 1946, and under governments headed by the Socialists or the MRP until May 1947. During that second period, the mobilization of energy by the Communist Party for the reconstruction of France was extremely effective. The party itself maintains a deep nostalgia for the period when it participated in power. Even today, when it wishes to describe how political life might be better in the future, what it refers to is the model of tripartism of 1946.

Although the de-Stalinization in the U.S.S.R. and the atmosphere of international détente facilitate its tasks, the party scarcely knows how to profit from its advantages. Despite the great mass of its adherents, the devotion of its militants, the skill of its propagandists who know how to tie the everyday difficulties of the housewife to the great world problems, the Communist Party appears old and sclerotic. Maurice Thorez became secretary general in 1930 at 30 years of age and kept his post until shortly before his death in 1964. The numerous internal purges, the refusal, incapacity, or inability to support an intellectual life analogous to that of the Italian party, the absence of precise political ends—all these have weakened the party. Its power to attract young people with a sense of social justice has diminished. Its power of mobilization has become insignificant in relation to the number of its members and its voters, even when it is a matter of acclaiming Mr. Khrushchev on an official visit to Paris. Contrary to the expectation of many observers, the arrival of General de Gaulle in power caused it to lose a good share of its clientele, for it declined from 5.1 and 5.5 million votes in 1951 and 1956 to 3.9 and 4 millions in 1958 and 1962.

The Communist Party remains nonetheless an essential factor in French political life. Its very presence transforms the nature of the problems to be solved. Until 1958 the existence of a powerful parliamentary group sometimes withdrawn into a shell, sometimes kept to one side, falsified the political game: the axis of the governmental majorities necessarily passed to the right of the arithmetical center of the Assembly. With the return of voting in single-member districts, the idea of constructing a barrier against the Communists at the run-off election also favors the Center-Right, to the detriment of a Left destined never to become a majority in the absence of the Communists—or to be dominated by them should they enter into the majority.

On the one hand, then, one might foresee the decline of conflicts (the end of decolonization, the effects of the détente between Washington and Moscow), the evolution of social groups toward participation in a bargaining opposition, the acceptance by the parties, since De Gaulle, of the necessity to confine themselves to a "democratic-reformist" opposition and even to a "policy opposition." France, pressed by technical civilization, moves toward the pacification of its political society. Yet one may also foresee the permanence of the Communist Party as a center of disturbance, uncertainties and confrontations in institutional matters, the pronounced pleasure of groups and even of parties in challenging the government and "democratic structural opposition," and so no "normalization" of French political society.

Each of these two forecasts has about an equal chance of being realized. This is why it is not ultimately possible to discover in the past or in the present or in the future an Opposition in France. There always has existed, there will exist in the foreseeable future, a variety of oppositions, diverse in type and perpetually intertwined.

10
ITALY:
OPPOSITIONS ON LEFT, RIGHT, AND CENTER

Samuel H. Barnes

Parliamentary opposition in Italy reflects general patterns present in other Western democracies plus some uniquely Italian characteristics. Analysis must begin with the following factors which condition the operations of the Italian parliamentary system:

the complex multiparty system

the historical experiences and institutional framework which have influenced Italian expectations and conceptions of opposition

the various cleavages in the body politic and their relation to political parties

the search for governmental stability in a system in which the opposition ranges from competition for office to the revolutionary alternatives of communist or fascist systems.

Opposition and the Party System

The Italian Republic is the sole remaining major European state with a classic multiparty parliamentary political system. Burdened like the French Fourth Republic with a Communist Party which receives almost one out of every four votes, the Italian system, unlike the French, is dominated by a powerful Christian Democratic Party which has received from just under half the votes cast in 1948 to a low in national elections of 38 per cent in 1963 (see Appendix Table 10.1). The position of the Christian Democratic Party near the center of the political spectrum, its long hold on office and deep penetration of the machinery of the state, and its firm doctrinal and organizational base—all these make it the governing party of Italy and the chief target of political opposition.

This opposition has been fragmented and largely unconstructive. The evolution of modern Italy has given rise to the typical socioeconomic cleavages of an urban industrial society without obliterating preexisting socioeconomic, regional, and historical divisions. Furthermore, ideological differences divide groups and regions which are otherwise similar. The present structure of political conflict reflects these various cleavages.

On the formal parliamentary level, Italian parties can be placed on a left-to-right continuum.[1] While such a continuum is inadequate for the analysis of many political systems, it does not greatly distort the realities of Italian politics; furthermore, it is a useful way of viewing Italian parties. On the left of the spectrum is the PCI. Although its functional role may be somewhat different, Communist espousal of an "Italian way to communism" still leaves it far from playing the formal role of a democratic opposition. Its neighbor on the spectrum and former ally, the PSI, has wavered between revolution and accommodation; the majority under Pietro Nenni accepted the existing democratic state and sought to work within it while the minority faction preferred a working alliance with the PCI. Opposition to Socialist participation in the Cabinet led to a withdrawal of much of the PSI left wing and the formation of the Italian Socialist Party of Proletarian Unity (PSIUP) in 1964. The PSDI differs from the majority in the PSI largely on the issue of the nature of its opposition: under the leadership of Giuseppe Saragat, the PSDI often supported and participated in postwar cabinets, while the PSI remained in opposition from 1947 until 1963. The tiny PRI likewise supported several postwar governments. The DC is in the center of the spectrum. The right is composed of the PLI, which is a constitutional conservative party of the "economic right," the monarchist PDIUM, and the neofascist MSI.

The parliamentary division of the parties simplifies reality, giving the parties a monolithic appearance which they do not in fact possess. The several dimensions of conflict which separate the parties also divide them internally, giving rise to factions which are continually subjected to the influence of wings of the other parties nearest them on the continuum. These factions are of importance in almost all of the parties, and particularly so in the governing parties, for they have often functioned as an internal democratic opposition. Thus the formal opposition and the real opposition must be distinguished, and an analysis of the latter must take into account the internal party factions.

1. The following abbreviations (taken from the parties' Italian initials) are used in this chapter:

DC	Christian Democratic Party
MSI	Italian Social Movement (neofascist)
PCI	Italian Communist Party
PDIUM	Italian Democratic Party of Monarchical Unity
PLI	Italian Liberal Party
PRI	Italian Republican Party
PSDI	Italian Social Democratic Party (Saragat Socialists)
PSI	Italian Socialist Party (Nenni Socialists)
PSIUP	Italian Socialist Party of Proletarian Unity (Vecchietti Socialists)

The PCI is the most monolithic of Italian parties. Its internal political divisions, while intriguing in themselves, are seldom relevant to the party's external politics. As already mentioned, the PSI was divided into a majority that wished to end its intransigence and play the parliamentary game and a procommunist minority which, while not opposing this in principle, set such a high price on Socialist cooperation that it was difficult for the Center parties to pay it. The departure of most of the minority into the PSIUP strengthened the unity of the PSI even though it weakened the party in Parliament. The evolution of the PSI greatly influenced its relations with the PSDI; indeed, a faction of the latter party returned to the former on the ground that Socialist acceptance of representative democracy rendered the PSDI unnecessary. While groups within both parties favored unity, bitter memories and personal ambitions hindered reconciliation. Even the small Republican Party is divided into factions that differ in their attitudes toward the "opening to the left" and clericalism.

Perhaps most important of all are the factions within the Christian Democratic Party. It contains a trade union faction, a reformist faction, an office-oriented majority, a traditionalist conservative faction, and several personal cliques operating both within and without these factions. The internal unity of the Liberal Party was enhanced by the schism of its radical members following the 1953 elections, leaving it in the hands of its more conservative members. The monarchist movement was long the toy of wealthy Southerners whose personal feuds led to the formation of rival monarchist parties, then the merger of the two, and, finally, in 1963 an electoral defeat which reduced the party to a fraction of its former parliamentary strength. The monarchist PDIUM represents no significant socioeconomic group or doctrine, and its decline is perhaps evidence of the growing rationalization of the Italian party system. The neofascist Italian Social Movement, like the Communist Party, opposed the constitutional system; but its 1963 national congress revealed a badly divided party, with one faction favoring intransigence and another accommodation with the system. So deep were the differences over the party's future role that the unity of the party was placed in jeopardy.

There are thus several levels of parliamentary opposition in Italy. There is the opposition of the parties which reject the constitutional order, such as the PCI and MSI. There are also often constitutional parties left outside the coalition, as has several times been the fate of the PLI. And there is the opposition within the governing parties of the factions that oppose the programs of the moment. This policy opposition differs from the internal maneuvering common to all political parties in the high degree of formal organization and recognition achieved by Italian party factions. Some single-party (*monocolore*) Christian Democratic minority cabinets accepted support where they could find it, from the Monarchists and even the MSI; and of course in this case the very concept of "opposition" becomes confused. While there has been some variation in the pattern of opposition, since 1947 the Christian Democrats have dominated the government and the PCI has been the largest of the opposition parties.

It is obvious that such a multiparty system with alternatives ranging from the PCI to the MSI differs greatly from the multiparty systems of most of northern Europe. Only France is perhaps roughly comparable to Italy, where the "monstrous trinity" of "disillusionment, skepticism, and indifference" have left a heritage of civic alienation.[2] Opposition in Italy taps a dimension of intensity not present in most of the other countries discussed in this book. These political divisions have deep roots in Italian history. Before we turn to a consideration of the contemporary saliency of these divisions in the polity and in Parliament we must examine this historical dimension.

Opposition in Perspective

PREFASCIST EXPERIENCES   In few countries of the Western world is the past so much a part of the present as in Italy. Its landscape, its cities, its monuments, its people are visible reminders of the continuity and change, the invasions and divisions, the greatness and decline which have made Italy both the museum and the laboratory of human achievement. In the arts the Italian past is a goad, a glorious and live tradition, a yardstick; in politics it is largely a burden, something to be overcome, a fountain of disunity and bad habits.

Italy was politically unified in the 1860s; its social and economic unity is still in the making. As a consequence of the hegemony of Piedmont, the achievement of unity seemed to many Italians merely the substitution of one alien, if Italian, rule for an Austrian, or Bourbon, or Papal one. The Liberal leaders of the new state imposed the constitution, the administrative machinery, and the debts of Piedmont on all of Italy. The South and the islands in particular, having known the harsher aspects of feudalism with few of its humane features, were to feel that liberalism was but a more modern—and more efficient—form of exploitation. The Liberal response to the South's opposition was centralization and force, soon supplemented by corruption: Liberal governments came to terms with the area and adopted its habits of buying off and frustrating opposition through the use of the machinery of the state and its local agent, the prefect. A career official responsible to the Minister of the Interior, the successful prefect produced votes for the friends of the government through the judicious exercise of discretion in awarding governmental

2. The phrase is from A. William Salomone, *Italian Democracy in the Making* (Philadelphia, University of Pennsylvania Press, 1945), p. 9.

favors and local improvements, the bribing and intimidation of opponents, the rigging of elections, and the careful cultivation of the local notables who organized the limited electorate as "clients." These practices, used mostly in the South, regularly provided the government with pliable majorities. They also left a heritage of cynicism, highly politicized administrative machinery, corruption, and the absence of civic pride and of vital local government.

On the national level the intrigues of the prefect, local notables, and leading parliamentarians made possible from the 1880s until the First World War a type of parliamentarianism known as *trasformismo*. This was a system in which prime ministers and cabinets remained in office by altering policies and personnel, when necessary, to fit the parliamentary majority. But this majority was itself largely the creation and creature of the Cabinet, thanks to the manipulation of elections as described above and of deputies through favors and, sometimes, outright bribery. Cabinets took their support where they could find it, whether right or left, thus making a coherent opposition impossible. These practices were facilitated by the small size of the electorate. In 1880 only the 2.2 per cent of the population which paid taxes or was educated could vote.[3] Due to the long withdrawal of Catholics from politics and the disenfranchisement of the lower classes, there was remarkable unanimity on socioeconomic questions in Parliament. Coupled with the practice of *trasformismo*, this agreement prevented the young state from developing a coherent parliamentary opposition.

The influence of Parliament on government policies varied greatly in the Liberal period. The king often exercised considerable influence, especially in foreign and military affairs. In addition, several leaders— Agostino Depretis (1881–87), Francesco Crispi (1887–96), and Giovanni Giolitti (1903–14)—so mastered the game of *trasformismo* that they were subjected to little meaningful parliamentary control. There were, of course, deputies who were in opposition to the government and the system. Radicals, reactionaries, and Mazzinian Republicans provided a steady flow of criticism. But they were few in number, divided among themselves, and repeatedly demoralized by defections to the majority. Moreover, they lacked a coherent social base. Only with the rise of socialism did a large opposition of principle emerge capable of withstanding the temptations of *combinazione*, of intrigue for personal advancement.

The genius of parliamentary politics after the turn of the century was Giovanni Giolitti. Cagy, experienced, open-minded, Giolitti appreciated the historical significance of the socialist movement and improvised a

3. Giovanni Schepis, "Analisi statistica dei risultati," in Alberto Spreafico and Joseph LaPalombara, eds., *Elezioni e comportamento politico in Italia* (Ivrea, Comunità, 1963), Tavola I, p. 384.

strategy for dealing with it. The socialists were to be domesticated by being incorporated into the parliamentary system through the expansion of the suffrage.[4] Their numbers were to be balanced by the cultivation of the Catholic masses who would also be enfranchised by the extension of the suffrage. The Catholic Church, likewise frightened by the growing strength of socialism, cooperated: the *non expedit* (the Papal prohibition on Catholics voting or holding public office) was relaxed in 1905 and 1913, and was abandoned following the First World War. There had been independent militant Catholic deputies for some time, and in the 1913 elections, in the absence of a Catholic party, a compact between Giolitti and the president of the Catholic Union, Count Gentiloni, promised Catholic support for those liberals who would favor religious schools and orders and oppose divorce.

Catholics and Socialists were not alone in opposing the Liberal system. The first Nationalists appeared in 1913; and just before the outbreak of the war, the Liberal era seemed to be coming to an end. With changes in the times and the electorate, the old techniques of manipulation and corruption no longer worked effectively. Gaetano Salvemini, calling Giolitti *il ministro della mala vita*, the minister of the underworld, bitterly denounced his hand in the corruption and intimidation of the 1913 election: "confronted not with a mere two or three thousand voters, but with ten thousand or more voters in a constituency to be 'managed,' he was forced to increase the dose of violence to ensure success."[5] Hence the Fascists were not the first to introduce violence into Italian politics: but with the advent of mass parties, mass violence was to be needed, and the Fascists were to be better organized for this than the Liberals.

By the elections of 1919, the transition from the Liberal system of *trasformismo* to the multiparty system was complete. In the Parliament chosen in that year the Socialists were the largest party (156 seats), followed by the Popular Party, a new reformist constitutional democratic party of the Catholic rank-and-file (100 seats). Universal manhood suffrage, proportional representation, and Catholic participation had produced, for the first time in Italian history, disciplined mass parties in Parliament which would not play the parliamentary game of *trasformismo*.

4. As early as 1903 Giolitti had invited a socialist leader to take a portfolio in his Cabinet, but he refused. See Salomone, *Italian Democracy*, p. 49. The Reform Act of 1882 gave the vote to literate males over 21 with no taxation requirement; the 1912 Reform Act added males under 30 who had served in the armed forces and all males over 30, including illiterates (i.e., quasi-universal manhood suffrage). Female suffrage was adopted in 1945. Proportional representation was first used in the 1919 elections.

5. "Introductory Essay," in Salomone, *Italian Democracy*, p. xiv. Salvemini's pamphlet, "Il ministro della mala vita," subtitled "Notes and documents on the Giolittian elections in Southern Italy," was written in 1909. Although conceived as propaganda and not scholarship, it nicely captures the essentials of the elections in the South in the Giolittian era. It is reprinted in a volume with the same title edited by Elio Apih (Milan, Feltrinelli, 1962), pp. 73–141. See also Robert C. Fried, *The Italian Prefects* (New Haven, Yale University Press, 1963), pp. 120–62.

For the extension of the suffrage and the participation of Catholics greatly increased the size of the electorate, and proportional representation enabled the parties to discipline their representatives by placing them lower on the list or eliminating them entirely. This had been difficult to accomplish in a single-member district where, in order to be assured of repeated reelection, the deputy had merely to retain the allegiance of the few hundred voters necessary for a majority of the restricted electorate.

There was now an opposition, or rather, there were several oppositions, for among the Socialists, Populists, Fascists, Nationalists, and Liberals in Parliament, only the Liberals had the experience and attitude of a governing party, and they were in a minority and divided among themselves. The Socialists, excited by the example of the Russian Revolution, vacillated between trying to duplicate it and settling down to parliamentary democracy. During the crucial year of 1919 the party seemed to do neither; it succeeded merely in frightening the middle classes and antagonizing its potential allies.[6] In 1921 the revolutionary wing broke away and formed the Italian Communist Party. The Populists were in a position in Parliament to be the arbiters of the system, but fear of socialism within the Catholic hierarchy cost the party first its independence and eventually its existence.

Fascist violence was viewed by many moderate Italians as a mere continuation of past practices by more effective means against a Socialist enemy which had first begun to employ mass violence. The role of fascism in the downfall of Italian democracy is well known. The errors of tactics and judgment committed by Socialist, Catholic, and Liberal politicians are also well documented. Why did the Italian political system fail to come to terms with its opponents? While no definitive answer can be given, some relative factors can be examined.

The unification of Italy was achieved under the guidance of the liberal aristocracy and the upper middle classes, and these groups continued to dominate politics for the remainder of the nineteenth century. These were without doubt the most enlightened groups in the country, and their relative unity made it easier to pursue coherent policies of centralization and economic development. Furthermore, the manipulation of elections, especially in the South, was a considerable improvement over an alternative device—force. Given the general poverty of Italy, its uneven modernization, and its divided loyalties, the achievements of the liberal state should be viewed with understanding and charity. If the liberal system was inadequate, it was no more inadequate than most other European political systems of the age. Neither France nor Germany, for example, really dealt satisfactorily with the claims of Catholics and Marxists during the

6. Daniel Horowitz has written that "the Socialist Party, with a choice between a policy of revolution and a policy of reform, chose the verbiage of revolution and the substance of neither." *The Italian Labor Movement* (Cambridge, Harvard University Press, 1963), p. 133.

period preceding the First World War. In the Giolittian era the Italian
political system made great progress toward overcoming its weaknesses,
and it is today often viewed as the golden age of Italian democracy. Its
weaknesses were judged severely by an age which combined high ideals
with an ignorance of what was to follow.[7] But the liberal system failed to
come to terms in time with the two major forces of present-day Italy—
Marxism and Catholicism. These two mass movements, and especially the
former, matured outside of and in opposition to the liberal state.

Despite late industrialization and the dominance of agriculture, Italian
civilization has been an urban civilization. Even the landowning aristocracy
has been oriented toward the cities. Consequently the urban proletariat
was not the creation of industrialization and Italian socialism has not been
dependent on the industrial worker. Some predominantly agricultural
regions have been radical strongholds and agricultural workers have provided many of the militants and voters of the left. Italian socialism has a
romantic strain perhaps traceable to its anarchist origins. It has historically
wavered between a maximalist program for a revolutionary reconstruction of society and a minimalist reformism often bordering on oppor-
tunism. The weakness of Italian trade unions and the low level of political
skills within the lower classes have robbed the movement of stability.
From Turati and Bissolati to Nenni, leaders who have moved toward
accommodation with the system have repeatedly found themselves out-
flanked on the left. Only after the turn of the century did the liberals
seriously study the *possibility* of coming to terms with the socialist
opposition: the extension of the suffrage (1912) and the adoption of
proportional representation (1919) were belated recognition of the *necessity* of coming to terms. Given the sharp cleavages between social classes
in Italy plus the traditional regional divisions and individualism, the task
of making a loyal parliamentary opposition out of a revolutionary movement was a formidable one. No country with a similar social structure
seems to have succeeded, even under much more favorable circumstances.
It is thus noteworthy that this seemingly indigestible electorate showed
signs of eventually becoming absorbed into the parliamentary system before fascism relegated the effort to the "might-have-beens" of history.[8]

7. Salvemini, who was a bitter foe and critic of Giolitti before the rise of fascism,
was to write in 1945: "I would have been wiser had I been more moderate in my
criticism of the Giolittian system. My knowledge of the men who came after
Giolitti in Italy as well as of countries in which I have lived during the last twenty
years has convinced me that if Giolitti was not better, neither was he worse than
many non-Italian politicians, and he was certainly less reprehensible than the Italian
politicians who followed him." "Introductory Essay," in Salomone, *Italian Democracy*,
p. xv.

8. H. Stuart Hughes suggests that Giolitti had succeeded in "domesticating" the
Socialists only to have them later regain "their revolutionary militancy." *The United
States and Italy* (Cambridge, Harvard University Press, 1953), p. 59.

The nature of the Catholic opposition to the liberal state was considerably different. It derived more from the Vatican's temporal politics than from the alienation of Catholics as such. To be sure, legitimists in the South, the Black Aristocracy of Rome, and pro-Austrian conservatives in the North continued their formal intransigence well into the twentieth century. On the other hand, many Catholics, the lower clergy included, applauded national unity and tried to lessen the impact of the *non expedit*. The prohibition on Catholic participation was not always respected, but it did prevent the organization of a Catholic political party. Catholics were active on the local level, however, first with the toleration and later with the approval of the hierarchy. With the rise of socialism and the expanding political activities of Catholics the need for national coordination was evident and gave rise to the Popular Party. While representing an opposition group in Italian society, the party was by no means committed to parliamentary opposition, and it formed with the Liberals and Socialists a potential large democratic majority in the Chamber. But the Catholics were internally divided, inexperienced, and lacking in self-confidence. The three democratic groups saw each other—not the Fascists and Nationalists—as the chief enemy.

It is not necessary here to assign responsibility for the failure of liberal democracy in Italy. But it should be noted that blame cannot be restricted to any single group. The Liberals made many mistakes. The Catholic withdrawal from politics deprived the system of a stabilizing force of potentially immense importance. The indecision of Italian Socialists likewise contributed to the disaster. And, finally, the madness of nationalism rampant in the first half of the twentieth century poisoned the system. In the tragedy of errors that destroyed Italian democracy there are many *personaggi*.

REPUBLICAN INSTITUTIONS AND THE LEGACY OF FASCISM   A widely read history of Italy tends to see fascism as a natural development out of weaknesses existing in the liberal state.[9] Certainly the interpenetration of party and state, corruption, elitism, violence, militarism, and absence of opposition characteristic of fascism all find their precedents in the earlier system. A more kindly interpretation would view fascism as a mere parenthesis in the evolution of liberal democracy in Italy. Perhaps the two points of view are not irreconcilable. The political system which emerged after the Second World War exhibits many characteristics of the prefascist system. The formal institutional structure has changed more than behavioral patterns. The Chamber of Deputies resembles that of the prefascist monarchy; the Senate, on the other hand, is now elected, not appointed, and is roughly similar in composition and powers to the lower house. Elections to the

9. Denis Mack Smith, *Italy: A Modern History* (Ann Arbor, University of Michigan Press, 1959), p. vii.

Senate and Chamber are by proportional representation. The Cabinet is
similar to the earlier one, but has lacked the stability of some prefascist
cabinets. A president has of course replaced the king. Several innovations
in the new constitution—the Constitutional Court, the High Judicial
Council, and the Economic and Labor Council—were implemented only
slowly, and 15 years after the constitution went into effect only five of
the proposed 19 regions were functioning. The Italian bureaucracy remains highly centralized, and political considerations are likely to enter
into any administrative action at any level. Interference by both the
Christian Democratic Party and the hierarchy of the Church in the administration reinforces the feelings of many Italians that the Republic is a
Christian Democratic *political system,* as previous ones were Fascist or
Liberal. The state machinery, in other words, is still viewed not as the
instrument of the collectivity but of the ruling party.

The most important difference between the Republic and the prefascist
constitutional monarchy lies not so much in institutional structures or
behavioral characteristics as in the lineup of political forces in Parliament.
The Catholic opposition, reinforced by economic conservatives and others
afraid of communism, has come to power. The descendents of the old
Socialists are now divided among the PCI, PSI, PSDI, and PSIUP. Unable
to find a mass base in an age of universal suffrage, the forces that provided
the old Liberal majority are divided among several parties. The old
clientele relationships of the South remain but the votes no longer go
exclusively or even predominantly to the PLI. The PRI survives precari-
ously from election to election, but its future is not bright. The Monarchists have no prefascist equivalent, although they are a primarily
clientelistic party not unlike the prefascist reactionary Southern cliques.
The MSI is a nostalgic reactionary party with more in common with
fascism in its early years and in its "purified" form under the Italian
Social Republic than with the long years of power and accommodation.
This revised lineup of parliamentary forces perhaps suggests greater
changes in the Italian political culture than have actually occurred. In
fact, most of the same groups which dominated the Italian economy,
society, and polity under the Liberal state and the Fascist state still occupy
commanding positions under the Republic. The range of groups participating in power, however, has broadened, and the range represented in
Parliament has broadened even more.

Among the many legacies of fascism were two of great significance to
our discussion. One was the discrediting of most of the groups and institutions formerly associated with legitimacy. The monarchy, the aristocracy, the bureaucracy, the judiciary, the business community, the military,
the educational system, and most of the old political groups had compromised with fascism in various degrees. The Roman Catholic Church

stood alone among the symbols of order at the end of the war. The Lateran Treaties of 1929 completed and formalized the reconciliation between the Church and unified Italy, and they did much to legitimize fascism. Religion and fascism, however, came increasingly in conflict, and at the end of the war the Church reaped a not completely deserved harvest of goodwill and prestige. It became the rallying point for the forces of order and conservatism, and, soon, of constitutional democracy itself. The Christian Democracy which emerged as the dominant force in Italian politics in the 1940s was considerably more than the prefascist Popular Party. While many Christian Democratic leaders had been active in the earlier party, the new party recruited from a much wider segment of the population. In the atmosphere of crisis and threatening revolution of the postwar period, the choice was often posed as being between God and Communism, and the Christian Democrats became the chief beneficiaries of the panic of conservative and middle-of-the-road voters.[10] As a result the party contained many disparate elements held together by fear, and the decline in its electoral appeal evident in the 1963 elections was perhaps due as much to the general relaxation of tension and the relative depolarization of Italian politics as to anything else.

The second political legacy of fascism was the myth of the Resistance. The Communists maintained the best underground organization during the Fascist years. Their discipline and sense of direction enabled them to exploit the Resistance movement better than the other parties. The Italian Resistance was almost exclusively a Central and Northern phenomenon, for the South was liberated quickly and was never under German control. This separate experience during a crucial moment in Italian history has greatly contributed to the political differences between North and South. The Resistance was not a Communist-led or -inspired movement; leaders and sympathizers of all the Center and Left parties participated in it. But the Italian Communist Party, like its French counterpart, had more than its share of martyrs, provided more than its share of the personnel and conspiratorial skill, and reaped more than its share of the material and symbolic rewards of liberation. The material rewards were dominant positions in local government and trade unions, and real property in the form of equipment, offices, weapons, and money. The symbolic rewards included the myth of Communist leadership of the great movement for

10. Gabriel Almond and Sidney Verba, using data from attitudinal surveys, have concluded that "Italy presents us with the curious anomaly of a political system in which the formal democratic constitution is supported in large part by traditional-clerical elements who are not democratic at all, and not even political in a specialized sense of the term. Opposed to the constitution is a left wing, which, at least in part and at the rank-and-file voter level rather than among the party elite, manifests a form of open partisanship that is consistent with a democratic system." *The Civic Culture* (Princeton, Princeton University Press, 1963), p. 160.

the regeneration of Italian society. The Resistance, in the areas where it existed, constituted one of the few genuinely popular mass political movements in the history of Italy, a country whose history has been made by its elites. It is unfortunate that its exploitation by the Left has forced the Christian Democrats to play down its significance, a policy that tends to reinforce the identification of the Resistance with the Left in the popular mind. Thus a legacy of fascism was the emergence of the Communist Party as a well-organized and -financed political machine, benefiting from the prestige of Russia, its own antifascism, and its role in the Resistance, all of which have given it a peculiar legitimacy even among many non-communists.

Opposition and the Polity

It is a truism of political science that different socioeconomic groups tend to be disproportionately represented in different political parties. How parliamentary opposition is related to the socioeconomic composition of the parties is one of our major interests. Regional, class, and ideological differences loom large in Italy; and of these differences, the class cleavage is probably the most important. For poverty makes mere survival a struggle and politics a grim zero-sum game in which the gains of one group correspond perfectly with the losses of another. Italy is experiencing rapid economic growth and social change at the moment, and the objective socioeconomic differences show signs of decreasing; but psychological attitudes change slowly and objective changes in differences are not immediately reflected in political behavior.

Gabriel Almond and Sidney Verba have written the following:

> The picture of Italian political culture that has emerged from our data is one of relatively unrelieved political alienation and of social isolation and distrust. The Italians are particularly low in national pride, in moderate and open partisanship, in the acknowledgment of the obligation to take an active part in local community affairs, in the sense of competence to join with others in situations of political stress, in their choice of social forms of leisure-time activity, and in their confidence in the social environment.[11]

This is undoubtedly a fair, if exaggerated, characterization. For a more detailed discussion we must note the political importance of regional, ideological, and social differences. Then we will examine the Italian political culture in general.

REGIONAL DIFFERENCES   Both economic and political considerations have led to the concentration of Italian industry in the North, especially in the

11. *The Civic Culture*, p. 402.

triangle formed by Milan, Turin, and Genoa. The North was closer to European markets and influences and more progressively administered at the time of unification; protective tariffs and government subsidies compounded this initial advantage. The standard of living is much higher in the North. The wages of industrial workers in the North approach those of the average Dutch worker. Moreover, the existence of alternative employment in an expanding economy has raised overall wages and led to a rapid influx into urban areas, into the provincial capitals as well as the large cities. In addition, Northern Italy has some of the nation's richest agricultural land; and there are many efficiently run large farms and smaller farms operated by owners and sharecroppers. The latifundia system of the South is absent. Many marginal farms have been abandoned; rural cooperatives and other self-help organizations have been developed; and educational possibilities have been extended. Among the political ramifications of these developments are reduced apathy, a higher degree of party and interest organization, less corruption in politics, and greater political sophistication and rationality.

Much of Southern Italy is still dominated by *la miseria* and a sense of hopelessness, alleviated only by emigration and remittances from abroad. Here the misfortune of poor land is compounded by the abundant population attempting to live off it. Fascist legislation which remained in effect until the mid-1950s made it legally difficult for most Southern peasants to leave their communes. Until the fall of fascism the situation of the South was largely hidden from the world and, indeed, from most Italians.[12]

Several coastal cities of the *Mezzogiorno*, such as Naples and Palermo, have long been administrative, commercial, and cultural centers. These and other areas have recently felt the impact of industrialization and economic development. Even the more developed areas of the South, however, suffer from poverty and overpopulation, while the interior of the lower part of the peninsula and of the islands remains barely touched by the economic boom, except for a loss of its males to the factories of Italy and Northern Europe.[13] Despite the beginnings of land reform and industrialization, the South remains economically backward. The political consequences are apathy, electoral volatility, and cynicism.

The interior is an area of large estates and small subsistence plots. The population lives in crowded hilltop towns and works the surrounding

12. Since the Second World War the plight of the Southern poor has been widely publicized by Carlo Levi, Ignazio Silone, Danilo Dolci, the studies published in *Nord e Sud*, and numerous other scholarly works.
13. It has been calculated that 2,235,000 persons left the South between 1952 and 1962. Half migrated abroad and half to Piedmont, Lombardy, Liguria, and, in lesser numbers, Latium. Some four-fifths of industrial investments are in the North, and almost four-fifths of investments made in the South are in agriculture or public works. *Annuario politico italiano, 1963* (Milan, Communità, 1963), pp. 225-26.

land. Some farm scattered plots which they themselves own; others till the soil as sharecroppers; still others hire themselves out as day laborers. But the man who owns his land may be poorer than a sharecropper, and all are susceptible to economic and political pressures at election time. The middle class is limited to professional men, civil servants, some agricultural managers, and some middle-sized landholders. As a group the Southern middle class has proved unprogressive and subservient to the small upper class, and efforts to create a prosperous rural middle class on owner-operated farms through land reform and government technical assistance have been disappointing.

Political parties in the South tend to be more individualistic than in the North; patron–client relationships are extremely important, and electoral shifts may reflect merely the change in loyalties of a local notable. Personalities are often more important than programs,[14] sentiment than reason, food baskets on holidays than year-round schools. Parties differ greatly in this respect, but they all are affected. The Left is somewhat less, and the Christian Democrats and Monarchists somewhat more, involved in this peculiar play of personalities and favoritism. Party organization is embryonic, associational life poorly developed or nonexistent, and political ignorance and apathy widespread. Regional parties sometimes take a line independent of the national party, as did the Sicilian Christian Democrats, and historic suspicion of outsiders applies equally to party organizers.

Central Italy, which starts north of Rome and extends to the Po Valley, is in the middle in behavioral as well as geographical terms. It is in general much poorer than the North and agriculture remains of great importance, although the balance is rapidly shifting to industry. Its poverty, however, has not been as demoralizing as in the South, and workers and peasants have long experience with political and other organizations for self-help. Central Italy contains the Tuscan, Emilian, and Romagnan strongholds of the Left. Moreover, the middle class is more numerous and progressive, and the upper class less reactionary than in the South. Consequently, Central Italy more closely resembles Northern than Southern Italy in its political behavior.

IDEOLOGICAL DIFFERENCES   The ideological divisions of Italian politics should be approached with considerable caution. Certainly they are overtly among the greatest in Western Europe, surpassing even those of France in their range and depth. Italian voters choose among a bewildering variety of ideological and political commitments—Marxist (communist

14. For example, Southerners are more than twice as likely to cast preference votes than Northerners (i.e., to vote for particular individuals on the party's list, rather than merely to vote for the party's slate as a whole). Schepis, "Analisi statistica," Tavola XXVI, p. 398 f.

and three socialist), liberal, fascist, traditionalist, integral Catholic, and social Catholic. These labels mask a variety of basic issues which crosscut the parties, such as democracy or totalitarianism, clericalism or laicism, Catholicism or secularism, laissez faire or government planning, the status quo or social change. It is probable that these policy choices are more fundamental than the ideological assumptions from which they are seemingly derived. For there is evidence accumulating that mass publics everywhere have extremely limited ideological perceptions; and, given the low level of education and political sophistication of the average Italian voter, it would be surprising if these findings did not also apply to Italy.[15] The role of ideology in Italian politics is consequently difficult to evaluate.

A tentative and preliminary analysis of the role of ideology should begin with social stratification and the educational system. Relatively few Italians receive a secondary education and even fewer attend a university. The potential audience for sophisticated ideological appeals is limited. The political elite, however, is well educated and, except for Communists (who are heavily lower class in origin), party leaders are not greatly dissimilar in educational and social background.[16] Italian higher education heavily emphasizes legal studies and the humanities, the manipulation of ideas and symbols, which encourage a tendency to view politics in abstract terms. Skill in the manipulation of symbols is an important source of influence for party elites in a country with traditional respect for learning combined with limited diffusion of it. But the importance of ideology can be exaggerated. For in all of the parties to the right of the Communists (and on the local level they too often "play the game"), ideological considerations do not prevent leaders who are secure in their party posts from entering into *combinazioni* inconceivable from the ideological viewpoint. Ideology is a weapon of particular importance in inter- and intraparty struggles, and is also a useful analytical tool in discussing some aspects of Italian politics; but it can easily confuse rather than clarify the reality of the Italian situation.

15. See Angus Campbell, Philip E. Converse, Warren E. Miller, and Donald E. Stokes, *The American Voter* (New York, Wiley, 1960), Ch. 9; and Philip E. Converse, "The Nature of Belief Systems of Mass Publics," in David E. Apter, ed., *Ideology and Discontent* (New York, Free Press, 1964), pp. 206–61. Little data is available for Italy on this point, but a study of the ideological perceptions of a group of PSI *members* by the author strongly reinforces the suspicion that Italians will conform to the patterns found by Converse.

16. Differences among leaders are in the direction one would expect, however: Monarchists tend to be higher in social class, Socialists lower, and Christian Democrats in between, although most are from the middle classes. For data on the background of Italian deputies (almost all top party officials are in Parliament, and most are deputies) see Luigi Lotti, "Il parlamento italiano, 1909–1963: raffronto storico," pp. 141–200; and Giovanni Sartori, "Dove va il parlamento?" pp. 312–46; both in Sartori et al., *Il parlamento italiano, 1946–1963* (Naples, Edizioni scientifiche italiane, 1963).

SOCIAL STRATIFICATION   Social class is a very important explanatory variable in Italian politics. Objective social differences are perhaps the greatest in democratic Europe, and the sense of social inequality is very strong. Moreover, the strength of the family plus economic stagnation have made social mobility difficult. As elsewhere, education is the key to social mobility, and higher education has been largely limited to those of means. Economic development is undoubtedly leading to an upgrading of Italian society as a whole, but the political results are not yet apparent.

The socioeconomic basis of Italian parties is blurred by two factors, the interclass nature of Christian Democracy and the division of each class's vote among several parties. The Christian Democratic party is truly an interclass party: in 1958 it received about 23 per cent of the votes of industrial workers, sharecroppers, agricultural workers, and other low income groups, according to estimates of Mattei Dogan.[17] But of these same groups, some 7 per cent voted for rightist parties and 70 per cent for the PCI, PSI, and PSDI. Moreover, a high proportion of the Christian Democratic working-class voters are women.[18] The PCI and PSI get about half their votes from the industrial working class alone. In the most heavily industrialized zones, however, the Communist portion of the industrial working-class vote falls to 38 per cent; thus the Communists are not necessarily stronger in the more industrialized areas.

There is further evidence of the association between communism and class in the Red Belt across Central Italy. Here a declining sharecropping system and the beginning of industrialization combine with a radical tradition to form the heaviest concentration of leftist voters in Italy. There seems to be a great income differential between Christian Democratic and leftist voters in agricultural categories, with the former coming from the higher income groups. According to the estimates of Dogan, large farmers vote overwhelmingly for the rightist parties; small and middle-sized

17. Taken from Dogan, "La stratificazione sociale dei suffragi," in Spreafico and LaPalombara, eds., *Elezioni*, pp. 407–74; and Dogan, "Les bases sociales des partis politiques en France et en Italie," paper presented at the Fifth World Congress of Sociology, Washington, D.C., September 2–8, 1962. These figures are estimates derived from a variety of sources and should be accepted with caution as indicative rather than definitive. Italian polling data are inadequate as a source of this kind of information because of the extremely large portion of respondents who refuse to divulge their party identification or vote to interviewers. See Almond and Verba, *The Civic Culture;* Pierpaolo Luzzatto Fegiz, *Il volto sconosciuto dell'Italia: dieci anni di sondaggi DOXA* (Milan, Giuffre, 1956); Alberto Spreafico, "Orientamento politico e identificazione partitica," pp. 689–732, and Paolo Ammassari, "Opinione politica e scelta elettorale," pp. 733–84, both in Spreafico and LaPalombara, eds., *Elezioni.*

18. Dogan, "La stratificazione sociale dei suffragi," p. 420; see also Dogan, "Le donne italiane tra il cattolicesimo e il marxismo," in Spreafico and LaPalombara, eds., *Elezioni,* pp. 475–94.

farmers support the DC; sharecroppers (very important in Central Italy) and farm workers provide the PCI and PSI with a strong agricultural following.[19]

The nonagricultural middle-class vote is likewise divided along social class lines, with about half the votes going to the DC and most of the rest being divided among the PLI, PRI, MSI, and PDIUM. Only the salaried lower middle class votes PCI and PSI in substantial proportions (30 per cent).[20]

The number of women in the Christian Democratic electorate should also be noted. In 1958 slightly over half the female electorate voted Christian Democratic, and they provided 63 per cent of the votes received by that party. As there are a million more women than men in Italy, this tendency assumes considerable importance.[21] Dogan attributes the Christian Democratic vote of women to religious and traditionalist impulses, rather than to economic or ideological conservatism.[22] He concludes that if only men had voted in 1958, the Communists and Socialists together would have received more votes than the Christian Democrats.[23]

POLITICAL CULTURE   The foregoing discussion has focused largely on the electorates of the various parties. The continuing relationships between parties, their members, and auxiliary organizations form another important source of information about the relationship between parliamentary opposition and social structure. The concept of political subculture is sometimes used as a form of shorthand to suggest the interconnected network of party, trade union, press, club, youth, recreational, and other organizations which cater to the associational needs of the party member from youth through old age, integrating him into the party, satisfying his needs for comradeship, and isolating him from contact with members of rival subcultures. The concept is useful in the Italian situation. The major parties and, with less success, the minor ones too are membership parties with extensive auxiliary organizations providing material and symbolic benefits to their members, ranking from the imposing formal structure of integral Catholicism to the individualistic emphasis on economic interests among the Liberals. The concept of subculture is useful—but it can be misleading. For the most important subcultural divisions of

19. Mattei Dogan, "Les bases sociales des partis politiques en France et en Italie" (note the limitations of these figures discussed in footnote 17).
20. Ibid.
21. *Annuario statistico italiano, 1962* (Rome, Instituto Centrale di Statistica, 1963), p. 15.
22. "Le donne italiane tra il cattolicesimo e il marxismo," p. 492.
23. Ibid., p. 478. However, this viewpoint is challenged by Joseph LaPalombara and Jerry B. Waters, "Values, Expectations, and Political Predispositions of Italian Youth," *Midwest Journal of Political Science*, 5 (1961), 54.

Italy are not primarily political, nor do the lines of cultural cleavage necessarily correspond to the party divisions. They are, however, related in interesting ways.

Perhaps politically the most important cultural heritage in Italy is that of the peasant. Largely cut off from opportunities for advancement and self-improvement, but living an essentially urban life, he has shaped the attitudes and expectations of the Italian form of communal individualism. In its extreme form this individualism has been labeled by Edward Banfield "amoral familism": "Maximize the material short-run advantage of the nuclear family; assume that all others will do likewise." [24] In areas where extreme poverty has not reduced the range of charity to the nuclear family, the extended family, godparent relationships, and associations have in various ways operated to reduce the uncertainty of a precarious existence. Increasingly, political organization is being adopted as a weapon in the struggle, and it is not surprising that those parties such as the Christian Democrats and Communists which have been most successful in exploiting face-to-face relationships and inserting themselves in the existing social fabric have been most successful in gaining loyal members.[25] This peasant heritage has important behavioral consequences. The industrial worker may still live in an agricultural zone, even in the North; he undoubtedly has relatives who remained behind to till the land; and he is at best only one or two generations away from the peasant state.[26] Many of the differences in Northern and Southern political behavior are to be explained by the greater advances made in the North in altering this peasant culture.

The traditional Italian middle class is a small, cultivated group which has proved capable of defending its class interests but has been less successful in carrying through either a thoroughgoing secularization of public life or a deep revolution in Italian social structure. It has oscillated between respect for clerical and aristocratic privilege and a vague liberalism. Like the lower classes it divides its vote between confessional and lay parties, the latter being the PLI, PRI, and PSDI rather than the PCI and PSI. The small aristocratic upper class has little political power, but it has greatly influenced the social and political attitudes of the insecure middle class. The numerically important subcultures are therefore those of the middle class and the lower class (industrial and agricultural, both largely

---

24. *The Moral Basis of a Backward Society* (Glencoe, Ill., Free Press, 1958), p. 85.

25. For claimed party membership (which should be treated with caution) of the Christian Democratic, Communist, and Socialist parties in 1960–62, complete with geographical and other breakdowns, see *Annuario Politico Italiano, 1963*, pp. 1262–69.

26. In 1936, 48.4 per cent of all employed Italians worked in agriculture, hunting, or fishing. The figure for the South was 57 per cent, rising to 75 per cent in the Abruzzi and in Basilicata. *Statistiche sul Mezzogiorno d'Italia, 1861–1953* (Rome, SVIMEZ, 1954), p. 46.

urban-based and peasant in background). The electorates of the parties to the left and right of the Christian Democrats fit more or less neatly into one of these political subcultures. But every party must share a subculture with at least one other party. And the Christian Democrats are firmly established in both subcultures.

For some purposes it might be convenient to view Christian Democracy as associated with a separate, nonclass-based subculture. But there is no evidence of great differences in outlook between one businessman who supports the PLI because of its economic conservatism and his colleague who votes Christian Democratic for business reasons and out of fear of communism, nor of differing basic attitudes between a landowning farmer who votes Christian Democratic to protect his farm and the sharecropper who votes Communist because he does not own land. The differences lie in perceptions of interests and how best to further them—not in *Weltanschauungen*.[27] This is not to deny the existence of a specifically Catholic subculture in Italy which would prefer an integral Catholicism, but it is far from being coterminous with Christian Democracy. Nor is the Communist Party, despite its size, able to isolate its members organizationally, except in some rural areas and some urban neighborhoods where the party has a virtual monopoly in lower-class milieux. But this is a monopoly over culturally deprived and socially isolated groups rather than over "true believers" in a competitive situation. And most PCI voters are doubtlessly not ideological communists. Finally, it should be noted that the level of political subcultural identification which exists, for example, in the Netherlands requires a degree of organization and politicization simply not present in Italy.

Although the level of associational activity in Italy is perhaps lower than in several other European countries, Joseph LaPalombara has discovered groups covering roughly the same fields of activity which would be found in the United States.[28] A major difference between Italian and American groups is the former's fragmentation along party or ideological lines. Thus there are Communist-Socialist, Christian Democratic, Social Democratic-Republican, and neofascist trade unions. Similar duplication is found in women's, students', veterans', and other types of organizations.

27. Hadley Cantril suggests that matched pairs of Christian Democratic and Communist voters differ in the relatively better fortune of the former: "Those who do *not* vote Communist are, by and large, people who in one way or another have had some breaks in life so that they have managed in their own eyes to get along well enough and more or less on their own." *The Politics of Despair* (New York, Basic Books, 1958), p. 125. For a study of *ex*-communists in Italy (and France, the United Kingdom, and the United States) see Gabriel Almond, *The Appeals of Communism* (Princeton, Princeton University Press, 1952).

28. "The Utility and Limitations of Interest Group Theory in Non-American Field Situations," *Journal of Politics, 22* (1960), 29–49.

Several of the most important interest organizations, however, speak for a relatively united segment of the population. Confindustria, the peak organization of industry, and Catholic Action, the lay affiliate of the Church, have no significant competitors in their fields. This is true also of a third organization, the Christian Democratic-oriented Association of Direct Cultivators (independent farmers), which has outdistanced its leftist and other rivals by more than nine-to-one in representation elections.

Catholic Action is of course wholly Christian Democratic in politics. With the party deeply indebted to the clergy and to the Civic Committees of Catholic Action for electioneering and propaganda, representatives of the Church and Catholic Action have long been able to count at least upon excellent channels of access and sympathetic consideration by the ministries and administration at all levels. With the growth of a more effective organization in the past decade, the party has been more independent. The importance of Catholic Action has also been reduced by the less aggressively partisan attitudes of the Vatican since the death of Pius XII, as well as the altered atmosphere under the opening to the left.[29]

The party alignment of Confindustria has been more complicated. During the De Gasperi era it was assured of good personal contacts with the government even if it seldom seemed very influential. Under his successors, however, the organization felt stifled and frustrated, and in 1958 it made an "incredibly amateurish and abortive" attempt to intervene in the elections on behalf of the Liberals.[30]

The historic identification of the Italian political system first with the Liberals, then with the Fascists, and today with the Christian Democrats has important ramifications for the operations of interest groups, and the feedback in turn reinforces the bitterness of opposition and the intensity of the political struggle. For the Christian Democrats largely exclude non-Christian Democratic-affiliated groups from influence on government. In general, those groups which can claim a "kinship" *(parentela)* relationship with Christian Democracy are granted favored access to decision-makers, whether in the party or in the ministries; others are largely excluded. Thus the Christian Democratic-oriented trade union, the Association of Direct Cultivators, and Catholic Action have privileged relationships which they assiduously cultivate and exploit. Interest groups not affiliated with Christian Democracy or one of its minor party allies are usually

29. Marcello Vigli, "I comitati civici nella nuova situazione politica," *Tempi moderni*, 10 (1962), 57–72. For a study of Italian Catholic Action by an American-trained sociologist see Gianfranco Poggi, *Il clero di riserva* (Milan, Feltrinelli, 1963).

30. LaPalombara, "The Utility and Limitations of Interest Group Theory in Non-American Field Situations," and "La Confindustria e la politica in Italia," *Tempi moderni*, 7 (1961), 3–16.

unable to participate meaningfully in the governmental process. They feel that only changing the system will alter this situation, hence the bitterness and negativism of opposition. It is not so much that significant *interests* go unrepresented in contemporary Italy; rather, the government determines who will be permitted to represent those interests vicariously. This is of course quite different from the model pluralistic society with a neutral state and free competition of interests.

This discussion of the bases of political conflict in Italy might be summed up as follows: Italian society is fragmented along a number of lines of cleavage. It is changing from the shape of an elongated pyramid common to developing countries to the normal curve characteristic of industrial society with most units clustered close to the midpoint. Some areas of the country still resemble the pyramid in social structure; others approach the normal curve. But attitudes still reflect the extreme class divisions of the earlier society, and only the Christian Democratic Party has substantial strength at most social levels. Other parties are largely tied to particular classes. However, no party is able to monopolize the voice of a class, as the classes themselves are fragmented along ideological and other lines. But there is little evidence that ideological considerations are foremost in motivating party choice within the mass electorate; rather, perceived interest and local considerations seem more important in choosing between parties. Interest organizations follow the lines of class and/or party, and those representing the opposition are largely blocked from the governmental process. The parties in Parliament are separated by the classes and ideologies they represent, the resulting gulf between their programs, and their mutual intolerance.

Opposition and Parliament

THE PROBLEM OF A MAJORITY   The Italian parliamentary system strongly resembles that of the Fourth French Republic, but the dominance of a single party makes the Italian system in reality quite different in a number of important particulars.[31] The absence of a strong democratic opposition party or parties eliminates the possibility of a democratic alternative government, while the strength of the extreme Left makes it impossible to rule out an undemocratic alternative.[32] And the interclass

31. The political process in Italy has received little attention. An important beginning based on extensive field work is LaPalombara's *Interest Groups in Italian Politics.* See also Norman Kogan, *The Politics of Italian Foreign Policy* (New York, Praeger, 1963); and A. Predieri, "La Produzione legislativa," in Sartori et al., *Il parlamento italiano,* pp. 205–76.

32. For a discussion of this and related issues, and a warning against simplistic single-cause explanations of parliamentary and electoral behavior, see Joseph La-Palombara, "Political Party Systems and Crisis Governments: French and Italian

nature of the dominant DC enables it to shift from one position to another as the mood of the electorate changes. Furthermore, many Christian Democratic leaders exhibit pragmatism, flexibility, willingness to compromise, and instinct for the politically popular and useful. The Christian Democratic Party thus in many respects forms half of a two-party system.

Although the PCI could provide the other half, its ideological and class bases make it an extremely unlikely candidate for the alternative government in a two-party system. It is possible that the changes in outlook implicit in the acceptance of the opening to the left by the DC may combine in the long run with the revisionist tendencies of the PCI to alter basically the role of the PCI in the system. It seems certain, however, that the intent of the architects of the opening to the left was rather to isolate and weaken the PCI, not to accommodate to it. The reasons for the opening to the left require attention.

The Christian Democratic Party is more than just another party, albeit a large one, which plays the parliamentary game of coalition building. Its size, its position at the center of the political spectrum, its close ties with dominant ecclesiastical, business, and interest group elites, and its long domination of the machinery of state give it a predominant position in Italian parliamentary politics. It is the center, the pivot of Italian politics, and for all practical purposes there is no majority possible without it. Consequently, the basic question of parliamentary politics in the Italian Republic has been: Who will support the Christian Democratic-dominated coalition? Parliamentary arithmetic dictates how many parties are necessary to a majority and the marginal utility of their votes, hence also the price that can be set as the outer limit to be considered; bargaining determines the concrete policies and personnel. A caveat should be entered here, however, in order to avoid misrepresentation: ideological barriers limit the range of parties which effectively engage in negotiations. Although some single-party Christian Democratic cabinets have tacitly depended upon the support of the rightist parties, the Monarchists and MSI have never been in the Cabinet. The PCI has not been represented in the Cabinet since 1947, and the PSI was likewise excluded from 1947 until 1963.

In the first legislature under the Republican Constitution (1948–53) the parliamentary majority of the Christian Democrats made coalition technically unnecessary; rather, De Gasperi's desire to strengthen the new Republic led to his inclusion of all the Center parties in the Cabinet. This

Contrasts," *Midwest Journal of Political Science*, 2 (1958), 117–39. For an excellent analysis of the Italian party system see Giovanni Sartori, "European Political Parties: The Case of Polarized Pluralism," in Joseph LaPalombara and Myron Weiner, eds., *Political Parties and Political Development* (Princeton, Princeton University Press, 1965).

Center coalition included the PSDI, PRI, and PLI in addition to the Christian Democrats. In 1950 the PLI dropped out; and in 1951 the PSDI also departed, leaving only the PRI still in the Cabinet with the DC. Following the elections of 1953, which resulted in a loss of seats for each of the coalition partners, the search for a majority became a paramount issue. The De Gasperi era had ended, and attempts by De Gasperi to form a single-party minority government failed. Giuseppe Pella succeeded in this for four months, but Amintore Fanfani failed in his bid to succeed him. A new Center was eventually formed with the PSDI and PLI which lasted through the ministries of Mario Scelba and Antonio Segni (January 1954–May 1957). A single-party DC Cabinet under Adone Zoli governed for the year before the elections of 1958.

The 1958 elections witnessed a mild revival of all the Center parties except the PRI. However, the difficulties of finding a majority increased. In particular, it was no longer possible for the Center-Left parties to coöperate with the PLI, which therefore went into opposition. Consequently, Fanfani began to speak openly of the need to enlarge the Center majority by seeking to woo the Socialists away from the Communists and into a new Center-Left coalition. But his government had the support of only the PSDI and *some* Christian Democrats: he resigned because of lack of support from members of his own party on secret ballots. A Christian Democratic *monocolore* Cabinet under Antonio Segni lasted 13 months, to be replaced by an unfortunate Christian Democratic government under Fernando Tambroni. Lacking a clear majority in Parliament, these governments were forced to court the favors of parties, or at least factions, outside the Cabinet. Tambroni depended upon the support of the Monarchists and MSI, and was forced to resign by violent antifascist demonstrations by Communists and Socialists. The extremists could accomplish in the streets what they could not accomplish in Parliament—the overthrow of a government—but only by capitalizing on the antifascist sentiments of the population. Tambroni was replaced in July 1960 by Fanfani, who began, or accelerated, an historic shift in Italian politics.

This new course, the opening to the left, had been long maturing in the thoughts and actions of several politicians of the Left-Center. In addition to Fanfani and other Christian Democrats, leading Social Democrats under Saragat and the Republican La Malfa led the campaign for the opening to the left. Its actual implementation was dependent upon the convergence of three separate but related developments. One of these, the weakening of the strength of the Center parties in Parliament, was largely a result of the other two—the changes in the policies of the Kremlin and the Vatican and their impact on Italian politics. Significantly, these developments were outside the Italian political system proper.

The succession of Christian Democratic *monocolore* cabinets resting upon the toleration of other Center and sometimes rightist parties served to dramatize the deterioration of the parliamentary situation. Not only did the DC not have a majority in Parliament: even with the PSDI and PRI there was no majority and these latter two parties would not enter into a coalition with the PLI. The Christian Democrats had dominated Parliament and the Cabinet since 1945. High office came naturally to their leaders; the skills required to maneuver between the demands of the masses, clergy, and conservatives equipped them well to face the challenge of new opportunities; if it proved necessary to shift to the left in order to retain office, the shift could and would be made.

This shift was facilitated by changes in the policies of the Catholic Church and in the organization of the party itself. Under the leadership of Pope John XXIII, the Vatican began to accommodate to some of the changes of the century. This led to a recognition of the strength of the Marxist parties in Italy. By no means did the Church either within or without Italy cease its opposition to Communism or leave Italians spiritually free to vote as they pleased. But an inevitable result was to reduce considerably the polarity of Italian politics and to facilitate a rapprochement between the PSI and the Center parties. Furthermore, the new Vatican policy involved something of a withdrawal of the Church and Church-related organizations such as Catholic Action from some of their more exposed positions in Italian public life. This withdrawal was paralleled and even preceded by the development of a Christian Democratic organizational structure based on a mass membership and forming a moderately effective electioneering machine which freed the party from its complete dependence on the Civic Committees of Catholic Action at election time. While leading Christian Democrats were not controlled by the apparatus of the party as was the case with some of the leftist parties, the party secretary, Fanfani, and his successor, Aldo Moro, were able to use the apparatus on behalf of the opening to the left in internal political struggles.

The crucial Christian Democratic Naples party congress of January 1962 approved the experiment of the opening to the left. Most Christian Democratic leaders bowed to the seeming absence of alternatives. They had extracted several guarantees, some public, some merely implicit. Antonio Segni, a moderately conservative Christian Democrat, was elected president in 1962 over the Social Democratic leader Saragat.[33] The new government had to be a programmatic one, that is, it was restrained by the coalition agreement, which provided for strict adherence to Italy's

33. Segni subsequently became very ill and eventually resigned; Saragat was named president in late 1964 after a long and bitter election. These events had important ramifications for the internal unity of the Christian Democratic Party and the survival of the coalition.

international agreements (the Atlantic alliance, in particular), limiting nationalization to the electric industry, and the establishment of the regions provided for in the Constitution but never authorized by Parliament. A start was made by the Socialist-supported Center-Left government of Fanfani before the elections of April 1963. But the anticipated entry of the PSI into the Cabinet following the election was delayed until the end of the year, for at the last minute some of the Socialist leaders got cold feet. The reason is related to the other development—changes in Soviet Communism.

Paradoxically, the PSI moved away from the PCI as the U.S.S.R. became more conciliatory and the Italian Communists "softer." Socialists suffered greatly from the memories of working-class divisions and ineffectualness which preceded the rise of fascism. The mystique of the Resistance and the hope of a working-class victory led them into an electoral agreement with the Communists in 1948. The PSI went into the election the equal of the PCI and emerged the junior partner. Following a period of recriminations and confusion, unity was restored under the leadership of Pietro Nenni, a popular prefascist leader who favored continued close ties, but not electoral alliances, with the PCI. A period of monolithic rule within the PSI began. Even during this period, however, Nenni spoke of the "Socialist Alternative," and his later espousal of autonomy for the PSI was but an extension of trends evident before the crucial year of 1956.[34] In that year Soviet intervention in Hungary and Khrushchev's denunciation of Stalin had a traumatic effect on Italian Socialism. Nenni returned his Stalin Peace Prize and strongly denounced Russian actions in Hungary. The party resolved that socialism was not possible without democracy and, further, that acquiring power democratically also involved a willingness to give it up when defeated in elections. Italian Communists have acknowledged the possibility of the working class coming to power peacefully; they have never suggested that political power, once attained, would ever be peacefully relinquished by Communists. The PSI majority thus values constitutionalism for its own sake. This was reflected also in the reestablishment of democracy within the party. The majority faction supported Nenni in his slow and sometimes agonizing journey from the "People's Bloc" to the Center. A minority faction favored retention of close ties with the PCI and feared a rapprochement with the PSDI and DC. Nenni's majority was not large, and from either necessity or choice he moved very cautiously.

The success of the PCI, the stagnation of the PSI vote, and the decline in the DC vote in the elections of April 1963 were variously interpreted as approval and rejection of the opening to the left. Nevertheless, following the elections Aldo Moro attempted to form a government which

34. See Zariski, "The Italian Socialist Party."

included the Socialists. At the last minute, Nenni's majority divided and the decision had to be postponed until after the PSI congress in October. This congress supported Nenni, and in December the long-gestating DC-PSI-PSDI-PRI government took office. The desertion of 25 PSI deputies and 13 senators (most of whom joined the PSIUP) did not prevent the government from securing a majority; and their departure indeed strengthened the position of Nenni in the PSI.

The coalition resolved for the time being the problem of a government majority. But it brought to the majority a party which was itself badly divided on the issue of participation and considerably different in outlook and size from the minor parties of the old Center coalition. The PSI continued to cooperate with the PCI in trade unions and numerous local governments; in many of these areas of activity it was extremely difficult for the Socialists to desert their long-time allies and to cooperate with Christian Democrats. The importance of personalities and face-to-face relationships at the grass-roots level added to their difficulties in this regard. In alliance with the PSDI and PRI (which reduced its conservative wing to impotence), the PSI was in a position to make demands which were difficult for moderate and conservative Christian Democrats to accept. Yet the PSI had to produce tangible results from participation or be cut down by leftist competitors. While relations between government and opposition entered a new phase with the opening to the left, by no means was a stable relationship between government and opposition worked out.

THE TACTICS OF OPPOSITION   The tactics of opposition in Italy range from very mild bargaining to semirevolutionary activity, and in Parliament from scholarly discourse within committees to obstructionism and even violence within the Chamber. The primary distinction to be made is, of course, between the Center opposition and that of the extremes.

The Center parties—and these generalizations apply equally to factions within a party—rely primarily upon the pressures they can bring to bear upon the majority to get what they want. They agree among themselves on many questions, especially in foreign affairs and constitutional matters, but agreement is a matter of convergence, rather than identity, of viewpoints. And on some of these basic issues there are disagreements, as on the implementation of the Constitution. The existence of several dimensions on which there is an underlying basic antagonism or even incompatibility of viewpoint results in a seeming conspiracy to ignore the issues completely as the price to be paid for government stability.[35] As a result,

35. This reflects an old tradition of Italian politics: Denis Mack Smith wrote of the late nineteenth century that, "Every government was a coalition, for no group was ever powerful enough of its own. This usually meant that when any real division or clash of principle emerged, it was driven underground in order to prevent the majority breaking up." *Italy*, p. 203.

some of the most pressing and obvious problems of Italian life are ignored, or treated ad hoc and without the attention they deserve.[36] Thus a basic conflict between the Christian Democrats and the lay Center parties exists in the field of church-state relations, but the issue is played down and sensitive related areas such as education, divorce, and clerical privileges get little attention. Anticlericalism pays no political dividends, and even the PCI treats the Catholic religion and the Papacy—though not all their representatives—with a peculiar respect. More important differences lie in the field of social and economic policy and in the competition for office, and it is of course difficult to separate these matters completely. The officeholding rather than policy orientation of much of the Christian Democratic leadership reinforces this tendency.

The classic Center stretching from the PSDI through the PLI left no constitutional opposition outside the Cabinet. Consequently, bargaining and the encouraging of outside support from business or farmers or Catholic Action or unions were among the principal tactics available to the internal factions within the coalition. Conservative Christian Democrats could bring pressure on the coalition through the Church and Catholic Action, the Liberals were supported by much of the business community, the Left by noncommunist unions, etc. Each party ran its own candidates separate from the others, so policy differentiation for electoral purposes was, in effect, an opposition tactic even within the coalition.

Anticommunism made it virtually a coalition *against* something rather than *for* something: the slightest relaxation of the sometimes hysterical tension of the era led to the disintegration of the alliance. First the PLI departed; although it returned for a short period, its electoral aim of uniting conservatives made participation unwise. Repeatedly, the other two parties also declined Cabinet positions. But the DC alone lacked a majority and had to depend upon the occasional support of other parties, occasionally including the extreme Right. In this situation, the distinction between government and opposition became confused. Cabinets sometimes resigned because of opposition by Christian Democrats on secret ballots. This was the fate of the first two Fanfani cabinets, for example. Thus the opposition from within the coalition had a wide range of tactics to employ, ranging from bargaining to the withdrawal of support on secret ballots and, sometimes, open revolt in Parliament and on votes. In Italy the outcome of parliamentary balloting cannot always be anticipated, and the absence of a formal majority often makes the results even more problematical. Italian parliamentary life consequently has a certain vitality seemingly lost by the assemblies of less volatile lands. Whereas administrative politics tends to replace parliamentary politics in countries which have achieved considerable consensus on basic issues, Italians feel that they are *governed* not *administered*. Basic decisions are made by the party

36. See A. Predieri, "La produzione legislativa."

leaders rather than Parliament as such. The outcome of votes can *usually* be precisely predicted. The individual deputy or senator counts for very little. But it would be a mistake to consider insignificant what goes on in Parliament.

While the extremist parties can seldom influence government policy through the more peaceful channels of bargaining, other possibilities are open to them. Parliament provides an excellent platform for these groups, as their spokesmen find a national audience and personal immunity provided them. Both government programs and government shortcomings—scandals in particular—provide the subject matter. Debate frequently becomes heated, and violence has at times broken out in the Chamber, especially involving Communists and neofascists. It is sometimes difficult to distinguish honest criticism from obstructionism, and the opportunities abound for the latter. The rules of procedure of committees, the Chamber, and the Senate do not, and probably cannot, completely eliminate the possibility of obstructionism in the legislative process.

The opposition can also exercise influence on the government from outside the formal structure. It has already been related how the Tambroni Cabinet resigned because of demonstrations of the extreme Left. Following the attempted assassination of Communist leader Palmiro Togliatti in 1948, the demonstrations reached an almost insurrectionary peak. Neofascists too have been involved in street violence. Labor disputes and protests have often been manipulated by the Left opposition to embarrass the government. It is increasingly difficult for the Communists to manipulate the unions for purely political aims, but there are sufficient economic issues which are political dynamite to make union activity a rewarding field for the opposition. Consequently, despite the absence of communication between government and opposition, the latter is not without means for influencing the former.

With the opening to the left, the Italian parliamentary system entered a new phase. The reduction of tension and the electoral decline of the DC made possible and necessary a modification of the old centrist formula. Ten years of instability had shown that even with the support of the PSDI, PRI, and PLI the parliamentary majority of the DC and its allies was intolerably slim, and also that the PSDI and PRI would not serve with the PLI. The DC consequently had to choose its allies either to its right or to its left.

The rightist solution appealed to many conservative Christian Democrats, and even to some moderates who saw Italy sliding into the instability of the French Fourth Republic. The stability of the systems of De Gaulle or even Salazar served as examples to some, and the possibility of a similar fate for Italy cannot be casually dismissed. Other Christian

Democrats, concerned with democracy and aware of some long-range trends in Italian society, rejected the rightist alternative in favor of a long-term effort to strengthen the constitutional system by incorporating the PSI into it. These leaders won a victory in 1962–63 with the maturation of the opening to the left. It is less certain that they won the war.

The Center-Left government isolated the PCI (and PSIUP) in opposition on the left, with the PLI, PDIUM, and MSI also opposing the government. Several factions within the coalition were not pleased with the 1963 formula. While the departure of most of the PSI minority into the PSIUP in 1964 strengthened the hand of Nenni, an important group of his followers preferred a more innovative program; and these policy preferences were shared by many Christian Democrats. Other important Christian Democrats also were not in sympathy with the experiment, for opposite reasons. Thus, as in the past, the outcome of factional struggles within the governing parties had great influence on the course of events. Equally important, as in the past, were the attitudes and behavior of the Vatican and the Communists, both Italian and Russian. The evolution of Italian politics was therefore only in part controlled by Italian politicians themselves.

11
PATTERNS OF OPPOSITION

Robert A. Dahl

If one reflects on the differences in the patterns of opposition in the ten countries examined here, the first, the most obvious, and yet the most striking conclusion is likely to be a new awareness of the great variety of different patterns of opposition in democratic systems. The answer to one of the questions posed in the first chapter is clear and unmistakable: there is no single prevailing pattern of opposition in Western democracies.

Can we make order out of the variety we have discovered? The patterns of opposition in the countries discussed in the preceding chapters —not to mention those in the score of democratic countries we have had to ignore—are too complex to repose easily within any classification scheme. Nevertheless, the simplification provided by a typology will prove useful in exploring some of the other questions set out in the first chapter. The present chapter will be devoted, therefore, to a search for a helpful way to classify the patterns of opposition revealed in this volume.

Oppositions, it appears, differ in at least six important ways:

1. The organizational cohesion or concentration of the opponents.
2. The competitiveness of the opposition.
3. The site or setting for the encounter between opposition and those who control the government.
4. The distinctiveness or identifiability of the opposition.
5. The goals of the opposition.
6. The strategies of opposition.

Let us examine each of these.

Concentration

Opponents of a government may display varying degrees of organizational cohesion; they may all be concentrated in a single organization, for example, or they may be dispersed in a number of organizations operating independently of one another.

Probably in no country, and certainly in no democratic country, are all the active opponents of government ever concentrated in one organization. If we concern ourselves with political parties, however, the situation is rather different. Because a political party is the most visible manifestation and surely one of the most effective forms of opposition in a democratic country, it is this particular form with which we have been most concerned in this book. However, the extent to which opposition is concentrated depends on the party system of a country. Although genuine one-party systems probably cannot exist and certainly do not now exist except where governments prohibit opposition parties, in a few countries where key civil liberties are by no means wholly impaired, as in Mexico, a single party has enjoyed a near monopoly of votes, or, as in India, of parliamentary seats. In each of these countries, although some opposition is concentrated in small parties, a good deal of opposition operates as factions within the dominant party. The highest degree of concentration of opposition exists in two-party systems, where the out-party has a substantial monopoly of the opposition. In multiparty systems, opposition is likely to be dispersed among several parties.

In the English-speaking world, all thought about opposition has been dominated, at least in this century, by simple two-party models—to which multiparty systems are a kind of unsatisfactory and probably temporary exception. And this view, so confidently held in Britain and the United States, has often been accepted even outside the English-speaking world.

Yet the facts themselves are enough to discredit such a parochial notion. To begin with, the system of two dominant parties has not been much imitated outside the English-speaking world and its zones of influence. Of 30 countries having in 1964 opposition parties, widespread suffrage, and governments based on relatively recent elections, only 8 would be considered "two-party systems" in the usual sense.[1] Of these 8 countries, all but 2 (Austria and Uruguay) are either English-speaking democracies or were launched politically under the influence of Britain or the United States.

Moreover, as our essays on Britain, the United States, and Austria make clear, even where there are only two dominant parties the patterns of opposition are often radically different. Indeed, in the English-speaking world, the British two-party system as we now understand it seems to

---

1. The eight countries are Australia, Austria, Panama, the Philippines, New Zealand, United Kingdom, the United States, and Uruguay. Even Australia is a highly doubtful case, since it can be included in the two-party class only if the coalition of the Liberal and Country parties is treated as a single party. The tests used to distinguish the two-party systems were somewhat arbitrary, but defensible. Two of the 30 countries, India and Mexico, were excluded because of one-party dominance. The other 21 countries were excluded because the proportion of third-party seats in one popularly elected chamber of the national legislature totaled more than 5 per cent. South Africa, which would have qualified as a two-party system by this test, was excluded from the list of 30 democratic countries because of its suffrage restrictions. A more carefully developed classification of party systems could not possibly change the size of the two-party category by much.

exist only in Britain and in New Zealand. In Australia, one of the two major "parties" is actually a coalition of two parties, while in Canada third parties have been much more significant than in either the United States or Britain.[2] The United States is a paradoxical case. The relative weakness of third parties throughout American history makes the United States an even more clear-cut example of two dominant parties than Britain; yet within this framework of two parties, as we have seen, the American pattern of dispersed opposition has nearly as much in common with some of the European multiparty systems as it does with the "concentrated" British pattern. Finally, as Allen Potter indicates in his essay, the British two-party system as we know it today has not existed for much more than the last four decades. Thanks first to the Irish Nationalists and then to Labor, Britain could scarcely be classified as a genuine two-party system for the 40-year period from about 1880 to 1920; while in the middle decades of the nineteenth century, the British pattern was rather similar to that of the United States: two heterogeneous parties with an executive drawing support from sympathetic elements in both parties.[3] Hence even in British experience the recent pattern is somewhat abnormal.

2. "In the thirteen elections to the Canadian Commons between 1921 and 1963, third parties (that is, parties other than the Liberals and Conservatives) secured over ten per cent of the total popular vote eleven times, and over 25 per cent five times. The low point was six per cent in 1930, and the high point 32 per cent in 1945. Although third parties have not been represented in the Commons in the same high proportion as they have in total votes, they have had enough M.P.s to keep either of the major parties from a legislative majority in six (including the two most recent) of the thirteen parliaments elected since 1921. These six parliaments, however, have sat for only 12 of the 43 years from 1921 to 1964, and during several of these 12 years the Liberals, as at present, have been just short of majority status." Leon D. Epstein, "A Comparative Study of Canadian Parties," *American Political Science Review, 58* (March 1964), 49.

3. *The Economist* observed on April 2, 1864:
The real danger of the present day is that which was pointed out by the great and gifted De Tocqueville. "There are no great topics now to divide parties. There is a concurrence almost unanimous between men of all parties. In consequence, men dispute on small subjects. The old contests of principle become faction fights, mere questions of persons. Governments are turned out perpetually upon questions of no intrinsic importance, just because the Opposition contrive to obtain a temporary and casual majority." Such in substance were the opinions of the great thinker, but they have not been borne out by the recent experience of this country. We have remarked with interest and pleasure that, during the last years of Lord Palmerston's Government, such passions and petty interests as De Tocqueville spoke of have never become predominant, that they have never even obtained substantial influence. The state of things has been most remarkable. The difference between the moderate supporters of the Ministry and its moderate opponents is of the very faintest kind; many men on opposite sides could as a wit has said, "change heads without its being noticed." No great question has arisen to divide or excite them. The Government has been maintained in office by a substantial coalition of the moderate men of both parties. Mr. Bright hates the Government; Mr. Newdegate hates it. But the Liberals who do not go as far as Mr. Bright, the Tories who do not go so far as Mr. Newdegate, by a tacit and informal alliance, have banded to-

In sum, it might be reasonable to consider multiparty systems as the natural way for government and oppositions to manage their conflicts in democracies, while two-party systems, whether resembling the British pattern or the American, are the deviant cases. It is conceivable, of course, that the deviant cases represent superior forms; yet multiparty systems exist in Denmark, Norway, Sweden, the Netherlands, and Switzerland, countries widely thought to have handled their political, social, and economic problems with at least as much skill, justice, and social peace as any other democracies.

In addition to the number of important parties, concentration has yet another dimension. Parties themselves vary enormously in internal unity, as measured, for example, by the way their members vote in parliament; what is formally a single opposition party may in fact disintegrate into a number of factions. Since there are variations in the degree of unity and factionalism among parties even within a particular country, it is difficult to characterize whole systems; in Italy and France the Communists have been highly cohesive in their voting in the parliament, whereas in both countries the other parties are much more divided among themselves.

In order to consider the bearing of concentration on patterns of opposition in the ten countries treated in this volume, it is helpful to combine these two dimensions into four simple categories: [4]

1. Two-party systems with a high degree of internal party unity, as in Britain.

2. Two-party systems with relatively low internal party unity, as in the United States.

3. Multiparty systems with relatively high internal party unity, as in Sweden, Norway, and the Netherlands.

4. Multiparty systems with low internal party unity, as in Italy and France.

To the extent that an opposition takes the party system of the country into account in selecting the strategy it will pursue, different party sys-

---

gether and maintained the Government. Lord Palmerston is in power because sensible persons of average opinions think he ought to be in power. The selection of a Prime Minister by what we may call the common element in the two opposing parties is a new improvement in representative government. It is the only mode in which a strong administration can be upheld in times when parties are equal—when no great question divides them. It is the only mode by which the great dangers which De Tocqueville spoke of can be eluded or escaped.
(Quoted in *The Economist,* April 4, 1964, p. 45.)

4. This scheme would be inadequate for many purposes, but it is sufficient to provide a rough guide to the degree of concentration of opposition in the countries treated in this volume. For a sophisticated treatment of the problem of classifying and analyzing party systems, see Giovanni Sartori, "The Theory of Parties Revisited," in L. Binder and D. Easton, eds., *Theory and Method in Comparative Politics* (Englewood Cliffs, N.J., Prentice-Hall, 1965).

tems should be associated with different strategies. Thus an opposition confronted with a party system of the first type is likely to behave somewhat differently from an opposition confronted with one of the other kinds of party systems. I shall return to this point in a moment.

Competitiveness

How competitive an opposition is depends partly on how concentrated it is. In this case "competitive" does not refer to the psychological orientations of political actors but to the way in which the gains and losses of political opponents in elections and in parliament are related. On the analogy of an equivalent concept in the theory of games, two parties are in a strictly competitive (or zero-sum) relation if they pursue strategies such that, given the election or voting system, the gains of one will exactly equal the losses of another.[5] Because in any given election the number of seats in a legislative body is fixed, whenever only two parties run competing candidates in an election they are necessarily engaged in a strictly competitive contest, since the seats gained by one party will be lost to the other. Applying the notion of strict competition to a legislative body presents some problems; but we can get around most of these by stipulating that two parties are strictly competitive in a legislature if they pursue strategies such that both cannot simultaneously belong to a winning coalition. As an empirical fact, of course, no legislature is strictly competitive all the time; some measures gain overwhelming or unanimous approval, while on others party leaders deliberately permit their followers to vote as they choose. In some legislatures, however, key votes are usually strictly competitive; votes on the formation of a government, votes of confidence, votes on the major legislative and budgeting measures submitted by the government, etc. We can regard parties as strictly competitive in parliament, then, if they are strictly competitive on key votes.

It might be conjectured that in a parliamentary or presidential system monopolized by two highly unified parties, competition would always be strictly competitive. The salient example is, of course, Britain. Yet the parties *could* deliberately decide to collaborate either in parliament or in elections, or in both. During most of two world wars the major parties in Britain agreed to substitute collaboration for competition: coalition cabinets were formed, and elections were delayed until after the end of the war. In Austria from 1947 onward, the People's Party and the Social-

5. This definition puts stress on the strategies of the parties rather than, as in the theory of games, on the objective characteristics of the game or contest itself. For a comparison, see R. D. Luce and H. Raiffa, *Games and Decisions* (New York, Wiley, 1947), Ch. 4; and A. Rapoport, *Fights, Games and Debates* (Ann Arbor, University of Michigan, 1960), Ch. 7.

ist Party formed a coalition government that left virtually no opposition in Parliament; yet at each election the two parties vigorously fought one another for votes. The most extreme displacement of competition by coalition has occurred in Colombia, where the two major parties deliberately entered into a pact to eliminate competition not only in Congress but in national elections; the agreement was intended to last through four elections and four terms of office for a total of 16 years.

Even in a system with two unified parties, then, strict competition is not inevitable. Yet the temptation to shift from coalition to competition is bound to be very great, particularly for the party that believes it could win a majority of votes.[6] Hence coalition in a two-party system imposes severe strains and probably tends to be an unstable solution. Whether, given these strains, the arrangement in Colombia will run the full 16 years therefore seems rather dubious.

In the United States, the two major parties are strictly competitive during presidential elections and for the most part during congressional elections; but in Congress party cohesion is weak as compared with Britain, and elements within one party enter into winning coalitions with elements of the other party even on key votes. In multiparty systems strict competition is unlikely; in fact unless one party can form a majority by itself, strict competition is actually impossible; for unless two parties are willing to enter into a coalition, no majority can be formed. Moreover, parties may not be strictly competitive even during elections, for they may enter into electoral alliances that limit competition in various ways, for example by uniting in some districts around a single candidate, as in runoff elections in France.

Thus the competitiveness of opposition (in the sense in which the term is used here) depends in large measure, though not completely, on the number and nature of parties, i.e., on the extent to which opposition is concentrated. The possibilities we have discussed, and for which examples actually exist, extend from a system in which the opposition is concentrated in a party that is strictly competitive both in elections and in parliament, through various systems in which opposition strategies are both cooperative and competitive, to systems in which the minority party that would ordinarily constitute the opposition coalesces with the majority party both in elections and in parliament (see Table 11.1).

6. One of the rare instances in the modern history of British parties when parliamentary party members revolted and displaced their leader occurred in 1922 when Conservatives turned against Austen Chamberlain because of his determination to continue the wartime coalition with the Liberals through the forthcoming election. (R. T. McKenzie, *British Political Parties* [London, Heinemann, 1955], pp. 83 ff.) In 1940, however, Neville Chamberlain resigned as Prime Minister because he was *unable* to form a wartime coalition; a few months later he gave up the leadership of the party (Ibid., pp. 47–49).

Table 11.1   Competition, Cooperation, and Coalescence:
Types of Party Systems

Type of system	Elections	Parliament	Examples
	Opposition in		
I. Strictly competitive	Strictly competitive	Strictly competitive	Britain
II. Cooperative-competitive			
A. Two-party	Strictly competitive	Cooperative and competitive	United States
B. Multiparty	Cooperative and competitive	Cooperative and competitive	France, Italy
III. Coalescent-competitive			
A. Two-party	Strictly competitive	Coalescent Coalescent	Austria, wartime Britain
B. Multiparty	Cooperative and competitive		
IV. Strictly coalescent	Coalescent	Coalescent	Colombia

Site

Because it seeks to bring about a change in the behavior of the government, an opposition will employ some of its political resources to persuade, induce, or compel a government to alter its conduct. The situation or circumstances in which an opposition employs its resources to bring about a change might be called a *site* for encounters between opposition and government.[7]

All ten of our systems offer oppositions the opportunity to challenge the government by influencing public opinion in order to increase support for themselves, by winning votes and parliamentary seats in elections, by entering into an executive coalition, by gaining support in parliament for legislation, by negotiating with other officials, and by negotiating with unofficial or quasi-official organizations.

The relative importance of these sites varies from one system to another. In some systems one site is relatively decisive: victory in that encounter entails a rather high probability of victory at the rest. But other systems may not offer a decisive site; an opposition may win an encounter at one site and lose at another.

In one sense, to be sure, public opinion is a decisive site in every democracy; for each democracy it would be possible in principle to specify some amount and distribution of opinions that would be decisive. Moreover,

7. Or an "arena"; cf. H. D. Lasswell and A. Kaplan, *Power and Society* (New Haven, Yale University Press, 1950), p. 78.

aside from the question of "decisiveness," influencing public opinion is highly important because success in that undertaking creates capital that can often be converted into influence at the other sites. Conversely, even if microscopic public backing is by no means always a fatal weakness, it is always a severe handicap, while outright public hostility greatly magnifies the difficulties of gaining influence at any site.

Nonetheless, the amount and distribution of public support required for an opposition to gain victory vary even among different democracies, and specifically among those analyzed in the preceding chapters. Unfortunately, the theoretical and empirical patterns have not, as far as I know, been at all worked out, and I shall not attempt to do so here. However, among the countries described in this volume it is possible to distinguish, in a rough way, four somewhat different patterns of "decisiveness."

First, in Britain, which is unique in this respect, parliamentary elections are relatively decisive. For a political opposition to succeed in changing important government policies, a condition that is ordinarily both necessary and sufficient is for it to win a majority of seats in a parliamentary election. By winning a parliamentary majority, the opposition is able to select the executive; and because of party unity the onetime opposition, now the new government, can count upon its majority in the House of Commons to support its policies. The consequences for opposition strategies are obvious. Ordinarily an opposition will concentrate on winning public opinion to its cause and its candidates so that it can win a future parliamentary majority. Every other use of its resources must be subordinated to this controlling purpose. Parliament itself is not, then, a site for genuine encounters so much as it is a forum from which to influence the next election. Parliamentary debate is not intended to influence Parliament as much as the public—and hence future elections; negotiations to enter into the Cabinet would, on the whole, be futile; and everyone knows it.

Second, in some countries where, unlike Britain, elections are not decisive (even though they are important) the formation of the executive is relatively decisive: an executive coalition is moderately sure of gaining the necessary parliamentary support for the policies the coalition agrees on; a group not in the executive coalition is much less likely to gain support for its policies. This pattern exists in countries with multiparty systems where the parties are cohesive in parliamentary voting, as in Holland and Italy, and also in the unusual Austrian two-party coalition system. In these countries the parties attempt to influence public opinion and win parliamentary seats in elections, but they take it more or less for granted that they cannot govern except as part of a coalition. Hence, unlike the British parties, they shape their strategy to take advantage of opportunities for bargaining their way into the current coalition, replacing it with a different coalition, or forcing new elections that are·expected to improve their bargaining position.

Third, some countries that might be placed in the second category because of the working of their parties and the regular governmental institutions have in fact moved closer to a system in which elections and the selection of the executive coalition are decisive only with respect to other *official* sites—parliament, the bureaucracies, local governments, and so on. But on a variety of key issues bargaining has been displaced from these official sites to "bargaining processes between the giant alliances of . . . associations and corporations," as Stein Rokkan says of the "two-tier system" in Norway. So important has this bargaining become in the Scandinavian countries that parliamentary democracy in the conventional sense has been to some extent replaced by a kind of democratic corporatism—or, if one prefers terms less tainted by undemocratic connotations, by a pluralistic democracy with highly organized associations.

The fourth group of countries bears some similarity to the third category because of the dispersed or pluralistic character of key decisions; what distinguishes these countries, however, is the fact that even among official sites none is decisive. For the absence of a decisive site has been produced by a deliberate dispersion of legal authority through constitutional devices such as federalism, separation of powers, and checks and balances. The United States and Switzerland are probably the extreme cases, though West Germany also falls into this category.

Distinctiveness

The distinctiveness of opposition in a political system is largely a result of the three factors we have just discussed: cohesion, competitiveness, and the relative importance of different sites.

In the classic model, the opposition is clearly identified. The principal sites for encounters between opposition and government are the national parliament, parliamentary elections, and the communications media; hence parliament enjoys a virtual monopoly over official, day-to-day encounters. There are only two major parties, both highly unified; hence the opposition is highly concentrated in a single party. Finally, the two parties are strictly competitive in parliament and in elections. As a result of all these conditions, opposition is so sharply distinguished that it is possible to identify unambiguously *the* opposition. In Britain, which has at various times most closely corresponded to this classic model, the distinctiveness of the opposition is symbolized by its very name, "Her Majesty's Loyal Opposition."

The United States and Switzerland both lie close to the opposite extreme. In the United States the sites at which conflict occurs between supporters and opponents of the conduct of government are scattered among the two houses of Congress, the bureaucracy, the White House itself, the courts, and the 50 states, to mention some of the main official sites. The two parties are decentralized; and in Congress they pursue cooperative–competitive strategies. Hence it is never easy to distinguish "opposition" from "government"; and it is exceedingly difficult, if not impossible, to identify *the* opposition. In Switzerland the opposition is perhaps even less distinctive, for in addition to the features that lessen the distinctiveness of opposition in the United States, the Swiss add a multiparty system, referenda, and a plural executive (the Federal Council), the members of which are drawn from all the major parties (including most recently the Socialists), and by tradition conduct themselves in a nonpartisan fashion.

Goals

Although it is obvious that oppositions differ in their goals, it is exceedingly difficult to reduce differences in goals to a manageable analytical scheme. Political actors, as we all know, have long-run aims and short-run aims, and their short-run goals are not necessarily deduced from their long-run goals; the short-run goals may so much dominate their choice of strategies that their "long-run" goals are, realistically speaking, nothing more than the outcome of their short-run goals. Everyone knows too that the ostensible goals of a political actor may not be his real goals; his public objectives may differ from his private objectives. There is no simple way to get round these complexities in the notion of aims or goals. The solution I have chosen is a deliberate oversimplification. I simply postulate that certain goals, whether long-run or short-run, public or private, are "dominant" or "controlling"; and I distinguish between (a) aims or goals and (b) strategies.

In the case of an opposition, the *controlling goals* are the objectives that the opposition seeks to arrive at by changing the conduct of the government. The *strategy* of opposition consists of the means it chooses to obtain these goals.

As to goals, an opposition may oppose the conduct of government because it wants to change (or to resist a possible change in) (1) the personnel of government; (2) the specific policies of government; (3) the structure of the political system; or (4) the socioeconomic structure. Although these are by no means sharply distinct categories, for the sake of simplicity we shall speak of them as if they were more clearly distinguishable than in fact they are. The seven most relevant patterns are shown in Table 11.2.

The fourth type exhibited in Table 11.2—political reformism that is not policy-oriented but is concerned with changes in the political struc-

Table 11.2 Patterns of Opposition: Goals*

Types of opposition	Opposition to the conduct of government in order to change (or prevent change) in				Example
	Personnel of govt.	Specific policies of govt.	Political structure	Socio-economic structure	
NONSTRUCTURAL OPPOSITION					
1. Pure office-seeking parties	+	−	−	−	U.S. Federalists 1815–30
2. Pressure groups	−	+	−	−	U.S. Farm Bureau Federation
3. Policy-oriented parties	+	+	−	−	U.S. Republican Party
LIMITED STRUCTURAL OPPOSITION					
4. Political reformism (not policy-oriented)	+ or −	−	+	−	Britain: Irish Nationalists; U.S.: Women's suffrage movement
MAJOR STRUCTURAL OPPOSITION					
5. Comprehensive political-structural reformism	+	+	+	−	France: RPF
6. Democratic social-structural reformism	+	+	−	+	Dem.-Socialist parties
7. Revolutionary movements	+	+	+	+	Communist parties

Symbols: + = yes
− = no

* Note that number 4, limited structural opposition, includes two subpatterns: i.e., either the presence or absence of opposition to the personnel of government. There are 16 theoretically possible patterns. The remaining 8 do not appear in the table because they were felt to be irrelevant or highly unlikely.

ture and perhaps in the personnel of government—has been, historically, a somewhat transitory kind of opposition in the Western democracies. The most important distinction is between systems that have relatively little structural opposition and those that have a great deal.

The United States has been something of a deviant case. As we saw in Chapter 2, opposition in the United States has been pretty much limited to the nonstructural varieties because of a rather widespread acceptance of the major political, economic, and social structures. By about 1815, the

Federalists had little left to quarrel with even on matters of government policy; their views became more and more indistinguishable from those of the leading Democratic-Republicans. A recent study of Federalism argues that

> the single most compelling motive for Federalists to engage in political activity after 1815 was the lure of public office both for its own sake and because it meant that they would once again participate in the day-to-day actions of government. Federalists had always believed themselves peculiarly fitted to rule and their exclusion from office was perhaps more noxious to them than their defeat on public issues.[8]

Although the Democrats and Republicans have not been, most of the time, purely office-seeking (despite their well-known reputation for being as alike as Tweedledum and Tweedledee), in opposition they tend to be policy-oriented and to avoid any challenge to the basic structures of American politics and society. And a great deal of opposition to the conduct of government in the United States manifests itself not in the parties but in the activities of pressure groups, which usually direct their energies to highly specific questions.

Is the United States, then, a gigantic unique case? Or is it the prototype which other stable democracies will tend to emulate? A good case can be made for both points of view. As the preceding chapters have shown, where major structural opposition exists it is for all practical purposes a monopoly of the Communists together with a much smaller element on the extreme Right. Whatever their "ultimate aims," the socialist parties (if we except the small left-socialist groups) have become essentially policy-oriented—in some cases with strong hankerings after the pleasures of office. This is most clearly evident in Germany, as Kirchheimer has shown in his essay, and in the Scandinavian countries, where the socialists, after more than a generation in office, have either carried out or renounced their major structural reforms and hence, like the Democratic Party in the United States, emphasize policies that would leave the major social, economic, and political structures of the country substantially intact or subject only to evolutionary transformations not directly induced by socialist policies.[9]

8. Shaw Livermore, Jr., *The Twilight of Federalism* (Princeton, N.J., Princeton University Press, 1962) p. 266. A contemporary, Edward Everett, said in 1828 that the lure of office in the United States was much greater than in England. "We have nothing to which the ambitious can aspire, but office . . . Office here is family, rank, hereditary fortune, in Short Everything, out of the range of private life. This links its possession with innate principles of our Nature; and truly incredible are the efforts Men are willing to Make, the humiliations they will endure, to get it."
9. See also Kirchheimer's pioneering contribution to this question, "The Waning of Opposition in Parliamentary Regimes," *Social Research* (Summer 1957), pp. 128–56.

Of the countries examined here, only in Italy and France is there today a relatively large structural opposition represented in parliament—or, for that matter, outside it. The decline of structural opposition in the other countries brings them, at least temporarily, closer to the situation that has prevailed in the United States throughout most of its national history.

Strategies

The specific strategies used by opponents in order to change (or to prevent possible change) in the conduct of government are of almost infinite variety. For they are the product of man's enormous capacity for ingenuity, including the special ingenuity of ambitious and unscrupulous men. Even if we confine our attention to democracies, with which we are exslusively concerned here, strategies that have been used at various times defy tidy classification.

Nonetheless, some patterns do emerge from our analysis so far. The strategy an opposition is likely to select depends, in part, on all of the characteristics that have been examined up to this point. Thus strategies obviously depend to some extent on goals: a revolutionary opposition is not likely to follow the same strategy as a pressure group. But as we have seen, given roughly similar goals a strategy that might make a good deal of sense in one system would be inappropriate in another. Putting goals momentarily to one side, then, one might deliberately oversimplify the actual variations in order to formulate the strategic imperatives of our various systems as follows.

Strategy I. Opposition will concentrate above all on strict competition by seeking to gain enough votes in elections to win a majority of seats in parliament and then to form a government (cabinet or executive) consisting only of its own leaders. This strategy is encouraged by a system characterized by two unified parties, where opposition is highly distinctive, and elections are decisive. The only system of this kind among our ten countries is Britain, where the strategy is in fact usually pursued by the opposition party.

Strategy II. An opposition will try to convert additional voters and to gain additional seats in parliamentary elections, but it will assume that it cannot win a parliamentary majority; hence it will concentrate heavily on entering into a governing coalition and gaining as much as it can by intracoalition bargaining. This strategy is encouraged by a system with more than two major parties that have a high degree of party unity, and where the selection of the government (i.e. cabinet or executive) is relatively decisive. This strategy is usually followed by oppositions in Belgium, France, Italy, and Holland.

Strategy III. An opposition will adopt all of Strategy II, but in addition it will assume that many important decisions will be made in quasi-official bargaining among giant associations; hence failure to get into the cabinet need not prevent it from gaining some of its goals by hard bargaining in these quasi-official encounters. This strategy is encouraged by multiparty systems in which Strategy II is appropriate but in which in addition there exists a rather highly developed structure of democratic corporatism. Strategy III is followed most notably in Norway and Sweden, perhaps, but also in the Netherlands and, to some extent, in a good many other countries as well.

Strategy IV. Oppositions will assume that gaining public support and winning votes in elections are both important but neither is always necessary or always sufficient, since any one of a great variety of sites may prove decisive in a specific case and none will prove generally decisive. Hence an opposition will adapt its specific tactics to its resources and to the most vulnerable site or sites. It may concentrate on pressure group activities, intraparty bargaining, legislative maneuvering, gaining favorable judicial decisions, actions at state and local levels, winning elections, or any combination of these. This kind of strategy is encouraged by a system in which constitutional rules and practice prevent any site from being decisive and where opportunities for preventing or inhibiting government action are numerous. The most notable examples of this strategy are provided by the United States; however, among our ten countries, West Germany also seems to approach it.

These, then, are four rather general strategies encouraged by the characteristics of the system in which opposition finds itself, or, more specifically, by what I have described as other elements in the pattern of opposition (concentration, competitiveness, distinctiveness, and sites) without respect, however, to the influence of goals.

Although the goals of an opposition influence its choice of strategies and tactics in ways too various to examine here, two additional strategies (or sets of strategies) may be encouraged in any democratic system where the opposition is motivated by certain kinds of goals.

Strategy V (really a set of strategies) is pursued by an opposition committed to the survival of the political entity when the opposition and the government believe that survival is seriously threatened by severe internal crisis, subversion, war, or the like. A great threat to the political entity encourages overtures by the government to opposition groups to enter into a broader coalition for the duration of the crisis; it encourages all oppositions committed to preserving the political entity (usually, therefore, all the nonrevolutionary oppositions) to adopt coalescent strategies. Coalescent strategies may vary somewhat from one system to another, but in general an opposition tries to enter into a coalition government on the most advantageous terms, seeks to confine conflicts within the cabinet and to prevent them from breaking out in parliament or in public, and keeps open the possibility of reverting to strict competition when the crisis has passed, or at the next election. This is the strategy pursued in Britain in both world wars, by the Swedish parties in the Second World War, and in Italy during the immediate postwar period. Austria is the most interesting example, however, for the coalescent strategy has been pursued by both the major parties long after the dangers that initially encouraged that strategy have declined; what now seems to preserve the strategy is a fear by both parties of the consequences, not so much for the survival of the polity as for the immediate benefits to the parties themselves should the arrangement give way to a competitive pattern.

Strategy VI (also a set of strategies) is often pursued by revolutionary oppositions committed to the destruction of the political entity or the main features of its constitutional system. The essence of this strategy is to use whatever resources the revolutionary opposition has available in order to disrupt the normal operation of political processes, to discredit the system, to impair its legitimacy, and, in general, to increase the vulnerability of the polity to seizure of power by the revolutionary opposition. This was the strategy pursued by the Nazis and the Communists in Weimar Germany. The failure of this strategy for the Communists and its success for the Nazis, the exigencies of Soviet foreign policy created by the threat of Nazi Germany, the wartime Allied coalition and postwar efforts to preserve that coalition all induced the Communist parties at various times to subordinate their revolutionary strategy to cooperative and coalescent strategies. In the intervening years since the end of the Second World War, the failure of revolutionary oppositions to gain or hold power in any European country without outside military assistance, the discrediting of Stalinism since Khrushchev's famous revelations at the Twentieth Party Congress in 1956, the increasing independence of European Communist parties from Soviet control, and the declining importance of the classic proletariat in expanding economies have evidently generated doubts within the two major Communist parties of Western Europe, those of France and Italy, as to the superiority of the revolutionary strategy over strategy II. Publicly, at least, the French and Italian Communist parties have come to emphasize strategy II—without, so far, yielding the advantages of a revolutionary strategy when it suits their purposes. Conceivably, the European Communist parties—the only important revolutionary oppositions now remaining in the Western democracies, even in Italy—may be undergoing a fundamental transformation of both goals and strategies, a change that will lead them to abandon revolutionary strategies in Western democracies. Yet it is much too early to leap to that facile conclusion. And even should the present Communist parties do so, it seems likely that a rival "Chinese" variety of Left-Communist would continue in both France and Italy to adhere to a revolutionary strategy, probably as a separate party.

To conclude, therefore, that the strategy of revolution is for all practical purposes dead in the Western democracies is, at the very least, premature.

Some Conclusions and Unsolved Problems

The main conclusions from the discussion in this chapter are, then, these:

First, there exist a great variety of different patterns of opposition in democratic systems.

Second, patterns of opposition differ, among other characteristics, in concentration, competitiveness, relative decisiveness of site, distinctiveness, goals, and strategies.

Third, a choice among strategies is partly determined for an opposition by all the other characteristics of the pattern. The influence of these other characteristics on strategies can be represented schematically as in Figure 11.1.

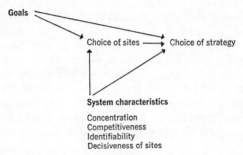

Figure 11.1. A Schematic Representation of the Influence of Various Characteristics of Opposition Patterns on the Choice of Strategies

Fourth, although this offers some explanation for the selection of opposition strategies, our analysis so far leaves the other characteristics pretty much unexplained. Evidently, then, a fuller explanation of differences in strategy would require some explanation of the differences that exist with respect to goals, concentration, competitiveness, identifiability, and site. Moreover, ideally one would want to account not only for present differences in these characteristics among our ten countries but also for any significant changes that have occurred, such as a decline in structural opposition.

These are formidable tasks. In the present state of knowledge, explanations will have to remain highly incomplete and conjectural. The aim of the next chapter is nevertheless to sketch out some explanations.

12
SOME EXPLANATIONS

Robert A. Dahl

To the question whether a standard pattern of opposition has developed in Western democracies, the answer is, as the preceding chapter shows, a confident no. Is there, however, one major factor that "causes" the variations in patterns from one country to another? Can we, to put the question a little differently, relate the differences in patterns to variations in some single factor? Here again the answer appears to be definitely in the negative.

It is possible to identify at least seven factors or conditions that help to account for differences in the patterns of opposition. The interplay of the seven factors is, unfortunately, doubly obscured, for not only is the relation between each of these conditions and patterns of opposition a complex one, but to complicate matters further the relations among the seven conditions themselves are unclear. As a start toward clarifying some of these relationships, therefore, I propose to advance several preliminary hypotheses:

1. Five primary conditions that help to explain patterns of oppositions are

   constitutional structure and electoral system;
   widely shared cultural premises;
   specific subcultures;
   the record of grievances against the government;
   and social and economic differences.

2. Two intervening factors that help to account for variations in patterns of opposition are highly (but perhaps not completely) dependent on the primary conditions. These are

   the specific patterns of cleavage, conflict, and agreement in attitudes and opinions;
   and the extent of polarization.

3. Within some limits that cannot be specified, each of the five primary conditions can vary independently of the others.

4. However, no one of the primary conditions (nor, of course, either of the intervening factors) can vary independently of the others without

limit. That is, if a change in one of those conditions is sufficiently great, it will occur only in association with changes in one or more of the other conditions.

5. Within a given country, a large change in one of the seven conditions increases the likelihood that the existing pattern of opposition will change in a specifiable way. As between two countries, a large difference with respect to one of these conditions is likely to be associated with a difference in patterns of opposition in the two countries.

6. Within a given country, two or more of these conditions may reinforce one another by promoting the same pattern of opposition; they may offset one another by promoting conflicting patterns; or they may be independent of one another. Differences in the patterns of opposition in two countries may therefore be accounted for by the way two or more factors interact with one another.

Constitutional Structure and Electoral System

Constitutional frameworks and electoral systems, it might be objected, have nothing to do with the characteristics of opposition; we must look instead to social, economic, cultural, or psychological factors. This kind of objection reflects a "reductionism" that seeks to reduce political factors to something more "basic," just as biophysicists seek to explain biology by evoking the "more basic" laws of physics. Yet just as biophysicists have encountered severe difficulties in reducing biology to physics,[1] to ignore the effects of constitutional and electoral institutions leaves one in serious difficulties. The American constitutional system, it was pointed out in Chapter 2, provides a complex array of positions from which a minority coalition can check presidential policies favored by a majority coalition in Congress. The constitutional framework thereby inhibits a high degree of concentration of all opposition groups, encourages diffusion, helps prevent clear identifiability, and reduces the prospects of strict competition. All these characteristics, in turn, favor the use of bargaining strategies. To take another case, if the present electoral system in Britain were replaced by one of the continental systems of proportional representation, the present degree of concentration, identifiability, and strict competitiveness of the opposition party surely would not continue to exist. For in the last half-century, no party in Britain has ever received a majority of popular votes.[2] Hence under most PR schemes, no one party could ever have formed a government during this period; all governments would necessarily have been coalition governments; in these circumstances strategies

1. Michael Polanyi, *The Study of Man* (Chicago, University of Chicago Press, 1959).
2. For 1910–51 see E. Lakeman and J. D. Lambert, *Voting in Democracies* (London, Faber and Faber, 1955), p. 35. For the period 1945–64, see the table in Potter, Chapter 1, p. 11.

of parliamentary bargaining (Strategy II) would have had a great deal
more utility for parliamentary opposition and the government than they
can possibly have under the present system, which, as we saw, strongly
promotes strict competition and concentration on elections (Strategy I).
To take a final example, the abrupt change in the pattern of opposition
from the Fourth Republic to the Fifth can be accounted for mainly by
the changed position of the chief executive. Indeed, there is good reason
to think that a return to the Constitution of the Fourth Republic would
to a considerable extent restore the previous pattern of opposition.

Several kinds of institutional arrangements seem to have a bearing on
patterns of opposition: the extent to which constitutional arrangements
effectively allocate independent political resources (sources of power) to
the chief executive, the legislature, and the courts (separation of powers),
and to geographical units (federalism); the relative magnitute of the political resources allotted to chief executive and legislature for influencing
one another; and the system of elections, whether single-member district
or some form of proportional representation. It is impossible to show that
any of these or any combination of them *totally* determines patterns of
opposition even in the short run, for to every plausible generalization of
this kind there seems to be an exception. Moreover, in the long run, constitutional and electoral arrangements themselves respond to other factors:
the pattern of opinions in a country may render some system of proportional representation far more acceptable than a single-member district,
winner-take-all system of elections.[3]

Yet the evidence does strongly suggest that different constitutional and
electoral arrangements raise or lower the likelihood of a particular pattern.[4] Thus constitutional separation of powers and federalism both create
a variety of alternative sites and reduce the possibility of an all-or-nothing
victory through elections; hence both tend to decrease the relative importance of electoral encounters as compared with encounters at other
sites. They also encourage decentralization in the control of parties [5] and

3. Giovanni Sartori, "The Theory of Parties Revisited," in L. Binder and D. Easton,
eds., *Theory and Method in Comparative Politics* (Englewood Cliffs, N.J., Prentice-
Hall, 1965); see also his "European Party Systems: The Case of Polarized Pluralism,"
in Joseph LaPalombara and Myron Weiner, eds., *Political Parties and Political Development* (Princeton, Princeton University Press, 1965), and John Grumm, "Theories of
Electoral Systems," *Midwest Journal of Political Science, 2* (November 1958), 357–76.

4. S. M. Lipset, "Party Systems and the Representation of Social Groups," *European
Journal of Sociology, 1,* No. 1 (1960), 50–85.

5. For a comparison of party organization in Australia (federalist) and New Zealand (unitary), see Gwendolyn M. Carter, "The Commonwealth Overseas: Variations
on a British Theme" in S. Neumann, ed., *Modern Political Parties* (Chicago, University of Chicago Press, 1956), pp. 58–105, especially at pp. 92–97. For a comparison
of two federal countries with substantially different party systems, see Leon D.
Epstein, "A Comparative Study of Canadian Parties," *American Political Science
Review, 58* (March 1964), 46–59.

thereby decrease the distinctiveness of the opposition and the chances for a strictly competitive contest between government and opposition. As a result of all these factors, both separation of powers and federalism confront an opposition with the alternative of carrying out a revolution to sweep the whole fragmented structure away, or else adopting a strategy for gaining goals by influencing the existing personnel of government rather than relying exclusively on winning elections and displacing the governing party or coalition. To increase the relative magnitude of the political resources available to the president, prime minister, or cabinet operates in the opposite direction. The more the power of the chief executive is increased relative to the power of legislators, the more an opposition will have to concentrate its efforts on the chief executive. This in turn increases the importance of winning elections in order to replace the executive. All three factors taken together generate pressures to concentrate the oppositions into a single coalition which, by its unity, has a chance to win the election; this in turn will emphasize the distinctiveness of opposition and push the system closer toward strict competition.

As to electoral arrangements, it is unnecessary to recapitulate that extensive controversy. The view that PR is a necessary condition for multiparty systems, and that single-member districts with plurality elections are a sufficient condition for a two-party system, is definitely untenable. Yet PR does seem to be a sufficient condition for more than two parties; none of the nations using a complete PR system for national elections has a two-party system, and if the reasoning about the United States and Britain employed a moment ago is correct, then both these countries would in all likelihood move toward multiparty systems if they were to adopt PR for national elections. PR decreases the concentration and distinctiveness of opposition; reduces strict competition and increases the need for cooperation; and thereby increases the rewards to be gained from bargaining strategies of various kinds. The argument of these paragraphs is summarized in Table 12.1.

Thus if constitution-makers wished to concentrate the opposition and encourage the existence of two distinct and strictly competitive parties each employing a strategy of winning elections in order to form a powerful one-party executive, they should recommend a parliamentary system without marked constitutional separation of powers; an executive with relatively great political resources in comparison with the legislature; a unitary rather than a federal system; and election of members of parliament by a relative majority of votes in single-member districts. However, constitution-makers in some countries would be well advised, as we shall see, to hesitate about adopting such a constitution because of its explosive potentialities if political attitudes were to become highly polarized. Conversely, if constitution-makers wished to diffuse the opposition into a

Table 12.1. *The Influence of Constitutional Structures and Electoral Arrangements on Patterns of Opposition*

Effects of:	Decisive-ness of one site	Concen-tration	Distinc-tiveness	Strict compe-tition	Concen-tration on Strategy I *
I. Separation of powers	—	—	—	—	—
II. Federalism	—	—	—	—	—
III. PR	—	—	—	—	—
IV. Increase in relative power of executive	+	+	+	+	+

+ = increase
— = decrease

* Strict competition, winning elections, and forming a one-party, noncoalition executive. See above, p. 344.

variety of different sites and parties and to encourage cooperative–competitive strategies with a strong emphasis on gaining entry into parliamentary coalitions, they should recommend proportional representation, a relatively weak executive, constitutional separation of powers, and federalism. However, the price of such a constitution might be a certain paralysis in the executive except in a country with rather high consensus —which, since it would have nothing to fear from a concentrated opposition, would have no great need to employ these constitutional devices in order to diffuse and fragment the opposition.

Widely Shared Cultural Premises

That we are examining the products of historical developments should serve as a warning. Our ten countries have had different histories: even Swedes and Norwegians do not share the same past. The history of a country is in this one respect analogous to the past of an individual: behavior at any given moment is a product of interplay between the present situation and what has already been learned from responses to earlier situations. In an individual, the sum total of these learned orientations is his personality; in a nation or a country, its culture.

Both notions are diffuse, and we are barely past the threshold of scientific knowledge about personality and culture, particularly as they bear on politics. Nonetheless, few students of comparative politics doubt that certain countries do have different political cultures: that leaders and a great part of the people differ from one country to the other in their orientations toward politics. For example, as Alfred Grosser suggests, underlying attitudes about opposing the government are rather different in France from what they are in, say, Britain or the United States. A

Frenchman, typically, is more disposed to oppose, less disposed to support the government—any government.[6]

Despite the slender evidence, the conjecture that patterns of opposition may have something to do with the widely shared cultural premises of a country is much too important to ignore. Our data—indeed, all existing data—do not permit one to do justice to the conjecture. We do not even know what weight to assign cultural factors as compared with others. But we cannot ignore them. What follows, then, is not a summary of findings but a sketch for a theory.

Four kinds of culturally derived orientations toward politics seem to have a bearing on patterns of opposition:

1. *Orientations toward the political system.* These orientations may be classified as allegiance, when attitudes, feelings, and evaluations are favorable to the political system; apathy or detachment, when attitudes, feelings, and evaluations are neutral rather than positive or negative; and alienation, when attitudes, feelings, and evaluations are unfavorable.[7] In the United States, Great Britain, Sweden, Norway, and (in a more complex way) Holland, the political culture evidently generates widespread allegiance. In West Germany (and perhaps Austria), it seems to generate detachment. In Italy and France, and possibly to some extent in Belgium, it generates alienation [8] mixed with a large measure of apathy.

2. *Orientations toward other people.* Beliefs that one can have faith and confidence in others, or conversely that one should exercise distrust and suspicion toward others, seem to be culturally rooted to some extent, even if there are great individual variations around the cultural norm. Though comparative evidence is scanty, Almond and Verba found sizable variations in "faith in people" among their samples in five countries: "the Americans and British tend to be consistently most positive about the safety and responsiveness of the human environment, the Germans and Italians more negative, and the Mexicans inconsistent." [9]

6. That the difference is one of degree and is subject to long-run changes is suggested by Bagehot's comment that "The natural impulse of the English people is to resist authority." *The English Constitution,* (New York, Dolphin Books, Doubleday, n.d.), p. 306.

7. These concepts are derived from the first systematic empirical study of political culture on a comparative basis: Gabriel Almond and Sidney Verba, *The Civic Culture,* (Princeton, Princeton University Press, 1963), pp. 21–22. The concept of allegiance was in turn derived from Robert Lane, *Political Ideology, Why the American Common Man Believes What He Does* (New York, Free Press, 1962), pp. 170 ff.

8. For Britain, U.S., Germany, and Italy, see Almond and Verba, *The Civic Culture,* Ch. 14, p. 402, and passim. For the others, the classification is a purely qualitative judgment based primarily though not exclusively on the essays in this volume.

9. *Ibid.,* p. 268. For example, the percentages agreeing that "most people can be trusted" were: U.S., 55 per cent; U.K., 49 per cent; Germany 19 per cent; Italy 7 per cent (Table 4, p. 267). Whether the expression in quotation marks has precisely equivalent meanings in the different countries is uncertain.

3. *Orientations toward cooperation and individuality.* Some cultures emphasize the virtues of cooperating with others, conciliating opposing views, compromise, willingness to submerge one's own special ideas in a larger solution. Other cultures stress the value of maintaining one's individuality, distinctiveness, the integrity of one's personality and ideas, preserving personal integrity by avoiding compromises. The political culture may, of course, stress these attitudes more—or less—heavily than the "general" culture. Though concrete evidence of cultural differences among our countries is difficult to find, it hardly seems open to doubt that in Sweden, Britain, and the United States, the political culture strongly emphasizes the virtues of compromise and conciliation and the possibility of compromising without threatening personal integrity; indeed, in these countries compromise is widely hailed as virtuous. In France and Italy, on the other hand, the virtue both to individuals and to groups of maintaining personal integrity and distinctiveness, even at the price of conflict, seems to be relatively more heavily stressed both in the general culture and in political life.[10]

4. *Orientations toward problem-solving.* Sartori has emphasized the importance of looking "at the underlying cultural patterns if we want to understand the difference between democracies of the Anglo-American type and, let us say, of the French type." [11] Englishmen and Americans, he argues, tend to be characterized by an empirical or (in a loose sense) pragmatic approach to problems, whereas among the French, Italians, and Germans,[12] a rationalistic approach is more likely to dominate thinking about politics. Sartori sketches the two orientations as follows:

10. Direct evidence is hard to find. One indirect piece of evidence for "cooperation" versus "individuality" is membership in voluntary organizations. Almond and Verba found such memberships much more frequent among Americans and Britishers than among Italians and Mexicans, *The Civic Culture,* pp. 301–06. On Italy, see also Arnold Rose, "On Individualism and Social Responsibility," in *European Journal of Sociology, 2,* No. 1 (1961), 163–69. For insights on French "individualism" see François Bourricaud, "France" in Arnold M. Rose, ed., *The Institutions of Advanced Societies* (Minneapolis, University of Minnesota Press, 1958), pp. 498 ff.

11. Giovanni Sartori, *Democratic Theory* (Detroit, Wayne State University Press, 1962), p. 233.

12. While a weakness in empirico-pragmatic styles of thought is often ascribed to Germans, other observers might not agree that their style is "rationalistic" in quite the sense of French and Italian "rationalism." Thus Deutsch and Edinger speak of "the two underdeveloped traditions of empiricism and equality: two muted themes in German culture . . . The mercantile traditions of empiricism, rationality, adaptability, and ease of compromise seem markedly underrepresented . . . German culture thus offers its members two quite different roles for imitation: on the one hand the obedient, dependable craftsman, and on the other, the bold, romantic knight and his intellectual cousin, the daring, demonic magician." Karl W. Deutsch and Lewis J. Edinger, *Germany Rejoins the Powers* (Stanford, Stanford University Press, 1959), p. 17.

While the empirical (empirico-pragmatic) mentality stays *in medias res*, close to what can be seen and touched, the rationalist mentality soars to a higher level of abstraction and hence tends to be far removed from facts. While the former is inclined to accept reality, the *raison* tends to reject reality in order to re-make it in its own image; while empiricism tends to be anti-dogmatic and tentative, rationalism tends to be dogmatic and definitive; while the former is eager to learn from experience and to proceed by testing and re-testing, the latter goes ahead even without tests; while the empiricist is not deeply concerned with rigorous coherence and distrusts long chains of demonstration, the rationalist is intransigent about the necessity for deductive consistency—and therefore, in the summing up, while the former prefers to be reasonable rather than rational, the latter puts logical rigor above everything and thus is rational even if it means being unreasonable. While the empirical approach takes the attitude that if a program does not work in practice there must be something wrong about the theory, the rationalist will retort that what is true in theory must also be true in practice—that it is the practice, not the theory, that is wrong.[13]

The extreme cases would then be represented in two hypothetical political systems:

Orientations to:	System I	System II
the political system	allegiant	alienated
other people	trustful	mistrustful
collective action	cooperative	noncooperative
problem-solving	empirico-pragmatic	rationalistic

13. *Democratic Theory*, p. 232. No better illustration of the "empirical" attitude toward political decisions could be found than Bagehot's description of the House of Commons:

it may seem odd to say so, just after inculcating that party organization is the vital principle of representative government, but that organization is permanently efficient, because it is not composed of warm partisans. The body is eager, but the atoms are cool. If it were otherwise, parliamentary government would become the worst of governments—a sectarian government. The party in power would go to all the lengths their orators proposed—all that their formulae enjoined, as far as they had ever said they would go. But the partisans of the English parliament are not of such a temper. They are Whigs, or Radicals, or Tories, but they are much else too. They are common Englishmen, and, as Father Newman complains, "hard to work up to the dogmatic level." They are not eager to press the tenets of their party to impossible conclusions. On the contrary, the way to lead them—the best and acknowledged way—is to affect a studied and illogical moderation . . . Nor indeed . . . are the leaders themselves of the House of Commons, for the most part, eager to carry party conclusions too far. They are in contact with reality . . . And the end always is, that the middle course is devised which *looks* as much as possible like what was suggested in opposition, but which *is* as much as possible what patent facts—facts which seem to live in the office, so teasing and unceasing are they—prove ought to be done.
Walter Bagehot, *The English Constitution*, pp. 181-83.

It seems reasonable to think that opposition in these two hypothetical systems would differ in the following ways:

In System I, opposition would stress the importance of:	*In System II, opposition would stress the importance of:*
maintaining a stable government	achieving goals, even if this leads to instability in government
adhering to the political and constitutional rules of the game	changing the rules if this is required by goals
making evolutionary changes by marginal adjustments	making major structural changes, possibly by revolutionary means
factual analysis rather than ideological consistency	ideological consistency rather than factual analysis

Perhaps the most interesting difference in these two contrasting cultural orientations is the extent to which they would encourage consideration by political elites and activists of major structural changes in society, economy, and polity. Because System I would deal only with marginal alternatives, proposals for major structural changes would receive slight attention. Thus System I might prove to be rigid if it were confronted by problems that could not be met satisfactorily by the existing structures. System II, on the other hand, would encourage political elites and activists to consider major structural changes; but the emphasis on deducing the program from an abstract ideology, and the willingness to violate or change the constitutional and political rules to achieve political goals, might so thoroughly fracture consensus that discussion—a "dialogue"— about the alternatives would, in practice, be impossible. The structural alternatives presented by different groups would not be analyzed and discussed as much as merely proclaimed: in the place of discussion, there would be a dialogue of the deaf.

The two systems, it should be said again, represent the extreme cases. In practice, concrete political systems, including the ten examined in this book, would fall short of the extreme types. Probably the United States comes closer than any of the other nine countries to our hypothetical System I; the orientations and the oppositional behavior ascribed to System I are, in fact, usually attributed to the United States. Present-day Britain, the Scandinavian countries, and Holland also seem to display the characteristics of System I. Italy and France, on the other hand, probably approach System II somewhat more closely than any of the other countries described in the preceding chapters.

Yet it bears re-emphasizing that while the evidence we have lends credence to these conjectures, our observations in this area are still mainly impressionistic. Much research remains to be done before we can be at all confident about the interplay between political cultures and patterns of opposition.

Subcultures

Almost any difference in behavior or beliefs can lead to the development of so many special patterns of thought, language, identity, and other forms of behavior that we can appropriately label these patterns as a subculture. Once it develops, a subculture often displays remarkable tenacity, for the levers of change cannot easily be manipulated by outsiders, and those inside the subculture are rewarded not for changing their way of life but for adhering to it.

Conflicts involving subcultures are likely to be especially intense, and therefore particularly difficult to manage, because they cannot be confined to single, discrete issues; to the person sharing the perspective of a subculture, conflict over a "single" issue threatens his "way of life," the whole future of the subculture. The historic conflict of anticlericals and Catholics over funds for parochial schools was surely not often perceived, on either side, as a simple, straightforward question of how to finance education: it was a matter of rival ways of life or fundamental notions about freedom. In the United States, the question of voting rights for Negroes has never meant simply whether Negroes should vote: the typical white Southerner has perceived this, or any other extension to Negroes of the rights and liberties enjoyed by whites, as a threat to "the South"—in short, to a way of life built directly upon the subjection of the Negro.

To some extent, all of the countries examined here are societies divided into subcultures. Occupation; social status; race, language, and ethnic group; religion; residence; size of community; and region—these are nodes, everywhere, around which cultural distinctiveness develops. But it is when the numbers who participate in a subculture are large, the differences sharp, and the subculture comprehensive that the effects on political conflict are greatest.

Not one of our ten countries has wholly escaped conflict exacerbated by differences among subcultures (or between a subculture and the dominant culture), and in six of the ten countries conflicts of this kind have—at least for a time—directly shaped the characteristics of opposition:

In *Britain,* the conflict over Ireland is now substantially ended, but while it endured it involved a subculture based on region, religion, and ethnic identity. The conflict proved to be incapable of solution within the framework of the British political system.

In *Norway,* the conflict, now diminishing, between "center" and "periphery," based on region, residence, occupation, language, and to some extent religion has been important in political life during much of this century.

In *Holland*, the conflict over religion has led to the division of Dutch society into three rather distinct communities.

In *Belgium*, the conflict between Walloons and Flemings reflects subcultures different in language, religious views in part, and region.

In *Austria*, the conflict between two *Lager* has dominated the political scene since the beginning of the Republic.

In the *United States*, the South has for nearly two centuries formed a distinctive regional subculture with profound effects on American political life.

Since opposition between a subculture and a government that represents a different subculture or the dominant majority culture is highly explosive, how have our countries responded to those conflicts?

In general, conflicts involving subcultures rarely seem to be handled—for long—by the normal political processes employed in other kinds of issues. For this sort of conflict is too explosive to be managed by ordinary parliamentary opposition, bargaining, campaigning, and winning elections. The chief ways in which these conflicts have been dealt with are these:

1. *Violence* and *repression*. This has been a response in Britain, in Belgium, and, most notably, in the United States, where violence has even erupted into a civil war. The possibility of violence and civil war always lurks as a special danger in countries with hostile subcultures; and this danger undoubtedly stimulates a search for alternative responses.

2. *Secession* or *separation*. This was the solution to the problem in Ireland. It was the solution sought by the South that eventuated in the American Civil War.

3. *Mutual veto* on government policies. In this case, each opponent can veto changes in the status quo involving his subculture. This is most clearly the system in Austria. But it is also characteristic of Holland and, to a considerable extent, Belgium and the United States.[14]

4. *Autonomy*. Autonomy may be granted to a regional subculture, as in the case of the South, which after about 1874–80 received, de facto, a grant of autonomy from Congress, President, and Supreme Court. Or, as in Holland, autonomy may be granted to subcultures that do not have a regional basis.

5. *Proportional representation* has been used to guarantee a subculture that it will be represented in parliament even though, as in Belgium, it does not receive much autonomy. And proportional representation in the broader sense of representing groups more or less in proportion to their numbers can be applied in all kinds of agencies and organizations, as in Belgium.

14. Passage of the Civil Rights Act of 1964 represents the first successful effort since the Reconstruction period to overcome Southern resistance in Congress to legislation protecting Negro rights.

6. *Assimilation.* This seems to be the evolutionary pattern in Norway. For a century and a half it was the characteristic response to ethnic group differences in the United States; but the process of assimilation has failed, so far, in the case of Negroes.

The Record of Grievance

The extent to which citizens of a country are allegiant or alienated depends in some measure on the way the government has responded to grievances in the past and is expected by citizens or subjects to respond in the future.

Reflecting on observations made during 1950–51 in the Provençal village of "Peyrane," Lawrence Wylie noted that

> there never has been a time since the beginning of Peyrane's history, when contact with organized humanity has meant anything but the exploitation and manipulation of the individual. The wandering hordes, the Romans, the feudal lords—including the neighboring papal rulers, the agents of Provencal counts and French kings, the nineteenth-century regimes set up by Paris, the twentieth-century bureaucracy centralized in Paris—all these form an unbroken past in the vague memory of the village. They all mean domination by a human power beyond the control of the individual. At best the domination has brought unsought modifications in living habits. At worst it has brought disaster. And so it has become conventional to think of human power as a plague to be classed with the plagues of nature: the odious government, the leveling mistral, the flooding Durance.[15]

If the citizens of the United States and Britain are much more confident than the citizens of Germany, Italy, and Mexico that they could do something to prevent the passage by the national legislature of a law they considered to be unjust or harmful, as Almond and Verba report,[16] surely these differences have something to do with the historic record of how grievances have previously been handled. To be sure, these differences in attitudes may now be embedded in the political cultures of these countries; but the political cultures themselves can be explained in part by the record of the past.

The burden of grievance is not, however, invariable in human societies. The institutions of a society generate a greater burden of grievance during some periods than in others; moreover, for a variety of reasons some societies evidently generate a smaller burden of grievances than others. Thus the accumulated burden of grievances may be low and allegiance high: either because the social and economic institutions of a country tend

15. *Village in the Vaucluse* (rev. ed. New York, Harper Colophon Books, 1964), p. 332.
16. *The Civic Culture,* p. 185, Table 1.

to generate a relatively small burden of grievance; or because, even though great grievances have been generated in the past, the government has responded to alleviate them.

Returning to the French village ten years later, Wylie was surprised to discover marked changes even in that brief period:

> As I went out into the country and talked to the farmers I realized the importance of the changed economic situation and state of mind of the farm people in the commune. They have a new awareness of their professional status and dignity, which is reflected in the growth of their professional organizations and in their sense of solidarity with farmers elsewhere . . . It was obvious that French farmers were in agreement that if they wanted action there was nothing to be gained by talking to elected officials . . . At last they had come to feel that their most effective political representatives were not the traditionally elected officers—deputies and senators—but farmers themselves who had been elected to office in professional organizations . . . Once there was no more hope of turning back, the inevitability of change was accepted, it at last became possible for people to devote their energy to seeking new solutions for their problems. People acquired a greater sense of freedom to act for their own welfare. The rejection of the old political system, the modernization of the farms, the tractor demonstrations, the development of farmers' organizations are, to a certain extent, manifestations of this changed spirit.[17]

For nearly a century the most insistent internal threat to the allegiance of citizens was the burden of grievance accumulated among the urban and (particularly in Italy) rural proletariats, a burden that threatened to alienate the working classes if the grievances were not heeded—or to alienate the middle classes if they were. The problem, then, was how to gain the allegiance of the working classes to democratic institutions without alienating the other social strata. This problem has not been solved in all ten countries: France and Italy in particular do not seem to have worked out a solution, though they may be in the process of doing so. In Germany (and perhaps in Austria) commitment to democratic institutions is untested by adversity and may still be somewhat weak; but working classes, at any rate, are as allegiant as other major social strata, and in this narrow sense a solution has been reached to the problem of political alienation among the working classes. In the remaining six countries, the problem has been solved, at least in the main. One of the significant developments of this century has been, then, the integration of the working classes into a large number of Western democratic systems and the decline in these countries of any serious threat to parliamentary democracy

17. *Village in the Vaucluse*, pp. 359, 362, 364.

generated by class conflict. The importance of this development for the future of oppositions can scarcely be exaggerated.

Even aside from France and Italy, however, the integration of the urban and rural workers into political life has not followed an identical pattern.[18] Despite the diversity of specific patterns, it is possible to clarify some of the major aspects of the process by drawing a simplified and abstract picture of how a political system might solve the problem of acquiring the allegiance of the working classes to democratic institutions without alienating the other strata, particularly the middle and upper strata. One might conjecture that the likelihood that this problem would be solved would be relatively high if the following conditions were met:[19]

1. As the urban (or rural) working classes increase in numbers and in demands on the political system, there already exists an operating parliamentary system supported by a large and allegiant middle class and led by an experienced and allegiant political elite.

2. These incumbents, the middle classes and their leaders, head off severe and prolonged frustration over the operation of the political system by peacefully yielding an increasing degree of participation in political life to the working classes by

the extension of the suffrage,

allowing the development of political leaders representing the working strata,

permitting the participation of these political leaders in political decisions,

and accepting their entry into the government.

3. Entrepreneurs and managers yield enough of the benefits made possible by more efficient technology and organization to reduce the frustrations that had been generated by social and economic conditions during early industrialism.

4. The government undertakes regulation or structural reforms in such a way as to reduce social and economic sources of frustration to people in working-class occupations, without, however, seriously alienating other social strata.

Six of our ten countries have, in varying degrees, satisfied these four general conditions: Britain, Belgium, Holland, Norway, Sweden, and the United States. Of these, the five European countries have followed a roughly similar development, while the United States has traced a different

18. Cf. Val R. Lorwin, "Working Class Politics and Economic Development in Western Europe," *American Historical Review*, v. *63* (January 1958), 338–51.

19. Although the formulation here is not identical with S. M. Lipset's, it has much in common with his. See his discussion of legitimacy and democracy in "Some Social Requisites of Democracy," reprinted in Nelson W. Polsby, Robert A. Dentler and Paul A. Smith, eds., *Politics and Social Life* (Boston, Houghton Mifflin, 1963), pp. 541–68, at pp. 554 ff.

path. In the five North European countries, a constitutional system with an elected parliament, middle-class support, and experienced leaders drawn from the middle classes or the aristocracy was already in existence when the urban and rural workers began to develop political consciousness and demands. In all these countries viable labor or socialist parties that drew increasing support from the working classes were formed in the years from about 1885 to 1905. By the end of this period or a few years later the right to vote was gained by most workers in all these countries.[20] Even the existing middle-class parties began to respond to the demands of the new strata, and they sometimes supported measures designed to eliminate, or at least to mitigate, the worst social and economic evils of unregulated capitalism: social security laws, legal support for trade unions, expansion of public education, and the like. These reforms did not, however, prevent the growth of the labor and socialist parties. During the First World War and after, socialist leaders began entering into coalition governments. Although the labor parties and their leaders participated initially only as junior partners in coalition governments, eventually they secured a large enough vote in elections and seats in parliament so that, as the largest or second largest party in the country, they were highly influential in the conduct of government—sometimes as the major opposition to the government, sometimes as a coalition partner, sometimes as the governing party. In the extreme cases, Norway and Sweden, the labor parties have governed for three decades; in Britain, their victory in 1945 enabled them to carry out most of their immediate program; in other countries, even when the labor parties are not currently participating in the governing coalition it is reasonable for them to expect that they may be able to do so within a few years.

Thus in these five countries the first two conditions mentioned a moment ago have been met, and in the process the working-class parties have acquired the sobering experience of governing their countries. Meanwhile, too, the third and fourth requirements have been met by both economic and social development and by government regulation and reform. In all five countries the labor parties have witnessed the attainment of a good many of their immediate objectives, while their ultimate goals for a socialist society have more and more become hypothetical and rhetorical.

In the United States the four conditions suggested earlier have been met—but according to a different timetable and in quite a different way. As in the five countries just mentioned, so too in the United States, well before rapid industrialization expanded the urban working class from a

20. On the development of political participation in Western Europe, see Stein Rokkan, "The Comparative Study of Political Participation: Notes Toward a Perspective on Current Research," in Austin Ranney, ed., *Essays on the Behavioral Study of Politics* (Urbana, University of Illinois Press, 1962), pp. 47–90.

tiny minority into a substantial proportion of the population, democracy was a going system of government, backed by a "middle class" (consisting predominantly of farmers) and operated by leaders skilled in the arts of managing the country's political institutions.

But the United States met the second condition by providing for participation of the emergent working classes in political life in a way that frequently leads European socialists to the conviction that this country has skipped "an inevitable stage of capitalist development" and that sooner or later (despite impressive and increasing evidence to the contrary) it will have to turn back and rerun its history according to the North European pattern. The essential difference is that unusual conditions in the United States permitted it to arrive at the same result—the integration of the working classes into the political system—without the mediating role of a specifically working-class party. The transition was far from peaceful. "American workers," Val Lorwin has said,[21] "had to fight bloodier industrial battles than the French for the right of unions to exist and to function." Nonetheless, in the United States the working classes have always been, on the whole, strongly allegiant to the political system;[22] and though many workingmen's or socialist parties have been created to appeal to urban workers, few have lasted more than a decade and none has ever attracted the continuing support of more than a small proportion of the working classes.

The reasons for this great difference between the United States and the European democracies with which it has much in common in other respects are complex. One was the fact that workers had already acquired full political rights long before an urban proletariat of any size came into existence; thus workers were never alienated from the political system as a result of being excluded from it. In addition, two national, "grass-roots" parties were already on the scene, ready, willing, and able to recruit workers or supporters. To call them "bourgeois" parties is to miss an important point. If they were "bourgeois"—American middle-class—in their orientations, they were by no means so in organization and recruitment. They were distinctly not elite parties of notables. Typically, they were organized all the way down to the poorest precincts of the large cities; and they had perfected techniques—in essence, rendering primitive social services—for gaining and holding the loyalty of their followers. A working-class party could offer distant collective goals; it could not compete in immediate individual palliatives for concrete grievances. Finally, in a very large country with a decentralized federal system of government and parties, many of the most pressing legislative demands of

21. Val R. Lorwin, "Reflections on the History of the French and American Labor Movements," *Journal of Economic History* (March 1957), p. 37.
22. In this respect the 15 men studied in depth by Robert Lane seem representative. See *Political Ideology*, Ch. 10, "The Alienated and the Allegiant," pp. 161–76.

the trade unions had to be met not by Congress but by the state legislatures. As early as the 1830s (Philip Taft has shown) union leaders had learned the disadvantages of a workingmen's party in such a system and the advantages of working through existing parties.[23]

If the United States diverged from the North European countries in the ways in which the working classes entered into political life, it also diverged somewhat in relying more heavily on meeting the third condition by private action than by government intervention to reduce working-class frustrations. When one takes state laws into account, however, the difference is much smaller. But probably the burden of grievance generated among workers by the operation of American social and economic institutions was less in the United States than among European workers: relatively high wages, rapidly rising standards of living, free public schools, and less rigid status barriers kept down discontent, drained off working-class leaders, fostered middle-class values, and encouraged trade union leaders to concentrate on gains through collective bargaining.

Finally, two additional features of American society no doubt helped the country to evolve its own peculiar solution. The strong emphasis on a common liberal democratic ideology so characteristic of American life impeded the growth of ideologically divergent parties. In combination with this ideology, the ethnic diversity of the industrial working classes helped to fragment their opposition by providing ethnic identifications that weakened working-class cohesion.

Thus both the United States and the five North European countries substantially met the four conditions suggested earlier. By different paths they managed to maintain the earlier allegiance of the middle classes while they gained the allegiance of the working classes.

None of the remaining four countries has, however, fulfilled these four

---

23. Only a state legislature could compel defaulting employers to pay wages earned, impose safety rules on hazardous occupations, and define minimum sanitary standards in work places. The state legislatures prescribed standards for schooling, voting, and minimum ages for working, the employment of women, and limitations of hours of labor in certain occupations . . . Union representatives appealing for legislative concessions understood that frequently only a beginning in the reform of a given problem could be made, and they were usually confident that additional improvements could be subsequently introduced. They also knew that the great majority of legislators were not ideologically committed to or opposed to many pieces of legislation sought by organized labor, and the members of legislative assemblies would respond to the pleas and pressures at slow or rapid rates depending upon the problem and the forces arrayed against labor on a particular issue. Promotion of an independent labor party would have necessitated the severance of relations with many members of the legislatures, who, assured of organized labor's political hostility, would have been more reluctant to support the bills labor annually or biennially presented to the legislatures.
Philip Taft, "Labor History and the Labor Issues of Today," *Proceedings of the American Philosophical Society,* 106, (August 1962), 306. See also the same author's "On the Origins of Business Unionism," *Industrial and Labor Relations Review,* 17 (October 1963), 20–38.

conditions. In Germany and Austria the first condition was not met; and because it was not met the whole problem was far more difficult to solve than in the United States and the five North European countries.

In Germany, as the working classes increased in numbers and in demands on the political system they were confronted not by a parliamentary system supported by a loyal and substantial middle class but by a recently created and almost powerless imperial legislature subservient to the Emperor and his Chancellor. A parliamentary system had to await the collapse of the Empire after the First World War; thus neither the middle classes nor the working classes underwent a sufficient period of tutelage in the politics of parliamentary democracy before the responsibilities of operating a republic were abruptly thrust upon them.

Since the first condition was not met, the second could not be. But in Germany the possibility of peaceful integration of the working classes was even more badly botched by the nature of the suffrage that was granted them. For although universal manhood suffrage was introduced in the Reich in the same year that Disraeli enfranchised a large part of the British urban working classes, Prussia itself maintained the three-class system introduced in 1849, which made a cynical joke out of working-class participation in public life. As Stein Rokkan has observed, "It would be difficult to devise an electoral measure more calculated to alienate the lower classes from the national political system than the one promulgated in Prussia in 1849." [24] Moreover, in granting universal manhood suffrage in elections to the imperial legislature, Bismarck's motive "was patently not to create a channel for the articulation of the interests of the economically dependent strata; the objective was to strengthen the policies of centralization by enlisting the support of the least articulate classes in German society . . . There is a wealth of evidence," Rokkan concludes, "to show that this constellation of institutions was highly dysfunctional: the extension of the suffrage appeared to encourage the participation of the lower classes, but the contrast between the two systems of elections made for widespread resentment and helped to isolate the workers in permanent opposition to the regime." [25]

In better circumstances, perhaps the Weimar Republic could have triumphed over this unpropitious past. But under the series of strains to which it was subjected, the task of solidifying the allegiance not merely of the working classes but (what proved more difficult) of the other strata as well was altogether too great, and it is not surprising that the Weimar Republic collapsed under the accumulated weight of postwar crises. The political and social origins of the First Austrian Republic were only slightly less foreboding, and its life almost equally short.

Today the working classes of Germany and Austria appear to be about

24. "The Comparative Study of Political Participation," p. 76.
25. Ibid., pp. 73, 76.

as fully integrated into, and as allegiant to, their democratic institutions as the other strata. In Germany, as Otto Kirchheimer indicates, class antagonism no longer serves as much of a political stimulus; and what was for generations considered the leading socialist party of Europe is now barely distinguishable in goals and strategies from the Christian Democratic Union. In Austria, coalition government and *Proporz* have provided the old enemies, the two *Lager*, with a very great stake in maintaining the system. The commitment to democracy may not be strong in either country; but allegiance is no weaker among the working class, evidence suggests, than among other major strata. It is not so much that the battle for allegiance has been won as that it has not been lost. The evidence of Almond and Verba seems to indicate that in Germany—and the same may be true in Austria—the population is neither alienated from nor allegiant to democratic institutions but rather indifferent or detached.[26]

Like Germany and Austria, the political development of France and Italy did not fulfill the four conditions suggested earlier. In both countries, the last two conditions were, at least until recently, met badly. In addition, Italy scarcely even fulfilled the first condition during the 60-year period of parliamentary government before fascism, for it failed to build up a large and allegiant middle class. Meanwhile, an extraordinary record, probably unparalleled in Western Europe, of violence and repression by the state against socialists, anarchists, trade unionists, and other workingmen's organizations must have strengthened the suspicion and hostility of the working classes toward parliamentary institutions. What is more, Italy arrived at the second condition rather late by maintaining a highly restricted suffrage until universal manhood suffrage was introduced in 1912: the result was an abrupt threefold swelling of the electorate. The First World War following upon the elections of 1913 and the rapid collapse of parliamentary government after the war meant that in Italy, as in Germany and Austria, the struggle for allegiance really began only two decades ago. So far, as Samuel Barnes' essay makes clear, the outcome remains in doubt.

Let me now draw this discussion together with three conclusions:

First, in seven of our nine European countries the politics of the working strata has converged toward a situation that has much in common with the traditional position of the American worker. An American is likely to consider desirable any change that brings European systems into conformity with his own. But the problem is not quite so simple.

For, in the second place, one cannot simply ignore the plain fact that, up to now, in Italy and France history has taken a different path. It is not yet clear, particularly in Italy, how the largest group of working-class voters, those who have voted for the Communists, are to be integrated peacefully into a viable political system.

26. *The Civic Culture*, pp. 428 ff.

Third, when the Left parties acquire a durable majority of votes, the problem of allegiance shifts from the working classes to the white-collar strata: lower middle classes, professional groups, businessmen. The problem would arise in Italy in its most extreme form if there were ever a coalition government in which the Communists participated. And for how long can a nation's second largest party, with the largest following of manual workers, be excluded from participating in the government? The problem is posed in much more moderate form in countries where the Left parties have become the largest parties and normally in control of the government: most notably Sweden, Norway, and the United States, where the parties representing the conservative middle classes have not been able to control the national government for the better part of the last three decades. To what extent will conservatives (whether in the Scandinavian or the radically different American sense) become politically alienated by their continuing exclusion from governing their countries? Certainly the American Right appears to be fully as hostile to the dominant tendencies in current American politics as the working classes of the United States ever were. And the strike of the Belgian doctors in 1964 shows to what length a professional group may go in opposing government policy.

Social and Economic Sources of Political Cleavage

An alternative though not necessarily contradictory way of describing and explaining these historical changes in the patterns of opposition in our ten countries is to attribute the changes in politics to long-run changes in social and economic factors, using these terms very broadly to include not only class, social status, and occupation but also such social factors as religion, ethnic group, and language. The political affiliations, loyalties, and attitudes of an individual, it might be said, are heavily dependent on his durable social and economic roles, functions, and affiliations: political cleavages are, according to this hypothesis, the expression of social and economic differences.[27] If the political behavior of various strata has become more alike in recent years, then this is because these strata have also become less distinct in their social and economic characteristics.

There is, surely, a great deal of truth in this explanation. The core of truth is to be found in the twin assumptions that social and economic differences usually are associated with differences in rewards and deprivations, in relative advantages and disadvantages; and that these differences in rewards and deprivations stimulate cohesion among those who are socially similar and conflict with those who are different. The difficulty with the explanation and the axioms on which it is founded is not so much

27. A special problem implicit or explicit in this kind of explanation, the relation of social and economic cleavages to "polarization," is dealt with below, at pp. 380–86.

that they are false as that they oversimplify a highly complex matter and thereby leave a great segment of political behavior unaccounted for.

To begin with, in the countries examined in this volume, the political affiliations, loyalties, and attitudes—in short, the political behavior—of individuals and groups cannot be traced to any single social or economic characteristic. Quite the contrary, political behavior is evidently influenced by a great variety of different social and economic characteristics.

The most important of these are differences with respect to economic position (in a broad sense), social position, religion, language or ethnic group, and region. Differences in economic position, ordinarily allied to differences in social position, are sources of conflict in all our countries. Religion is usually an important source of differences in political behavior in countries with sizable Catholic populations, because religious commitments generate differences in political attitudes between Catholics and Protestants or between Catholics and anticlericals, as in France, Italy, and Belgium. Differences in language or ethnic identification have been critically important in Belgium and the United States. And regional differences—associated often with some of the others—have been significant in the United States, Norway, Belgium, and, to some extent, Italy.

Second, some social differences are associated with differences in relative advantage, and hence with political behavior, in some countries but not in others. Differences in language are one of the commonest sources of cleavage in all parts of the world. In Belgium, as Lorwin points out, the bitterness between Walloons and Flemings arises not only from the language difference but also from the fact that language has been associated with a pattern of inequalities in occupations, education, social class, prestige, and opportunities to rise in Belgian national life. In Switzerland, on the other hand, although there are often abrasive relations at the cantonal level, conflict between German- and French-speaking Swiss has been largely avoided in national politics, evidently because few persons in either language group feel that they have been unfairly treated in Swiss national life as a result of their language.

Third, the ways in which different socioeconomic factors are related to one another do not produce a single pattern of cleavage in the different countries, but a great profusion of patterns. In a rough way it is possible to distinguish three patterns:

a. *Countries highly homogeneous except for social standing and economic position (which are highly correlated).* Among our countries these are Protestant nations where religious differences have ceased to be salient, and where ethnic, language, and regional differences have left only slight traces. Britain and Sweden fall most clearly into this class; Norway is a somewhat marginal member because of the declining but not insignificant influence of region, religion, and loyalty to the rural language. Because these differences are at a minimum, the most salient differences are those in occupations, incomes, and social standing—socioeconomic status. As a consequence, in countries like Britain and Sweden the political parties reflect more clearly than in other countries the differences in the class composition of their followings; the labor-socialist party draws the bulk of its strength from blue-collar workers, while the middle-class parties (or party) receive considerably more votes in the middle or upper strata than does the labor-socialist party. In this sense there is a higher degree of "status polarization" in politics than in other countries. But, as we shall see, this polarization is probably statistical rather than psychological.

b. *Countries in which several kinds of socioeconomic differences coincide and thus reinforce one another.* One of the surprising results of our inquiry is that this pattern does not exist in anything approaching a pure form in any of our ten countries. This may well be because a pattern of this kind would lead to such severe conflicts that a parliamentary system would founder. In each one of our countries where several different kinds of socioeconomic differences stimulate political conflicts, the planes of cleavage in one conflict do not coincide exactly with those in other conflicts—fortunately for the survival of the system. However, some countries approach this pattern more closely than others.

Belgium falls most clearly—even if imperfectly—into this category, for there, as we have seen, two of the three main planes of socioeconomic cleavage do coincide to some extent. The explosive nature of the question of the Negro in the United States also stems in considerable part from the fact that the most pronounced line of cleavage, that between North and South, goes hand in hand with differences in ideologies, economic issues, social systems, and regions.

c. *Countries in which several kinds of socioeconomic differences crosscut one another.* It is in this case that the effects of "overlapping memberships," "conflicting identifications," and "cross-pressures" so much discussed in the literature of American political science may occur.[28] Thus a Dutch Catholic worker may have a strong sense of his identity both as a Catholic and as a member of the working class. Potentially, then, he is in conflict with non-Catholics on religious matters and with nonworkers on economic issues. Both his class and his religion are durable features of his life. As a worker living in a working-class ambience he finds common ground with other workers, be they Catholic or non-Catholic; as a Catholic living among Catholics he feels solidarity with other Catholics,

28. For a summary and critique as of 1958 see Robert E. Lane, *Political Life* (Glencoe, Free Press, 1959), pp. 187–203. The overlapping membership model particularly as it applies to the United States is examined by William C. Mitchell in "Interest Group Theory and 'Overlapping Membership,'" a paper prepared for the 59th Annual Meeting of the American Political Science Association, New York City, September 1963.

whether bourgeois or workers. He therefore has an incentive, particularly
if his identification with each group is strong, to seek (or to accept at the
behest of his leaders) ways of reducing conflict within each group. His
desire for group solidarity may stem from psychological needs, from a
fear of the collective consequences of internal divisions, from a strategy of
influence in politics and economic life, or from all of these and other
reasons. Whatever the reasons, though responses other than compromise
are possible, he is likely to be receptive to compromises on questions involving religion or economic matters, for conflict threatens to divide a
group whose solidarity he wants to maintain.

Although socioeconomic differences help to account for patterns of
opposition, they leave a good deal unexplained. Even in a country with
such sharp social and economic differences as Italy, political conflict is by
no means purely a matter of conflict among different social and economic
groups. Industrial workers evidently divide their votes among Communists, Socialists, and Christian Democrats. Even in a homogeneous
country like Britain, where socioeconomic status has greater influence
because of the weakness of other kinds of social distinctions, a third of the
workers vote Conservative. Or again, compare the fate of the labor parties
in Britain and Sweden. In Britain, the most urbanized and industrialized of
our countries, the Labor Party has spent most of its history in opposition;
while the middle classes are rather solidly united in a Conservative Party
which, thanks to the support of its working-class voters, managed until the
election of 1964 to remain in office for all except 6 years out of the
previous 30. In Sweden, less urban and industrial than Britain, the Socialist
Party not only wins the support of two-thirds or more of the working
class, as the Labor Party does in Britain, but also gains a quarter of its
votes from nonworking-class groups.[29] Thanks to middle-class support it
has been in office for 30 years, and it is the bourgeois parties that have
formed the opposition.

Why do socioeconomic factors account for only a part of the variation
in patterns of opposition? Principally, it seems, because the causal chain
from one's socioeconomic position to one's overt political action is long
and tenuous; and each link in the chain may be weak enough to be broken
by the pull of other forces. A pure social determinist might postulate a
causal sequence in which one's overt political acts are completely determined by one's socioeconomic position.

$$\left\{\begin{array}{l}\text{Objective}\\\text{s-e position}\end{array}\right\} \xrightarrow{a} \left\{\begin{array}{l}\text{Subjective}\\\text{identifications}\end{array}\right\} \xrightarrow{b} \left\{\begin{array}{l}\text{Political}\\\text{opinions}\end{array}\right\} \xrightarrow{c} \left\{\begin{array}{l}\text{Overt political}\\\text{acts}\end{array}\right\}$$

But we know that each of these links can be so weak that it cannot bear
the weight of the others. Whenever objective differences in socioeconomic

29. Above, p. 127, Table 4.1.

positions are blurred and ambiguous, as they are, for example, among clerical workers, then there may be only a weak correlation between socioeconomic position and subjective identification; hence while a majority of white-collar workers might identify themselves as middle class, a sizable minority might see themselves as working class. Moreover, for a variety of reasons subjective identifications vary in strength; and if one's identification with one's occupational group is weak, they may not have much to do with one's political opinion—as was probably the case with the wirer in a California radio factory who said: "Well, I work for a living so I guess I'm in the working class." [30] Finally, political opinions may be weakly related to overt political acts, particularly among people who are uneducated, who are unable to conceptualize abstract political ideas, or who are not interested in politics.

The link at *c*, between political opinions and overt political acts, is usually stronger among educated persons, intellectuals, and political activists than among the general population; conversely, however, among these very groups, the links at *a* and *b* connecting objective position, identifications, and political opinions are somewhat weaker than among the general population. Thus with the general population the breakdown in the hypothetical causal chain of the social determinist is likely to occur closer to the terminal end, at *c* or *b*; but among the political elites, the break is more likely near the beginning, at *a*.

The determinist's chain of causation is thus rather easily broken by the intrusion of factors that he assumes are irrelevant or extraneous. The British middle classes may not agree in their ideas more than the Swedish middle classes; but in Sweden PR encourages the middle classes to distribute their votes among several parties, whereas in Britain the single-member district and plurality elections make it simple for them to concentrate their votes on the Conservative Party. Other factors also have an opportunity to express themselves, as we shall see in a moment.

Specific Patterns of Attitudes and Opinions

I have already referred to attitudes and opinions in order to explain patterns of opposition. Widely shared cultural premises consist of attitudes, feelings, and evaluations held, presumably, by a substantial proportion of leaders and the general population. Subcultures are relatively distinctive sets of attitudes, opinions, and values that persist for relatively long periods of time in the life of a country and give individuals in a particular subculture a sense of identity that distinguishes them from individuals in other subcultures.

In this section, however, I am not concerned with the widely shared

30. V. O. Key, *Public Opinion and American Democracy*, (New York, Knopf, 1961), p. 141, n. 5.

attitudes that go into a general political culture nor with the *content* of political attitudes found in specific subcultures or other distinctive groups; I am concerned only with the *patterns* of cleavage and consensus formed by the ways in which political attitudes are distributed over the population of a country. What follows is an effort to draw together a tentative theory to explain how four factors may increase or decrease the incentives of political leaders to pursue conflicting goals and strategies (or, conversely, conciliatory goals and strategies).

These four factors are:

The *distribution* of opinions on political questions—specifically whether the distribution is single-peaked or bimodal.[31]

The *coincidence* of opinions among different individuals, that is, the extent to which individuals who agree on one question agree on others.

The *salience* or *intensity* of opinions on different questions.

The institutional means for aggregating opinions, and specifically the *party system.*

Let us begin with the last factor, for a belief widely expressed in the literature of political science is that a two-party system has a moderating influence on the selection of goals.[32] In a two-party system, it is often said, the government party and the opposition tend to converge toward common ground because both parties compete for the great mass of voters whose opinions on political questions differ only very little: the center. Yet this hypothesis assumes that there *is* a great mass of voters responsive to "centrist" ideas and proposals. But this might not be the case. If not, our hypothesis is that a two-party system would not necessarily lead to conciliation and compromise but might actually intensify political conflict. Suppose that opinion on some critical political question[33] were distributed along a continuum from the extreme left to the extreme right, as

31. Obviously there are many other distributions; but to add others not only increases the complexity of exposition but takes theory well beyond the limits of the data at hand.

32. Assertions about the moderating effects of a two-party system are surely among the oldest and most widespread in the modern study of political parties, and a number of writers on parties have provided explanations derived implicitly from the assumptions and argument in these paragraphs. See in particular A. Lawrence Lowell, *The Government of England* (2 vols. New York, Macmillan, 1908) and *Public Opinion and Popular Government* (New York, Longmans, Green, 1913); and E. E. Schattschneider's discussion in *Political Parties* (New York, Farrar and Rinehart, 1942) on "the moderating effect of the attempt to create a majority" in a two-party system (pp. 85 ff.). Lowell recognized the possibility that the distribution of opinion necessary for a two-party system to have a moderating effect might not exist: in this case, however, it was not a "true public opinion" and it would be impossible to conduct the government "by a true public opinion or by consent" (*Public Opinion and Popular Government*, p. 11).

33. I use the word "question" deliberately in this discussion to include issues, candidates, ideology, or any other matter on which political opinions exist.

in Figure 12.1.[34] Suppose, further, that the distribution were unimodal and similar to the familiar bell-shaped pattern (Figure 12.1); that political leaders were more or less familiar with the distribution of opinion; and that they were anxious to win elections by adopting a position on this

I. Moderation

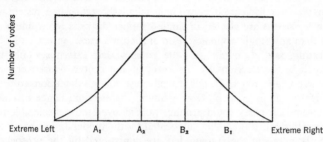

Figure 12.1. Effects of Distribution of Opinion on Two Parties

issue that would gain them maximum popular support. Suppose, now, that the ideologues of Party A were to advocate an extreme left-wing policy represented by the position A_1. The leaders of Party A would see that this extreme position would very likely cost them nearly all of the votes of people whose opinions were to the right of A_1, provided only that Party B were astute enough to take a position slightly to the right of A_1; hence if Party A were to take a position A_1, it might retain its extreme left wing but would probably lose votes catastrophically to Party B. In precisely the same way, if the ideologues of Party B were to advocate B_1, the party leaders would see how heavy a price they might ultimately pay in order to satisfy their extremists. Thus both parties would have strong incentives driving them toward positions close to the middle that have the support of the preponderant majority of citizens, say A_2 and B_2. If the parties were to adopt A_2 and B_2, most voters would feel that the policy adopted by the government was an acceptable one no matter which party were to win the election. And compromises between the two parties would not be par-

34. Spatial models, like those used in the exposition that follows, derive indirectly from Harold Hotelling, "Stability in Competition," *Economic Journal*, *39* (1929), 41–57, but became an explicit basis for a theory of party competition in Anthony Downs, *An Economic Theory of Democracy* (New York, Harper, 1957). They were also employed in my *A Preface to Democratic Theory* (Chicago, University of Chicago Press, 1956), pp. 93 ff., which set out some of the argument that follows. The unrealistic character of some of the assumptions made in using spatial models has been severely criticized by Donald E. Stokes in "Spatial Models of Party Competition," *American Political Science Review*, *57* (June 1963), 368–77. Stokes' criticisms are, I think, valid.

ticularly difficult, since positions A_2 and B_2 are not, after all, very far apart.

The effect of party competition in this situation would be to reinforce moderate or central opinion. By responding to the moderates and proposing moderate policies, the parties would help to strengthen moderate opinions and moderate leaders, which in turn would reinforce the tendencies of the parties to adopt moderate positions.[35] The moderating effects of party competition are likely to be particularly strong in a system under which legislators are elected in single-member districts by winning more votes than any single opponent. For in such a system, an extremist party advocating, say, A_1 might gain the votes of left extremists only to be swamped in the elections by the votes of the center. Moreover, an extreme left-wing party at A_1 might well cause enough defections to prevent a moderate left party at A_2 from winning the election; hence to vote for the extreme left party could produce policies even more intolerable to the left extremists than the policy advocated by the moderate left party. Consequently voters at the extreme left are confronted by the prospect that they will not only throw away their votes by supporting a party that advocates their views but they may well help to bring about a victory of a party on the right. Similar reasoning applies, of course, to the right.[36]

Even under a system of proportional representation with, let us say, four parties, dominant coalitions would tend to move toward moderation. For the moderate center parties would stand the best chance of winning the most votes; by winning the most votes they would acquire the most seats; and thus they would have the greatest influence in a governing coalition. Indeed the two moderate parties might well combine to form a governing coalition. But even a moderate party that considered the prospect of forming a coalition with the party on its extreme flank would hardly find it worthwhile to bargain away its own policies for those of its lesser partner simply to gain the support of the smaller party; for to do so would cause the moderate party to lose the bulk of its supporters to its moderate rival. Consequently the moderate parties would bargain from positions of strength, the extreme parties from positions of weakness.

The preceding analysis is probably correct, at least roughly. Yet it rests entirely on the assumption that opinions do in fact have a single mode. And there is no reason at all to rule out the possibility of radically different

35. In this discussion "moderate" means no more than being near the center of some distribution of opinions. In this sense, "moderation" has no intrinsic or necessary virtues and implies no psychological qualities in the "moderate" person or the supporters of a "moderate" party.

36. All these arguments were used, in less formal language, by moderate opponents of Senator Goldwater in their unsuccessful attempt to block his nomination by the Republican Party in 1964. The election demonstrated, I think, that their arguments were correct.

distributions of opinions. For example, some great question might divide the opinions of citizens into two camps as in Figure 12.2. Now a center scarcely exists; and the ideologues of moderation labor under the same handicaps as the ideologues of extremism under the single-peaked dis-

II. Extremism

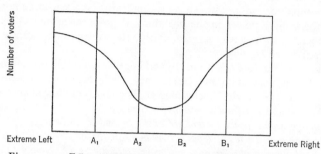

Figure 12.2. Effects of Distribution of Opinion on Two Parties

tribution. To the contention of moderates in Party A that they should hold to position A_2, the left will argue that the great bulk of Party A's support lies toward the extreme; and if Party A takes a moderate position it might well see its support sapped by another party of the left. And so, too, on the right. Once again, the single-member district system with plurality elections reinforces the cleavage in opinion. If, for example, a moderate left party were to adhere to its traditional position of centrist moderation, it would run the risk that a new party would arise and advocate a position to the left of A_2. Such a party would be likely to swamp the old moderate left party (as Labor in Britain did with the Liberals.) [37] Thus when opinion is bimodal a two-party system based on single-member districts and plurality elections is likely to intensify rather than to mitigate conflict either by inducing the existing parties to shift to the extremes or by generating a new extreme party (and thus ceasing, at least temporarily, to be a two-party system). For a center party will, in time, be reduced to a corporal's guard by the effects of the election system. Indeed, it is altogether likely that with a bimodal distribution of political opinions a two-party system may intensify conflict even more than a multiparty system and proportional representation might do.

To be sure, a multiparty system cannot create moderation and conciliation where they do not exist. With proportional representation, the for-

37. Cf., for example, John Bonham, *The Middle Class Vote* (London, Faber and Faber, 1954), pp. 149 ff., and Ivor Jennings, *Party Politics, The Growth of Parties* (Cambridge, Cambridge University Press, 1961), pp. 250 ff.

mation of extreme parties would be inevitable; and by making it difficult for the center parties to form a viable coalition the growth of support for extreme parties would increase the chances for coalitions influenced by the extremes. This was the problem of Weimar Germany, and it is to some degree the situation in Italy. Yet where polarization is less than complete, proportional representation and multiple parties may help a center to survive as long as any significant number of left-center, center, and right-center opinions persist. Thus the center parties may manage to retain some bargaining power in the coalitions of government and opposition and thereby to weaken, at least partly, the strength of incentives to antagonism and conflict.

One must therefore qualify the hypothesis that two-party systems necessarily foster moderation and compromise while multiparty systems encourage antagonism and severe conflict. We conclude instead that *when voters' opinions are (and are thought to be) unimodal, both a two-party system and a multiparty system are likely to lead to moderation and compromise among the leading parties. When, on the other hand, opinion is strongly polarized in a bimodal pattern, two parties, each striving to retain the support of the extremists on its flank, will only exacerbate a conflict; and in multiparty systems the center parties will decline in votes and influence.*

So far in this discussion I have implicitly assumed that it is possible to characterize opinions on all important questions or conflicts by means of a single, summary distribution. Thus if Smith is to the "left" and Green to the "right" of Jones on one question, Smith will be to the left and Green to the right of Jones on other questions. But of course this is not necessarily the case.[38] The extent to which the opinions of individuals or groups coincide from one question to another may vary; and these variations are likely to encourage different patterns of opposition.

Thus the relative strength of incentives for conciliation and antagonism does not depend only on whether opinions are unimodal or bimodal, but also on the extent to which opinions coincide from one political question to another, that is, on the extent to which individuals or groups who agree (or are close to one another) on one question agree on other questions.

If there is a high degree of coincidence, so that individuals who agree on one political matter agree on others, then the effect is evidently quite straightforward: *high coincidence reinforces the effects of unimodal or bimodal distributions of opinion.*

If people who are moderate on one question are moderate on others, and if most people are moderate on every question, then the incentives of party leaders to engage in a search for moderate policies are, of course, very much increased. If, on the contrary, people who are at opposite

38. Cf. Stokes, *Spatial Models of Party Competition*, p. 370.

extremes on one question are likely to be at opposite extremes on all questions, and if most people are extremists, then moderate, conciliatory parties or coalitions will be even more likely to yield to intransigent political groups implacably at odds with one another.

If the effects of high coincidence seem clear, the effects of low coincidence are complex. To begin with, as compared with high coincidence, low coincidence of opinions increases the number of different clusters of persons with divergent opinions. Each of these "opinion-clusters" is potentially a separate political following—potentially, therefore, the basis of a separate political movement, whether pressure group, faction, or party. The point may be clarified by using Belgium as an example.

Belgians, as Lorwin has shown, have been at odds over three sets of questions. If we consider them as pro–con questions for ease of exposition, then in Belgium an individual might be characterized as:

either pro-labor or pro-property;
either anticlerical or pro-Catholic; and
either pro-Walloon or pro-Flemish.

Because three dichotomous attributes can be combined in eight ways, in principle every Belgian might be located within one of eight possible combinations; for example, individual *A, B, C, D*, etc. might be:

A: pro-labor/anticlerical/Walloon
B: pro-labor/Catholic/Walloon
C: pro-property/anticlerical/Walloon
D: pro-labor/Catholic/Flemish
etc.

At one extreme, coincidence among the opinions of Belgians might be maximally high. Individuals who agreed on one question would agree on the others; those who disagreed on one would disagree on the others. Thus by knowing how a Belgian stood on one of these questions one could predict perfectly how he would stand on the other two. Under the particular conditions of our example, this would mean that every individual would fall into one of two opinion-clusters. (Technically, one cluster might be empty, but we ignore that possibility.) For example, all Walloons might be pro-labor and anticlerical; and all Flemings Catholic and pro-property. In this case, the society, and presumably political life, would be polarized.[39] At the other extreme, coincidence among opinions might be at a minimum, so that if two persons agreed on one issue (if, for example, they were both Walloons) nothing could be predicted as to their opinions on the other issues. Hence all eight opinion-clusters might be

---

39. This result follows from the particular example. Conditions could be specified under which maximally high coincidence would mean complete unanimity.

represented in the population. Each would be a potential foundation for a separate political movement antagonistic to all the others.[40]

Yet low coincidence does not necessarily produce this kind of fragmented antagonism among opinion-clusters. In some circumstances, as we shall see, low coincidence may strengthen incentives for conciliation. The extent to which incentives for conciliation (or antagonism) are strengthened (reduced) appears to depend on two additional factors: the salience of a political question or intensity of opinions, and the available institutional means for aggregating opinions.

Suppose that in Belgium there were not only a low coincidence of opinions but that all three questions evoked extremely intense views on the part of everyone. In this case each opinion-cluster would tend to become a separate political movement, and it would be extremely troublesome for leaders to build political coalitions combining two clusters. For example, Catholics would split down the middle over labor and property and Walloon Catholics would split with Flemish Catholics. There would be four distinct Catholic parties, or four distinct factions within one Catholic party. If everyone held to all three of his opinions strongly, compromise would be impossible. Each question would involve a straight fight between a rigid majority and a rigid minority. And a majority that held together on one question would collapse completely on the next.[41]

It is quite possible, however, that one of the three questions in Belgium might be more salient than the others. In the simplest case, the same question would be salient to everyone, and therefore the other two would be less important to everyone. Suppose, for example, that everyone in Belgium believed that language was the overarching problem. In this case, the leaders of the Walloon community might profitably search for support among both socialists and pro-property Walloons, among both anticlerical and Catholic Walloons; and so, too, with the Flemish leaders. Hence while conflict over language would doubtless grow more intense, the possibilities of conciliation on the other questions would increase, since everyone would have some incentive to reduce conflict on these questions.

But there is still another possibility: although everyone might believe that one of the three issues was the most important, different individuals might rank the importance of the issues in different ways. To one citizen,

40. This is equivalent to "the superposition of dualisms" of Maurice Duverger, *Les Partis Politiques* (Paris, Colin, 1954), pp. 260–65.

41. Discussions of the effects of cross-cutting cleavages in mitigating conflict usually ignore this possibility. The usual assumption, at least in recent American political science, seems to be that cross-cutting cleavages inevitably have a unifying rather than a disintegrating effect. But the analysis here indicates that unifying effects cannot occur if all the cleavages are felt with equal intensity. Conciliation is encouraged by cross-cutting cleavages *only* if some cleavages are less significant than others (as is shown in the paragraphs that follow).

the language question would be dominant; to another, Catholicism; to a third, socialism. When opinions are held in this fashion, the possibility of building coalitions of different opinion-clusters is evidently considerably increased. For example, it would now be easier to unite strongly pro-labor Walloons to whom anticlericalism is of secondary importance with fervent Catholic-Flemish workers who might otherwise support the Christian Social Party. Thus there would be a tendency for each opinion-cluster to yield somewhat on secondary issues in order to gain support on primary questions. Hence heterogeneous coalitions or parties might develop; and party leaders would exert great efforts in trying to conciliate their diverse followings.

The extent to which a nation with strong cleavages may be held together in part by its cleavages is perhaps best illustrated by the Netherlands. Abstractly considered, the Netherlands would surely be counted a prime candidate for political disintegration, since the country must bear not only some class antagonism but an even more profound cleavage over religion. Yet the very way in which the one conflict is superimposed on the other probably helps to reduce the potential for conflict. A Catholic party, as Hans Daalder shows, unties both working- and middle-class Catholics. The Protestant parties also cross class lines for their support. Although the Socialist and Liberal parties have had only modest success in gaining support among Catholics and orthodox Protestants, they do nonetheless persist in striving for votes among these religious groups and the liberal Protestants; consequently, less because of their actual support than because of the support they hope to acquire, Socialists and Liberals are a moderating influence on religious cleavages. Taken together, then, the efforts of the parties help to knit the community together.

As the Dutch example suggests, the effects of low coincidence cannot be explained simply by the salience of the questions among the various opinion-clusters, but also by the way in which political institutions encourage people in the different opinion-clusters to unite in coalitions. The most important of these institutions is, no doubt, the political party. If we assume that the number of important parties is not solely a function of the various patterns of opinion we have been describing but also of election systems, historical events, tradition, and the weight of institutions, then the effects of low coincidence of opinions (and hence the existence of a number of different opinion-clusters) will depend *in part* on the number of parties.

The matter, it must be admitted, is somewhat unclear. However, there is some reason for thinking that where political opinions do not coincide and are unequally salient, a two-party system strengthens incentives for conciliation and reduces incentives for conflict. The reasoning is often applied to the United States, which seems to meet the requirements for our hypothesis: low coincidence, unequal salience, and two major parties. Given low coincidence, the two parties are bound to be heterogeneous—as indeed they are in the United States. There, as we have seen, the co-incidence of opinions is too low to permit homogeneous parties. But these very circumstances create strong incentives for conciliation and compromise. For party leaders have nothing to gain from yielding entirely to one opinion-cluster: They cannot possibly gain majorities in Congress or win presidential elections by that strategy. Hence they must devote unremitting effort to building coalitions of different opinion-clusters not only in order to win elections but also to pass legislation. A major preoccupation of the American politician is therefore to persuade any given opinion-cluster to give way on its secondary demands in order to gain—if only temporarily—the support of other opinion-clusters for its primary demands. Given the unequal salience of opinions on different questions among different opinion-clusters, politicians stand a fair chance of succeeding in their efforts at conciliation.

How different are the effects of a multiparty system? Given the same conditions—low coincidence and unequal salience—the same process could, presumably, lead to similar results. Moreover, if a government is to receive the support of a majority in parliament, presumably the process must and will take place. Yet it does seem rather likely that the incentives for conciliation as compared with conflict are stronger if there are only two parties. For one thing, with two parties the process of conciliation is necessary not only in the legislature (as in a multiparty system), but also in nominations and elections. For another, in a two-party system a good deal of the process of negotiation takes place among politicians of the same party rather than among politicians of different parties; in this case the incentive to arrive at a viable compromise is strengthened, not weakened, by party loyalties.[42]

This somewhat abstract discussion of the effects of different factors on incentives for conciliation or conflict is summarized in Table 12.2.

Polarization

It is a common assumption, one by no means confined to Marxists, that urbanization, industrialization, the growth of national economies, and other features associated with social and economic modernization tend to result in a high degree of political polarization. A contradictory and more recent hypothesis is that, beyond some range, in Western societies modernization leads to a decrease in political polarization.

---

42. This is a specific application of a familiar proposition. Drawing on George Simmel, Lewis Coser has formulated a number of propositions about conflict that are relevant to the discussion in this section. Thus "Conflict with another group leads to the mobilization of the energies of group members and hence to increased cohesion of the group." *The Functions of Conflict* (Glencoe, Free Press, 1956), p. 95.

Table 12.2 Some Factors That Affect Incentives for Conciliating or Pressing Conflicting Opinions

Factors that strengthen incentives for conciliating conflicting opinions	Factors that strengthen incentives for pressing conflicting opinions
1. All uni-modal distributions of opinions.	1. All bimodal distributions.
2. High coincidence of uni-modal distributions.	2. High coincidence of bimodal distributions.
3. Low coincidence, if of unequal salience.	3. Low coincidence, if of equal salience.
4. Two-party system: a. If opinions are uni-modal. b. If opinions have low coincidence but unequal salience.	4. Multiparty system: a. If opinions are uni-modal. b. If opinions have coincidence but unequal salience.
5. Multiparty system, if opinions are distributed bimodally with high coincidence.	5. Two-party system, if opinions are distributed bimodally with high coincidence.

To test either hypothesis is, unfortunately, difficult. To begin with, the term "polarization" is used in various ways. Typically, it is intended to refer to the extent to which a population is divided politically into two antagonistic camps distinguished by differences in socioeconomic characteristics.

Unfortunately, the concept is bristling with difficulties, for it combines at least three different notions that need to be distinguished.

1. It contains the idea of a dimension of bipolarity, dualism, a U-shaped distribution, the extent to which a population is divided into two categories. A measure of dualism might be the proportion of a population contained in the two largest categories.

2. It also contains the idea of a dimension of distance between the two largest categories. The greater the distance the more polarized the society.

3. Finally, it contains the idea of different characteristics with respect to which bipolarity or dualism might exist. The most important of these are:

a. Social and economic characteristics. Socioeconomic dualism, then, would be a measure of the extent to which a population is divided into two categories by class, status, language, religion, income, wealth, etc. A country where everyone considered himself a member either of the working class or the middle class would be completely dualistic with respect to these class categories.

b. Psychological, emotional, or affective characteristics. Psychological or affective dualism would require a measure of the extent to which a population is divided into two antagonistic or hostile groups.

c. Political characteristics. Political dualism would be measured by the extent to which a population is divided into groups distinguished by differences in political behavior—ideology, political goals and demands, party memberships or identifications, and voting. In the simplest case, a country

where everyone voted either for Party *A* or Party *B* would be (by definition) completely dualistic with respect to voting.

Since the three main dimensions are logically independent, and the
three types of characteristics are also logically independent of one
another, managing the concept of polarization is inordinately difficult.[43]
A moment's reflection will reveal the vast variety of different patterns
that might be regarded as examples of polarization. Indeed, the concept is
so complex that it has seemed advisable to avoid the term "polarization"
wherever possible in the discussion that follows and to refer instead to
some specific patterns. Among a very much larger number of theoretical
possibilities, it is useful to imagine four different general situations in
which a high degree of political dualism might exist.

   1. *Political dualism unrelated to social or affective dualism.* To offer a
hypothetical example, this would exist in the United States if everyone
identified strongly with either the Democratic or Republican parties, or if
everyone adhered either to a liberal or a conservative ideology, or to an
isolationist or interventionist foreign policy; if, however, there were little
antagonism between the two groups; and if there were little or no
correlation between party loyalties or ideology and occupation, income,
religion, etc.

   2. *Political dualism closely related to a social dualism, but not to affective dualism.* This would exist in Britain if all manual workers were
socialists and people in nonmanual occupations were conservative; and if
there were little antagonism between the two groups.

   3. *Political duality closely related to affective duality but not to any
social dualities.* This would exist in France if everyone were strongly pro-
or anti-De Gaulle; if there were very great antagonism between Gaullists

43. See, for example, *The American Voter*, where the concept of polarization is
discussed at some length and used fruitfully in exploring American survey data without, however, escaping some ambiguity (pp. 338 ff.). The authors begin by defining
polarization in psychological terms, i.e., in terms of antagonism: "The condition of
active discord between social strata [is] *status polarization*" (p. 338, their italics).
"Status polarization, then, refers to the degree to which upper and lower status groups
in a society have taken up mutually antagonistic value positions" (p. 339). They then
go on to suggest that status polarization (or, in terms of the distinction above, psychological dualism) is a function of a certain kind of social dualism, namely with respect
to social class: "We can say in a rough way that *variation in the status polarization
of a society reflects variation in the intensity and extent of class identification among
its members.* When polarization is high most of the citizenry must have perceived a
conflict of interests between strata and have taken on class identifications with fair
intensity. When polarization is low, either few people are identifying or extant
identifications are weak, or both" (p. 339, their italics). The measures they use do not,
however, bear directly on the question of antagonism; for they measure "status
polarization" by using indices of occupation in some cases (Figure 13–2, p. 347, and
Figure 13–6, p. 358), and "subjective status" or class identification in others (Figures
13–3, p. 352; 13–4, p. 354; 13–7, p. 364; 13–8, p. 367). Thus while they define "status
polarization" in psychological terms, they do not in fact measure antagonism. A.
Campbell, P. Converse, W. Miller, and D. Stokes, *The American Voter* (New York,
Wiley, 1960).

and anti-Gaullists; and if these differences were not correlated with social status, income, occupation, region, etc.

4. *Political dualism closely related to both social and psychological dualisms.* This is full-scale political polarization. It would exist in France if, in the example just given, the last condition did not hold and instead the middle classes and farmers were uniformly Gaullist while the working classes were uniformly anti-Gaullist.

It is obvious that each of these patterns of political dualism is significantly different from the others. What has been called "status polarization" sometimes refers to the second, sometimes to the last. Political polarization might refer to the third or fourth, but it might also refer to the first. Yet the consequences for oppositions, as well as for government, would surely be very different in each case.[44] Keeping these various possibilities in mind, what conclusions can we draw from the experiences of the countries examined in this volume? Although the data are hardly sufficient for solidly based generalizations, some tentative conclusions are suggested by the evidence at hand.

1. Objective status differences seem to be on the decline throughout Western Europe. Rising incomes, the redistributive effects of tax and welfare measures, increased consumption, standardization of consumer goods, expansion of white-collar occupations, and increased education (among other things) all contribute to a blurring of status differences and

---

44. The notion of political polarization is troubled by still other problems that we cannot pursue here. In particular, there are formidable problems of constructing satisfactory indices and measures. Since each characteristic—social, psychological, political —is a broad category, one problem is to choose a satisfactory attribute or set of attributes within that category. In discussions of social dualism, the attribute most frequently referred to is class or status, for which occupation, income, education, class identification, etc. are used as indicators. But status polarization is only one type of social dualism, though an important one; for a society may also divide along other lines—religion, ethnic group, region, for example. Indices of psychological polarity are difficult to construct. Gabriel Almond and Sidney Verba in *The Civic Culture* offer some highly interesting possibilities; how one political group views another—positive, negative, and neutral qualities (Tables 1–6, pp. 125 ff.); and psychological distance between parties as indicated by willingness to have one's son or daughter marry across party lines (Tables 7–11, pp. 132 ff.). Political duality is also broad; indicators might include party identifications or orientation to candidates, though these are all complicated by simple differences in the number of alternatives presented to voters in two-party and multiparty countries; by differences in policy preferences, ideology, and other attitudes.

In order to find the degree of relationship between political duality and social or psychological dualities, measures of correlation are needed. In principle, a wide variety of standard statistical measures of correlation might be applied. In practice, however, few are satisfactory because of limitations in the data. The authors of *The American Voter* suggest a simple straightforward Index of Status Polarization. Robert Alford uses the same index, calling it the "Index of Class Voting." Curiously, however, Alford objects to the index suggested in *The American Voter*, even though his own is identical to it in all but name (see *The American Voter*, Figure 13.1, p. 345, and Alford, *Party and Society* (Chicago, Rand-McNally, 1963), pp. 79 ff.) Alford uses his Index of Class Voting to compare Australia, Britain, Canada, and the United States.

the enlargement of middle strata who shade off into the skilled working class on the one side and the wealthy upper strata on the other.[45]

2. Political duality as reflected in political attitudes, aspirations, and loyalties varies a good deal among our countries; but once sharp differences in political attitudes also seem to be declining. Nearly all the essays in the volume emphasize the decline of socialism as a distinctive ideology; as Otto Kirchheimer has indicated in his essay, the change may have been greatest—it is, at any rate, the most remarkable—in Germany, the home of the classic European Social Democratic Party. Strong loyalties to different political parties do, of course, persist; but as the experience of the United States demonstrates, party loyalty may be strong and yet have little to do with differences in ideology or policy. While the United States is no doubt the extreme case, the essays in this book suggest that European democracies are moving toward a somewhat similar situation.

3. It would be hasty to conclude, however, that the same pattern is emerging in the United States and the European democracies: that is, the first pattern suggested a moment ago, where political duality, even where it exists, is unrelated to social differences or psychological antagonism. There are two difficulties with this hypothesis.

First, the relation between status or occupation and party preference does not seem to have declined in Europe. Indeed, Lipset concludes:

> A comparative look at the pattern of working-class voting in contemporary Europe reveals that with the exception of Holland and Germany, the leftist parties secure about two-thirds or more of the working-class vote, a much higher percentage than during the depression of the 1930's . . . The leftist working-class parties have increased their strength in most of Europe during the 1960's. It is clear, therefore, that the easy assumption made by many, concerning American as well as European politics, that greater national affluence would mean a weakening of electoral support for the left is simply wrong.[46]

Second, the English-speaking and European democracies exhibit no single pattern. Sizable differences occur from one country to another in the extent to which status or occupation is related to party preference. Alford, who applied an Index of Class Voting to voting surveys taken from 1952 to 1962 in the four major English-speaking democracies found that:

> Class voting is almost always above zero; only one Canadian survey falls below that mark. Great Britain is consistently higher than Australia

45. See particularly the essay by Otto Kircheimer, above. And the essays by R. Bendix, R. Dahrendorf, M. Crozier, D. Lockwood, and Raymond Aron in *European Journal of Sociology*, 1, No. 2 (1960), 181–282.

46. S. M. Lipset, "Class Conflict and Contemporary European Society, Daedalus" in S. R. Graubard, ed., *A New Europe* (Boston, Houghton Mifflin, 1964), pp. 337–69.

in the 1952–62 period . . . Australia is consistently higher than the United States . . . The United States is consistently higher than Canada, except for one 1948 Canadian survey . . . Canada always has the lowest level of class voting with the single exception mentioned.[47]

Moreover, there is no consistent pattern of change. In Britain, as Alford shows, the "electorate remains sharply divided along class lines. No decline of the differences between classes as such or of the political predispositions connected with occupational status has occurred." On the other hand, in Norway, as Rokkan has demonstrated, an interesting change has occurred since the 1890s, for the Labor Party has gradually increased its support among the lower manual strata at the expense of all other parties, and in this sense political behavior has become more closely related to social cleavage. But the Labor Party also receives a good deal of support from the middle and upper strata. In this respect, the pattern of incomplete polarization is the reverse of that in Britain.[48]

4. Yet if status polarization is not decreasing, most of our essays indicate that psychological dualism in political life—i.e., antagonism and hostility —has sharply declined since the interwar period. In this case, too, differences remain. The presence of large Communist parties in France and Italy produces (and doubtless is produced by) a higher level of antagonism between a large proportion of the population (and of political elites) than is true in the other countries.[49] And in the United States the level of hostility over racial issues obviously has remained high, although the antagonism has historically been sharpest between the Southern and Northern wings of the same party.

5. None of the countries examined in this book closely approaches the pattern described a moment ago as full-scale political polarization, where sharp political, socioeconomic, and psychological dualisms all coincide. In Italy, political antagonisms are probably higher than in any of the other countries; indeed, it is difficult to see how its parliamentary system could withstand much higher psychological voltages. But even in Italy, as Barnes points out, socioeconomic status is quite imperfectly correlated with political cleavages, and the political groups around the center have been able, so far, to prevent political life from turning into a straight conflict between Communists on the Left and anti-Communists on the Right. In

47. "The index of class voting was computed by subtracting the percentage of non-manual workers voting for 'Left' parties from the percentage of manual workers voting for 'Left' parties. For Great Britain, the Labor party was used; for Australia, the Australian Labor party; for the United States, the Democratic party; for Canada, the CCF (or NDP) and Liberal parties" (p. 102, Table 5–2).

48. Above, pp. 89 ff. See also Stein Rokkan, "Geography, Religion and Social Class: Cross-Cutting Cleavages in Norwegian Politics," S. M. Lipset and S. Rokkan, eds., *Party Systems and Voter Alignments* (New York, Free Press, 1965).

49. Almond and Verba report that "Italian respondents show a far sharper (psychological) polarization between right and left than do the Americans, British and Germans" (*The Civic Culture*, p. 128).

Britain, Sweden, and Norway, where socialist and nonsocialist parties reflect differences in occupations, incomes, and status a good deal more strongly than the two major parties in the United States, the effects of socioeconomic differences on political life are, as we have seen, greatly attenuated because one of the largest parties in each of these countries has a socially heterogeneous following: thus in Norway the socialists draw as much as 40 per cent of the votes of the nonmanual workers, while in Britain a third or more of the manual workers support the Conservatives, and a quarter or more of the voters in nonmanual occupations have supported Labor. In these countries, moreover, psychological antagonisms appear to be exceedingly low.

How can we account for the absence of full-scale social-psychological polarization in these countries?

First there are the various factors, frequently mentioned in these essays, that are associated with economic "modernity," the growth of national communications, the blurring of class lines, etc.

Second, in some countries the effects of cross-cutting social characteristics have probably reduced both social and psychological dualities in political life.

Third, and paradoxically, it is in these countries, where political dualism along status lines has been most evident, that a long-run reduction in antagonisms and hostilities has been most notable. Political differences are most likely to reflect status differences, as we have seen, in highly homogeneous countries like Britain and Sweden where other differences—religious, ethnic, geographical—are comparatively slight. Yet this very homogeneity facilitates peaceful evolutionary reforms that blunt the edge of class hostilities.

Finally, it must always be kept in mind that our Western democracies. like other nation-states, are the products of an historical process during which extreme polarization has worked its drastic cures. In this book we have studied the survivors; we might have studied the casualties; we might, conceivably, be examining future casualties. Full-scale polarization is obviously an unstable condition for any polity, and particularly for a representative one. Extreme polarization of political life will be reduced somehow. Perhaps the strongest polarizing forces in modern times have been those of religion, language, and ethnic identity. If these forces do not polarize political life in most Western democracies today, this is only because they did so earlier. Typically they worked their drastic cure by destroying the political system: either by a separation into different countries, so that the cleavages became international rather than national, as with the separation of Ireland from Britain or Norway from Sweden; or by the creation of a one-party authoritarian or totalitarian states, as in the case of Fascist Italy, Nazi Germany, and Franco Spain.

13
EPILOGUE

Robert A. Dahl

To one who believes in the essential worth of a democratic polity, how much opposition is desirable, and what kinds? What is the best balance between consensus and dissent? Even among democrats there is not much agreement on the answers to these questions.

It is easy to see why. These questions seem to demand nothing less than a complicated assessment of democracy itself. Or to put the matter more precisely, one can judge the desirability of different patterns of political opposition only by employing a number of different criteria that would be used if one were appraising the extent to which a political system as a whole achieves what are usually considered democratic goals or values.

Eight of these standards seem directly relevant in judging different patterns of opposition. In comparison with other possible arrangements, one might ask, to what extent does a particular pattern maximize:

1. Liberty of thought and expression, including opportunities for dissenting minorities to make their views known to other citizens and policy-makers?
2. Opportunities for citizens to participate in political life?
3. When political conflicts occur, control over the decisions of government by majorities (rather than minorities) of citizens, voters, and elected officials?
4. Rationality in political discussion and decision-making, in the sense of increasing understanding by citizens and leaders of the goals involved and the appropriate means? [1]
5. Consensus in political discussion and decision-making, in the sense that solutions are sought that will minimize the size, resentments, and coercion of defeated minorities, and will maximixe the numbers of citizens who conclude that their goals have been adequately met by the solution adopted?

---

1. Cf. Bagehot, who refers to "one of the mental conditions of Parliamentary Government, by which I do not mean reasoning power, but rather the power of hearing the reasons of others, of comparing them quietly with one's own reasons, and then being guided by the result." *The English Constitution*, p. 44. See also p. 280.

6. The peaceful management of conflicts and the minimization of political violence?

7. Resolution of urgent policy questions, in the sense that the government directs its attention to any question regarded as urgent and important by a substantial proportion of citizens or leaders, and adopts solutions satisfactory to the largest number of citizens?

8. Widespread confidence in and loyalty to a constitutional and democratic polity?

A number of other criteria might be advanced, but these are enough to give an idea of the magnitude of the problem of evaluation. What is most obvious and most important about these criteria is that, like most standards of performance for complex achievements, they conflict with one another; if a political system were to maximize one of these ends it would probably do so only at considerable cost to some of the others. Moreover, because different individuals disagree about the relative importance of different goals, they disagree as to what is the best solution in general, and even for a specific situation. How then can one prescribe an optimal balance among competing goals, when the goals are nonquantitative and imprecise, and when one man's optimum may be another man's prison? Nor are these the only sources of disagreement. The eight criteria conflict with one another; there is a certain tension among them; we cannot maximize one goal beyond some range without sacrificing another goal.

In spite of all these obstacles to finding an "optimal solution," it is possible to clarify some of the costs and gains of different solutions, actual or proposed. Let me start by examining the tension created by wanting—as most good democrats do—freedom, dissent, and consensus.

Freedom, Dissent, and Consensus

The first criterion listed above emphasizes opportunities for dissent; and it is no doubt their concern for this goal that explains, in the main, why liberals and radicals have usually been keenly sensitive to problems of political opposition. For to look at any political system from the point of view of an opposition inclines one to stress the virtues of dissent, of *opposing*. Yet the last criterion in our list emphasizes the virtues of stability; and the penultimate criterion, the importance of resolution and dispatch, avoiding deadlock, paralysis, impotence in government. Sensitivity to these criteria leads one to be concerned with the high costs of unlimited dissent and to stress the importance of consensus, particularly if governments willing to protect dissent are to survive.

There are, we all know, many varieties of freedom. One variety of freedom exists to the extent that every citizen has opportunities to engage in political activities without severe social and governmental constraints. In all political systems this freedom—let me call it Freedom of Political

Action—is, like other freedoms, limited by government and society; yet it is the differences in these limits that distinguish libertarian from authoritarian systems. In libertarian systems (like the ten described in this book), the right to dissent from the views of government—to oppose the government—is a vital form of Freedom of Political Action. And political oppositions are a crucial expression of this Freedom.

Yet the very existence of dissent and political opposition is a sure sign that someone is constrained by government to do or to forbear from doing something that he would like to do and very likely feels he has a moral right, or even an obligation, to do. To feel politically free because one obeys laws one believes in, to obey a government one approves of, to obey governmental policies one wants or agrees with—here is a second variety of freedom. Since this variety, like the other, bears no accepted name, let me call it Freedom in Political Obligations.

Now if the existence of political opposition is evidence of Freedom of Political Action, it is also a symbol of the Unfreedom in Political Obligations [2] of those opposed to the government. I expect that some readers will now move a well-known objection. Even citizens who are opposed to the laws enforced by their government may nonetheless yield their implicit consent, provided these laws are adopted by procedures they regard as legitimate; in this sense, their Freedom in Political Obligations is not diminished by their need to obey specific laws to which they object. Let me recognize the force of this familiar argument and put it to one side as irrelevant here. I do so in order to distinguish (1) a polity in which a large and permanent minority accepts the constitutional procedures and arrangements, yet detests the policies of government, which seems to it tyrannical in what it does if not in the way it acts; from (2) a polity in which agreement is so extensive that minorities are microscopic and evanescent, and no one ever feels much injured by the laws he is obliged to obey. In the first case, members of the outvoted minority might accept the obligation to obey the laws because these were adopted according to legitimate constitutional processes, and yet feel constrained to obey laws they hold wrong. In the second case, they would feel no such constraint.

If you will allow me this distinction, it follows, I think, that in a democratic system where Freedom of Political Action is widely enjoyed, the less the dissent, the greater the Freedom in Political Obligations. In fact the only system in which every citizen would be completely free in his Political Obligations would be one in which political consensus was perfect; for no citizen would then feel constrained by government to do something he believed he should not do. The more extreme the dissent permitted, the greater the range of Freedom in Political Action; yet the

2. The notion of "unfreedom" is defined in Felix E. Oppenheim, *Dimensions of Freedom* (New York, St. Martin's Press, 1961), Ch. 4, "Unfreedom."

more numerous the extreme dissenters, the greater the number who are (at least temporarily and perhaps indefinitely) Unfree in their Political Obligations.

Let me try to make these abstractions more concrete by comparing a high-consensus system like Sweden with a low-consensus system like Italy. In a high-consensus system most citizens are only moderately opposed, if at all, to the character and conduct of government; by comparison, in a low-consensus system a great many more people are strongly opposed to the conduct and even the form of the government. The proportion of citizens who feel themselves coerced or constrained by government, and thus Unfree in Political Obligations is, naturally, much larger in the low-consensus systems than in the high-consensus ones.

Yet an extreme dissenter may enjoy more freedom to express his dissent in a low-consensus system like Italy than in a system with considerably more consensus like the United States. For (aside from any other reasons) the very magnitude of extreme dissent in Italy and France limits the extent to which dissent is coerced by social and governmental actions; in the United States, however, where extreme dissent is so small that it can be coerced at less cost, social and governmental constraints are rather powerful. Thus in the United States opportunities for discussing one's views with others, attending meetings, reading newspapers sympathetic to one's cause, joining in a like-minded party, and voting for like-minded candidates are extensive for most citizens—but not, often, for the extreme dissenter.

Thus a low-consensus country like Italy may actually provide more Freedom of Political Action (to Communists, Monarchists, and Fascists, for example) than a country like the United States where there is considerably higher consensus. Is low consensus a better guarantee of political freedom, then, than high consensus? Hardly, for a low-consensus system greatly increases the amount of Unfreedom in Political Obligations among its citizens. What is more, widespread Unfreedom in Political Obligations is inescapable as long as consensus remains low; for even if the Outs were to displace the Ins, their positions would only be reversed. The Freedom in Political Obligations of the one-time Outs would now be greater; but so would the Unfreedom in Political Obligations of the one-time Ins. Then, too, a low-consensus system is much more likely to impose other costs such as deadlock, political violence, constitutional instability, and destruction of democracy itself.

If, then, the most desirable long-run solution for a low-consensus country would be to increase consensus, surely the most desirable long-run solution for a high-consensus country would not be deliberately to foster extreme dissent! An obvious alternative solution would be to reduce the legal obstacles that limit the Freedom of Political Action among dissenters until they are legally on a par with all other citizens. This is, in fact, the solution adopted in a number of high-consensus countries. In this respect, the United States is a somewhat deviant case: most other stable democracies have not imposed as severe a set of legal and social obstacles to political dissent as exist in the United States.

Rationality, Dissent, and Consensus

If freedom of dissent is thought (by most libertarians and democrats) to be a desirable freedom in itself, advocates of libertarian democracy have usually contended, as John Stuart Mill did, that an opportunity for the expression of dissenting opinions is also a necessary (though definitely not a sufficient) condition for "rational" political action. The citizens of any country, in this view, need dissenters and oppositions in order to act wisely, to explore alternatives, to understand the advantages and disadvantages of different alternatives, to know what they want and how to go about getting it. Yet there is a certain conflict, one not always recognized, between the conditions required for a relatively rational consideration of alternatives, and the existence of extensive dissent or extensive consensus.

Where dissent is slight, the alternatives presented by political leaders for consideration among themselves and by the voters are likely to represent relatively small marginal changes. For in a society where nearly everyone is already rather satisfied with the conduct of government, alternatives profoundly opposed to existing government policy are not likely to be generated, proposed, or considered. Changes are likely to come about by paying attention to a relatively small number of marginally different alternatives to existing policies, examining a limited set of possible consequences, comparing the results of whatever changes are made, and making whatever further modifications are suggested by subsequent experience: in short, by incremental action.

Although incrementalism evidently seems to a great many people a less rational process than comprehensive and deductive approaches, in fact it offers great advantages as a process for relatively rational change.[3] The characteristics and effects of existing policies and institutions are more easily, more accurately, and more confidently known than for hypothetical policies and institutions. The effects of small changes are usually much easier to predict than the effects of large changes. Current processes generate information about effects, and since this information can be fed back to policy-makers, changes can be reversed, accelerated, or altered. In practice, moreover, peaceful change is usually highly incremental.

3. Cf. the discussion in R. A. Dahl and C. E. Lindblom, *Politics, Economics, and Welfare* (New York, Harper, 1953), pp. 82 ff., and the much more highly developed theory in C. E. Lindblom and D. Braybrooke, *A Strategy of Decision* (Glencoe, Free Press, 1963), Chs. 5 and 6, and C. E. Lindblom, *The Intelligence of Democracy* (Glencoe, Free Press, 1965).

Partly for this reason, no doubt, incremental change is the characteristic method of democracies: liquidation of the Kulaks and the Great Leap Forward would not have been carried out by parliamentary governments.

Yet if high-consensus societies can profit from the advantages of incremental change, they run an opposite danger. Where there is little dissent, both political leaders and citizens escape the compulsion to weigh the relative advantages offered by a comprehensive, large-scale change, even when a large-scale change might prove less costly in the long-run than either the status quo or a series of incremental changes. The history of politics is writ large with the results of costly timidities that have produced too little, too late.

Reflecting that incremental responses have frequently failed to match the magnitude of a challenge, one is tempted to conclude that sharp political conflict, clashing ideologies, and even low consensus are needed for a rational examination of alternatives. Yet the historical record seems to offer little support for this view. For intense conflicts create their own irrationalities, particularly when conflict is fortified by ideology. It is a reasonable hypothesis that the greater the discrepancy between the goals of the parties to a conflict, the more that problem-solving and persuasion are likely to give way to bargaining and coercion.[4] The true believer does not judiciously appraise the arguments of the infidel. Has the clash of ideologies in France and Italy provided a more "rational" examination of alternatives than the low-tension conflicts and unideological analyses among Britons and Swedes?

In sum, high-consensus polities are able to give relatively rational consideration to small changes but they are prone to ignore the possible advantages of radical changes in the status quo. Low-consensus polities may find it difficult to profit from the advantages of incremental changes; yet posing radically conflicting alternatives to citizens and leaders is accompanied by the irrationalities of ideological controversy.

Is it possible to have the best of both worlds? A society where dissent is low enough to encourage a relatively calm and objective appraisal of alternatives, and yet sufficient to make sure that radical alternatives will not be ignored or suppressed? Among our ten countries, if Italy lies at the one extreme, the United States is at the other. Possibly some of the north-European democracies come closer to the balance we seek. Yet if their high-consensus endures and increases, will not they, too, suffer the disadvantages of weak dissent?

Dispersion, Concentration, and Majority Rule

Does the two-party system offer a solution? Probably no other cure is so often proposed for the ailments of a sick polity. Does it not solve the

---

4. James G. March and Herbert A. Simon, *Organizations* (New York, Wiley, 1958), 129 ff.

problem of how to balance a large measure of consensus with a satisfactory amount of rational dissent? For cannot one party embody the values of stability and consensus, and the other the values of change and dissent?

The only country where a two-party system of this kind has ever endured in a relatively clear form is Britain, which does, I believe, exhibit many of the virtues claimed for the two-party system. Should it be more widely copied?

Unfortunately, the two-party system presents two imposing difficulties as a general solution. It is evidently not viable in many countries. And even if it were, it would not in all circumstances produce the results found in Britain.

The very rarity of the two-party system, a fact heavily stressed in an earlier chapter, argues that the existence of such a system requires an unusual combination of circumstances. The absence of one or more of these circumstances greatly reduces the likelihood that a two-party system will exist, or, if it does exist, that it will have the results expected of it.

The conditions under which a two-party system would provide an optimal solution for meeting the eight goals listed earlier probably include these:

1. The parliament is sovereign in law and in fact.

2. Within parliament, the principle of majority rule is applied to decisions.

3. Among citizens, and markedly among political activists, there exists a high degree of consensus on the desirability and legitimacy of the first two conditions; on the other characteristics of the constitutional system; on the rights, liberties, and duties of individuals and groups; and on a great many social and economic goals, institutions, and arrangements.

4. On all questions about which there are conflicting views, and for which governmental action is regarded by some people as desirable, most citizens divide into only two great clusters of opinion. These opinions, though stable for long periods, are not rigidly fixed but change with time, as does the size of the two opinion-clusters.

5. There are two political parties, and neither of these parties is, or expects to be, indefinitely out of office.

In these circumstances, two unified parties, each having a program and policies directed toward one of the two great clusters of opinion and competing actively for office, meet a great many of the criteria listed earlier. As long as most conflicting opinions fall into one of the two great clusters, the two-party system would provide an outlet for expressing views, including criticizing the government (Criterion 1), and opportunities for citizens to participate in political life (Criterion 2). Any fair system for apportioning parliamentary seats would insure that the government would represent the larger opinion-cluster rather than the smaller (Criterion 3). The existence of two divergent sets of public attitudes bounded by extensive consensus would facilitate rationality in political discussion and decision-making (Criterion 4), by insuring that alternatives would be posed, providing a reasonably clear choice to voters, and enabling a rather high degree of coherence of policies and programs. Rationality would also be enhanced because an opposition's past experience in office and its expectation of future responsibility as the governing party would encourage its members to avoid demagogic and irresponsible appeals for unworkable and unrealistic solutions. The existence of widespread consensus and the experience and expectation of governing would help to minimize the resentments of the opposition and the need for coercion (Criterion 5) and also to insure that conflicts would be peacefully resolved (Criterion 6). Policy questions uppermost in the minds of any large group of people would almost certainly be brought forward by one of the two parties; and in due time each party would have an opportunity to enact its own solution (Criterion 7). Finally, all these conditions taken together would surely go very far toward creating widespread loyalty to democracy and constitutional government (Criterion 8).

It is easy to see why the two-party model, especially in the idealized form in which it is often described, has charmed so many political observers. Yet the conditions I have just specified are an unusual combination; they have not always existed even in Britain.

In the first place, as we have already seen (Chapter 12), if a society is polarized into highly antagonistic camps, then the two-party system might actually increase the intensity of conflicts by wiping out the mediating center.

Second, opinions may fall into more than two clusters, as they generally do in Belgium, Holland, Italy, and the United States. In these circumstances, there would have to be more than two parties; or, as in the United States, the two parties would not be highly unified. Moreover, if a system of disciplined parties existed, it could produce flagrant contradictions with several of our criteria. Specifically, the application of the principle of majority rule and parliamentary sovereignty could lead to minority government, negate majority rule, and thus violate Criterion 3. For if a faction in one party, even if it were a majority faction, could use the instruments of party discipline to impose its policies on that party, and if that party had a majority in parliament, then the policies adopted by the government and agreed to by the parliamentary majority might well be policies preferred only by a minority and opposed by a majority of the whole country. When there are more than two large clusters of opinions it would be necessary, in order to satisfy our criterion, for different majority coalitions to form on different issues. Thus a multiparty system or two heterogeneous parties without strong discipline would be preferable

Third, the government and the opposition parties might not alternate in office. In this case, an opposition might find demagogic and unrealistic appeals increasingly attractive. Even if, as Nils Stjernquist's essay shows, the problem of a permanent opposition is not at all peculiar to a two-party system, there is nothing inherent in the dynamics of a two-party system that guarantees an alternation between the two parties.

A system with two disciplined and strictly competitive parties, one controlling the government and the other providing a concentrated focus for opposition, is not always, therefore, a desirable solution. The circumstances under which it is the optimal solution may be, in fact, rather uncommon. The typical solution of democracies is not concentration but dispersion, not strict competition but bargaining and coalescent strategies. Given the conditions of political life in most countries, quite possibly this solution is preferable; for it is often possible where the other solution is not, and it may come somewhat closer to satisfying our various criteria.

Majority Rule, Minorities, and Organized Pluralism

Every solution to the problems of opposition that focuses upon party systems runs the danger of neglecting a palpable fact of political life: many important decisions are not made in parliament. To the extent that an opposition concentrates on elections and parliamentary action, it may be powerful in unimportant encounters and feeble or even absent when key decisions are made.

As the extent of governmental intervention and control in social and economic affairs has expanded, the work of parliaments has also multiplied. But even with the enormously increased work load of parliaments and the much greater weight and range of the effects that laws passed by parliament now have on social and economic behavior, the *relative* importance of parliaments in making important decisions has not increased in the same proportion; the "decline of parliaments" has become a familiar topic and a source of concern.

No single curve could summarize the historical changes in the power of various parliaments. But in a number of countries two kinds of developments have helped to increase the *relative* importance of other sites. One is a pronounced growth in many Western democracies in the power of a plebiscitary executive who acquires great political resources by winning a national election. Although this development is clearest in the United States and the Fifth French Republic, the rise of highly disciplined parties has led by a different route to similar results in Britain, Norway, Sweden, Austria, and a number of other democracies. In France and the United States, the Constitution, laws, and political practices grant extensive discretionary power and authority to an elected chief executive; in the other countries, if a party or coalition wins a majority of seats in parliament, party discipline insures that it will form a government whose policies cannot, for all practical purposes, be defeated by opponents in parliament. Although the development is highly uneven and the pattern is markedly different from one country to another, the importance of the legislature as a site for encounters between opposition and government is reduced to the extent that a plebiscitary executive (whether president or cabinet) has acquired the power to make key decisions without much restraint by parliament.

The other development that creates a powerful rival for parliament is the one stressed by Stein Rokkan in his chapter on Norway: the evolution of national bargaining among employers, trade unions, and other interests has led to a process for making decisions of great economic and social importance over which parliaments and sometimes even executives exercise scant control.

What these two developments have in common is the creation of highly strategic sites outside parliament—rivals to parliamentary power. Where they differ is in the importance of national elections. For if the rise of a plebiscitary executive has reduced the relative influence of parliament, that development has, if anything, made elections even more crucial. Yet because the concrete alternatives open to voters are few and simple in comparison with the great range of problems confronting a modern state, an election furnishes a vague mandate at best; and at worst it simply allows winners and losers to provide their own interpretations of the election returns.

Bargaining with the executive, bargaining among private and public bureaucracies, negotiations among the great national associations, all these provide ways of supplementing, interpreting, offsetting, and even negating the election returns. This is exactly the source of both the advantages and the dangers of organized pluralism and national bargaining.

Organized pluralism meets many of the criteria for opposition in a democracy that I proposed at the beginning of this chapter. For example, because it often enables key groups to arrive at decisions they find more acceptable than decisions imposed by legislature or executive order, bargaining is an instrument for gaining consensus and enlarging the area of Freedom in Political Obligations. It provides additional sites for effective expression of views, dissent, criticism. Often it insures that the specialized knowledge of the groups most deeply involved in some activity will be brought to bear on a solution. Yet if it has many advantages—and it is in any case inevitable in every modern libertarian industrial society—organized pluralism creates two problems that have not yet been solved anywhere. For one thing, since all resources except the vote are unequally distributed, some minorities (one thinks of the uneducated poor in the United States) may not have much in the way of political resources to bargain with: they have the ballot—and little else. In addition, to the extent that parliament is excluded from the process and elections provide only a vague and rather uncertain control over national leaders, there is no political institution in which majorities weigh heavily that can control the great bargained decisions by means of public review, appraisal, opposition, amendment, or veto.

Perhaps organized pluralism would weaken democracy in a small city–state, as Rousseau and his admirers would argue, for it encourages a citizen to take only a fragmentary view of his interests. And faction has always been the mortal disease of the city–state. Yet in the modern nation–state, it is difficult to imagine an alternative to organized pluralism that would not leave the plebiscitary executive and the official bureaucracies without effective oppositions, criticism, and control.

What is not yet perfectly clear, however, is how organized pluralism and national bargaining are to be reconciled with systems in which political equality and majority rule are major principles of legitimacy.

Oppositions in Western Democracies: The Future

There is a tension, then, among our goals, a tension that seems to be inescapable. The demands imposed by the values of democracy are extraordinarily severe.

To one who accepts these values, one perennial problem of opposition is that there is either too much or too little. The revolutionary parts of the world have a surplus of poverty and a deficit of order. The authoritarian countries have a surplus of order and a deficit of political freedom. Some of the Western democracies are achieving a mounting surplus of riches and consensus.

To be concerned over the decline of structural oppositions in most Western democracies may very well be an anachronism, a throwback to nineteenth-century styles of thought, on a par with a nonrational faith in the virtues of a balanced budget or the conviction that a seven-day workweek is indispensable if the working classes are not to become dissolute from having too much spare time on their hands. Should we not begin instead to adjust our minds to the notion that in the future—or at least in that short-run future into which it is not wholly senseless to extrapolate present trends—a great many Western democracies will have rather high levels of agreement and not much structural opposition?

That a large number of democracies have won the battle for the allegiance of their citizens among all social strata is, surely, a satisfying victory to anyone who believes in the values of a democratic polity. Yet it is difficult to disregard the sense of disquiet that follows hard upon one's awareness that severe criticism of social and economic structures has all but disappeared from the political life of many Western democracies—or else has become a monopoly of political forces like the Communists and the Radical Right whose allegiance to democratic values is, to say the least, doubtful. If the growth of extreme dissent can endanger a democratic system, universal but quite possibly superficial and irrational "consensus" may also be undesirable, for reasons I have just been exploring.

But is the trend evident in so many Western democracies over the past several decades toward greater consensus likely to continue? Might it level off, or even be reversed?

No way of conjecturing about the future, as Bertrand de Jouvenel has remarked, is more compelling than the temptation to project recent trends, "to suppose that tomorrow is going to differ from today in the same way that today differs from yesterday." [5] And as M. de Jouvenel also reminds us, it is the extrapolation of recent trends that has so often led men who understood their own time well to miss completely the large changes and abrupt reversals that transform the future into something radically different from the past. Suppose, then, that we make two assumptions about the future: that there will be no holocaust, an assumption without which it would be futile to speculate about the future of politics; and that Western societies will continue to develop greater affluence, higher consumption, reduction of poverty, wider educational opportunities, and steadily increasing technical and technological resources. Under these conditions, what can we conjecture about the future of oppositions in Western democracies?

To begin with, even the growth of affluence does not automatically wipe out conflicts over the distribution of the national income and opportunities of all kinds. There is no reason to assume a decline in the familiar conflicts among different interest groups, each striving to insure that its members gain a satisfactory share. Indeed, since a just or satisfactory share probably cannot be defined so as to command general assent, and since any particular allotment reveals itself more and more clearly nowadays to be a product of political decisions and less and less an act of God, nature, or the inexorable operation of economic laws, conflicts over the distribution of income might, if anything, become more numerous even if less intense.

International policies will also remain, surely, subjects of conflict. Since there is small chance that international politics will diminish in importance and salience in the next half century, and since judgments of alternative policies and proposals will necessarily rest on highly controversial assessments of very great risks, gains, and costs, a variety of foreign policies, military affairs, treaties, regional and international organizations and alliances all promise a steady flow of internal conflict.

In many cases, conflicts over international politics and the distribution of national income and opportunities may not generate anything more

5. *L'Art de la Conjecture* (Monaco, Editions de Rocher, 1964), p. 82.

than the kinds of policy oppositions with which we are already familiar in Western democracies. To this extent the future looks rather like the immediate past that has been described in the essays here. Yet this may not be the whole picture. For these two kinds of conflicts need not necessarily entail only narrow group interests or technical matters. The more the distribution of incomes and other opportunities is thought to be subject to determination by government, the more relevant may become the ancient and evidently inextinguishable controversies over the issue of equality versus differential rewards. And conflicts over international affairs will in some cases involve nothing less than alternative views of how the nation, the civilization, even the species itself are most likely to survive or perish.

Yet neither of these kinds of issues inevitably entails structural oppositions. Are there possible sources of alienation in Western democracies that might foster new structural oppositions? Since alienation has lately become a fashionable topic, let me hasten to add that I do not mean to imply anything about social or psychological alienation, whatever these may be. I speak only of political alienation. A citizen is alienated from his political system to the extent that he has unfavorable feelings, evaluations, and attitudes toward it. I assume that a citizen might be alienated from the political system in which he lives without necessarily being neurotic, rootless, excessively anxious over his social standing, or otherwise much different in personality and social characteristics from his fellow citizens. In short, I wish to leave completely open the murky empirical question of how political alienation may be related, if at all, to strictly social and psychological factors.

Among the possible sources of alienation in Western democracies that may generate new forms of structural opposition is the new democratic Leviathan itself. By the democratic Leviathan I mean the very kind of political system the chapters in this book have described, a product of long evolution and hard struggle, welfare-oriented, centralized, bureaucratic, tamed and controlled by competition among highly organized elites, and, in the perspectives of the ordinary citizen, somewhat remote, distant, and impersonal even in small countries like Norway and Sweden. The politics of this new democratic Leviathan, as we have seen so often in the past chapters, are above all the politics of compromise, adjustment, negotiation, bargaining; a politics carried on among professional and quasi-professional leaders who constitute only a small part of the total citizen body; a politics that reflects a commitment to the virtues of pragmatism, moderation, and incremental change; a politics that is un-ideological and even anti-ideological.

The traditional opposition to the new democratic Leviathan has come from critics on the Right. In most European countries this traditional opposition has been greatly enfeebled. In the United States, I suggested in Chapter 2, a Radical Right has become alienated from the existing political system, for the principal leaders in the American system—whether in the Administration's coalition or nominally in opposition—accept policies, express views, and engage in conduct that the Right passionately rejects as evil; being a minority and unable to win national elections (and not many state or local elections) the Right has steadily suffered the humiliation of political impotence and rejection.

Is it likely that the wheel of history may make a full turn, that opposition to the democratic Leviathan may arise from a new quarter? There are already faint signs, not only in the United States but in high-consensus European systems like Sweden, Norway, and Britain, that many young people, intellectuals, and academics reject the democratic Leviathan—not because it is democratic but because, in their view, it is not democratic enough: this new Leviathan is too remote and bureaucratized, too addicted to bargaining and compromise, too much an instrument of political elites and technicians with whom they feel slight identification. Political isolation, alienation, and rebellion among youth, intellectuals, and academics are not, of course, new. Yet in the past half century the Left has, on the whole, sought to channel these feelings into support for policies and programs that have encouraged, not retarded, the development of the new democratic Leviathan. Is it not possible, however, that political alienation will increase, and that a new Left—if one can stretch traditional terms to cover the case—might channel these feelings into radical efforts (the shape of which we cannot foresee) to reconstruct the Leviathan to a more nearly human scale?

None of the three possible sources of future oppositions that I have been describing can be reduced, I imagine, to strictly technical questions. Although most issues involving the distribution of incomes and opportunities, international politics, and the democratic Leviathan have strictly technical aspects, few of them can be settled by strictly technical answers. The position one takes must depend in part on nontechnical factors —on values more implicit than explicit, psychological orientations and predispositions, identifications, feelings of hate, hostility, fear, jealousy, pride, self-confidence, respect, solidarity. If factors of this kind are to play a part, then there is good reason for expecting that political conflict will encourage the birth of new ideologies. For political elites and involved citizens alike will sense a need for broad, integrated views of the world to provide guidance, validity, and authority for their judgments on specific issues. And it will be surprising if these views of the world do not differ considerably in their perspectives, goals, evaluations, and assumptions about the nature of man and society.

Yet should these conflicting issues and ideologies develop it seems unlikely that they will be strongly associated, at least in the democracies examined in this book, with the familiar social and economic character-istics that have done such yeoman service in social theory in the recent past. For differences in political demands will probably become in large measure detached from general socioeconomic factors. At one end of the scale, new oppositions may reflect no more than conflicts among shifting coalitions of interest groups. At the other extreme, conflicting demands are likely to be attached to relatively durable orientations, perspectives, "mentalities," political philosophies, or ideologies that are related only casually to the kinds of social forces that have played such an important part in the political life of Western democracies in the past century.

In short, differences in basic political ideas and evaluations are likely to become more and more important in explaining differences in political behavior and therefore in patterns of opposition. Yet these crucial differ-ences in political ideas and evaluations will probably be less and less trace-able to differences in social and economic characteristics. In this sense, political ideologies, far from waning, will be ascendant.

To be sure, the traditional ideologies that have played so great a role in Western politics in the past century show every sign of being well on the way to ultimate extinction. But democracies have not eliminated all causes of political conflict; and if we agree with James Madison that "the latent causes of faction are sown in the nature of man," then democracies will not and cannot eliminate all causes of political conflict. If democ-racies cannot eliminate all the causes of conflict, is it not reasonable to expect that with the passage of time the clash of governments and oppo-sitions, indeed of one opposition with another, will generate—and will be generated by—new political perspectives that we cannot now accurately foresee?

APPENDIXES

APPENDIXES

Chapter 4. Sweden

Appendix Table 4.1. Distribution of Riksdag Seats, 1922–1965 [1]

	1922		1925		1929		1933		1937		1941	
	LH[3]	UH[3]	LH	UH	LH	UH	LH	UH	LH	UH	LH	UH
Conservatives	62	41	65	44	73	49	58	50	44	45	42	35
Liberals	41	38	33	35	32	31	24	23	27	16	23	15
Center Party	21	18	23	18	27	17	36	18	36	22	28	24
Socialists	93	50	104	52	90	52	104	58	112	66	134	75
Communists	7	1	5	1	8	1	2	—	5	—	3	1
Other	6	2	—	—	—	—	6[6]	1[6]	6[6]	1[6]	—	—
Total	230	150	230	150	230	150	230	150	230	150	230	150

	1945		1949		1953		1957		1959		1961		1965	
	LH	UH	LH	UH	LH	UH	LH	UH	LH	UH	LH	UH	LH[4]	UH[4]
Con.	39	30	23	24	31	20	42	13	45	16	39	19	33	26
Lib.	26	14	57	18	58	22	58	30	38	32	40	33	43	26
Cen.	35	21	30	21	26	25	19	25	32	22	34	20	36	19
Soc.	115	83	112	84	110	79	106	79	111	79	114	77	113	78
Com.	15	2	8	3	5	4	6	3	5	2	5	2	8	2
	—	—	—	—	—	—	—	—	—	—	—	—	—	—
Other	230	150	230	150	230	150	231	150	231	151	232	151	233	151

1. The years selected are those immediately following the years when elections to the Lower House were held. It may be observed that the distribution of Upper House seats generally fluctuates in some degree from year to year owing to the annual renewal of one-eighth of its membership. Underlined figures indicate a majority of seats.

2. LH—Lower House.

3. UH—Upper House.

4. The three MBS-representatives are divided up into their original parties, i.e. one Conservative, one Liberal, and one Centrist. The last-mentioned was not accepted by his Parliamentary group in 1965.

5. One of the new Conservative members in the Upper House also belonged to the MBS.

6. Representatives of the Kihlbom group, which in 1929 was excluded from the Communist Party.

Appendix Table 4.2. The Parliamentary Support of the Government, 1922–1965

Year	LH [1]	UH [2]	JD [3]	Prime Minister	Party	Period
1922	92 [4]	50	142 [4]	Hj. Branting	Socialist	Oct. 13, 1921–Apr. 19, 1923
1923	92 [4]	50	142 [4]			
1923	62	41 [4]	103 [4]	E. Trygger	Conservative	Apr. 19, 1923–Oct. 18, 1924
1924	62	43 [4]	105 [4]			
1924	98 [4]	52	150 [4]	Hj. Branting	Socialist	Oct. 18, 1924–June 7, 1926
				(to Jan. 24, 1925)		
1925	103 [4]	52	155 [4]	R. Sandler		
1926	104 [4]	52	156 [4]			
1926	33	34	67	C. G. Ekman	Liberal	June 7, 1926–Oct. 2, 1928
1927	33	32	65			
1928	33	31	64			
1928	65	49 [4]	114 [4]	A. Lindman	Conservative	Oct. 2, 1928–June 7, 1930
1929	73	48 [4]	121 [4]			
1930	73	48 [4]	121 [4]			
1930	28	24	52	C. G. Ekman	Liberal [6]	June 7, 1930–Sept. 24, 1932
				(to Aug. 6, 1932)		
1931	28	23	51			
1932	28	22	50	F. Hamrin		
1932	89 [4]	55	144 [4]	P. A. Hansson	Socialist	Sept. 24, 1932–June 19, 1936
1933	103 [4]	58	161 [4]			
1934	101 [4]	61	162 [4]			
1935	101 [4]	62	163 [4]			
1936	100 [4]	65	165 [4]			
1936	37	22	69	A. Pehrsson-Bramstorp	Center	June 19, 1936–Sept. 28, 1936
1936	137 [4]	87	224 [4]	P. A. Hansson	Socialist/Center	Sept. 28, 1936–Dec. 13, 1939
1937	147 [4]	88	235 [4]			
1938	150 [4]	89	239 [4]			
1939	150 [4]	93	243 [4]			
1940	221 [4]	148 [4]	369 [5]	P. A. Hansson	Socialist/Center/Conservative/Liberal	Dec. 13, 1939–July 31, 1945
1941	226 [4]	148 [4]	374 [5]			
1942	226 [4]	148 [4]	374 [5]			
1943	226 [4]	148 [4]	374 [5]			
1944	226 [4]	147 [4]	373 [5]			

Year	Lower House	Upper House	JD	Prime Minister	Party	Period
1945	214[4]	147[4]	361[5]			
1945	114[4]	83	197[4]	P. A. Hansson	Socialist	July 31, 1945– Oct. 1, 1951
				(died Oct. 6, 1946)		
1946	114[4]	84	198[4]			
1947	114[4]	86	200[4]	T. Erlander		
				(from Oct. 11, 1946)		
1948	114[4]	85	199[4]			
1949	111[4]	84	195[4]			
1950	111[4]	81	192[4]			
1951	111[4]	79	190[4]			
1951	141[4]	104	245[4]	T. Erlander	Soc./Center	Oct. 1, 1951– Oct. 31, 1957
1952	141[4]	104	245[4]			
1953	135[4]	104	239[4]			
1954	135[4]	104	239[4]			
1955	135[4]	103	238[4]			
1956	135[4]	103	238[4]			
1957	124[4]	104	228[4]			
1957	105[4]	79	184[4]	T. Erlander	Socialist	Oct. 31, 1957–
1958A	105[4]	79	184[4]			
1958B	110[4]	79	189[4]			
1959	110[4]	79	189[4]			
1960	110[4]	78	188[4]			
1961	114	77	191			
1962	114	77	191			
1963	114	77	191			
1964	114	78	192			
1965	113	78	191			

1. The Lower House had 230 members 1922–56, 231 members 1957–60, 232 members 1961–64, and 233 members from 1965. The Speaker was not allowed to vote before 1961. Thus in the period 1922–56 the government needed support from at least 115 members to command a majority, in the period 1957–60 from at least 116 members, and from 1961 from at least 117 members. Underlined figures indicate possession of a majority.

2. The Upper House had 150 members from 1922 to 1957 and 151 members from 1958. The Speaker was not allowed to vote before 1961. Thus in the period 1922–57 the government needed support from at least 75 members to command a majority, and from 1958 from at least 76 members.

3. JD = joint divisions. Needed to command the majority: 1922–57 at least 190 members, 1958–60 at least 191 members, 1961–64 at least 192 members, and from 1965 at least 193 members.

4. The total number was one more, but this member was the Speaker and as such not allowed to vote.

5. The total number was two more, but these two members were the Speakers and as such not allowed to vote.

6. One small group of Liberals stood outside the government.

Appendix Table 4.3. Percentages of Total Vote Cast for Each Party in the Elections to the Lower House, 1921–1964

	1921	1924	1928	1932	1936	1940
Cons.	25.9	26.1	29.4	23.5	17.6	18.0
Lib.	18.8	16.9	15.9	11.7	12.9	12.0
Center	11.1	10.8	11.2	14.1	14.3	12.0
Soc.	36.4	41.1	37.0	41.7	45.9	53.8
Comm.	4.6	5.1	6.4	3.0	3.3	3.5
Other	3.2	—	0.1	6.0[1]	6.0[1]	0.7

	1944	1948	1952	1956	1958	1960	1964
Cons.	15.9	12.3	14.4	17.1	19.5	16.5	13.7
Lib.	12.9	22.8	24.4	23.8	18.2	17.5	17.1
Center	13.6	12.4	10.7	9.4	12.7	13.6	13.4
Soc.	46.6	46.1	46.1	44.6	46.2	47.8	47.3
Comm.	10.3	6.3	4.3	5.0	3.4	4.5	5.2
Other	0.7	0.1	0.1	0.1	0.0	0.1	3.3[2]

1. Mainly voters for the Kihlbom group, which in 1929 was excluded from the Communist Party.
2. KDS 1.8% and MBS 1.5%.

Appendix Table 4.4. Participation in the Elections to the Lower House, 1921–1964 (in percentages)

1921	1924	1928	1932	1936	1940
54.2	53.0	67.4	67.6	74.5	70.3

1944	1948	1952	1956	1958	1960	1964
71.9	82.7	79.1	79.8	77.4	85.9	83.9

Chapter 5. Belgium

Appendix Table 5.1. School and Preschool Population by
Sponsorship of School, Public and Private, and Level
of Instruction, 1960–1961

	Public	Private	Total
Preschool	140,008	265,127	405,135
Primary	437,064	481,758	918,822
Secondary	209,801	316,931	526,732
University, higher technical institution, normal school	20,394	31,605	51,999
Total	807,267	1,095,421	1,902,688

Note: Almost all private elementary and secondary schools are
Catholic institutions. Some nominally public primary schools
(notably in Flanders) are Catholic institutions under municipal
aegis. One major private university, the University of Brussels
(5,047 students), is not Catholic.

Source: Ministry of Economic Affairs and Ministry of National
Education and Culture, *Annuaire Statistique de l'enseignement,
1960–1961* (Brussels, 1962), pp. 20–21.

Appendix Table 5.2. School and Preschool Population
by Sponsorship of School and Language, 1960–1961

	Public	Private
French	465,095	335,528
Flemish	336,141	759,324
German	6,031	569
Total	807,267	1,095,421

Source: *Annuaire statistique de l'enseignement,
1960–1961*, pp. 20–21.

Appendix Table 5.3. Membership of House of Representatives, by Party, During the Period of Taxpayers' Suffrage—Selected Years, 1847–1892

Year	Population (to nearest thousand)	Voters	Abstentions %	Total	Catholics	Liberals
1847	4,338,000	46,000	27	108	53	55
1848 (D)	4,359,000	79,000	33	108	25	83
1856	4,529,000	44,000	28	108	63	45
1857 (D)	4,577,000	91,000	15	108	38	70
1864 (D)	4,941,000	104,000	19	116	52	64
1870 (D)	5,088,000	107,000	26	124	72	52
1878	5,477,000	92,000	28	132	60	72
1884	5,785,000	125,000	16	138	86	52
1892 (D)	6,195,000	137,000	16	152	92	60

Note: Because of the difficulties in attributing party affiliations, there are no figures here for the years between 1831 and 1847. The House was renewed by half every two years, except when the entire House was dissolved. (D) indicates dissolution of the House. I have chosen the years in which there was a change of majority or a renewal of the whole House. Compulsory voting was not introduced until 1893.

Sources: Jean Temmerman, *Droit Public* (Brussels, École Royale Militaire, 1963), pp. 122–23, and John Gilissen, *Le Régime représentatif en Belgique depuis 1790* (Brussels, 1958), pp. 188–89.

Appendix Table 5.4. *Election Results and Membership of House of Representatives, by Party, During the Period of Universal Suffrage with Plural Voting, 1894–1914* [a]

Year	Voters [b]	Valid Votes [b]	Seats, Total	Catholics Votes [b]	Catholics Seats	Liberals Votes [b]	Liberals Seats	Socialists Votes [b]	Socialists Seats	Liberal-Socialist (joint tickets) Votes [b]	Daensists [e] Seats
1894(D)	1,355,000	1,922,000	152	963,000	104	537,000	20	311,000	28	33,000	—
1896	694,000 [c]	928,000	152	489,000	111	202,000	13	34,000	28	174,000	—
1898	715,000 [d]	997,000	152	428,000	112	212,000	13	277,000	27	30,000	—
1900 (D)	1,473,000	2,053,000	152 [f]	994,000	86	502,000	34	461,000	31	—	1
1902	1,154,000	1,639,000	166	842,000	96	370,000	34	380,000	34	—	2
1904	774,000	1,115,000	166	487,000	93	283,000	42	301,000	29	—	2
1906	786,000	1,173,000	166	636,000	89	250,000	46	72,000	30	182,000	1
1908	814,000	1,201,000	166	518,000	87	223,000	43	272,000	35	149,000	1
1910	836,000	1,274,000	166	677,000	86	280,000	44	85,000	35	195,000	1
1912 (D)	1,746,000	2,622,000	186	1,337,000	101	306,000	44	243,000	39	693,000	2
1914	878,000	1,335,000	186	572,000	99	327,000	45	405,000	40	—	2

a. The House was renewed by half every two years, except when dissolution caused a renewal of the whole House. (D) indicates a dissolution.

b. Rounded off to nearest thousand.

c. Some 27,000 voters, with 41,000 votes, did not vote because the Catholic ticket was uncontested in one arrondissement.

d. Some 36,000 voters, with 54,000 votes, did not vote because the Catholic tickets were uncontested in two arrondissements.

e. The Daensists were Flemish Christian Democrats or leftish Catholics.

f. Proportional representation first went into effect in 1900.

Source: Gilissen, *Le Régime représentatif*, pp. 190–91.

Appendix Table 5.5. Votes for House of Representatives, by Party, During the Period of Equal Universal Suffrage, 1919–1961 [a]
(as percentages of total number of valid ballots)

Year	Soc.	Comm.	Lib.	Flem. Nat.	Rex	Cath.	Diss. Cath.	Misc.
1919	36.6	—	17.6	2.6	—	36.6	2.1	4.4
1921	34.8	0.05	17.8	3.0	—	37.0	4.3	3.0
1925	39.4	1.6	14.6	3.9	—	36.1	2.5	1.8
1929	36.0	1.9	16.6	6.3	—	35.4	3.2	0.6
1932	37.1	2.8	14.3	5.9	—	38.6	0.2	1.1
1936	32.1	6.1	12.4	7.1	11.5	27.7	1.1	2.0
1939	30.2	5.4	17.2	8.3	4.4	32.7	—	1.8
					UDB			
1946	32.6 [b]	12.7	9.5 [b]	—	2.2	42.5	—	0.5
1949 [c]	29.8	7.5	15.3	2.1	—	43.6	0.1	1.8
1950	35.6 [b]	4.7	12.0 [b]	—	—	47.7	—	—
1954	38.6 [b]	3.6	13.0 [b]	2.02	—	41.1	0.9	0.6
1958	37.1 [b]	1.9	11.8 [b]	2.0	—	46.5	—	0.7
1961	36.7	3.1	12.3	3.5	—	41.5	—	2.9

a. Abbreviations:
  Soc.—Socialist Party (Workers Party until 1940; Socialist Party after 1945)
  Comm.—Communist Party
  Lib.—Liberal Party (Party of Liberty and Progress since 1961)
  Flem. Nat.—Flemish nationalist parties (Flemish People's Union since 1954)
  Cath.—Catholic Party between the wars; Christian Social Party since 1945
  Diss. Cath.—Dissident Catholic tickets
  UDB—Belgian Democratic Union
  Misc.—Miscellaneous
b. In 1946, 1950, 1954, and 1958, the Socialist and Liberal parties ran joint tickets in Limbourg and Luxembourg provinces. I have assigned to each party a percentage of the joint vote based on the rather stable percentages obtained by their separate tickets in those provinces in 1939 and 1949. The possible error is unimportant, as the total involved each year is only about 2 per cent of the total national vote for all parties.
c. Women's suffrage introduced in national elections in 1949.
Sources: R. E. De Smet, R. Evalenko, and W. Fraeys, *Atlas des élections belges, 1919–1954* (Brussels, Institut de Sociologie, 1958), *Annexe*, pp. 10–11, for 1919–54, except for estimates referred to in footnote b, and Ministry of Interior for 1958 and 1961.

Appendix Table 5.6. Seats in House of Representatives, by Party, During the Period of Equal Universal Suffrage, 1919–1961 (in number of seats immediately after each national election)

Year	Soc.	Comm.	Lib.	Flem. Nat.	Rex	Cath.	Diss. Cath.	Misc.	Total
1919	70	—	34	5	—	73	—	4	186
1921	68	—	33	4	—	76	4	1	186
1925	78	2	23	6	—	75	3	—	187
1929	70	1	28	11	—	71	6	—	187
1932	73	3	24	8	—	79	—	—	187
1936	70	9	23	16	21	61	2	—	202
1939	64	9	33	17	4	73	—	2	202
					UDB				
1946	69	23	17	—	1	92	—	—	202
1949	66	12	29	—	—	105	—	—	212
1950	77	7	20	—	—	108	—	—	212
1954	86	4	25	1	—	95	1	—	212
1958	84	2	21	1	—	104	—	—	212
1961	84	5	20	5	—	96	—	2	212

Abbreviations: See Appendix Table 5.5.
Sources: R. E. De Smet, R. Evalenko, and W. Fraeys, *Altas des élections belges, 1919–1954, Annexe*, pp. 14–15, for 1919–54, and Ministry of Interior figures for 1958 and 1961.

Appendix Table 5.7. Distribution of Votes Within Linguistic Regions, by Party, as Percentages of Valid Ballots for House of Representatives, 1961

	Total Vote (to nearest thousand)	PSC	Soc.	Lib.	Comm.	Flemish People's Union	Others	Total
Flanders	2,867,000	50.9	29.7	11.6	1.0	6.0	0.8	100
Wallonia	1,695,000	30.1	47.1	11.8	6.5	—	4.5	100
Brussels	668,000	28.0	41.6	17.0	3.6	1.7	8.1	100
German-speaking cantons	35,000	71.1	13.0	11.3	0.5	—	4.0	99.9
Belgium	5,265,000	41.5	36.7	12.3	3.1	3.5	2.9	100

Source: William Fraeys, "Les Résultats des élections législatives du 26 mars 1961," *Res Publica, 3*, No. 4 (1961), p. 394.

Appendix Table 5.8. Distribution of Electoral Support Within Parties, by Linguistic Region, as Percentages of Each Party's Total Vote for House of Representatives, 1961

	PSC		Socialists		Liberals		Communists	
	Votes	%	Votes	%	Votes	%	Votes	%
Flanders	1,460,000	66.2	852,000	44.1	332,000	51.1	28,000	17.3
Wallonia	511,000	23.4	798,000	41.3	199,000	30.7	110,000	67.9
Brussels	187,000	8.6	278,000	14.4	114,000	17.6	24,000	14.8
German-speaking cantons	25,000	1.1	5,000	0.2	4,000	0.6	—	—
Belgium	2,183,000	100.0	1,933,000	100.0	649,000	100.0	162,000	100.0

Source: Calculated from Fraeys, Table 5.7. All votes rounded off to nearest thousand.

Appendix Table 5.9. Party Experience in Government Coalitions and Opposition, 1918–1940, 1944–1963 [a]

	Duration (months)		
Duration of cabinet coalitions, by party of Prime Minister	Nov. 21, 1918– May 28, 1940	Sept. 26, 1944– Sept. 30, 1963	1918–63
Governments headed by:			
Catholic [b]	232	124	356
Socialist	9	104	113
Catholic and Socialist	11	—	11
Liberal	6	—	6
Total	258	228	486
Duration of cabinets, by party composition			
Catholic-Socialist-Liberal [b]	110	3	113
Catholic-Liberal	134	40	174
Catholic-Socialist	13	58	71
Socialist-Liberal	—	50	50
Catholic (one party)	1	50	51
Catholic-Socialist-Liberal-Communist	—	8	8
Socialist-Liberal-Communist	—	19	19
Total	258	228	486

(*continued on p. 415*)

Appendix Table 5.9. (Cont'd.)
Major parties in government and in opposition

	1918–40 Months	1918–40 % of period	1944–63 Months	1944–63 % of period	1918–63 Months	1918–63 % of period
Catholic Party (PSC)						
In government	258	100	159	70	417	86
In opposition	—	—	69	30	69	14
Socialist Party						
In government	123	48	138	61	261	54
In opposition	135	52	90	39	225	46
Liberal Party						
In government	244	95	120	53	364	75
In opposition	14	5	108	47	122	25

a. Excludes the period of government in exile in World War II.

b. Including the Van Zeeland governments of 1935–37, whose Prime Minister, although of Catholic tendency, was not yet a member of the Catholic Party.

Source: Calculated chiefly from information in *Guide des Ministères, 1963–64* (Brussels, 1963), pp. 80–93 (which does not give party affiliations), and Carl-Henrik Höjer, *Le Régime parlementaire belge de 1918 à 1940,* (Uppsala, Almqvist, 1946).

Appendix Table 5.10. Population of Belgium, by Regions, 1910–1961

Region	1910 Inhabitants (in 000's)	%	1920 Inhabitants (in 000's)	%
Flanders	3,506	47.2	3,500	47.2
Wallonia	2,893	39.0	2,828	38.2
Brussels	1,023	13.8	1,078	14.6
Belgium	7,422	100.0	7,406	100.0

Region	1930 Inhabitants (in 000's)	%	1947 Inhabitants (in 000's)	%	1961 Inhabitants (in 000's)	%
Flanders	3,886	48.0	4,272	50.2	4,711	51.3
Wallonia	3,001	37.1	2,940	34.5	3,038	33.1
Brussels	1,205	14.9	1,300	15.3	1,439	15.6
Belgium	8,092	100.0	8,512	100.0	9,189	100.0

Note: Totals do not always add up due to rounding of numbers of components.

Sources: Conseil Economique Wallon, *Le Rapport Sauvy* (Liège, 1962), p. 7, for 1910–47, and census figures for 1961.

Appendix Table 5.11. School and Preschool Population by Language and Level of Instruction, 1960–1961

	French	Flemish	German	Total
Preschool	152,574	251,435	1,126	405,135
Primary (ages 6–12)	397,827	515,854	5,141	918,822
Secondary (ages 12–18)	222,058	304,341	333	526,732
University, higher technical institutions, normal schools	28,164	23,835	—	51,999
Total	800,623	1,095,465	6,600	1,902,688

Source: *Annuaire statistique de l'enseignement, 1960–1961*, pp. 14–15.

Chapter 6. The Netherlands

Appendix Table 6.1. The Franchise in the Netherlands, 1853–1963

Year	Number of enfranchised persons	Percentage of total adult males until 1910, total adult population since 1920	Qualifications: age and sex
1853	83,561	11.0	Over 23; male only
1870	103,538	11.3	"
1880	122,481	12.3	"
1890	295,570	26.8	"
1900	569,768	49.0	Over 25; male only
1910	854,539	63.2	"
1920	3,250,247	97.6	Over 25; all adults
1930	3,884,489	98.1	"
1940	4,721,113	98.5	"
1948	5,433,663	96.6 *	Over 23; all adults
1963	6,748,611	98.6	"

* Decline mainly attributable to disenfranchisement of convicted National Socialists.
Source: Central Bureau of Statistics, *Statistiek der Verkiezingen* (1963), p. 8.

Appendix Table 6.2. *Dutch Cabinets and Party Composition of Lower House of Parliament, 1888–1965* [1]

— = Party members in government
— = Conditional support without direct representation in Cabinet

Years	Cabinet	Duration in months	Election year	Total seats, lower house	Socialists	Radicals	Center	Liberals	Conservative	Catholics	Chr. Historicals	Anti-Revolutionaries	Others	Potentially definite government supporters [2]	Parties not in government [2]
1888–1891	Mackay	40	1888	100	1			46		25		27	1	52	48
1891–1894	Van Tienhoven	32½	1891	100		1		53		25		21	–	54	46
														Government ended by dividing all parties over franchise	
1894–1897	Röell	38½	1894	100		3		57		25		15		Conservative-Liberal government with no clear opposition	–
1897–1901	Pierson	48	1897	100	2	4	35		13	22	6	17	1	52	48
1901–1905	Kuyper	48½	1901	100	6	9	18		8	25	9	23	2	57	53
1905–1908	De Meester	30	1905	100	6	11	25		9	25	8	15	1	36	64

Nonreligious parties — Religious parties

For 1905–1908 De Meester: Liberal minority government defeated in December 1907 followed by minority government of religious parties (48 seats) which obtained majority at next election

Years	Election in months	Election year	seats, lower house	Communists	Socialists	Radicals	Liberals Center	Liberals Conservative	Catholics	Chr. Historicals	Anti-Revolutionaries	Others	Potentially definite government supporters[2]	Parties not in government[2]
1908–1913 Heemskerk	66⅔	1905	100		6	11	25	9	25	8	15	1	48	52
		1909	100		7	9	20	4	25	10	25	—	60	40
1913–1918 Cort van der Linden	60	1913	100		15	7	22	10	25	10	11	—	39(54)	46
													Liberal minority government which became War Cabinet with support of all democratic parties	
1918–1922 Ruys De Beerenbrouck	48	1918	100	2	22	5	6	9	30	7	13	6	50	50
1922–1925 Ruys De Beerenbrouck	34½ (13 + 21½)	1922	100	2	20	5	*Fusion of Liberals*	10	32	11	16	4	59	41
													(Intermediate Cabinet crisis, when Socialists, Radicals, and minority of Catholics rejected Navy bill)	
1925–1926 Colijn	7	1925	100	1	24	7		9	30	11	13	5	54	46
1926–1929 De Geer	41	1925	100	1	24	7		9	30	11	13	5	54	46
													Intermezzo Cabinet of "nonpoliticians" from all parties, except Socialists and Communists; both government and opposition uncertain	

Years	Cabinet	Duration in months	Election year	Total seats, lower house	Communists	Socialists	Radicals	Liberals	Catholics	Chr. His-toricals	Anti-Revolution-aries	Others	Potentially definite government supporters [2]	Parties not in government [2]
						Nonreligious parties				Religious parties				
1929–1933	Ruys De Beeren-brouck	45%	1929	100	2	24	7	8	30	11	12	6	53	47
1933–1937	Colijn	49 (26 + 23)	1933	100	4	22	6	7	28	10	14	9	65 (Intermediate Cabinet crisis caused by Catholic opposition)	35
1937–1939	Colijn	25	1937	100	3	23	6	4	31	8	17	8	56	4
1939	Colijn	½	1937	100	3	23	6	4	31	8	17	8	Cabinet of "strong" men of orthodox Protestant and Liberal background dismissed by combined vote of Catholics, Socialists, and Radicals	
1939–1940	De Geer	13	1937	100	3	23	6	4	31	8	17	8	68 Became War Coalition under dissident Anti-Revolutionary Ger-brandy, 1940–1945	28

Years	Cabinet	Duration in months	Election year	Total seats, lower house	Communists	Socialists 1940-1945 1945-1946	Liberals	Catholics	Chr. Historicals	Anti-Revolutionaries	Others	Potentially definite government supporters [2]	Parties not in government [2]
						Nonreligious parties			Religious parties				
1940-1946	WAR CABINETS IN EXILE AND "NATIONAL" GOVERNMENT 1945-1946 (PROGRESSIVE-ORIENTED)					NO PARLIAMENT EMERGENCY PARLIAMENT							
1946-1948	Beel	25	1946	100	10	29	6	32	8	13	2	61	39
1948-1952	Drees	49 (31+18)	1948	100	8	27	8 ---	32	9	13	3	68(76)	34
	(Intermediate Cabinet crisis caused by Liberal vote against Liberal Minister of Foreign Affairs)												
1952-1956	Drees	49 (32½+17)	1952	100	6	30	9	30	9	12	4	81	19
	(Intermediate Cabinet crisis caused by disagreement about housing policy)												
1956-1958	Drees	26	1956	100	4	34	9	33	8	10	2	85	15
			1956	150	7	50	13	49	13	15	3	127	23
	(Socialist ministers resigned in December 1958 when majority in Parliament rejected tax bill)												

					Nonreligious parties				Religious parties					
Years	Cabinet	Duration in months	Election year	Total seats, lower house	Communists	Pacifist Socialists	Socialists	Liberals	Catholics	Chr. Historicals	Anti-Revolutionaries	Others	Potentially definite government supporters[a]	Parties not in government[2]
1958–1959	Beel	5	1956	150	7		50	13	49	13	15	3	77 (90)	60
													Rump Cabinet presiding over tactical dissolution of Parliament	
1959–1963	De Quay	50 (19 + 31)	1959	150	3	2	48	19	49	12	14	3	94	56
													(Intermediate Cabinet crisis in December 1960, through dissension about housing policy)	
1963–1965	Marijnen	20	1963	150	4	4	43	16	50	13	13	7	92	58
1965–	Cals		1963	150	4	4	43	16	50	13	13	7	106	44

1. Before 1888 party affiliation and party composition of cabinets were too undefined to permit tabular representation.

2. The detached relations of government and Parliament which prevail in the Netherlands causes both parliamentary support and parliamentary opposition to be somewhat fluid. Governments with a fairly narrow official basis have in practice enjoyed considerable support from parties not represented in the government, while nominal government supporters have often opposed particular cabinets on particular issues.

Source: D. Hans, *Parade der Politieke Partijen* (Putten, n.d.), pp. 102, 103; Central Bureau of Statistics, *Statistiek der Verkiezingen, 1963; Parlement en Kiezer,* Yearbook, 1963-1964, List of cabinets and ministers since 1848.

Appendix Table 6.3. Percentages of Total Number of Valid Ballots Obtained by Parties in Elections for Lower House of Dutch Parliament Since Introduction of Proportional Representation and Universal Suffrage, 1918–1963

	1918	1922	1925	1929	1933	1937	1946	1948	1952	1956	1959	1963
1. Protestant parties												
Anti-Revolutionary Party	13.4	13.7	12.2	11.6	13.4	16.4	12.9	13.2	11.3	9.9	9.4	8.7
Christian Historical Union	6.5	10.9	9.9	10.5	9.1	7.8	7.9	9.2	8.9	8.4	8.1	8.6
Staatkundig-Gereformeerde Partij	0.4	0.9	2.0	2.3	2.5	1.9	2.1	2.4	2.4	2.3	2.2	2.3
2. Catholic Party	30.0	29.9	28.6	29.6	27.9	28.8	30.8	31.0	28.7	31.7	31.6	31.9
3. Liberals												
Liberals	10.0	9.3	8.7	7.4	6.9	4.0	6.4	8.0	8.8	8.8	12.2	10.3
Radicals	5.3	4.6	6.1	6.2	5.1	5.9	—	—	—	—	—	—
4. Socialists												
SDAP	22.0	19.4	22.9	23.8	21.5	22.0	—	—	—	—	—	—
Labor Party	—	—	—	—	—	—	28.3	25.6	29.0	32.7	30.3	28.0
Pacifist Socialists	—	—	—	—	—	—	—	—	—	—	1.8	3.0
5. Communists	2.3	1.8	1.2	2.0	3.2	3.3	10.6	7.7	6.2	4.8	2.4	2.8
6. Other parties with seats	8.3	2.4	3.5	3.2	6.4	6.3	—	1.3	2.7	—	—	2.9
7. Other parties without seats	2.2	7.1	4.9	2.9	4.0	3.9	1.1	1.6	2.0	1.4	2.0	1.5

Source: Central Bureau of Statistics, *Statistiek der Verkiezingen*, 1963, p. 13; and calculations by R. P. van den Helm.

Appendix Table 6.4. The Relation Between Religious and Nonreligious Parties in the Netherlands (combined percentages of all valid ballots, including votes for dissident parties)

	1918	1922	1925	1929	1933	1937	1946	1948	1952	1956	1959	1963
All Protestants[1]	21.9	27.7	26.0	25.9	27.1	29.0	23.5	24.8	23.3	21.2	20.4	20.4
All Catholics	30.0	30.9	29.8	30.4	29.5	29.4	30.8	32.3	31.4	31.7	31.6	31.9
Total: Religious Parties	51.9	58.6	55.8	56.3	56.6	58.4	54.3	57.1	54.7	52.9	52.0	52.3
All Liberals[2]	15.3	14.5	14.8	13.6	12.0	9.9	6.4	8.0	8.8	8.8	12.2	11.0
All Socialists and Communists[3]	25.9	21.6	25.3	26.8	26.7	26.1	38.9	33.4	35.5	37.5	35.1	33.8
Total: Liberals, Socialists, and Communists	41.2	36.1	40.1	40.4	38.7	36.0	45.3	41.4	44.3	46.3	47.3	44.8
Others[4]	6.9	5.3	4.1	3.3	4.7	5.6	0.4	1.5	1.0	0.9	0.7	2.9

1. Includes also Christian-Democratic Union, which fused with Socialists in 1945.
2. Includes also Vrijzinnig-Democratische Bond (Radical Party), which fused with Socialists in 1945.
3. Includes SDAP/Labor Party, Revolutionary Socialists, Pacifist Socialists, Communists.
4. Mainly interest parties and rightist groups, including National Socialists, Fascists, and Boerenpartij (Peasant Party).
Source: Calculated by R. P. van den Helm from data of Central Bureau of Statistics.

Appendix Table 6.5. Religious Divisions in the Netherlands, 1849–1960

	Roman Catholic	Dutch Reformed (Nederlands) Hervormd)	Orthodox-Reformed (Gereformeerden)	Other Protestants	Jewish	Others	No church
1849	38.1	54.6	1.3	3.3	1.9	0.8	0.01
1859	37.1	54.9	2.0	3.1	1.9	0.8	0.1
1869	36.5	54.7	3.0	2.9	1.9	0.8	0.1
1879	35.9	54.5	3.5	3.0	2.0	0.8	0.3
1889	35.4	48.6	8.2	2.9	2.1	1.2	1.5
1899	35.1	48.4	8.1	2.9	2.0	1.1	2.3
1909	35.0	44.2	9.4	3.0	1.8	1.7	5.0
1920	35.6	41.2	9.1	2.7	1.7	2.0	7.8
1930	36.4	34.3	8.7	2.2	1.4	2.4	14.4
1947	38.5	31.0	8.6	1.8	0.1	2.8	17.0
1960	40.4	28.3	9.3	1.5	0.1	2.0	18.4

Source: Central Bureau of Statistics, Jaarcijfers.

Appendix Table 6.6. Percentage of Children Attending Government and Private Schools in the Netherlands, 1860–1960 *

	Attending government schools		Attending private schools		
1860	78		22		
1870	76		24		
1880	75		25		
1890	70		30		
1900	69		31		
1910	62		38		
1920	55		45		
		Protestant	Catholic	Other	All
1930	38	25	36	2	62
1940	30	26	42	2	70
1950	27	27	44	2	73
1960	27	27	44	2	73

* In the analysis of this table it should be remembered that Catholics and orthodox Protestants have tended to have larger families over most of this period. According to J. P. Kruyt, Verzuiling (Zaandijk, 1959), p. 25, roughly 35% of parents send their children to Catholic schools, 28% to Protestant schools, and 37% to nonreligious schools (calculation for 1957).

Source: 1860–1890: Calculated from Verslag van de Staat der Hoge, Middelbare en Lagere Scholen over 1890–1891, Bijlage II. 1900 to date: Central Bureau of Statistics, Zestig Jaren Statistiek in Tijdreeksen, 1959, p. 31.

Chapter 7. Germany

Appendix 7.1

The following remarks contain some comments on a Hamburg public opinion poll[1] which, diffuse and ambiguous as it may be, throws some light on popular attitudes toward the German political system. To what extent is the German population at large conscious of the turn its political establishment has taken and how is it reacting to it? In November 1960, at the time when the SPD shift was already in full swing, a poll in Hamburg, Germany's biggest and one of its most cosmopolitan cities, asked what it would mean if the opposition were to take over the government: would it make a significant difference? Fifty-seven per cent failed to see that such a change would constitute a major event. A total of 5 per cent of the entire sample visualized the SPD's taking over the federal government in a positive light. They emphasized that such a change would not impinge on the democratic foundation of the system. All others evaluated the "no-change" situation in a more skeptical light: 17 per cent replying that the new *equipe* would anyhow have to go on as before; 13 per cent laying stress on the ideological similarities of the two major parties; and 10 per cent stressing the foreign policy commitments already incurred. Thus a great part of the German population seems to be increasingly aware of the limited significance of a change in the parties holding the reins of government. When a similar question was put in 1952, the number of those doubting the importance of a change was only 36 per cent.[2] This insight into the strictly limited meaning of governmental change was most conspicuous among those less than 30 years old: 63 per cent.

In the light of this skeptical attitude toward the meaning of political change, the continued high electoral participation (86.9 per cent throughout the country in 1965) remains puzzling. The rise in the invalid vote, at

1. Wolfgang Hartenstein and Günther Schubert, *Mitlaufen oder Mitbestimmen* (Frankfurt, Europaische Verlangstalt, 1961), p. 103.
2. *Jahrbuch der Öffentlichen Meinung, 1947–1955* (1956), p. 262. For the Hamburg figures see Hartenstein and Schubert, pp. 49–52.

its apex at 4 per cent in 1961 (2.4 per cent in 1965), possibly expresses a small nucleus of discontent with the political system, but it means little if held against such participation figures.[3]

A small indication of an interesting motivation for electoral participation is furnished by the reaction to the Hamburg poll question asking whether someone politically totally uninterested should vote. Among the 52 per cent who felt that such a person should nevertheless vote, a good 39 per cent felt that voting is a duty (p. 37); they thus look at voting as one of the many interconnected types of activity which modern society imposes on its citizens before releasing them to their private pursuits.[4]

That the act of voting may not itself connote meaningful participation in public life is clear from another group of answers. Asked how they would react if a law were to be passed unfavorable to their class of people, only 20 per cent replied in terms of some collective measure they would want to take. That unionists would figure prominently in this group (with 36 per cent) was to be expected. But voting for either of the two big parties has apparently no relation to one's preparedness to secure one's rights by some form of collective action (22 per cent for the SPD, 21 per cent for the CDU); 12 per cent would take individual steps, most of them (9 per cent) by contacting the competent authorities. Interestingly, only 2 per cent thought of voting as a form of response to legislation threatening their interests. This shows to what extent parties remain abstract entities to the citizens, scarcely related to their own life situations; 22 per cent would just gripe, having the feeling of powerlessness in the face of official action, and 33 per cent would not go beyond passive resignation (pp. 43–48).

However, this remoteness from the political process—the feeling of an outside event taking place way beyond their own life sphere and, while impinging on them, scarcely accessible to influence by them—does not result in any hostile attitude toward official institutions and belief systems. Quite the contrary, with one characteristic exception, official values are upheld with a good deal of intransigence against potential deviants. Even in Protestant Hamburg only 50 per cent of the people would allow an adversary of established religion to make a public speech and only 23 per cent would allow him to teach in an institution of secondary education (p. 60). Significantly, political deviationists would do much worse. Only 29 per cent would allow a public speech by someone attacking one of the

3. On the political significance of the invalid vote see R. Stiefbold, "The Significance of Void Ballots in West German Elections," *American Political Science Review,* 59 (1965), p. 391.

4. See also Sidney Verba, "Germany: The Remaking of Political Culture," in Lucian Pye and Sidney Verba, eds., *Political Culture and Political Development* (Princeton, Princeton University Press, 1965), which evaluates related German material.

official dogmas of the Federal Republic by accepting the Oder-Neisse line; only 18 per cent would allow such a dangerous character to teach in a high school. Professional people (55 per cent), skilled workers (46 per cent), and those with college education (60 per cent) would be more liberal in this respect. Among white-collar workers and public servants only 40 per cent, and among unskilled workers only 33 per cent (pp. 59–63), would be that liberal.

In one field both urban background and the experience of the '30s and '40s have produced a clear choice for tolerance and constitutionalism. A neighbor suspected of communism would be denounced to the authorities by only one out of three of those questioned, and by only one out of four among younger groups and skilled working-class families.

While the picture is far from uniform, some points seem to be beyond dispute. Integration of the population into the political system is not very far advanced, and there is some indication, as suggested by the answers to the question on the significance of political change, that the petering out of general political debate seems to have contributed to the characteristic distinction between the "we" and "they," the people and the rulers. Non-integration does not necessarily mean cleavage, especially under the

Appendix Table 7.2. Voting in Bundestag Elections, 1949–1965

	1949	1953	1957	1961	1965
Electorate and participation					
Registered voters (in millions)	31.2	33.2	35.4	37.4	38.5
Percentage turnout	78.5	86	87.8	87.5	86.8
Invalid (list) votes as percentage of votes cast	3.1	3.3	3.8	4	2.4
Valid (list) votes cast (in millions)	23.7	27.6	29.9	31.5	32.6
Party strength as percentage of valid votes cast					
CDU/CSU	31	45.2	50.2	45.3	47.6
SPD	29.2	28.8	31.8	36.3	39.3
FDP	11.9	9.5	7.7	12.7	9.5
DP	4	3.2	3.4	.1	—
BHE	—	5.9	4.6	—	—
BP	3.1	.8	.9	—	—
Z	4.2	1.7		—	—
KPD	5.7	2.2	—	—	—
DRP	1.8	1.1	1	.8	—
WAV	2.9	—	—	—	—
Others	6.2	1.6	.4	4.8	3.6

Abbreviations:
  CDU/CSU—Christian Democratic Union and Christian Social Union
  SPD—Social Democratic Party   FDP—Free Democratic Party
  DP—German Party   BHE—Refugee Party   BP—Bavarian Party
  Z—Center Party   KPD—German Communist Party
  DRP—German Rightist Party   WAV—Economic Reconstruction League

favorable economic circumstances of today. Official values, especially in the field of national interest, are upheld. They give way clearly only where the official value system suffers from internal contradiction between substantive and procedural goals—between the danger of communism and the need for constitutional safeguards—and where the substantive threat seems less real than past popular experience and the ensuing desire to safeguard one's privacy against all intrusion. More recent polls centering on the *Spiegel* affair would confirm the intensive concern for individual rights and procedural guarantees.

Appendix Table 7.3. Composition of the Federal Government at the Time of the Federal Chancellor's Election, 1949–1965

Date of vote	Composition of coalition	Strength of government coalition by individual factions	Total coalition strength	Strength of SPD faction and other opposition	Total number of Bundestag members entitled to vote *
Sept. 15, 1949	CDU/CSU FDP DP	139 52 17	208	131 plus 63 of small parties mostly in opposition	402
Oct. 9, 1953	CDU/CSU FDP DP GB/BHE	243 48 15 27	335	151	487
Oct. 22, 1957	CDU/CSU DP	270 17	287	169 plus 41 FDP temporarily not in the government	497
Nov. 7, 1961	CDU/CSU FDP	242 67	309	190	499
Oct. 16, 1963	CDU/CSU FDP	242 67	309	190	499
Oct. 20, 1965	CDU/CSU FDP	245 49	294	202	497

* Berlin members (19 since 1952) delegated by the Berlin City Assembly do not appear in these figures.

Source: The material for the pre-1965 tabulation has been furnished by members of the Institute for Political Science (Chair II) of the Institute for Technology at Darmstadt, Germany.

Explanations of Appendix Tables 7.2 and 7.3

Appendix Table 7.2 tells the story of the increasing concentration of votes on the three parties represented exclusively in the Bundestag since 1961.

Appendix Table 7.3 explains the story of government and opposition in terms of their respective strengths at the most important time of parliamentary history, the moment of the election of the new Chancellor. It shows that, with the exception of the first Bundestag and the third Bundestag, opposition and SPD were synonymous. Thanks to the workings of economic deprivation, a still fairly liberal election law, and old habits, the first Bundestag counted eight parties with 10 members and more. In 1953 there was a short-lived emergence of the Refugee Party, prohibited from running by fiat of the occupation authorities in 1949. But with this exception incipient prosperity helped along by a stricter election law eliminated the radical Right and Left and started the process of party concentration. By 1957 only four parties were left, with the fourth existing merely by sufferance of what was then the majority party. In the same year the FDP temporarily joined the ranks of the opposition. In the three-party system operating since 1961, the so-called opposition is restricted to the solitary ranks of the SPD.

Appendix Table 7.4. Analysis of Party Preferences (1963) in Answer to the Question: Which of Today's Parties Do You Like Best?
(in percentages)

	CDU/CSU	SPD	FDP	Others	No clear-cut answer
Total	33	34	8	2	23
Men	28	38	9	2	23
Women	38	30	6	2	24
Age groups:					
16–21	31	29	8	2	30
21–25	39	27	5	2	27
25–30	29	42	8	1	20
30–50	33	37	6	2	22
50–65	31	32	8	3	26
Older than 65	41	31	9	1	18
Monthly family income after deductions					
Below DM 400	38	26	6	3	27
400–600	31	39	7	2	21
600–800	31	39	6	1	23
800–1200	35	32	9	2	22
More than 1200	41	22	14	2	21
Professional categories					
Workers and agricultural laborers	26	43	4	2	25
White-collar	38	29	8	0	25
Officials	36	35	8	1	20
Self-employed and professions	37	21	16	3	23
Farmers	46	10	15	1	28
Retired	38	34	6	2	20

	CDU/CSU	SPD	FDP	Others	No clear-cut answer
Educational level					
Grade school (8 years)	32	36	6	2	24
Junior high (10 years)	40	27	13	0	20
Senior high, college, graduate school	32	22	18	4	24
Denominational structure					
Protestants	25	37	10	2	26
Catholics	49	27	3	1	20
Others: unaffiliated or no data given	19	41	10	5	25

Source: Appendix to *Emnid informationen*, No. 33, of August 12, 1963.

Appendix Table 7.5. Professional Affiliation or Background of Members of the Fourth Bundestag (as percentage of total membership)

	CDU/CSU	SPD	Total
Independent entrepreneurs	5.9	1	5.2
Business executives	6.4	5.9	6.5
Managers of Business associations	4.4	1.5	3.8
Retailers, innkeepers, etc.	4.4	1.5	3.1
Artisans and employees of artisan organizations	3.6	2	2.9
Farmers and employees of farm organizations	18.3	1.5	11.5
Employees and workers	4.8	7.4	5.6
Party functionaries	2.4	12.3	6.5
Functionaries of labor organizations	7.2	15.8	9.6
Lawyers and accountants	8	5.4	7.6
Academic professions, clergy, physicians, and architects	5.9	7.9	6
Publishers and journalists	3.6	11.8	6.9
Employees of public enterprises and officials	22.7	23.1	22.3
Housewives	2.4	2.9	2.5

Source: Deutsche Industrieinstitut Publication, No. 7 (July 3, 1962), p. 14.

Explanations of Appendix Tables 7.4 and 7.5

Appendix Table 7.4 has little meaning in terms of predicting voters' future decisions as such a large part of the sample (23 per cent) remains undecided. But it is of value for the correlation between party preferences and a variety of social characteristics of the electorate. In spite of a number of crosscurrents the tabulation confirms the continued existence of a working-class subculture with some, however attenuated, form of SPD loyalty (43 per cent). It is most marked among male non-Catholic workers in the 25- to 50-year age group, among people who never went beyond grade school and whose family income stays within the 400 to 800 DM limit. The lower-level SPD interest among the lowest income group (26 per cent) runs parallel to a high degree of political apathy or indecisiveness (27 per cent). It belongs to the same syndrome as lower SPD interest among women (30 per cent as against 38 per cent for the CDU) and among Catholics (27 per cent against 49 per cent CDU).

Other inquiries would show that the white-collar workers not only have a higher income than workers, but that even in the same income categories there is a marked difference in consumer goods preference (see Richard F. Hamilton, "Affluence and the Worker: The West German Case," in *American Journal of Sociology*, 71 (1965), 144–52, and Hans Paul Bahrdt in *Gibt es noch ein Proletariat?* Marianne Feuersenger, ed., Frankfurt, 1962, pp. 15–33). Both income differentials and different consumer habits are reflected in the appreciable difference in party preference (29 per cent SPD as against 38 per cent CDU). SPD and CDU are running neck-and-neck among officials (35 per cent SPD as against 36 per cent CDU); this reflects not only the fact that railroad men and postal clerks, for example, count as officials but also the fact that a sizable number of city and state administrations are SPD-governed. However, it should be noted that SPD strength remains appreciable throughout with both white-collar workers and retired people (38 per cent) suggesting a continued basis for the party's present attempt to cast a wide net for a multiplicity of social groups. Only among farmers has it scarcely any clientele (10 per cent). The same tabulation would show the precariousness of the social basis of the third party: with 14–18 per cent, the FDP has some position only among higher income groups, self-employed, professionals, farmers, and persons educated beyond grade school—mainly Protestant.

Appendix Table 7.5 shows that the professional background of members of the Bundestag is to some extent in keeping with party attractiveness to various social groups. The small percentage of agricultural representatives in the SPD faction corresponds to the generally poor response the SPD has among farmers (1.5 per cent as against 18.3 per cent for the CDU). Conversely, labor organization functionaries appear in more than double strength among the SPD as compared with the CDU 15.8 per cent as against 7.2 per cent. The fact that the SPD is to some extent still a membership party whereas CDU recruiting is handled by tributary and ancillary organizations is reflected in the drastic difference in the number of full-time party functionaries in the Bundestag: 12.3 per cent for the SPD as against 2.4 per cent for the CDU. Many of the 11.8 per cent publishers and journalists among the SPD ranks, too, are likely to be connected with party or related enterprises. However, the most important professional category in the Bundestag—evenly distributed among all parties—are employees of public enterprises and civil servants: 22.3 per cent. It is this element—emphasizing continuity, shared interests, proper procedure as well as administrative experience needed for the planning and running of extensive public services in the huge agglomerations of population—which is most characteristic of the German parliamentary scene.

Chapter 8. Austria

Appendix Table 8.1. *Voting Percentages for Parliamentary Elections When Social Democrats Were in Opposition*

	1920	1923	1927	1930
Government				
Christian Socials	42	45	—	36
Pan-Germans	17	13		
Heimwehr (fascist)	—	—	—	6
Schober bloc	—	—	—	—[b]
Total	59	58	49[a]	42[b]
No. of seats	*113*	*92*	*85*	*80*
Opposition				
Social Democrats	36	39.5	42	41
Agrarian League	—	2.5	6	—
Others	5	—	3	3
Schober bloc	—	—	—	—[b]
Total	41	42	51	44[b]
No. of seats	*70*	*73*	*80*	*83*

a. There was a common list for government parties.

b. The total vote for Schober-bloc candidates (Pan-Germans and Agrarian League) was 12 per cent. Nine of the elected members sat with the government, 10 with the opposition.

Appendix Table 8.2. *Voting Percentages for Parliamentary Elections Under Coalition Regimes*

	1919	1945	1949	1953	1956	1959	1962
People's Party (CS in 1919)	36	50	44	41	46	44	45.5
No. of seats	*69*	*85*	*77*	*74*	*82*	*79*	*81*
Socialists (SD in 1919)	41	45	39	42	43	45	44
No. of seats	*72*	*76*	*67*	*73*	*74*	*78*	*76*
Communists	—	5	—	—	—	—	—
No. of seats		*4*					
Coalition	77	100	83	83	89	89	89.5
No. of seats	*141*	*165*	*144*	*147*	*156*	*157*	*157*
Freedom Party (Pan-Germans, 1919, Independents, 1949, 1953)	18	—	12	11	7	8	7
No. of seats	*26*		*16*	*14*	*6*	*8*	*8*
Communists	—	—	5	5.5	4	3	3
No. of seats			*5*	*4*	*3*		
European Federalists	—	—	—	—	—	—	.5
Others	5	—	—	.5	—	—	—
No. of seats	*3*						
Opposition	23	—	17	17	11	11	10.5
No. of seats	*29*		*21*	*18*	*9*	*8*	*8*

Appendix Table 8.3. Party Strength in Chamber Elections
(percentage of vote)

Chamber of Labor	1949	1954	1959
(total)			
SPÖ	64	69	68
ÖAAB (ÖVP)	14	16	19
Communists	10	10	6
Freedom Party	12	2	4
Nonparty	—	3	3
Chamber of Labor			
(manual workers only)			
SPÖ	66	73	74
ÖAAB (ÖVP)	11	11	14
Communists	11	11	7
Freedom Party	12	2	3
Nonparty	—	3	2
Chamber of Commerce	1950	1955	1960 *
(contested elections only)			
ÖWB (ÖVP)	77	79	79
FWV (SPÖ)	16	16	8
Others	7	5	13
Chamber of Agriculture	1949–51	1954–58	1959–63
(aggregate of provincial			
elections)			
ÖBB (ÖVP)	82	85	83
ABB (SPÖ)	9	10	11
NB (Freedom Party)	8	4	5
Others	1	1	1

* Contested *and* uncontested election (FWV figures would be somewhat higher if total were for contested elections only).
Sources: H. P. Secher, "Representative Democracy or 'Chamber State,'" *Western Political Quarterly*, 13 (1960), 890–909; *Wiener Zeitung*, October 18, 1959; compilations in archive of ÖVP.

Appendix Table 8.4. Party Strength in Presidential
Elections
(percentage of vote)

	1951 1st ballot	1951 2nd ballot	1957 (and 1965)	1963
SPÖ	39	52	51	55.5
ÖVP	40	48	49	40.5
VdU	15.5	—	—	—
KPÖ	5	—	—	—
EFP	—	—	—	4
Others	.5	—	—	—

Chapter 10. Italy

Appendix Table 10.1 Elections—Chamber of Deputies
(percentage of total vote, with number of seats in parentheses)

	1946 Constit. Assembly	1948 1st Legislature	1953 2nd Legislature	1958 3rd Legislature	1963 4th Legislature
PCI	18.9 (104)		22.6 (143)	22.7 (140)	25.3 (166)
		31.0 (183)			
PSI	20.7 (115)		12.7 (75)	T4.2 (84)	13.8 (87)
PSDI	—	7.1 (33)	4.5 (19)	4.5 (22)	6.1 (33)
PRI	4.4 (23)	2.5 (9)	1.6 (5)	1.4 (6)	1.4 (6)
DC	35.1 (207)	48.4 (304)	40.0 (262)	42.3 (273)	38.3 (260)
PLI	2.8 (16)	3.8 (19)	3.0 (13)	3.5 (17)	7.0 (39)
PDIUM (and other Monarchist parties)	—	2.8 (14)	6.9 (40)	PMP 2.6 (14) PNM 2.2 (11)	1.7 (8)
MSI	—	2.0 (6)	5.8 (29)	4.8 (24)	5.1 (27)
Other parties	18.1 (90)	2.4 (5)	2.9 (3)	1.8 (4)	1.3 (4)
Total	100.0 (555)	100.0 (573)	100.0 (589)	100.0 (595)	100.0 (630)

Source: Through 1958, "Analisi statistica dei risultati," Schepis, Tavola XII; for 1963 results, *Tempi moderni, 13* (April 1963), 75.

BIBLIOGRAPHY

Chapter 1. Great Britain

The development of the institution of organized parliamentary opposition is traced in Archibald S. Foord, *His Majesty's Opposition 1714-1830* (Oxford, Oxford University Press, 1964), but the period from the 1780s is inadequately covered. History is treated as background to present political institutions in John P. Mackintosh, *The British Cabinet* (London, Stevens, 1962). The most recent editions of Walter Bagehot, *The English Constitution* (Fontana Library ed. London, Collins, 1963), and A. V. Dicey, *Introduction to the Study of the Law of the Constitution* (10th ed. London, Macmillan, 1959), contain introductions by R.H.S. Crossman and E.C.S. Wade, respectively, referring to developments since the authors' times.

On the landed aristocracy and the "governing class" in the nineteenth century see F.M.L. Thompson, *English Landed Society in the Nineteenth Century* (London, Routledge, 1963), and G. Kitson Clark, *The Making of Victorian England* (London, Methuen, 1962). On the rise and decline of "movement politics" see Donald Read, *The English Provinces c. 1760-1960* (London, Arnold, 1964).

On the crises before the First World War see Roy Jenkins, *Mr. Balfour's Poodle* (London, Heinemann, 1954); Harold Nicolson, *King George the Fifth* (London, Constable, 1952); Robert Blake, *The Unknown Prime Minister* (London, Eyre and Spottiswoode, 1955); and A. P. Ryan, *Mutiny at the Curragh* (London, Macmillan, 1956). For the history of the Labor Party and Governments see Carl F. Brand, *The British Labour Party* (Stanford, Stanford University Press, 1964); G.D.H. Cole, *A History of the Labour Party from 1914* (London, Routledge, 1948); Margaret Cole, *The Story of Fabian Socialism* (London, Heinemann, 1961); Ralph Miliband, *Parliamentary Socialism* (London, Allen and Unwin, 1961); and R. Bassett, *Nineteen Thirty-One* (London, Macmillan, 1958).

On Parliament see Sir Ivor Jennings, *Parliament* (2nd ed. Cambridge, Cambridge University Press, 1961). On the electoral and party systems see D. E. Butler, *The Electoral System in Britain Since 1918* (2nd ed. Oxford, Oxford University Press, 1963); R. T. McKenzie, *British Political Parties* (2nd ed. London, Heinemann, 1964); and the Nuffield College studies of British general elections since 1945, especially the latest, D. E. Butler and Anthony King, *The British General Election of 1964* (London, Macmillan, 1965). On organized groups and pressure politics see S. E. Finer, *Anonymous Empire* (London, Pall Mall Press, 1958), and Allen Potter, *Organized Groups in British National Politics* (London, Faber, 1961).

On the social setting see Anthony Sampson, *Anatomy of Britain* (London, Hodder and Stoughton, 1962), and *Anatomy of Britain Today* (London, Hodder and Stoughton, 1965) and W. L. Guttsman, *The British Political Elite* (London, Macgibbon and Kee, 1963). On politics in the social setting see Jean Blondel, *Voters, Parties, and Leaders* (London, Penguin, 1963); Richard Rose, *Politics in England* (Boston, Little, Brown, 1964); and Samuel H. Beer, *Modern British Politics* (London, Faber, 1965). The contributors to *The Twentieth Century* (October 1957) special number on "Who Governs Britain?" answer or evade the question in a variety of ways.

Chapter 2. *The American Oppositions*

Probably no political system has ever had so much written about it as that of the
United States. A reader who wishes to pursue the topics discussed in this chapter
should consult the various works cited in the footnotes. There are also a number of
short works that provide excellent overviews of certain aspects of American politics
and good critical bibliographies:

Fred I. Greenstein, *The American Party System and the American People* (Englewood
Cliffs, N.J., Prentice-Hall, 1963); Nelson W. Polsby, *Congress and the Presidency*
(Englewood Cliffs, N.J., Prentice-Hall, 1964); Robert E. Lane and David O. Sears,
Public Opinion (Englewood Cliffs, N.J., Prentice-Hall, 1964). David Truman's now
classic *The Government Process* (New York, Knopf, 1953) is rich in bibliographical
references. Two standard works cited in the footnotes that are of central importance
to this chapter are Angus Campbell et al., *The American Voter* (New York, Wiley,
1960), and V. O. Key, *Public Opinion and American Democracy* (New York, Knopf,
1961). One should also consult Seymour M. Lipset, *Political Man* (Garden City, N.Y.,
Doubleday, 1960) and his *The First New Nation* (New York, Basic Books, 1963).

Chapter 3. *Norway*

GENERAL HISTORY: There is no dearth of narrative histories of Norway but very
little serious work on developments after 1905. The standard history of the first three
decades after 1814 is Sverre Steen's five-volume *Det frie Norge* (Oslo, Cappelen,
1951–62). In contrast to other general histories this is well annotated and documented.
Useful summaries of further developments are found in W. Keilhau's three volumes
(8–10) of the series *Det norske folks liv og historie gjennom tidene* (Oslo, Aschehoug,
1931–35), and his *Det norske folks historie i vår egen tid* (Oslo, Aschehoug, 1938).
More recent summaries are found in M. Jensen, *Norges historie fra 1660 til våre dager*
(Oslo, Gyldendal, 1949; pocket ed. Universitetsforlaget, 1964), and in the multivolume
series edited by T. Dahl, *Vårt folks historie*, vols. 5–7 (Oslo, Aschehoug, 1963–64). A
useful collection of essays on a variety of aspects of national development is *Dette er
Norge*, vols. 1–3 (Oslo, Gyldendal, 1964).

Among English-language histories Karen Larson, *A History of Norway* (Princeton,
Princeton University Press, 1948), is particularly useful for earlier periods but highly
inadequate for an understanding of developments since 1905.

POLITICAL HISTORY: The standard work on the history of Parliament is *Det norske
Storting gjennom 150 år* (Oslo, Gyldendal, 1964), vols. 1–4. The first volume, by Alf
Kaartvedt, covers the *ancien régime* until 1869. The second volume, by Rolf Danielsen,
covers the critical period from 1870 to 1908 and constitutes the first thorough analysis
of the changes in procedures and alignments brought about through the great struggle
over constitutional principles in the '70s and '80s. The volume by Tim Greve on the
period since 1905 leaves much to be desired.

A leading interpreter of nineteenth-century political developments in Norway is
Jens Arup Seip. His most important contributions are: *Det opinionsstyrte enevelde*

(Oslo, Universitetsforlaget, 1958), an illuminating analysis of the absolutist heritage and of the early conceptions of representation and popular sovereignty; "Det norske system," *Historisk tidsskrift 39* (1959), 1–58, an analysis of the influence of Saint-Simonian ideas on the policies of the leading officials; *Et regime foran undergangen* (Oslo, Tanum, 1945), a pathbreaking analysis of the strains within the official leadership in the decade before the breakdown of the *ancien régime; Fra embetsmannsstat til ettpartistat* (Oslo, Universitetsforlaget, 1963)—essays on the development of the Norwegian system from a regime of king's officials to the rule of one party.

A work of major importance for an understanding of developments in the '80s is Alf Kaartvedt, *Kampen om parlamentarisme 1880–84* (Oslo, Universitetsforlaget, 1956).

A Swedish work on the period 1905–35 is still a major source of information: Arne Björnberg, *Parlamentarismens utveckling i Norge sedan 1905* (Uppsala, Almqvist and Wiksell, 1939).

There are hardly any detailed analyses of the politics of the years between the two world wars. A thoroughgoing account of the controversies over foreign and military policy and their importance for the development of party alignments in the Storting is found in Nils Ørvik, *Sikkerhetspolitikken 1920–1939* (Oslo, Tanum, 1960–61).

On World War II and its aftermath see especially M. Skodvin, *Striden om okkupasjonsstyret i Norge* (Oslo, Universitetsforlaget, 1956); T. Chr. Wyller, *Nyordning og motstand* (Oslo, Universitetsforlaget, 1958); and *Frigjøringspolitikk* (Oslo, Universitetsforlaget, 1963).

CONSTITUTIONAL COMMENTARIES: The basic work on the Constitution of 1814 is still T. H. Aschehoug, *Norges nuværende Statsforfatning*, vols. 1–3 (Christiania, Aschehoug, 1875–85). The standard textbook is F. Castberg, *Norges statsforfatning*, vols. 1–2 (3d ed. Oslo, Universitetsforlaget, 1964). A summary presentation is given in J. Andenæs, *Statsforfatningen i Norge* (Oslo, Tanum, 1945 and later eds.).

An important review of constitutional developments is given by T. Eckhoff in "Utviklingslinjer i norsk statsstyre og forfatningsrett," *Tidsskrift for Rettsvitenskap*, 77 (1964), 171–231.

A summary presentation in English of the Constitution and the principal organs of government can be found in J. A. Storing, *Norwegian Democracy* (Boston, Houghton Mifflin, 1963). This conventional text is unfortunately marred by a few inaccuracies and misinterpretations.

ELECTIONS AND PARTIES: A review of Norwegian research on elections and parties is given in S. Rokkan and H. Valen, "Parties, Elections and Political Behaviour in the Northern Countries," pp. 103–36 in O. Stammer, ed., *Politische Forschung* (Cologne, Westdeutscher Verlag, 1960).

Analyses of early electoral developments are presented in S. Rokkan and H. Valen, "The Mobilization of the Periphery," pp. 111–59 in S. Rokkan, ed., *Approaches to the Study of Political Participation* (Bergen, Christian Michelsen Institute, 1962), and in S. Rokkan, "Geography, Religion and Social Class," in S. M. Lipset and S. Rokkan, *Party Systems and Voter Alignments* (New York, Free Press, 1967).

An excellent review of early party developments is found in R. Danielsen's chapter on Norway in "Framveksten av de politiske partier i de nordiske land på 1800-tallet," pp. 131–50 of *Problemer i nordisk historieforskning* (Oslo, Universitetsforlaget, 1964). A useful contribution to the analysis of the growth of urban party organization has been published by Ulf Torgersen in the collective volume edited by E. Allardt and Y. Littunen, *Cleavages, Ideologies and Party Systems* (Helsinki, Westermarck Society, 1964).

The official party histories published since the 1930s (the latest ones are for the

442

Labor Party, 1887–1962, and for the Communist Party, 1923–40) contain very little
serious analysis. On the development of the Labor Party there is useful information in
H. Lange, *Fra sekt til parti* (Oslo, Universitetsforlaget, 1962); K. Langfeldt, *Moskvatesene i norsk politikk* (Oslo, Universitetsforlaget, 1961); and I. Roset, *Det norske
Arbeiderparti og Hornsruds regjeringsdannelse i 1928* (Oslo, Universitetsforlaget,
1964).

The best introduction in English to the study of parties and electoral behavior in
Norway is H. Valen and D. Katz, *Political Parties in Norway: A Community Study*
(Oslo, Universitetsforlaget, 1964). For a broader treatment of regional variations, see
the paper by S. Rokkan and H. Valen in E. Allardt and Y. Littunen, eds., *Cleavages,
Ideologies and Party Systems,* and S. Rokkan, "Geography, Religion and Social Class."
The findings of the long-term program of electoral research at the Christian Michelsen Institute in Bergen and the Institute for Social Research in Oslo are being published
in a series of reports in English and in Norwegian. Particularly detailed accounts of
electoral arrangements, party organization, candidate recruitment, turnout, and the
ecology of the vote will be given in forthcoming volumes by S. Rokkan, H. Valen,
et al., in the series *Valg i Norge.*

MOVEMENTS AND ORGANIZATIONS: There is no general work on the growth of popular
movements and interest organizations. A useful *aperçu* is given in Sverre Steen's collected essays, *Tusen års norsk historie* (Oslo, Cappelen, 1958), pp. 182–86. For a quick
review of the growth of "organizational society," see T. Chr. Wyller, *Nyordning...,*
Sect. 3.

The standard works on the unions are G. Ousland and A. Skar, *Fagbevegelsen i
Norge,* vols. 1–3 (Oslo, Tiden, 1949), and W. Galenson, *Labor in Norway* (Cambridge,
Mass., Harvard University Press, 1949). Cf. also the latter's chapter on Scandinavia in
W. Galenson, ed., *Comparative Labor Movements* (New York, Prentice-Hall, 1952).
On white-collar unions, see specifically E. Fivelsdal, *Funksjonærenes syn på faglige
og politiske spørsmål* (Oslo, Universitetsforlaget, 1964). On the employers' associations:
E. Petersen, *Norsk Arbeidsgiverforening 1900–1950* (Oslo, Arbeidsgiverforening, 1950).
On farmers' organizations: O. A. Johnsen, *Norges Bønder* (Kristiania, Aschehoug,
1919); G. Werner-Hansen, ed., *Norges Bondelag 1896–1956* (Oslo, Bøndernes Forlag,
1956); and J. Tveite, *Jord og gjerning* (Oslo Selskspet Norges Vel, 1959). On the
Folk High School movement: Erica Simon, *Réveil national et culture populaire en
Scandinavie* (Paris, Presses Universitaires, 1960). On consumer cooperatives: I. Debes,
Forbrukerkooperasjonens historie, vols. 1–2 (Oslo, Norges Kooperative Landsfortund,
1956).

A Register of Norwegian associations and organizations has been prepared by J.
Moren at the Christian Michelsen Institute and is scheduled for publication in 1966.
The growth of "corporatist" bodies of consultation and decision-making has been
described by J. Moren in *Organisasjonene og forvaltningen* (Bergen, Norges Handelshøyskole, 1958).

THE MASS MEDIA: The political role of the press has been analyzed in S. Rokkan and
P. Torsvik, "Der Wähler, der Leser und die Parteipresse," *Kölner Zeitschrift für
Soziologie, 12* (1960), and in S. Høyer, "Pressens økonomiske og politiske struktur,"
Tidsskrift for samfunnsforskning, 1964 (4), 221–42.

THE CENTRAL DECISION-MAKING ORGANS: The basic works on Parliament are T. Lindstøl,
Stortinget og Statsrådet 1814–1914, vols. 1–4 (Kristiania, Steenske, 1914); V. Haffner
and K. Bjørnstad, *Stortinget og Statsrådet 1915–45* (Stortinget, 1949); and the already
cited 150-year history, *Det norske Storting gjennom 150 år,* vols. 1–4. On legislative
procedure the indispensable manual is V. Haffner, *Om Stortingets lovbehandling og
Stortingets voteringsordning* (new ed. Oslo, Universitetsforlaget, 1964).

On the Cabinet a straightforward reference work is J. Debes, *Det norske Statsråd 1814–1949* (Oslo, Cammermeyer, 1950). A useful description of its procedures is given in K. Bloch, *Kongens Råd* (Oslo, Universitetsforlaget, 1963). A standard history of the central bureaucracy is H. K. Steffens, *Den norske Central-administrations Historie 1814–1914* (Kristiania, Stenersen, 1914). A team of young historians and political scientists is currently preparing an analytical history of developments department by department from 1814 to 1964.

Knut D. Jacobsen's *Teknisk hjelp og politisk struktur* (Oslo, Universitetsforlaget, 1964) presents a major breakthrough in the study of processes of administrative change in Norway; it deals with the development of administrative machinery for agriculture from 1874 to 1899.

Useful compendia for students are Per Stavang, *Parlamentarisme og maktbalanse* (Oslo, Universitetsforlaget, 1964), and Ulf Torgersen, *Norske politiske institusjoner* (Oslo, Universitetsforlaget, 1964).

Chapter 4. Sweden

BIBLIOGRAPHY: E. Håstad, "Swedish Political Science," in *Contemporary Political Science* (Paris, UNESCO, 1950), pp. 150 ff.; Sarah Thorelli, "Political Science in Sweden," *American Political Science Review, 44* (1950), 977 ff.; L. Frykholm, "Swedish Legal Publications in English, French and German 1935–60," *Scandinavian Studies in Law, 5* (1961), 155.ff.

PERIODICALS: *Statsvetenskaplig Tidskrift* (Lund) from 1897; *Scandinavian Political Studies* (Helsinki) from 1966.

GENERAL WORKS: I. Andersson, *A History of Sweden* (2d ed. Stockholm, Natur och Kultur, 1956); E. Lundberg, *Business Cycles and Economic Policy* (London, Allen and Unwin, 1957).

CONSTITUTIONAL PROVISIONS, SWEDISH GOVERNMENT AND POLITICS: *The Constitution of Sweden,* Documents published by the Ministry for Foreign Affairs, 1953 (also in French); N. Andrén, *Modern Swedish Government* (Stockholm, Almqvist and Wiksell, 1961); B. Arneson, *The Democratic Monarchies of Scandinavia* (New York, Van Nostrand, 1939); E. Fahlbeck, N. Herlitz, and N. Stjernquist, "Die Entwicklung des öffentlichen Rechts Schwedens in den Jahren 1933 bis 1953," *Jahrbuch des öffentlichen Rechts,* N.F.(4) 1955; R. Fusilier, *Les Monarchies parlementaires* (Paris, Éditions Ouvrières, 1960); W. Haller, *Der schwedische Justitieombudsman* (Zürich, Polygraphischer Verlag, 1964); N. Herlitz, *Sweden: a Modern Democracy on Ancient Foundations* (Minneapolis, University of Minnesota Press, 1939); E. Håstad, *The Parliament of Sweden* (London, Hansard Society, 1957); H. Tingsten, *The Debate on the Foreign Policy of Sweden 1918–1939* (London, Oxford University Press, 1949); D. A. Rustow, *The Politics of Compromise: A Study of Parties and Cabinet Government in Sweden* (Princeton, Princeton University Press, 1955); D. Verney, *Parliamentary Reform in Sweden* (Oxford, Clarendon Press, 1957).

R. Malmgren, *Sveriges grundlagar och tillhörande författningar med förklaringar* (9th ed. Stockholm, Norstedts, 1965); N. Herlitz, *Svenska statsrättens grunder* (2d ed. Stockholm, Norstedts, 1956); R. Malmgren, *Sveriges författning, en lärobok i svensk statsrätt,* vols. 1–2 (Malmö, 1941–52); Författningsutredningen, "Sveriges statsskick, 1. Lagförslag, 2. Motiv, förslag till regeringsform, 3. Motiv, förslag till riksdagsordning," *Statens offentliga utredningar,* 1963, Nos. 16–18 (Stockholm, Ministry of Justice,

1963); G. Heckscher, Svensk statsförvaltning i arbete (2d ed. Stockholm, Studieförbundet Näringsliv och Samhälle, 1958); N. Herlitz, Grunddragen av det svenska statskickets historia (6th ed. Stockholm, Norstedts, 1964); H. Meijer, Kommittépolitik och kommittéarbete (Lund, Gleerups, 1956) (with an English summary); O. Nyman, Parlamentarismen i Sverige (4th ed. Stockholm, Bokförlaget Medborgarskolan, 1963); Sveriges Riksdag, vols. 1–17 (Stockholm, 1931–38).

POLITICAL PARTIES AND ORGANIZATIONS: R. Fusilier, Le Parti socialiste suédois (Paris, Éditions Ouvrières, 1954); G. Heckscher, "Interest Groups in Sweden," in Interest Groups on Four Continents, ed. H. W. Ehrmann (Pittsburgh, University of Pittsburgh Press, 1958); T. L. Johnston, Collective Bargaining in Sweden (London, Allen and Unwin, 1962); F. Schmidt, The Law of Labour Relations in Sweden (Stockholm, Almquist and Wiksell, 1962).

G. Heckscher, Staten och organisationerna (2d ed. Stockholm, KF:s Bokförlag, 1951); H. Johansson, Folkrörelserna och det demokratiska statsskicket (Lund, Gleerups, 1952); O. Ruin, Kooperativa Förbundet 1899–1929 (Stockholm, Rabén and Sjögren, 1960) (with an English summary); T. Vallinder, I kamp för demokratin, rösträttsrörelsen i Sverige 1886–1900 (Stockholm, Natur och Kultur, 1962) (with an English summary); J. Westerståhl, Svensk fackföreningsrörelse (Stockholm, Tidens förlag, 1945).

IDEOLOGIES AND RELIGION: C. A. Hessler, Statskyrkodebatten (Stockholm, Almqvist and Wiksell, 1964) (with an English summary); H. Tingsten, Den svenska socialdemokratiens idéutveckling, vols. 1–2 (Stockholm, Tidens förlag, 1941).

ELECTIONS AND MASS MEDIA: Official Statistics of Sweden: The Elections to the Riksdag During the Years 1961–1964 (Stockholm, Central Bureau of Statistics, 1965); A. Y. Pers, The Swedish Press (Stockholm Forum, 1963); H. Tingsten, Political Behavior: Studies in Election Statistics (London, King and Son, 1937); C.-G. Janson, Majoritetsval (Stockholm, 1958); C.-G. Janson, Mandattilldelning och regional röstfördelning (Stockholm, 1961) (with an English summary); L. Sköld, Kandidatnominering vid andrakammarval (Stockholm, 1958) (with an English summary); B. Särlvik, Opinionsbildningen vid folkomröstningen 1957 (Stockholm, 1959) (with an English summary); G. Wallin, Valrörelser och valresultat, andrakammarvalen i Sverige 1866–1884 (Stockholm, 1961) (with an English summary); J. Westerståhl and C.-G. Janson, Politisk press: Studier till belysning av dagspressens politiska roll i Sverige (Gothenburg, Political Science Institute, University of Gothenburg, 1958) (with an English summary).

Chapter 5. Belgium

GENERAL HISTORY: J.-A. Goris, ed., Belgium (Berkeley, University of California Press, 1946); J. A. van Houtte et al., eds., Algemene Geschiedenis der Nederlanden, vols. 9–13 (Zeist and Antwerp, Standard Boekhandel, 1956–58); Henri Pirenne, Histoire de Belgique, vols. 5, 6, and 7 (2d ed. Brussels, Lamertin, 1921, 1926, and, for vol. 7, 1948); J. Deharveng et al., eds., Histoire de la Belgique contemporaine (3 vols. Brussels, Dewit, 1928–30).

POLITICAL HISTORY: Frans van Kalken, La Belgique contemporaine (2d ed. Paris, Colin, 1950); Carl-Henrik Höjer, Le Régime parlementaire belge de 1918 à 1940 (Uppsala, Almqvist and Wiksell, 1946); E. R. Arango, Leopold III and the Belgian Royal Question (Baltimore, Johns Hopkins Press, 1963); Msgr. A. Simon, works cited in footnote

2, especially *Le Parti Catholique Belge, 1830–1945* (Brussels, Renaissance du Livre, 1958); Léon Delsinne, *Le Parti Ouvrier Belge des origines à 1894* (Brussels, Renaissance du Livre, 1955); K. van Isacker, *Werkelijk en Wettelijk land . . . 1863–1884* (Antwerp, Standaard Boekhandel, 1955); sections in various volumes of G. D. H. Cole, *History of Socialist Thought* (5 vols. in 7, London, Macmillan and St. Martin's Press, 1953–60), and of Carl Landauer, *European Socialism* (2 vols. Berkeley, University of California Press, 1959). See also the recent book by Jean Meynaud, Jean Ladrière, and François Perin, for the Centre de Recherches et d'Information Socio-Politiques, *La Décision politique en Belgique: Le pouvoir et les groupes* (Paris, Colin, 1965), and Theo Luykx, *Politieke Geschiedenis van Belgie* (Brussels, Elseviér, 1964).

POLITICAL INSTITUTIONS AND ELECTIONS: André Mast, *Les Pays du Bénélux* (in series *Comment Ils Sont Gouvernés*) (Paris, Librairie Générale du Droit et de Jurisprudence, 1960); Raymond Fusilier, *Les Monarchies parlementaires* (Paris, Editions Ouvrières, 1960); John Gilissen, *Le Regime représentatif en Belgique depuis 1790* (Brussels, Renaissance du Livre, 1958); R. E. De Smet, R. Evalenko, and W. Fraeys, *Atlas des élections belges, 1919–1954* (Brussels, Institut de Sociologie, 1958); Institut Belge de Science Politique, a number of works, especially its *Aspects de la Société Belge* (Brussels, Librairie Encyclopédique, 1958), *Le Contrôle parlementaire de l'action gouvernementale* (Brussels, Librairie Encyclopédique, 1957), *Le Problème des grandes agglomérations en Belgique* (Brussels, Librairie Encyclopédique, 1957); and articles on "La campagne électorale de mars 1961," in *Res Publica, 3,* no. 4 (1961); Felix Oppenheim, chapter on Belgium in Sigmund Neumann, ed., *Modern Political Parties* (Chicago, University of Chicago Press, 1956); Jan Dhondt, "De evolutie van de partijen tussen de twee wereldoorlogen," *Res Publica, 4,* no. 4 (1962), 370–80; and T. H. Reed, *Government and Politics of Belgium* (Yonkers, World Book Co., 1924).

SOCIAL MOVEMENTS: B. S. Chlepner, *Cent ans d'histoire sociale en Belgique* (Brussels, Institut de Sociologie Solvay, 1956); Léon Delsinne, *Le Mouvement syndical en Belgique* (Paris, Sirey, 1936); and R. Rezsohazy, *Origines et formation du catholicisme social en Belgique, 1842–1909* (Louvain, University of Louvain, 1958).

REGIONAL AND LINGUISTIC PROBLEMS: S. B. Clough, *A History of the Flemish National Movement* (New York, R. H. Smith, 1930); A. W. Willemsen, *Het Vlaams Nationalisme, 1914–1940* (Groningen, Wolters, 1958); *Revue Nouvelle*, special number August–September 1961; Telemachus, "De Spanning tussen de Taalgroepen: een sociologische benadering," *De Maand, 6* (1963), 332–44 (French version in *Revue Nouvelle*, Oct. 15, 1963, 303–14); and M. van Haegendoren, *De Vlaamse beweging: verweer en aanval!* (Hasselt, Vlaamse Pockets, 1964).

CURRENT ANALYSIS of parties, interest groups, social movements: periodic and other reports of the Centre de Recherche et d'Information Socio-politiques, 1959—.

BIBLIOGRAPHY: Most complete historical bibliography in the volumes of the *Algemene Geschiedenis* (see under General History); *Res Publica*, current bibliography in each issue and special bibliography on political parties, 1830–1962, in vol. 5, no. 4 (1963); and extensive annual bibliographies on Belgian history by Jan Dhondt and associates in *Revue du Nord* (Lille) and *Revue belge de philologie et d'histoire*.

Chapter 6. The Netherlands

GENERAL HISTORY: The most recent and complete general history, J. A. van Houtte et al., eds., *Algemene Geschiedenis der Nederlanden* (Utrecht, W. de Haan, 1949–55), is not available in English. But extensive data can be found in the writings of P. J. Blok, *History of the People of the Netherlands* (5 vols. New York, Putnam's, 1898–1912); *Britain and The Netherlands*, papers delivered at the Anglo-Dutch Historical Conferences (2 vols. London, Chatto and Windus, 1960, and Groningen, Wolters, 1964); Pieter Geyl, *The Revolt of The Netherlands, 1555–1609* (2d ed. London, Benn, 1958); *The Netherlands in the Seventeenth Century*, Parts I and II (London, Benn, 1961–64), and *History of the Low Countries—Episodes and Problems* (London, Macmillan, 1964); E. Kossmann, *In Praise of the Dutch Republic: Some Seventeenth-Century Attitudes* (London, 1963); G. J. Renier, *The Dutch Nation: An Historical Study* (London, Allen and Unwin, 1944); and I. Schöffer, *A Short History of The Netherlands* (Amsterdam, Allert de Lange, 1956).

In addition, a number of works on the Netherlands were published in English during or just after the Second World War: see A. J. Barnouw, *The Dutch—A Portrait Study of the People of Holland* (New York, Columbia University Press, 1940), and *The Making of Modern Holland* (New York, Norton, 1944); B. Landheer, ed., *The Netherlands* (Berkeley, University of California Press, 1943); J. Veraart, *Holland* (London, Macdonald, 1944); and especially B. H. M. Vlekke, *The Evolution of the Dutch Nation* (New York, Roy, 1945).

POLITICAL HISTORY: The most important study of institutions in the time of the Dutch Republic is S. J. Fockema Andreae, "De Nederlandse Staat onder de Republiek," *Verhandelingen der Koninklijke Nederlandse Akademie van Wetenschappen*, Nieuwe Reeks, 68 (Amsterdam, 1960). The development of the Dutch States-General is described by a number of authors in S. J. Fockema Andreae and H. Hardenberg, eds., *500 Jaren Staten-Generaal in de Nederlanden* (Assen, Van Gorcum, 1964). For the history of politics in Parliament see W. J. van Welderen Baron Rengers, *Schets eener Parlementaire Geschiedenis van Nederland, 1848–91*, new edition by C. W. de Vries and new volumes by De Vries, W. H. Vermeulen and L. G. Kortenhorst, *1891–1918* and *1945–46* (5 vols. The Hague, Nijhoff, 1948–56), and P. J. Oud, *Het Jongste Verleden* (6 vols. Assen, Van Gorcum, 1948–51), covering the period 1918–40. An excellent analysis from orthodox Protestant perspective is given by P. A. Diepenhorst, *Onze Strijd in de Staten-Generaal* (2 vols. Amsterdam, Dagbl. en Drukkerij De Standaard, 1927–29).

GENERAL PARTY HISTORIES: H. Daalder, "Nederland," in section on political systems in *Repertorium van de Sociale Wetenschappen*, vol. 1: *Politiek* (Amsterdam, Elsevier, 1958), pp. 213–38; D. Hans, *Parade der Politieke Partijen* (Putten, Terwee, nd. [1938?]); C. E. van Koetsveld, *Het Ontstaan, de Beginselen en de Geschiedenis van Onze Politieke Partijen* (Utrecht, Jac. C. van der Stal., 1904). On the orthodox Protestants, J. A. de Wilde and C. Smeenk, *Het Volk ten Baat, de Geschiedenis van de A. R.-Partij* (Groningen, Jan Haan, 1949); on the Catholics, N. de Rooy and L. J. Rogier, *In Vrijheid Herboren* (The Hague, Pax, 1953). There is little literature in English on Dutch socialism: G. D. H. Cole's treatment in *History of Socialist Thought* (London, Macmillan, 1953–60) is often erroneous.

For Dutch sources see the literature mentioned in the footnotes to Chapter 6 and the full bibliography in Fr. de Jong Edz, *Om de Plaats van de Arbeid* (Amsterdam, De Arbeiderspers, 1956).

POLITICAL INSTITUTIONS AND PARTY SYSTEM: In English: R. C. Bone, "The Dynamics of Dutch Politics," *Journal of Politics, 24* (1962), 23–49; H. Daalder, "Parties and Politics in The Netherlands," *Political Studies, 3* (1955), 1–16, and *The Relation Between Cabinet and Parliament in The Netherlands*, report to the International Political Science Association (Rome, 1958); B. W. Schaper, "Religious Groups and Political Parties in Contemporary Holland," in *Britain and The Netherlands, 1,* 204–20; Amry Vandenbosch and S. J. Eldersveld, *Government of The Netherlands* (Lexington, University of Kentucky Press, 1947). In French: Raymond Fusilier, *Les Monarchies parlementaires* (Paris, Éditions Ouvrières, 1960), Ch. VI; André Mast, *Les Pays du Benelux*, in series *Comment Ils Sont Gouvernés* (Paris, Librairie Générale du Droit et de Jurisprudence, 1960). In Dutch: see especially the thorough constitutional law treatises by R. Kranenburg, C. W. van der Pot, and P. J. Oud.

SOCIAL STRUCTURE AND VERZUILING: A. N. J. den Hollander et al., eds., *Drift en Koers: een halve eeuw sociale verandering in Nederland* (Assen, Van Gorcum, 1962); J. P. Kruijt, *Verzuiling* (Zaandijk, Heijnis, 1959); and special issues on *Verzuiling* of *Sociologische Gids*, vol. 3, no. 2 (1956), and *Socialisme en Democratie*, no. 1 (1956).

ELECTIONS AND POLITICAL BEHAVIOR: A full bibliography and data on elections and the electoral system are given in G. H. Scholten and G. Ringnalda, chapter on the Netherlands in S. Rokkan, ed., *An International Guide to Electoral Statistics* (forthcoming). In English, see Hans Daudt and Henk de Lange, *Youth and Politics in The Netherlands*, and L. van der Land et al., *Voting in The Netherlands: A Panel Study in an Amsterdam Suburb*, both reports to the International Political Science Association (Geneva, 1964); A. Hoogerwerf, *Protestantisme en Progressiviteit* (Meppel, Boom, 1964) (with English summary); and English summary to *De Nederlandse Kiezer* (The Hague, Staatsdrukkerij 1956). In French, see J. Barents and J. J. de Jong, *Partis politiques et classes sociales* (mimeo. Paris, Association Française de Science Politique, 1955). In German, see Georg Geismann, *Politische Struktur und Regierungssystem in den Niederlanden* (Frankfurt, Athenäum Verlag, 1964) (with many data, if a one-sided analysis).

BUREAUCRACY: A. van Braam, *Ambtenaren en Bureaucratie in Nederland* (Zeist, W. de Haan, 1957).

INTEREST GROUPS: A. D. Robinson, *Dutch Organized Agriculture in International Politics, 1945-1960* (The Hague, Nijhoff, 1961); John P. Windmuller, "Post-War Wage Determination in The Netherlands," *Annals of the American Academy of Political and Social Science, 310* (1957), 109-22 (with full bibliography).

For contemporary developments, see the English-language journal *Delta: A Review of Arts, Life and Thought and in The Netherlands*, 1958 to date.

Chapter 7 Germany

In addition to the books and articles listed in the notes, the following writings are germane to our subject.

ARTICLES: O. K. Flechtheim, "Zur Frage der Innerparteilichen Demokratie," *Neue Kritik*, No. 8 (1962); W. Hennis, "Parlamentarische Opposition und Industriegesellschaft," *Gesellschaft, Staat Erziehung*, No. 5 (1956); S. Landshut, "Form und Funktion der Parlamentarischen Opposition," *Wirtschaft und Kultursystem* (Rüstow Festgabe), ed. G. Eisermann (Zurich and Stuttgart, Eugen Rentsch Verlag, 1955); H. Kremer and L. Meunier, "Gemeinsamkeit ist eine Zier . . . ein politische Portrait Willy Brandts," *Der Monat, 17*, No. 197 (February 1965), pp. 5-15; E. Krippendorf, "Das Ende des Parteienstaats," *Der Monat*, No. 160 (1962), pp. 64-70; G. Loewenberg, "Parliamentarism in Western Germany: The Functioning of the Bundestag," *American Political Science Review, 55* (1961), pp. 87-102; J. Seifert, "Innerparteiliche Opposition," *Frankfurter Hefte*, No. 11 (1960); D. Sternberger, "Über Parlamentarische Opposition," *Wirtschaft und Kultursystem* (Rüstow Festabe), ed. G. Eisermann (Zurich and Stuttgart, Eugen Rentsch Verlag, 1955).

BOOKS: Douglas A. Chalmers, *The Social Democratic Party of Germany* (New Haven, Yale University Press, 1964); K. W. Deutsch and L. J. Edinger, *Germany Rejoins the Powers* (Stanford, Stanford University Press, 1959); L. J. Edinger, *Kurt Schumacher: A Study in Personality and Political Behavior* (Stanford, Stanford University Press, 1965); Th. Eschenburg, *Institutionelle Sorgen in der Bundesrepublik Politische Aufsätze 1957–1961* (Stuttgart, Kurt E. Schwab Verlag, 1961); A. Faul, ed., *Wahlen and Wähler in West Deutschland* (Villingen, Ring Verlag, 1960); J. Habermas, *Struktur der Öffentlichen Meinung* (Neuwied, Luchterhand, 1962); U. Kitzinger, *German Electoral Politics* (Oxford, Oxford University Press, 1959); M. G. Lange, ed., *Parteien in der Bundesrepublik* (Stuttgart and Düsseldorf, Ring Verlag, 1955); U. Lohmar, *Innerparteiliche Demokratie* (Stuttgart, Ferdinand Enke Verlag, 1963); Theo Pirker, *Die SPD nach Hitler* (Munich, Rütten and Löning, 1965); C. Schmid, *Politik und Geist* (Stuttgart, Ernst Klett Verlag, 1961); R. Wildenmann, *Macht und Konsens als Problem der Innen- und Aussenpolitik* (Frankfurt-Bonn, Atheneum Verlag, 1963).

DOCUMENTS: *Verfehlt die Opposition Ihre Aufgabe?* (Does the opposition fail to do its job?). Debate between Rudolf Augstein, publisher of *Der Spiegel*, and Heinz Kühn, SPD Land chairman for Rheinland-Westphalia, at Freiburg University, January 19, 1965. Reprinted as an insert in *Der Spiegel*, February 20, 1965.

Chapter 8. Austria

The only English-language books on the Second Republic are Richard Hiscocks, *The Rebirth of Austria* (London and New York, Oxford University Press, 1953) and Gordon Shepherd, *The Austrian Odyssey* (London and New York, Macmillan, 1957). For the politics of the First Republic, see Mary MacDonald, *The Republic of Austria, 1918–1934* (London and New York, Oxford University Press, 1946), and Charles A. Gulick, *Austria from Habsburg to Hitler* (2 vols. Berkeley, University of California Press, 1948). Catholic politics in the First Republic is discussed in Alfred Diamant, *Austrian Catholics and the First Republic* (Princeton, Princeton University Press, 1960), and Socialism in the First and Second Republics in Kurt L. Shell, *The Transformation of Austrian Socialism* (New York, State University of New York, 1962).

The following are the most rewarding volumes in German: for the political history of the First Republic, and a discussion of the *Lager*, Henrich Benedikt, ed., *Geschichte der Republik Österreich* (Vienna, Verlag für Geschichte und Politik, 1954); for a Socialist account of the Second Republic, Adolf Schärf, *Österreichs Erneuerung* (Vienna, Wiener Volksbuchhandlung, 1955); for a Catholic account, mostly of the First Republic, Eduard Ludwig, *Österreichs Sendung im Donauraum* (Vienna, Österreichische Staatsdruckerei, 1954); for a critical account of the Coalition, Alexander Vodopivec, *Wer regiert in Österreich?* (2d. ed. Vienna, Verlag für Geschichte und Politik, 1962); and for a penetrating critique of Austria's political ethos, Günther Nenning, *Anschluss an die Zukunft* (Vienna, Europa-Verlag, 1963).

Austria's major political monthlies are *Die Zukunft* (SPÖ) and *Österreichische Monatshefte* (ÖVP). The cultural monthly *Forum* has significant articles on politics. All three are published in Vienna.

Chapter 9. France

Extended critical bibliographies can be found in F. Goguel and A. Grosser, *La Politique en France* (Paris, Colin, 1964) and in A. Grosser, *La Quatrième République et sa politique extérieure* (Paris, Colin, 1961).

The most detailed institutional study of present France is Pierre Avril, *Le Régime politique de la 5. République* (Paris, Librairie Gale. de Droit, 1964) (bibliography).

On the very important problem of legitimacy at different moments, see *L'Affaire Henri Martin*, Commentaire de J. P. Sartre (Paris, Gallimard, 1953); Michèle Cotta, *La Collaboration* (Paris, Colin, 1963); Jacques Duquesne, *L'Algérie et la guerre des mythes* (Paris, Desclée, 1958); Otto Kirchheimer, *Political Justice* (Princeton, Princeton University Press, 1961); *Le Procès de l'attentat du petit Clamart* (Paris, A. Michel, 1963); *Le Procès du Maréchal Pétain* (2 vols. Paris, A. Michel, 1949); Jacques Weygand, *Le Serment* (Paris, Flammarion, 1960) (novel).

On the attitudes of political and social organizations (with historical and sociological explanations), see Gérard Adam, *La CFTC 1940–1958: histoire politique et idéologique* (Paris, Colin, 1964); Axel von Campenhausen, *L'Église et l'état en France* (Paris, Éd. de l'Épi, 1964); Georges Dupeux, *La Société française 1789–1960* (Paris, Colin, 1964) (bibliography); Raoul Girardet, ed., *La Crise Militaire française* (Paris, Colin, 1964); Annie Kriegel, *Le Congrès de Tours* (Paris, Julliard, 1964), and *Aux Origines du communisme* (2 vols. Paris, Mouton, 1964); M. de La Fournière and F. Borella, *Le Syndicalisme étudiant* (Paris, Éd. du Seuil, 1957); Maurice Labi, *La Grande division des travailleurs: la première scission de la CGT* (Paris, Éd. Ouvrières, 1964); Jean Meynaud, *Nouvelles études sur les groupes de pression en France* (Paris, Colin, 1962); Jean Meynaud and A. Lancelot, *La Participation des français à la politique* (Paris, P.U.F., 1961); René Rémond, *La Droite en France* (Enlarged ed. Paris, Aubier, 1964); Jean-Daniel Reynaud, *Les Syndicats en France* (Paris, Colin, 1964); Gregor Siefert, *La Mission des prêtres-ouvriers* (Paris, Éd. de l'Épi, 1963); Georges Vedel, ed., *La Dépolitisation, mythe ou réalité* (Paris, Colin, 1962).

Chapter 10. Italy

The literature on Italian politics is voluminous. This bibliography can only suggest how the interested reader can begin to acquaint himself with available materials, especially those in English.

Numerous studies of the historical and economic background are available. Useful introductory bibliographies on Italian history can be found in general histories of Italy such as that of Denis Mack Smith, *Italy: A Modern History* (Ann Arbor, University of Michigan Press, 1959). For an introduction to the Italian economy see Shepard B. Clough, *The Economic History of Modern Italy* (New York, Columbia University Press, 1964). There is no good general book on the socio-cultural context of Italian politics; an excellent beginning in a work directed to another problem is Joseph LaPalombara, *Interest Groups in Italian Politics* (Princeton, Princeton University Press, 1964), pp. 1–102. For an introduction to the sociological literature see Filippo

Barbano and Mario Viterbi, *Bibliografia della sociologia italiana (1948–1958)* (Turin, Edizioni Romella, 1959).

Although the number of empirical studies published is growing each year, works on Italian politics are largely legalistic, philosophical, historical, or polemical. Many significant works (few of them based on empirical research) have been cited in the notes to the chapter on Italy and will not be repeated here. Two general works in English are John Clarke Adams and Paolo Barile, *The Government of Republican Italy* (Boston, Houghton Mifflin, 1961), and Norman Kogan, *The Government of Italy* (New York, Crowell, 1962). An extremely useful volume for the student of Italian politics is the *Annuario politico italiano*, compiled by the Centro Italiano Richerche e Documentazione and published by *Comunità*. It contains a review of the past year's politics, biographical and statistical information, and an extensive bibliography of Italian books and articles of political relevance published during the previous year.

There is no general work on Italian parties either in English or Italian. An introduction is Carlo Morandi, *I partiti politici nella storia d'Italia* (Florence, Felice Le Monnier, 1963); the text ends with the advent of fascism, but the excellent bibliography contains references to publications issued through 1962. Some useful studies in English of the postwar PCI are the following: Aldo Garosci in Mario Einaudi, Jean-Marie Domenach, and Aldo Garosci, eds., *Communism in Western Europe* (Ithaca, N.Y., Cornell University Press, 1951); Norman Kogan, "National Communism vs. the National Way to Communism—An Italian Interpretation," *Western Political Quarterly, 11* (1958), 660–72; Giorgio Galli, "Italy," in Walter Laqueur and Leopold Labedz, eds., *Polycentrism* (New York, Praeger, 1962), pp. 127–40; and Galli, "Italy: The Choice for the Left," in Leopold Labedz, ed., *Revisionism* (New York, Praeger, 1956), pp. 324–36.

The best introduction in English to the postwar Socialist Party is Raphael Zariski, "The Italian Socialist Party: A Case Study in Factional Conflict," *American Political Science Review, 56* (1962), 372–90. On the Christian Democratic Party see Mario Einaudi and François Goguel, *Christian Democracy in Italy and France* (Notre Dame, University of Notre Dame Press, 1952). For an evaluation of neofascism see R. Taylor Cole, "Neofascism in Western Germany and Italy," *American Political Science Review, 49* (1955), 131–43.

On the Church in politics see A. C. Jemolo, *Church and State in Italy 1850–1950* (Oxford, Blackwell, 1960); Richard A. Webster, *The Cross and the Fasces* (Stanford, Stanford University Press, 1960); and Leicester C. Webb, *Church and State in Italy, 1947–1957* (Melbourne, Melbourne University Press, 1958).

The Italian Resistance is treated in Charles F. Delzell, *Mussolini's Enemies: The Italian Anti-Fascist Resistance* (Princeton, Princeton University Press, 1961). On the political situation at the end of the Second World War see Norman Kogan, *Italy and the Allies* (Cambridge, Harvard University Press, 1956).

CONTRIBUTORS

SAMUEL H. BARNES is associate professor of political science, University of Michigan. He has contributed articles to *The American Political Science Review, The Journal of Politics, The Review of Politics, Industrial and Labor Relations Review,* and *The Journal of Conflict Resolution.* He is completing a study of communications and participation in an Italian Socialist federation. In 1962–63 he held a Fulbright lectureship at the University of Florence, Italy.

HANS DAALDER, professor at the University of Leiden, the Netherlands, is a former Rockefeller Fellow in Political Science (1960–61) at Harvard and Berkeley. He has published (in English) *Cabinet Reform in Britain, 1914–1963,* and various articles on Dutch politics, the military in the emerging countries, and Marxist theories of imperialism.

ROBERT A. DAHL is Sterling Professor of Political Science, Yale University. His publications include *A Preface to Democratic Theory; Who Governs? Democracy and Power in an American City; Modern Political Analysis;* and (with C. E. Lindblom) *Politics, Economics, and Welfare.*

FREDERICK C. ENGELMANN, professor of political science, University of Alberta, Edmonton, Alberta, Canada, has written articles on political parties, Canadian politics, and Austrian politics.

ALFRED GROSSER is director of studies and research at the Fondation Nationale des Sciences Politiques, professor at the Institut d'Études Politiques, University of Paris, visiting professor at the Bologna Center, S.A.I.S., The Johns Hopkins University, and, in 1965, Kratter Visiting Professor of Modern European History, Stanford University. His most recent books are *La Quatrième Republique et sa politique extérieure; The Federal Republic of Germany; La Politique en France* (with François Goguel); and *La Politique Extérieure de la Ve République.*

OTTO KIRCHHEIMER, Dr. jur., professor of government, Columbia University, died in November 1965. His recent publications included *Political Justice* and *Politik und Verfassung;* he was a co-author of "The Spiegel Case," in *Politics in Europe* (Carter-Westin, eds.)

VAL R. LORWIN, professor of history, University of Oregon, is the author of *The French Labor Movement* and has written a number of articles on American, international, and comparative labor history and French and Belgian politics.

ALLEN M. POTTER is professor of government, University of Essex, England. His publications include *American Government and Politics* and *Organized Groups in British National Politics.*

STEIN ROKKAN is director of research for comparative politics, Christian Michelsen Institute, Bergen, Norway. He has been a visiting professor at Yale and the University of Manchester. He was co-editor and co-author of the UNESCO publication *Democracy in a World of Tensions* and has contributed a number of reports on electoral research: *Approaches to the Study of Political Participation; Regional Contrasts in Norwegian Politics* (with H. Valen), *Party Systems and Voter Alignments* (edited with S. M. Lipset), *International Guide to Electoral Statistics* (edited with J. Meyriat). He is currently a member of the Executive Committee of the International Political Science Association.

NILS STJERNQUIST is professor of political science, Lund University, Sweden. His published works deal mainly with Swedish and Danish government and politics.

INDEX